CAMBRIDGE LIBRARY

Books of enduring schola

The Naval Chronicle

The *Naval Chronicle*, published in 40 volumes between 1799 and 1818, is a key source for British maritime and military history, and is also sought after by those researching family histories. Six instalments per year were produced (and often reprinted with corrections) by Bunney and Gold, later Joyce Gold, in London, and bound up into two volumes per year. Printed economically, on paper of varying weights and often with very small type, the extant copies have been heavily used over the course of two centuries, present significant conservation challenges, and are difficult to find outside major libraries. This reissue is the first complete printed reproduction of what was the most influential maritime publication of its day. The subjects covered range widely, including accounts of battles, notices of promotions, marriages and deaths, lists of ships and their tonnages, reports of courts martial, shipwrecks, privateers and prizes, biographies and poetry, notes on the latest technology, and letters. Each volume also contains engravings and charts relating to naval engagements and important harbours from Jamaica to Timor, Newfoundland to Canton, and Penzance to Port Jackson.

Volume 13

Volume 13 (1805) reveals how, following Napoleon's coronation as Emperor and the outbreak of war with Spain, fears of invasion grew stronger. Parliament greatly increased expenditure on the Navy, but the lengthy lists of ships lost or captured on all sides show that resources were stretched. Topographical reports concentrate on French controlled ports, and literary and historical content in this issue was considerably reduced.

Cambridge University Press has long been a pioneer in the reissuing of out-of-print titles from its own backlist, producing digital reprints of books that are still sought after by scholars and students but could not be reprinted economically using traditional technology. The Cambridge Library Collection extends this activity to a wider range of books which are still of importance to researchers and professionals, either for the source material they contain, or as landmarks in the history of their academic discipline.

Drawing from the world-renowned collections in the Cambridge University Library, and guided by the advice of experts in each subject area, Cambridge University Press is using state-of-the-art scanning machines in its own Printing House to capture the content of each book selected for inclusion. The files are processed to give a consistently clear, crisp image, and the books finished to the high quality standard for which the Press is recognised around the world. The latest print-on-demand technology ensures that the books will remain available indefinitely, and that orders for single or multiple copies can quickly be supplied.

The Cambridge Library Collection will bring back to life books of enduring scholarly value (including out-of-copyright works originally issued by other publishers) across a wide range of disciplines in the humanities and social sciences and in science and technology.

The Naval Chronicle

Containing a General and Biographical
History of the Royal Navy of the United
Kingdom with a Variety of Original Papers on
Nautical Subjects

VOLUME 13: JANUARY-JUNE 1805

EDITED BY JAMES STANIER CLARKE
AND JOHN MCARTHUR

CAMBRIDGE UNIVERSITY PRESS

Cambridge, New York, Melbourne, Madrid, Cape Town, Singapore,
São Paolo, Delhi, Dubai, Tokyo

Published in the United States of America by Cambridge University Press, New York

www.cambridge.org
Information on this title: www.cambridge.org/9781108018524

© in this compilation Cambridge University Press 2010

This edition first published 1805
This digitally printed version 2010

ISBN 978-1-108-01852-4 Paperback

This book reproduces the text of the original edition. The content and language reflect
the beliefs, practices and terminology of their time, and have not been updated.

Cambridge University Press wishes to make clear that the book, unless originally published
by Cambridge, is not being republished by, in association or collaboration with, or
with the endorsement or approval of, the original publisher or its successors in title.

Monument erected to the Memory of Captain Montagu, in Westminster Abbey.

THE
Naval Chronicle,

FOR 1805:

CONTAINING A

GENERAL AND BIOGRAPHICAL HISTORY

OF

THE ROYAL NAVY

OF THE

UNITED KINGDOM;

WITH A

VARIETY OF ORIGINAL PAPERS

ON

NAUTICAL SUBJECTS:

UNDER THE GUIDANCE OF SEVERAL
LITERARY AND PROFESSIONAL MEN.

VOLUME THE THIRTEENTH.
(FROM JANUARY TO JUNE.)

In Native Vigour bold, by Freedom led,
No path of Honour have they fail'd to tread:
But whilst they wisely plan, and bravely dare,
Their own Achievements are their latest care.
HAYLEY.

London:

PRINTED AND PUBLISHED BY I. GOLD, SHOE-LANE.

And sold by Messrs. LONGMAN, HURST, REES, and ORME, Mr. SYMONDS, and Mr. WALKER, Paternoster Row; Mr. WHITE, Fleet-street; Messrs. VERNOR and HOOD, Poultry; Mr. ASPERNE, and Messrs. RICHARDSON, Cornhill; Messrs. A. & J. BLACKS and H. PARRY, Leadenhall-street; Messrs. CROSBY and Co., Stationers' Hall Court; Mr. OSTELL, and Mr. LAW, Avemaria-lane; Mr. MOTTLEY, Portsmouth; Mr. HAYDON, Plymouth; Messrs. NORTON and SON, Bristol; Mr. ROBINSON, Liverpool; Messrs. MANNERS and MILLER, Mr. CREECH, and Mr. CONSTABLE, Edinburgh; Mr. ARCHER, Dublin; and the principal Booksellers in the different Seaport Towns throughout the United Kingdom.

MDCCCV.

TO

THE RIGHT HONOURABLE

SAMUEL

LORD VISCOUNT HOOD,

&c. &c. &c.

THIS THIRTEENTH VOLUME OF THE

Naval Chronicle

IS RESPECTFULLY DEDICATED

BY THE EDITORS.

PLATES IN VOLUME XIII.
From Original Designs.

PLATE.	Page
HEAD PIECE to Vol. XIII. A correct Portrait of the ROYAL SOVEREIGN YACHT, launched at Deptford in 1804. Engraved on Wood by NESBIT, from a Drawing by POCOCK...............	1
CLXVIII. PORTRAIT of WILLIAM HUNTER, Esq. Lieutenant of Greenwich Hospital. Engraved by RIDLEY from a Painting by ABBOT, in the possession of JOHN M'ARTHUR, Esq. of York Place.......	1
CLXIX. SKETCH of the FRENCH COAST about BOULOGNE, with the situation of the French Flotilla when attacked by Captain Owen's Squadron in August, 1804. Engraved from a Drawing made by an Officer present at the different Attacks,...................	53
CLXX. PORTRAIT of the CLEOPATRA Frigate, of 32 guns, in three different positions. Engraved by MEDLAND from a Drawing made by Mr. POCOCK in the year 1781...........................	61
CLXXI. PORTRAIT of the late Sir WILLIAM JAMES, Bart., Commodore in the Hon. East India Company's Service. Engraved by RIDLEY from a Painting by Sir JOSHUA REYNOLDS....................	89
CLXXII. VIEW of DUNKIRK. Engraved by RICKARDS from a Drawing taken on the Spot by F. GIBSON, Esq., F.A.S.................	117
CLXXIII. PORTRAIT of PHILIP D'AUVERGNE, Duke of BOUILLON, Commodore in His Majesty's Service. Engraved by RIDLEY from an original Miniature.......................................	169
CLXXIV. VIEW of MARSTON ROCK, near Durham. Engraved by WELLS from a Drawing made on the Spot by AMOR..................	201
CLXXV. PORTRAIT of Admiral Sir RICHARD ONSLOW, Bart. Engraved by ORME, Engraver to His Majesty........................	249
CLXXVI. VIEW of ST. KITTS in the West Indies. Engraved by MEDLAND from an original Drawing by POCOCK..................	283
CLXXVII. PORTRAIT of Sir RICHARD BICKERTON, Bart., K.C., Rear-Admiral of the Red Squadron. Engraved by RIDLEY, from a Drawing by MAYNARD, copied from the original Painting by an Italian Artist at Malta..	337
CLXXVIII. Second VIEW of TORBAY. Engraved by MEDLAND from a Drawing by ANDERSON.....................................	385
CLXXIX. PORTRAIT of RICHARD RODNEY BLIGH, Esq., Admiral of the Blue Squadron. Engraved by RIDLEY from a Painting by OPIE	425
CLXXX. The HYDROGRAPHER, (No. 1,) consisting of a Series of Islands, Harbours, and Bays, from Drawings by AARON ARROWSMITH	474
CLXXXI. The FRONTISPIECE to Vol. XIII, being a Representation of the Monument erected in WESTMINSTER ABBEY to the Memory of Captain JAMES FLAXMAN, R.A., Sculptor.—Engraved by H. R. COOKE from a Drawing by MAYNARD	489

PREFACE

TO THE THIRTEENTH VOLUME.

NEVER, since we first went out of Dock, in the year 1799, have we witnessed so tremendous a Gale, as that which has continued, nearly throughout the whole of our thirteenth Cruise; and, as the old song says,

> HARDER YET, IT YET BLOWS HARDER!
> Now again the BOATSWAIN calls.

It has indeed been dirty weather: but we have endeavoured that it should not blind our eyes: whilst the good old Ship the BRITANNIA strained in every timber, and gave some awkward rolls, we strove to keep our little Packet *steady*, and to preserve whatever of value was thrown out, during the Tempest. Our Vessel was hardly large enough to stow it all away, though we removed many of our Bulk-heads; which brought on us angry and threatening words from some of our Passengers. Who must forgive us, if amidst the bustle and anxiety that has prevailed, we have lost something of our usual courtesy and condescension.

The NAVAL CHRONICLE, like all other Periodical Works, that have the smallest connection with the Political World, must sometimes vary the limits of the different subjects it embraces. And as, from its very name, it undertakes to chronicle the Naval Events of the Year, it must have a reference to the Naval Columns of the Public Prints, and to the Naval Debates of the British Senate. Nor does it follow from this, that we are negligent in procuring Philosophical Papers, Naval Literature, or Hydrographical Information. All of these in their turn, and due season, have their proper place allotted: if they occasionally are passed by, their omission arises from the Tide of historical Events; many of which, if not noticed in our pages, may probably never reach the future Historian: for as we have already said, on our Wrapper, we must, in some respects, *look towards Posterity.*

In a former Preface we promised to insert the late " Admiral Knowles's Correspondence on Ship Building." This, with some other similar declarations, may seem to have been neglected: but our Readers shall eventually find us as good as our word. We have lately reprinted Admiral Sir C. Knowles's Memoir for the fifth time, and with considerable additions. That of Lord Howe has gone through many impressions, and is again out of print: we request, that such additions may be sent to us, as may have offered themselves to our Subscribers.—Though we wish not to run into the egotism of the age, it is a duty we owe ourselves, to declare; that we have often kept back

PREFACE.

Biographical Memoirs of considerable interest, as relating to some of the principal Characters of the day, with the hope of rendering them more full and correct; until sometimes, the more rapid pen of other periodical Works has prevented, or rather preceded us, in the publication of them. Memoirs of Lord BARHAM, and Sir CHARLES POLE, have long been on our table; and we had hoped, before this, to have received from a Friend to our CHRONICLE, the Memoir which he promised of the late gallant and Hon. Captain PAGET, who commanded the Romney.

Our thanks, for assistance in the following pages, are principally due, among others, to the Gentleman who sent us the *Robinson Crusoe* Life of Lieutenant Hunter; to Mr. G. Matthew, for his Letter from Llwyn (page 51.).—To the Gentleman who sent the Letter, that was written by an Officer on board the Fury, (page 53).—To our old Correspondent, who dates from Great Queen-street, Lincoln's-inn-fields, (page 116: In answer to whose queries, we have to mention *Pepys' List of the Royal Navy.*)—To Mr. Gibson, (page 117), for his account, and view of Dunkirk; for a Paragraph relative to Sir Home Popham, (page 137).—For a Letter from Mr. E. Hoppe, maker of the new Sextant and Compass, (page 196.) To *Amor*, for his View of Marston Rock, (page 200.) For Hints for Improving the Navy, by a Well-wisher (page 268).—For the justification of a brave Man's Character, by himself, (page 272).—For the origin of the Infernal, as used in the Expedition against the Enemy in the autumn of last year, (page 275.)—For the State of the efficient Force of the British Navy by F. F., at Upper Clapton, (page 365.)—And for Mr. Tucker's Letter, however long, (page 368.)—The third Number of *Spanish Naval State Papers* was not inserted in the Appendix, owing to the great press of other Articles.

They who sometimes too hastily condemn us, and who scruple not to pester us with Letters, either complaining of the arrangement of our Pages, or urging, with too much impatience, an immediate attention to such particular Articles, as appear the most interesting to themselves; have little idea of the difficulty and anxiety of our labours. The NAVAL CHRONICLE, without any exception, is the cheapest Periodical Work, for its Size, Paper, and Embellishments, that ever appeared in Europe. We have found it extremely difficult to continue it at its present low price, when so many others are vended at the same, though on a smaller Paper, and without Engravings. Nor do we insert this with any idea of advantage to ourselves: but to silence, a little, that spleen, or discontent, which, as we have not merited, we are sorry to draw upon us.—The thirteen Columns we have raised, if they are not always of the *Corinthian* Order, will serve to increase the stability of more splendid Monuments; and will hereafter be often pilfered, as they have been, to set off the works of those, who would otherwise search in vain for such Materials.

Engraved by Ridley from an Original Picture

WILLIAM HUNTER ESQ.R
Lieutenant of Greenwich Hospital

Pub by I. Gold, 103, Shoe Lane, 1. Feb.y 1805.

The Royal Sovereign Yacht, built at Deptford, and launched there during the summer of 1804. After which she attended on the King at Weymouth, commanded by Sir Harry Burrard Neale. This Yacht is of larger dimensions than any that had been previously built; and is a remarkably good Sea Boat.

BIOGRAPHICAL MEMOIR OF
LIEUTENANT WILLIAM HUNTER[*],

OF GREENWICH HOSPITAL:

An intimate Friend of the Poet FALCONER.

> " THE WEDDING GUEST SATE ON A STONE,
> HE CANNOT CHUSE BUT HEAR;
> AND THUS SPAKE ON THAT ANCYENT MAN
> THE BRIGHT-EY'D MARINERE:
> LISTEN STRANGER!" ———
> 　　　　　(*Rime of the Ancyent Marinere*[†].)

The following simple Narrative contains the life of a Veteran who, though not altogether successful in his Naval Career, yet has uniformly *run with Patience the race that was set before him*. It was originally drawn up to gratify the curiosity of a Friend; and it is alone owing to the importunity of friendship, that so correct a delineation of a British Seaman is now presented to

---

[*] Brother to Captain Hunter, late Governor of New Holland.
[†] See NAVAL CHRONICLE, Vol. II, p. 328.

the public. May it prove a powerful antidote to the discontent which frequently increases their natural irritability, and overcome that despondency which has sometimes induced Officers to tax their country with ingratitude.

I WAS born in the City of Edinburgh on the 6th of May, O. S., 1731, and having from my cradle an abhorrence of a sedentary life, I went to sea at the early age of twelve years with my Father, in the Britannia Merchantman fitted out from Leith belonging to the London Trade. After making several voyages both in her and in the Ships James and John, the latter was taken up as a Transport, and ordered with many others to proceed to Aberdeen, under convoy of his Majesty's Ship Fox, of 20 guns, commanded by Capt. Beaver; who was under orders there to embark some Troops that were destined to oppose the progress of the Rebels, already in the vicinity of Edinburgh. Having received the Troops and thirty-two Horse on board, we landed them at Dunbar, and then proceeded for Leith; when a violent Gale came on about N.W. and obliged us to anchor under Inch Keith Island*, nearly opposite to Leith. The Fox was lost during the night on the Sands of north Berwick, and every soul perished. We arrived providentially at Leith; when, wishing for a little relaxation on shore, I quitted the John, and remained a short time with my Father.

About this time the battle of Preston was fought, and the town swarmed with Rebels. I remained at home until after the battle of Falkirk, when I again grew weary of a quiet life, and longed to be at Sea. It happened that my Uncle, who was Purser of the Lizard Sloop, then on the Bristol Station, wrote to my Father and requested I might be sent; as the Captain had promised to rate me Mid: they accordingly equipped me in all haste, and I embarked with no small degree of exultation on board a Ship that was bound for London. If not the most prosperous, it was at least one of the happiest Cruises in my

---

* It is half a league long, and half a mile broad, and has an Harbour towards each quarter; round its coasts are shoals of fish, and abundance of oysters.

life. I had a letter in my chest from my Father to a fair-weather Friend of his in town, who was requested to advance me a small sum to defray my expenses to Bristol: though disappointed in this supply, I was resolved not to knock under; so, having no other alternative, I forthwith shipped myself, in the year 1746, on board the Neptune Letter of Marque, then lying off Irongate Stairs, bound for the Mediterranean, commanded by Capt. Charles Betson, with a complement of forty-five men, at thirty-five shillings a month. Having completed our Cargo, we sailed through the Downs with a fair wind; off Beachy, or as Seamen call it, the Seven Cliffs, it took us a-head: kept plying to windward; but during the night in standing to the northward we struck on the Owers, a bank at S.E., half S. from Culver Cliff, about five leagues from the east end of the Isle of Wight. We got the Ship off; but making much water, we proceeded with her to Portsmouth, and got her docked. Eleven feet of keel were put on; and it was providential that the damage happened in the after part where there was but little dead wood, for otherwise the Ship would have foundered. On her leaving dock, having got our guns and stores again on board, we sailed through the Needles with a fair wind. Nothing occurred until half across the Bay of Biscay, when we observed a Ship in chase of us considerably a-stern: this she continued for two days; on the third we lost sight of her.

Every thing in these Seas was new to me; and long before we came in sight of the celebrated Rock of Gibraltar, I had forgot my disappointment, and felt as happy, perhaps happier, than if I had obtained a supply of money: though poor, I felt I was independent; and confiding in a bountiful Providence, I *took no thought for the Morrow.* We discharged our lading at the old Rock, and proceeded to Minorca; but had scarcely made that Island when a Zebec appeared in chase. We still continued our course, supposing her to be a Spaniard: accordingly prepared for Action. At eight in the evening she began to fire her prow Guns at us, a compliment which we immediately returned with our stern Chasers. The Zebec had much the advantage of us in sailing: we soon commenced close

Action, which continued for two hours and an half; when she boarded us with an hundred and eighty men. Not being exactly prepared for such a visit, and having neither cutlasses nor pikes, we were reluctantly compelled to jump down the Hatchways in order to save ourselves from their fury. Such of our companions as could not escape from the Quarter Deck, were either killed, or wounded in a most dreadful manner: our Captain and Supercargo were literally cut to pieces. When the Algerines discovered that we were English, their violence abated, particularly as they had been towed out of Mahon Harbour that very morning by some of our Men of War's Boats. To add to our distress, a violent gale had come on; all our rigging was shot away, and the Ship lay in such a Trough of the Sea, that we were in great danger of losing her Masts. The gale did not cease until the fifth day after our Capture; when they sent their Boats on board for our men. The Algerine Captain came with them, and to our great surprize exerted himself to repress, and even to chastise that love of plunder which his followers had indulged. Having put our Ship into as good a condition as we could, we were permitted to proceed to Port Mahon Harbour; and on our arrival were put into quarantine. The Admiral, hearing what had passed, sent two of his Surgeon's Mates to assist in the care of our wounded, many of whom were in a most deplorable state. On being released from quarantine, they were sent to Bloody Island, and but few returned.

By the death of Captain Betson, the command of the Neptune devolved on Mr. Stephen Munday, chief Mate; under him, therefore, we sailed for Leghorn, and after continuing there for several weeks without obtaining Pratique, at length bent our course for the last place of destination, Smyrna. During the passage, not being able to weather Strombolo, we bore up in an heavy gale of wind, and ran to leeward of that Island; but had nearly been lost before we passed the Faro of Messina. Off the celebrated Island of Candia we anchored for one night. At Smyrna we repaired the Ship; took in a lading of fruit; and touching at Gibraltar for water, arrived safely in England after a voyage of eleven months.

The Shore was pleasant enough after so long an absence; but, as Tom Tackle was poor, his Finances urged an immediate departure from it. I accordingly entered on board the John and Zachariah, bound to St. Kitts, then lying off Stone Stairs in the River, Joseph Inches, Master. Our first Convoy was the Advice, of 50 guns, Capt. Haddick, under whom we sailed from the Downs to the Motherbank; and there waited, until another Convoy was appointed to Cork, the Loo, of 40 guns. Barbadoes was the first land we made. On our arrival at Basse Terre, St. Kitts, we took in a lading of sugar, and sailed for Sandy Point.

It was at this place that a trifling circumstance again set me adrift: the Captain had struck me, and as I felt without cause; I determined therefore to leave him; but my mode of executing this intention was as singular, as it was rash and perilous. One Sunday evening, it being calm weather, I began by turning all the Beef out of the Steep Tub, which I destined for the conveyance of my clothes: then having lowered it down over the side, and myself with it, I swam with all my might towards the shore. Here I found a tremendous Surf running; my poor tub was upset, and a young Shark wishing to make his supper of me, I was obliged to practise every stratagem in my power to save myself, and the only shirt I had left. At length I succeeded in terrifying my enemy, and reached the shore without any other hindrance.

I was now blest with all the liberty and freedom of choice the most enthusiastic Philosopher could desire: but however captivating such blessings may be in idea, I preferred the discipline of a seafaring life, and making what haste I could, went to Deep Bay, where I shipped myself on board the Constantine; a large Sloop laden with rum for Ireland. I now crossed the Atlantic to Dublin, and then again to Basse Terre where I was discharged. It was now a long time since I had been cheered by the smiles of a Parent; friends I had none; of money I had little enough: but I had commenced my Career as a Sailor, and was not to be daunted by finding I was left alone to make my fortune. With these ideas I again shipped myself, without loss of time, on board the Brig Lucretia, Captain

Watts, bound for Charlestown, South Carolina, with a cargo of rum and sugar. After a passage of about twelve days we returned laden with rice and Indian corn; when I took an amicable leave of my Captain. Being heartily tired of the West Indies, I employed myself in drogging * sugar, until a Ship should offer that was bound for old England. During this interval I fell in one day with my old acquaintance of the Zachariah, just arrived from America, whose Steep Tub I had capsised in the surf. He upbraided me for leaving him, though his own violent behaviour was the cause.—I retorted the language of truth and sincerity; and having thus had my Say, and finding he wanted hands, I at length consented to go again with Captain Inches. We loaded with sugar and rum, and arriving safe at Hull, were all discharged. My old Master, indeed, wished me to remain until he was ready for another voyage, but my finances would not admit of paying a lodging for four or five months.

Not finding any immediate employment at Hull, I resolved to seek for it in the port of London: but I was out in my reckoning, for I there found Sailors as plenty as Shingles on Deal Beach. The only resource that now offered was an old acquaintance of my father, who kept a lodging-house for Sailors, and had received many favours from my family: here, at least, I expected a kind reception. The Master of the house was from home; but the daughter was not wanting in hospitality, until, in the frankness of my heart, thinking Honesty was the best Policy, I made known my real situation: adding, that I would honestly pay her father whenever it was in my power. To my astonishment and dismay, I found that tenderness does not always predominate in the female character, at least in the civilized part of the globe: the countenance of mine hostess immediately changed, and I remained in no very pleasant state of mind until her father appeared.

The night was considerably advanced when the Master of the house arrived. His daughter took care that his heart should not be taken by surprise; and the natural hypocrisy of his character prompted him what conduct to pursue. I at first received a broadside of unmeaning civility; was desired to sit down, and

---

* A drogger is a Shallop, or Schooner, employed to convey sugar from the Plantations to the Merchantmen.

asked if I had got a lodging. I replied, that "Thinking my father's friend would provide me with one, I had not inquired for any." This staggered his politeness, but did not alter a feature of his countenance: his protestations of regard were renewed with fresh warmth, nothing was ever so unfortunate as my arrival; he expected a young man every minute to whom his only bed was engaged; had he but known it before it would have made him too happy; "*but as it is, I am obliged, reluctantly obliged, my dear Mr. Hunter, to say I have no room. So late at Night too!—Let me advise you, my dear Sir, to make haste, for otherwise you may not get admittance any where.*"

Indignation raised my otherwise dejected spirits, which were not exactly prepared for such a mixture of unmeaning protestation and selfish distrust; and as the House door closed in no very gentle manner upon me, I resolved never again to cross its inhospitable threshold. It was now Midnight. The streets of Wapping offer nothing very inviting that could induce a man to choose them as a place of repose. For some minutes I walked on like one who had been stunned by a sudden blow; until a watchman roused me from my reverie by exclaiming, "*Whither are you bound, Friend?*" Even his hoarse voice seemed kind, after the treatment I had received; and I immediately answered, "*To look for just such a man as you are; for a Watch House is the only Lodging I am likely to procure to night.*" The man stared in my face; and finding I was in earnest, conducted me to that drear abode; where I however found a good fire, and slept very comfortably until the morning. Having thus recruited my spirits, I thanked the honest Watchman and Constable; and then worked a Traverse through and across all the lanes in Wapping to find a lodging suitable to my circumstances. Nor was it long before I discovered one in a well-known Alley: the terms were adapted at least to my pocket. I was to pay one shilling per week for sleeping on a bed of flocks, about half an inch thick; my food consisted of sheep's feet, or as they are more fashionably styled, Sheep's trotters. I remained six weeks in this Sky parlour; when, notwithstanding all my economy, my purse began to grow as contracted as my stomach. This induced me to try what the India House might produce, for I resolutely persevered in giving the inhospitable dwelling of my father's friend, a good Birth. My efforts were successful; and having obtained a letter from Captain Egerton, which made me truly happy, I bade adieu to my Sky parlour, and Sheep's trotters, and went on board the Lynn East Indiaman, then lying at Deptford. We sailed to Gravesend to complete our lading, and then proceeded on the voyage to Bengal. Every thing went on favourable until our arrival in that river; when in proceeding up, I experienced another trial for my strength of mind: off Fults the Ship grounded on a quicksand, and was completely wrecked. With the rest of the Ship's Company I was again at liberty to go just where I pleased: but Providence had now blessed me with a Friend, who lightened every difficulty which it was my duty as a Christian to surmount.

In this Ship I first commenced an acquaintance with that worthy, warm-hearted, and benevolent Seaman, Mr. William Locker*, who died Lieutenant-Governor of Greenwich Hospital. We made the best of our way to Calcutta; and, as he was going home in the Lapwing, Captain Chyne, I procured a recommendation from my Commander, to be received on board the same Ship; in which Mr. Spearing †, at present one of the Lieutenants of Greenwich Hospital, was Midshipman.

The first day, after leaving St. Helena, we fell in with a shoal of Dolphins, and in a few hours caught five hundred; when the Captain ordered us to desist. We then proceeded on our voyage, until we struck soundings in the English Channel. Our anchors being unstocked, as is the custom in Indiamen, (which, by the bye, I think very absurd and wrong,) we found great difficulty in guying and steadying them, in order to get the anchors in the stocks; owing to the heavy rolling of the Ship: for it blew hard at S.W.; and, with thick hazy weather, we had a very heavy

---

* A Biographical Memoir was given of Governor Locker, in our 5th Vol. page 97.

† See NAVAL CHRONICLE, Vol. XII, page 281.

Sea. We at length placed the Anchors where the sheet and spare ones ought to be; and having bent the cables, anchored in the Downs: our passage from St. Helena was made in six weeks and three days. We next proceeded for the River, and arrived at North Fleet about the 22d of March, 1750, when all hands were again discharged. Captain Francis Cheyne was the best, and most complete Seaman, I ever sailed with; and I profited accordingly: there was not any thing done, or that could be done on board a Ship, but what he was perfect master of.

Nothing is more trying to a Seaman, both in the King's, and in the Merchant's Service, than the manner in which the best and ablest hands are turned adrift, the moment their labours are no longer required. Well would that man deserve of his Country, who should suggest some remedy to this custom: he might not only remove the necessity of Pressing, but establish a continual supply of able Seamen, who would be ready to embark at the shortest notice. For want of this, how many Boys are reduced to beggary; and then driven to the most desperate resources for a livelihood. The professional life of a Seaman renders him thoughtless and improvident; and when he is thus suddenly turned adrift from the Element to which he has been accustomed, he literally feels, as the old Adage expresses it, *like a Fish out of water.*

I now again, to avoid the Spectre of an empty purse, went to London, and engaged myself to work as a Rigger; in which employ I continued for several months; until an offer came across me of going out to South Carolina, in a very handsome little Ship called the Live Oak, and I believe the first ever constructed with that invaluable timber. Our Voyage was concluded in a few months; when I was again adrift, and again engaged myself to work as a Rigger.—And here let me advise other young men, who like me stand alone in the world, to follow my example *Let what will happen, my Boys, Head up! and bear it.* My worthy friend Mr. Locker one day came to my relief, and as I well remember in the year 1752. He told me that he was going out in the Houghton East Indiaman, the

Hon. Richard Walpole*, Commander; and begged that I would once more be his Shipmate. I accordingly procured an order from Captain Walpole to be received on board, and sailed from Gravesend to the Downs; where, owing to the negligence of our Pilot, the Houghton struck on the North Sand Head; and had she not been a new Ship, must have been lost. She thumped with so much violence as to lift her Masts; but as the tide fell our striking ceased. The weather was at this time so severe, that I had nearly been frozen to death whilst on service, in carrying out the Stream Anchor: for never did I suffer more from cold. With the next flood we hove the Ship off, and then ran into Plymouth to dock her. Proceeding on our Voyage, we arrived at the Isle of Java, and took in store of wood and water; sailed through the Straits of Sunda and Banca with the Monsoon in our favour; received a Pilot at Macao, and, passing through the Bocca Tigris up Canton River, moored at Wampoo. Here we took in our cargo, floored with china, and then chests of tea; and the Trade Winds having shifted in our favour, proceeded to Prince's Island on our Voyage home. In the Houghton I finished my career in the Merchant Service.

It was now long since I had been cheered by the sight of a relation; and being very desirous of once more receiving my worthy Father's blessing, I prepared to enjoy that support. It was in a Collier that I worked my passage down to Sunderland; whence I walked, in about two days, to Edinburgh, that method of travelling suiting me best. As I approached the well-known haunts of former days, every Tree, and Cottage, seemed to claim an acquaintance with me; and even to this day, when I recollect what I felt on first beholding my Father, I forget that I am an old man: Our joy cannot be expressed. I had as many

---

* The Honourable Captain Richard Walpole, of the Houghton East Indiaman was Son of the late Horatio Lord Walpole, Brother to the present, and Nephew to Sir Robert Walpole, afterwards Earl of Orford. The Hon. Capt. Townshend, R.N., took Mr. Walpole first to Sea, and died during that Voyage. Capt. R. Walpole particularly distinguished himself in an action with the French about 1756. We hope on some future occasion to give a life of this distinguished Officer from original materials; which have escaped the researches of Mr. Coxe.

stories to tell my Father and Sisters, as ever the lady fabricated in the Arabian Nights to save her head. For upwards of twelve months I continued to enjoy domestic happiness, to which I had so long been a stranger; and I heightened my relish for it, by employing some of my leisure in the study of mathematics. By means of Euclid's Elements I became master of angles; was particularly struck with the value of the forty-seventh proposition; and at length, without any instructor, made such progress, as afterwards proved of the most important service to me in my profession.

It was now the year 1755, when a dispute arising between this * Country and France, I felt anxious to return to my duty as a Seaman. The late Sir James Douglas, who died an Admiral, was a school-fellow of my father's; and then commanded the Bedford†, fitting out at Chatham. On receiving a letter from my father, Captain Douglas sent us a ticket to prevent my being impressed, with an order to enter on board the Bedford, and to bring with me as many men as I could procure. I took a passage for myself, and what followers I had obtained, in one of the London Traders: but the night before we sailed, the Regulating Officer at Edinburgh and Leith, Captain John Ferguson, impressed all the hands that were on board the Vessel. The Master of the London Trader shrugged up his shoulders, and felt unable to proceed on his Voyage: however, he at length consented to put to Sea, if I would find men to navigate his Ship. I accordingly sent those on board that were engaged for the Bedford, and arrived with them in six days at the rendezvous.

On reaching Chatham I was informed by the First Lieutenant, that as the Bedford was not yet ready to receive the *gentlemen* MIDS, we had permission to sleep on shore; but must come on board every morning. This was Nuts to many of them whose purses could afford it: mine contained only ten shillings; five of

---

* War was not declared until the 17th of May, 1756.

† In the list published by Beatson for 1755, the Bedford is assigned to Captain Thorpe Fowke, who was not appointed to her until some time afterwards.

which were engaged to pay for the freight of my Chest and Bedding, by the Chatham Hoy. I was sadly mortified in being thus thrown aback, at the very beginning of my career in the King's Service, and racked my invention to devise if possible a good excuse for slinging my hammock on board: but fearing that my real situation might thus be exposed to some high flying Midshipmen, I at length devised the following expedient; having previously discovered, on comparing notes, that one of my Messmates was in the same predicament. Amidst the beauties of Chatham Hill, we were particularly struck with a fine Haystack: this we knew must have a lee-side. It was fortunately fine weather; and with the Hay to cover us, though it was not then so much the fashion to sleep on straw, as it has since been, our Lodging was tolerably good, whilst it lasted: for the owner of the stack, having occasion for his Hay, soon removed our bed clothes. In this dilemma, necessity became again the mother of invention. We recollected that below the Dock Yard a wooden Bridge had been placed over the marshy ground, for the convenience of people going to Upnor; and that upon this bridge a small house, or shed, had been placed for shelter in case of rain. There we took up our nightly abode, and a rare cold one it was; the sides of our dormitory being made of old Ship planks, with the trunnel holes left in them. When the last night of our roughing it out arrived, Mr. John Willock, the First Lieutenant, a most worthy Officer, told us, he had received the Captain's order for us to sleep on board; and never did I so much feel the luxury of a warm bed: they who have only slept on beds of Eider down, can have no conception of what I felt; nor ever will, unless they first resort, as I had done, to an Haystack and an Hovel.

As the Bedford was but badly manned, and even the few hands we could muster were poor Orkney Fishermen, Captain Douglas requested the Mids to exert themselves in rigging the Ship: this order produced considerable emulation among us, and was particularly pleasing to me, and my Haystack Chum, since it gave us an opportunity of vying with our young gentry. When the Ship was ready to proceed to Blackstakes, our Carpenter found a defect in the Fore-Mast, which was accordingly condemned, unrigged, and taken out by the Sheer Hulk; and another rigged, and fitted for Sea the same day. This was considered as brisk work; more especially when done by Mids, who were employed at the Mast Head on this Service. We waited in the Downs for orders, and sailed thence as convoy to the Straits, with the Princess Louisa, of 60 guns, Portland, 50, and Bristol 50. After a tolerable passage we anchored in Tangier Bay; and having taken in water at Gibraltar, sailed to the eastward as far as Cape de Gatt, where the Phœnix, Hon. Capt. Augustus Hervey, took charge of the Merchant Vessels; the Bristol returned with us to the Rock. During our stay there, whilst I was one day watering at the ragged Staff*, I observed the Sea suddenly to recede, or fall, very fast: our Boat immediately grounded on some rocks; and being apprehensive of her bilging, I started the water casks. Before this was half done, the Sea rose again very rapidly. I could hardly believe the evidence of my senses; and not being able to explain so strange an event, proceeded to refill my casks, thinking that *Davy's Locker* was bewitched. After my return to the Ship I found her shake, as if she had touched the ground. I threw the Lead, but found the same depth of water as when we came to anchor: It then occurred to me that a dreadful earthquake must somewhere have taken place. We soon sailed for Cadiz, where the water had risen to an amazing height; and having smuggled all the money on board that was in our power, proceeded to Lisbon; where we found the town in ruins, and its wretched inhabitants living in tents by the river's side †.

We freighted our Ship with as much money as we could procure, and sailed for England; when we were soon put under the

---

* So called from the Stump Mast that was fitted into the Launch, when sent to get water, in order to hoist the Casks in and out.

† This dreadful Earthquake began at Lisbon, on the 1st of November, 1755, about ten minutes past ten in the morning. The Sea rose six feet every fifteen minutes, and then fell as much; this flux and reflux lasted until the next morning. It was not felt at Gibraltar until the 17th of November, at half an hour past eleven in the forenoon. The greatest shocks at Lisbon were on the eighth, and eleventh. A very particular account is given in the Gentleman's Magazine, Vol. XXV, pages 554 and 587.

command of Admiral Boscawen, who had lately arrived from Halifax, to relieve Sir Edward Hawke* off Brest. The threats of invasion had been made by the French, who immediately after the declaration of war collected a formidable number of flat-bottomed Boats for that purpose, and greatly alarmed our Government. On our second return from the Western Squadron to refit, Captain Douglas left us, and Captain Thorpe Fowke succeeded him. We sailed under Admiral Holburne from St. Helens, April 16, 1757, the troops destined for North America were to embark at Cork; which having done, we left that harbour on the 7th of May, and arrived at Halifax on the 9th of July. During our passage we carried away our main-mast, and with it one of the greatest rogues that ever entered on board a Man of War, called *Spanish Tom:* the rascal, however, though born to be hung, a punishment which he afterwards underwent, was not born to be drowned. At the time the accident happened he was stationed in the main-top, and was precipitated with it to a great depth in the Ocean: he however rose like a cork, and to our astonishment survived. On our arrival at Halifax we took the Arc en Ciel's † main-mast for a fore-mast, and proceeded with the rest of the Admiral's Fleet on a cruise off Louisbourg. We stood in close with the harbour, and saw a number of Ships of War lying there: then returned to Halifax, re-victualled our Fleet, and appeared again off Louisbourg ‡ to block up the enemy.

---

* Here again Mr. Beatson seems guilty of an inaccuracy in saying, Vol. II p. 97, that Admiral Boscawen did not join the Western Squadron until the return of Sir E. Hawke, in May.

† L'Arc en Ciel, of 50 guns, was taken in 1756, after a sharp action, by the Litchfield and Norwich. She had on board 578 men; one hundred and ninety of whom were Soldiers. The late Comptroller of the Navy, Sir Henry Martin, was made Post in her.

‡ The French force in Louisbourg at this time, and Admiral Holburne's Line of Battle, are inserted in our Naval Anecdotes, from Mr. Beatson's valuable Memoirs, who adds, Vol. II, p. 151, " It has often been matter of wonder, that M. de la Mothe, with a Fleet so much superior to Admiral Holburne's, did not pursue the British Fleet when it retired from before Louisbourg, and block it up in the harbour of Halifax; but our surprise will cease, when it is considered, that M. de la Mothe's orders were expressly for the protection of Louisbourg. Besides,

This attempt to shut up the powerful French Fleet in Louisbourg, was made in consequence of the arrival of Captain Francis Geary, in the Somerset, of 64 guns; with the Devonshire, 64, Capt. W. Gordon; the Eagle, 60, Capt. Hugh Palliser; and the York, 60, Capt. Hugh Pigot. But the whole was frustrated by a dreadful Hurricane which blew dead on shore: it began at east, in the evening of September 23*, and during the night veered round to the south; and thus continued with a violence that had never been surpassed, for the time it lasted, until eleven o'clock the next morning; when it got round to the north. The Tilbury ran on shore, and was wrecked about two leagues from Louisbourg: her Captain and most of her Crew perished. The Ferret Sloop foundered, and every soul went to the bottom. Our Ship, like most others, was dismasted. When the gale first came on, there were but little hopes that any of the Fleet would be saved, as we were only thirteen leagues' distance from the land. Had not Providence favoured us with a shift of Wind of eight points, it would have been all over with us. Many of the disabled Ships were sent to England under Sir Charles Hardy and Commodore Holmes. We were ordered to take the Prince Frederic in tow; and proceeded with her to Aqua Forta in Newfoundland: the Admiral returned with the other Ships to Halifax, and thence to England; leaving the command to Lord Colvill in the Northumberland. Having fitted the Prince Frederick with jury masts, we returned home with a large Convoy. During our passage another hard gale came on at S.W. The Convoy was totally dispersed, and never joined company; and the Prince Frederick again rolled away her masts. On our arrival at Plymouth, where the Bedford was docked, I found a considerable degree of party spirit had arisen in consequence of the conduct of Admiral Holburne, and

---

it was a most positive instruction given to the French Commanders, to avoid as much as possible the coming to action with the British Fleets, or even single Ships, unless the superiority should be so decidedly in their favour, as to give a certainty of victory.

* Beatson says it was the 24th. We mention this, and other similar variations in the printed narratives that have appeared, in order to preserve the accuracy of Naval History. But not in the least to find fault with the respective Writers of it; who did not enjoy the opportunities of information we possess.

Lord Loudown, who commanded the land forces. One of the best answers that appeared, was a letter from a gentleman at Bristol, dated September the 17th; an extract from which is preserved *. This ingenious writer concluded with the following postcript:—" No Captain of a Man of War ought to be consulted about wintering in Halifax: not one of them will give his vote for it, as there are no public diversions there: *Nor should any Man be listened to who deals in Navy Jobs.*"

The year 1758 is ever memorable to a Seaman, for the Bill that was then brought forward, and passed under the auspices of the Hon. Mr. George Grenville, enabling our honest Tars to remit money with care, and safety, to their families.—Government had resolved that the operations in America should commence with the siege of Louisbourg. The gallant Admiral Boscawen, who on the 5th of February had been promoted Admiral of the Blue, was appointed to command the Fleet, having under him Admiral Sir Charles Hardy, lately made a Rear-Admiral of the White, and Commodore Philip Durell. These two Officers sailed previous to the remainder of the Fleet; the first early in January, and the other in February. We followed with the Admiral on the 19th of the same month, having a number of Transports in company. For the better preservation of the Soldiers' health, this prudent Commander made a southern passage, by getting into the Trade Winds, which ran down great part of our longitude: we made Madeira, Teneriffe, and the Bermudas; and having arrived at our destination, left Halifax on the 28th of May, and with a Fleet of 157 Sail stood for Gabreuse Bay, the general rendezvous.

The success of this Attack † is well known. I witnessed the landing of our brave troops under a most tremendous fire of cannon and of musketry. We thought as much of this exploit at the time, as we have since of the landing in Egypt; and it is a singular coincidence, that although General Amherst so ably supported Admiral Boscawen in this Expedition, the chief Commander in America was an ABERCROMBIE. On the capitulation of Louis-

---
* Gentleman's Magazine, Vol. XXVII, page 463.
† For further particulars, see Biographical Memoir of Admiral Boscawen, Vol. VII, page 202.

bourg our Ships went into the harbour; and soon afterwards the Admiral sailed for England with a part of the Squadron, leaving the remainder to winter in America under Rear-Admiral Durell, who had been promoted in the month of August. By this Admiral's order Captain Fowke discharged me into the Flag Ship the Princess Amelia.

We remained some weeks in Louisbourg Harbour; but whilst there, were hardly secure from a gale of wind which blew with much violence. Our anchor came home, and the Captain ordered the sheet anchor to be cut away; when, observing that our Men were cutting the stopper in a very awkward manner, I ran forward, seized the axe, and cut it away myself.—This was not lost on Captain Bray, and from this time I became a great favourite of his, as well as of the Admiral. We wintered at Halifax; and waited there until the ensuing spring, for the arrival of Admiral Boscawen our successor on the Station, with a powerful reinforcement.

The year 1759, termed by Paul Whitehead *Annus Mirabilis,* or *the year of wondrous Feats,* was particularly brilliant both in Naval and Military Events, as that Poet described it in Stanzas well known to Seamen—

" Of Roman and Greek
  Let Fame no more speak,
How their Arms the Old World did subdue;
  Through the Nations around
  Let our trumpets now sound,
How Britons have conquer'd the new.

East, West, North, and South,
  Our Cannon's loud mouth
Shall the rights of our Monarch maintain;
  On America's strand
  Amherst limits the Land,
Boscawen gives law to the Main "

The French, irritated by their constant defeats, were again reduced to the necessity of threatening England and Ireland with a formidable Invasion. But they soon found cause, particularly from our achievements in America, to lay aside their gasconading accounts of Flat Bottomed Boats* on a new construction, which were to steal across the Channel in a dark night, and to carry all before them.

Admiral Boscawen was succeeded in North America by Vice-Admiral Saunders; who sailed from England on the 17th of February, with General Wolfe, in order to co-operate with him in an expedition against Quebec. This was only one of four grand Expeditions in America, planned originally by the Earl of Loudoun, which this year, 1759, were carried into effect. Sir Charles Saunders, I remember, had his Flag on board the Neptune, of 90 guns, Captain Broderick Hartwell; and Admiral Holmes, who left England a few weeks before him, on board the Dublin; a name which I hope will one day be again revived in our Dock Yards. This Fleet arrived within sight of Louisbourg on the 21st of April; but found that harbour so choaked up with ice, that the Admiral was obliged to proceed to Halifax.

We were sent early in May with a Squadron to the small Isle de Coudre, situated in the midst of the River St. Lawrence, about 20 leagues below Quebec; in order to intercept some French Transports, and Victuallers, who had proceeded up the † River. During the passage Captain Simcoe of the Pembroke, 60 guns, died in the Gulf, and was succeeded by Capt. John Wheelock: one of our Lieutenants was sent for the time being to command the Pembroke, and Admiral Durell‡ ap-

---

* The following Pasquinade was afterwards posted up in the most public parts of Paris:

        Batteaux plats à vendre.
        Soldats a louer,
        Ministre a pendre,
        Generaux à rouer!
        O France! le sexe femelle
        Fit toujours ton destin;
        Ton bonheur vint d une Pucelle,
        Ton malheur vient d'une Catin.

† Admiral Saunders, in his dispatches of Sept. 5, says, "Before Admiral Durell got into the River, three Frigates, and seventeen Sail, with provisions, stores, and a few recruits, got up; and are those we are so anxious if possible to destroy."

‡ Admiral Durell, in February, 1759, had been promoted Rear-Admiral of the Red.

pointed me to act in his stead. As we proceeded up this noble River, which is the largest in North America, I was particularly struck with its beauty. At its mouth it is full thirty leagues wide, if measured from Cape Rosiers; and is thence navigable as far as Quebec, upwards of four hundred miles from the Ocean. Some make it forty leagues wide, by probably measuring from the Bay, and Point, of Gaspee, which are a little to the South. Above this latter Bay is a steep broken rock, with an opening in the middle of it, through which a small Sloop might sail: it is on this account called *The pierced Island*. On our arrival at the Isle de Coudres, the Squadron anchored in the afternoon with great difficulty; as the tide runs at the rate of nine knots an hour. It is generally the custom to keep in the North Channel; though the southern, which is called the Pass of Ibberville, from a General of that name, is not near so dangerous. According to report, an earthquake in 1663 overturned a mountain, and threw it on this Isle, which it increased by one half; and, in place of the mountain, a dangerous gulf was sunk. Admiral Durell did not allow me to remain idle. Observing several Canoes and a large Launch on the beach, he ordered three Boats to be manned and armed, to destroy them; which I did accordingly: but, on returning to the beach, found them, to our surprize, all high and dry. The water had fallen six feet in the course of an hour.

Our situation became now extremely perilous; and as we could only launch one Boat at a time, and were much exposed to an attack from the woods by the Indians, I every moment expected a retaliation from the Natives, whose Scalping Knives were not suffered to rust for want of use. Our companions on board the Princess Amelia had been informed of this danger, by Mons. de Vitney, the Pilot; who coming on deck, and hearing the service we had been sent on, declared that we should run the utmost risk of being cut off. The Admiral immediately made our signal to return, but it was too dark to see it. In this dreadful state of uncertainty and obscurity, we laboured hard to get the Boats afloat, and at length succeeded, without any molestation from the Natives; who, being panick struck, we found had fled into the woods. It was now a difficult, and most arduous task, with such a tide running, to reach our respective Ships: I therefore particularly cautioned the Officers in the other two Boats, to beware of getting *athwart Hawze*, and to go on board the first Ship they could reach:—they missed every Ship, and being carried down with the whole Ebb Tide, could not return until the morning. Our Boat had better success; we were fortunate enough to get on board and relieved the Admiral from his anxiety.

The next service in which I was employed was to sound the River in the Barge: we were soon attacked by nine Canoes, which we beat off. The Admiral on this placed me for greater security in an armed Schooner prize; and by the time I had finished the Soundings, Admiral Saunders entered the River on board the Hind, 20 guns, Captain Robert Bond. I was sent to meet him, and to furnish* instructions for passing the Straits of Coudre; which being done by the 23d of June, Admiral Saunders gave me his orders to hasten down to Captain Alexander Schomberg of the Diana, 32 guns, who had charge of the first division of Transports, and to give him directions how to proceed up the River. On my return the Princess Amelia was sent up to the Isle Madame, where she remained stationary during the siege; and Admiral Durell was ordered to send an Officer with two Petty Officers, and one hundred Men, in order to assist in the preparatory operations. I was now superseded as acting Lieutenant in the Princess Amelia.

Before Admiral Saunders † advanced further up the River, he shifted his Flag from the Neptune into a Ship of less burden, the Stirling Castle, 64 guns, Captain Michael Everitt. In this Ship he proceeded up the River with the first division of the Fleet and Transports, on the 26th of June; and anchoring

---

* Beatson appears not to have known this circumstance, when he says, Vol. II. page 359, That Admiral Durell, on his arrival in the River, hoisted French colours in consequence of which a number of Pilots went on board, and, being detained, afterwards proved of great service in navigating the Fleet under Admiral Saunders up the River.

† The reader is referred, for further particulars, to our Biographical Memoir of Sir Charles Saunders, Vol. VIII, p. 10.

off the Island of Orleans *, a little below Quebec, immediately prepared to land the Troops, which was done the next morning. Soon afterwards a heavy gale came on, which did much damage to the Transports, and swamped many of the Boats. Our Boats were afterwards variously employed, until the plan was finally fixed on the first of July; when Admiral Saunders moving up between the Points of Orleans and Levi, on the ninth prepared to land on the North Shore, below the falls of Montmorenci; having placed his Majesty's Sloop, the Porcupine, 14 guns, Capt. John Jervis, and the Boscawen, armed Ship, 16 guns, Capt. Charles Douglas, in the Channel between Orleans and the North Shore, to cover the Boats. The Troops were obliged to continue in the Boats until it was near low water, when there was a flat hard sand to land them on. While we were lying on our oars, the French were not idle in saluting us with shells, but they did no damage. On the 18th of July, two Men of War, two armed Sloops, and two Transports, among which were the Sutherland, 50 guns, Captain Rouse, with Admiral Holmes' Flag, and the Squirrel, 20 guns, Captain Hamilton, passed Quebec without any loss, and got into the upper River. I was also ordered to pass the Town, with eighteen more, our oars being all muffled: during which our batteries on Point Levi kept up an heavy fire. We stopped at Major Goram's Post, joined the Ships, and proceeding up the River, endeavoured to land at a village named Point au Tremble, but the French were too strong. We then attempted the other side, St. Antoine, where we met with little opposition; raised a redoubt on high ground, and left in it a party of Marines: we then advanced still higher up the River, and landed at Dechambo, where we destroyed some magazines. We were thus employed for nearly eighteen days before we again repassed Quebec. On the 31st of July preparations were made for an attack. Two light armed Transports had been

---

* When James Cartier discovered this Island he found it overgrown with vines, and called it the Isle of Bacchus. The Normans who settled here, introduced wheat and excellent fruits. Its lands, all cultivated, rise like an amphitheatre before the view.

prepared by the Admiral to be lain on shore, as a defence against the Batteries. One of them was not of the least use after she was aground; but the other was conducted, and placed with the utmost judgment by an able Seaman, who had also been employed to survey the River, Mr. James Cook, then Master of the Pembroke; afterwards so eminently distinguished, and lamented, as a Circumnavigator * The Boats of the Fleet were filled with Grenadiers. Two Brigades under Lord Townshend, and General Murray, were in readiness to pass the Ford; and to facilitate the passage, the Centurion, 50 guns, Captain William Mantel, had been placed by the Admiral in the Channel. Many of the Boats grounded on a ledge, and were some time in getting off. We at length, however, landed under a most tremendous fire. Our men were dreadfully exposed; and not able to make the least impression on the enemy, who had a breast Work even with their chins. Fortunately a tremendous clap of thunder, succeeded by an heavy shower of rain, occasioned a cessation in their firing, and gave our men time to retreat: but the night had now set in, with a severe storm, and the tide had risen very much. The division under Lord Townshend were obliged to ford below the Falls, and were up to their shoulders in crossing. The Indians now swarmed down to murder such of the wounded as could not be brought off, and to † scalp the

---

* This circumstance is not mentioned, either in the General's, or Admiral's, public letters. It even escaped Dr. Kippis, who notices in Capt. Cook's Life, his services in the River St. Lawrence, and his excellent chart of it.

† The following noble instance of generosity is related of an Officer who fell in this unsuccessful attack. As the naval and military operations were so much combined, we trust our readers will be pleased with its insertion. Captain Ochterlony, and Ensign Peyton, both of the *Royal Americans*, were left wounded at a little distance from each other on the field of battle; the Captain mortally, but the Ensign had only his knee-pan shattered. Soon afterwards an Indian came running down, in order to scalp the former; which, being perceived by Ensign Peyton, he crawled to a musket that was loaded, and shot the Savage. The same danger then threatened him by the approach of another Indian, whom he wounded with a bayonet, and after some struggling pinned to the ground. At length a Grenadier came back to the Captain, in order to bear him off the field : but he declined his assistance; exclaiming, *Thou art a brave fellow ! but your kindness will be lost on me, I am mortally wounded; and the bayonet, or the scalping knife, would now be a mercy. Go yonder to Ensign Peyton, and carry him off, he may live !* The Grenadier obeyed, and conveyed him safe through a severe fire.

dead. After landing such of the wounded, as we could secure, at the Hospital in the Isle of Orleans, I returned to the Shrewsbury, 74 guns, Capt. Hugh Palliser.

At the beginning of September I was sent for by Sir Charles Saunders, and informed, that he intended to send me home in the Rodney Cutter, of four guns, commanded by the Hon. Capt. Ph. J. Percival, with his own and General Wolfe's dispatches. The Admiral also added, that he had recommended me to Lord Anson for promotion. I received my orders on the 5th, and immediately got into the Boat which was waiting to carry me on board my old Ship the Princess Amelia, that I might be ready by the time the Cutter dropped down. I then received Admiral Durell's letters, who also gave me a very flattering certificate.

Though my mind was buoyed up with the thoughts of promotion, I left the busy scene I had so long witnessed, with regret; particularly as a most eventful crisis seemed daily approaching. The Town and Citadel of Quebec surrendered on the 18th of September; so that I only missed that triumph of my Countrymen, by thirteen days. During my Voyage home nothing material occurred for some time; until one day, as we were scudding before the Wind in an heavy Gale from the S.W. I observed a most tremendous Sea coming, which threatened to break on board us. In order to divide it, and take us end on, I immediately called out to the Man at the Steerage, *put the Helm a-port!* I was standing in the Companion, when suddenly it struck us with such violence as made me think it would turn the Cutter end-over-end. It shifted the casks in her Hold, and, knocking me down, washed the Man away from the Helm, and nearly overboard. We had in all but † thirteen hands, and even these were below. Myself and the Helmsman were the only persons on deck; and we could not open the Scuttle to let our Shipmates out, as it was entirely under water. The Vessel lay like a Log—her sails all split and flying into

---

* This Expedition in great measure owed its success, next to the gallantry of the Officers concerned in it, to the information given by a Mr. Paulet   See NAVAL CHRONICLE, Vol. XII, p. 388.

† The complement of the Cutter was forty Men.

shreds It was therefore plain, that it was all over with us, unless by some means we could right again. We therefore instantly cut away every thing from the lee-side, that could, be got at; and endeavoured to bring that side to windward, that the Sea might strike her deck, and once more set her right: By our repeated exertions, and the assistance of Providence, this was at length effected. I then lay to; finding the Vessel too small to scud in such a Sea. The weather becoming more moderate, we proceeded safely on our Voyage until we struck soundings in the Channel; but it still blew strong at S.W. We ran into Portsmouth Harbour, and landed Captain Perceval with the Express. Owing to what I have now related, General Wolfe's Letter, though written eighteen days before the taking of Quebec, only arrived in town two days before the news from Brigadier Townshend, of that City's capitulation. The close of it, is so just an encomium on the perseverance and zealous co-operation of the Naval Men, who were concerned in the Expedition, that I shall here insert it. " I should not do justice to the Admirals, and the Naval Service," says that General, " if I neglected this occasion of acknowledging how much we are indebted for our success to the constant assistance and support received from them; and the perfect harmony and correspondence, which has prevailed throughout all our operations, in the uncommon difficulties which the nature of this Country, in particular, presents to military operations of a great extent, and which no Army can itself solely supply; the immense labour in Artillery, Stores, and Provisions; the long-watchings and attendance in Boats; the drawing up our Artillery by the Seamen, *even in the heat of action;* it is my duty, short as my Command has been, to acknowledge, for that, how great a share the Navy has had in this successful Campaign."

Admiral Holburne, who commanded at Portsmouth, ordered me to drop the Cutter up-abreast of Common Hard; and there I remained, without ever receiving a single word from the Admiralty, for some weeks. This was not quite so pleasant, and I began to think that Admiral Saunders had *hummed* me about my promotion. To increase my satisfaction, I was sent for by Admiral Holburne, and told to strike the Pendant; my Men were to be sent on board his Flag Ship, the Royal Sovereign: Being now adrift, and having received several invitations from Captain Percival, I thought I would e'en go and look him up at his Father's, the Earl of Egmont.—Was introduced, and received kindly. Upon which I informed his Lordship what Sir Charles Saunders had promised to do for me; with my apprehensions, that either the Admiral, or Lord Anson, had forgot me. Lord Egmont immediately sent his son to inquire at the Admiralty, and in about six weeks, whilst I was on a visit to my old and worthy friend Admiral Durell, at Portsmouth, a letter from Captain Percival informed me of my promotion, 1760. Upon this I immediately made for London, and took up my Commission for the Sutherland, 50 guns, Captain Rouse, who had been at the siege of Quebec: his Ship was then repairing at Chatham. When I joined I found but one Officer on board, Lieut. Norman, who left the Ship on my arrival. I could only muster thirty-five men, although the whole complement was on the books; and my orders were to fit the Ship out as soon as possible. I therefore borrowed men from the other Ships, and with their exertions soon sailed to Blackstakes, for the guns, powder, and shot. During our passage to the Downs Captain Rouse was taken very ill; I therefore waited on the Admiral, Sir Piercy Brett, on our arrival, and by his orders took a Convoy round to Portsmouth.—Admiral Holburne immediately sent the Commissioners' Yacht out to Spithead to bring Captain Rouse on shore, where he died in a few days. We remained without any Captain for five or six weeks: when finding I had a sad lazy Crew to deal with, most of whom had been on shore all the time the Ship was fitting, I applied to the Admiral for leave to exercise them; and thus they were brought into some order.

Captain Benjamin Clive was next appointed our Commander, under whom we sailed for Quebec; having taken a Convoy of several Victuallers in charge at Cork. On our arrival in the Spring of 1760, we found Commodore Lord Colvill Commander in Chief, on board the Northumberland, 70 guns, Capt. William

Adams, and the rest of his Squadron, which had wintered in America; and also the Squadron under Commodore Swanton, in the Vanguard, 70 guns. Three distinct Expeditions had been planned; all of which were ultimately to unite in laying siege to the City of Mont Royal, or * Montreal, situated on an Island formerly called Ville Marie, sixty leagues above Quebec, in the River St. Lawrence; which is there about a league in breadth, and contains several Islands. General Amherst, who had wintered at New York, had the conduct of the military; and under him, Capt. Joshua Loring, of the Royal Navy, commanded the armed Vessels; a body of Indians were under the discipline and humane restraint of Sir William Johnston, Bart.: and General Murray commanded at Quebec. On the side of the French, the Chevalier de Levis seconded the Marquis de Vaudreuil in the military department, and Mons. de Rigaud was Governor of Montreal. During the winter, the Commander in Chief had established a Naval Force above Montreal, on the Lake Ontario; and had built two fine Vessels at Niagara, the Onondaga, 18 guns, and the Mohawk, 16 six-pounders. At Oswego, also, he had constructed Row Gallies, Floating Batteries, and a number of Whale Boats.

On the ninth of May, the Lowestoffe Frigate, commanded by Captain Deane, had arrived in the Bason, and brought the joyful intelligence to General Murray; whose Garrison had suffered severely during the winter from an inveterate scurvy; that Commodore Swanton was approaching with a Fleet from England. On the night between the 16th and 17th of May, Mons. de Levis raised the siege of Quebec and retired, leaving his camp standing. On the 13th of June, the Troops under General Murray had embarked for Montreal, in forty Transports, escorted by Captain Deane, with the Penzance, 44 guns, the Diana, 36, the Porcupine, 16, and the Gaspee Schooner, 8 guns, without waiting for the reinforcements which we had in convoy.

Our Ship was ordered to proceed up the River to Point Platoon, and there to remain. On our arrival, we found that the

---
* It received this name from a Mountain of great height, rising about the middle of the Island, which it commands; and thence the appellation of the Royal Mountain.

western side of the River still held out; for after the boasting letter which *M. Vaudreuil* had addressed to the Captains of the Canadian Militia, the poor devils had nothing left for it but to contest every spot to the last moment.—" If the English make any attempt, said that vaunting Officer, it can have no other object than the ambition of their Generals; we are thoroughly prepared to repulse them with spirit." Having several skirmishes with the inhabitants, I got a Boat called a Battoe, and, hoisting her on board the Sutherland, had her fitted with a six-pounder. This annoyed the enemy considerably whenever they attacked our sounding parties.—On the 8th of August the Squadron under Captain Deane passed Trois Rivieres, about half way between Quebec and Montreal; and, having removed a strong Boom placed across the River, anchored on the twelfth off Sorrel, where the enemy had a strong post: The Diana remained below Trois Rivieres to keep up the communication. Lord Rolls, with the Troops from Louisbourg, followed General Murray up the River on board a small Squadron conducted by Lieutenant Garnier of the Navy, who was sent on this service by Lord Colvill: and about a league from Trois Rivieres, Lieutenant Garnier was superseded.

The passage of the Rapids of Richlieu is extremely perilous, and can only be accomplished by the utmost skill and courage. These Rapids are four in number—Cotau de lac; Hattures des Cedres; Buisson; and Trou et la Cascade: of these the two last are the most tremendous. About noon on the 31st of August a division of our army had passed the first. The next day, the Rapids being full of broken waves, the Boats rowed in single file, and kept at a distance: notwithstanding which precaution a Corporal and three Men were drowned. The weather on the third came on so bad that our army was obliged to halt. On the fourth, at day break, they began a navigation beyond measure dangerous; the enemy deemed it impracticable. Though the weather was favourable, we lost eighty-four Men, forty-six Batteaux, seventeen Whale Boats, and a Row Galley: but our men were soon rewarded for all their fatigue and anxiety. On the seventh of September, Colonel Bougainville, and another Officer, came in the morning to one of the Out Posts with a letter, to parley: at twelve o'clock proposals for a Capitulation arrived; and on the ensuing day, the eighth, the articles were agreed to and exchanged. Our good Commander Capt. Clive being in an ill state of health, changed into the Trident, 64, with Captain Julien Legge; and we sailed under him to Halifax, where we wintered.

Early in the ensuing spring, 1761, being the senior Officer on that Station, we received our orders to proceed to New York, with the Faulkland, Capt. Drake, Repulse, Capt. Allen, and Lizard, Capt. Drake; and then taking a Convoy of Transports with Troops on board, Lord Rollo, Commander, to sail for the West Indies. On our arrival at the Leeward Islands we were attached to the Squadron under Commodore Sir James Douglas, with his Pendant on board the Dublin, Capt. Gascoigne; and on the sixth of June anchored in the Road of Roseau, Dominica. Two Officers were immediately dispatched with a summons to M. Longprie, the Governor; who, after trifling with us, by sending two of the principal inhabitants on board the Dublin to treat about a Capitulation, declared in the afternoon, that the inhabitants would defend themselves. Our Ships therefore moved in close to the shore, and having come to an anchor with springs on their cables, soon silenced the batteries. The Troops landed under cover of our fire, and the next day became masters of the Island.—Sir James Douglas was succeeded at the end of the year by Rear-Admiral Rodney; who had been appointed by Mr. Pitt to co-operate with the force which he had provided, to attack all the French West India Islands. Admiral Rodney arrived at Barbadoes on the 22d of November; where he was joined by Sir James Douglas, and a part of his Squadron. As soon as we had taken in our water and provisions, we sailed under Sir James to block up Martinico. Admiral Rodney arrived from Carlisle Bay on the 5th of January, 1762, and joined us on the seventh, with an armament consisting of sixteen Sail of the Line, many Frigates, Sloops of War, Bomb Ketches, Hospital Ships, and Transports; on board of which were upwards of 13,000 land forces.—But I have not time to describe that variety of fatigue, which Seamen had the glory of cheerfully sharing with the Army, in this memorable attack: suffice it therefore to add , that on the 12th of February Martinico yielded, like Louisbourg, Quebec, and Montreal, to British valour; and soon afterwards Granada, St. Lucia, and St. Vincent. I must now repair to a still more stupendous instance of British Heroism. Having been almost frozen amidst the severe cold of North America, I now, after a genial thawing at the Leeward Islands, was nearly roasted at the Havana. Fortunately, like other Seamen, I was happily blest with an accommodating, amphibious sort of constitution. If we cannot blow Hot and Cold with the same mouth, we are frequently reduced to endure the extremes of each with the same body, and that too very suddenly.

Upon the reduction of Martinico, Captain Legge changed into the Temple, 70 guns, and Captain Everitt into our Ship†; and after the arrival of Sir George Pocock in the West Indies, we sailed under his Flag; first to Jamaica, and afterwards to the Havana. Our Captain was ordered, with the Cerberus Frigate, Captain Webber, and Lurcher Cutter, to sound the Bay of Matanzas, and report its survey. Captain Everitt appointed me to this service, in the Cutter. As soon as I had obtained sufficient knowledge of that Bay, I sent the Soundings on board; adding, that with the leading marks which accompanied it, the Ships might run in and anchor; which they afterwards did. On the 26th of July, 1762, I received the following letter from my Captain—

SIR,

I have yours, with the enclosed Soundings, &c.; and as the Coxswain tells me he learns from the Cutter there are no Vessels or Craft of any kind in the Bay, I think the Cutter will be a sufficient safeguard to the Boats; viz. the Sutherland's Barge, and Yawl, and the Cerberus's Barge, whose Lieutenant has directions, which accompany this, to stay and assist you in taking a Sketch of the Bay, from the Eastward round to the bottom of the Bay to the west Point. And you are to endeavour to come at the strength of the Castle; and when you have a nearer view of it, to take a Sketch of it.—And be very particular in your Soundings, Bear-

---

See Biographical Memoir of Lord Rodney, Vol. I, page 362.
† See Vol. VIII, page 455.

ings, and what Distance from it. This you are to do with the utmost prudence and caution, and not to suffer any body to land for fear of their being cut off. I send you the Master in the Barge, who is to be employed on this Service. If any strength should hereafter appear, let the Lurcher Cutter attend the Boats at a proper distance. In the mean time we shall lay off and on. You are to use the utmost dispatch on this Service, and join me with the Boats as soon as possible. It will also be necessary that you consult with the Lieutenant of the Cerberus, how that Castle may be atracked by Ships, and in what manner they are to bring up; and how near they can get to it.

I am your humble Servant,

MICHAELL EVERITT.

P.S. I much approve of the regular method you have taken in setting down the Soundings. Also endeavour to come at the height of the Castle, as near as you can.

On my return from this Service, I was sent on shore with a party of Men to assist the operations going on against the Morro; and this was the most fatiguing duty I ever underwent. My Sky Parlour, and Sheep's Trotters at Wapping, were luxury when compared to it. The ground was our only resting place in the woods; and even that was rendered a bed of torture by multitudes of Scorpions, Centipedes, and Tarantulas. Our wretched beverage was brackish water, and though our Men were dreadfully afflicted both with the flux and scurvy, their only food was Salt Beef: Most devoutly did we all rejoice, when the Morro was taken by Storm, and the Havana surrendered. The Sutherland, which had only sixteen of her guns remaining mounted, had the honour of conveying the Admiral to Spain:—our poor old Ship had but a single bottom, and that was perforated through and through by the worms: we however landed the Admiral and our prisoners, in perfect safety at Cadiz to the utter astonishment of their countrymen, who thought the Havana impregnable; and, after wishing they might *live a thousand years,* so that they did not bring us again into such a place to fetch them away, we sailed for England and were paid off, on the peace, at Chatham.

---

* August 13, 1762. To record the bravery of Don Louis de Velasco, who fell in defending the Morro, his King ordered that there should always be a Ship called Il Velasco, in the Spanish Navy.

It was at this period of my life that I became acquainted with poor Falconer, whose genius survives in his beautiful Poem of the Shipwreck; and which has at length been given to the * public with a correctness and elegance, worthy of its inestimable value. He was at this time on board the Royal George, and was paid off at the same time with the Sutherland. My Brother was a Midshipman with him in the same Ship. The Ode on a Storm, which is mentioned in Falconer's Life †, as having been repeated by him with particular pleasure, has appeared in the Naval Chronicle ‡, and most beautiful it is. I never could discover the Author. In addition to the information which I gave Mr. Clarke, I have only to add—that the Brother of the *Miss Hicks*, whom Falconer married, was one of the Physicians of Westminster Hospital, and married a lady who was Laundress to the King. Dr. Hicks's widow is still alive, but I could never ascertain what became of Mrs. Falconer: she certainly must possess Letters and Papers relative to her husband, which would be of great value to the literary World; and probably a Portrait of him. At the Peace I returned once more to my worthy Father in Scotland, and remained there on half-pay for about five months: when, to my great joy, I received a Letter from the Secretary of the Admiralty, Mr. Philip Stephens, informing me, that the Earl of Egmont, then First Lord of the Admiralty, would appoint me Lieutenant of the Ramilies ‖ Guard Ship, commanded by his Son the Hon. Captain Percival. Our meeting, after so long an absence, was cordial on both sides, and I found him the same gay eccentric character, who had so often led both himself and me into a thousand hair-breadth escapes. He was never fond of his Profession; and before he died, which was about eight years ago, had smarted severely for his dissipation. Captain Percival was buried at *Charlton*, in Kent; and, previous to his death, commanded the Mary Yacht.

---

* Edition printed by Miller, 1804. The Designs by Pocock; with a Life and corrected Text by the Rev. J. S. Clarke, F. R. S. See Vol. XI, pages 305 and 466.
† Page 22.
‡ Vol. VII, page 158.
‖ The Ship in which Admiral Byng had his Flag in the Mediterranean; and which on the day of his execution, (Monday, March 14, 1757,) about half an hour before he suffered, broke her mooring chain, and only held by her bridle.

In the month of December, 1763, I was sent from on board the Ramilies to Hull, with a party of Seamen, to navigate the Glory Frigate, of 32 guns, to Portsmouth, which had lately been launched at the former place. It was to this Ship, that poor Falconer in the ensuing year was appointed Purser. She was commanded in the year 1770 by Captain John Ruthven, and was afterwards called the Apollo*. On my arrival at Hull I met Mr. Collingwood, the Master-Attendant of Deptford Yard, who had come, by order of the Navy Board, with thirty Riggers and Yachts' Men, to get the Glory ready : But on going on board to examine her, I found she had only ninety tons of ballast, which was not sufficient at such a season of the year. I made Mr. Collingwood observe that she heeled considerably with the Wind: upon which he put more on board, but still not enough. As we were badly manned, with little else than Yachts' Men and Watermen, I reefed the Courses and Topsails before we got under weigh. When in sight of Cromer, whose Bay, from its rocky Coast, is called by Seamen the *Devil's Throat*, the Wind took us a-head, and would not allow of our fetching Yarmouth Roads. Our Ship also being in no disposition to beat to windward, and it beginning to blow hard, we were under the necessity of close reefing our top-sails ; and even then she lay on her beam-ends.—Her Rigging being all new, was not sufficiently set up. Our situation every moment became more and more critical. It still blowing harder, we could not bear our Courses ; were therefore obliged to hand them, and let the Ship drift under the balanced Mizen. Providentially we had an experienced Pilot, well acquainted with the North Sea. I observed to him, on looking at the Charts, that if the Wind did not shift, we must drive on the Lemon and Ower Sands, which lie on the Coast of Norfolk, about nine leagues from Haseborough. He replied, that when we came into nineteen fathoms Water, we must endeavour to put the Ship before the Wind, and push for the Swash ; when the Lead should be kept going all the time : This was our only alternative to save the

---

* See Appendix, No. II, p. 3, Vol. XI. The Apollo, there mentioned, was lost April 2, 1804. (Ibid. Vol. p. 392.)

Ship, and our lives; but, to increase our distress, there was not a Man besides the Pilot and myself, who could heave the Lead. At this dreadful instant the Wind, thank God! shifted several points in our favour; so that we drove clear of those dangerous Shoals. The Gale also gradually abated; when making what sail we could, we brought our Ship to an anchor off Mock Beggar Church, about midway between Winterton and Haseborough. While lying there we experienced another heavy gale; but it was off the land and only made the Yachts' Men and lubbers sick: we rode with three Cables an end. Having at length a fair Wind we passed through Yarmouth Roads, and anchored in the Downs; but, on leaving it, made several ineffectual attempts to get to Portsmouth; when the Wind shifted round to the S.W. and blew a perfect Hurricane. Many of the outward-bound Ships then riding in the Downs were lost, and I fear but few of their Crews saved. We were detained by frequent heavy gales for fifty-three days; until by orders of the Navy Board we stood up the Medway for Chatham, where to our general satisfaction we arrived after a Voyage of two months.—I wish the Service was well rid of names which are taken from Grecian and Roman History, and often unintelligible to Seamen: When so many gallant Officers have lost their lives in the Service, why do we prefer JUNO and VENUS (who by-the-bye were little better than Soldiers' Trulls) to the sacred names of our Naval Heroes? But the former I am told are classic terms, and therefore preferable. Be that as it may: the fatigue and anxiety I had undergone, owing to the age and infirmities of the Master Attendant, sent me to sick quarters; and it was two months before I was able to return on board the Ramillies.

A Guard Ship being thought too idle a life for so young and inexperienced an Officer as Captain Percival, Lord Egmont placed him in a more active Ship, the Tweed, 32 guns, then on the Newfoundland Station. I was removed with the Captain and we sailed together to join our Ship in September, 1764. Commodore Palliser ordered us to Cadiz and Lisbon, to bring home the Merchants' money on our arrival at Sheerness, we remained there until the month of May, 1765; when Captain Percival, being dissatisfied with the Tweed, asked his father for the Aquilon Frigate, 28 guns. In this Ship we again sailed for Newfoundland; but carrying away the main-mast, and springing the bowsprit on our passage, were sent home to refit. We afterwards made a second Voyage to Cadiz and Lisbon for money, and on our return were both appointed to the Launceston, designed for the Virginia Station. Captain Percival soon gave up this Ship for a Yacht; when we parted, and Captain John Gell, a most excellent Seaman and Officer, became my Commander. The Launceston was now ordered to receive on board the Flag of my worthy Friend Admiral Durell; who applying for me to the Board, I received the following letter from Mr. Marsh, dated Admiralty, 12th April, 1766:—

SIR,

I am ordered by my Lord Egmont to acquaint you, that you are to be one of Admiral Durell's Lieutenants, and that he has recommended you *in a very particular manner to the Admiral for Promotion.*

We sailed for Spithead, and hoisted the Blue Flag at our fore-top-mast head. The present Sir Robert Calder was First Lieutenant, though junior to both myself, and another Officer, Mr. Nourse. Calder, on his first appointment to the Ship, had been only third; upon which I wrote a letter of remonstrance to Lord Egmont. During our passage the Admiral was taken ill, and died the second day after our arrival at Halifax.—With him I lost such a friend as I never recovered: That Tide, which Shakspeare says is in the affairs of men, now began gradually to ebb, until at last it laid me up, high and dry, in Greenwich Tier.

After the death of Admiral Durell we remained at Virginia, until Commodore Hood took the command on that Station. We had long been off the ground, without heaving down, and our Sheathing was all eat away by the worms; the Commodore therefore ordered us to Halifax. Then returning to our Station, where we remained some time, the Conquestadore sailed for England, and was paid off at Portsmouth.

On the dispute that arose between us and Spain, respecting the Falkland Islands, I was again commissioned for the Conquestadore after remaining about eleven months on half pay, at the request of the Earl of Egmont, who was daily expected to return to the Board. We hoisted her Pendant at Woolwich; and after being stationed at the Nore as a receiving Ship, were commanded by the present Sir Andrew Hammond; who conducted her to the next place of destination, and was superseded by Capt. John Falkingham. I had only been six weeks in the Conquestadore when I experienced another severe loss, by the death of my only friend, Lord Egmont*, on the fourth of Dec. 1770. I now drifted bodily to leeward; and on being paid off, which happened when I had been about half a year on board, I felt myself a complete Wretch, without interest, and without resources.

It was not however the first time in my life. Fortunately my mind was as tough as a piece of old Junk. I e'en therefore went to work resolutely; and wrote to Mr. Stephens for employment, who got me appointed to the Lizard, fitting at Portsmouth for North America, commanded by Captain Charles Inglis. So passing again the Atlantic, I chewed my Quid of bitterness somewhat more sedately at Boston.

Here we wintered under Admiral Montague, whose Flag was on board the Captain. In the spring we sailed to Charlestown; and then coasted along Georgia, and Florida, as far as St. Augustin, about eighty leagues from the Gulf of Florida, or Channel of Bahama. Our Captain frequently landed on the different Islands, to survey the growth, size, and scantling of the Live Oak Trees: we then returned to the Admiral, who ordered us to Rhode Island. There, during the year 1773, I was appointed to command the Gaspee Brig, then fitting at Halifax.

---

* His Lordship was called to the House of Peers, May 7, 1762, by the title of Lord Lovel and Holland, of Enmore, Somersetshire. He was succeeded by his eldest Son, then a Colonel in the Foot Guards.

I made all dispatch to join her, and arrived in the month of June. When I reached Boston, the Admiral gave me his orders to cruise six weeks in that Bay. On my return I was stationed at Rhode Island, where I continued all the summer. In the fall of the year, when my Brig was laid up for the winter season, I suddenly received directions to proceed round to Boston without a moment's loss of time: immediately got her ready, and with much difficulty sailed over the Shoals. But owing to the season of the year, with heavy gales, and a severe frost; the Wind also sometimes at N.W., at others N.E., with great falls of snow, so as not to be able to see the length of the Vessel; we were nine weeks on our passage, which might have been accomplished in two days during summer. However, by perseverance we got safe to Boston, where we remained for the winter; during which we experienced great difficulties, by repeatedly drawing our anchors, and driving down the Harbour; where, if we had not provisions sufficient on board, we must all have perished, although so near the shore. At one of these times our anchors hooked the ground, and brought the Vessel's head to the tide, crushed our windlass to pieces like a bunch of matches, and had nearly hauled out our bows, had we not cut the cable. As soon as the ice broke up, we were warped up by the Active Frigate, and hauled alongside of Long Wharf. Finding the Vessel very leaky, the Admiral ordered us into Three Point Channel: when the Carpenters came to inspect us, her bows were found quite rotten:—this was a very providential circumstance, in favour of the Gaspee's Company of thirty Men; for had we been acquainted with the real state of our Barkie's Bows, we should not have slept quite so easy as we did. She had only been kept afloat by a covering of plank on her bows; and what was more surprising, not above nine months before, the Master Builder of Halifax had reported her sound and fit to run for six or seven years, without requiring any repair of consequence.

The Gaspee being ready for Sea, I was ordered to the Gulf of St. Lawrence, to superintend the Fisheries; and this I found a very pleasant and interesting Service. I generally called at

Halifax on my return, which was in October, for any stores I stood in need of, and thence joined the Admiral at Boston.

And here I beg leave to digress a little. The Admiral had often seen a young gentleman, of the name of * Coffin, very active on board the Merchant Ships, whose father I well knew; and thinking that he would make a good Seaman, the young man's inclination being so decidedly for that way of life, the Admiral sent him with me to try him. Of all the young men I ever had the care of, none answered my expectations equal to *Isaac Coffin*. He pleased me so much, that I took all the pains in my power to make him a good Seaman; and I succeeded to the height of my wishes: for never did I know a young man acquire so much nautical knowledge in so short a time. But when he became of use to me, the Admiral thought proper to remove him. We parted with considerable regret.

In consequence of instructions which I received from the Admiral on the 16th of April, 1774, I sailed from my Station, along the coast of Nova Scotia, into the Gulf of St. Lawrence, to prevent smuggling, and again to superintend the Fisheries. When the season was over, I was to return to Boston, and place myself under the command of Admiral Greaves in the Preston, who directed me to proceed up the Bay of Fundy, between New England and Nova Scotia, and there to cruise during the winter, to prevent the notorious practice of smuggling. This Navigation is the most dangerous that is to be found in America, especially in that inclement season, being a rocky iron-bound Coast. I strictly followed my instructions, running from one port to another; and if I found the Wind shift to the N.E. (when there constantly come on heavy falls of snow, so as not to be able to see half the length of the Vessel,) I was obliged to push for an Harbour. On this Service I continued until the following unfortunate circumstance took place—We were lying in Falmouth Harbour, very near the Town; when, by the neglect of the watch, four men jumped into the Cutter, and made for the shore. I was in my cabin at the time; and hearing the rattling of oars looked out of the windows, con-

---

* See Memoir of this Officer, Vol. XII, page 1.

ceiving their intention was to desert. Upon my coming on deck, with the Master, our muskets loaded, we called to them to return; which they not complying with, I fired, and killed one man. The rest got safe to land, and were received by some hundreds of the inhabitants. I then borrowed a Boat of a Merchant Ship there, and recovered our own, otherwise she would have been hauled on shore and burnt. On the next day the Select Men, as Magistrates, wrote to me, desiring to know what was to be done with the body of John I atty? I offered to send for it, and to bury him according to the custom of the Navy: this however they refused. During the night they hailed; threatening that they would board us with two light Schooners, and execute the whole Crew. I was not alarmed at their threats, being prepared to give them a warm reception: but, as I observed we were lying within a Cable's length of the shore, and the Master having represented to me that they were very busy in an old fort, as he imagined going to mount some guns in it; and that the navigation where we lay was narrow; I thought it necessary to move the Brig a mile lower down, where we had room to work the Vessel, in case of an attack. There we lay very quiet. I then wrote to the Admiral, informing him of every circumstance: but my letters were intercepted, and even published to the enemy, with every addition they could invent; although the Master of a Vessel. who was about sailing to Boston, offered to deliver them to the Admiral himself.

Having therefore this, and other difficulties, to encounter, I ventured to quit my Station without order, and ran for Nantasket Road; where I wrote to the Admiral, apologising for the liberty I had taken, and requesting he would order a Court Martial. The Court assembled; and having tried the Master and myself, we were honourably acquitted. When the Admiral delivered me his order to resume the Command of the Gaspee, he at the same time gave me instructions to write to the Select Men, and inform them, that if they did not deliver up the Deserters, I was empowered to impress every Man I found on the Water. This gave the Inhabitants great uneasiness, as they could not produce the Men; they having all sailed in a new

Vessel for England.—I continued on this very disagreeable Service until the 1st of March, 1775, when, to the joy of all hands, I received orders to resume my old Station in the Gulf of St. Lawrence, and superintend the Fisheries. After moving from place to place, until our provisions ran short, we sailed for Quebec. On my arrival, the Governor, Sir Guy Carleton, informed me, of his having received intelligence, that the Rebels were coming across Lake Champlain to attack the Settlement; that he had ordered two Vessels to be built at St. John's, and armed for the protection of the Colony; and therefore wished me to go and examine them. I immediately sailed up the River to Montreal, where I left the Gaspee; crossed to Lepriere, and then to St. John's, where I found the Vessels in Timbers with no prospect of their being ready in time. The Rebels at that moment were not above twenty or twenty-five miles from me: we made every exertion, and got one launched on the 3d of September, 1775, being by far the nearest finished:—she was called the Royal Savage. We got also another Vessel, intended for a Row Galley, but so badly formed for that Service, that one of the Thames Ballast Lighters would have rowed as fast. The Enemy were at Isle aux Noix, where they had a strong post; and on the 11th we remained all night at Quarters. On the 17th, their Fleet appeared, and anchored at Point Daniel: two Gundolas came down and fired at us, which we returned from our South Redoubt, with shot and shells; this soon made them retreat. On the next day the Gundolas mounted an heavy twelve-pounder, and pointed it at us; we returned it with ten or twelve field-pieces that we had on board. I must observe, that the Royal Savage was not by any means constructed as a Vessel of War, her Decks being arched, like Merchant Vessels, instead of being quite flat: so that when we had occasion to fire, with a little elevation; owing to this arching of the Deck, it was very difficult to bring the gun to an horizontal line; being often obliged to heel the Vessel.

By the 18th of September, 1775, the enemy had cut off our communication with Montreal, and were busily employed in building gun and mortar batteries: the South Redoubt fired several shot and shells in the wood, where we thought they were at work. On the 21st a Batteau drifted from Point Daniel, and we picked her up; soon afterwards another drifted down, which we also took possession of: one man was asleep in it, with two casks of pork, some muskets, and paddles. We cut her down for a Floating Battery, and putting a field six-pounder in her, employed her on different Services. On the 25th the Rebels unmasked a battery of two twelve-pounders on us, from a distance of eight hundred yards on the west side of the River, which we returned: but the shot falling short, Capt. Williams, of the Artillery, from the Redoubt, told us that our fire had no effect. The enemy continued to attack us for above three quarters of an hour afterwards; wounded our mainmast, shot away much of our rigging, and once hit us between Wind and Water. We were therefore under the necessity, as soon as dark, to haul the Vessel on shore. Having stopped the leak, we got her out again before day break, so that the enemy knew not what damage they had done. On the 27th they threw a number of shot and shells, but did us no injury, notwithstanding they were so near us. On the 30th they began again at day light; when a shot came through the bows of the Row Galley, that was fitting alongside, and broke a Shipwright's arm, which occasioned his death. And upon this all refused to work any more in the line of fire. We were thus every day saluted with shot and shells, which sunk the Batteau; one thirteen inch shell came so near us as to gull our whale, and, bursting under water, the pieces struck our bottom. October 11th, the enemy opened a Battery on the east side of the River, which was very narrow: this Battery, when completed, occasioned the reduction of St. Johns, by the number and weight of its calibre; the Royal Savage was soon sunk. November the first, a Flag of Truce came from the enemy to summon us to surrender: Hostilities ceased on the night of the third, and we surrendered, agreeable to Capitulation. As soon as the Batteries were got ready to take all the garrison on board, we proceeded up the River to

their camp, where we remained for sometime : then moved up to l'Isle aux Noix, slept there all night, and in the morning proceeded with a fair Wind to cross Lake Champlain. We arrived shortly at Crown Point, where we rested, and then set off for Ticondaroga. Here we continued several days, at the end of which we were ordered to go to Lake George; crossed it, and landed at the Fort of that name. We lived at this Fort, until conveyances were procured to remove our baggage down to Albany : as for my part, I had only what I carried on my back. Every thing being at length ready, we continued our journey; passed Fort Edward through Serra Toga, crossed the river at Half Moon, and slept one night at Stone Arabia, or new City, as they called it; then embarked in Boats, and arrived at Albany, where we continued until the Congress had fixed upon our destination : The Artillery, and thirteen Seamen, were ordered to pass the River and proceed to the Government of Connecticut. Myself, and the remainder, after many days travelling, came to a village called Canaan, and lodged there several weeks; but as that place could not supply us with such necessaries as we stood in need of, I resolved to write to Governor Trumbull of that Colony, for leave to be moved down to Hartford, or Withersfield, where we could supply ourselves with such things as we wanted. The Governor was so obliging as to give orders for my removal, and the other Officers, to Withersfield; a beautiful village on the side of Connecticut River. We remained in it about fifteen months, when we were exchanged and sent to New York. My men were then put on board such Ships as the Admiral, Lord Howe, appointed: not one of them ever deserted, though often tempted. I am sorry to say this was not the case with the Soldiers, many of whom were left behind. I took passage for England in a Transport. On my arrival in town, I informed the Admiralty of my return from Captivity; at the same time claiming, as I thought, my right, promotion : but receiving no answer, I waited on Lord Sandwich, and presented him the following
MEMORIAL OF MY SERVICES—

MEMORIAL OF LIEUTENANT WILLIAM HUNTER, LATE COMMANDER OF HIS MAJESTY'S BRIG GASPEE, TAKEN BY THE REBELS IN THE RIVER ST. LAWRENCE, IN THE YEAR 1775,

Sheweth,

That your Memorialist came into the Navy the fourth of June, 1755, and served in the Ships whose names* are undermentioned, in the Channel Service, America, and the West Indies, during the War, and since the Peace.

That your Memorialist was at (and had an active part allotted him in) the reduction of the following Places ; viz. *Cape Breton, Quebec, Montreal, Dominica, Martinico* with its Dependencies, and the *Havana.*

That your Memorialist was made an Officer the 24th of January, 1760, soon after he came home in the Rodney Cutter with an Express from Quebec ; and has ever since been almost constantly employed on Foreign Service.

That your Memorialist was taken Prisoner by the Rebels with the Garrison of St. John's, in Canada, the third of November, 1775 ; where he had been at the request of General Carleton, as will appear by Memorials presented some time ago to your Lordship and the Board ; and was detained Prisoner for fifteen Months : which unlucky event deprived him of the command of the Gaspee, with the loss of his Property then on board, as well as the loss of his time.

That Mr. Ezekiel Williams, Sheriff of the County of Hartford, before your Memorialist was released by exchange, extorted from him Bills at an exorbitant rate for the subsistence they allowed him while he was a Prisoner ; notwithstanding they had declared from the beginning, that the Congress had given orders for two Dollars a week being allowed to each Officer.

That your Memorialist lost all his friends by the death of the late Earl of Egmont, Thomas Orby Hunter, Esq. and Admiral Durell, whose Lieutenant he was when appointed to the Command in North America.

Your Memorialist humbly hopes, having lost his other Friends, that your Lordship will take his Services, Sufferings, and Losses into consideration ; and, as he is now ready to serve, that you will give him Promotion as has been done for those who were

---

* Bedford.   Ramillies.   Conquestadore.
Princess Amelia.   Tweed.   Lizard.
Rodney Cutter.   Aquilon.   Gaspee.
Sutherland.   Launceston.

his junior Officers, and as such employed in Canada, where they did not show more zeal to promote his Majesty's Service, nor had any superior claim to urge, than your Memorialist : who further begs leave to remind your Lordship, that Mr. Chace, who commanded the Gaspee when taken from the Enemy, has been promoted to the rank of Lieutenant in England.

To the Right Hon.
The Earl of Sandwich.

When his Lordship had looked it over, he merely said, *You may send one into the Board!* I did so; but without any effect. I therefore became heartily sick of applying any more; and felt it very degrading to dance attendance, and fee old Cerberus, when my Services might have claimed attention. But being still fond of a Profession I had for such a number of years been employed in, I could not endure an idle life, or change it for another. So I at length waited again on Lord Sandwich, and tendered my Services, wherever he might think proper. He looked at the list, remarked *that I was an old Officer;* and then replied, *We will employ you still.* Flattering myself, from some hints he gave me, that I might expect Promotion, I the next morning received a note from the Admiralty, informing me there was a Commission, waiting at the Office, to take up. To my astonishment and surprise, it was only as *Second Lieutenant* of the Cumberland, Captain Joseph Peyton. After having passed between 23 and 24 years in actual Service as an Officer, I conceived this to be both degrading and unjust; more especially as I had been employed in Services under the Admiral, where great responsibility was required. However, as I was always zealous for the welfare of my Country, and very fond of my Profession, I took up my Commission, and repaired to the Ship; and I must acknowledge that I never sailed with a more zealous Commander. But he was not a pleasant Officer to serve under; his temper being very petulant and warm: yet at the same time he was the most upright, honourable man I ever knew. The First Lieutenant not having joined, I did all in my power with the few Men I could muster to forward my Captain's wishes; and in a short time had the Cumberland ready for Spithead; when the First Lieut. came on board and we were placed under the command of Admiral Keppel. As soon as the Fleet was collected we sailed on the Channel Service, and saw the French Fleet; but could not bring them to action until the morning, when the Wind shifted so as to enable our Fleet to fetch them. Further particulars of that ever memorable day I leave to better judges. All I shall say is, that the Admiral was brought to trial and honourably acquitted. We next cruised under the command of Sir Charles Hardy, with the Fleet. On our return to Portsmouth I received a letter that informed me of my Father's death.

This event quite unmanned me! Until I lost my worthy Father, though I sincerely loved him, I had never been sufficiently sensible of what I should feel when he was no more. Often, amidst perils and agitation of my mind, I felt relief, though far distant, by knowing I had a Father—And if my Reader cannot understand my sensations in this respect, I, alas! have not words to express them.

I wrote to be superseded, and quitted a Ship as well conditioned as any in the Navy. I then went into the North, and after a few months, returned to London, bringing with me credentials from the Lord Provost and Magistrates of Edinburgh, recommending me in the strongest manner to Sir Lawrence Dundas, their Member; requesting him to use all his influence with the First Lord of the Admiralty to get me promoted: but these letters were of no kind of service. I was therefore thrown in the back ground again: but, being determined to be employed, accepted of an appointment to the Impress service in London, through the interest of my friend Mr. James Dyson, Solicitor of the Admiralty; and on this duty I continued for the war, viz. two years and a month: That being concluded, I returned for thirteen months to Scotland, with two * children on my half pay, which amounted to 54l. per annum.

---

* Penelope, one of the daughters of Lieutenant Hunter, was married to Lieutenant H. Kent, Jan. 22, 1794. This brave Officer was employed under the Transport Board for several years; and after having performed many Voyages, to the Continent, North America, and the West Indies, he lost his life in Egypt when commanding his Majesty's Ship Dover, leaving his wife with three young female children.—*Note by the Editor.*

Thus finishes my professional Career; for when the gallant veteran Earl Howe was placed at the head of The Board, my younger Brother Captain John Hunter, of the Royal Navy, late Governor of New South Wales, applied to him, to appoint me Lieutenant of the Royal Hospital of GREENWICH, in the room of Lieutenant Larcock deceased. His Lordship willingly complied, and I accordingly succeeded to Lieutenant Larcock's Birth on the 15th of October, 1787, satisfied and happy. Here, after plowing that turbulent and inconstant element the Ocean for forty-four years, I have since led a life, which if it affords but little variety, is not exposed to Uncertainty, or Dependence. Ambition, indeed, once flattered me I should have risen higher in my Profession; and there have been times that I felt my Services merited Promotion. When I have heard, as, thank God! I have lately often done, the shout of Victory, I rode uneasy at my Moorings; and experienced a pang, that after so many years of Service I should in my old age be unknown, and unnoticed: But the Squall never lasted long. Amidst all my Fortunes I have preserved that Sheet Anchor which no Man taketh from me—*A firm belief in an overruling Providence, and a constant reliance upon* HIM WHO STILLED THE WAVES.

Whilst this Life was in the press the following corrections have been received from Lieutenant Hunter—

In some of the impression of the first sheet (p. 3, lines 10 and 11) an error was made in the punctuation. It should have been, " We sailed through the Downs with a fair Wind; off Beachy, or as Seamen call it the Seven Cliffs, it took us a-head."

Page 3, line 19. *For* little dead wood, *read* much dead wood.
Page 4, line 16. *For* our Men *read* their Men.
Page 8, line 21. In some of the impression, *for* Cleyne, *read* Chyne.
Page 15, line 14. The Bedford was not dismasted, though said to have been so in all the printed narratives that have appeared. Her Masts were saved by knocking out the wedges.

NAVAL ANECDOTES,
COMMERCIAL HINTS, RECOLLECTIONS, &c.

NANTES IN GURGITE VASTO.

NAVIGATION OF THE THAMES.

IN the Regulations recently issued on this subject, it is ordered,

" That the Colours of all Foreign Vessels are to be hoisted immediately on their entering Bugby's Hole; to remain up till they arrive at their appointed Stations. The Colours are likewise to be hoisted when the Vessel leaves her moorings on going down the River.

" That all Commanders of Foreign Vessels do muster their Crew every evening at sun-set; and not suffer any of them to go on shore after that time till sun-rise: and in case any of their People desert, or are discharged, immediate information must be sent to the London Schooner, off Greenwich.

" That all Pilots, or Watermen, are expressly directed not to move any Foreign Vessel between London Bridge and Bugby's Hole, after dark in the evening, till sun-rise the next morning, ander any pretence whatever.

" That all Coal and other Barges pass up and down the River singly, (not lashed together,) with one able Man at least in each Craft; and to continue constantly on board whilst on duty.

" That Ships letting go an anchor in the stream to check them n their Births, shall not let it remain there longer than the following slack water, unless by permission.

" That no Ship, loaded in the whole, or in part with timber, nemp, pitch, tar, rosin, or other Naval Stores, be permitted to come or lie above Limehouse Hole, to discharge.

" That all Vessels shall strike their yards and top-masts vithin six hours after they shall respectively have arrived at their noorings; and continue so struck till within forty-eight hours of heir departure, between the 21st of September and the 21st of March following.

" That no Vessel whatever, after having made fast to her Staon, must remove without permission from the Harbour Master n duty.

" That no Ship or Vessel shall intersect any tier, but must ake the outside birth of any Ship in the Stream.

THE *Rotterdam Courant*, of the 18th November, 1804, contained this singular Letter.

" We have been desired to insert the following, addressed to the Conductor of the *Delft Courant*:—I have seen, with the utmost surprise, in your *Courant* of the 9th inst. a tedious and impudent article, inserted by you, as an extract of a letter from an English Officer on board the Chiffone Frigate. I have also seen with no less astonishment, that you, in inserting that account, have taken the trouble to alter the false spelling of my name, which is well known to you; and have in many other respects entirely adopted the brutal abuse of that calumniator from the Thames, without explaining circumstances full as well known to you as my name; unless it be possible that you are ignorant of the Naval Actions I have fought off St. Domingo and Teneriffe; and that, in the latter of these actions, I wrung NELSON's sword out of his hand, and made myself master of it—a trophy, which surely no man, who only fights upon paper, can acquire . . . . but, however this may be, it ill becomes a Batavian newswriter to pretend not to know, that I, on the 19th of September, 1803, with the Schooner Unie, carrying only four small guns, fought an action with the English Cutter the Princess Augusta, carrying 14 guns, eight-pounders, which only saved herself by flight, from being captured by boarding, for which I was already disposing my Crew. Further, that I, on the 3d of May last, in the Corvette de Bataufche Trouw, carrying 18 guns, fought upwards of three hours, the British Frigate the Amethyst, of 46 guns, of heavier metal than mine, in such a manner, that she was obliged to bend all her sails, and to sheer off: nor would she have escaped even then, but for all the rigging and canvas of my Corvette being so cut, that it was impossible to pursue the English Frigate, and to take her by boarding, as they had already began to prepare to surrender and strike their colours, of which there is evidence extant.

It is incredible, Mynheer, that any English Officer, who was in the latitude where this action was fought, and even in the port which the said English Frigate was obliged to enter, in order to repair, and where it appeared, beyond contradiction, that she had lost upwards of eighty men, should dare to put me upon a level with the heroes of the quill, whose field of battle is a sheet of paper, and their arms a pen; who receiving the wages of venality, are directed by vice only.

Therefore Mynheer, I call upon you to inform me of the name of the person who signed this pretended letter, and the person or persons who gave it you, or an extract from the same; otherwise I must consider and treat yourself as the author of this piece of impudence, and as the insertion of an article which no newswriter, who values a good name, would ever permit himself to propagate.

I request, moreover, that my present letter be inserted in length in the next number of your Paper. I think I may conclude that you will not refuse me this satisfaction, and thereby prevent my being obliged to adopt less pleasant measures, to show you what a public writer owes to himself and to his own country, as well as to its defenders."

Amsterdam, Oct. 10th, 1804.   (Signed)   "ST. FAUST."

METALLIC RIGGING.

A PATENT has been obtained, by Mr. Slater, of Huddersfield, for manufacturing cables, shrouds, stays, and other articles, for the rigging of Ships, of materials never before used for the purpose.

" My invention, says the patentee, consists in the substitution of metals in lieu of hemp in the fabrication of cables, shrouds, stays, and other articles for the rigging of Ships, which is to be applied in the form of chain-work, and which every workman in chain-work knows how to apply without farther instructions."—He then adds, that he claims no discovery in the construction of chains, but in the application of them to the rigging of Ships, of whatever form, metal, or metallic substance, they may be constructed.

Observations.—This invention is intended chiefly for standing-rigging; and the links of the chains are made of a short oval form, thick in proportion to their size, and every two nearly touching in the centre of the third, in which they are inserted. The weight of the different articles to be the same as that of the cordage now in use. The mast-heads are to be surrounded with a plate of rolled iron or copper to keep the shrouds from chafing. One leg of a pair of shrouds is to be received through a large link in the other, just at the place where the present kind are seized; and they are to be set up with dead-eyes and lanniards, as in the present manner. The fore-stays are to be hooked where they are now seized, and the back-stays fitted in the same manner as the shrouds.

The advantages are :—1. The duration of one suit of rigging would exceed that of any Ship made of the best materials. 2. As there would be no sensible stretching, it would obviate a serious inconvenience, by which many a Ship has lost her masts, and ultimately both cargo and hull; as it is often impossible to set the shrouds up in a heavy gale, or even to secure them in any manner that will preserve the masts. 3. This substitute for cordage will never require any mechanical stretching, and will be always pliant and easy to handle. 4. In time of action this kind of rigging will be much less liable to be cut with shot, from its greater cohesion, elasticity, and slipperiness; and, in case of its being cut, may be much more easily repaired with string, which will last during the action, and afterwards, by a new link or links. 5. This kind of rigging has a much lighter and more beautiful appearance to the eye; and, when blacked with lamp black and pitch, is effectually preserved from rust. The first cost is not much greater than of that now in use, and, when worn out, it can be re-manufactured; of course, the saving to this country would be immense, if it were adopted in the British Navy.

Such are the advantages which the patentee describes as resulting from the application of chain-work to the rigging of Ships. He is, however, aware it may be objected that the metal of which the chains are composed will have a tendency to attract the electric fluid. In answering this objection, he observes, and justly, that when the fluid does strike the metal, it will follow every turn it makes till it reaches the surface of the earth or water, which is a strong reason for the adoption of metallic rigging, as in the case of a Ship being struck with lightning, the shrouds having small appendages to let down, it would be easily conducted into the water without injury to the Crew, Ship, or cargo, except a man happened to be on the shrouds where, or leading from where it fell. And it is presumed, that accidents of this kind would more seldom happen than they even do at present, as the men upon deck, in the tops, and on the yards, would be almost entirely secure; and in climates where the surrounding atmosphere is pregnant with the electric fluid, no accumulation could take place, as the rigging would be continually conducting it harmless to the surface, in the same manner as a chain suspended from the conductor of an electrical machine, and resting on the ground, would prevent a person touching it from receiving a shock. The chain-work may be made of iron or copper.

BUTTON WORN BY THE OFFICERS AT GREENWICH HOSPITAL*.

BY an order of King William III, this button was first worn on the Uniform of the Officers of Greenwich Hospital, and represents a Naval Crown.

---

* An Engraving of this Button is under the Portrait of Lieutenant Hunter, prefixed to his Memoir.

EXHORTATIONS AND INJUNCTIONS TO THE SHIP'S COMPANY
OF HIS MAJESTY'S SHIP DIADEM.

AS every well-disposed Sailor must be convinced, that neither comfort nor happiness can exist in a dirty, disorderly Ship, Sir Home Popham hopes, that the Ship's Company will consider themselves interested in keeping the Ship clean, and stimulating each other to do the duty of their respective Stations with cheerfulnes and alacrity. It will always be his most anxious wish to study their comfort, and promote their happiness, by every mode in his power, consistent with the rules of the Service; in granting leave at a proper time, or any other indulgence that can be pointed out; and they may rest satisfied, that the most rigid attention will be paid to each article of provision, and the greatest care taken of the sick; but he expects from the Ship's Company—

The readiest obedience to all orders given by their superior Officers.

1. That the instant the hands are called, they are to come up without a moment's loss of time.
2. That they finish every point of duty with the greatest alacrity.
3. That while it is carrying on, they observe the strictest silence.
4. That they keep themselves clean, sober, and honest.
5. That they are never to throw any dirt or slops out of the ports, or over the sides; and whenever they see any yarns about the rigging, they are to pick them off.
6. That they endeavour to discover skulkers and thieves.
7. That they are neither to swear, or use any blackguard expressions, unworthy a British Sailor.
8. That they are neither to gamble, to fight, or to quarrel.
9. That they study as much as possible the credit of the Ship, particularly on detached Service.
10. That every Sunday they are dressed in their best clothes for muster and prayers; and that at church service they behave themselves devoutly, and as becometh brave Seamen and good Christians.

CHRONOMETRICAL REGULATION.

MR. JAMISON, time-piece-maker to the Commissioners of the Navy, has invented a machine, whereby the error of a time-keeper may be ascertained at Sea without observation. The great purpose of this invention is to prove whether the chronometer of a watch has varied from its given rate at the Royal Observatory, or any other place, the situation of which is known, so that the navigator will have the same advantage of comparison as he would by a regulator on shore.

CORRESPONDENCE.

SIR,

YOU having done me the honour to insert in your NAVAL CHRONICLE my proposals for giving Vessels another form, and rigging them in a manner different from the present mode, I am induced to solicit a further extension of your kindness, and beg once more to occupy a page of your interesting Publication.

Had the Venerable, which was lately lost in Torbay, been constructed something like the Sketch given in your CHRONICLE of November last, I flatter myself she would not have been cast away. It seems it was necessary for that Ship, in working out of Torbay, to stand on towards the Brixham side, until she approached so close to the land, that, when she came to be put about, the rocks to the leeward were so near, if the Vessel missed stays, she must drive on them, there not being sufficient room to wear—accordingly, she missed stays, drove on the rocks, and was lost*.

Now with the utmost diffidence, for I know very little of the practical part of Seamanship, I will ask those who do, whether, if that Ship, *formed and rigged even as she was*, with the following additions, might not have been brought safe out of such a dangerous situation? Had there been a gaft placed on the foreside of the fore-mast, just above the fore-yard; the same on the main and mizen masts, each of them supporting a Schooner-like sail; and the same on the foreside of the top-masts. If these sails, when the Ship was falling off, after missing stays, could have been immediately spread, all the other sails clewed up, and furled as fast as possible; the yards braced in such a manner as to have the least power in pressing the Ship to leeward; the rudder placed in a direct line with the keel; and the Ship had been provided with a light, yet wide rudder, hung to the stern, so contrived as to have been turned back against it. Had the Ship been thus equipped, she might then, in my opinion, have sailed back stern foremost, have cleared the rocks, and have been brought to safe anchorage in the middle of the Bay. I am aware that it may be thought, the draught of water abaft being so much superior to that forward, the Vessel would not answer the helm at the bows; yet by a judicious management of the sails, the Ship might have been kept on the wind, stern foremost for some

---

* I do not know that this was the exact situation of this Ship, but from what I read in the Papers, it appeared to be something like it.

time, and probably the rudder at the stern-post would have assisted in doing it: by being turned in a contrary direction to which it is usually moved, to answer the same purposes. Ships may be provided with sails in the manner above described, with another of a jib-like shape, from the taffrel to the mizen-masthead; and when they are imbayed, and it becomes necessary to work to windward, and tack often, those gafts and sails might be got up, before they get under weigh, and ready to be used in case of necessity. Suppose a Ship thus provided, and in the situation before mentioned, probably if the sea ran high, and there was reason to fear the Ship might miss stays, it would be the best way not to attempt it; but throw all the sails aback, and instantly set the Schooner sails, &c. and the moment the Ship's head-way is stopt, to trace round the yards, and furl the sails. By adopting this method, she might make less lee-way, before her motion, stern first, commenced, than if she had failed in stays: but both should be tried, and that mode abided by, in extreme peril, which causes the Ship to drive least to leeward; for it might so happen that a few feet to windward might save a fine Ship and the lives of some hundreds of brave Men. The lower stay-sails may in all likelihood be made useful sails in going stern first; by carrying the sheets to the weather gun-wale, but the leech rope must be very strong. Experience would soon make Sailors masters of this kind of sailing.

To the proposal for partitioning Vessels, to render them less liable to sink, there appears to me to be two principal objections. First, If the bulkheads were to be firmly fixed to the sides and floor timbers, when the Ship strained much, in carrying sail, or in a heavy Sea, the seams of the planks might open so wide, as to frustrate the ends for which they were erected. Secondly, Such partitions firmly fastened, might prevent the Ship from sailing so fast as others. I have been informed a Vessel sails the faster for being loose. Thus the chief art seems to lie in contriving a bulkhead that will stop water, and not bind the Vessel tighter together than usual;—and this I imagine may easily be accomplished. I shall say nothing of the manner in which I conceive it should be formed, as able mechanics must be better qualified for the task.

Llwyn, 19*th Dec.* 1804. GEORGE MATTHEW.

ERRATA.

In Vol. XII, page 296, 24th line from the top, after the word expense add a semicolon, and for *than* read *then*.

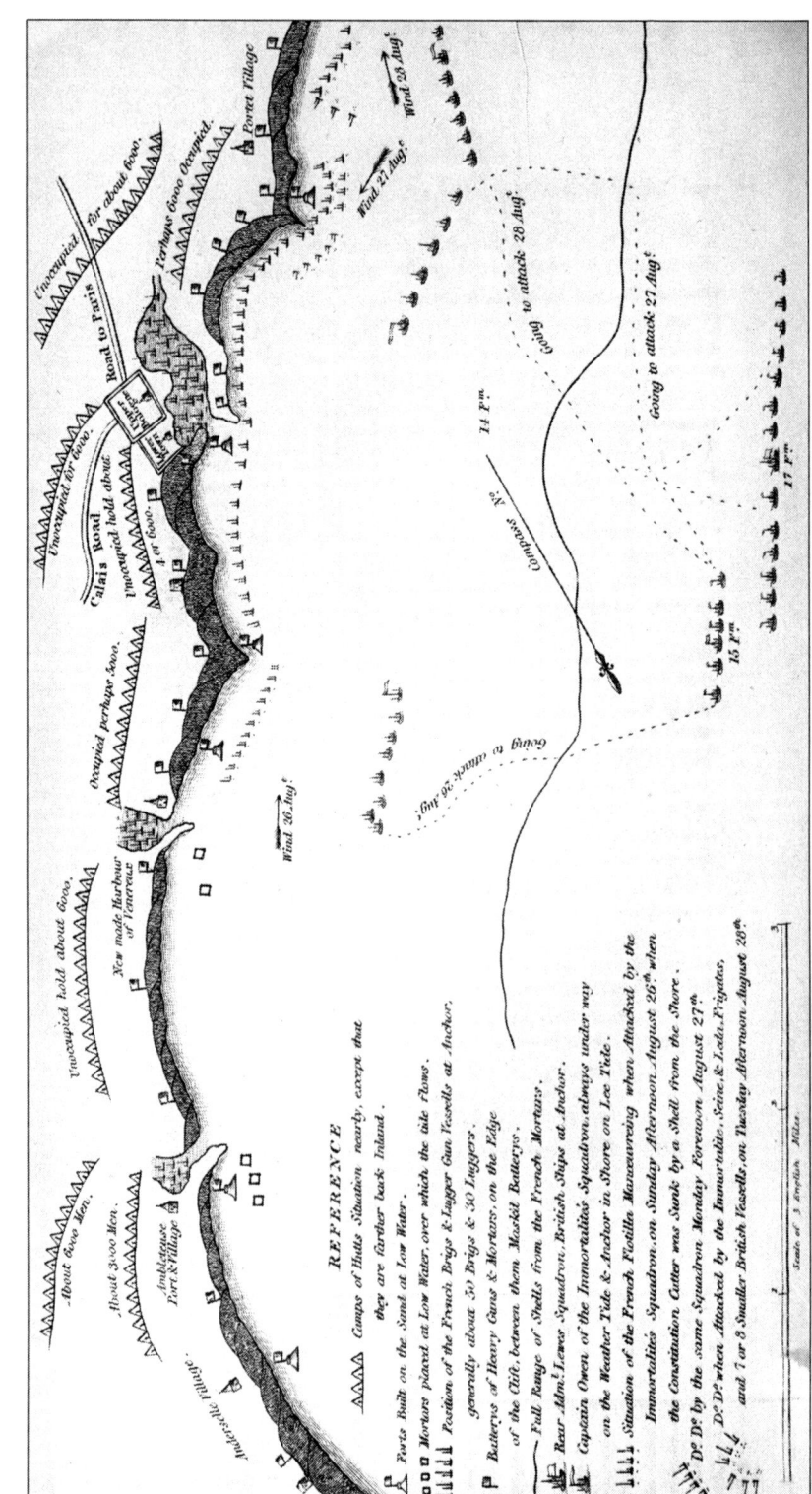

PLATE CLXIX.

THE following letter was written by an Officer belonging to the Fury, to his friend in London, who has transmitted it for insertion in the NAVAL CHRONICLE.

MY DEAR FRIEND, *Fury, Sheerness, Sept.* 3, 1804.

I shall most readily comply with your request, in giving you some farther accounts of our operations at Boulogne, which I will accompany with a rough sketch; my draft you are not to criticise, as it is sent only to give you some little idea of the place; and as you say you cannot go to see Boulogne, I send something like it to you. I took the angles to amuse myself; and if it amuses you a little, I owe it you for your obliging attention. I see your newspapers are all filled with accounts of the French Gunboats beginning their operations by an attack on our Squadron— no such thing; I believe they will never be caught at that work; however, on Sunday, August 26, in the evening about four, the Brigs and some few Luggers got under weigh, I suppose to *manœuvre dans la rade en face des Anglois*, and worked to windward, between Boulogne and Vernuel, by way, I have no doubt, of decoying our Vessels under their tremendous Batteries, as they know well whenever they make the slightest movement the Immortalité's Squadron always annoys them; (the Sailors call them the fire eaters' Squad.) The French Gun-brigs never stood half gun-shot out, and the moment they saw our little Squadron dash in, they stood in, and the whole time that our Vessels were firing at them they kept as close down along shore as possible, and in as little water as could float them, returning to their secure anchorage. Our Squadron was the Immortalité Frigate, 36 guns, Harpy, 18 guns, three Gun-vessels, and a Cutter. Theirs, *sixty* Brigs, *thirty* Luggers, and *all the Batteries* within range. A shell from the shore sunk the Constitution Cutter, without other loss, as all were taken out by the Boats of the Fleet; the Harpy was also struck by one, which killed a man and sprung one beam, but she still remained off Boulogne. On Monday, the 27th, many of their Brigs got under weigh again, and worked down by short tacks against a light westerly Wind to Portet, and as soon as the Immortalité's Squadron showed their head toward them, they stood back close along shore to their anchorage, our Vessels firing and receiving the fire of the Batteries as they passed them. A few shot struck our Vessels, with no other injury than to wound the bowsprit of the Bruizer Gun-brig. On Tuesday, about 14 or 15 Brigs only weighed, with a light westerly Wind, and worked down beyond Portet, with the latter part of the ebb, when the Wind changed against them. Our Ships this day lay longer at anchor in hopes to entice them to venture out of their leading strings. The Immortalité, Seine, and Leda Frigates, with seven or eight other smaller Vessels, weighed, and came on them a little before they got quite close to their shore, although well under their Batteries, and I should suppose they must have suffered most on that day (the result of which I did not hear, having gone up off Calais.) Several times the whole of these Brigs had nothing to oppose them but a Gun-brig *(English)*; they however never ventured the least out to give battle. The sight on the Sunday was beautiful beyond description; the whole range of clifts was covered with Soldiers, Bourgeois, and women, to view the action; their Brigs fired but little, but the whole coast seemed a continued fire; they no doubt expected John *Anglois* to take the bull by the horns, for their Batteries were all prepared, and even began before our Ships got within range, and fired also after they were without, and when their Brigs were safe, they fired from them a great while, I suppose as a *feu de joie* on having sunk an English Cutter. On the Wednesday they lay fast, being calm. On Thursday came on a top-gallant-breeze at low water, and I believe they were very glad when the tide would admit of their taking shelter in their own ports, and we than stand for ours. On the Monday, August 27, they had more Vessels out than ever before, 69 Brigs, two Sloops, and 110 Luggers, from Boulogne and Vimereux. This thinned the harbour of Boulogne so much, that only small Vessels seemed to remain, though I have no doubt they have full 600, and some of them very small. The Luggers and some few Brigs went in that night, as they are very cautious of keeping more out than will conveniently go in in one tide; generally about 50 Brigs and 30 Luggers. The Brigs have many of them wheels in their chains, either for field pieces or waggons. The late actions rather more confirm me in opinion that *one* of our *larger* Vessels would sink the *whole* of their *Flotilla*, and I almost think either of our Frigates would do for them; if they can be kept from boarding, any one of them would destroy them; and their Brigs are too heavy, as well as the greater part of the Luggers, to row across the Channel in a calm. I believe *Emperor* NAP. must have been at Boulogne on the Sunday, if not on all the days of action, and I think he has seen (if so) sufficient to convince a *reasonable* man of the impracticability of succeeding in bringing over an army in those small craft. Yet I think he trusts in an attempt by his Brest Fleet, or a division of it, evading our Channel Fleet, and coming up Channel to Boulogne, and whilst their Ships are engaging our Ships, make the attempt with his Flotilla; even this would be thought madness by another man, yet some such scheme must be in his head, or he can have no idea at all of getting them over.

The French Troops quartered in their camps are constantly employed about their harbours of Ambleteuse and Vimereux, and I judge from the length of time they have been at them that they cannot make them answer their expectations, as they have not more than 30 or 40 Luggers in all. The Fury is come to Sheerness to take out her mortars; whether they are going to convert her to a Sloop of War I do not know, being just anchored only.

Yours sincerely, &c.

NAVAL LITERATURE.

WE are happy to announce to our Readers that Mr. M'ARTHUR's original Work on *Naval Courts Martial*, which has been several years out of print, is now in the press of Mr. Strahan, the King's printer, and will make its appearance in the month of February. We understand that the plan of the work is entirely changed, and contains the *principles* and *practice* of *Military Courts Martial* as well as *Naval*; and which must be extremely interesting to both Services at the present crisis. The author has not only traced the institution of *Naval* and *Military Laws* to their origin and first principles; but he has also illustrated all doubtful cases by the received practice and usage in the *Naval* and *Military Services*, as well as by the Common and Statute law of England, and the practice of civil and criminal Courts, with the coincidence and variance in *Naval* and *Military* laws, the forms preparatory to trial, rules of evidence, and proceedings of Courts Martial to judgment and execution. The work has also an invaluable Appendix, of the most approved practical forms and precedents, with the opinions of learned Counsel, more especially of his Majesty's law Officers, and the Judge Advocate General, on all remarkable cases in both Services for the last fifty years: and to which is added an interesting chronological list of trials by Courts Martial in the Navy, under the existing laws, namely, since the year 1750, specifying the nature of offences and purport of sentences, thereby exhibiting a scale of Military crimes and punishments. The whole forming a complete Code of Naval and Military Jurisprudence; and it may justly be considered a book of authority and reference, adapted as well to the library of the Lawyer, as to that of the Naval and Military profession *."

---

* The work in its original and comparatively imperfect form has been often quoted in the Courts of Law; and it was first noticed the very week of its publication, June 1792, in the cause tried before Lord Loughborough, Common Pleas, Sergeant Grant *v.* Sir *Charles Gould,* then Judge Advocate General.

CORRECT RELATION OF SHIPWRECKS.

[Continued from Vol. XII, page 480.]

No. VIII.

Ha! total Night, and Horror, here preside;
My stunn'd ear tingles to the whizzing tide;
It is their funeral knell! and gliding near,
Methinks the phantoms of the Dead appear.
But lo! emerging from the watery grave,
Again they float incumbent on the wave;
Again the dismal prospect opens round,
The wreck, the shore, the dying, and the drown'd.

FALCONER.

LOSS OF THE SEVERN.

THE most detailed account of the loss of his Majesty's Ship Severn, commanded by Commodore d'Auvergne, Prince of Bouillon, which has come to hand, is contained in the following letter from Guernsey, dated on the 26th of December, 1804:—

It was noticed some days since, that the Severn, lying in Grouville Bay, had suffered very much in a heavy gale of Wind; that she drifted, touched on a rock, and injured her bottom, broke her rudder, and one fluke of her sheet anchor, which was supposed not to have been a good one. At the first it was intended that she should have gone to England to be repaired. Unfortunately she did not; and a violent gale of Wind with severe frost set in from N.E., which blew directly on shore—a shore without shelter, and full of dangerous rocks. Wednesday night, the 19th instant, at one o'clock, she cut away her main-mast: next morning her mizen.—About twelve o'clock she was seen driving on shore, having parted all her anchors. Never was a more anxious scene. The tide was out, which left a strand of near a mile from the redoubts. Here were assembled in fearful agitation all the military in barracks at Grouville, consisting of 1500 men, besides some of the inhabitants of the island. Among these was Commodore the Duke de Bouillon. He was obliged to witness the fate of his Ship. Almost close on the sands, she was seen drifting on the sunken and craggy points of a rock. Every exertion was made by the Commander on board, Lieutenant d'Auvergne, (brother to the Prince,) to turn her head off. It was truly distressing to see the unavailing efforts made to get up something of a sail to the point of the foremast that was standing. As she came near the rock the terror of the spectators increased. Insensible to the most piercing cold and violence of the storm, and up to their knees in water, they stood holding their hands out to the people on board, so near did the Ship drift, as if they could catch and save them; while she continued firing gun after gun for assistance that she could not receive. Such was the fury of the Wind and Waves, that inevitable destruction seemed to await the unfortunate Crew. By the uncommon exertions of the military, some Boats were got, and dragged along the sands with great difficulty, and then attempted to be, in despite of the elements, forced to Sea. Officers and Men were seen up to their waists in water, striving in this virtuous contest who should arrive with the succours first, but all in vain. The Boats were obliged to return from many vain attempts to reach the Ship, which was now fast on the rock. In this dreadful suspense two Boats from the Alcmene, who rode out the storm and were to windward, reached the Severn. Ropes were got to the shore, and by five in the evening every creature (above three hundred) were landed in safety. One man only remained on board, and would not, it is said, quit the Ship. About eleven o'clock at night she got off the rock, and the spring tide carried her close in to the shore. Next day (Friday) the Wind continued almost as fierce and cold as before. Parties from the 18th and 69th, to the amount of 300 men, were employed all day in getting her stores out. Saturday the same. She is now quite a wreck, and lies, when the tide is out, quite dry. It is not supposed that she ever can be got off. It was very fortunate that, in all this disastrous period, no life was lost, nor did any accident happen to the men: they are mostly lodged in an empty barrack at Grouville.—During the storm a Cutter was drove on shore, and was near being lost. Considerable fears were entertained for the Alcmene; she, however, rode out the storm; and on Saturday, the weather being moderate, she got round to St. Hilliar's.

LOSS OF THE TARTARUS.

Particulars of the Loss of his Majesty's Ship Tartarus, Captain WITHERS, *off Margate, on the 20th Dec.* 1804.

" WE had rode out in safety the heavy gale of the 19th ult.; but, on the 20th, at six in the evening, a heavy squall parted our cable, and drove us upon those dangerous sands in Margate Roads, from which no Ship was ever known to be saved.

" Our signals of distress were heard at Margate; but it being then low water, no Boats could get off to our assistance till about twelve o'clock, when two Luggers were manned with twelve men each (the Lord Nelson and Queen), which, after encountering a tremendous Sea, with a violent gale from E.N.E., got, about one o'clock, near the Tartarus; but, on account of the heavy surf, could not approach the Ship, without the risk of being immediately sunk; they were therefore obliged to anchor at some little distance, within two fathoms water. The Tartarus lowered one of her Boats, into which were put the sick, the women, and children, to the number of 20; but the Boat, in endeavouring to reach one of the Luggers (the Lord Nelson), grounded on the sand, and the people gave themselves up for lost. The Queen, at the imminent hazard of the lives of her own people, immediately slipped her cable, and ran alongside the Boat, in six feet water, and had the good fortune to save the whole. During this, another Boat was sent off from the Ship with prisoners, which reached the Lord Nelson in safety. A rope was carried with her to draw her back to the Ship; but she was dashed to pieces in the attempt. Another (the only remaining Boat) was then lowered from the Ship, with two men in it, and immediately sunk; one of the men was drowned, and the other, with great difficulty, saved.

" In this situation, it being impossible for the Luggers to approach the Ship, the Captain directed them to return to Margate with those they had saved, and to endeavour to procure further assistance. This was almost three o'clock, and it was not till two o'clock of the afternoon of the next day, Friday, (during the whole of which time the Ship was momentarily expected to fall on her beam ends,) that the Luggers were able to return with two other Boats. The weather having moderated, they laid themselves alongside of us, and took out the remainder of the Crew, to the number of seventy, who were obliged to be slung by ropes from the yard-arms into the Boats.

" Soon after we left the Ship, she fell on her beam-ends, and the Sea made a fair breach over her. Next morning nothing was to be seen but her masts."

LOSS OF THE SPEEDY.

THE subjoined account of the supposed loss of the Speedy Schooner, in his Majesty's Service, on the Lake Ontario, is copied from the *Upper Canada Gazette* of the 3d of Nov. 1804 :—

The Speedy, Capt. Paxton, left this port on Sunday evening, the 7th of October last, with a moderate breeze from the N.W., for Presque Isle, and was descried off that island on the Monday following, before dark, when preparations were made for the reception of the Passengers; but the Wind coming round to the N.E., it blew with such violence as rendered it impossible for her to enter the Harbour, and very shortly after she disappeared. A large fire was then kindled on shore as a guide to the Vessel during the night; but she has not been seen or heard of; and it is with the most painful sensations we have to say, we fear she is entirely lost. Inquiry, we understand, has been made at almost every part on the Lake, but without effect; and it is concluded that this unfortunate Vessel must have upset, or foundered. It is reported, that several articles, such as the compass box, hen-coop, and mast, known to have belonged to this Vessel, have been picked up on the opposite side of the Lake. The Passengers on board the ill-fated Speedy, as near as we can recollect, were, Mr. Justice Cochrane, Robert J. D. Gray, Esq. Solicitor General, and Member of the House of Assembly; Angus Macdonnell, Esq. Advocate, also a Member of the House of Assembly; Mr. Jacob Herchmen, Merchant; Mr. John Slegman, Surveyor; Mr. George Cowan, Indian Interpreter; James Ruggles, Esq.; Mr. Anderson, Student of Law; Mr. John Fisk, High Constable; all of this place. The above gentlemen were proceeding to the district of Newcastle, in order to hold the Circuit, and for the trial of an Indian (also on board the Speedy) for the murder of John Sharp, late of the Queen's Rangers. It is also said, that, exclusive of the above Passengers, there were two servants on board, and two children of parents whose indigent circumstances necessitated them to walk by land. The Crew of the Speedy consisted of five Seamen, three of whom had left large families, exclusive of Captain Paxton, who had also a large family. The total number on board is supposed to have been 20.

Detail of the Loss of the Ship Anne, Captain KNIGHT, *on a Reef of Rocks, five Leagues to the northward of the southernmost Souhelepar Islands.*

APRIL 19th, 1804, at 11 P. M. the Seacunny of the watch called out that he saw the land, and before any body else could distinguish it, being very dark, saw the appearance of breakers a-head—put the helm down immediately, for the purpose of bringing her head to the westward; but before it could be effected, the Ship struck on a reef of rocks, sand, and stones—furled all the sails to prevent her going further on the reef—hoisted out the Boats, and run the stream anchor out to the north, to keep her from forging a-head on the reef—sounded astern of the Ship, and found the deepest water to the N.N.W.—carried the small bower anchor out in a N.N.W. direction, and let it go in four fathom rock, sand, and stones—hove a great strain on the small bower, and finding that she did not go off, left off heaving, and sent the people below to heave out the stones, and stave the salt-water casks forward.

At twelve, the appearance of a squall from the southward, loosed all the sails, and hoisted them: at half past twelve a heavy squall from the southward, with heavy rain, hove all a-back, and kept heaving a great strain on the small bower, but without effect. Sent the people below again for the purpose of heaving up the stones ; and at half past one, having lightened her considerably, hove again the small bower, but without effect—sent the people below again to heave out the remainder of the stones ; but instead of doing that, and exerting themselves, and doing what was necessary for the safety of the Ship, many of them began to plunder what they could lay their hands on, saying, that there was no danger, the land being very near. At three, hove again on the small bower, but without effect, and pumping out the water started. At four, the Gunner reported four feet water in the hold ; still kept heaving, and at day-light the water had gained on the pumps to eight and a half feet; a heavy swell setting in, the Ship began to strike very hard, and observed several large pieces of sheathing, and other parts of her bottom, come up alongside.—At five the rudder unshipped, and carried away the greater part of the stern, and stove in the counter on the starboard side, the water being within one foot of the twin decks. At half past five, the Ship being bilged, fell over on her starboard beam-ends : finding nothing further could be done for the safety of the Ship, left off pumping : the Captain then ordered the Syrang and Lascars to get the masts and sails in the Boats, also some rice and water for the people, which they refused to do, saying there was plenty on the island, and began to plunder the great cabin, and the Officers' chests and trunks, during which time the Captain being below for the purpose of securing his papers, he heard one of the Lascars (Mahomed) saying to some of those who refused to get the provision in the Boat, that when we got on the island they would take the first opportunity of killing the Captain, Officers, and Seacunnies, and seizing the Boats, and going to the Malabar Coast.

In consequence of which the Captain was resolved to quit the wreck as soon as possible, with as many of the other party as the

CORRECT RELATION OF SHIPWRECKS. 61

Boat could carry, and to leave the Pinnace for the rest, with instructions to follow us; during this time the Seacunnies had got the Long-boat's mast and sails in, with a small quantity of water and biscuit; and at seven, after consulting with the Officers of the Ship, who were of opinion that nothing further could be done, quitted the wreck in the Long-boat with the following people, for the purpose of making the best of our way to the Malabar Coast: at the same time the Pinnace left the wreck, but was soon out of sight; when we quitted the wreck she was laying on her starboard beam ends, and nearly full of water.

A List of the People saved in the Long-boat.

Thomas Knight, Commander; John Wheattall, Pilot for the Red Sea; Edward Greaves, 2d Officer; John Lunardy, Gunner; four Seacunnies, and six Natives.—Total, 14.

An account of the reef on which the Anne struck, whose bearings were taken at day-light—the extremes of the reef bore from S.W. to E.N.E., the southernmost of the Souhelepar Islands bore S.E. by W., and the northernmost ditto E.S.E., distance from the southernmost about six leagues, and from the northernmost about four or five—the extreme length of the reef ten or twelve miles, of which reef no mention is made in any of the charts on board.

PLATE CLXX.

MR. POCOCK in this Design has given a minute Portrait of the Cleopatra Frigate, of 32 guns, in three different Positions. She was built by Mr. James Hilhouse, of Bristol, and launched in December 1779.

The original Drawing was made in the year 1780, for her then Commander, the Hon. George Murray.

In the principal Portrait she is described lying-to, with her main-top-sail aback.

DIMENSIONS OF THE ROYAL SOVEREIGN* AND ROYAL CHARLOTTE YACHTS.

	Sovereign.		Charlotte.	
	Feet.	In.	Feet.	In.
Length on the deck	96	1	90	1
Keel for tonnage	80	9	72	$2\frac{1}{2}$
Breadth extreme	25	7	24	7
Depth in hold	10	3	11	2
Tonnage	280	$0\frac{18}{94}$	232	0

* See the Engraving, by Nesbit, page 1.

CHRONOLOGICAL SKETCH
OF THE
MOST REMARKABLE NAVAL EVENTS
OF THE YEAR 1804.

JANUARY.

1. ADMIRAL Cornwallis, who had been driven off Brest by a tremendous gale of Wind on the 24th and 25th of December, sailed again this day from Torbay, and resumed his station before the enemy's port.

2. Accounts received of the loss of the Suffisante Man of War in Cork harbour, on the 25th ult.

Dreadful storms on our coasts for several days, by which much damage was sustained by our Shipping.

6. Accounts received of the successful attack made by the Immortalité Frigate and Archer Gun-brig, upon a Flotilla of the enemy's Gun-boats, Galliots, Transports, &c. to the number of 50 Sail, proceeding from Boulogne to Dunkirk, of which they took several Sail, and drove many others on shore.

18. The Settlement of Goree, on the coast of Africa, taken by a French Expedition from Cayenne.

26. Intelligence was received of the evacuation of the French part of St. Domingo by General Rochambeau and the troops under his command. This event took place on the 28th of November, in consequence of a Capitulation between Rochambeau and the Black General Dessalines. At the same time Admiral Duckworth captured the French Shipping, consisting of three Frigates, several smaller Ships of War, and a number of Merchantmen. It was afterwards learned that this event was followed by the most shocking cruelties, all the white inhabitants of Cape François, and other places, of which the Blacks obtained possession, being massacred.

31. Strong rumours prevailed the whole of this month, of the enemy being daily expected to make his threatened attempt for the invasion of this country; but our Squadrons, notwithstanding the continued tempests, constantly braved the enemy in the mouths of his own harbours, while the whole country, armed and unanimous, anxiously awaited the long-menaced invasion of our shores, confident of the utter destruction of the foe.

FEBRUARY.

15. Captain Nathaniel Dance, Commodore of the China Fleet, was attacked by a French Squadron of Ships of War under the command of Admiral Linois, which the British Indiamen beat off.

MARCH.

7. Lord Camelford received a mortal wound in a duel with Mr. Best. His Lordship languished until the 19th.

8. Goree taken by Captain Dickson, of his Majesty's Ship Inconstant.

15. Mr. Pitt made an important motion relative to the Naval Defence of the Country, on which a long discussion arose. When the House divided, there were for the Administration of Mr. Addington 201; for the Opposition 180.—Majority for Ministers, 71.

27. L'Egyptienne French Frigate Privateer, of 36 guns, and full of men, captured by the Hippomenes Sloop of War, Captain Ripley. L'Egyptienne had received a severe drubbing four days before from the Osprey Sloop, Captain Younghusband.

The Magnificent, Captain Jarvis, wrecked on the French coast, and 86 of the Crew made prisoners.

APRIL.

2. The Apollo Frigate, and about 40 outward-bound West Indiamen, lost off Cape Mondego, on the coast of Portugal.

25. Accounts received of the surrender of Curaçoa to his Majesty's arms.

MAY.

5. The Dutch Colony of Surinam taken by Major-General Sir Charles Green and Commodore Hood, and several Ships of War delivered up to the captors.

12. Launched at Deptford the Royal Sovereign Yacht, a Vessel of 35 tons, beautifully ornamented, and built for the accommodation of the Royal Family.

— The Vincego, Captain Wright, having run ashore on the French coast, was taken possession of by the enemy, and Captain Wright sent to Paris by General Julien, under the charge of being connected with the pretended conspiracy against Buonaparté.

JUNE.

3. The French accounts received here of Linois' attack on Bencoolen, and the destruction of the Company's Pepper Magazines.

JULY.

9. Accounts from Gibraltar, of the 4th ult. stating a partial action between Lord Nelson's Squadron and the Toulon Fleet, in which the latter sheered off.

11. A gallant attack made on some French Vessels at la Vaudour in Hieres Bay, by the Boats of the Sea Horse, Narcissus, and Maidstone Frigates, under the command of Lieutenant Thompson, when a number of the enemy's Vessels were destroyed.

20. A spirited attack made by the Squadron under the command of Capt. Owen, of the Immortalité Frigate, on part of the Boulogne Flotilla, in a gale of Wind, when a number of the enemy were driven ashore and destroyed.

Accounts received of a dreadful storm at Newfoundland, on the 11th May, in which above 80 Vessels were lost.

25. The first account received, by the Calcutta Man of War, of the repulse of Linois' attack, by the homeward-bound China Fleet, under Sir Nathaniel Dance, in the Straits of Malacca.

28. A Gazette account published of the bombardment of Havre, by a small British Squadron, on the 23d inst.

AUGUST.

6. Admiral Lord Duncan died suddenly on his way to Edinburgh.

19. Accounts of a dreadful storm, and overflowing of the river Aar, in Germany, by which a number of villages were entirely overwhelmed and destroyed, with their inhabitants.

The blockade of the Elbe announced by an official communication from Lord Harrowby.

31. Rumours prevailed the whole of this month, apparently corroborated by the enemy's movements, that an immediate attack would be made upon our coasts.

SEPTEMBER.

10. A violent tempest in the West Indies, at Charlestown (South Carolina), and other parts of the coast of North America, in which a vast number of Vessels were destroyed.

19. A number of letters from persons in this country to their friends in India, which were found on board the Admiral Aplin Indiaman, captured by the enemy, were published in the French Official Journal, the Moniteur, from which they were re-translated by the London Papers of the 29th inst.

26. A communication made by Lord Harrowby, to a Committee of the London Merchants, in the Spanish trade, respecting some disputes subsisting between this Country and Spain, which might terminate in hostility.

OCTOBER.

1. Mr. Magee, a Surgeon's Mate in the Navy, went into the Three Goats public-house, Vauxhall Turnpike, where, in a fit of phrenzy, he stabbed the servant maid, wounded several men, and cut his own throat.

3. On the night between the 2d and 3d, an experiment was made by Lord Keith, with fire Vessels called *coffers*, which exploded among 150 of the Boulogne Flotilla. This experiment was made on a limited scale; and Lord Keith, in his dispatch, stated, that a combined operation of a similar nature would hold forth a reasonable prospect of a successful result.

5. Four Spanish Frigates were stopped off St. Mary's, by a British Squadron, consisting of the Indefatigable, Medusa, Lively, and Amphion, when an engagement took place, in the course of which one of the Spanish Frigates blew up, and the other three, richly laden, were taken.

11. A letter from Lord Nelson received by the Lord Mayor of London, declining the thanks of the Corporation of London, voted for himself, while Sir Richard Bickerton and the minor Flag Officers were passed unnoticed.

16. Accounts received of the destruction of Makey, a Malay settlement, on the coast of Sumatra, on the 13th of April, by a British Squadron.

17. The Contre Amiral Magon French Brig Privateer, of 18 guns, commanded by the celebrated Captain Blackeman, of Dunkirk, captured by the Cruizer Sloop of War, Captain Hancock.

18. Accounts received of the capture of the three Spanish Register Ships, from Pio de la Plata, to Cadiz, laden with treasure, by a Squadron of British Frigates under Captain Moore, and of the destruction of a fourth.

23 and 24. An extensive attack was made by the Immortalité Frigate, and Basilisk Gun-brig, with a division of the enemy's Flotilla, proceeding from the eastward towards Boulogne, in which great damage was done to the enemy's Vessels. The Conflict Gun-brig lost, by approaching too near in pursuit of the enemy.

NOVEMBER.

2. Accounts received of a dreadful hurricane in the Island of St. Kitt's, and several other Islands in the West Indies, in which a vast number of Ships were lost, principally foreign.

7. The two French Frigates, so long blockaded at New York by the Leander and the Cambrian Frigate, escaped through the passage called Hell's Gate.— Jerome Buonaparté and his wife, it is said, had embarked in the Frigate called the Didon.

8. The Matilda Spanish Frigate brought into Portsmouth; she was captured on her Voyage from Cadiz to Rio de la Plata by the Medusa, Captain Gore.

21. Accounts from Rotterdam of the 15th, stated the order of the First Consul to seize all the Ships, with their cargoes, if containing British merchandize, after fourteen days.

22. The Romney, of 50 guns, lost off the Texel.

24. The Venerable, of 74 guns, lost in a gale of Wind, in Torbay.

25. The Amphitrite, a fine Spanish Frigate, captured by the Donegal, Captain Sir Richard Strachan.

DECEMBER

9. An attack with explosion Vessels was made, under the direction of Sir Home Popham, on Fort Rouge, at the entrance of Calais Harbour, by which the Fort was considerably damaged.

15. The Channel Fleet, under Lord Cornwallis, which having been at different times partially driven off the French coast, and was now in Torbay, sailed to resume the blockade of Brest.

20. An Embargo laid on all Ships belonging to Spain, or bound to that country.

— The Blonde, of 32 guns, wrecked in a gale of Wind in Torbay.

21. The Severn, of 44 guns, lost in the same gale, in Grouville Bay.

30. Intelligence received of Reprisals and Sequestration of British property on the part of Spain.

NAVAL HISTORY OF THE PRESENT YEAR, 1805.
(December—January.)
RETROSPECTIVE AND MISCELLANEOUS.

RIGHT HON. LORD MELVILLE—*First Lord of the Admiralty.*
SECRETARIES. { *William Marsden, Esq.*
{ *John Borrow, Esq.*

THE re-union which has taken place between Mr. Pitt and Mr. Addington was celebrated under the immediate auspices, and in the very presence of the greatest personage in the kingdom.

Mr. Addington stands on high ground: he is the decided favourite in the closet, and may now be regarded as the King's confidential servant.

The naval force which the present Board of Admiralty has destined for the protection of the Coast of Ireland, will put that part of the United Kingdom perfectly at ease with regard to any attempt from the French. In addition to the Hibernia, the largest Ship ever built in this country, seven or eight Sail of the Line are appropriated for that Station; among which are the Thunderer, the Princess Royal, the Prince of Orange, the Goliath, and the Raisonable.

In the Secret Expedition there are to be employed 800 artillery with battering cannon; the 9th, 10th, and 13th regiments of cavalry; a Brigade of Guards; and a proportion of Regiments of the Line.

The correspondence between our Court and the Courts of St. Petersburg and Stockholm is conducted with uncommon activity. Messengers are constantly in waiting at Gottenburgh, to forward all dispatches to and from England. That negociations of the most important nature are at present pending between those two Northern Courts and the Government of this Country, we have conclusive reasons to infer, not only from the critical state of Europe, but from the peculiar character of the war in which we are engaged. England, Russia, and Sweden, are the only powers which have, as yet, manifested any disposition to combat, or controul, the phrenzied and immeasurable ambition of Buonaparte.

The private expenses of Buonaparté for his coronation are calculated at 80 millions, (3,500,000l.) hitherto not paid in cash, but in *bons* on the imperial treasury, which are already at a discount of 12 per cent.

EMBARGO ON SPANISH SHIPS.

AT the Court at the Queen's Palace, the 19th December, 1804, Present, the King's Most Excellent Majesty in Council.

Whereas information has been received that an Embargo has been ordered to be laid upon all British Ships in the ports of the kingdom of Spain; it is this day ordered by his Majesty, by and with the advice of his Privy Council, that no Ships or Vessels belonging to any of his Majesty's subjects be permitted to enter and clear out for any of the ports of Spain, until further orders: And his Majesty is further pleased to order, that a General Embargo or Stop be made of all Spanish Ships and Vessels whatsoever, now within, or which hereafter shall come into any of the ports, harbours or roads, within the United Kingdom of Great Britain and Ireland, together with all persons and effects on board the said Ships and Vessels; but that the utmost care be taken for the preservation of all and every part of the cargoes on board any of the said Ships, so that no damage or embezzlement whatever be sustained.

S. COTTRELL.

The Mercury, a large Spanish Ship from la Plata, has been sent into Baltimore in Ireland, by the Phœnix Frigate.

Government has exchanged the Dutch Captain Blys Van Tuslong, late Commandant of the Dutch Marine Forces, captured at Surinam, for the Hon. Captain Colvill, late of the Romney; and as a cartel for the exchange of prisoners has been opened between the two Governments on the most liberal footing, there is no doubt that the British now in Holland will very soon be restored to their country and friends.

Extract of a letter from Captain William Williams, of the Brig St. Joseph, 12 guns and 22 men, bound to Africa, to his owners; dated at Sea, 20th July, 1804, (lat. 4° 34' S. long. 11° 58 E.

"I take the first opportunity that has offered, to inform you, that in lat. 46° 56' N. long. 13° 18' W. we fell in with a French Brig Privateer of 16 guns, and apparently full of men, which we engaged for two hours, and beat her off; the action began at half past nine A.M. and lasted till half past eleven, when the Privateer sheered off and made all the sail she could from us. We received no damage whatever in the action, as most of her shot went over us. She had several of our shot in her quarter, and some through her fore and aft main-sail, which we could very plainly see; but what other damage she got I cannot inform you. She kept in sight for two days after, but did not think proper to come within gun-shot of us a second time: she was a long low Brig, sailed remarkably fast, and apparently had been out but a very short time: all the people I had on board behaved in the action as well as I could expect."

A letter from an Officer on board his Majesty's Ship Fisgard, dated off Cape St. Vincent, Nov. 28th, says—"We cannot desire a better Station; we heard of hostilities with Spain on October the 15th, and on that very day we captured two Ships. Lord Nelson received from us the first intelligence.—We have already taken twelve Ships, and entertain hopes of as many more. Yesterday we fell in with the Donegal, Capt. Sir R. Strachan, who has taken a large Spanish Frigate, the Amphitrite, after a chase of 46 hours, and 15 minutes' action, in which the Spanish Captain was killed: the prize was from Cadiz, with dispatches for Teneriffe and the Havana, laden with stores. The Amphitrite Frigate, of 42 guns, was one of the finest Frigates in the Spanish Navy. The Donegal chased the Amphitrite for several hours, sometimes gaining upon her, and sometimes losing; at length the Amphitrite carried away her mizen-top-mast, which enabled the Donegal to come up with her. A Boat was then dispatched by Sir Richard for the purpose of bringing the Spanish Captain on board. Some difficulty arose from neither party understanding the language of the other; at length Sir Richard acquainted the Spanish Captain, that, in compliance with the orders he had received from his Admiral, he was under the necessity of conducting the Amphitrite back again to Cadiz, and he allowed the Spanish Captain three minutes to determine whether he would comply without compelling him to have recourse to force. After waiting six minutes in vain for a favourable answer, the Donegal fired into the Amphitrite, which was immediately answered with a broadside. An engagement then ensued, which lasted about eight minutes, when the Amphitrite struck her colours. During this short engagement the Spanish Captain was unfortunately killed by a musket ball. The Donegal has also captured another Spanish Ship, supposed the richest that ever sailed from Cadiz, her cargo reported worth 200,000l."

Another letter, dated November 29, adds—"We have this day taken a large Ship from the River de la Plata."

They had captured the following Ships previous to the 3d of December:

Nostra Signora del Rosario, value	£.10,000
Il Fortuna	8,000
St. Joseph	12,000
La Virgine Assumpto	6,000
Apollo	15,000
Signora del Purificatione	40,000
Fawket	1,100
Gustavus Adolphus	1,000
A Settee	600
A Ship, with naval stores	40,000

A courier arrived at Cork, Dec. 12, from Baltimore with intelligence, that a large Spanish Ship called the Mercury, from the river la Plata, with a very valuable cargo, a considerable part of it specie, had arrived in the harbour, detained and sent in by the Phœnix Frigate.

COURT OF KING'S BENCH, DECEMBER 12.

RACK and others v. MACKAY.

THIS and three other actions were brought against the defendant, the Captain of a Man of War, by the plaintiffs, as privileged Seamen on board the Ocean, who claimed Protection. The proceedings were interrupted by Mr. Gibbs, who said the actions were not brought for the sake of damages, but to teach Naval Officers in the Impress Service that they must respect protections; and added, that he would be content with a shilling damages in each cause.

Lord Ellenborough observed, that it was very handsomely done on the part of the plaintiffs, and he hoped it would have the desired effect.—Verdict for the plaintiffs—Damages 1s.

Advice has been received by Government, that the fast-sailing Cutter, in which Major-General Sir John Moore, K.B. had embarked, landed him safely at Lisbon: the object of this secret mission is to learn, through the local investigation made by this gallant and discerning Officer, whether any, and what aid can be given to effect the security of that endangered country.

The Renommée Frigate, which has undergone a complete repair in Messrs. Perry's Dock-yard, will be completed in the course of a few days, when she will be ordered into commission.

Bantry Bay, Dec. 22.—His Majesty's Ship Thunderer grounded yesterday about the fall of night, close to Bere Island. In the dreadful gale of yesterday she rode hard, and snapped her cable; by which accident she shored. Fortunately she has struck upon a muddy place, and there is hope that she may be got off. She fired signal guns of distress repeatedly last night. His Majesty's Ship Princess Royal, of 98 guns, is anchored off the western harbour of Beerhaven, waiting only a change of Wind to come in.

Castlebar, Bantry Bay, Dec. 24, 1804.

Yesterday the Princess Royal, which had been off our Coast, arrived here, to take on board the guns, stores, and shot of the Thunderer; and this day the Goliath, with a Frigate, name hitherto unknown, and a Transport, came in to take out the remainder of the stores. It is still thought, when the Thunderer is lightened, she will be got off, as she lies in a soft bed, and there is good discipline on board, the Crew being ready to second the Officers in every exertion.

Dublin, Jan. 3. His Majesty's Ship Thunderer was at last got off the place at Bere Island, where she had grounded, and now rides safely at anchor in deep water. Besides the powerful Squadron now in Bantry Bay, there are British Ships of War cruizing off all the head-lands from the Shannon to Cork harbour.

Cork, Dec. 31. By our Correspondent at Bantry, we are informed of the arrival of his Majesty's Ship Prince of Orange, with Rear-Admiral Drury's Flag, to join the Squadron at Beerhaven, consisting of the Princess Royal, Goliath, and Thunderer. The Dryad and Rossario were also at Beerhaven.

The Dauntless, a new Sloop of 18 guns, recently launched at Hull, is ordered to Sheerness to be prepared for immediate Service.

The Spanish Ship captured by the Neptune, of Greenock, is estimated to be worth 500,000l.

The Dock-yard at Woolwich has been visited by Mr. Churchman, accompanied by Mr. Whidbey, the superintendant, who are employed by Government in making observations on the gradual rising of the tide waters of the Thames. There were made at this place one whole year's observations, commencing on the 4th of May, 1761; and, according to the register, they were continued during the arrival of our most gracious Queen at Harwich, the 8th of September. The orders from the Admiralty were to send an account of the spring and neap tides at this port, after keeping an exact account of the perpendicular rise from low to high water on each tide, taking notice of the course of the Wind on each day of the month, and whether morning or evening tide. The cell at the bottom of the single dock gates was a fixed mark, and the depth the water ebbed below it was added to the height that the next tide flowed above it, which gave the perpendicular flow of each tide. Now it is ascertained that, since the year 1761, there have been two new set of dock gates, on account of the old ones going to decay: the first was said to be somewhere about the year 1766, and the last in 1783. On paying particular attention to the cell of the dock gates at low water, it did not appear above the surface, but a considerable piece of timber was observed under water, but above the cell; and although the difference between high and low water remains nearly the same, both high and low water marks are about four feet perpendicular higher than was the case in 1761, which remains to be confirmed or not, by corresponding observations to be made in different parts of the United Empire. Capt. Vancouver, or rather Mr. Whidbey, informs us, Vol. III, pages 293 and 294, that on the N.W. coast of America, in his two last excursions, several places were seen where the Ocean was evidently encroaching very fast upon the Land. (See NAVAL CHRONICLE, Vol. I, page 406.)

December 31, the day appointed for launching the Hebe Frigate, at his Majesty's Yard, at Deptford, her Royal Highness the Princess of Wales signified her intention of honouring the Launch with her presence. At a quarter past one o'clock her Royal Highness arrived, attended by two Ladies: they were conducted on board the Royal Sovereign Yacht, and very politely received by Admiral Douglas; the Volunteers of the Yard saluted her Royal Highness as she passed, and the Band of the Tower Hamlets Militia played " *God save the King.*" At half past one the Frigate dashed into the water, amidst an immense concourse of spectators, the Band playing " *Rule Britannia.*" Immediately after the Launch her Royal Highness went into the state-room, and after taking some refreshment, landed, and left the yard greeted by the huzzas of the spectators. The Frigate is pierced for 36 guns, but rated only at 32; she is already coppered, and will be speedily rigged and fitted for Sea; she is built of fir, and has been but little more than four months under hand.

It is with extreme pleasure we announce to the public, that a plan for a Light-House, intended to be erected on Flamborough Head, is now invented on a very peculiar construction; and submitted to the inspection of the Trinity Houses, Ship Owners, Underwriters, and Merchants of London, Newcastle, Hull, and other ports. We believe that it meets with the general approbation of all who are concerned in the preservation of property, and the lives of Mariners at Sea, and that it will be carried into effect. The plan is the invention of B. Milne, Esq. Collector of his Majesty's Customs at the port of Bridlington. It is to be constructed with two lights revolving on a horizontal plane, seventy feet from the ground, reflected by concave mirrors; appearing to the Mariners at Sea alternately seventy feet asunder, and then as one light, by eclipsing each as they pass round, every five minutes; by which means they will be distinguishable from all other lights on the coast. Those perilous rocks at Flamborough Head may then be passed with safety. The lights being continually seen, and distinctly known by all Mariners, even of the least experience, must prove of the greatest utility to the navigation on that coast.

In Cork the slaughtering season ceased on Christmas-eve. An immense quantity of the finest beef has been saved for the use of the Navy, and notwithstanding the great consumption of the article, the price continued throughout the season to the public infinitely lower there than we can purchase beef or pork in our markets.

In consequence of a representation from the Lords Commissioners of the Admiralty, of the necessity of a Sub-Lieutenant on board such of his Majesty's armed Brigs as are commanded by Lieutenants, (and to which we alluded in our last, Vol. XII, page 510,) an Order of Council has been directed to them, authorizing their Lordships to employ Midshipmen who have served their time, and passed their examination, as Sub-Lieutenants on board the said Brigs accordingly. Their pay to be 4s. per day. The above is in orders, and was made known to all the Ships at Sheerness.

As a feature in the British naval character, the following is worthy of notice: His Majesty's Ship the Buckingham being appropriated solely for the reception of Dutch prisoners of war, her Ship's Company, consisting of a detachment of the Royal Marines and some Seamen, gave up the whole of their provisions, beer, &c. on Christmas Day, to the Dutch prisoners, in consideration of the humanity and kindness with which they understood the Romney's Officers and Ship's Company had been treated by the Dutch on the loss of that Ship on their coast: an acknowledgment which the prisoners most thankfully enjoyed in every sense of the expression. On New Year's day they were regaled by the Officers of the Ship on account of the same consideration.

During the late gales, a Vessel from Gottenburgh, laden with various merchandise, was driven ashore between Blackeny and Cley, and soon after became a wreck: four of the Crew, consisting of nine men, unfortunately perished. A large box, which had been observed floating on the Sea, has since been picked up by some beachmen, one of whom was near losing his life in his exertions, with two others, to bring it on shore. It contained a number of gold rings, several dozen bottle slides, some silver waiters, and other articles, which are now in the possession of T. W. Coke, Esq. as Lord of the Manor. Several barrels of spermaceti oil have also come ashore.

On the 1st of January was launched from Mr. Tanner's Yard, at Dartmouth, a beautiful Ship of War, of 26 guns. This is the third Ship which has been launched for Government from the same Yard within the last six months. There are above 200 Ship Carpenters and other Artificers in Mr. Tanner's employ; and four or five more Vessels will be launched before the summer Such are the peculiar advantages of this private Yard, that a 74 could be launched in any tide.

The news of the Spanish Declaration of War was communicated to Lloyd's Coffee-house in the following note from Mr. Hammond:

(COPY.)

"Downing-street, Jan. 7, 1805.

"I am directed to acquaint you, that War was declared, on the part of his Catholic Majesty, against Great Britain, on the 12th of December last.

"I am your most obedient humble servant,

(Signed) "GEORGE HAMMOND.

"To the Masters of Lloyd's."

DECLARATION OF WAR AGAINST SPAIN.

AT the Court at the Queen's Palace, the 11th of January, 1805, Present, the King's Most Excellent Majesty in Council.

WHEREAS his Majesty has received information that the King of Spain has issued a Declaration of War against his Majesty, his Subjects, and People; his Majesty, therefore, being determined to take such measures as are necessary for vindicating the honour of his Crown, and for the vigorous prosecution of the War in which he finds himself engaged, is pleased, by and with the advice of his Privy Council, to order, and it is hereby ordered, that General Reprisals be granted against the Ships, Goods, and Subjects of the King of Spain, so that as well his Majesty's Fleets and Ships, as also all other Ships and Vessels that shall be commissioned, by Letters of Marque, or General Reprisals, or otherwise, by his Majesty's Commissioners for executing the Office of Lord High Admiral of Great Britain, shall and may lawfully seize all Ships, Vessels, and Goods belonging to the King of Spain, or his Subjects, or others inhabiting within the territories of the King of Spain, and bring the same to judgment in any of the Courts of Admiralty within his Majesty's dominions; and, to that end, his Majesty's Advocate-General, with the Advocate of the Admiralty, are forthwith to prepare the draft of a commission, and present the same to his Majesty at this Board, authorising the Commissioners for executing the Office of Lord High Admiral, or any person or persons by them empowered and appointed, to issue forth and grant Letters of Marque and Reprisals to any of his Majesty's Subjects, or others whom the said Commissioners shall deem fitly qualified in that behalf, for the apprehending, seizing, and taking the Ships, Vessels, and Goods belonging to Spain, and the Vassals and Subjects of the King of Spain, or any inhabiting within his Countries, Territories, or Dominions; and that such powers and clauses be inserted in the said Commission, as have been usual, and are according to former precedents; and his Majesty's said Advocate-General, with the Advocate of the Admiralty, are also forthwith to prepare the Draft of a Commission, and present the same to his Majesty at this Board, authorising the said Commissioners for executing the Office of Lord High Admiral, to will and require the High Court of Admiralty of Great Britain, and the Lieutenant and Judge of the said Court, his Surrogate or Surrogates, as also the several Courts of Admiralty within his Majesty's Dominions, to take cognizance of, and judicially proceed upon all and all manner of Captures, Seizures, Prizes, and Reprisals of all Ships and Goods that are or shall be taken, and to hear and determine the same; and, according to the course of Admiralty, and the Laws of Nations, to adjudge and condemn all such Ships, Vessels, and Goods, as shall belong to Spain, or the Vassals and Subjects of the King of Spain, or to any others inhabiting within any of his Countries, Territories, and Dominions; and that such powers and clauses be inserted in the said Commission as have been usual, and are according to former precedents; and they are likewise to prepare and lay before his Majesty at this Board a draft of such instructions as may be proper to be sent to the Courts of Admiralty in his Majesty's foreign Governments and Plantations, for their guidance herein; as also another draft of instructions for such Ships as shall be commissionated for the purposes afore-mentioned.

Eldon, C.	Hawkesbury.
Montrose.	Ellenborough.
Camden.	W. Pitt.
Mellville.	W. Grant.
Sidmouth.	Charles Morgan.
Castlereagh.	Evan Nepean.
Mulgrave.	

WESTMINSTER, JANUARY 15, 1805.

THIS day his Majesty came to the House of Peers, and being, in his royal robes, seated on the Throne with the usual solemnity, Sir Francis Molyneux, Gentleman Usher of the Black Rod, was sent with a message from his Majesty to the House of Commons, commanding their attendance in the House of Peers. The Commons being come thither accordingly, his Majesty was pleased to make the following most gracious Speech:

My Lords, and Gentlemen,

SINCE the end of the last session, the preparations of the enemy for the invasion of this kingdom have been continued with incessant activity; but no attempt has been made to carry their repeated menaces into effect.

The skill and intrepidity of my Navy, the respectable and formidable state of my Army and Militia, the unabated zeal and improved discipline of a numerous Volunteer Force, and the general ardor manifested by all classes of my Subjects, have, indeed, been sufficient to deter them from so presumptuous and desperate an enterprize. While this spirit continues to animate the country, and its voluntary exertions for its own defence subsist in their full vigour, we need not fear the consequences of the most powerful efforts on the part of the enemy: but let us never forget that our security has arisen from the resolution with which we have met and provided against the danger, and that it can be preserved only by steady perseverance and unremitting activity.

The conduct of the Court of Spain, evidently under the predominant influence and controul of France, compelled Me to take prompt and decisive measures to guard against the effects of hostility. I have, at the same time, endeavoured, as long as it was possible, to prevent the necessity of a rupture; but, in consequence of the refusal of a satisfactory explanation, my Minister quitted Madrid, and War has since been declared by Spain against this country.

I have directed a copy of the Manifesto, which I have caused to be prepared on this occasion, to be laid before you, together with such papers as are necessary to explain the discussions which have taken place between Me and the Court of Madrid. You will, I trust, be convinced by them, that my forbearance has been carried to the utmost extent which the interests of my dominions would admit; and, while I lament the situation of Spain, involved in hostilities contrary to its true interests, I rely with confidence on your vigorous support in a contest which can be attributed only to the unfortunate prevalence of French counsels.

The general conduct of the French Government on the continent of Europe, has been marked by the utmost violence and outrage, and has shown a wanton defiance of the rights of neutral territories, of the acknowledged privileges of accredited ministers, and of the established principles of the law of nations.

Notwithstanding these transactions, so repugnant to every sentiment of moderation and justice, I have recently received a communication from the French Government, containing professions of a pacific disposition. I have, in consequence, expressed my earnest desire to embrace the first opportunity of restoring the blessings of peace on such grounds as may be consistent with the permanent safety and interests of my Dominions; but I am confident you will agree with Me, that those objects are closely connected with the general security of Europe; I have, therefore, not thought it right to enter into any more particular explanation without previous communication with those Powers on the Continent, with whom I am engaged in confidential intercourse and connexion, with a view to that important object, and especially with the Emperor of Russia, who has given the strongest proofs of the wise and dignified sentiments by which he is animated, and of the warm interest he takes in the safety and independence of Europe.

Gentlemen of the House of Commons,

I have directed the estimates for the public service to be laid before you. I regret the necessity of any additional burdens being imposed on my people; but I am sure you will be sensible how much their future safety and happiness depend on the vigour of our exertions, and that in the mode of raising the supplies you will continue to show your anxiety for the support of public credit, and for restraining as much as possible the accumulation of the national debt.

My Lords and Gentlemen,

In considering the great efforts and sacrifices which the nature of the contest requires, it is a peculiar satisfaction to Me to observe the many proofs of the internal wealth and prosperity of the country. It will, I am sure, be your great object to maintain and improve these advantages, and at the same time to take all such measures, as by enabling Me to prosecute the war with vigour, may afford the best prospect of bringing it to a safe and honourable termination.

Gazette Letters,

Copied verbatim from the LONDON GAZETTE.

ADMIRALTY-OFFICE, JAN. 8, 1805.

Copy of a Letter from Commodore Sir Samuel Hood, K.B. Commander in Chief of his Majesty's Ships and Vessels at the Leeward Islands, to William Marsden, Esq.; dated on board the Centaur, Carlisle Bay, Barbadoes, 7th November, 1804.

SIR,

I HEREWITH enclose a copy of a letter from Captain Nourse, of his Majesty's Ship Barbadoes, stating the capture of the Napoleon French Privateer, mounting 18 guns, and 150 men. This circumstance is highly flattering to the Merchants of Barbadoes, who presented this Ship to his Majesty, as it was her first cruise, only four days at Sea, and gives us hopes of the most essential aid to the protection of the trade. I have the honour to be, &c.

SAMUEL HOOD.

SIR, *His Majesty's Ship Barbadoes, at Sea, Oct. 17, 1804.*

I have the satisfaction to inform you, that his Majesty's Ship Barbadoes, under my command, at three A.M. this morning fell in with a strange Sail in the latitude of 17° 40′ N. long. 59° 54′ min. W. and, after a chase of thirteen hours, the latter part some little firing from her stern and our bow chasers, she struck her colours, and proved to be the Napoleon French Privateer, formerly the Duke of Kent Packet, from Guadaloupe, commanded by Suyrvens Pitot, Enseigne de Vaisseau, mounting 18 guns, two of which were thrown overboard during the chase; she had 150 men on board, was out nine days, on her first cruise, and had not made any captures. I am, &c.

Commodore Hood, Commander in Chief.

JOSEPH NOURSE.

ADMIRALTY-OFFICE, JAN. 22, 1805.

Copy of a Letter from the Right Honourable Lord Keith, K.B. Admiral of the Blue &c. to William Marsden, Esq.; dated on board the Ardent, off Ramsgate, the 21st Instant.

SIR,

I transmit, for their Lordships' information, a copy of a letter from Captain Elphinstone, of his Majesty's Ship the Greyhound, to Captain Laroche, of the Melpomene, reporting the capture of another of the enemy's Privateers that have lately infested the Channel; and from which their Lordships will have the satisfaction of observing, that Mr. Dalyell, acting Lieutenant of the Rattler, and Mr. Donaldson, the late acting Commander of the Folkstone, are alive, and likely to recover. I am, &c.

KEITH.

SIR, *Greyhound, at Sea, Jan. 19, 1805.*

Cruising in conformity to your orders, I yesterday fell in with, and, after an eleven hours' chase, captured the French Lugger Privateer le Vimereux, Jan B. Pollet, Captain, armed with 15 guns, and having on board a complement of 69 men. She sailed from St. Vallery en Caux (to which port she belonged) on Thursday, and had taken nothing. She is a remarkable fine Vessel, about sixty tons burthen, nearly new, and sails so well, that had we not been greatly favoured by frequent changes of Wind, I believe all our efforts in pursuit of her would have been fruitless.

It was against this Lugger that the gallant, although unfortunate attempt was made by the Boats of his Majesty's Sloop Rattler and Folkstone Lugger; and it is with great satisfaction I learnt, that the Lieutenants of the Rattler and Folkstone were still living, and, although severely wounded, that there is very great expectation of their recovery. I remain, &c.

C. ELPHINSTONE.

Christopher Laroche, Esq. Melpomene, off Havre.

FOREIGN REPORTS.

MEDITERRANEAN, AND ADJACENT ATLANTIC.

Vice-Admiral Lord Viscount NELSON.
Rear-Admiral Sir R. BICKERTON, Bart.

*C*ADIZ, Nov. 1. —Violently as the Fever has raged, it is remarkable that our Harbour, which was never more full of Ships, has been entirely spared. General Moreau will sail to America in the Spring; he leads here a very retired life.

Constantinople, Oct. 26.—Two English Frigates have arrived in this Harbour, appointed to convoy the Vessels laden with Corn for the Black Sea, destined for Malta, where there is now a great scarcity. A French Privateer of eight guns, and 64 Men, has likewise arrived, which has been detained thirty days at Tenedos, by the Governor of that Island. The Captain of the Privateer demands 60,000 Piastres as an indemnity. The Porte in the mean time has sent a Courier to Tenedos to learn the true cause of the detention. The Porte, as we understand by another Letter, is labouring, as far as the adoption of new regulations can effect it, to new model the constitution of its Naval and Military Force. Barracks are ordered to be constructed for the reception of Sailors; the British discipline is to be introduced into the Turkish Marine; and a permanent and formidable Military Force is to be trained according to the system of the most martial among the other Powers of Europe.

Letters received from Malta state, that all the Vessels in that Port were actively preparing for the embarkation of Troops from that Garrison, upon a secret Expedition: it was generally conjectured that its destination was for Egypt, or Sicily.

Genoa, Nov. 29.—According to Letters from Nice, an embargo has been laid on all Swedish Ships in the French Ports in the Mediterranean Sea, as at Marseilles, &c.

FROM THE FRENCH PAPERS.

Barcelona, Nov. 30.—The port of Barcelona has been blockaded by a strong division of Admiral Nelson's Squadron since the morning of Sunday the 18th instant. We can plainly distinguish, at three leagues' distance, four Ships of the Line, first rates, and three large Frigates, which sometimes come within cannon-shot. The Captain-General of Catalonia caused a notice to be inserted in the Papers of yesterday (Tuesday), that the English Commander had received orders to sink all Vessels belonging to Spain, or her Allies, which were not of 100 tons burthen to take all those of 100 tons or upwards; and to burn all such as should be moored or anchored on the Coast. Those orders are began to be executed. A Vessel, which has been dispatched to Port Mahon with a company of Artillery, was captured on her return. The English have also taken three Transports having on board 1000 Men of the Regiment of Castilian Volunteers, destined for the same place; the women have been sent back to Barcelona. It is expected that Barcelona will be bombarded, especially since we have learned, that, exclusive of the seven Ships of War by which the Port is blockaded, there are a great number of others cruising on every part of the Coast, among which it is supposed there are a number of Bomb-Vessels. For these four days past, Lord Nelson has been exercising the most cruel hostilities in sight of our Port, which may now be looked upon as very closely blockaded. A Regiment of Castilian Volunteers, who were on their way to Mahon, on board small Vessels, together with six Merchantmen, have already been captured by them; and that at the very moment when our unfortunate Country was struggling with famine, pestilence, earthquakes, &c.; and all this without any previous Declaration of War. Lord. Nelson made an official communication to our Captain-General, that he had received orders from the Admiralty, to sink every Spanish Vessel of an hundred tons and under; to send the others to Malta; and to set fire to the Ports and Havens of Spain; and that at a moment when our Country, relying on the faith of treaties, was collecting together its few remaining Forces to contend against the different calamities with which we are afflicted.—Nelson's Squadron has just captured, in sight of our Port, a Schooner of the Royal Navy, which had conveyed a hundred Artillerymen to Mahon. We are likewise just informed, that they burnt a Spanish Ship that fondly imagined itself to be in safety in the Port of Palemos, which seems to confirm the orders which Lord Nelson declares he has received: but two or three days ago, one of his Frigates came in here for Provisions, to which no obstacle was made; such was our confidence in the faith of Treaties.—*Moniteur.*

Letters from Malaga, down to the 27th November, confirm former statements relative to the seizure of British Vessels in that Port. The Spanish Government seem determined to retaliate for the capture of their own Vessels, and have already gone so far as to seize some of their own Vessels, with their cargoes, because they were loaded in England. The Mariana, a Spanish Vessel from Bristol, was seized on the 25th November at Malaga, with a cargo of English produce. The Little Amy, Captain Lander, an English Vessel, was also embargoed, with two others, laden with cod fish, from Newfoundland.

Letters from Barcelona, dated Dec. 8, say, "The Declaration of War against

England has been signed and proclaimed by sound of trumpet. Our Spanish Government have proceeded even to this measure of self-defence with great reluctance. We abhor our task-masters, but unfortunately have no other alternative, but submission, or Gallic subjugation!"

Jan. 5.—Dispatches were received from Lord Nelson, cruising off Barcelona, dated Dec. 4th, brought by the Ambuscade Frigate. His Squadron had detained many Spanish Ships, among whom was a very rich Vessel from Buenos Ayres.

FRANCE.

(CHIEFLY FROM THE FRENCH PAPERS.)

ATTACK ON FORT ROUGE.

The English, under cover of a very thick fog, directed a Fire-ship on the night of the 8th inst. against Fort Rouge, which protects the entrance of the Port and the Road of Calais; which blew up, within a short distance of the Fort and the Jetty Head. The explosion was so great, that some windows were shattered in the Town. The Fort, however, sustained no damage, except that some articles in the inside were shook, or put out of their places. The Men who were upon guard were knocked down, but only one of them received a contusion in the arm. The Jetty was a little damaged; but we have reason to expect that they who directed the Fire-ship were worse treated, as some musketry and two cannon-shot were fired on them previous to the explosion. We could also perceive frequent signals to recal the Sailors employed in navigating this *infernal* machine, who, most probably, have been overwhelmed by the waves.

By letters from Bourdeaux, intelligence has been received at Paris, that the French Frigate the City of Milan, had fortunately arrived at Martinique, and landed 500 Soldiers there. The City of Milan is one of the finest Frigates in the French Navy; she carries 44 guns. The same letters state, that the last intelligence from Guadaloupe represent that Colony as being in a most prosperous state.

SPAIN.

As the Spaniards have hitherto carried on, almost exclusively, the Commerce of the Levant, there are many Ships of that nation in the Ports of Turkey; an Aviso has therefore been sent from Barcelona, by order of the Court of Madrid, to inform them of the change in Politics, that has taken place.

As soon as War was found to be inevitable, orders were dispatched by the Spanish Court to Cadiz to forward the earliest possible intelligence, on the subject, to the Colonies. Two Frigates accordingly sailed for this purpose, but they were both intercepted: one of them was the Amphitrite, captured by Sir R. Strachan's Ship after a short engagement. The other was detained by one of our Cruisers for twenty-four hours, and then liberated. The Captain was allowed to return into Cadiz Harbour, with an assurance, however, that the Frigate would, if again seized in an attempt to escape, be considered a good prize. It does not appear that any other Vessel had been fortunate enough to escape, so that intelligence of a rupture cannot reach the Spanish Colonies till a considerable time after our Cruisers were fully apprised of the event. By Letters from several of the Spanish Ports, it would seem that in a number of instances the orders for laying an Embargo on British Ships and property were very tardily executed. In consequence of this, the loss sustained by our Merchants would be inconsiderable. At other Ports, however, the orders were executed with the utmost severity. At Bilboa, in particular, such activity was shown, that the seizure will be to a considerable amount.

The Spaniards complain bitterly of the severity with which the orders for the detention of their Ships had been executed on the Mediterranean Station. It is natural enough to lament an activity by which they have already suffered so severely, though no one can attach blame to our Naval Commanders.

Madrid, Nov. 22.—The English Charge d'Affaires departed from hence on the 14th inst. for Lisbon, and on the 19th General Bournonville arrived here to resume his former post at our Court. We do not, however, learn that any orders have been sent, ordering our Ambassador to quit the Court of London, notwithstanding intelligence has been received that Admiral Cochrane, on the northwest coast, is imitating the conduct of Nelson along that of Catalonia. The Frigate Sabina, from Mexico, having on board about three millions of piastres, which was refused entrance at Cadiz, on account of the epidemy, is safely arrived at Vigo. The Vengenza and Ruffina, which are got safe into Port, had each the like quantity of treasure on board.

Among the many evils which England suffered from the treacherous neutrality of Spain, there was none more striking than the injury which our Commerce sustained from the Spanish Ports being made nests of Privateers from France. They had so regulated the manner of condemning prizes, and sending prize goods to France, that, after a prize had been sent into a Spanish port, the captors were as secure as if it had reached a French port. As soon as ever the cargo was condemned, it was unloaded, and instead of being ventured any more in the same Ship, it was sent to some French port, or the Bay of Biscay, in very small Vessels, bearing the Spanish or Portuguese Flag. Those Vessels, from their diminutive size, kept usually so close to the shore, that our Cruisers could not follow them: but even if any of them did fall in with our Cruisers, they had an additional security: however strongly it might be suspected that the property they carried was enemy's goods, yet the value of each of these small Vessels, separately, was not worth the expense of sending them into port for adjudication, and it has already been ascertained that no Vessel bearing a neutral Flag can be lawfully destroyed at Sea by our Cruisers. Under these circumstances our brave Sailors were obliged to see, daily, prize goods going peaceably to the ports of France, which never could have been ventured out of the port they were first sent into, if it had not been the respect which this Country always paid to a neutral Flag. The injury that this Country has suffered by these practices is of a double nature: in the first place, a great deal of British property has already found its way into French ports, which would have been recaptured, if it had not been for the pretended neutrality of Spain; 2dly, the number of French Privateers has very much increased, by the facilities so afforded them of bringing in their prize-goods without risk. In fact, Spain is the favourite situation for the privateering speculations of the French—their Crews are not pressed there, as in France, to man the Fleet; and, among a number of similar instances, it can be proved that the Braave Privateer, of 16 guns, which has made about 20 valuable prizes, never yet entered a French port since she got her commission. The Spanish ports have been for a long time past the general asylum and rendezvous of French Privateers and their prizes.

HOME REPORTS.

NARROW SEAS.

ADMIRAL HON. W. CORNWALLIS.
Vice-Admiral Sir C. COTTON, Bart.
Vice-Admiral C. COLLINGWOOD.
Vice-Admiral Sir R. CALDER, Bart.
Rear-Admiral Sir T. GRAVES, K.B.
Rear-Admiral Earl of NORTHESK.

Dover, Dec. 16. The French Lugger Privateer formerly mentioned as having taken a Brig, arrived here on Friday evening, about eight o'clock; The is named the Cruiser, of 15 guns, of different calibres, and 55 men, and was taken by the Favourite Sloop of War, Captain Foote, after a sharp chase; the Frenchmen supposed nothing could catch her, she sailed so fast: she was going $11\frac{1}{2}$ knots an hour, when taken. One of the Crew informs me, there are two others of the same kind, one of the same size as this, and another larger. She had taken five Vessels since she was first fitted out, and is a very handsome Vessel. The Crew report that there are upwards of 7,000 Gun-vessels, Transports, &c. at Boulogne, Calais, Dunkirk, and Ostend; but I think this account must be exaggerated. They say all the houses without the gates at Calais, on the Quay, under the Cour de Gain Wall, are converted into guard-houses, and every means adopted to strengthen both Boulogne and Calais from a sudden attack. It is much to be hoped the Favourite Sloop will be continued on her Station off Brighton, as she sails so fast, to counteract the depredations of the other two Luggers. Nothing but a fast Vessel like her can catch them.

18. The Starling Gun-brig got on shore near Calais, in a thick fog, and Lieutenant Shotton, who commanded her, finding it utterly impracticable to get her off, had the precaution to blow her up, and brought away all her Crew in the Cutter and the Jolly-boat.

Penzance, Dec. 18. Arrived the Spanish Ship Dido, from the River de la Plata, and the Schooner la Lindes, from Goracius, both detained by the Fisgard Frigate, who has detained thirteen other Vessels.

Brixham, Dec. 20. We have had a violent gale of Wind about E. by N. for several days. Yesterday a Torbay Sloop drove from her moorings, out of Torr Road, and went on shore near Livermead Sands, and will soon go to pieces; she belongs to a poor Fisherman; Crew saved. Another Torbay Sloop went on shore in Start Bay, and it is feared the Crew are all lost. The Frigate Nemesis, Captain Somerville, who was left here to take charge of the Venerable's stores, was to have been relieved by his Majesty's Ship Blonde, Capt. Faulknor, who came in here on Monday; but it has blown such a gale ever since, her Boat could not reach the shore, nor any go off. This morning at day-light the Blonde Frigate was discovered in great distress, having parted both her bowers, and riding to her sheet anchor, her colours hoisted Union downwards; no Boat could venture off to assist them. About nine A.M. she cut away her main and mizen-masts, to ease the Ship, which was scarce completed before she parted her last cable; they got the forestays on her, and run her into Goodrington Sands, within a mile from where the Venerable was lost; some hundreds of men from Brixham flew to their assistance. They also took two large lively Smuggling Boats, which would live almost in any Sea, and dragged them round from Brixham, four miles. Then seven daring Brixham Sailors, much to their praise, ventured off in the midst of the breakers, took out the Captain's lady with all the rest of the women and children first, and brought them on shore safe; amounting to 114 men, and 18 women; then took a rope on shore, and continued to haul on shore and on board till they had saved every soul of them. The greatest praise is due to the Brixham men. If the gale continues the Blonde will go to pieces next tide, as her rudder is gone already; and great fears are entertained for the Nemesis, which rides forecastle in Sea. Pray Heavens assuage the storm! I have just been an eye-witness of this melancholy scene, and assisted in saving all I could. The Blonde was last from Lymington Creek, where she has been Guardship.

Torbay, Dec. 22. The storm continues at E. by N. with unabated fury. The Nemesis Frigate (thank God!) continues to ride it out. The Blonde Frigate is not yet gone to pieces, and great hopes are entertained, if the weather abates, she might be preserved. Capt. Faulknor, in a masterly Seaman-like manner, run her in on the Sands, within her length of a reef of rocks, then gave a yield to the shore, and laid her athwart. Captain Faulknor and some other Gentlemen intend to have a Medal engraved for those seven men who ventured off in their Boat.

24. His Majesty's Ship Nemesis, Captain Somerville, has rode the storm out thus far very well, having had her yards, top-masts, and every thing that possibly could be struck, snug on deck, that she appeared almost like a Lugger at a distance. Yesterday it moderated a little, and every appearance of the gale's being over, she began to get up yards and top-masts, and her Boat being able to come on shore, it was found she had drove a little in the gale, having broke her sheet anchor off in the shank. The brave Brixham young men, who had so gallantly preserved the Crew of the Blonde, and to whom the preference was given to weigh her anchors by Captain Faulknor, were immediately ordered by our Navy Agent to weigh the Blonde's sheet anchor, and carry it on board the Nemesis; but before they could accomplish it last night the Wind and Sea prevented them. This morning, at dawn, the Agent sent them off again, with an anchor from the shore, as it came on to blow, with a heavy Sea again from the east; but before they could

teach the Ship, the anchor got loose by the pitching of the Sloop, and was likely to go through her bows: they were necessitated, with great reluctance, to return. The Wind and Sea increasing, the Nemesis' yards and top-masts are again struck; she rides quite easy, being well in from tide's way. The old Brig Nelly is entirely gone to pieces, and the poor Fishermen have suffered considerably in their Craft.

Dover, Dec. 25. During the late gale, the Immortalite Frigate was left alone off Boulogne, and, as the Wind blew off shore, between 20 and 30 of the enemy's large Gun Boats came out, but were afraid to attack her. Captain Owen took out the Crew of a Swedish Dogger, that had been ashore on the French coast, and was nearly sinking.

Torbay, Dec. 27. The Wind is again increasing to a whole gale at E. by S.: the Nemesis Frigate continues to ride it out exceeding well. In my last I wrote you that the Nemesis had parted her sheet anchor, and that the same brave Brixham men, who saved the Blonde's Crew, had taken a Sloop to carry off an anchor to her, but were obliged to return. Christmas-day they took a larger Sloop, and much to their credit accomplished their design, and delivered it safe to her bows, although there was such a violent Sea. One of the brave fellows broke his hand-spike in heaving up, and bruised himself much; the others had near swamped their Boat along-side, but returned, thank God! all safe.

THE LATE GALE AT GUERNSEY.

His Majesty's Ship Thisbe, Captain Sheppard, sailed from Portsmouth the 12th of December, and, after chasing a French Lugger Privateer, of 16 guns, close into Dieppe, arrived at Guernsey on the 16th; it blew so hard that the Privateer's lee-guns were quite under water; and although within half gun-shot, the Thisbe unfortunately could not get her guns to bear: the Privateer carried such a press of sail that she was almost under water during the chase. On Monday, the 17th, the Thisbe, lying at anchor in Guernsey Roads, received orders to proceed to Jersey, with an anchor and cable for his Majesty's Ship Severn.· At about two, the Niobe Frigate, Captain Scott, came in and anchored close a-head of the Thisbe; and, although every exertion was made in veering cable, she fell on board the Thisbe, which Ship was obliged to veer two cables to get clear of the Niobe: she, however, carried away the Thisbe's figure head, and did her some damage. At about four, the Niobe attempted to weigh, to get clear, but fell a-board the second time, and sprung the Thisbe's bowsprit, which obliged the Thisbe to veer to three cables; but, being so near the rocks, was forced to cut and make sail, and anchor without the Niobe. The next day it came on to blow very strong from the eastward, which obliged the Thisbe to let go the sheet anchor, and, having no other cable on board but that before mentioned for the Severn, bent that to the spare anchor, and had it ready for letting go. At about eleven that night it blew an Hurricane, and in half an hour after the best bower cable parted: the only anchor they had remaining was then let go, with the Severn's cable bent to it, which brought the Ship up within half a cable's length of the rocks. Almost immediately the Niobe and Sylph cut away their masts; and at one in the morning, the gale increasing, and the Thisbe pitching very heavy, the fore-mast was cut away, which eased her very much. She continued riding so till ten o'clock, and, no appearance of the gale ceasing, the main-mast was cut away. About four in the afternoon the gale abated, the sheet anchor was attempted to be got up; but the cable parted, being cut to pieces with the rocks, and when the other anchor was hove up, it was found that, if the gale had continued two hours longer, the Thisbe must inevitably have been lost and all the Crew drowned.

PLYMOUTH.

Vice-Admiral W. YOUNG.
Rear-Admiral J. SUTTON.

THE getting out of a Man of War from Plymouth, in hazy weather, so as to avoid the buoys, merely by sound of *drum*, at each of them, is unquestionably a great trial of nautical skill; but to some military persons it would sound queer to hear of a 98-gun Ship being *drummed out of harbour.* This was also done at Portsmouth with the Prince of Wales, of 98 guns (See Portsmouth Report, January 5.)

Dec. 15. The Queen Charlotte, Mudge, which arrived on Thursday, brings the pleasing account of the safe arrival in the Chesapeak of the Revolutionaire, 44 guns, from Spithead.

Yesterday in the gale of Wind, the Fame, of 36 guns (late la Blonde), Captain Hosier, lying in Hamoaze, parted from her cables, and went on shore near Devil's Point; but the tide flowing, she swung off with much damage, and is now near the West Mud. There were drowned on Thursday last, in the Beaver Transport, on her being wrecked on the rocks near Yealm Point, in the gale of Wind, two men, a woman, and a child. Great credit is due for the assistance rendered by Lieutenant Dundas, of la Musette, of 24 guns, Guard-ship in Yealm River, and a detachment of the Plymouth, or Prince of Wales's own Royal Volunteers, Lieutenant Colonel Hawker, in their endeavours to save the people and stores of the Transport.

16. Yesterday at noon Vice-Admiral Sir C. Cotton, Bart. shifted his Flag from the Prince, of 98 guns, to the San Josef, of 112 guns, his old Flag-Ship; the Ship and yards were manned on the occasion, and his Flag was cheered when run up to the fore-top-gallant-mast-head. This morning the Prince, of 98 guns, sailed to join the Channel Fleet, under Admiral Cornwallis, in Torbay. Went into the Sound, and sailed for Milford, with convoy, the Caroline, hired armed Brig, of 14 guns, Lieutenant Derby. Sailed for the Eastward, the Morristown, of 14 guns, with convoy; the Spartiate, of 84 guns, Captain Sir F. Laforey, Bart. now in Hamoaze, fitting for her Station off Ferrol, is to take on board twelve months' provisions and stores for that part of the world, and from thence up the Straits.

17. Came in from the Westward, the Windsor Castle, of 98 guns, and the Queen of 98 guns, with the Crescent, of 36 guns. The Temeraire landed Captain Kelly, and sailed again immediately.

18. The Squadron under Vice-Admiral Sir T. Graves were left all well by the Queen, on the 15th instant. The enemy in the roads of Rochefort and l'Orient as usual. This Squadron experienced dreadful weather, and in the fury of the gale on Thursday night last, the Queen was forced to bear away for this port; but the gale abating, she spoke the Squadron, all well, after the gale, and brought dispatches and letters from the Squadron. The Queen has been on the Rochefort Station fifteen weeks and four days. There were five persons lost when the Rover Packet was wrecked last Thursday night on the rocks of Yealm Point, east of the Slimer Rocks. The Ship parted midships. Two men and the Mate jumped from the bows, but were drowned, with the Mate's wife. Captain Rutledge, with his usual humanity, tried to get ashore, with the Mate's child in his arms, but was washed on shore senseless, and the child perished.

20. Last night it blew a dreadful gale of Wind at S. S.E. with a great surf in Cawsand Bay. The Men of War having good ground, rode out well till this morning; when the Malta, of 84 guns, drove from her anchors, and was obliged to veer away more cable, and touched some rocks in the Bay, but brought up again very soon. A Victualling-Office Hoy, with provisions for the Fleet in Cawsand Bay; the Boats of the Pay-Office, going to pay the Dreadnought, of 98 guns, six months' wages; and several others, with stores and cordage, were all obliged to bear away and return, as the gale was tremendous.

22. It has blown one of the hardest gales of Wind since Monday at S.S.E. and E. N.E. experienced for many years along this coast. The Men of War in Cawsand Bay have weathered it without damage. The Malta, of 84 guns, Captain Butler, though she struck slightly, by the exertions of Officers and Crew, did not receive any damage: Mr. Penn, King's Pilot, with some Cawsand men, ventured out to her assistance, though their Boat was nearly blown out of the water.

24. Yesterday there was a great fall of snow. Friday, though it blew so hard at E.N.E., being appointed for a review of the Cawsand Sea Fencibles, 150 fine fellows and hardy fishermen were mustered at eleven A. M. by Rear-Admiral Phillips, Inspecting Admiral of the Sea Fencibles on the coasts of Devon and Cornwall. They were ready for the great gun and pike exercise; but, after their muster on Maker Heights field, the Admiral dismissed them, as it blew such a Hurricane the men could not stand at the guns. He was much pleased with their appearance, and returned them his thanks by Captain Winne, of the Royal Navy, their commanding Officer. 7

The order of Council for an embargo on all Spanish Ships in this port, and its dependencies, was put in force yesterday, and four Spanish merchantmen were in consequence boarded by the Officers of the Customs. The Spanish Men of War are also placed in a similar situation, and their cargoes of sundries are landed, and under directions and care of the Collector of the Customs of this port. From the late violent easterly Winds, the convoy from Milford, and the west of Cornwall, have been much retarded, to the great detriment of the trade of this town and dock.

26. Went into the Sound the Uranie, of 44 guns, Honourable Captain C. Herbert; she sails on a cruise in a few days. Came in from a cruise the Niobe, of 44 guns, and a very large Frigate, much disabled in her masts and rigging: she has rigged up a jury fore-mast and fore-top-mast; her bowsprit appears sprung: she has also a jury main-top-mast. She went directly up into Hamoaze to refit.

27. This day the Thisbe, of 28 guns, arrived from Guernsey under jury masts. The Pigmy was towed into Guernsey Pier a mere wreck with the Sylph; a gentleman of Guernsey, assisting in hauling on, had his thighs dreadfully fractured, owing to a hawser giving way, and two Seamen had their legs broke; several other accidents likewise occurred.

29. Went up the harbour to refit the damages she received in Guernsey Roads, in the Hurricane of the 19th at E.N.E. the Thisbe, of 28 guns. The Ariadne, of 24, and the Merlin of 18 guns, which came in yesterday morning, were obliged to bear away from their Station off Havre de Grace, as it blew dreadfully direct on that part of the coast of France. Came in the Chichester, of 44 guns, from the Straits; she brings nothing new. Sailed to join the Channel Fleet the Dreadnought, of 98 guns, Vice-Admiral Collingwood. This afternoon were landed from the Malta, of 84 guns, Captain Buller, lately arrived from off Ferrol, several barrels, containing nearly 60,000 dollars in silver, consigned from merchants in Spain to their correspondents in London. They were deposited in Russel's waggon warehouses previous to their being sent to London under a proper escort.

January 2, 1805. Yesterday being the first day of the new year, the blocks were fixed on the slip from whence the Hibernia, of 120 guns, was launched on the 17th of November last; and the keel of a new Ship, of the same class, was laid down, under the direction of J. Tucker, Esq. Master-Builder, and his Assistants, of this Dock-yard, which is to be called the Caledonia, of 120 guns; she is to be finished in two years from this date. Came in and went up the harbour to get spare anchors and cables, the Lord Nelson Defence Ship, Captain Halsted, blown out of the Downs in the late gales of Wind at E.N.E. She parted all her anchors, but fortunately bore away for this port. Letters from Milford Haven state the safe arrival of the Caroline Brig, of 14 guns, Lieutenant Derby, after experiencing very terrible gales of Wind; but owing to her being so clever, tight, and well found a Vessel, she did not strain a spun-yarn. She is to cruise to the Southward as soon as Lieutenant Derby receives his orders. She is a beautiful fast-sailing Vessel of her class. Came in the Albacore, 18 guns. She experienced the fury of the late Hurricane at E.N.E. on the coast of France, and rode out the gale with one anchor, having parted two cables just after it began to blow. When the gale abated, she weighed her remaining anchor and bore away for this port, and has received new anchors and cables; she sails for her Station off Havre de Grace and along the French coast, this evening or to-morrow, at day-light. Went up the harbour at two P.M. the Phœnix, 44 guns.

4. A few days since a fire broke out on board a Transport, laden with sails, near the Calder Basin of the Dock-yard, but it was soon put out, with only the burning of the sails. The orders are to be strictly enforced in future, that no fires are to be kept on board any Navy Transport or any other Vessel that may be loading or unloading stores in the above Basin, which is directly opposite the sail lofts and warehouses on the south side of the Dock-yard.

This morning came in, having thrown her guns overboard in a gale of Wind, the Rattler, Capt. Francis Mason, 18 guns; also from off the Coast of Spain, under a press of sail, the Indefatigable, 44 guns, Capt. G. Monro; she came to in the Sound, and lay-to for two hours, till the return of a Boat from shore, which landed a gentleman from her at the Pier. He set off express in a post-chaise from the Prince George Tavern, Foxhall Quay, at 11 A.M. The gentleman was not at all communicative, but expressed great anxiety to set off on his journey: as soon as the Boat which brought him ashore from the Indefatigable returned to the Ship, she made sail again directly. Went down into the Sound, the Amphion, 40 guns, Capt. Sutton.

5. Arrived from a cruise off the coast of Spain, the Diamond, 36 guns, Capt. Elphinstone, with a most beautiful Spanish Corvette, the Infanta Carlos, from the Havana, was dispatched for Corunna; laden on the King of Spain's and Merchants' account with a valuable cargo, and 120,000 dollars in specie. Before she struck, three of her men were killed. The Diamond has taken two other Spanish prizes, not yet arrived. Came in from Milford Haven, the Caroline, 14 guns, Lieutenant J. Derby; she convoyed up off this port a large South Sea Whaler, very leaky, and having overshot this port, she went into Dartmouth: the Crew has since got into Catwater. Sailed for Dartmouth, with jury-masts, yards, and Naval Stores, a Navy Transport, for the Martin, of 18 guns, a new Sloop of War, building at Dartmouth. At eleven P.M. this morning, the Pickle, of 14 guns, Lieutenant Lapontiere, express from Ferrol in only 49 hours, brought dispatches from Rear-Admiral Cochrane, of importance, which were directly forwarded to the Admiralty express. Came in the Neptune, of 98 guns, Capt. T. Williams, from the Fleet off Ferrol; she left Admiral Cochrane all well about ten days since, and would have been into this port before, but for the violent gales of Wind at E.N.E. Came in the Santa Margaretta, of 36 guns, Capt. Rathbourne, from a cruise, and the Plover, of 18 guns, Capt. Hancock: also a large timber Ship, from America, with masts, yards, and spars; and a large Dantzick Ship, with deals, balk, &c. for the Dock-yard.

7. Came in the Naiad, of 36 guns, Captain Dundas, from a cruise off the Coast of Spain, with a large rich Spanish Ship, bound to a Port in Spain, with 200,000 dollars on board; besides a valuable cargo of sundry dry goods. She immediately went up the Harbour and had nearly been ashore: but wearing steady, she got safe up to her moorings. Sailed for Spithead the Chichester, of 44 guns, which was reported to have sailed for the Straits; but it appears she was blown down Channel by the late easterly Winds. Sailed to join the Channel Fleet, the San Josef, of 112 guns, Vice-Admiral Sir C. Cotton, Bart. with bullocks and vegetables.

8. The Aigle, of 44 guns, Captain Wolfe, arrived yesterday in the Sound from a long Cruise. The Aigle, in her late Cruise, in a violent gale of Wind, ran down the Flying Fish, of 10 guns, but fortunately all the Officers and Crew were saved on board the Aigle. The Naiad, of 36 guns, Captain Dundas, sailed last night on a Cruise to the Westward. Last night there was a hot press in the Harbour and in Catwater, and many useful hands were picked up and sent on board the Flag Ship.

PORTSMOUTH.

Admiral G. MONTAGU.
Rear-Admiral Sir ISAAC COFFIN.

Dec. 11. Arrived his Majesty's Ship Avenger, from Newfoundland. Sailed the Leopard Man of War to the eastward.

16. Sailed the Melampus Frigate, to join the Channel Fleet. The Mercury Frigate, Hon. Captain Bouverie, has made a signal for a Convoy to the Mediterranean. Admiral O'Brien Drury has hoisted his Flag on board his Majesty's Ship Princess of Orange.

17. Arrived the Orpheus Frigate, Aurora armed Ship, Swift and Hector Sloops of War, with a large Fleet of outward-bound Vessels under Convoy, from the Downs. Sailed the Merlin Sloop of War, on a Cruise. The Venus, of London, bound to Africa, upset this morning, seven leagues to the eastward of the Isle of Wight; three men were drowned, and the remainder were picked up by the Rebecca, of St. Helen's. Orders came down to make prizes of all Ships bearing the Spanish Flag; in consequence of which the Merlin Sloop, Captain Brenton, sailed with dispatches for our Cruisers on the Coast of France.

18. The Decade Frigate, Captain Rutherford, unmoored to proceed off Cherbourg. Arrived the Eugenie Sloop of War, from the Downs. Came into Har-

bour his Majesty's Ship Aurora. Arrived the Hecla Bomb, from a cruise; Prospero Bomb, Aurora and Osborne armed Ships, from the Eastward. Sailed the Chichester Frigate, from St Helen's, where she has lain as a Guard Ship for some months, to the Westward, with sealed orders; and Merlin Sloop of War, on a Cruise.

20. Arrived the Greyhound Frigate, Captain Elphinstone; and the Steady Gun-Brig, from a cruise; Eugenie, Harlequin, and l'Utile, Sloops of War, from the Eastward. Went out of Harbour the Arethusa Frigate to the Eastward, to be refitted.

21. Sailed to join the Russian Squadron at Corfu, four Sail of Russian Ships of War, under a Commodore, which have been lying at Spithead some time; also the Mediterranean Convoy, under the Mercury Frigate.

22. This morning sailed Rear-Admiral O. Drury, as Second in Command on the Coast of Ireland, where an additional strong Squadron is to be stationed. The Princess Royal, of 98 guns; the Goliath and Thunderer, of 74 guns, from the Channel Fleet; and the Raisonable, Captain Barton, from Spithead, are to reinforce this Squadron.

24. Sailed the Unicorn, of 32 guns, Captain Hardyman, and the Swift Sloop of War, with the Fleet under their Convoy, consisting of 200 Sail, for the West Indies; also the Harrier, with Dispatches for the East Indies. Wind E.

26. Sailed for Spithead the Euryalus, Captain Blackwood. Arrived a Spanish Ship, detained and sent in from Cowes by his Majesty's Ship Royal William; this Ship had discharged her Cargo at Cowes, and was loaded with Coals, and ready to sail. On Tuesday, the 18th inst. the English Brig Golden Grove, Captain G. Pearce, from Tortola, bound to London, was towed into Cowes by the hired armed Schooner Princess Charlotte, Captain F. Husband. Great praise is due to Captain Husband, for the promptitude, zeal, and perseverance with which he assisted this Vessel, which had lost all her Sails in a tremendous gale of Wind, lost her main-yard, and sprung her top-mast, and had all her rigging shattered, with only two Men and the Captain able to keep the Deck.

29. The Triumph, of 74 guns, Sir R. Barlow, was paid off on Wednesday, at this Port.

Jan. 2, 1805. The fog has been so thick, that it cannot be ascertained whether any Ships have arrived at Spithead; notwithstanding which, the Prince of Wales, of 98 guns, and Hecla Bomb, went out of Harbour with little Wind, as did several large Transports. Sir Robert Calder is arrived, to hoist his Flag on board the Prince of Wales. The Poullet Frigate, being ordered on a particular Service, has dropped down to Stokes Bay to receive her water, as there is too much Sea at Spithead to take it on board there; this is an unusual proceeding: she is now ready for Sea. Captain Sayer took the command of the Proselyte Frigate, this morning, in the room of Captain Hardinge. she is bound to the West Indies, with Convoy. The Majestic armed Ship remains with a Convoy for the Downs. The Wind is getting round from N. E. to nearly W.

3. All the Men of the Triumph are turned over to the Barfleur, of 98 guns, Captain Martin; she has made the signal to go out of Harbour. The very thick fog still continues; Spithead has not been visible these two days, but there are no Ships arrived or sailed. The Royal Marine Court-Martial on Captain Meredith, of that Corps, resumed its sittings this day in the Marine Barracks. Sailed the Manly Gun-Vessel, Lieutenant White, for the Downs. At ten o'clock last night, the Monarch, of 74 guns, Captain Searle, the Flag Ship of Lord Keith, arrived at Spithead, from the Downs, to be refitted: as the weather was very thick, she ran into shallow water near the Owers: she is to be repaired at Spithead. Also the Merlin Sloop, Captain Brenton, from off Havre.

5. The Raven Brig, Capt. Layman, has made the signal for a Convoy to the Mediterranean. Governor Beckwith this day embarked on board the Proselyte Frigate, Capt. Sayer, which will sail to-morrow for Cork and the West Indies. Yesterday afternoon the Ambuscade Frigate, Capt. Durban, arrived here with Rear-Admiral Campbell, from the Mediterranean, who has resigned his command.

in consequence of an ill state of health. We are, however, happy in being able to state, that the Admiral is much recovered since he left the Station. The Ambuscade passed through the Gut of Gibraltar on the 15th, when the Sophie Sloop was cruising, and the Swiftsure was lying in the Bay. The Donnegal, Sir R. Strachan, had passed through the Gut to join the Fleet. On the 16th she spoke the Ruby and Agamemnon, cruising on the Coast of Spain; and for the last fortnight has had very heavy gales of Wind. On Tuesday last she fell in with the Channel Fleet, 100 leagues to the westward of the Lizard. Lord Nelson's baggage was removed to the Superb, Capt. Keats, ready for his return to England. He may be daily expected. Capt. Elliott, of the 61st Regiment, is the only passenger in the Ambuscade. She was a month on her passage, in consequence of adverse Winds; having left Lord Nelson cruising to the north east of Barcelona, on the 4th of December. The number of captures made by his Lordship at that date has been greatly exaggerated, it not exceeding seven or eight, and some of those were of small value. A Spanish South American Ship had, however, made the probable amount of detained property more than 150,000l. A private letter by the same conveyance, dated the 21st Dec. states, that a Midshipman and two Seamen belonging to the Northumberland, had been detained by a guard of Spanish Soldiers as they were walking in the fields near Ferrol; but on the receipt of a Flag of truce from Adm. Cochrane, they were immediately released. The British Officers had declined going ashore, as they had been accustomed to do; and whenever it was necessary to send in Flags of Truce, they were accompanied by Gun-boats. One of our Boats, while trowling off Ferrol, was fired at from the Batteries, under an opinion that she was taking soundings, but when the mistake was discovered, an apology was sent to the Admiral. At the date of these dispatches, our Squadron consisted of the Northumberland, Neptune, Montague, Illustrious, Terrible, Repulse, Minotaur, Ajax, and several Frigates. A fog, unusually thick, has prevailed here this week. On Wednesday (and it should be noticed as a novel effort of nautical zeal and skill) the Prince of Wales, of 98 guns, was led out of the harbour to Spithead, by a drum being sent from the Ship, and beat at the different buoys, when the atmosphere was so dense that she could not be distinctly seen, even when passing the platform.

The extraordinary working of the imagination which acts on the mind, and causes a walking in the sleep, was attended with very melancholy consequences to Lieutenant and Adjutant Wills, of the Portsmouth division of the Royal Marines, who, about two o'clock, took the lamp out of the window, unfastened and got out of it, walked along the colonnade, and fell into the Barrack-yard, a height of about twelve feet, which broke the small bones of his ancles, and fractured his head. It is with much satisfaction we learn that the consequences are not likely to prove fatal.

7. The whole of the men in the Dock-yard at Portsmouth, to the full number of 3000, were last week regaled with a pot of strong beer each; the donor or donors of which have hitherto withheld their names from publicity.

8. Wind West. Came into harbour the Sylph Brig, to make good the damage she received by being driven on shore at Guernsey. The Avenger Sloop went out of the harbour this morning. The Court Martial on Captain Meredith, of the Royal Marines, closed this morning. The sentence awaits the approval of the Lords of the Admiralty. Came up to Spithead the Polyphemus, from the Mediterranean.

9. Sailed the Proselyte Frigate, with a Fleet of outward-bound West Indiamen, under convoy for Cork. Sailed also the Firm Gun-vessel, on a cruise. The Prince of Wales of 98 guns, Vice-Admiral Sir Robert Calder, was paid this morning. The Polyphemus, Capt. Lawford, has captured the Guerra Spanish Frigate, off Cape St. Vincent's, which is hourly expected to arrive. She is valuably laden, supposed at about two millions, in specie and merchandise. The Polyphemus has a number of Spanish prisoners on board, which were taken out of between thirty and forty prizes, which are sent into Gibraltar.

13. Wind Southerly. Arrived the Rattler Sloop, Captain Francis Mason, from a cruise.

Promotions and Appointments.

(December—January.)

His Majesty by his Royal Commission has been pleased to appoint Sir Charles Middleton, Bart.; Admiral Sir Roger Curtis, Bart.; Rear-Admiral Domett; Mr. Fordyce, of the Land Revenue Office; and Mr. Serle, of the Transport Board; to examine and report upon the improvements suggested by the Commissioners of Naval Inquiry. Mr. Thompson, Naval Officer at Leith, is appointed Secretary to the Commission.

Sir Evan Nepean, Bart. is appointed one of the Lords of the Admiralty.

Captain George Sayer, to the Proselyte Frigate, *vice* Hardinge; Captain Mends, to the Sea Fencibles in Ireland; Luke F. Nagle, Esq. to be Surgeon of the Barfleur; Mr. Mitchell, to be Purser of the Gladiator; Captain Simpson, to the Moselle; Captain Carden, to the Driver.

An Order in Council has directed, that Midshipmen who have served their time, are to be employed as Sub-Lieutenants on board of such armed Brigs as are commanded by Lieutenants; for which service their pay will be 4s. per day; and when they are not in Commission, are to receive half pay. They will be allowed their rank; and their uniform is to be that of the undress which the Lieutenants now wear.

Captain J. W. Loring is appointed to the Aurora Frigate; Captain Malbon to the Hebe, a new Frigate. Hon. Lieutenant H. Duncan, to the command, *pro tempore*, of the Bittern Sloop, *vice* Corbett, indisposed.

Samuel Curry, Esq. late Secretary to Vice-Admiral Patton, whilst commanding in the Downs, but now one of the Lords of the Admiralty, is promoted as Purser of his Majesty's Frigate Arethusa, to the Crown, of 64 guns, now lying in ordinary at Portsmouth. Captain Inman, to the Utrecht; Captain Granger to the command, *pro tempore*, of the Malta, *vice* Bullen; Mr. Pritchard, Midshipman of the Ville de Paris, and son of Mr. Pritchard, who commands a division of Ships in ordinary at Portsmouth, is made a Lieutenant. Captain E. P. Brenton, to the Amaranthe; Captain Forbes, to the Merlin.

To be Sub-Lieutenants,—Mr. George Harris, of the Medusa, to the Clinker;. Mr. C. Hill, to the Acute; Mr. J. Darby, to the Bouncer; Mr. N. Row, to the Aimwell; Mr. W. L. Patterson, to the Rover.

Lieutenants Irwin, Skinner, and Down, of the Royal Yachts, are promoted to the rank of Commanders.

The Lords Commissioners of the Admiralty have been pleased, in consideration of his long and meritorious services, to restore to his rank in the Navy, and appoint to his Majesty's Ship Prince George, Lieutenant James Buchannan, of Gosport, who was about two years since dismissed from his Majesty's Ship Peterell, for being a short time off the deck in his watch.

Captain G. Losack, to the Prince George, of 98 guns, instead of Captain Yorke; Captain Lobb to the Pomona, a new Frigate; Lieutenant Grant, who lately commanded the Hawke Cutter, an old, brave, and scientific Officer, is promoted to be a Commander; and Lieutenant Bogue is appointed First Lieutenant of the Weymouth; Captain Hardinge, to the Valorous, a new Frigate: Sir T. Livingstone, to the Renommee Frigate; and Captain Seator, to the Mediator.

Mr. John Wilby, Purser of the Scorpion Sloop, is promoted to the Jamaica Frigate.

Lieutenant Tremlett is appointed to the command of the Phosphorous Fire-Vessel at the Nore.

Captain Drummond is appointed to the Dryad, *vice* Giffard, who resigns from ill health; Captain Gore retains the command of the Medusa; Captain Davie to the Favourite, *vice* Foote; Captain Westbeach to the Hermes; Captain Woolcombe to the Amelia, *vice* Lord Proby, deceased. The Rev. Mr. Souter to the Prince of Wales; Mr. Macdonald, to be Surgeon of the Colossus.

The King has been pleased to grant unto Sir Rd. Bickerton, Bt. Rear-Adm. of the Red Squadron of his Majesty's Fleet, his Royal License and permission to accept and wear the insignia of the Ottoman Imperial Order of the Crescent (of the superior degree), transmitted to him by the Grand Signior. And the Order of the Crescent having been instituted by his Majesty's Ally the Grand Signior, in commemoration of the signal and important services rendered to the Ottoman Empire, by the glorious achievements of the British arms in Egypt; the King has further been pleased by warrant under his Royal Signet and Sign Manual, to grant unto the said Rear-Admiral Sir Richard Bickerton, his Royal License and permission, to bear, in allusion thereto, a Crescent, and certain other appropriate honourable augmentations to his family arms, together with supporters; the same being first duly exemplified according to the laws of arms, and recorded in the Herald's Office.

Captain Bouchier is appointed Lieutenant-Governor of Greenwich Hospital, in the room of the late Sir Richard Pearson.

BIRTHS.

Jan. 1, 1805. At Swansea, the Lady of Captain New, of the Navy, of a daughter.

The Lady of Captain J. Baker, of the Navy, of a son.

MARRIAGES.

Dec. 17. At Weande, near Plymouth, Major Bevan, of the 28th Regiment of Foot, to Miss Dacres, eldest daughter of Admiral Dacres.

23. Captain Winthrop, of the Ardent, to Miss Farbrace, of Dover.

24. At Ryde, Captain Hill, of the Orpheus, to Miss Bettesworth, daughter of Captain Bettesworth, of the South Hants Militia.

Lately, at Barbadoes, Commodore Hood, to the Hon. Miss M'Kenzie, daughter of Lord Seaforth, Governor of Barbadoes.

Jan. 12, 1805. At Southweald, in Essex, by the Rev. Dr. Bullock, Captain Charles Finling, of the Royal Navy, to Miss Sarah Bullock, youngest daughter of William Bullock, Esq. of Wealside House.

Lieutenant E. Young, of the Royal Marines, to Miss Perfect, daughter of W. Perfect, Esq. M.D. of West Maling.

At Rochester, Captain T. Young, of the Royal Marines, to Mrs. G. Wynch, widow, daughter of the above-named W. Perfect.

Lord Viscount Duncan, son of the late Admiral Lord Viscount Duncan, to Miss J. Dalrymple, daughter of the late Sir H. H. Dalrymple, Bart. of Bargany and North Berwick.

At Buckland, Captain Rolles, of the Navy, to Miss Rawbone, daughter of the Rev. Dr. Rawbone, Rector of Hatford.

Captain Kerr, of the Navy, to Miss C. Maule, daughter of the late C. Maule, Esq.

OBITUARY.

Nov. 22. At Gibraltar, Doctor Bird, Physician to the Naval Hospital there.

Dec. 17. At Huntingdon, Thomas Furbor, late of the Royal Hospital School, Greenwich, of which he was Master nearly thirty years.

26. Sir Samuel Hales, Bart. of Mundell, Lincolnshire, Lieutenant in the Royal Navy.

29. Two young men were found dead in a West Indiaman, outward bound, lying off Woolwich. It is supposed they had drank too much spirits, and fell asleep, when they became frost bitten.

The same night, two lads belonging to a Collier, waiting in a Boat for their Captain, at Stone-Stairs, Ratcliffe-Cross, were found in the arms of one another, nearly expiring, through the inclemency of the weather. They were taken to a public-house, where, with much difficulty, they recovered.

30. An Officer of the Navy, in shooting birds, at Fratton, near Portsmouth, as he inadvertently attempted to divide the briars with the butt end of the piece, being on full cock, the trigger caught a bramble, and the contents of the gun were discharged through the Lieutenant's heart, who instantly expired.

From the effects of a cold, Lieutenant Urquhart, of the Royal Marines, of his Majesty's Ship Euryalus. He was buried on Thursday in Portsmouth Garrison Chapel, with the accustomed military honours.

31. Mr. J. Callaway, Midshipman of his Majesty's Ship Montagu, and son of R. Callaway, Esq. of Portsmouth, aged 17. The spirit and talents of this youth were promising of his becoming a future ornament to the profession in which he was engaged. He had just served his time as a Midshipman.

A Seaman's body, supposed to have been drowned some time since, was hauled up, fastened by his clothes to the anchor fluke of a Man of War lying in Barnpool.

Jan. 2, 1805. At her mother's house, in Lower Eton-street, the wife of Captain Liardet, of the Royal Marines.

18. At Clifton, Miss Church, eldest daughter of the late Captain Church, of the Navy.

26. At Greenwich Hospital, Sir R. Pearson, Lieutenant-Governor of that Institution; on whom the honour of Knighthood was conferred for his bravery in action with Paul Jones, while in command of the Serapis. We hope, with the assistance of some of our Friends, to be soon able to present our Readers with the Memoirs of this worthy Officer.

Lately, aged 80, Mrs. E. Hall, mother to the Rev. J. Hall, Chaplain of the Royal Naval Hospital at Haslar. Her remains were deposited in the family vault, at Ledbury, Herefordshire.

Lately, suddenly, Captain C. B. Jones, of the Navy, at Swansea.

Lately, of the pestilential fever, at Gibraltar, aged 24, Robert Palgrave, Esq. Register of the Court of Admiralty there, and late of Coltishall, near Norwich.

A Seaman of the Spartiate, of 84 guns, refitting in Hamoaze, fell from the main-yard, and was killed on the spot. It is supposed his hands were benumbed with the excessive cold, and lost his hold.

Mr. John Mitchell, Harbour Master at Sunderland. He went on a visit to a friend at Hilton Ferry; and on his return in the evening, it is supposed owing to the darkness of the night he had mistaken his way, as he was found at the bottom of Clagshiff Rock on Thursday morning; over which it is believed he fell, as his head seemed very much bruised.

At Bridgenorth, Mr. Owen Davis, Chart Maker, in the 80th year of his age; who, it is well known, spent more than 600l. in one public-house in that town, in the course of the last forty years, though he was seldom known to spend more than 1s. in any one day.

Mechain, the Astronomer, Member of the First Class of the National Institute, who was sent to Spain by the Government to make observations. He was born at Lyons, on the 16th of August, 1744. On the 18th August, 1774, the Academy approved of his first Memoir on an Eclipse which he had observed at Versailles on the 11th April. He then belonged to the Marine Arsenal, in which situation he executed immense calculations for the improvement of Charts. He discovered and calculated several comets. He gained the prize of the Academy in 1782, on the comet of 1661, the return of which was expected in 1790; and he was received into that body the same year. He was made Editor of the *Connoissance des Temps*; and since 1788, that work has assumed a new perfection; it has been every year enriched with the labours of M. Mechain. In 1792 he was employed in the great work of the Meridian from Dunkirk to Barcelona, conjointly with M. Delambre. He returned from it in 1798. But, to complete that work, he wished to continue it as far as the Balearian Islands; and he set out for them in 1803. He had already with vast difficulty recognised all the Stations, and terminated three, when he was cut off on the 4th September, by a fever which prevails every year on the coast of Valencia, by reason of the morasses produced from the overflowing of the rivers.

At Plymouth, Miss de Courcy, daughter of the Hon. Captain de Courcy, of the Navy.

At Taplow Lodge, Bucks, the seat of P. C. Bruce, Esq. M. P., Mr. R. Bruce, of the Royal Navy, aged 20.

Lately, at Mount Merrion, near Dublin, Mr. G. Battier, late of his Majesty's Ship Resolution, which, with the Discovery, circumnavigated the Globe with Captain Cook. This intrepid Mariner was present with the unfortunate Captain at the fatal period of his death, and made a bold and vigorous defence against the savages in the Island of Owyhee.

Lloyd's Marine List

OF

SHIPS LOST, DESTROYED, CAPTURED, AND RECAPTURED, &c

FROM JULY 13, TO SEPTEMBER 11, 1804.

ACCOUNTS from Jamaica, dated 5th of May, state that a Guineaman, bound to that Island, is taken by a French Privateer, and carried into Cuba.

The Eliza, Atkinson, of and for N. Brunswick, from Jamaica, is taken off Cuba by a French Privateer.

The Alliance, Kefner, from Stockho m to Dublin, with Iron and Deals, is lost off Southwold. The cargo expected to be saved.

The Calliope, Nash, from Jamaica for Virginia, is lost on Florida Reef.

The Regulator, Burkitt, from New York to Jamaica, was taken 2d of April, and carried into Cuba.

The New York, King, from New York to Amsterdam, is put into Boston, leaky.

The Brothers, Lambert, from Poole to Bristol, is put into Falmouth, having lost her bowsprit, sails, &c. in a gale the 7th July off the Lizard.

The Nancy, Scott, from Liverpool to St. Andrews, went on shore and sunk near N. Brunswick, 7th May.

The Dwina, ———, from Hull, and the East Lothian, ———, from Aberdeen, are lost at Greenland. Crews saved.

The Active, Brade, from ———, is lost at the Bahamas. People saved.

The Zephyr, Jackson, from Gibraltar and Lisbon to Cork, taken on the 9th of June off Cape Clear by the Augereau Privateer, is carried into Muros.

The Nymph, Collins, from Liverpool to Lynn, was taken 23d of April, and carried into Boulogne.

A Ship, supposed to belong to Shields or Scarbro,' was taken by a French Privateer 6th of July off Southwold.

The Dolphin, Hellegren, from Malaga to Embden; the Mercury, Janson, from St. Remo to Tonningen; the Courier, Hasplairs, and the Sophia, Alhey, both from Cette, are detained and sent into Gibraltar.

The Caroline, Prince, from Honduras, is totally lost near Tonningen; 245 pieces of manogany saved.

The Adeonas, from Stockholm to Nantes, is detained by l'Entreprenante Cutter, and sent into Portsmouth.

The Pearl, Stephenson, from Hull to Jamaica, is taken by a Privateer, and supposed to be carried into Guadaloupe.

The President, Wells, from the C pe of Good Hope to a Market, is sent into Cork by the Lapwing Frigate.

The Bourdeaux Packet, Hedeluis, from Philadelphia to Bourleaux, is detained by the Rosario Sloop, and sent into Cork 13th July

The Ocean, Prit hard, from Massachusetts to St. Bartholomews; and the Two Brothers, Nichols, from Guadaloupe to New York, were sent into Bermuda 24th May, by the Driver Sloop of War.

The Minerva, ———, from London and Lisbon to Honduras, has been taken by a French Privateer, retaken by the Blanche Frigate, and arrived at Jamaica 23d of May.

The Anna Bella, Maclean, is seized at Cape Coast, Africa, by the Inconstant Frigate, for illicit trade.

The American Ship New York, ———, from Liverpool to New Orleans, has been taken by a French privateer, retaken by the Tartar Frigate, and carried into Jamaica.

The Hercules, ———, from Guernsey to Honduras, is lost near Honduras.

The Surprize, Renshaw, from the Cape of Good Hope to Philadelphia, is lost near Bermuda.

The Duke of Kent Packet, from Falmouth to Barbadoes and Jamaica, is taken, and carried into Guadaloupe.

The Mary, Wood, from Teignmouth to Newfoundland, w s c ptured on the 17th of April on the Banks of Newfoundland, by a French Privateer, of 18 guns.

The Ariel, Rivetfon, of Liverpool, with Coals, for Petersburg, is lost on Sand Hammer.

The Sisters, Knoll, from Boston to Jamaica; and the Morning Star, from Jamaica to Charleston, are taken by French Privateers, and sent for Cuba.

The Providence, ———, of 80 tons, from Swansea to London; and the Gratitude, ———, of 200 tons, laden with iron, are reported to be captured, and carried into Boulogne.

The Vrow Hermina, Bowman; Juno, Gulzeet; Frau Margaretta, Roloff; General Van Bloucher, Ruyle; Jong Oune and Brower, Ruyle; Nicka, Riecka, Four Brothers, Stemmings; Jong Peter Casper, Jobs; Gute Hoffnung, ———; Piepersburg, ———; from Riga to Embden, with masts, are detained by the Scorpion and Lynx Sloops, and Censor Gun Brig, and sent into Yarmouth.

The William and Margaret sloop, Bishop, bound to Plymouth, sprung a leak 21st of July, near the Isle of Wight, and was quitted by the Crew; but she had not sunk when they lost sight of her.

The American Ship Thomas, ———, from Bourdeaux to Norfolk, Virginia, is detained by the Busy Brig, and carried into Barbadoes.

The Exchange, ———, from Waterford to London, having sprung a leak, foundered near Scilly 20th July. Crew saved by the John, arrived at Liverpool from Charleston.

The Providence, Lownsbro, from Jersey to Petersburg; and the Mary, ———, from Emsworth to Hull, have been taken, and were retaken on the 7th July, by the Nile Cutter, of Hastings, near Boulogne.

The Packet of Embden, from Bourdeaux, is detained by the Lion Cutter, and arrived at Portsmouth.

The Emerald, Eccles, from Liverpool to Africa, is taken.

The Albion, Randall, from Waterford to London, was captured 22d July off Fairlee, by a Lugger Privateer, retaken on 23d by the Stag Revenue Cutter, and carried into Ramsgate.

The Sally, Child, from St. Domingo to Philadelphia, is taken by a French Privateer, in the Crooked Island Passage.

The Frances Lewes, Ewers, of Philadelphia, from Telemachus, ———, of Norfolk; the Delight, ———, of Charleston, are taken by French Privateers, and carried into the Havana.

The Peggy, Sinclair, from London to Demerara, is totally lost near Demerara.

The Active, Rasor, from Jamaica to London, was captured 1st May, near Cuba.

The American Brig Speedwell, ———, from Boston to Havre, is detained by the Favourite Sloop, and sent into Portsmouth.

The del Peys, de la Bella, from Malaga, is on shore in the Eyder, but expected to be got off.

The Hambro Ship ———, Derks, from Bourdeaux, is totally lost at the mouth of the Eyder.

The Nancy, ———, from St. Vincent's to Liverpool, has been taken and retaken off Grenada.

The Sir Sidney Smith, Wheele, from London to Tobago, put into Oporto 8th July, in distress, with five feet water in her hold.

The Young Nicholas, Horry, from Honduras to London, last from Savannah; failed from Savannah on the 8th July, and was taken the next day by a French Privateer, and sent for Guadaloupe. Captain Horry arrived at Liverpool in the Daphne.

The Vittoria, Mirabito, from Malta to Trieste, is taken by a French Privateer in the Port of Trieste.

The Argo, Williams, from Petersburg, is arrived in the River, after being stranded on the Island of Lessoe.

The Paul and Elizabeth, Raven, from Christiana to London, is carried into Yarmouth Roads, by a Winterton Boat, with much damage, having been on Happesburg Sand.

The St. Bartholomew, Willberg, from Stockholm to Dublin, is carried into Margate by the Boatmen, with loss of rudder, and some damage to her keel, having been on the Long Sand.

The Henry, Reynolds, from Charleston to London, which put into Virginia in distress, has been condemned, and the Cargo sold.

LLOYD'S MARINE LIST OF SHIPS LOST, &c.

French Papers state that the Atalante, Jenkins, from Jamaica to London, is taken and carried into Bourdeaux, by the Minerva Privateer of that Port.

The Mary, Garmock, from Belfast to Copenhagen, is on shore near Kirkwall.

The Fleet arrived in the Downs from China, sailed on the 5th February, in company with eleven Country Ships and Gangus Brig, and on the 14th, off Pulo Auro, fell in with a Squadron under the French Admiral Linois, consisting of the Marengoe, of 84 guns, Belle Poule and Semillante, heavy Frigates; a Corvette, of 28 guns; and a Batavian Brig of 18 guns, which engaged them for a considerable time, and then sheered off. On the 28th, in the Straits of Malacca, met the Albion and Sceptre Men of War, who convoyed them to St. Helena, where they arrived the 9th June, and sailed from thence the 18th, under protection of the Plantagenet Man of War.

The William Heathcote, Phillips, from Demerara to Liverpool, was captured 4th August off Ireland, by a French Privateer.

The Atalanta, Jenkins, from Jamaica to London, is taken by a French Privateer, and carried into Bourdeaux.

The Ranger, Williams, from Demerara to London, is on shore off South End.

The Traveller, ———, from Aberdeen to London, was taken off Fifeness 29th July, retaken by the Hebe armed Ship, and is arrived at Leith.

The Active, Ewing, from London to Dundee, sprung a leak off Cromer, and was deserted by the Crew.

The Hawke, Bryant, from Monteveldo, put into Lisbon last month leaky, and has been condemned.

The Anna, Harmitage, from Hull to London, foundered near Yarmouth. People saved.

The Ranger, Leishman, from London to Honduras, was taken the 9th May, by the Department de Nord French Privateer. Captain Leishman, and part of his Crew, were landed on the Island of St. Domingo, and since arrived at Jamaica.

The Sloop Lucy, Burrell, from Bermuda, is captured near Jamaica.

The Caroline Frigate arrived at Bengal the end of February, with two French Privateers she had captured.

The N. S. de Conception, ———, from Amsterdam to Cadiz, was detained and sent into Gibraltar 7th July, by His Majesty's Ship Ambuscade.

The Adeona, Richards, bound to Memel, went on shore in Carmarthen River 7th August, and received considerable damage.

The Golden Grove, Burden, from Newcastle to Jamaica, was taken on the 9th May, off Jamaica, by a French Privateer, by which she was plundered, and then given up. The next day she was captured by another Privateer, and carried into St. Jago de Cuba the 14th; and on the 20th the Privateer took the Golden Grove out to sea and burnt her, as the Spanish Governor would not permit the Ship to lay in that Harbour, nor suffer the Crew to be landed.

The Brig Betsey, of Jersey, bound to the West Indies, has been taken and retaken the 24th July by the Mary, Captain Temple.

The Brig Tartar, of New York, mounting 10 guns, was taken by a French Privateer off Hencaga on 5th July.

The Schooner Eagle, of New York, bound to Jamaica, was taken 20th June by a French Privateer.

The George, M'Leven, of Liverpool, was captured 24th May, at Gaboon, by the Vengeance Privateer.

The Lucy Maria, ———, from Bengal to China; the Henrietta, ———, from Ballanbangan to Madras; and the Brig Ranier, ———, of Madras, are reported to have been taken previous to the 28th of February, by Linois' Squadron.

The Ranger, Leishman, from London to Honduras, is retaken by one of his Majesty's Ships, and carried into Jamaica, and sold.

The John and Mary, ———, of Sunderland, coal laden, was lost on Hasbro' Sand, 13th August.

The Fortitude, Gidney, from Liverpool to Malta, was taken by the Esperance French Privateer, and carried into Malaga 16th July.

The Hannah, Garrett, from Sunderland to Whitby, is on shore at the West Pier, Whitby.

The Ariadne, Flott, late M'Bride, captured by the Dutch on the Coast of Africa, has been retaken by the Alexander of Liverpool, and arrived at Liverpool.

The Eagle, Ramsay, from London, is captured on the Coast of Africa, by two French Privateers, after a severe engagement.

The Margaret, Napier, from Shields to Grenada, was taken 22d April by a French Privateer. Since retaken and carried into Berbice River.

The following Vessels from Riga with masts, are detained and sent into Yarmouth, viz. Experiment, Meyners, by the Lord Nelson Cutter; Aftrea, Gelhaur, by the Ferreter Gun Brig; Ignatus, Bakker, by the Scorpion Sloop; Enterprise, Martin, by the Fanny Armed Sloop. The Ferreter has also detained and sent into the Fryherinna, Wardeur, from Stockholm to Dieppe.

The Carl Gustaff, Neilson, from Stockholm to Dieppe, is detained by the Melpomene Frigate, and sent into Portsmouth.

The Jonge Ayr, Vanderdyn, from Hull to Catwyk, is detained by the Minerva Privateer, of Hull, and carried into Grimsby.

The Delight, Johnson, from Hull to Yarmouth, foundered off Cromer the middle of this month.

The William Heathcote, Phillips, from Demerara to Liverpool, was captured on 4th August by the General Augereau French Privateer, of 12 guns and 90 men, after a severe conflict, in which Captain Phillips, his son, a passenger, and one Seaman, were killed; the Mate, one Passenger, and seven Seamen, wounded; the Privateer had three men killed, her Captain and five men wounded. The William Heathcote was recaptured on 9th August by the Nautilus Sloop of War, and is brought into Plymouth.

The Blonde French Privateer, of 30 guns and 240 men, is taken by the Loire Frigate, and arrived at Plymouth.

The Port of Pillau, Christianson, from Petersburg to Dieppe; and the Three Brothers, Wietelman, from Calais to Christiansand, are detained and sent into Dover.

The Sloop King of Prussia, ———, from Prussia to Bilboa, is detained, and sent into Portsmouth by the Rose Cutter.

The President, ———, from the Cape of Good Hope, last from Cork, detained by the Lapwing Frigate, went on shore on the Goodwin Sands 28th August, but was got off by the Deal Boats.

The Kilberry, Sinclair, from St. Michael's to Liverpool, was captured 3d August, and carried into Rochefort the 18th, by the Pursuivante French Frigate.

The Venus Privateer, of Nantes, mounting 16 guns and 72 men, was taken on the 22d August by the Union, from Bengal; she had been out 11 days from a Spanish Port, and made two captures.

The Dispatch and the Rodney Droghers, belonging to Grenada, were cut out of a Bay in that Island on the 9th July, by a French Privateer; and the Mary Cutter run on shore to prevent being captured; and it was supposed would be lost.

The Brig Amiable Julia, of 116 tons and 6 men, from Sunderland to Newhaven; and the Brig Friends, of 135 tons and 7 men, from Dartmouth to Sunder and, are stated in the French Papers to be taken by the Prosper Privateer of Boulogne, and carried into Dunkirk.

The Esther, of Whitehaven, and the Beaver, of Liverpool, both bound to Barbadoes, are taken in the West Indies.

The Margaret, Goodwin, for London, was lost in Manchioneal Harbour, Jamaica, on 12th July.

The Sybil, Head, from London and Madeira to Demerara, has been taken, retaken, and carried into Barbadoes.

The Juno, Sowdon, from Newcastle to Jamaica, is captured, and carried into Guadaloupe.

The American Schooner Linnet, from Barbadoes to Virginia, has been captured by the French, retaken by a Frigate, and carried into Jamaica.

The Rambler, Ritch, from Boston to Rotterdam, was run down off Newfoundland by the Ulysses, Morgan, from London to New York. Crew saved.

The Mercurius, Hindler, from Dantzic to London, is stranded on Bornholm. Part of the cargo and materials saved.

The Beaver, Christie, from Africa to the West Indies, has been taken, retaken, and carried into Antigua.

The Charlotte, Merron, from Tortola and St. Thomas's to Jamaica, was captured 22d June, after a long engagement, and carried to Porto Rico.

The Brig l'Espoir, ———, from Martinique to America, in ballast, was taken by the Lilly Sloop of War, and carried into Bermuda 25th June. The Lilly was taken 15th July on the Coast of Virginia by a French Privateer, after an engagement of two hours and a half.

The Brig Surprise, ———, from Grenada to Trinidada, is lost near Grenada.

The Abeona, ———, from Labradore to Quebec, is lost.

The Reindeer, Cattrall, has been on shore on Bornholm, but got off after throwing a part of her Cargo overboard.

The Lucy Maria, Dawes, from Bengal to China, was taken previous to the end of February by Linois' Squadron in the China Seas.

The American Ship Joseph, Grant, from Buenos Ayres to Embden, detained and carried into St. Kitt's some time since, by l'Eclair Sloop, has been sold to discharge a Bottomry Bond.

[*To be continued.*]

SIR WILLIAM JAMES BART
Commodore in the Honble East India Comp^y Service
Chairman of the Court of Directors &c

BIOGRAPHICAL MEMOIR OF THE LATE
COMMODORE SIR WILLIAM JAMES, Bart.
IN THE HON. EAST INDIA COMPANY'S SERVICE,
Chairman of the Court of Directors, &c,

" So I LEFT MY POOR PLOUGH TO GO PLOUGHING THE DEEP."
Dibdin.

WE have been gratified in learning, that our biographical sketch of the " gallant *Merchant* Commodore DANCE" has not been condemned as an innovation, but has rather been deemed a just tribute to that spirit of invincible valour, which so universally pervades both the Royal and Mercantile British Navy. The actions of another Merchant, whose birth indeed was humble, but whose high achievements were splendid, will more fully illustrate the truth of this remark; and prove unto the French, that if we are a Nation of Shopkeepers, the spirit of commerce has no tendency to abate the natural and inherent Valour of an Englishman.

The origin of Commodore Sir William James is enveloped in obscurity. Whether this may have proceeded from that feeling which revolts at the retrospect of poverty, it would now be difficult, if not impossible, to determine. That such feelings are frequently incidental both to families and individuals, is too true; since it too often has deprived us of the means of marking the progress of naval merit, from its first dawn, to its meridian splendour. Even Johnson was not invulnerable to its influence. That truly great philosopher, though endowed with sentiments too noble and elevated to permit any attempt at deceit, dwelt with pain on the poverty of his early years.

Respecting the earliest period of Sir William James's life, all that is known with certainty is, that he was a native of Wales; that his parents were extremely poor; and that, consequently, their offspring had many difficulties to struggle with. We are not convinced that this statement is fully to be relied on: but it has been generally understood that he was born near Milford Haven, in 1721; and that, for some time, he there followed the occupation of husbandry, in the humble station of a Ploughboy; and that such occupations have a tendency to confirm an heroic character, we have the authority of our Bible to affirm; " Thy servant," said the young Shepherd unto Saul, " kept his Father's sheep, and there came a lion and a bear, and took a lamb out of the flock; and I went out after him, and smote him, and delivered it out of his mouth: and when he arose against me, I caught him by his beard, and smote him, and slew him: Thy servant slew both the lion and the bear—The Lord who delivered me out of the paw of the lion and out of the paw of the bear, he will deliver me out of the hand of this Philistine."

That spirit of enterprise, which has formed so many heroes, in modern as well as in ancient days, was probably stimulated in this youth, by the constant sight of the Ocean, and this at an early period of his life.

From the information of his widow, the late Lady James, her husband became a Sailor at the age of twelve years; but without friends, and without interest: and a period of more than twenty years elapsed before he obtained the command of a Ship. He indeed commenced his career in the Merchant Service; but in the year 1738 he served under the gallant Captain, afterwards Admiral Lord Hawke, in the West Indies. It is imagined that he was not entered as a Midshipman, but acted in some other subordinate station, which he had obtained rather by good behaviour than by interest.

Some years after this, Mr. James procured the command of a Ship in the Virginia trade. But fortune was not yet auspicious to his wishes; for in this service he was taken prisoner by the Spaniards, and carried to the Havana, which has been the grave of so many Englishmen. From a dungeon in the island of Cuba, both himself and his men were at length released; but their emancipation only led to fresh calamities. Having embarked on board of a Brig for the colony of South Carolina, a very hard gale of Wind came on the second day after their departure; and the Vessel, which it is supposed was not adapted to encounter the occasional Hurricanes of those latitudes, strained so much, that the most imminent danger ensued. The pumps were set to work; and the people employed at them were incessantly occupied in bailing out the water; but, though every possible exertion was made, the Vessel could not long be kept afloat.

Despairing of any other means of safety, Mr. James and seven of the Crew got into the Boat, taking with them a little bag of biscuits and a keg of water; soon after this, the Brig went down, and disappeared. What became of the rest of the Crew is not mentioned; but, from this account, it is too probable that they were consigned to a watery grave.

In the Brig's small Boat, Mr. James and his companions remained twenty days: exposed, not only to the dangers of the Winds and Waves, but experiencing the slow approaches of famine, and dying a thousand deaths amidst their protracted existence. The supply of fresh water being unfortunately very scanty, was regularly distributed, in equal portions, from the Commander's snuff-box. Their bread also, from being wetted with the Sea, which, during two whole days, made a breach over them, became scarcely eatable.

Being unprovided with a compass, they had no idea where they were, or towards what part they were driven. The appearance, however, of any land would have been grateful; but twenty days elapsed before they were blessed with so delightful a prospect. Cuba at length appeared;—the very same island whence they had so recently set out; and the spot which they first reached was not ten miles distant from their old prison. But a prison had no longer any horrors for them; they readily, and even cordially, delivered themselves up to the Spaniards, who received them once more into captivity; and it is not a little remarkable, that but one out of the eight perished. All of them, however, were afflicted by the hardships which they had experienced, and for a considerable time they were deprived of the use of their limbs. Having at length found means to return to England, in the year 1747 Mr. James entered into the service of the EAST INDIA COMPANY.

About the same period, he first entered into the marriage

state, and his wife kept a public-house in Wapping, bearing the sign of the " *Red Cow.*"—An amiable trait in Mr. James's character may be mentioned here with much propriety. After having tasted the fruits of prosperity, he returned to Wales, and earnestly inquired after a young woman, with whom, while they were yet children, he had interchanged a promise of marriage. He bantered her for not keeping her word; performed some acts of friendship towards her husband; and presented his *quondam* sweetheart with a gown, which he had brought with him for that purpose.

The East India Company, at the period when Mr. James first entered into its service, was merely a petty, trading association. A few obscure merchants of Leadenhall Street were at that time the feudal tenants of the Mogul, who never dreamed of being the SOVEREIGNS OF HINDOSTAN.

Before we proceed with Mr. James, it may not perhaps be amiss, briefly to state the origin, rise, and progress of that establishment, which, in its embassies and governments, may now be considered as eclipsing the splendour of eastern nations.

History furnishes us with reason for believing, that, as early as the days of the great Alfred, England had a circuitous, but not regular communication with India. The spices, however, and other commodities of the East, found their way into this island by foreign bottoms; at first through the Red Sea, by Alexandria, and afterwards by the way of Trebizond, Damascus, and Aleppo, which increased the trade of the free cities of Venice, Genoa, Pisa, &c. Those goods were not only vended in all the countries bordering upon the Mediterranean, but were sent to England, Germany, and the Netherlands, and all over the Baltic, which afforded great encouragement to the traffic of Bruges, the depositary of northern commodities.

The first person who proposed to establish the East India Trade in England, is recorded to have been a Mr. Robert Thorne, a Merchant of London, who had settled at Seville, in Spain. Having resided there many years, he had gained considerable knowledge respecting the state of both the East and West Indies. About the year 1527, this gentleman made an application on the subject to his Majesty, KING HENRY THE VIIIth, to whom he represented the vast advantages which would accrue to the nation by opening a direct commerce with the East Indies. Mr. Thorne's scheme, however, does not appear to have been considered in any other view than as a project too bold to be carried into effect. The first person who threw any real light upon this navigation was Sir Francis Drake, in the year 1578. The next year a Mr. Stevens went from Lisbon to Goa, by the Cape of Good Hope; and, in 1586, the famous Candish made his voyage round the world. This clearly opened a passage to these parts; and, in 1591, Captain George Raymond, in a Ship of his own, called the Penelope, accompanied by two others, the Merchant Royal and the Bonaventure, sailed for the East Indies. Before they reached the Cape of Good Hope, the Crews became so very sickly, that it was found necessary to send one of the Ships back to England with the invalids; another was lost with all its Crew in a gale of Wind; and the Bonaventure, commanded by Captain Lancaster, having stopped at an uninhabited island, probably St. Helena or Ascension, on her return home, a part of the Crew mutinied and ran away with the Ship, while the Captain and the rest were on shore seeking for refreshments. Here they remained three years, when a Ship fortunately arrived and relieved the survivors from their miserable situation, several having actually perished for want.

Favourable accounts continuing to be received from India, as to the facility with which the English might establish factories, and commence a regular trade thither, several Merchants, and other monied men, at length conceived a desire to open such a commerce. In pursuance of this wish, they applied to QUEEN ELIZABETH for a charter, which her Majesty was pleased to grant on the 31st of December, A.D. 1600, in the forty-third year of her reign.

The petitioners for this establishment, and to whom the privilege was granted, were, Sir John Hart, of London, Knt. Sir John Spencer, of London, Knt. Sir Edward Michelburn, Knt. William Candish, Esq. Paul Banning, Robert Lee, Leonard

Holiday, John Watts, John Moore, Edward Holmden, Robert Hampson, Thomas Smith, and Thomas Campbell, Citizens and Aldermen of London, and upwards of two hundred persons more, named in the royal grant.—They were formed into a body, corporate and politic, by the title of *The Governor and Company of Merchants of London, trading into the East Indies.*

In the following year, 1601, the above society fitted and sent out five Ships, from one hundred to six hundred tons burden, the command of which was given to Captain Lancaster, who has been already mentioned.

For some time the respective partners in this concern appear to have traded with separate stocks, though only in the Ships belonging to the whole Company. In 1612, they joined their stocks into one common capital; and though their charter had not as yet been confirmed by Parliament, it was considered to be sufficiently valid, and no one presumed to interfere with their trade. At this time their capital amounted to about 740,000l., and the shares were as low as 50l. Their trade was in general successful, notwithstanding some heavy losses, which were chiefly sustained through the malice of their rivals, the Dutch. In process of time, however, it came to be understood, that a royal charter could not by itself convey an exclusive privilege to traders, and the Company was reduced to distress by the multitude of interlopers who carried off the greater part of their trade. They continued in this dilemma during the latter part of the reign of CHARLES THE IId, the whole of JAMES THE IId's, and part of that of WILLIAM THE IIId. In 1698, a scheme was formed, and a proposal was made to Parliament for advancing the sum of 2,000,000l. to Government, on condition of the subscribers being formed into a new Company, with exclusive privileges. The original Company endeavoured to prevent the appearance of such a formidable rival, by offering Government 700,000l., nearly the whole amount of their capital; but such were at that time the exigencies of the State, that the larger sum, though at eight *per cent.* interest, was preferred to the smaller at four *per cent.*

Thus were two Companies formed, the interests of each necessarily clashing one with another. Through the negligence of those who prepared the act of parliament, the partners of the new Company were not obliged to unite in a joint stock; and, in consequence of this, a few private traders, whose subscriptions scarcely exceeded 7200l., insisted on a right of trading separately at their own risk. A sort of third Company was thus established; and by their contentions one with the other, all three were brought to the verge of ruin. On a subsequent occasion, in 1700, a proposal was made to Parliament, for putting the trade under the management of a regulated Company. This, however, was opposed; but, in 1702, the companies were in some measure united by an indenture tripartite, to which the Queen was a party; and, in 1708, they were, by act of parliament, perfectly consolidated into one Company, by the title of THE UNITED COMPANY OF MERCHANTS TRADING TO THE EAST INDIES. Into this act it was thought proper to insert a clause, allowing the separate traders to continue their traffic till Michaelmas, 1711; but at the same time empowering the Directors, on three years' notice, to redeem their capital of 7200l., and thereby convert the whole capital of the Company into a joint stock. By the same act, in consequence of a new loan to Government, their capital was augmented from 2,000,000l. to 3,200,000l.; and, in 1743, another million was advanced to Government. But the latter being raised, not by a call upon the proprietors, but by selling annuities and contracting bond-debts, it did not augment the stock on which a dividend could be claimed.

From 1708, or at least from 1711, this Company, being free from all competitors, and fully established in the monopoly of English commerce to India, carried on a successful trade; making, from their annual profits, a moderate dividen to the proprietors.

In a short time, however, whether fortunately or otherwise we shall not pretend to decide, an inclinaton for *war* and *conquest* began to take place among the serva ts of the Company; which, though it put them in possession o extensive territories, and immense *nominal revenues*, yet embarrassed their affairs to such a degree, that they have not, to this ay, been fully able to recover themselves.

We have thus briefly exhibited the origin and progress of the East India Company, down to the period when Mr. James first entered into its service. To trace them farther, would in this place be an irrelevant digression; we shall therefore return to the immediate subject of our memoir.

Mr. James performed two Voyages in the capacity of chief Mate; and having evinced much good conduct, and displayed considerable talents, he was appointed to the command of a new Ship, equipped for war, and called the *Guardian*, from the situation in which she was destined to be employed, and which led to her Captain's future fortune and preferment.

Soon after this he sailed from Bombay, with orders to protect the trade on the Malabar coast, then greatly annoyed by the depredations of Angria, and other Pirates, who seem to have done occasionally by Sea what the Moors and Europeans did by land; that is, they attacked those who were weaker than themselves; with this difference, however, that the naval marauders, instead of being at enmity with only one foe at a time, lived by the indiscriminate plunder of all who happened to be less powerful than themselves.

The founder of the Angrian dynasty was Conagee Angria, an adventurer in the time of Aurengzebe, who, having been entrusted by the Mahrattas with the command of the port of Severndroog, betrayed his trust declared himself independent of his Master, extended his terriories 120 miles along the coast, and as far inwards as the Ghauts; while Negroes, Mussulmans, and renegado Christians, flocking to his standard, this Corsair and his successors became formidable by their power and depredations. The extensive tract thus occupied, reaching nearly from Bombay to Goa, is caled the *Pirate Coast**. We learn from Pliny, that the Ronan East India Trade was subject to the inroads of the inhabtants, who seem, at that time, to have been Arabians; and, accoding to the accurate Rennel, no situation can possibly be betteradapted to the purposes of naval depredation; for, though the eneral outline of coast appears strait and

---

* Ptolemy gives a list of the ports, and he terms the natives Ανδρων πειδατων.

uniform, the Shore is every where niched with Bays and recesses. The multitude of small Ports affords secure asylums, while the elevated island stations, affording an extensive view to Seaward, have fitted this neighbourhood to be the chosen seat of piracy. The shallowness of the Harbours, and the strength of the country within, are well calculated to protect the free-booters from extirpation; and indeed afford such security, that, after all our victories, they are nearly as numerous at this day as ever, and will probably continue to infest the Indian Seas as long as there is any commerce to be preyed upon. While their fellow Corsairs of Barbary are compelled to rove at a distance from their own Shores in search of booty, here the prizes come within sight of the Coast, and the *grabs* and *gallivats* may lie secure in Port until it be discovered whether the opportunity for obtaining booty be favourable.

During the time that the Mogul empire remained prosperous, care was taken to repress the outrages of these men, and Dunda Rajapore* was the name of the Harbour at which Aurengzebe's Fleet rendezvoused for that purpose, under the command of the *Siddee*, or High Admiral, who, like the *Comes Littoris Saxonici* of our own island, was employed to repel the incursions of rovers of all kinds.

One of the principal of their fastnesses was called Bancoote, or Victoria, the latter of which names it still retains. Severndroog, Sunderdoo, and Vingorla, are so many rocks situated in lat. 15° 22 30", six or seven miles from the Shore. There are also Kennary, and Gheriah, the capital of Angria, situated nearly midway between Bombay and Goa. This, indeed, might be termed the Algiers of the Indian pirate coast; and had, for about fifty years, been formidable to all the nations of Europe. The English East India Company had kept up a naval force for the protection of their trade, at the rate of more than 50,000l. annually, but scarcely found that sum adequate to the purpose.

In the year 1717, an unsuccessful attempt had been made, by the presidency of Bombay, against the Forts of Gheriah and

---

* *Vide* PENNANT's *Hindostan*, Vol. I, page 104.

Kennary; another attempt was also made, in 1722, against Fort named Coilabley, about fifteen leagues south of Bor...y; but this also miscarried, through the cowardice and treachery of the Portuguese, who pretended to assist the English. In 1735, Gheriah was unsuccessfully attacked by a Dutch armament of seven Ships, two Bomb-ketches, and a numerous body of land forces. All this time the piracies of Angria proceeded, and not only trading Vessels, but even Men of War, belonging to different nations, were captured by him.

The nature of the service in which Captain James was now employed, afforded him almost daily opportunities of ascertaining the strength, learning the habits, and even contesting the powers of these marauders. During the two years which were occupied by him in conveying the Merchant Ships from Bombay and Surat to the Red Sea, the Gulf of Persia, and along the Malabar Coast from the Gulf of Cambay to Cape Comorin, he was frequently attacked by the Vessels of the different piratical States. At one time, when he had nearly seventy Sail under his protection, he was assailed by a large Fleet of Angria's Frigates and Gallivats, which were well provided with guns, and full of men.

Having formed the Line with his little Squadron, consisting of the Guardian, Bombay Grab, and Drake Bomb-ketch, he engaged the enemy, and kept them in close action, while his Convoy got safe into Tellicherry. In this conflict, during which the hope of victory animated one side, and the thirst for plunder inflamed the other, and which seems, on the part of both, to have been vigorously disputed, the brave English Commander sunk one of the enemy's largest Gallivats, and compelled the remainder to take shelter in Gheriah and Severndroog.

In order to illustrate the above action, and to convey some idea of the general mode of piratical warfare adopted in the East, it is here requisite to describe the two species of Vessels peculiar to these parts; *viz.* Grabs and Gallivats.—The former have generally two masts, though some have three, according to their burden, which is from a hundred and fifty to three hundred tons. They are constructed so as to draw but little water, being very broad in proportion to their length; but narrowing from the middle to the end, where, instead of bows, they have a prow, projecting like that of a Mediterranean Galley, and covered with a strong deck level with the main-deck of the Vessel, from which it is separated by a bulk-head that terminates the forecastle. As this construction subjects the Grab to pitch violently when sailing against a head Sea, the deck of the prow is not enclosed with sides like the rest of the Vessel, but remains bare, so that the water which comes upon it may pass off without interruption. Two pieces of cannon are mounted on the main-deck under the forecastle, carrying balls of nine or twelve pounds, which point forwards through port-holes that are cut in the bulk-head, and fire over the prow : the guns of the broad side are from six to nine-pounders. The Gallivats are large Rowboats, built like the Grabs, but smaller; the largest scarcely exceeding seventy tons burden. They have two masts, the mizen slightly made, and the main-mast bearing one large triangular sail. In general they are covered with a spar-deck made of split bamboos, and carry only paterreroes fixed on swivels, in the gunwale of the Vessel; but those of a larger size have a fixed deck, on which they mount six or eight pieces of cannon, from two to four-pounders. They are furnished with forty or fifty stout oars, by which they may be moved at the rate of four miles an hour.

In these parts, the land breezes do not extend more than forty miles out at Sea, so that the trading Ships are obliged to keep within sight of land; and there was not a Creek, Harbour, Bay, or mouth of a River along the whole Coast of his dominions, where Angria had not erected fortifications, both as stations of discovery, and as places of refuge to his Vessels.—He had commonly a Fleet of eight or ten Grabs, with forty or fifty Gallivats, which slipped their cable and put out to Sea as soon as any Vessel had the misfortune to come within sight of the place where they lay. If the Wind blew with any strength, their construction enabled them to sail very swiftly; but if the weather were calm, the Gallivats rowed and towed the Grabs. As soon as they came within gun-shot of their supposed prey, they assembled astern, and the Grabs began the attack, firing at first only at the masts, and choosing the most advantageous positions for this purpose. If the Vessel happened to be dismasted, they then drew nearer, and battered her on all sides till she struck; but if the defence were obstinate, they sent a number of Gallivats, with two or three hundred Soldiers in each, who boarded from all quarters sword in hand.

From the spirited conduct of Captain James, in his important defeat of this common robber, it may readily be supposed that he derived additional preferment. Accordingly, in the beginning of 1751, after a period of only four years' service, and but two from his first promotion to a Ship, he was appointed *Commander in Chief* of the East India Company's Marine Forces, and hoisted his broad Pendant, as Commodore, on board of the Protector, a forty-four gun Ship.

Notwithstanding their late defeat, the continued depredations of the pirates had rendered the navigation of single Vessels extremely hazardous; and, during the month of February, 1754, three Dutch Ships, of 50, 36, and 18 guns, were burnt or taken by their Fleet.

This last success encouraged Angria so much, that he began to build Vessels of a larger size, and boasted that he would be master of the Indian Seas. The Mahrattas, however, implored the assistance of the English against their common enemy, and it was at length resolved to commence an attack against him, and to destroy some of his principal settlements. Accordingly, on the 22d of March, 1755, Commodore James was sent from Bombay, with the Protector, of 44 guns, the Swallow, of 16 guns, the Triumph and Viper Bomb-vessels, and a Squadron of Mahratta Grabs and Gallivats under his command. His instructions were, not to hazard his Ships by attacking any of the pirate's Forts, but to blockade the Harbours while the Mahratta army carried on their operations by land. On the 28th of March the Commodore received information, that Tullagee Angria's Fleet was at anchor in the Port of Severndroog; he therefore made sail thither, with the precaution of arriving just at day-light on the 29th, being apprehensive that, otherwise, instead of coming to an action, they would endeavour to escape. This proved to be the case; for, on sight of the Protector, they precipitately slipped their cables and ran out to Sea. As there was but little Wind, they employed their Gallivats to row them out of danger, an advantage which enabled them to gain greatly on the Protector, though she was by far the best sailing Vessel of the Squadron. The Sea-Wind, however, setting in, the Protector came up with them so fast, as to be within random shot; when, finding themselves so closely pursued, they stemmed for the Shore, and at length drew the Commodore so low down from his station, that he was obliged to leave off the chase. He was much chagrined at this disappointment, particularly so, on account of the timidity and dilatory behaviour of his allies, the Mahrattas, who could not by any means be induced to follow him.

Commodore James immediately made sail again for Severndroog, which he reached on the 1st of April. On his arrival he found that the Mahrattas had invested three of the Forts, but after a very strange manner; their cowardice having deterred them from approaching nearer than two miles, and even at that distance they were entrenched up to the chin, to secure themselves from the enemy's fire, which they returned with only one four-pounder. Provoked at their pusillanimous behaviour, and anxious for the honour of the British arms, the Commodore determined on going beyond his orders. The next day he employed Boats to reconnoitre and sound round the Harbour and Forts, and finding water enough for the small Vessels to bombard, and for the Protector to cannonade, he ran in within a hundred yards of the Fort called Severndroog. The attack commenced; and in the course of the day about eight hundred shot and shells were expended. At night a deserter arrived with the information, that the Governor and eight people were killed in the Castle, that several others were wounded, and that the shot and shells had done considerable damage. The Commodore, however, learning from this deserter, that it would be impossible to make an effectual breach on the side of the great Fort where he then was, the walls being at least fifty feet high, nearly eighteen thick, and most part cut out of the solid rock, thought it proper to quit his station. Finding that the water to the eastward was deep enough to admit the Protector and the other Vessels to go in to open on all the Forts, *viz.* one of 42 guns, two of 24 guns each, and the outer one of 50 guns, which was built upon the island, and at first sustained the principal attack; early in the morning of the 3d he hauled the Protector within half musket shot, having a foot more water at the lowest ebb than the Ship drew, and renewed the attack. During the time he was getting the Ship's broadside to bear, by means of springs, &c. the enemy fired briskly on him; but the compliment was soon heartily returned to the farther Forts, with the lower-deck guns; and to the nearer, with those of the upper-deck, two and three at a time, holding an incessant fire, seconded by the Swallow and the Bomb-vessels. By this conduct, in about four hours the enemy's fire was pretty well silenced; and, at noon, a great part of the parapet of the north-east bastion of the outer Fort, where the Protector lay, and the work itself, were in ruins. At the same time a shell successfully exploded, and set fire to one of the Store-houses, which the Commodore perceiving, he prevented the enemy from extinguishing the flames, by constantly pouring in his grape-shot and musketry. It raged so fiercely, that in an hour's time one of the Magazines blew up. The fire was thus effectually communicated through the Fort, where it continued to burn, without interruption, till eleven at night, when their grand Magazine blew up with a great shock.

The people, to the number of about 1000, now abandoned the place, embarked in eight large Boats, and attempted to make their escape to another Fort, named Goa, but were all intercepted and made prisoners by the English.

The whole besieging force being then directed against Goa, a white Flag was soon hung out as a signal to surrender. The Governor, however, did not think proper to await the event of a capitulation, but without delay passed over to Severndroog, where he entertained the hope of being able to maintain his ground, notwithstanding the ruinous state of the fortifications. The fire was now renewed against this Fortress; and the Seamen having cut a passage through one of the gates with their axes, the Garrison soon surrendered. At the same time, two other Forts, which were besieged by the Mahrattas, hung out Flags of Truce and capitulated; and thus were four of Angria's Forts, which for many years had been deemed impregnable, subdued in one day.

These successes were followed by the surrender of Bancoote, a strongly fortified island, of which the English retained possession. The other Forts were delivered up to the Mahrattas.

Next to Gheriah, Severndroog had always been considered the strongest of Angria's possessions. On landing, a number of Stores was found belonging to the Derby Indiaman, which had been captured and carried in thither. The Stores of the Dutch Ships, which had been destroyed in the preceding year, were also found in this place.

These brilliant achievements of Commodore James, while they considerably heightened the fame which he had previously acquired, added greatly to the glory of the British name in the East.

The success of the expedition against Severndroog served greatly to facilitate another of the same kind, of still greater magnitude. On the arrival of Commodore James at Bombay, the usual station of his Fleet, he found Rear-Admiral Watson there with a considerable force. The Government conceiving this to be an excellent opportunity for annihilating the power of Angria, consulted with that Officer on the best means of accomplishing so desirable an event. It was at length determined, that Commodore James, who had so recently proved himself a skilful Commander, should now display his talents as a Seaman. In consequence of this resolution, he set sail for Gheriah, the capital of Angria's dominions; arrived in its neighbourhood towards the dusk; stood in close under the walls; and, in the course of the night, fitted out his Boat, in which he himself took all the soundings, examined all the bearings, and made himself intimately acquainted with the various channels leading to this celebrated Fortress.

Having effected all this in the course of a few days, he returned to Bombay, and gave in his report to Admiral Watson.—The attack being immediately determined on, the necessary Troops, Stores, &c. were embarked with all possible dispatch, and Lieutenant Colonel, afterwards Lord Clive, was appointed to command the land forces.

About the 7th of February, 1756, the united Squadron sailed from Bombay; and, on the 11th of the same month, it appeared before the walls of Gheriah, having been joined in the neighbourhood by the Fleet of the Mahrattas, who were concerned in the expedition as allies, consisting of four Grabs and forty Gallivats.

The land force of the Mahrattas amounted to seven or eight thousand men, under the command of Rhamagee Punt, who had not only made himself master of one Fort, but was then actually treating for the surrender of Gheriah itself. Angria had quitted the place; but he had left his wife and family behind, under the protection of his brother-in-law, who commanded in the Fort.

Admiral Watson, immediately on his arrival, sent the Governor a formal summons to surrender, to which was returned a peremptory refusal, with a declaration, that he would defend the place to the last extremity.

Arrangements were consequently made for an immediate attack; and, on the afternoon of the 12th, Admiral Watson, finding that the Mahrattas, from whom he had received no assistance, were trifling with him, weighed anchor and stood into the Harbour with the Fleet in the two following divisions:—

Division ordered to attack the Forts and Batteries.

Ships.	Guns.	Men.	Commanders.
Bridgewater	24	160	Captain W. Martin.
Tiger	60	400	—— T. Latham.
Kent	70	595	Charles Watson, Vice-Admiral of the Blue. Captain H. Speke.
Cumberland	66	530	George Pocock, Rear-Admiral of the Red. Captain J. Harrison.
Salisbury	50	300	—— J. Knowles.
Protector *	44	300	Commodore James.

* Company's Ship

Division to attack Angria's Fleet and the Dock-Yard.

Ships.	Guns.	Men.	Commanders.
Kingfisher	16	100	Captain H. Smith
Revenge *	28	200	
Bombay Grab *	28	200	
Guardian *	26	160	
Drake, Bomb *			
Warren, do.*			
Triumph, do.*			
Viper, do.*			
Dispatch, do.*			

As they entered, the English Fleet sustained a very heavy cannonade from the Batteries of the place, and a number of large Grabs moored close under them. The enemy's fire, however, slackened very considerably, soon after the Ships which were ordered to attack had got into their stations.

The post of honour seems on this occasion to have been assigned to Commodore James; as he stood in with the Protector, and led the principal division of the Squadron to the attack, while the Frigates and Bomb-ketches formed the other.

The Ships of the Line, calculated from their weight of metal to make a quick and lasting impression, now commenced a heavy fire; and, between four and five in the afternoon, a shell fell into the Restoration, an armed Ship which Angria had some time before taken from the East India Company. The explosion set her on fire, and the flames quickly communicating to the rest of the piratical Fleet, the whole of them was completely and expeditiously destroyed.—Between the hours of six and seven in the evening, a shell which was thrown into the Fort set that on fire also; and, for a short interval, the cannonading ceased on both sides.

Admiral Watson suspected that the Governor would prefer surrendering the town to the Mahrattas, rather than to the English; and in this suspicion he was confirmed by the arrival of a deserter, who informed him, that Angria had sent orders to

---

* Company's Ships.

his brother-in-law, not on any account to suffer the English to come in. In consequence of this, the Admiral requested Colonel Clive to disembark the Troops, that he might be ready, in case of emergency, to take possession of the place.

The bombardment of the Citadel having re-commenced, it was continued with the greatest spirit, and the Line of Battle Ships were warped in close enough to the walls to batter in breach. After this arrangement had been made, the Admiral humanely sent in a Flag of Truce, inviting the Governor to surrender. The proposal, however, was still rejected; and on the following day, the 13th, the English Squadron renewed its attack with the utmost vigour. About one o'clock in the afternoon the principal Magazine of the Fort blew up. This accident had such an effect on the spirits of its defenders, that, about four, they displayed a white Flag, as a signal for parley: but the terms of surrender could not yet be agreed on. The Admiral insisted that the English Troops should be let in, and that the Colours of the enemy should be taken down; but this being refused, the assault re-commenced, and was continued with unremitting ardour till a quarter past five. At that time the white Flag was once more hoisted, and the Governor thought proper to surrender on such terms as Admiral Watson himself had proposed.

Angria's Flag was immediaiely struck; the British Colours were hoisted in its room; a detachment of sixty men took possession of the Fort that night; and, on the following morning, the whole of our Forces marched in.—Thus was possession obtained of a Fortress, which, from its appearance, might have been considered proof against the utmost efforts of an assailant. All the ramparts were either cut out of the solid rock, or built with stones of at least ten feet long, laid endways. The whole of the loss which was sustained by the English amounted but to nineteen men killed and wounded; and the damage of the Shipping was so trivial, that the whole Fleet might have proceeded to Sea again in four-and-twenty hours, had there been a necessity for its so doing.

As a proof that Admiral Watson's precaution, in desiring Colonel Clive to land with the Troops, was absolutely necessary, it may be mentioned, that the Mahratta Chiefs tampered with the British Officers who commanded, offering them a bribe of fifty thousand rupees, if they would permit them to pass and take possession of the Fort. It is scarcely requisite to say, that this proposal was rejected with becoming disdain.

Upwards of two hundred pieces of cannon, six brass mortars, and a considerable quantity of ammunition, with valuable effects and specie, to the amount of 120 or 130,000l., were found in the Fortress. The Fleet which was destroyed consisted of eight Grabs and one Ship, with two others on the Stocks, one of which was intended to mount 40 guns, and a considerable number of Gallivats.

There were in the Fort above 2000 people, 1300 of whom bore arms. Among the prisoners were Angria's wife and children, his mother, his brother-in-law, and the Commander in Chief of his Grabs.

The conduct of Admiral Watson towards the unfortunate relatives of Angria exhibits his character in too amiable a point of view for us to suffer it to pass unnoticed.

On his entering their apartment, the whole family, shedding floods of tears, fell with their faces to the ground. When raised, the mother of Angria told him, in an affecting tone, that " the people had no king, she no son, her daughter no husband, their children no father." On his replying, that " they must look upon him as their father and friend," the youngest boy, about six years of age, seized him by the hand, and, sobbing, exclaimed, " Then you shall be my father!" The brave Admiral was so affected with this artless but pathetic address, that the tears rolled down his cheeks, while he assured them that they might depend on his protection and friendship.

Great as the treasure appears that was found at Gheriah, it fell infinitely short of the expectations of the victors; for, however regardless Angria had been respecting the fate of his family, he had taken care to remove the greater part of his immense property.

Six hundred European and native Soldiers were left to garrison the Fort; and, as an additional protection, four armed Vessels, belonging to the East India Company, remained in the Harbour, which was extremely well situated for commerce.

All the other Forts belonging to Angria soon submitted; his power on the Coast of Malabar was entirely annihilated; and the English Squadron returned in triumph to Bombay.

Soon after this, while cruising off the Malabar Coast, Commodore James descried, and gave chase to, a French Ship called l'Indienne, from the Mauritius. She was greatly superior to his own, both in guns and men; but, in a short time after having been brought to action, she struck and was carried into Bombay.

An adventure, in which considerable science was displayed, next engaged his attention. He had long supposed, that, by getting out of the course of the Trade Winds, it was possible for a Vessel to reach a latitude where variable gales prevailed, and that, by such means, a communication might be kept up between different parts of the Company's Settlements at all times of the year. He accordingly resolved to attempt this discovery, in which he fortunately succeeded. Sailing from Bombay in a clear Ship, in the midst of a contrary monsoon, he steered from land, got into favourable weather, and arrived on the Coromandel Coast, to the surprise of the whole Settlement, after a Voyage nearly as short, in point of time, as had commonly been made during a fine season.

Pennant informs us, in his *History of Hindostan**, " that in effecting this passage, the Commodore crossed the equator in the meridian of Bombay, and continued his course to the southward as far as the tenth degree, and then was enabled to go as far to the eastward as the meridian of Atcheen Head, the N.W. extremity of Sumatra, from whence, with the N.W. monsoon, which then prevailed in the Bay of Bengal, he could with ease gain the entrance of the Ganges, or any port on the Coromandel Coast."—The track is laid down in Arrowsmith's Map of the World.

This event was not only attended with agreeable results as a speculation, but was actually pregnant with practical benefits;

---

* *Vide* Vol. I, page 260.

for it was Commodore James who, on this occasion, not only carried the first intelligence of the War with France, which had been received at Bombay by an over-land dispatch from England, but, at the same time, brought five hundred Troops to the assistance of Bengal; by which Admiral Watson and Colonel Clive were enabled, in March 1757, to take Chandenagore from the enemy, and thus ruin their trade and consequence in the East.

In the month of September, in the same year, our Officer commanded the Company's Frigate Revenge, which was stationed to cruise off Pondicherry, in company with his Majesty's Frigate the Triton. A strong Squadron of French Ships, however, chased them from the Coast, of which circumstance the Commodore duly apprised Admiral Pocock, who, on the demise of his friend Admiral Watson, had succeeded to the command in that part.

In the year 1759, having obtained a considerable fortune by his share of the prize-money of Severndroog, Gheriah, &c. as well as by the profits resulting from his own mercantile transactions, the Commodore returned to his native Country, purchased an estate at Eltham in Kent, and soon after (his former wife being deceased) married Miss Goddard, a Lady of a very respectable family in Wiltshire. On his arrival in England the East India Company presented him with a handsome gold-hilted sword, on the blade of which his exploits were enumerated. Government, however, did not at this period reward his merits; and it was not until his naval trophies were nearly faded in the remembrance of his contemporaries, that he was honoured with a title. Indeed it is extremely probable, that, had he not occupied situations of some importance at home, in which he had an opportunity of conferring favours, none would ever have been received.

On their arrival in England, most gentlemen who have obtained fortunes in India aspire to the management of the Company's affairs. Commodore James accordingly became a candidate for the Directorship, and not only procured a seat, but was appointed, first, Deputy Chairman, and then Chairman, offices of great consideration, and to which considerable influence is necessarily attached.

At length, on the 25th of July, 1778, his Majesty was pleased to confer upon him a baronetage. He was also returned in Parliament for West Looe, a Cornish borough; was elected one of the Elder Brethren, and Deputy Master, of the Trinity House; a Governor of Greenwich Hospital; and, whenever he was not obliged to remain out by rotation, was re-appointed, during more than twenty years, a Director of the East India Company.

Having been accustomed to an active life from his earliest youth, his mind was always employed on schemes of general importance. When Louis the XVIth took part with the American Colonies, and a war in consequence ensued between England and France, Sir William, ever attentive to the affairs of the East India Company, and anxious for the general interests of his Country, planned the annihilation of the enemy's power in India, by the capture of Pondicherry, which, according to his suggestions, was taken, but restored at the Peace. This may be mentioned as an instance, among a variety of others which might be named, of the advantage that must necessarily arise to the Company, from its Directors being possessed of a local knowledge of India.—The Company were so conscious of Sir William's superior merit on this occasion, that they presented him with a valuable service of plate.

His health at length began to decline; and, in consequence of the fatigues to which he had been exposed, and the unhealthy climates in which he had resided in early life, his constitution evinced palpable symptoms of premature decay. There was something melancholy and awful in the circumstance of his death. Immediately before his daughter's marriage some presages of apoplexy were discovered; and on the 16th of December, 1783, the very day that that ceremony, which had his full assent, took place, he fell down in a fit and expired, at the age of sixty-two.

Lady James, his widow, who is also since dead, determined to erect a monument to his memory on the northern brow of Shooter's Hill; and, being a woman of considerable taste, she was resolved to effect her purpose in a manner that could not fail to attract the notice of every traveller who passed into Kent. By way of perpetuating the memory of the capture of Severndroog, the year after the death of its victorious assailant, she caused a castellated building to be erected, after a design by Mr. Jupp, the summit of which is upwards of one hundred and forty feet higher than the cross of St. Paul's cupola. It consists of three stories, and is surmounted by battlements. The inside is fitted up in an appropriate manner, with arms, partisans, shields, daggers, javelins, &c. proper to the various nations of the East; and the whole is so contrived as to impress the mind with the belief, that it is the identical armory appertaining to Angria. In the room above this, the naval actions and enterprises of the Commodore are beautifully painted on the ceiling; and from the windows there is a most admirable view of London, the Thames, the Shipping, and the adjacent country. This Monument of Lady James's affection may be seen in a clear day from many parts of the metropolis, and from the tops of most of the public buildings. The spot on which it has been placed possesses so commanding an aspect, that it has been selected for the site of a telegraph, which communicates on one side with the Admiralty, and on the other with the Flag-ships at the Nore.

On a tablet over the entrance of the building, which is generally known by the appellation of Lady James's Tower, is the following inscription:—

THIS BUILDING WAS ERECTED

M,DCC,LXXXIV,

BY THE REPRESENTATIVE OF THE LATE

Sir WILLIAM JAMES, Bart.

To commemorate that gallant Officer's achievements in the East Indies, during the command of the Company's Marine Forces in those Seas; and in a particular manner to record the Conquest of the Castle of SEVERNDROOG, on the Coast of Malabar, which fell to his superior Virtue and able Conduct, on the 2d day of April, M,DCC,LV.

In the same Vault with Sir William James, the body of General Goddard, who distinguished himself by his achievements in India, lies also interred, by the care of the late Lady James, to whom he was nearly related. Descended from an ancient family in Wiltshire, but born to little or no fortune, he determined to form one in Asia, when only between sixteen and seventeen years of age: he accordingly embarked for India, and served under Generals Sir Eyre Coote and Lawrence, on the Coast of Coromandel. He afterwards served during twenty years in Bengal, and performed a most arduous march across the peninsula of India, which, from Calpy to Surat, is a distance of eight hundred miles, as measured on the General's own map by the late Mr. Pennant, who compares it to the famous expedition of Xenophon.

Sir William James was succeeded in his title and estate by his eldest son, who then became Sir Richard James; and, on his decease, by his youngest, who also died, on the 16th of November, 1792, at the early age of eighteen. Sir Richard James, the second Baronet, was the son of Sir William, by a native of Asia. He entered into the service of the East India Company, and was a Captain at the time of his father's death. He was the first person born in Hindostan, who succeeded to the hereditary honours of England.

Lady Rancliffe, the only daughter of Sir William, died on the 18th of January, 1797; and his widow, Lady James, died soon afterwards.

Sir William was attentive to the increase of his fortune: yet he was generous, and even munificent. On one occasion he made a present to a friend, which, had it been converted into money, would have produced the sum of two thousand pounds.

From the detailed account which we have given of Sir William James's services in India, it may easily be perceived, that he was an able Seaman and an excellent Commander; and that, to the professional qualities which he possessed, he united those of an enlightened superintendant, and a faithful guardian of the affairs of a Company which he had long served, and to the flourishing state of which he had materially contributed.

HERALDIC PARTICULARS.

The arms which were furnished by the Herald's College to Sir William James, were in strict allusion to his achievements, as follow:—

Azure, on a chevron or, between three lions or, passant, guardant, and ducally crowned, three fired Bombs proper.

CREST.—A Fort on fire, the Flag struck.

NAVAL ANECDOTES,
COMMERCIAL HINTS, RECOLLECTIONS, &c.

NANTES IN GURGITE VASTO.

ANECDOTE OF CAPTAIN WILLIAM CHAMBERS.

SIR Frederick Haldimand, who was Governor of Canada during the American war, was remarkable for having every apartment in his house kept with peculiar neatness. At that mansion which is appropriated to the Governor, he had formed one large room, in which he held his levees; and to avoid the dust and soil unavoidably brought in by the Officers, &c. he would not, on any account, suffer it to be carpeted, but had it carefully scoured every morning. In Canada it is customary, during the winter season, in order to prevent slipping on the ice, to wear on the feet a sort of patten, called *caulks*. Captain Chambers, who then acted as Commodore on the Lakes in Canada, entered the General's room without any precaution, and with his caulks made several indentions on the floor. The Governor, much irritated, cried out—"My God! my God! Commodore! your *caulks* will ruin my floor!" The Commodore immediately replied—"D—n your deck, 'tis no deck for me if it will not bear *caulking!*"

LORD ANSON'S EXPEDIENT TO PREVENT A SHIP FROM DRIVING.

THE Terrible, of 74 guns, Captain Richard Collins, which was attached to the Squadron under Admiral Saunders at the taking of Quebec, would probably have been lost in the River St. Lawrence, but for the following expedient of a Warrant Officer then on board. When the Ship drove from her anchors, he secured one of the Ship's guns to two small anchors, as had formerly been done by Anson in the Centurion, and thus kept her fast.

ROYAL WILLIAM.

IN addition to what we have already said of this venerable Ship (Appendix, No. I, Vol. I,) may be added, that when commanded by Captain Hugh Pigot at the taking of Quebec in 1759, she brought home the lamented remains of General Wolfe; which were landed from her at Portsmouth, on the 17th of November, in the same year, under a discharge of minute guns from all the Ships at Spithead.

List of the French Fleet at LOUISBOURG, *in* 1757, *under the Command of* M. BOIS *de la* MOTHE.

Ships.	Guns.	Commanders.
Le Duc de Bourgoyne	84	M. Bois de la Mothe.
L'Etonnant - - - -	80	M. de Beaufrement.
Le Formidable - - -	80	
L'Hector - - - -	74	M. de Revest.
Le Defenseur - - -	74	
Le Diademe - - - -	74	
Le Superbe - - - -	74	
Le Glorieux - - - -	74	
Le Heros - - - - -	74	
Le Dauphin Royal -	70	
L'Achille - - - - -	64	
Le Vaillante - - - -	64	
Le Sage - - - -	64	
L'Inflexible - - - -	64	
L'Eveille - - - - -	64	
Le Belliqueux - - -	64	
Le Celebre - - -	64	
Le Bizarre - - -	64	

FRIGATES.

	Guns.		Guns.
La Brune - - - - -	36	La Hermoine* - - -	36
Le Bien Acquis - - -	38	Le Fleur de Lys - -	36
La Comette - - - -	30	La Fochine, *flute* -	36

When Admiral Holburne sailed for Louisbourg, he gave out the following Line of Battle †:

The KINGSTON *to lead with the starboard, and the* DEFIANCE *with the larboard, tacks on board.*

Frigates to repeat Signals.	Ships.	Guns.	Commanders.	Division.
	Kingston - -	60	William Parry.	
	Captain - -	64	John Amherst.	Sir C. Hardy,
Hunter.	Invincible - -	74	John Bentley.	Rear-Admiral
	Nassau - -	64	James Sayer.	of the White.
	Sutherland -	50	Ed. Falkingham.	
	Tilbury - -	60	Henry Barnsley.	Fra. Holburne,
	Northumberland	70	Lord Colvill.	Vice-Admiral
	Newark -	80	William Holburne.	of the Blue,
Portmahon.	Orford -	66	Richard Spry.	Commander
	Sunderland	60	George Mackenzie.	in Chief.
	Centurion - -	50	William Mantle.	
	Nottingham	60	Samuel Marshall.	
	Bedford - -	64	Thorpe Fowke.	Chas. Holmes,
Ferret.	Grafton - -	70	Thomas Cornewall.	Commodore.
	Terrible - -	74	Richard Collins.	
	Defiance -	60	Patrick Baird.	

* Taken by our Cruisers on her return to Europe in the Autumn of 1757.
† See Note on Memoir of Lieutenant William Hunter, page 14.

ADMIRAL LINOIS.

(From the Revolutionary Plutarch.)

" THIS Officer was made a Lieutenant in the Royal Navy during the American War, and in 1789 emigrated with several of his comrades to Italy, and in the ensuing year to Spain. In 1791 he returned to France, and the following year was promoted Captain of a Frigate. On the first of June he commanded one of the French seventy-fours, which with difficulty ran away from Lord Howe, and escaped into Brest. He was in consequence imprisoned by the furious Jean Bon St. Andre, and remained so until the death of Robespierre.

" Under the Directory he was employed first at Brest, and afterwards at Toulon; and in 1800 was advanced by Buonaparté to the rank of Admiral. In the following spring he declined the command of the Fleet that carried succours to Egypt, and Gantheaume was appointed. Nothing but a great want of Naval Officers prevented him from feeling the Corsican Despot's rage at this refusal. On the 6th of July, 1801, he was engaged with Sir James Saumarez off Algesiras (See Vol. VI, pages 110 and 194), and again on the 13th, when he was defeated, though his superiority was immense, and escaped safe into Cadiz.

" At the Peace of Amiens, Linois was appointed to command the French Expedition to reinforce their Troops at the Isles of France and Bourbon, and to take possession of Pondicherry: an appointment he obtained from having formerly served in that part of the world under the Count de Suffrein.—His contest with Sir Nathaniel Dance soon followed: General Decaen, Governor of the Isle of France, denounced Linois to the vengeance of the Corsican, in a dispatch inserted in the Moniteur, Sept. 16, 1804. This Officer is between forty and fifty years of age, a gentleman by birth, and from his youth educated for the Navy."

COOKE, THE BLIND SEAMAN.

OUR readers will recollect the case of Cooke[*], the blind Seaman, who was robbed by his comrade in his way from Sheerness to London. About the beginning of December he returned to his friends at Bridgewater, totally blind, and pronounced to be incurable by the highest professional authorities in London. As a last resource, he was placed under the care of Mr. Sully, Surgeon to the Dispensary lately instituted at Wiveliscombe, who applied the

---

[*] See Vol. XII, page 306.

galvanic influence for three days to the organs of sight. Cooke was afterwards brought to Bath, and examined by Mr. Creaser, and other professional Gentlemen, who found, on the fullest and most satisfactory inspection, *that the sight of one of the patient's eyes was restored to him.*

Copy of a Letter transmitted from the Swedish Consul, London, to THOMAS HOGG, *Esq. Appledore:—*

SIR, *London, Jan.* 8, 1805.

" Having received official information from the Royal College of Stockholm, that an embargo has been laid on Swedish Ships at Antwerp, and likely to extend not only to France, but to all countries under its dominion, I have to request you will make this circumstance known to all Swedish Captains in the Ports of Barnstaple and Bideford, and warn them from attempting to enter any French Ports under present circumstances. I remain respectfully,

SIR,
Your most obedient servant,
" CLAES GRILL, Swedish Consul."

To Thomas Hogg, Esq. Appledore, Swedish Vice-Consul for Barnstaple and Bideford Ports.

MR. EDITOR,

IT is a just remark, that the memory of the brave should never perish, which sentiment I am persuaded you and your numerous readers will fully assent to; and as your CHRONICLE is open for the express purpose of rescuing from oblivion traits of gallantry, I request a corner in one of your valuable pages to transmit to posterity the heroic behaviour (not of a British Tar) but of a true British Game Cock, in the ever-memorsble 1st of June, 1794. The account made its appearance in a pamphlet some time ago, and on mentioning the circumstance to a friend of mine who was in the Marlborough at the above-mentioned period, he informed me that the account was strictly true.

I remain, Sir, yours, &c.

Great Queen Street, CHANTICLEER.
Lincoln's Inn Fields, Jan. 28, 1805.

BRITISH GAME COCK.

A COCK that had been purchased by the present Admiral Berkeley, when Captain of the Marlborough, of 74 guns, for the purpose of being kept as his live stock, greatly distinguished the

undaunted spirit attached to the English breed, during the time the above Ship was engaged in close action with the French Fleet on the glorious 1st of June, 1794. By being ordered on the boldest service against the enemy, she became totally dismasted, and was reduced to a mere wreck. At the time her main-mast went, the Cock alluded to flew upon the stump and began to flutter his wings and to crow with exulting boldness. So singular a circumstance attracted the attention of the brave Tars, who became reanimated by the example, and fought with additional bravery until Victory crowned them with her laurel. This undaunted Cock was preserved until the Ship reached Plymouth; when, in remembrance of his valour and the glorious occasion, he was presented to Lord Lenox, who placed him in a walk, where he to this day struts with a silver collar round his neck descriptive of his worth, proudly supporting his honour and the gallant behaviour of the British Fleet.

P. S. I should thank any of your Correspondents if they can inform me where I can meet with a List of the English and Dutch Navies during the Wars between England and Holland, in the times of Cromwell and Charles the IId, and a List of the loss of Ships taken and destroyed on each side: also if it be possible to find out the names of the Ships that were destroyed at Toulon during its siege in Queen Anne's Reign, when it was blockaded by the British Fleet under the meritorious Admiral Sir Cloudesley Shovel; the French lost eight capital Men of War in this business, which were either sunk or destroyed, but History has not given their names. Should you or any of your Correspondents be able to throw any light on this subject, it would give much satisfaction to your sincere wellwisher, C.

PLATE CLXXII.

MR. EDITOR,

AGREEABLY to your request I have sent you a Drawing of Dunkirk, which was taken by myself on the spot, so you may depend on its accuracy. What is below, you are welcome to curtail, alter, or enlarge upon, as you think proper. Yours,

F. GIBSON

DUNKIRK, or Drynkerk, that is, the Church upon the Downs, was originally a small Hamlet with a Church. Its advantageous situation upon the German Ocean, induced Baldwin,

Earl of Flanders, to enlarge and surround it with walls. By the Emperor Charles V it was further strengthened by a Castle, of which hardly a vestige remains. In 1658, Mareschal Turenne having routed the Spanish Army under Don John of Austria, the City of Dunkirk surrendered to him after eighteen days open trenches. It was then delivered to the English by Mazarine's treaty with Cromwell, who made Lockhart its Governor.

In 1662, Charles II sold it to the French for five millions of livres. Louis XIV employed the Chevalier de Ville to fortify it in the most formidable manner, by erecting a strong Citadel, ten large Bastions with Half-moons towards the Country, and numerous Forts and Batteries to the Sea. The Harbour was then deepened, and made capable of receiving Vessels of 70 guns.

All these Fortifications, with the Moles, Sluices, and Fort Louis, were demolished, and the Harbour filled up by virtue of the Treaty of Utrecht; but they have been occasionally restored, though not effectually, till the close of the late American War, when the former stipulations against the improvement of Dunkirk were rescinded, and the residence of British Commissaries no longer rendered necessary.

Dunkirk is a large well-built Town, extremely regular: the principal Church, dedicated to St. John, stands in the great Square. It is detached from its Steeple by the intersection of a Street. A noble Pediment, supported by six Corinthian Columns, was lately erected at the west end of the Church, and faces the insulated Tower.

The interior is occupied by fifteen Altars.—Over that dedicated to St. George, is seen an excellent painting of the Military Saint, by Rubens.

On the summit of the Steeple is erected a small House, in which Guards are placed every evening, alternately relieving each other. Four bells differing in tone, are hung, one at each corner of the Tower. Should the Centinel perceive a fire in any part of the Town, he immediately strikes the Bell that hangs in the pinnacle pointing to that quarter, which being heard by the Guard stationed at the Foot of the Tower, the alarm is immediately given to the inhabitants to repair to the place.

The Church of the Carmelites has a good appearance; it is constructed of brick, the pilasters and cornice of freestone.

In Dunkirk were lately two English Nunneries; one of Benedictines, receiving the relatives of people of opulence; the other, a retreat for the children of those of the lower order, denominated Poor Clares.

The Convent of the Capuchins was chiefly supported by the mendicant brethren, who attended the inns and public markets to collect eleemosynary charity.

In addition to these, we may reckon the black Beguin Nuns, a most laudable order, who, by their vows, are obliged to attend the sick poor, and even to collect alms for them.

The Grande Place is spacious, and surrounded by elegant buildings; amongst which the Hotel de Ville is most conspicuous, though the interior is not remarkable for any thing that merits a particular description.

Volti Subito.—In this square the principal market is kept. That appropriated to the sale of fruits and vegetables is held in a remote quarter of the town.

The Exchange is situated at a small distance from the Hotel de Ville, in which, as is usual on the Continent, a small Fair is held for the sale of books and toys.

The Governor's Hotel is a handsome pile of the Tuscan Order, the extent of the front being nearly 200 feet. The houses of the principal citizens are solidly constructed of stone; and in those a great degree of uniformity prevails. The Sale de Comedie is embellished with a beautiful frontispiece, supporting an entablature of the Ionic Order, and forms an agreeable cross termination of a wide street: the inside is elegantly and conveniently fitted up: in the coved ceiling over the orchestra was *once* seen a masterly painting of the late unfortunate Louis XVI, supported by Fame, with the inscription of *In hoc Numine felix;* but this inscription is now obliterated—*Tempora mutantur.*

In summer the people amuse themselves by a promenade on the Mall: it contains four acres of ground, regularly planted with trees and furnished with benches. The English Nunnery fronts the Military School, those two buildings forming two sides of the square.

The Harbour of Dunkirk is by no means so formidable as has been represented; but that it is of detriment to the trade of Great Britain, by its being a receptacle for Privateers and Smugglers, cannot be denied. It may likewise be allowed that the Bason may be deepened to 20, 30, or even 40 feet, and be made capable of receiving first rate Ships of War: but what purpose can this answer while the shifting nature of the Beach renders the shallows that accumulate round the Jetty-heads immoveable? and should those Jetties be extended a mile further into the Sea, the Sludge from the Harbour would most probably follow them.

Before the demolition at the Peace of Utrecht, the great Sluice, the site of which is now covered with buildings, opened directly fronting the Harbour, and scoured the Channel in a strait line: at present it takes an oblique direction; and the stream, by passing two acute angles, forming eddies, its utility is in a great measure lost.

Another great disadvantage arises from the Tide setting across the mouth of the Harbour and parallel with the Flemish Coast. The entrance of Dunkirk is defended by several strong Batteries, furnished with heavy cannon, particularly those on the Jetty-heads and the Risbank Forts, which stand in the water.

Dunkirk, in latitude 51° 1' N., and longitude 2° 26' E., lies three miles east from Mardyke Harbour, 10 miles E. ½ N. from Gravelines, and seven leagues E. ½ S. from Calais: it may be easily known by the height of its great Steeple, which, in clear weather, may be seen five or six leagues off.

To sail into Dunkirk you must bring the innermost Beacon a handspike's length open to the eastward of the outer one, and steer with them so until you get into the Channel between the two Jetties, which will bring you safely into Harbour.

The Entrance or Bar of Dunkirk is nearly dry at low water: the tide rises from 10 to 14 feet. At the Bar it flows full and change 45 minutes past eleven, but in the Road the flood continues to run till three o'clock.

F. G.

P.S. For more particular directions, *vide* "Sailing Directions for the North Sea," published by Laurie and Whittle, No. 53, Fleet Street.

CORRECT RELATION OF SHIPWRECKS.
[Continued from page 61.]

No. IX.

Again the dismal prospect opens round,
The wreck, the shore, the dying, and the drown'd.

FALCONER.

LOSS OF THE SHIP NABBY.

The following Account of the Loss of the Ship NABBY, *of Portland, has been communicated to us:—*

"ON the 19th of December, 1804, the Ship Nabby, Philip Crandell, Master, sailed from Liverpool for Boston, with a Cargo of salt, crates, dry goods, &c. with the Wind at E.S.E. On the 21st the Ship sprung a leak, which continued to gain upon them, notwithstanding both their pumps were kept constantly going. Finding the leak still increasing, they hauled their Wind in order to gain a Port. Standing along by the Wind, they made Mizen-head, on the western Coast of Ireland. Not being able to gain to windward of it, and then having six feet water in the hold, and the Men much fatigued with three days and nights' incessant pumping, they tried for Beerhaven, in Bantry Bay.

" By this time the Ship became water-logged, and the Wind still a-head, they determined upon gaining the Shore, and saving, if possible, a part of the Cargo. Accordingly, on the 25th, in the morning, they ran into a small Cove on the south side of the Bay, and let go their anchor in eight fathoms water, about 25 yards from the Shore. They then loaded their Boat with provisions and part of their effects, and sent them on Shore, where they were left in the care of the Mate and one Man.

" While they were loading a second Boat, the country people began to collect on the Shore, to the amount of about two hundred Men and Women. Immediately on the arrival of the Boat again on Shore, which contained all the effects of the Officers and Crew, together with all the Ship's papers, the inhabitants attacked the defenceless Crew, and inhumanly robbed them of all their clothes, papers, and money, and from some of the Crew their hats from their heads, and shoes from their feet. Not content with this, they proceeded on board the Ship, where all they could lay their hands upon fell a prey to their rapacity, threatening those who opposed them with instant death. About dark the robbers left the Ship, and carried their spoil into the mountains, when the Crew left her also, and proceeded to a miserable hut in the mountains, where they passed a most melancholy night. Early in the morning of the 26th, Richard Donovan, Esq. a gentleman living eight miles from where the Ship was lost, came to their assistance, and conducted the whole Ship's Company to his house. To the benevolence and humanity of this worthy gentleman, and his humane family, they are indebted for the preservation of their lives, without whose friendly assistance they must inevitably have perished. Early on the morning of the 28th, David Mellefont, Esq. of Bantry, together with Captain Scott and Lieutenant Griffin, with a party of forty Soldiers, went from Bantry in order to search for the stolen property; upon the approach of whom the robbers immediately left their huts and fled to the mountains.

To this gentleman and to Jonas Baldwin, Esq. they are also much indebted for their active and benevolent exertions."

LOSS OF THE BRIG FLORA.

Distressing Particulars of the Loss of the Brig FLORA, *of Philadelphia,* T. BURROWS, *Master, on a Whaling Voyage to Cayenne.*

THE following melancholy statement is extracted from *The New York Chronicle:—*

The Flora sailed from Philadelphia, in good order and well conditioned, on September 28th, with a Crew, consisting of Thomas Burrows, Master; Jacob Olderburg, Mate; William Davidson, Supercargo; John Nevan, Samuel Badcock, William Story, Joseph Wilder, Seamen; Josiah Smith, James Cameron, Boys; and Josiah Anderson, Steward. Nothing particular happened till Friday, the 12th of October, lat. 28° 50′ N., long. 54° W., the Wind began to blow hard from the N.E., the gale continuing to increase, accompanied by thunder, lightning, rain, and a heavy Sea, the pumps constantly going. Next day at two A.M. finding it impossible to lie-to any longer, determined to cut away the main-mast and scud before the Wind; but before that could be done, was struck with a Whirlwind, which hove the Brig on her beam ends. Joseph Wilder, being in the forecastle, was drowned; the main-mast went by the board, the hatches burst off, the Vessel filled with water, and the Cargo floating out at each hatchway—for our preservation we endeavoured to lash ourselves to the main-chains; but the Sea breaking furiously over us, William Davidson, William Story, and the two Boys, were washed away. The foremast now went by the board, and day coming on, we beheld a most awful sight, mast and spars hanging to the Wreck, and the Cargo coming out of the hold washed over us. At this time we shipped a Sea, which stove in the stern, and the Cargo broke out of the cabin; at nine A.M. we took to the bowsprit, when William Story and William Cameron drifted aboard on the canboose; the Boy shortly after died. The latter part of the day the gale began to abate, but a heavy Sea continued. On Monday William Story died. We continued in this dreadful situation until Friday the 19th of October, when we discovered a large Ship to leeward; made all the signals we could, but in vain. On the 20th several kegs of butter came out of the forecastle, one of which we immediately opened and fed on, which greatly increased our thirst. On the 21st the Mate went out of his senses, and a Schooner passed to leeward so near that we could see every Man on deck, but they took no notice of us. On the 23d the Mate died; his blood we drank, and devoured part of his flesh; with the remainder we caught a large shark, which proved a great relief to us. On Wednesday, the 24th, at sun-rise, saw a Brig standing towards us. At ten A.M. she hove-to, and hoisted out her Boat to our assistance, and we were taken on board in a weak condition. The Vessel proved to be the Snow Thames, Captain Burton, from Madeira to New Providence, and then in lat. 25° N., long. 59° W. To the humane attention of the Officers and Passengers we feel ourselves much indebted, and thus publicly express our thanks.

LOSS OF THE DORIS FRIGATE.

Particulars of the Loss of the DORIS *Frigate, communicated by an Officer of that Ship.*

ON the night of the 12th of January, as the Doris was proceeding to Quiberon Bay, through the Benequet Passage, she struck upon a sunken rock, called the Diamond Rock, and in consequence made so much water that Captain Campbell was obliged to throw all her guns, and every weighty article, overboard. During the following day it blew a tremendous gale at S.W., but the weather moderating on the day following, they gained upon the leak, which was under the fore-foot, and in the evening she sailed for England with a fine breeze, accompanied by the Felix. In the night, however, it blew hard from the N.W. with a heavy Sea, which tore off the soldering which had been put under her bottom to stop the leak, and the water gushed in with such violence, that every exertion to keep it under proved ineffectual; she became water-logged, would not answer her helm, and had drifted considerably to leeward during the night.—In this predicament, Capt. Campbell finding it impossible to keep her above water, determined to abandon her, and accordingly brought her to an anchor— " Our situation," says our informant, " was very critical; we were on the most dangerous part of the Coast, between a reef of rocks off Crozie (near the mouth of the Loire), called le Four, and a rock called the Turk: there was an excessive heavy swell running, and we could see the breakers directly astern, about three miles distant. Happily the Wind abated, or we all must have perished. At this time a Danish Brig was drifted in by the tide, and part of our people were put on board her, with orders to proceed for England; the rest, including the Captain and most of the Officers, in all 117, got on board the Felix, with a few portable articles. Captain Campbell then set the Doris on fire; in a short time the after Magazine blew up (the fore one had been drowned), and she immediately went down."

LOSS OF THE
EARL OF ABERGAVENNY, EAST-INDIAMAN.

THE melancholy account of the loss of this valuable Ship was received in London on the morning of Thursday, February 4. An Officer, who was one among the fortunate number saved from the Wreck, brought the unhappy tidings to the India-House, and we communicate them from his relation.—On Friday, the 1st of February, the Abergavenny, Captain Wordsworth, sailed from Portsmouth, in company with the Royal George, Henry Addington, Wexford, and Bombay Castle, for the East Indies, under Convoy of the Weymouth Frigate. The weather proved very unfavourable after their sailing, and the Wind being strongly adverse, induced them to make the best of their way for Portland Roads. After encountering a severe gale of Wind on Friday night (during which they parted Convoy), the five Indiamen reached the entrance of the Roads on Tuesday, about noon, when the Wexford, having been appointed Commodore, made signal for those Ships which had Pilots on board, to run for Port. At this period the Abergavenny had not been supplied with a Pilot, and therefore was compelled to wait a few hours for that purpose. About three P.M. having obtained one, she bore up for Portland Roads. The weather had become tolerably moderate, and notwithstanding a strong ebb tide was setting in, no disaster was at this time apprehended, it being conceived that the Pilot knew the Coast well. In a few minutes, however, the Ship's Company learned their dangerous situation, the Ship having struck on the shambles of the Bill of Portland, about two miles from the Shore. Captain Wordsworth and his Officers were, notwithstanding, of opinion, that the Ship might be got off without sustaining any material damage, and accordingly no signal guns of distress were ordered to be fired for upwards of an hour and an half afterwards, when twenty were discharged. All this time the people were free from alarm, and no idea prevailed that it would be necessary to hoist out the Boats to be ready to take the Crew on Shore in case of necessity. About five P.M. things bore a more unfavourable aspect: the Carpenter announced that a considerable leak was discovered near the bottom of the chain-pumps, which it was not in his power to stop, the water gushed in so fast. The pumps being all in readiness, were set a-going, and a part of the Crew endeavoured to bail her at the fore hatch, but all their attempts to keep the water under were in vain.

At six P.M. the inevitable loss of the Ship became more and more apparent; other leaks were discovered, the Wind had increased to a gale, and the severe beating of the Vessel upon the rocks threatened immediate destruction. The Captain and Officers were far from shrinking from the perils around them. They gave their orders with the greatest firmness and coolness, and by their proper conduct were enabled to preserve subordination. As the night advanced, the situation of all on board became the more terrible; the Misses Evans, and several other Passengers, entreated to be sent on Shore; but this was impossible. It was as much as all the Ship's Company could do to keep the Vessel afloat. In order to induce the Men to exert their utmost powers at the pumps, the Officers stood by cheering and encouraging them, by giving them allowances of liquor. At 7 P.M. the Ship's Company being almost exhausted, it was thought advisable to fire fresh signal guns, in hopes of obtaining Boats from the Shore, to save as many of the people on board as possible. In the mean time the Purser, Mr. Mortimer, was dispatched, in one of the Ship's Boats, with the papers and dispatches, in order to save them. The Third Mate, a cousin of the Captain, and of the same name, accompanied the Purser, with about six Seamen.

One Boat came off from the Shore, which took on board the Misses Evans, Miss Jackson, Mr. Rutledge, and Mr. Taylor, a Cadet, all Passengers. Mrs. Blair, companion to the Misses Evans, chose, in spite of all entreaties, to remain on board : indeed there were many who would have made the same choice, so little hope was there of the Boat contending successfully against the high Sea in so dark a night.

It was now about nine o'clock, and several Boats were heard at a short distance from the Ship, but they rendered no assistance to the distressed on board. Whether this were owing to their being employed in the humane purpose of saving those who had clung to pieces of wreck (upon which many had ventured from the Vessel), or because they were engaged in plunder, is a matter which has not yet been ascertained.

The dreadful crisis was now approaching—every one on board seemed assured of his fate; some gave themselves up to despair, whilst others endeavoured to collect themselves, and employed the few minutes they had left in the best of purposes—that of imploring the mercy of their Creator. At ten o'clock the Ship was nearly full of water, and as she began gradually to sink, confusion commenced on board. A number of the Sailors begged ardently for more liquor, and when it was refused, they attacked the spirit-room, but were repulsed by their Officers, who never once lost sight of their character, and continued to conduct themselves with the utmost fortitude. One of them was stationed at the spirit-room door, with a brace of pistols, to guard against surprise, and there remained even while the Ship was sinking. A Sailor was extremely solicitous to obtain some liquor from him, saying, "It will be all as one an hour hence."—"Be that as it may," replied the Officer, "let us die like Men." It is a circumstance hardly to be accounted for, that, in the midst of all this distress, the Boats were never attempted to be hoisted out. About two minutes before the Ship went down, Mr. Baggot, the Chief Mate, went to Captain Wordsworth, and said, "We have done all we can, Sir, she will sink in a moment." The Captain replied, "It cannot be helped—God's will be done."

When the Passengers and Crew were acquainted with their situation, they made several efforts to save their lives; some laid hold of pieces of the Wreck, and committed themselves to the mercy of the waves. A Mr. Forbes stripped off his clothes, and being an excellent swimmer, plunged into the Sea, and was one of those who were picked up by a Boat from the Shore. A great number ran up the shrouds. At about eleven o'clock a heavy Sea gave the Vessel a sudden shock, and in an instant she sunk to the bottom, in twelve fathoms water. Many of those unfortunate persons who had run up the shrouds for safety, were unable to sustain the motion of the Vessel in going down, and suffered with their unfortunate companions below. Between eighty and ninety persons, however, were still able to maintain their situation, and were ultimately saved. For some time after the Vessel had gone down, she kept gradually sinking deeper in the sand, insomuch, that several persons were under the necessity of climbing higher up the masts. The highest mast was estimated to be above the water about twenty-five feet, and the persons aloft could plainly discover the end of the bowsprit.

When the Ship sunk, she did not go down in the usual way that Vessels do, by falling first upon her beam ends; this deviation was supposed to have arisen from her being laden with treasure and Porcelain ware. She had 70,000l. in specie on board, and nearly 400 persons. The Crew consisted of 160 Men, and there were between 50 and 60 Passengers; the rest were Recruits for his Majesty's and the Company's Service: about 30 Chinamen were also on board. The total number of the drowned is estimated at 300.

Several Boats were heard paddling about the Wreck at half past eleven o'clock; and although they were hailed by the unfortunate persons on the shrouds and masts, they could not be prevailed upon to take them on Shore. The reason which was afterwards assigned for this apparently inhuman conduct, was, that they were fearful that every person on board, being eager to save himself, the whole would attempt to jump in, overload the Boats, and sink them.

About twelve o'clock, a Sloop that had been attracted to the spot by the signal guns, came to anchor close to the Ship, sent a Boat, and took off all the persons we have mentioned as being above water, about twenty at a time, and conveyed them to Weymouth. So far were the people from crowding improperly into the Boat, that they got off the shrouds one by one, and then only as they were called by the Officers who were with them. When it was supposed that every person was brought off, and the Boat was about to depart for the last time, a person was observed nearly at the top of a mast in the shrouds; he was called to, but did not answer; one of the Officers, much to his credit, returned, and there found a Man in an inanimate state, arising from the piercing cold weather. The Officer brought him down on his back, and took him ashore; the person proved to be a Surgeon; every possible care was taken of him, but his recovery was extremely doubtful. The whole value of the Cargo is estimated at 200,000l. Nothing was saved except the dispatches and some valuable prints, which had been sent out for General Lake. Captain Wordsworth, at the moment the Ship was going down, was seen clinging to the ropes. Mr. Gilpin, one of the Mates, used every persuasion to induce him to endeavour to save his life, but all in vain; he did not seem desirous to survive the loss of his Ship. The exertions of Cornet Burgoyne, and the Mates, were most exemplary; they did all that human means could effect.

The Abergavenny was of about 1200 tons burthen, and was destined to Bengal and China. She was to have laden at Bengal with cotton for the China market. The Passengers were unusually numerous. Forty sat down daily at the Captain's table, and above fourteen at the third Mate's. The first and third Mates were on Shore when the Abergavenny left Portsmouth, and paid forty guineas for a Boat, which enabled them to join the ill-fated Ship. Captain Wordsworth was a Man of remarkably mild manners, and of a cool and temperate disposition. Mr. Baggot, the Chief Mate, possessed a similar character; he made no attempt to save his life, but met the fate of his Captain with the same composure. The names of the persons said to have been saved are:—

Mr. W. G. E. Stewart, 2d Mate; Mr. Joseph Wordsworth, 3d ditto; Mr. Thomas Gilpin, 4th ditto; Mr. John Clark, 5th ditto; Mr. H. Mortimer, 6th ditto; Mr. Davie, Surgeon; Mr. Stewart, Purser; Mr. Abbot, Gunner; Mr. Addwater, Carpenter; Mr. White, Midshipman and Cockswain; Messrs. Pitcher, Rason, Yates, and Barnett, Midshipmen; W. Akers, Ship's Steward; W. Ivers, Boatswain's 2d Mate; C. Dunn and J. Williams, Gunner's Mates; A. Barret, C. Boyd, J. Palmer, G. Thompson, and J. Thomson, Quarter Masters; D. Lundie, Baker; J. Parsons, J. Swinie, and M. Bonge, Seamen; and J. Thompson, Chinese Servant.

Passengers.—Thomas Evans, Esq. senior Merchant; Miss Evans; Miss Jackson; Mr. Rutledge; Cornet Burgoyne, 8th Light Dragoons; Dr. Maxwell; Mr. Evans's black Servant; Messrs. Baillie, Gramshaw, C. Taylor, Thwaites, and Johnson, Cadets.

Exclusive of the above-mentioned persons, about twenty Soldiers, and from forty to fifty of the Petty Officers, and others of the Ship's Company, were saved, whose names have not yet been ascertained.

The total number saved is reckoned at from ninety to one hundred persons.

The following letter, since received from an Officer on board (Mr. Clark), states with precision the immediate causes of the Abergavenny striking on the Shambles:—

ON the 5th inst. at 10 A.M. being about ten leagues to the westward of Portland, the Commodore made signal to bear up; did so accordingly; at this time having main-top-gallant-mast struck, fore and mizen ditto on deck, jib-boom in, and the Wind about west south-west. At three P.M. got a Pilot on board, being about two leagues to the westward of Portland: ranged and bitted both cables. At about half past three called all hands, and got out the jib-boom at four o'clock. While crossing the east end of the Shambles, the Wind suddenly died away, and a strong tide setting the Ship to the westward, drifted her into the breakers; and a Sea striking her on the larboard quarter, broached her to with her head to the northward, when she instantly struck, it being about five o'clock; let out all reefs, and hoisted the top-sails up, in hopes to shoot the Ship across the Shambles. The Wind shifting to the north-westward, the surf driving us off, and the tide setting us on alternately, sometimes having four and a half, at others nine fathoms. Continued in this situation till seven o'clock; at about half past seven o'clock she got off. During the time she was on the Shambles, had from three to four feet Water, pumps constantly going. Finding she gained on the pumps, it was determined to run her on the nearest Shore. At eight o'clock the Wind shifted to the eastward. The leak continuing to gain upon us, having 10 or 11 feet water, found it expedient to bail at the fore scuttle and hatchway. The helm being hard a starboard, the Ship would not bear up, she being water logged; but still had a hope we could keep her up till we got her on Weymouth Sands: cut the lashing of the Boats, could not get the Long-Boat out without laying the main-top-sail aback, by which our progress would have been so retarded, that little hope would have been left us of running her aground; and there being several Sloops in sight, one having sent a Skiff on board, and took away two Ladies and four or five Passengers, and put them on board their Sloop, at the same time promising to return and take away a hundred or more people, at different trips, to the Sloop; but finding much difficulty in getting back to the Sloop, did not return. About this time the third Officer and Purser were sent on Shore in the Cutter to get assistance from the other Ships: continued pumping and bailing till eleven o'clock, when she sunk. The last heave of the lead was in eleven fathoms water, having fired guns from the time she struck till she went down. At two in the morning Boats came off and took the people from the Wreck, about seventy in number. The tops of all the masts were above water.

NAVAL LITERATURE.

The Narrative of Captain DAVID WOODARD *and four Seamen, who lost their Ship while in a Boat at Sea, and surrendered themselves up to the Malays, in the Island of Celebes; containing an interesting Account of their Sufferings from Hunger and various Hardships, and their Escape from the Malays, after a Captivity of Two Years and a Half; also an Account of the Manners and Customs of the Country, and a Description of the Harbours and Coast, &c. Together with an Introduction, and an Appendix, containing Narratives of various Escapes from Shipwrecks, under great Hardships and Abstinence; holding out a Valuable Seaman's Guide, and the Importance of Union, Confidence, and Perseverance, in the midst of Distress.* 8vo.

IT appears, from this Narrative, that Mr. Woodard, who is an American, sailed from Boston in America, for the East Indies, in 1791. After his arrival there, he was employed in making country Voyages, in different Country Ships, until January, 1793, when he sailed as Chief Mate in the American Ship Enterprise, bound from Batavia to Manilla. In passing through the Straits of Macassar, the Wind and Current were both against them, and they were obliged to beat up the Straits for six weeks, in which time they fell short of provisions. A Vessel being perceived, at the distance of about four leagues, Mr. Woodard and five Seamen were sent on board of her to purchase a supply. It being nearly sun-set when they reached the Vessel, they staid on board all night, and left her the next day, without water, or provisions of any kind, excepting a bottle of brandy. All their efforts to descry or recover their own Vessel were in vain; and, having been without sustenance for several days, they surrendered themselves to the Malays, in the Island of Celebes. Previously to their surrender, however, the Malays had barbarously murdered one of these unfortunate Men. They were detained as prisoners for two years and a half, during which time they experienced many hardships and misfortunes, being kept destitute of clothes, short of provisions, and without most of the comforts of life. Mr. Woodard and his four surviving companions, after many efforts and disappointments, at length effected their escape, and arrived at Macassar, almost exhausted by distress, fatigue, and want of nourishment. They there experienced the most liberal and friendly treatment from the Governor, the Hon. William Pitts Jacobson, and from Mynheer Alstromer, the Dutch East India Company's Captain, who supplied them with clothes and money, and dispatched them in a Proa to Batavia.

This volume is dedicated to Captain Hallowell, of the Royal Navy, by Mr. Vaughan, the Editor, who obtained the materials from Captain Woodard about eight or ten years ago.

The *Introduction*, though well intended, and containing some useful remarks for the benefit of Seamen, in cases of Shipwreck, &c. is by far too diffuse. In point of composition, it has no claim to praise; and the substance might have been condensed into a much smaller compass.

The first part of the work comprises the whole of Mr. Woodard's Narrative. It excites considerable interest, and will be read with satisfaction by Seamen in general. The second part consists of a description of the Island of Celebes, its Harbours, Rivers, Towns, &c. &c. The third is composed of miscellaneous information respecting Mr. Woodard, who, since his misfortunes, has commanded different Merchant Vessels, and now lives in retirement, on a farm, in America, his native country.

The Appendix might, with much propriety, be published in a cheap and detached form, as it is merely a collection of cases, tending " to show the frequency and extent of abstinence, and the importance of perseverance and subordination in moments of distress."

From the third part of this performance, which, on the whole, is entitled to commendation, we shall take the liberty of copying the following letter from Captain Woodard to Mr. Vaughan, as it contains some nautical intelligence that is worthy of attention:—

DEAR SIR, *Manilla, February,* 1803.

I embrace this opportunity of writing to you. I am now returning from a long Voyage; and during my route I have paid a visit to Chili, Peru, and Mexico, and up the Gulf of California further than any English Vessel was known to be; and was visited by the Governor and Head Men of New Mexico, and treated in the most civil manner. I made a discovery of a fine Port up the Gulf, and a good Harbour, which I think would be of use to the Public in general. It lies in lat. 28° N. and is good anchoring, and a safe Harbour against all Winds; and, I think, deserves a place in your Naval Gazetteer. It is called Port Guimor; and lies in lat. 28° N. on the east side of the Gulf of California. Care must be taken, sailing up the Gulf, not to come too near the east Shore, as there are several points on that side, and subject to heavy Squalls from the high land that lies back. Keep the west Shore in view till in lat. 27° 45′ N. and then steer in east till you bring a high ridge of rugged land to bear N.N.E. and a small island plain in sight, which bears from the point of high land west; then steer for the easternmost part of the high land, which will appear as if there was a River that divides it from the other high land; but it is nothing more than a tract of low land, that begins at the Sea, and runs back thirty or forty miles. As you draw near the land, you will begin to raise the tops of the trees. The Harbour lies on the east point of the high land. It is surrounded on the north and west part, to S.S.W., by very high land; and on the east by this low land, as above; and on S.E. by Pelican Island, which is high and bold. In going into the Harbour you must leave Pelican Island on the starboard hand. The passage is narrow, but perfectly safe, and good anchorage. In a calm, the course in is N.N.W. till you open a large white house; then let go the anchor in five fathoms: mud and sand. The Town is but small, and lies about ten miles up the Bay. You must moor N.W. and S.E. It is a good place for refreshments, and very cheap.

NAVAL HISTORY OF THE PRESENT YEAR, 1805.

(January—February.)

RETROSPECTIVE AND MISCELLANEOUS.

VARIOUS were the Conjectures which the sudden Pacific Message of BUONA-PARTE occasioned to the moment when our last Retrospect went to Press. But we have little room for Conjectures, especially those of a Political nature. It is most probable that the *soi-disant* Emperor was either terrified by the formidable alliance we had made with the Northern Powers; or else, in some degree, hoped to paralyse our exertions, by dazzling us with the prospect of Peace previous to the meeting of Parliament. The sudden capture of the Spanish Ships has called forth the virulence of party, and been strangely misrepresented by many writers. In our last Volume, among the Naval Anecdotes, we inserted a justifiable precedent for such a measure; and our readers will find this subject discussed more at large in the Naval Debates that took place on the King's Speech; in the Declaration of War made by our Government; and in the Spanish State Papers *.

Sir John Orde has made some valuable Spanish captures. The Crews of three of the captured Ships have been sent to Lisbon, the Ships to Gibraltar. The Camilla, of 20 guns, has taken a valuable Spanish Ship, and sent her into Gibraltar.

It is said to be in the contemplation of Government, to send splendid Embassies to the distinguished Courts of Europe, in order to fix the basis upon which a new Political Balance can be established for all its powers and dependencies. Lords Macartney, Malmesbury, St. Helens, and Auckland, have been named as being likely to be employed in these missions.

The Consecration of Buonaparté reminds us of the Bon Mot of the celebrated Lord Peterborough.—On being asked, when in France, " *Si on sacrois les Rois en Angleterre?*"—replied, " *Oui, on les sacre—ct les massacre aussi!*"—What says the Corsican to this?

Jan. 24. The new COMMISSION under the Great Seal has commenced its labours at the Office in Craven Street, Strand, the purport of which is to form a complete Digest of regulations and instructions for the civil department of the Navy.

Orders have been given to break up the Duquesne, of 74 guns, at Chatham.

There are at present in commission, exclusively of Cutters, armed Brigs, Gunvessels, &c. (of which the number is immense), 694 Ships, of which 105 are of the Line, 24 Fifties, 137 Frigates, 431 Sloops of War. Besides these, there are receiving Ships, those repairing for Service, in ordinary and building, of different descriptions, 211, of which about 80 are of the Line; making the grand total, exclusive of the smaller description of Ships of War, 905 Sail.

The preparations for the intended Expedition are carrying on with great activity. It was at first intended that it should have sailed before this time. A great many Transports are assembled at Cowes and Spithead—the Cavalry are in the Isle of Wight, the Infantry at Spithead; the former will embark at Southampton Water, the Infantry at Portsmouth. It was generally believed, that Portugal was the

---

* See Appendix, No. I.

destination of the expedition; but since General Moore's return, who is stated to have delivered it as his opinion, that though the country might be defended, it would require a very large body of Troops, Ministers are said to have abandoned the idea. Some of the Transports are engaged not to go beyond a certain latitude; others are engaged to go wherever it shall be deemed proper to send them. The object of the expedition is very properly kept a profound secret.

It has long been a subject of complaint, that no fixed adequate provision was made for Surgeons and Surgeons' Mates in the Navy. That complaint has now been remedied by Lord Melville; and we understand that Surgeons, after ten years' service, are to be allowed 20 shillings a day full pay—Surgeons' Mates are to be allowed full pay, and half pay in proportion, after a shorter period of service than ten years.

The following excellent Vindication is extracted from the COURIER of Jan. 26:—Were we not entreated by his friends, we should feel ourselves called upon by justice and patriotism to repel the charges made against a gallant Naval Officer in *The Morning Chronicle*, of Saturday last. That paper asserts, that *" Officers who had just as good means of intelligence and observation as Admiral Cochrane,"* deny what he writes home; it adds, that *" he makes an assertion in respect to the armaments for which no evidence can be discovered, and which is utterly improbable."* This impeachment of his testimony, though severe, might have passed without notice, if his conduct had not been imputed to the basest motives. It is pretended that his honour or veracity are not discredited by an insinuation, that on the subject of the armaments in Ferrol, *" he might not be impartial. He knew to whom he was writing. He had the natural prejudices of a Sailor for a Spanish war."*

The insinuations made, or rather the direct charges advanced, against this brave Officer, are—that he was not an impartial reporter of the Spanish armaments; that he sent false reports to suit the designs of the British Ministers; that he was desirous of involving his country in a war with Spain, from the sordid motive of obtaining prize-money; and that he must have reported falsely with this view, since other Officers, who had as good means of intelligence and observation, deny what he writes home.—" He makes assertions for which there is no evidence, and which are utterly improbable," all it seems for the lucre of Spanish dollars; or, as it is more artfully said, " from the natural prejudices of a Sailor for a Spanish war." Greater crimes could not be imputed than these. If Admiral Cochrane could send home false intelligence, if he could vamp up a story to enable Ministers to involve Britain in an unnecessary war, he must be the most base and servile creature in the English Navy; but if he could fabricate accounts of armaments which had no existence, or if he could grossly exaggerate those which were on foot, " from the natural prejudices of a Sailor for a Spanish war;" that is, from avarice, and in the hope of making rich captures; if he could involve his country in a war with such sordid designs; if he could thus be the means of shedding the blood of thousands, and expending millions of the money of his fellow-subjects, that he might fill his own pockets—then is he more base and wicked than language can express. That we may not be accused of misrepresentation, the whole of the article is copied*.

---

* Admiral Cochrane says there were armaments at Ferrol; but with all deference for that excellent Officer, we apprehend that it is not to discredit either his honour or veracity to say, that in this instance *he might not be impartial. He knew to whom he was writing. He had the natural prejudices of a Sailor for a Spanish war;* not to mention that the preparations for Biscay, which even Mr. Frere does not insist to be of a general hostile character, may have led him into an error on

The public will judge whether it contains the inuendos we describe. We trust that an apology will be made for it. In the haste of newspaper writing, unguarded expressions sometimes escape, which are disapproved of on reflection; but they do not cut the less deep, or spread the less calumny, because they were not intended. Custom has privileged detraction against our Statesmen; but the slander of a rancorous Coalition Faction should not be suffered to blacken the moral characters of our Naval Defenders. While they are fighting our battles abroad, we are bound to protect their reputation at home; and no man is better entitled to this protection than Admiral Cochrane: he is one of the oldest Officers in the Service; one of the most brave and amiable; and one of the most moral of Men. On the American Coast last war, with a small Frigate and two Gun-brigs, he beat three large Frigates, took one, and destroyed another. This is one of the most brilliant actions on record. He was Captain of the Ajax in Sir Ralph Abercrombie's expedition to Egypt. There he had the chief care in debarking the Troops and covering the landing. This service he performed with a degree of skill and enterprise that stamped him one of our ablest Naval Commanders, and probably pointed him out lately as a proper Officer to watch the Port of Ferrol. By all persons employed on the Egyptian expedition, Admiral Cochrane was beloved and admired. He is not only brave and enterprising, but gentle, humane, and religious. He commonly does the duty of Chaplain on board his own Ship: his Crew are remarkable for their good conduct, and they adore him. This is not the Man who would betray his country into a war to fill his own pockets.

Greenock, Jan. 24. Three o'clock. A little after eight o'clock this morning, the Tourterelle Frigate put to Sea; the anchors of the other Ships were a-trip, and were just going to follow, when a person of the name of Brown, from Craignish, arrived in town, and brought accounts that the Ship which created so much noise turned out to be his Majesty's Ship Brilliant, Captain Barrie. This information was first obtained by Colonel Campbell, of the Craignish Volunteers, who boarded her on Monday; and was informed by Captain Barrie, that the reason of his not allowing any Boats to come alongside was, that lately when passing through the Sounds seven of his Crew had deserted in the Boats belonging to the Islands.

Immediately on Browne's reaching town, the Princess Elizabeth, Captain Beatson, was sent after the Tourterelle, and it is said she got sight of her as she was passing the Cumbraes, and brought her to by signal guns. The Volunteers who had embarked as Marines on board of the other Ships, are just now landing.

---

this head. But is there a word proved of preparations at Carthagena, at Cadiz, &c.? Not a single fact is proved by any *assertion*. Besides, we cannot help stating, that we know that Officers who had just as good means of intelligence and observation as Admiral Cochrane, deny that there were, after the preparations for Biscay (which were countermanded), any preparations of a general hostile appearance. Admiral Cochrane, in his dispatch of the 11th of September, makes an assertion for which we see no evidence whatever, and indeed which is utterly improbable; viz. "There does not remain any doubt that the intentions of the French, Spanish, and Dutch Ships of War are to act together; and as three First-rates are expected from Cadiz, their Lordships, I hope, will approve of my concentrating the force I have under my orders!!" Now who does believe, or can believe, that previous to the 11th Sept. 1804, the French, Spanish, and Dutch Ships had any intention of coming out and acting hostilely together? Then what sort of intelligence is this? Yet what hasty, precipitate, and criminal orders were founded on it.

Jan. 26. Government, actuated by motives which do it honour, have just issued instructions to our Naval Commanders, not to molest any neutral Vessel going with supplies of grain to Spain, during the present distress of that unfortunate country, even though the grain should belong to our enemy.

Hull, Jan. 28. On Wednesday morning the Hull Packet, bound from this Port for Lynn, returned hither with only one Man on board. The Master and the rest of the Crew having gone to Grimsby on Monday to buy fresh provisions, were unable to make the Vessel again, in consequence of the boisterous weather. The great fatigue and anxiety which he underwent, during this period, may be easily conceived; but, by perseverance, he succeeded in bringing the Vessel safely back into Port, after parting from anchors and cables.

Orders have been issued on Saturday last, to the Transport Board, that all the private property belonging to the Officers and Men of the captured Spanish Frigates, whether in money or goods, should be forthwith restored to the owners. These acts certainly reflected credit on Administration, and should be promulgated in every quarter of Europe.

Jan. 31. The London Docks opened for the reception of Shipping and Merchandize. The Corporation of London, we understand, attended in their municipal paraphernalia; and a great number of the Nobility and Gentry of the first rank honoured the ceremony with their presence. Every preparation had been made by Mr. Rennie, the principal Engineer and Manager of the Dock, preparatory to its being opened this day, for the reception of Shipping, when the buoys in the Dock were all examined, and the flood-gates and hinges all eased. At a late hour on Tuesday night the Engineer took advantage of the tide and a strong current; and, aided by several hundred workmen, removed the floating-bridge from its station, which was placed across the entrance of the Dock, below Hermitage Bridge, level with the River Thames. This Bridge being, since the commencement of the Dock, erected to prevent the water coming in, in case of accident, by the breaking of the banks, when towed from its moorings, was carried by the strong current of the tide through the swivel iron-bridge, through the double locks, and into the right-hand side of the outer bason. In less than three quarters of an hour after the removal of the bridge, the water rushed into the Dock so rapidly, it rose, in the outer bason, to the height of nineteen feet three inches; and, in the inner bason, to eighteen feet. The swivel bridge was built upon a new construction, and is made of cast iron, formed to open in the centre on swivels; it is forty feet span, and 15 broad. The road-way from the bridge to the entrance of the outer bason is a hundred feet. The outer bason is five acres, which leads to the inner Dock by two locks, about fifty feet apart; and the Dock twenty acres. The spring-tide depth of the inner Dock, when full, will be twenty feet, and the outer bason twenty-three. The whole of this immense work is surrounded with a circular road, and a wall thirty feet high. A more minute account of this great Commercial Establishment shall appear in the course of the present Volume.

The sailing of the Rochefort Squadron took place on the night of the 11th of January. The following morning about five o'clock they were seen by the Felix Schooner standing to the north-west, under top-gallant-sails, the Wind then S. by W. The Felix was at one time within half gun shot of the enemy, but at nine a squall came on from the northward, in which she lost sight of them; at ten it cleared up, and she again saw them from the mast-head steering N.W., and then in lat. 45º 50' N., long. 1º 52' W., about fifty leagues from the Isle Dieu. On the 12th they were perceived by one of our Cutters, standing to the northward, apparently having sustained much damage in their masts, sails, and yards. The Schooner proceeded to Quiberon Bay, in quest of Sir T. Graves; and not finding him there, again put to Sea, but did not meet him until the 16th following, at which period he was wholly uninformed of the escape of the enemy. The Wind then blew so hard from the S. W. that the Admiral was unable to take the course the enemy had steered; and he was compelled to return to Quiberon Bay. On the 16th the Tonnant saw the top-mast of a very large Ship adrift off Belleisle, and the Admiral was informed by the Master of an American Schooner that he had seen the French Squadron off the Penmarks, and that one of the Ships was dismasted. On the 20th the Felix was sent to reconnoitre Basque Bay, and found there only one Vessel, supposed to be a Frigate. An heavy gale was then blowing into the Roads, and prevented a more minute examination. The Colossus, which had anchored outside the Isle of Rhee, was compelled to cut her cable, and with difficulty got off the Shore; she joined Sir T. Graves on the 23d, and on the 24th he stood to the N.N.W. to join the Ushant Fleet; his Squadron then comprised Foudroyant, Windsor Castle, Hero, Mars, Colossus, and Bellerophon.

Without pretending to give any opinion on the conduct of Sir Home Popham, for which he has been arraigned before Parliament, (the Debate on which will be given at length in our next,) we shall at present only insert part of a paragraph, which appeared in the Courier. What we have omitted is a violent attack on the character of Earl St. Vincent; which, whether just or unjust, can have no place in our CHRONICLE:—

" The late Admiralty Board directed the Naval Commission of Inquiry especially to report to it on the repairs of the Romney, &c. from certain Papers in the Navy Office. The Commission was directed to make an *ex parte* Report, without calling upon Sir Home to know if he could explain away or rebut the charges It has hitherto been the practice, when any Officer has been implicated in improper proceedings, to send for him to state the charges to him, and to ask if he is desirous of saying any thing in his justification?—then, if the Officer chooses, he can call evidence, or produce testimony to repel the charge. But the Commission, in Sir Home's case, was expressly directed to make an *ex parte* Report, without attempting to inquire whether the documents on which they proceeded could be answered by other evidence. The Report was, of course, such as might have been expected.

" Hearing what was going forward, Sir Home, with the feelings of conscious innocence, went to the Admiralty Board, and entreated that he might be allowed to answer the charge, but he was afforded no opportunity of doing so. He solicited a copy of the Report, and was told by the Admiralty Board, that it had given directions to the Navy Office to furnish him with a copy. On applying to the Navy Office, he was told they had received no orders to give him a copy of the Report, but they had been instructed to show him the documents on which it was founded, and they promised to do so. On applying for these documents afterwards, he was told they were mislaid, and he could not obtain a sight either of them or of the Report. In this way he was deprived of any authentic information to which he might reply, while in the most injurious and exaggerated rumours, his character was whispered away. He went to his public duty to command a Squadron on the Coast of France, still unable to obtain a copy of the Report of the Naval Commission; but he had not been long there, when he found that this very Report, accompanied by scurrilous comments, in the shape of a Pamphlet, had been anonymously conveyed into the hands of every Officer under him in the Squadron he commanded! This most malicious step was, no doubt, taken to render Sir Home obnoxious and contemptible in the eyes of his Officers, because he had zealously, skilfully, and with considerable success, attempted to make an impression on the enemy at Boulogne, by means of Vessels filled with combustibles. Some of the admirers of the late Admiralty Board could not bear, we suppose, to see the present Admiralty make superior and successful exertions to annoy the enemy. The success of the combustible coffers was conceived to be a reproach to the late Admiralty, and hence some of its friends attacked Sir Home Popham, the chief conductor of those machines.

" But no sooner had Sir Home Popham possession of the Pamphlet, anonymous as it was, than he set about answering it. On applying to the Booksellers, no one would venture to publish it. The Newspapers were filled with Trials and Speeches about prosecutions carried on by Earl St. Vincent for libels. Sir Home was therefore obliged to sustain the anonymous slanderer's fire, without being able to return it. Mr. Kinnaird, however, has very kindly procured him an opportunity of defending himself; and considering the illiberality with which he has been treated, we hope he will be able to give his enemies a sound drubbing."

FROM THE LONDON GAZETTE,

26TH JANUARY, 1805.

DECLARATION.

FROM the moment that Hostilities had commenced between Great Britain and France, a sufficient ground of War against Spain, on the part of Great Britain, necessarily followed from the Treaty of St. Ildephonso, if not disclaimed by Spain.

That Treaty in fact identified Spain with the Republican Government of France, by a virtual acknowledgment of unqualified vassalage, and by specific stipulations of unconditional offence.

By the articles of that Treaty, Spain covenanted to furnish a stated contingent of Naval and Military Force for the prosecution of any War in which the French Republic might think proper to engage. She specifically surrendered any right or pretension to inquire into the nature, origin, or justice of that War. She stipulated, in the first instance, a contingent of Troops and Ships, which, of itself, comprised no moderate proportion of the means at her disposal; but in the event of this contingent being at any time found insufficient for the purposes of France, she further bound herself to put into a state of activity the utmost force, both by Sea and Land, that it should be in her power to collect. She covenanted that this Force should be at the disposal of France, to be employed conjointly or separately for the annoyance of the common enemy; thus submitting her entire power and resources to be used as the instruments of French ambition and aggression, and to be applied in whatever proportion France might think proper, for the avowed purpose of endeavouring to subvert the Government, and destroy the national existence of Great Britain.

The character of such a Treaty gave Great Britain an incontestable right to declare to Spain, that unless she decidedly renounced the Treaty, or gave assurances that she would not perform the obligations of it, she would not be considered as a neutral power.

This right, however, for prudential reasons, and from motives of forbearance and tenderness towards Spain, was not exercised in its full extent; and, in consequence of assurances of a pacific disposition on the part of the Spanish Government, his Majesty did not, in the first instance, insist on a distinct and formal renunciation of the Treaty. It does not appear that any express demand of succour had been made by France before the month of July One Thousand Eight Hundred and Three; and on the first notification of the War, his Majesty's Minister at Madrid was led to believe, in consequence of communications which passed between him and the Spanish Government, that his Catholic Majesty did not consider himself as necessarily bound by the mere fact of the existence of a War between Great Britain and France, without subsequent explanation and discussion, to fulfil the stipulations of the Treaty of St. Ildephonso, though the articles of that Treaty would certainly give rise to a very different interpretation. In the month of October a Convention was signed, by which Spain agreed to pay France a certain sum monthly in lieu of the Naval and Military succours which they had stipulated by the Treaty to provide; but of the amount of this sum, or of the nature of any other stipulations which that Convention might contain, no official information whatever was given.

It was immediately stated by his Majesty's Minister at Madrid to the Spanish Government, that a subsidy as large as that which they were supposed to have engaged to pay to France, far exceeded the bounds of forbearance; that it could only meet with a temporary connivance; as, if it was continued, it might prove in fact a greater injury than any other hostility. In reply to these remonstrances, it was represented as an expedient to gain time, and assurances were given which were confirmed by circumstances, which came to his Majesty's knowledge from other quarters, that the disposition of the Spanish Government would induce them to extricate themselves from this engagement, if the course of events should admit of their doing so with safety.

When his Majesty had first reason to believe that such a Convention was concluded, he directed his Minister at Madrid to declare that his forbearing to consider Spain as an enemy must depend in some degree upon the amount of the succours, and upon her maintaining a perfect neutrality in all other respects; but that it would be impossible for him to consider a permanent payment, to the amount of that which was stated to have been in agitation, in any other light than as a direct subsidy of War. His Majesty's Envoy was directed, therefore, first to protest against the Convention, as a violation of neutrality, and a justifiable cause of War; secondly, to declare, that our abstaining from hostilities must depend upon its being only a temporary measure, and that we must be at liberty to consider a perseverance in it as a cause of War; thirdly, that the entrance of any French Troops into Spain must be refused; fourthly, that any Naval preparation must be a great cause of jealousy, and any attempt to give Naval assistance to France an immediate cause of War; fifthly, that the Spanish Ports must remain open to our Commerce, and that our Ships of War must have equal treatment with those of France. His Majesty's Minister was also instructed, if any French Troops entered Spain, or if he received authentic information of any Naval armaments preparing for the assistance of France, to leave Madrid, and to give immediate notice to our Naval Commanders, that they might proceed to hostilities without the delay that might be occasioned by a reference home.

The execution of these instructions produced a variety of discussions; during which his Majesty's Minister told Mr. Cevallos, in answer to his question, whether a continuance of such pecuniary succours to France would be considered as a ground of War, and whether he was authorised to declare it? that he was so authorised, and that War would be the infallible consequence.

It was, however, still thought desirable by his Majesty to protract, if possible, the decision of this question; and it was therefore stated in the instructions to his Minister at Madrid, that as the subsidy was represented by the Spanish Government to be merely a temporary measure, his Majesty might still continue to overlook it for a time; but that his decision in this respect must depend upon knowing the precise nature of all the stipulations between Spain and France, and upon the Spanish Government being determined to cause their neutrality to be respected in all other particulars. That until these questions were answered in a satisfactory manner, and the Convention communicated to him, he could give no positive answer whether he would make the pecuniary succours a cause of War or not.

Before the receipt of these instructions, dated January 21, 1804, the report of some Naval armaments in the Ports of Spain had occasioned a fresh correspondence between his Majesty's Minister and the Spanish Government. In one of the notes presented by the former, he declares, that if the King was forced to begin a War, he would want no other declaration than what he had already made. The answers of the Spanish Government were at first of an evasive nature; his Majesty's Minister closed the Correspondence on his part by a note delivered on the Eighteenth of February, in which he declares that all further forbearance on the part of England must depend upon the cessation of all Naval armaments, and a prohibition of the sale of Prizes in their Ports: and unless these points were agreed to without modification, he had orders to leave Madrid. On the second of these points a satisfactory answer was given, and orders issued accordingly; on the first, a reference was made to former Declarations. To the question about disclosing the Treaty with France, no satisfactory answer was ever given. As however no Naval preparations appeared to be proceeding at that period in the Ports of Spain, the matter was allowed to remain there for a time.

In the month of July One Thousand Eight Hundred and Four, the Government of Spain gave assurances of faithful and settled neutrality, and disavowed any orders to arm in their Ports; yet, in the subsequent month, when these assurances were recent, and a confident reliance reposed in them, the British Charge d'Affaires received advices from the Admiral commanding his Majesty's Ships off the Port of Ferrol, that reinforcements of Soldiers and Sailors had arrived through Spain for the French Fleets at Toulon and Ferrol. On this intelligence two Notes were presented to the Spanish Ministers, but no answer was received to either of them. Towards the end of the month of September, information was received in London from the British Admiral stationed off Ferrol, that orders had actually been given, by the Court of Madrid, for arming, without loss of time, at that Port, four Ships of the Line, two Frigates, and other smaller Vessels; that (according to his intelligence) similar orders had been given at Carthagena and Cadiz, and particularly that three First Rate Ships of the Line were directed to sail from the last-mentioned Port; and, as an additional proof of hostile intentions, that orders had been given to arm the Packets as in time of War.

Here then appeared a direct and unequivocal violation of the terms on which the continuance of Peace had been acquiesced in; previous notice having been given to the Spanish Government, that a state of War would be the immediate consequence of such a measure, his Majesty on this event stood almost pledged to an instant commencement of hostilities: the King, however, preferred a persevering adherence to the system of moderation so congenial to his disposition: he resolved to leave still an opening for accommodation, if Spain should be still allowed the liberty to adopt the course prescribed by a just sense of her own interests and security. It is here worthy of remark, that the groundless and ungrateful imputations thrown out against his Majesty's conduct in the Spanish Manifesto are built upon the foundation of this forbearance alone. Had his Majesty exercised, without reserve, his just rights of War, the representations so falsely asserted, and so insidiously dwelt upon, could not have been even stated under any colourable pretext: the indulgence, therefore, which postponed the actual state of War, was not only misrepresented, but transformed into a ground of complaint, because the forbearance extended to the aggressors was not carried to a dangerous and inadmissible extreme. In consequence of the intelligence above stated, directions were sent to his Majesty's Minister at Madrid to make representations and remonstrances to the Spanish Court, to demand explanations relative to the existing Conventions between Spain and France; and, above all, to insist, that the Naval armaments in their Ports should be placed on the same footing as they were previously to the commencement of hostilities between Great Britain and France: And he was further directed, explicitly to state to the Spanish Government, that his Majesty felt a duty imposed upon him of taking, without delay, every measure of precaution; and, particularly, of giving orders to his Admiral off the Port of Ferrol to prevent any of the Spanish Ships of War sailing from that Port, or any additional Ships of War from entering it.

No substantial redress, no satisfactory explanation, was afforded in consequence of these repeated representations; whilst, under the cover of his Majesty's forbearance, the enemy had received considerable remittances of treasure, together with the facility of procuring other supplies.

Every circumstance of the general conduct of Spain was peculiarly calculated to excite the vigilant attention of the British Government—the removal of Spanish Ships out of their Docks, to make room for the accommodation of the Men of War of France—the march of French Troops and Seamen through the Spanish Territory—the equipment of Naval armaments at Ferrol—the consideration that the junction of this armament with the French Ships already in that Harbour would create a decided superiority of numbers over his Majesty's Squadron cruising off that Port—the additional Naval exertions, and the consequent increase of expense which this conduct of Spain necessarily imposed upon Great Britain. All these together required those precautions, both of representation and action, to which his Majesty had immediate recourse. While official notice was given of his Majesty's intention to adopt those necessary measures, the Spanish Government was, at the same time, assured that his Majesty still felt an earnest desire to maintain a good understanding with Spain; but that the continuance of such a state of things must be subject to the condition of abstaining, on their part, from all hostile preparations, and on making, without hesitation or reserve, that full and explicit disclosure of the nature and extent of the subsisting engagements with France, which had hitherto been so frequently and so fruitlessly demanded.

The precautions adopted by his Majesty were such only as he deemed indispensably necessary to guard against the augmentation by Spain of her means of Naval preparation during the discussion, and against the possible consequences of the safe arrival of the expected American treasure in the Spanish Ports: an event which has more than once, in former times, become the epoch of the termination of discussions, and of the commencement of hostility on the part of Spain.

The orders issued by his Majesty on this occasion to the Admirals commanding his Fleets, afford the most striking example of a scrupulous and indulgent forbearance; the most strict limitation was given, as to the extent and object of the measures proposed; and the execution of those orders was guarded with the strongest injunctions to avoid, by every means consistent with the attainment of their object, any act of violence or hostility against the Dominions or Subjects of his Catholic Majesty. The hostile preparations in the Harbour of Ferrol rendered it necessary, in the first instance, that a reinforcement should be added to the Squadron cruising off that Port; and orders were at the same time conveyed to the British Admirals, to send intimation to the Spanish Government of the instructions they had received, and of their determination, in consequence, to resist, under the present circumstances, the sailing either of the French or Spanish Fleets, if any attempt for that purpose should be made by either of them.

His Majesty's pleasure was at the same time signified, that they were not to detain, in the first instance, any Ship belonging to his Catholic Majesty, sailing from a Port of Spain; but to require the Commander of such Ship to return directly to the Port from whence she came; and only, in the event of his refusing to comply with such requisition, to detain and send her to Gibraltar or to England.

Further directions were given not to detain any Spanish homeward-bound Ships of War, unless they should have treasure on board; nor Merchant Ships of that Nation, however laden, on any account whatsoever. That, in the prosecution of those measures of precaution, many valuable lives should have been sacrificed, is a subject of much regret to his Majesty, who laments it as an event produced alone by an unhappy concurrence of circumstances, but which can in no degree affect the merits of the case. The question of the just principle and due exercise of his Majesty's rights rests upon every foundation of the laws of nature and of nations, which enjoin and justify the adoption of such measures as are requisite for defence, and the prevention of aggression.

It remains only further to observe, that if any additional proof were requisite of the wisdom and necessity of precautionary measures, that proof would be found even in the declaration relied upon in the Manifesto of Spain, in which its Government now states itself to have contemplated, from the beginning of the War, the necessity of making itself a party to it, in support of the pretensions of France, expressly declaring, that "Spain and Holland, who treated conjointly with France at Amiens, and whose interests and political relations were so closely connected with her, must have with difficulty refrained from taking part against the injuries and insults offered to their ally."

It will further appear, by a reference to the dates and results of the several representations made by his Majesty's Charge d'Affaires at the Court of Spain, that the detention of the Spanish Treasure Ships never was in question during the discussions which preceded his departure from Madrid. That ground of complaint therefore, which has since been so much relied upon, formed no part of the motive of the previous hostile character so strongly manifested by the Spanish Court in their mode of treating the points in discussion, nor (as will appear in the sequel) of the final rupture of Negotiation at Madrid.

On the Twenty-sixth of October, One Thousand Eight Hundred and Four, his

Majesty's Charge d'Affaires presented a Note to the Spanish Minister, in which the following conditions were insisted upon as preliminary to the appointment of a Minister from Great Britain, who might treat of the adjustment of other matters which remained for discussion. The conditions were three. First, that the orders given at Ferrol, Cadiz, and Carthagena, should be countermanded, as well for the equipment of Ships of War in any of those Ports, as for their removal from from one of those Ports to another. Secondly, that not only the present armaments should be discontinued, but that the establishment of Ships of War in the different Ports should be replaced on the footing on which they stood at the commencement of hostilities between England and France. Thirdly, that a full disclosure should be made of the existing engagements, and of the future intentions of Spain with respect to France. From the period above mentioned to the Second of November, several official Notes passed between his Majesty's Charge d'Affaires and the Spanish Minister, consisting, with little variation in their tenor, of urgent demands of satisfaction on the one side, and of evasive and unsatisfactory replies on the other. After repeated delays and reiterated applications, his Majesty's Charge d'Affaires received his Passports on the Seventh of November, and departed from Madrid on the Fourteenth of that month. During the whole of this Negotiation no mention was made of the detention of the Spanish Treasure Ships, nor does it any where appear that an account had been received at Madrid of that transaction. It is evident therefore, notwithstanding the attempt made by the Spanish Court to avail itself of that event, in the Manifesto which has been since published, that the state of War must equally have arisen between Great Britain and Spain, had the detention never taken place, and that, in point of fact, the rupture ultimately took place upon grounds distinct from, and totally unconnected with, that measure.

The leading circumstances which characterise the reiterated abuse of his Majesty's moderation, were each of them of a nature to have exhausted any less settled system of lenity and forbearance. Succours afforded to his enemies; explanations refused or evaded after repeated demands; conditions violated, after distinct notice that on them depended the continuance of Peace. Such has been the conduct of the Spanish Court; and it is, under these circumstances, that his Majesty finds the domineering influence of France exerted, and the Spanish Nation in a state of declared and open War.

His Majesty appeals with confidence to all Europe for the acknowledgment of his exemplary moderation in the whole course of these transactions. His Majesty feels with regret the necessity which places him in a state of hostility with Spain; and would with heartfelt satisfaction observe, on the part of that Country, the assumption of a more dignified sense of national importance, and a more independent exercise of Sovereign rights.

His Majesty would indeed be most happy to discover in the Councils of Spain a reviving sense of those ancient feelings and honourable propensities which have at all times been so congenial to the Spanish Character, and which, in better times, have marked the conduct of its Government. His Majesty will, on his part, eagerly embrace the first opportunity, thus offered, of resuming a state of Peace and Confidence with a Nation which has so many ties of common interest to connect it with Great Britain, and which he has hitherto been ever disposed to regard with sentiments of the utmost consideration and esteem.

Downing Street, January 1805.

PROCLAMATION BY THE KING.

GEORGE R.

WHEREAS alarming accounts have been received that the infectious disease (which, with a malignancy equalling if not exceeding that of the plague, has occasioned a dreadful mortality in several parts of Spain, and in our Town and Garrison of Gibraltar,) has spread and extended itself to parts of the Coast of the Mediterranean; and whereas, from the season of the year in which it has continued its ravages in those places where it has already appeared, there is no good ground of confidence or hope that the comparative coldness and the temperature of this climate can afford any obstacle to its introduction and progress in our Kingdom:

And whereas we feel it to be incumbent upon us to employ such means as, under the protection and favour of Divine Providence, may be best calculated to guard our loving Subjects against the visitation of so dreadful a calamity, we have thought fit, by and with the advice of our Privy Council, to issue this our Royal Proclamation; and we do herein, by and with the advice of our said Council, most strictly enjoin and command all our loving Subjects, and more especially those residing at any of the Sea-port Towns, or in any other places on the Coasts of this Kingdom, whether they may themselves be liable to quarantine or otherwise, as they tender the preservation of their own lives, and the safety and welfare of all the Inhabitants of this Kingdom, most scrupulously to observe all the laws of quarantine which now are or may hereafter be in force, and all orders made by us, with the advice of our Privy Council, or by our Privy Council, under the authority thereof: and particularly most carefully to avoid any communication with any Ship or Vessel, or with any person or persons coming therein, from or through the Mediterranean, or from the West Barbary, on the Atlantic Ocean, or from Cadiz, or other parts of Spain without the Streights, lying to the southward of Cape St. Vincent, or from any place to which, by our Royal Proclamation, by and with the advice of our Privy Council, or by our orders in Council, the laws of quarantine are, or may hereafter, be extended; or with any Boat or person therein, coming from or having been on board any such Ship, until such Ship, Vessel, or Boat, with the Crews and Persons on board, and the goods, wares, and merchandizes imported therein, shall have performed their quarantine, in such places and manner as are or shall hereafter be directed in that behalf, and until they respectively shall have been duly discharged therefrom: And we do further strictly exhort, enjoin, and command all Magistrates and persons in authority, and all others our loving Subjects, without loss of time, to give information to us, through our principal Secretary of State for the Home Department, or to our Privy Council, of any persons that they may know or believe to have offended against any of the said laws or orders; and we do hereby warn all persons whom it may concern, that we have given the strictest orders for enforcing, with the utmost rigour, the most punctual observance of the laws of quarantine, and all the orders, rules, and regulations relating thereto, it being our firm determination, upon serious consideration of the great extent of misery and calamity which a single instance of improvidently neglecting any of these regulations may bring upon our loving Subjects, to cause the several Penalties which the law has provided, or may provide, to be inflicted upon all those who may be guilty of any offence against the same:

And whereas it is also necessary to take the utmost precaution to prevent the spreading of infection, in case the said malignant disease, or any other of a contagious nature (which God, in his mercy, avert!) should unhappily manifest itself in any part of our United Kingdom, notwithstanding the precautions taken to guard against the introduction thereof, we have thought fit, by and with the advice of our said Council, to take measures for the establishment of a Board of Health, to consist of Men, able, learned, eminent, and experienced in the study and practice of physic, together with persons most capable, from their knowledge of the Ports of our Kingdoms, to afford assistance in the forming of regulations respectively applicable to the local circumstances of the said Ports; such Board to be authorized and directed to prepare and digest the best rules and regulations for the speedy and effectual adoption of the most approved methods of guarding against the introduction and spreading of infection, and for purifying any Ship or House, or any place in which any contagious disorder may have manifested itself, and to communicate the same to all Magistrates, Medical Persons, and others of our loving Subjects, who may be desirous, and may apply to be made acquainted therewith; and we most strictly enjoin and command all Magistrates and persons in authority, all Medical Persons, and others our loving Subjects, especially those within the Maritime Counties, to give immediate notice to us, through our principal Secretary of State for the Home Department, or our Privy Council, in case any person or persons should be attacked with any fever attended with new and uncommon symptoms, such as to afford ground for apprehension that such fever is of the same nature as the disorder prevailing in several parts of Spain, and in Gibraltar, in order that the most immediate and effectual measures may be taken, as well for affording due and necessary assistance and relief to those afflicted with the same, as for preventing the contagion from spreading amongst our loving Subjects.

Given at our Court at the Queen's Palace, the sixth day of February, one thousand eight hundred and five, and in the forty-fifth year of our Reign.

GOD save the KING!

Gazette Letters,
Copied verbatim from the LONDON GAZETTE.

ADMIRALTY-OFFICE, JAN. 29, 1805.

Copy of a Letter from Rear-Admiral Russel to William Marsden Esq.; dated on board his Majesty's Ship Monmouth, in Yarmouth Roads, the 28th January, 1805.

SIR,

PLEASE to inform my Lords Commissioners of the Admiralty, that the Swan Cutter arrived here yesterday with the Dutch Privateer mentioned in my letter of yesterday. I enclose Lieutenant Wallace's letter to me on the subject.

I am, &c. T. M. RUSSEL.

His Majesty's Hired Cutter Swan, at Sea,
SIR, *January 26, 1805.*

I beg leave to inform you, I this day gave chase to a Cutter rigged Vessel, and after a few hours' chase, came up with and took the Flip Privateer, belonging to Holland, having on board eighteen Men. She sailed from Holland on the 19th instant, had taken only one Brig, which Brig I retook yesterday and sent into Yarmouth Roads. I beg leave to remain, Sir, &c.

W. R. WALLACE.

*Thomas Macnamara Russel, Esq. Rear-Admiral
of the Red, &c. &c. &c.*

ADMIRALTY-OFFICE, FEB. 1, 1805.

Copy of a Letter from the Right Honourable Lord Keith, K.B. Admiral of the Blue, &c. to William Marsden, Esq.; dated on board his Majesty's Ship the Ardent, off Ramsgate, the 31st of January, 1805.

SIR,

I enclose, for their Lordships' information, an extract of a letter from Captain Owen, of his Majesty's Ship Immortalité, to Vice-Admiral Holloway, acquainting him that a division of the enemy's Flotilla arrived at Boulogne on the 29th instant, from the westward; and that one of them (a Lugger) had been cut off by the Harpy. I have the honour to be, &c.

KEITH.

Extract of a Letter from Captain Owen, of the Immortalité, off Boulogne, to Vice-Admiral Holloway, dated 29th of January, 1805.

A division of seventeen Brigs, three Schooners, four Sloops, a Dogger, and six Luggers, arrived this morning from the westward; and although I got close enough to exchange shot with the body of them, the Wind and lee-tide enabled them to haul close to the Beach, and pass in that manner. One Lugger had carried away her fore-mast, and was cut off by the Harpy, whose fire she returned before she struck. I have sent her to the Downs with the Bruiser.

ADMIRALTY-OFFICE, FEB. 9, 1805.

Copy of a Letter from Commodore Sir Samuel Hood, K.B. Commander in Chief of his Majesty's Ships and Vessels at the Leeward Islands, to William Marsden, Esq.; dated on board the Serapis, at Barbadoes, 16th December, 1804.

SIR,

I transmit, for the information of the Lords Commissioners of the Admiralty, the copy of a letter from Captain Nourse, of his Majesty's Ship Barbadoes, giving an account of the capture of l'Heureux French Privateer, of ten guns and eighty Men. I am, &c.

SAMUEL HOOD.

SIR,   *His Majesty's Ship Barbadoes, at Sea, November, 1804.*

I have the honour to inform you, his Majesty's Ship under my command this day captured l'Heureux, a French Privateer Sloop, of ten six-pounders (thrown overboard during the chase) and eighty Men, out nine days from Guadaloupe, and had made no capture. I have the honour to be, &c.

JOSEPH NOURSE.

To Commodore Hood, Commander in Chief,
&c. &c. &c.

Copy of another Letter from Commodore Sir Samuel Hood, K.B. to W. Marsden, Esq.; dated on board the Serapis, at Barbadoes, 16th December, 1804.

SIR,

I have the satisfaction to send to their Lordships the copy of a letter from the Honourable Captain Cadogan, Commander of his Majesty's Sloop Cyane, giving an account of the capture of the Buonaparté Brig Privateer of 18 guns and 150 Men, after a few minutes' running fight, which Captain Cadogan appears to have executed with judgment. I have the honour to be, &c.

SAMUEL HOOD.

SIR,   *His Majesty's Sloop Cyane, off Antigua, 12th Nov. 1804.*

I have the honour to inform you, that, on the 11th instant, at three A.M. off the Island of Mariegalante, after a short chase and running fight of thirty minutes, I had the good fortune to come up with and capture le Buonaparté, a very fine

Privateer Brig, pierced for 22 guns, mounting 18 long French 8-pounders, and 150 Men. I am happy to add that we have received no material damage in our masts or hull, and have only a few Men hurt, occasioned by the explosion of a cartridge on the main-deck. We found the Buonaparté in a very shattered condition, having lost her fore-mast, bowsprit, and top-masts, in an action with three English Letters of Marque, three days previous to her capture. I should not do justice to my feelings were I to omit expressing my thorough satisfaction at the steady and determined conduct of all the Officers and Crew of the Cyane; and although the state of the Vessel was such as not to call forth any extraordinary exertions on their part, I feel confident that whenever chance may give them an opportunity, they will do ample justice to the character which in my opinion they so justly deserve. I have the honour to be, &c.

GEORGE CADOGAN,

Samuel Hood, Esq. Commodore, and Commander in Chief, &c. &c. &c.

Copy of a Letter from Captain Lord Mark Robert Kerr, of his Majesty's Ship Fisgard, to William Marsden, Esq.; dated at Sea, the 24th of December, 1804.

SIR,

I enclose, for the information of my Lords Commissioners of the Admiralty, the copy of a letter which I have forwarded to Lord Viscount Nelson.

I have the honour to be, &c.

M. R. KERR.

MY LORD,   *His Majesty's Ship Fisgard, at Sea, Dec. 22, 1804.*

I beg to inform you, that, according to your orders, I proceeded and joined Sir Richard Strachan, Bart. off Cape St. Mary's, and was by him sent into Lisbon to complete. On my return from that Port to join your Lordship, in lat. 37° N., long. 13° 40' W., I captured a French Ship Letter of Marque, le Tigre, (formerly the Angola of Liverpool,) from Cayenne to Cadiz; pierced for 16 guns, and having fourteen mounted; viz. twelve 18-pound carronades, and two brass guns, 4-pounders, (and four in her hold,) ballasted in mahogany and dry wood, having on board 40 Men. She was out 56 days, and had captured an English Brig from London to St. Michael's; whose Master and Crew we found on board.

I have the honour to be, &c.

M. R. KERR.

ADMIRALTY-OFFICE, FEB. 16, 1805.

Extract of a Letter from Vice-Admiral Rainier, Commander in Chief of his Majesty's Ships and Vessels in the East Indies, to William Marsden, Esq.; dated in Mangalore Road, the 10th of March, 1804.

Three Privateers have been captured by his Majesty's Ships, as follow:

L'Espiegle, of two guns, by Dedaigneuse.

Le Passe par Tout, (Chasse Marée), of two guns and six swivels, by St. Fiorenzo.

Les Frères Unis, of eight guns, by the Caroline.

ADMIRALTY-OFFICE, FEB. 19, 1805.

Copy of a Letter from the Honourable William Cornwallis, K.B. Admiral of the White, &c. to William Marsden, Esq. dated on board the Ville de Paris, off Ushant, the 13th of February, 1805.

SIR,

I have the honour to enclose, for the information of the Lords Commissioners of the Admiralty, a letter to me from Captain Poyntz, of the Melampus, and one from Lieutenant Nicholson, commanding the Frisk Cutter, giving accounts of the capture of the enemy's Gun-vessels therein mentioned.

I have the honour to be, &c.

W. CORNWALLIS.

SIR, *Melampus, Off Ushant, Feb.* 13, 1805.

I have the honour to inform you, that I, this morning, fell in with and captured two Gun-brigs, carrying two long 24-pounders, and one 18-pounder each, having on board 50 Men, the greater part Soldiers; also four Luggers, mounting one long 18-pounder each, manned with 25 Men, mostly Soldiers.

These Vessels are part of 27 of the same description, from Bourdeaux to Brest; two more were captured (Lugger rigged) early the same morning by the Rhoda and Frisk armed Cutters. I have the honour to be, &c.

To the Honourable William Cornwallis, S. POYNTS.
&c. &c. &c.

His Majesty's Hired Cutter Frisk, at Sea,
SIR, 13th *February,* 1805.

I have the honour to acquaint you, that, at daylight yesterday, (the Rhoda Cutter in company,) I discovered ten Sail of the enemy's Gun-vessels and Luggers had come through the Passage du Raz, and the Wind blowing fresh to the eastward, they were not able to get to windward: I immediately gave chase to the weathermost, a Lugger, and at half-past seven (Point du Raz S.S.W. distant five miles) I captured her, and sent her to Plymouth. She proves to be No. 288, Gun-vessel, mounting one long 24-pounder, with 25 Men, 20 of whom are Troops of the 44th Regiment, commanded by Mons. P. Roux, Enseigne de Vaisseau. At half-past eleven the Melampus hove in sight to leeward.

I have the honour to be, &c.

The Honourable William Cornwallis. JAMES NICHOLSON.

Imperial Parliament.

HOUSE OF LORDS, TUESDAY, JAN. 15.

NAVAL DEBATES.

(Invasion—Spanish Frigates—Message respecting Peace.)

LORD ELLIOT, who rose to move the Address, observed, that notwithstanding all the boasted preparations of France, the Invasion with which we had so long been threatened had not yet been undertaken. It must certainly be matter of satisfaction to their Lordships and the nation at large, that the wise measures adopted by his Majesty's Government had deterred the enemy from any attempt of the kind; for, though no man could entertain any apprehension for the result, the landing of any considerable hostile force could not fail to be attended with disagreeable consequences, in a country abounding with wealth, and long accustomed to internal tranquillity. But if this consideration afforded satisfaction, it was also a just ground of pride, when it was recollected that we were not indebted for this delay to any moderation on the part of the enemy, or to any deficiency of preparation on his part. It was the effect of the wisdom of his Majesty's Councils—of the vigour and unanimity of Parliament in support of the War—of the strength and discipline of our military and naval force—of the confidence and energy of the people. He had little to say in adverting to the second point of his Majesty's Speech. When the documents respecting the conduct of the Court of Spain were laid before Parliament, their Lordships would have an opportunity of coming regularly to the discussion of that subject. At present they were not called upon to pronounce any opinion. He must however make this observation, that the forbearance which his Majesty's Ministers had already displayed with respect to Spain, afforded the strongest evidence that they had not acted hostilely till hostility became unavoidable. Spain had ever since the commencement of the War been affording to France the means of carrying on the contest against us. It was not, therefore, merely the question of justice, which their Lordships would have before them, in considering the rupture with Spain, but that of its expediency, as well as the manner in which it has taken place. The general conduct of the French Government afforded little hope of any sincere desire on its part for Peace. The language of that Government was now, however, very different from that which it used at the commencement of the War, when it was boasted that England could not contend single-handed with France.—That boast was now given up, and an anxious desire for Peace substituted in its stead. He could not pretend to explain the views with which these overtures were made. The enemy might have various motives. He might hope to embarrass the Government, to create divisions in Parliament, or discontent in the country, by exciting too eager a desire for Peace.

Lord *Gwydir* seconded the Address. Though the Noble Lord who had just sat down had left him little to say, he could not help noticing the imposing situation in which this country stood at the present moment. Safe at home, and respectable abroad, his Majesty might now, indeed, listen to propositions from the enemy. After two years, he found all his threats of invasion impracticable, and saw this country placed in a very different situation from what it was at the commencement of the War. He has not dared to undertake the great expedition with which he vainly hoped to subject a free and loyal people; but finds his Fleets and his Flotillas confined to his Shores, and compelled to seek shelter under his Batteries. With regard to the rupture with Spain, he was convinced that when the documents on that subject were laid before the House, their Lordships would find that the measure was indispensable. Explanations had been demanded of the Court of Spain, and refused, and new engagements had been made between that Court and the French Government, under an offensive treaty entered into with the enemy. It could not, therefore, be said, that Ministers had been precipitate in their conduct towards Spain, unless it was to be contended that the convenience of the enemy only ought to be consulted, and War entered into or not, just as it suited him. Were his Majesty's Ministers, by their forbearance, to permit the enemy to receive from another Power supplies, which were to be employed with the avowed view of effecting the ruin of this country? As the nature of the communication from the enemy was not known, the Address very properly did not pledge their Lordships to any thing beyond what the interests of humanity and the welfare of the country required. They well knew, that no Peace could be secure which was not founded on the permanent and immutable interests, not only of the British Empire, but of all the States of Europe. It was not a Peace of mere words, a hollow and fallacious treaty like the last [*a cry of Hear! Hear! from the Opposition*] that could give safety or confidence to the country. It was necessary not to forget the lessons of experience so recently received. The concessions imprudently made, in concluding the last Peace, had induced the enemy to regard Great Britain as a vanquished nation.—At last it was found that the country had no alternative but Peace with degradation, or Hostilities with honour. The people indignantly rejected the profered disgrace, and unanimously approved the War.—If the propositions made by the enemy be sincere and honourable, great indeed and sudden must have been the change which has taken place in his disposition. But whatever ground there may be to hope for Peace, the country must be prepared for War. If farther sacrifices were necessary, they would be cheerfully made; for no sacrifices could be too great, when compared with the importance of the objects to be attained. Impressed with these views, he was proud to second the Address which his Noble Friend had proposed.

Lord *Hawkesbury* thus concluded his speech :—One observation more, however, he would take the liberty of making. It related to the order for detaining the Spanish Frigates. It was important to be understood, that that order was not the cause of the War. That transaction, which he would contend was justifiable on every principle of the Law of Nations and of self-defence, had nothing to do with the question of War or Peace with Spain. The fact was, that previous discussions had taken place; that, previous to that event, his Majesty's Minister had demanded distinct explanations on certain points from the Cabinet of Madrid. It was also a fact, that his passports were demanded and received, and his mission completely at an end before the news of the detention of the Frigates reached the Court of Spain. He did not mean to state this as the justification of the detention of the Spanish Frigates, but he thought it necessary to take this opportunity of declaring that the War did not spring from that cause. The situation of the country was truly a proud one. The War was commenced with a declaration, that the whole force of France was to be employed in a descent on the British Shores. Looking at the preparations the enemy has made, it must be evident that this was no inconsiderable unmeaning boast; yet two years have passed away, and no attempt has been made to carry it into execution. The spirit and energy of this country has rendered all the plans of the enemy abortive. The military and naval force of the country, now actually embodied, amounts to between 6 and 700,000 Men; a force which, either taken positively, or with respect to the population, is greater than any other country of a similar extent ever maintained. It was only by keeping up this force that the country could be rendered invulnerable. It was by the spirit and energy of the country that permanent security was to be obtained, and he was happy to declare that spirit and energy never were so high as at the present moment.

Lord *Grenville* had but a word or two to say upon two points of the Speech, and with respect to the overtures from France. It was impossible to say more than the Address did, without the nature of the communication, and the proposed terms were known; but it was with great satisfaction he heard that it was resolved to pay due attention to our future security, which could only be gained by also consulting the security of the rest of Europe. He could not, however, agree with the Noble Lord, that the mere naked fact of some of the treasures of Spain being destined for France, a sufficient proof of the justice of our cause. He hoped and trusted that the documents to be produced, would prove us in the right of our conduct. Never let us suffer the just rights of our own country to be invaded, but at the same time let not our selfish feelings make us forget the rights of others. With respect to other topics that have fallen from Noble Lords this day, I shall not detain you with any observations now. The state of our force, the magnitude of our preparations, and the security which we enjoy, will all be the subject of future discussion. In the mean time I cannot hear it made the source of self-congratulation, and of panegyric, that we have been near two years at War, and yet have not been invaded. I confess that this is no great cause of triumph—and I hope that we shall reap other laurels from the strength, spirit, and zeal of our Armies and Navies, than the mere boast that the enemy has not landed on our Shores. My Lords, I concur in the Motion for the Address, and I again express my sincere satisfaction at the sentiment which has been so unequivocally declared today, that it is only in communion with the great powers of Europe that we can listen to any terms of pacification with the Government of France.

HOUSE OF COMMONS.

Mr. *Fox* thus concluded an admirable speech:—One word he should say on the subject of that transaction, respecting which his Majesty had given directions to lay certain Papers before the House. As it was impossible to anticipate their contents, it would be but to prejudge the question to say any thing now on that subject. Yet he could not but admit, that on the first view, the capture of the Spanish Frigates, as Frigates, appeared a measure unseemly to the honour of the nation. If that could be done away by a statement of facts, he should rejoice in the circumstance. But he was sure there never had been a time when it was more necessary that the honour and integrity of the nation should be maintained pure and inviolate. In the Speech, the outrages committed by the French Government had been adverted to, and he was ready to admit that the outrages were undoubted, and such as could not fail to call forth the unqualified disapprobation of every one who set any value upon the laws of nations, and the established rights of civilized society. But if, after having engaged in the War, we were disposed to change the ground of the War; if we meant to stand for right and moderation, we should take care to be clear of any imputation of violence; if we were to engage in a new War on a new ground, we should prove to the world, whilst we were advocating justice and moderation, we were ourselves just and moderate. We should act so that surrounding nations might not perceive that acts of violence and outrage were committed on both sides; that they should not conclude that two great nations vie with each other only in outrage, aggressions, and violence, and that the smaller independent States were to be the sacrifice. He hoped and trusted that this subject would be fully and satisfactorily explained. He was confident, that when the question should be under discussion, they would come to its consideration without any partiality to our own Government, or the exclusive interests of our country, without any prejudice against the cause of Spain; and that they would look upon themselves as bound to prove to the world, that in entering into this War, we had acted under the influence of necessity, and in conformity with the strict and immutable principle of the laws of nations. He had thought it necessary to say thus much previous to the question being put, in explanation of his sentiments with respect to the matter of the Speech.

The *Chancellor of the Exchequer* declared, he should only advert to those points which had been touched upon by that Hon. Gentleman, and principally the first he had mentioned, in which he had expressed a doubt as to the propriety of calling on the House to approve the wisdom of his Majesty's determination not to make any further communication with respect to the pacific propositions, until he should communicate with certain Powers, and especially with the Emperor of Russia, of whom his Majesty had spoken in terms which he trusted would afford satisfaction to every Member of that House. He agreed that it was impossible for the House, by its vote of this night, to pledge itself implicitly to any measure founded on the communication in his Majesty's Speech. But if his Majesty expressed his confidence that the House would concur in every measure necessary for the security of the Empire, if he particularly directed their attention to certain points arising out of the wise, noble, and magnanimous conduct of the Emperor of Russia, which were important to the security and independence of Europe, he trusted that all those who were of opinion that the commanding situation of this country would have a considerable influence on the state of Europe, would agree to the magnitude and independence of such considerations, and the necessity of communicating with that august Monarch. There would be another occasion for inquiring into the grounds of his Majesty's determination, when the documents would be before the House, and it would be regular for them to consider the question. Then it would be open for every gentleman to inquire into the grounds on which this determination rests, and to shape his conduct accordingly. It would be obvious to every Hon. Member, that there were certain periods in the connexions between states, when it would be imprudent and impolitic to publish or explain altogether the nature of them; and he trusted that Gentlemen would not look upon him as called on to give a further explanation on this subject, than was contained in the Speech.

Mr. *Windham* will obtain the gratitude of Naval Men, by the notice which he took of the situation of Captain Wright:

" As to the aggressions on the part of France, and the acts of violence of its Government, those circumstances referring to the communication which had recently been made, and his Majesty's Speech alluded to, laid the foundation of a more extended view of the subject. It was clear that France had been guilty of a violation of the Law of Nations, which we ought by no means to lose sight of, particularly in the instance of Captain Wright, a Gentleman in the British Navy, taken fighting on board his own Ship. Without the smallest pretext, he had been withdrawn from the operations of the laws of War, and for a long time confined a close prisoner at Ghent, where probably he still remained. He did not wish for any answer or observation from the Chancellor of the Exchequer upon this subject at present. He only mentioned it that Ministers might know it would hereafter be a matter of discussion. He only wished to recall it to their minds, to show that it was a subject which was in the minds and hearts of the people of this country; and to recommend it to them, if the French Government were doing any thing to tamper with the person to whom he had alluded, to make every necessary inquiry. He hoped that the case of that Gentleman was one of the objects of this very communication on the part of the French Government. If not, he trusted it would be brought in aid of their endeavours to bring about a reconciliation, if they were sincere. If the means of obtaining satisfaction on this point failed, he expected Ministers would have recourse to reprisals against persons who should be in similar situations in this country. It was not necessary to dwell further upon the time of the House."

JANUARY 16.

The Ninth Report of the Commissioners of Naval Inquiry was presented by Mr. Williams, Secretary to the Board of Naval Inquiry.—Ordered to lie on the table, and be printed for the use of the Members.

Mr. *Rowe*, from the Commissioners of Customs, appeared at the Bar, and presented, pursuant to Act of Parliament, certain Accounts with respect to prohibited East India Goods imported, exported, and warehoused; and also to Naval Stores imported from Russia; together with a List of the Officers of the Customs. Ordered to lie on the table.

JANUARY 22.

On the motion of Mr. Huskisson, the following Estimates were ordered to be laid before the House; and that an Address should be presented to his Majesty, &c. pursuant to said Order.

An estimate of the ordinary Expenses of the Navy, for the year 1805, including an estimate of the Half Pay of Officers of the Navy and Marines, who had been employed during the last War.

An Estimate of the probable Expense of Building and Re-building of Ships in his Majesty's Dock-yards, above the wear and tear, &c.

An account of the Navy Debt on the 31st December, 1804.

An Estimate of the Expense of the Transport Service for the year 1805, and also of the money that may be wanted for hiring Transports for the same period.

JANUARY 23.

The House went into a Committee of Supply, and Sir Evan Nepean moved the following Resolutions, viz.

That the number of 120,000 Seamen be employed for the service of the year 1805.—That a sum not exceeding 2,886,000l. be granted for the payment of these Seamen.—That a sum not exceeding 2,964,000l. be granted for victualling them.— That 4,680,000l. be granted for wear and tear of Vessels; and that 390,000l. be granted to his Majesty, for Ordnance and Sea Stores.

Mr. *Johnstone* wished to know what number of Seamen and Marines were now in the Service. About eight months ago he understood the number to be about 100,000.

Sir *Evan Nepean* said, he could not exactly state the precise amount, but, according to the best of his information, he supposed the number of Seamen and Marines to be about 107,000 or 108,000. The several Resolutions were agreed to; the House resumed, and the Report was ordered to be received to-morrow.

JANUARY 25.

A Person from the Commissioners of Excise and Customs in Scotland, presented an account of the number of Vessels employed in the Coasting Trade of Scotland.

An account of the number of Vessels from Scotland, employed in the Fisheries in Davis's Straits.

Also, from the Commissioners of the Northern Light House, an abstract of their Accounts, and an account of the duties for its support.

JANUARY 31.

SIR HOME POPHAM.

Mr. *Kinnaird* gave notice, that he should, on Tuesday next, move that there be laid before the House certain documents from the Report made by the Navy Board to the Lords of the Admiralty, respecting certain repairs due to the Squadron of Ships under the command of Sir Home Popham in the Red Sea, consisting of the Romney, the Nassau, and le Sensible; and if, when those Papers should be laid before the House, they should be found to contain such matters as he was taught to expect, he thought it fair to give notice that he should follow up the inquiry to its utmost extent.

NAVAL INQUIRY.

Mr. *Giles*, adverting to the Commission of Naval Inquiry, stated, that, according to the Act under which that Commission was constituted, it was to continue for two years, from the 22d of December, 1802, and to the end of the then next Session of Parliament. As this Session did not commence as early as usual, and as the time specified expired on the 22d of last December, he apprehended that, according to the letter of the Act alluded to, the existence of the Commission for Naval Inquiry would terminate a year sooner than was originally intended. He therefore wished to know whether it was the intention of any of his Majesty's Ministers to bring forward a Bill for the continuance of this Act to the period originally designed?

No answer being returned, Mr. Giles announced his intention of moving on Monday fortnight for leave to bring in a Bill for the purpose of continuing the Act referred to.

Sir *Evan Nepean* presented an account of the Navy Debt for 1804.

QUARANTINE.

Mr. *Rose* presented the Bill for the amendment of the *Quarantine Act*. The Bill having been read a first time,

Mr. *Rose* thought it his duty to call the attention of the House to the provisions contained in it. The Bill passed in 40th Geo. III had placed the performance of Quarantine under various regulations, which were to be performed according to orders to be issued by his Majesty in Council, in virtue of powers vested by that Act. At present it was intended to increase these powers, so that the necessary precautions may be applied, not only in case of plague but of every other infectious disease. The Bill now before the House went also to give similar powers with respect to Vessels on board of which any infection may have broken out at Sea, though that Vessel may not have sailed from an infected place. This Bill also was designed to give powers to force back, on board their Ships, persons escaping from Quarantine; or to put them to death if they should resist such force: also a clause to indemnify his Majesty's Privy Council, for their conduct with respect to Vessels which arrived from Gibraltar, and part of the Crew of which had landed under circumstances certainly very much to be compassionated. The Vessel had come from Gibraltar to Falmouth, whence she was ordered round to Stokes Bay, the place appointed for the performance of Quarantine; but in coming round she was wrecked, and part of the Crew escaped to a Village near Chichester, where they were discovered at a Public-House, and sent back to the proper place for performing the remainder of their Quarantine. The Bill was ordered to be read a second time.

Mr. *Kinnaird* gave notice, that in addition to the Papers he had alluded to, (Jan. 31,) it was his intention to move to-morrow for an account of the repairs of his Majesty's Ship Romney, at Sheerness, in the year 1800; also an account of the repairs of the Ships in the Red Sea, under the command of Sir Home Popham; and copies of the Letters of Marquis Wellesley on that subject.

PRINCE OF WALES ISLAND.

Mr. *Johnstone*, in rising to move the House on this subject, thought it sufficiently proved, that he did not mean to trouble the House causelessly, when he stated, that on a ballot at the India House, relative to the proposed establishment at that Island, there were 325 out of 736 against the question; which was thus carried by a majority of only 86. The papers he meant to move for were merely such as were necessary to put the House in possession of the subject. He then moved for a copy of Lord Castlereagh's Letter, dated 9th Sept. 1804, to the Chairman of the Court of Directors, relative to the Prince of Wales Island, with the enclosures contained in that Letter; also Copies of the estimates of building 74 gun Ships, and 36 gun Frigates, at Bombay; Copies of the Letters of Sir A. Snape Hammond to the Chairman of the Court of Directors, relative to Prince of Wales Island; also an account of the proceedings of the Board of Controul, and the Court of Directors, relative to an establishment on that Island, so far as the same may be disclosed without detriment to the public service.—Ordered.

NAVAL INQUIRY.

Mr. *Creevy* said, that understanding a Commission had been issued, granting great and extraordinary powers to those to whom it was addressed, for acting on the reports of the existing Commission of Naval Inquiry, he should move —"That an humble address be presented to his Majesty, praying that his Majesty would be graciously pleased to order the proper Officer to lay before the House a Copy of the Commission lately issued by the Crown to Sir Charles Middleton, and others, authorising them to act according as they should deem right, with respect to certain subjects contained in the reports of the Commissioners of Naval Inquiry."

The *Chancellor of the Exchequer* said, this Commission did not answer either to the description given of it in the motion, or to that which the Hon. Gentleman gave in the observation with which he prefaced the motion. The Hon. Gentleman had described the Commission as giving large discretionary powers; it gave no such powers, it limited precisely the powers it gave, and the objects of these powers. The Commissioners were only empowered to digest and report to the Admiralty the best means of carrying into execution such reforms as should appear to them to be proper, in consequence of the Reports of the Commissioners of Naval Inquiry. This was the whole of the discretion granted to them. He had no objection to the production of the Commission; he only said thus much, to prevent its being understood that such an unlimited discretion was given as the Hon. Gentleman supposed. A copy of the Commission was ordered.

We shall continue to pay every attention to such parts of the Parliamentary Debates as are connected with the Naval History of the present period: but perhaps from the press of other articles this will be repeated at intervals: only being careful that it may tend to form a complete historic narrative when the Volume is completed.

FOREIGN REPORTS.

EAST INDIES.

Admiral P. RAINIER.
Sir EDWARD PELLEW.

BY private letters from Bencoolen, we find, that the Expedition which had been fitted out at that Settlement, had sailed for Mouchie, and dropped anchor before that Fort on the 14th April last.

Our demand against the Rajah of the place not having been acceded to, the Ships were moored within pistol shot of the walls of the Fort, and, after battering for some time, the place was stormed with the loss of about 50 killed and wounded on our part.

The Ships suffered a little in their masts and rigging; 83 pieces of cannon were found in the Fort.

The terms granted to the enemy were the same offered to them previous to the storm, viz.—to make good the value of the Ship Crescent, plundered at Muchie some time since, and to reimburse us the expense of the Expedition fitted out against them: these terms were finally agreed to, and six Chiefs delivered up as hostages for their due performance.

It may not be uninteresting to the Public, to know by what means the Prince of Wales Island came into the possession of the East India Company. The late Captain Light formed an alliance with a daughter of the King of Quedda—this Island was given to him as her portion. After some time, the King of Quedda conceived the growing importance of this Island, with the Trade, worth contention. He, therefore, made hostile demonstrations, which Captain Light most ably diverted, by pecuniary arrangement, which secured it to the Company. We have now, the more effectually to establish our security, obtained a cession of a part of the opposite Coast.

A Ship of 74 guns, of teak wood, is ordered to be built at Bombay, for his Majesty's Navy.

WEST INDIES.

Admiral Sir J. T. DUCKWORTH, K. B. *Jamaica.*
Rear-Admiral J. R. DACRES.

A NAVAL Hospital is to be established at Barbadoes, for the purpose of receiving the Seamen on that Station.

Two of our Guineamen, the Ann and Diana, of Liverpool, have been captured by the French Privateer la Dame Ambert, and carried into Guadaloupe. She fell in with them 100 leagues to windward of Barbadoes, and engaged them both at the same time; having boarded one, the other attempted to escape; but the Privateer immediately pursued and came up with her. The Ann and Diana had been both under Convoy, and were armed Ships, the one carrying 22, and the other 18 guns; but they were much encumbered with slaves, having nearly 600 on board. The Privateer mounted sixteen 12-pound carronades, and was full of Men.

Barbadoes, Nov. 16.—It is with great satisfaction that I inform you of the capture of the Buonaparté Privateer, which has done so much mischief to our Trade in the West Indies for a considerable time past. You may recollect, that in my last I gave you a circumstantial account of a severe engagement which had taken place near Barbadoes, between this Privateer, and the Ceres, Penelope, and Thetis, Merchantmen, and in which the Privateer was so ill treated, that she lay like a log in the water. Information of her situation being given at Barbadoes by the Merchantmen, a stout Privateer was sent in quest of her, which, however, had not the good fortune to fall in with her. In the course of a day or two afterwards, the Cyane Sloop of War met with her in a very shattered condition, as she was making the best of her way to Guadaloupe to refit, and without difficulty made a prize of her, and carried her into Antigua on the 11th of November.

Nov. 26.—The blockade of the Island of Curacoa was raised on the 16th of October, after an Officer from an English Frigate had been on Shore to exchange Prisoners.

FROM THE JAMAICA GAZETTE.

Oct. 20. The French National Lugger Hazard, from Guadaloupe, bound to Curacoa, a prize to the Echo Sloop of War, arrived here on Tuesday evening.

Nov. 3.—On Tuesday se'nnight, a Seaman was apprehended at the Old Harbour, by the Officers belonging to l'Hercule Tender, charged with being one of the Crew of the Hermoine Frigate at the time of the mutiny. Several deserters from his Majesty's Ships were apprehended at the same time.

The Blanche Frigate, Captain Mudge, arrived the same day from a cruise off St. Domingo, with a Spanish Schooner, which she detained; and a French Schooner, from France, bound to St. Domingo, with dispatches (which have been saved,) for General Ferrand.

The Morne Fortunée Brig which arrived at Barbadoes on the 22d October, and at Jamaica the 30th, carried out to our Naval and Military Commanders, intimation of the probability of a rupture with Spain. Orders were in consequence given for the detention of all Spanish Vessels, and several were accordingly stopped by the Blanche, Echo, and Suffisante.

The Penguin Frigate is arrived with the Fleet from Portsmouth.

The following Decree has been issued by his Imperial Majesty of Hayti:—

" Jaques, Emperor of Hayti, directs the following Ordinance to be carried into effect throughout his Dominions:—All Vessels, to whatever Nation belonging, that shall introduce spirituous liquors into this Island, shall be liable to pay a duty of two dollars per gallon on the liquor thus imported.

" By the Emperor,

" *Boisrond Tonnere.*"   " DESSALINES."

The following Letters respecting the Action between the Merchant Ship Thetis, and the Buonaparté Privateer, of 20 guns, are particularly interesting.

" *On board the Ceres, Bridge-Town, Barbadoes, Nov. 10, 1804.*

" I am happy to inform you of my safe arrival here, in company with the Penelope and Thetis. The day we came in we fell in with the Buonaparté* French Privateer, of 20 guns, which bore down upon us, and commenced a very heavy fire, which we returned as warm as possible. She attempted to board the Thetis, and, in the act, lost her bowsprit, and soon after her foremast went over the side —a fortunate circumstance, as I understand she was the terror of the West Indies. She sent a challenge here by an American, the day before we arrived, to any of our Sloops of War to fight her. We understand she had beaten off one of them.—The action was very smart for about two hours: we began firing at nine o'clock in the morning, and did not leave off till half after twelve. My Ship was on fire three times by neglect of the people with their cartridges. She once got on fire in the Cabin; but by the exertions of the Crew, it was soon extinguished. They behaved with the greatest spirit; and, I believe, would have fought to the last, though one half of them were Foreigners. I had several shot in the hull, and my rigging and sails were very much cut. The small shot and grape came on board us like hail, though they did not hit one Man. I had two Men blown up by the cartridges taking fire, who are very much burnt."

" *On board the Penelope, Bridge-Town, Barbadoes, Nov. 10, 1804.*

" I arrived here safe, after a passage of thirty-three days, in company with the Ceres and Thetis, and shall be detained here some time to refit; having on the 8th inst., in lat. 13º 26′ N., long. 57º 30′ W., had an engagement with the Buonaparté Privateer, of 22 guns, and 250 men, for three hours; in which engagement we had ten of our guns dismounted, which I must repair here, and likewise replenish our powder. I suppose I shall be ready for Sea by the 13th. I am sorry to say Mr. Lindo was killed in the engagement; and his poor wife is very disconsolate. I wish her to return home from hence, but she refuses. I send this by the Burton, of Liverpool, who is now under weigh, or otherwise would be more particular. The Action commenced at nine A. M., and we engaged until half past meridian, when we left off chase. The Privateer lost her bowsprit and foremast in attempting to board the Thetis, who had two Men killed and five wounded."

The following is a copy of the Captain's letter to his owners:—

" Messrs. SUART, HEESMAN, and Co.

" GENTLEMEN, " *Barbadoes, Nov. 10. 1804.*

" I arrived here, in company with the Ceres and Penelope, last evening. On the 8th instant, at seven A.M. seeing a strange Sail and a suspicious one (being Commodore) I made a signal for an enemy, and to haul our Wind on the larboard tack to meet her. At nine we met; she kept English colours flying till after firing two broadsides. Seeing him attempt to lay us alongside to leeward, thought it better to have him to windward, so wore Ship on the other tack; he was then on our quarter, and lashed himself to our mizen chains: the contest then became desperate for one hour; they set us on fire twice on the quarter deck, with stink pots and other combustibles, and made four very daring attempts to board, with at least eighty Men, out of their rigging, foretop, and bowsprit, but were most boldly repulsed by every Man and Boy in the Ship. At the conclusion, a double-headed shot, from our aftermost gun, carried away his foremast by the board; that took away his bowsprit and main-top-gallant-mast. He then thought it was time to cast us off. Not less than fifty Men fell with the Wreck. We then hauled our Wind as well as we could, to knot, splice, and repair our rigging for the time; which gave the other Ships an opportunity to play upon the enemy; but being a little to leeward, had not so good an effect. A short time afterwards, wore Ship for him again, with the other Ships, and engaged him for about an hour more; but

---

* Probably the same Ship that had a gallant action with the Hippomenes. See Vol. XII, page 492.

finding it impossible to take him, owing to his number of Men, and no Surgeon to dress our wounded, I thought it best to steer our course for this Island.

" Her name is the Buonaparte, of 20 9-pounders, and upwards of 200 Men. I had 18 6-pounders, and 45 Men, 19 never at Sea before, Boys and Landmen.

" As to the behaviour of my whole Crew, to a Man they were steady, and determined to defend the Ship whilst there was one left alive. I had two killed and nine wounded; their names are at foot.

" On our arrival, Commodore Hood paid us every attention, sent the Surgeon and Mate to dress the wounded, also Men to assist the Ship to anchor, and gave me a written protection for my Crew.

" I cannot conclude without mentioning the gallant and spirited conduct of Mr. Dobbs, a Midshipman (Passenger with me), who acted as Captain of Marines, and during the Action fought like a brave fellow, as well as exciting in the minds of the Crew unconquerable zeal.

" We are much shattered in our hull, sails, and rigging; it will take us two days before we can be ready for Sea.

" I remain, in haste, Gentlemen,
" Your very obedient servant,
" JOHN CHARNLEY."

" LIST OF THE KILLED AND WOUNDED.

" Killed.—Thomas Duncan, Seaman; James Donaldson, Landman.

" Dangerously wounded.—James Knipe, Carpenter; William Cane, Seaman; John Dale, ditto; Pat. Murman, Landman; Robert Newton, Apprentice.

" Slightly wounded.—Robert Lambert, Second Mate; John Bishop, half Seaman; James M'Donald, Seaman; Daniel M'Carty, Cook's Mate."

Another letter from Captain Charnley to his friend in Lancaster, dated Barbadoes, Nov. 13, mentions that the wounded Men were in a fair way of recovery, and all went into the Royal Hospital that day. He says, " the Buonaparté Privateer is the completest Ship in these Seas. She made too certain of us. Freers, my first Mate, behaved most gallantly, and fought like a lion; so did Lambert, my second Mate. Indeed I cannot say enough for every Man and Boy in the Ship; the greatest part of them stripped and fought naked, and I am sure would have died sooner than have been carried. There was one hour's hard work, I assure you: I was near going frequently, as they fired several musket balls through my clothes."

The *Barbadoes Mercury* of November 10, gives a similar account to the above, under the head,
" DEFEAT OF BUONAPARTE, *not the great!!!*
" BUT
" *Celebrated Privateer of Guadaloupe.*"

The Lieutenant-Governor Nugent opened the General Assembly on the 23d of October, 1804, at Jamaica, with the following Speech:—

" *Gentlemen of the Council,*
" *Mr. Speaker, and Gentlemen of the Assembly,*

" It gives me the highest gratification to meet you under auspices so much more favourable for the Island than on former occasions, the seasonable rains having providentially returned to reward your industrious exertions; and I have also to congratulate you upon the early attention paid by the British Government to the safety of Jamaica, by the removal of the numerous French Prisoners to Europe, under circumstances of peculiar difficulty and embarrassment.

" I am commanded to acquaint you, that the War which was so unjustly provoked by the ambition of France, is directed with increased energy by that Power for the overthrow of the British Empire. His Majesty, however, feels the fullest confidence, from the justice of his cause, and the spirit and liberality of his subjects, that all the attempts of the enemy will be completely defeated, and his arms ultimately crowned with success. He derives this confident expectation from the blessing of Providence, from the unexampled zeal of his subjects in forming themselves to the use of arms, and their undiminished cheerfulness in submitting to the extraordinary burthens which public exigencies have occasioned.

" *Mr. Speaker, and Gentlemen of the Assembly*,

" His Majesty feels a similar confidence in your attachment; his attention will be always extended to your safety and protection, and he doubts not that he shall receive such support from your liberality, as will enable him to fulfil those objects with the smallest possible burthen to the subjects of the United Kingdom, who are already so deeply charged by the expenses of a War, which, if disastrous to Great Britain, must necessarily be so to Jamaica.

" *Gentlemen of the Council,*
" *Mr. Speaker, and Gentlemen of the Assembly,*

" I have only to renew my assurances of hearty co-operation with you in every measure which may best promote the welfare, and tend to the security and tranquillity of this Island."

The answer of the Council is a direct echo to the Speech, without particularly alluding to the contributions they might be called on for. The House of Assembly, in their Answer, observes, " that they reflected with pleasure, that they had always contributed their full proportion to the expenses of the State." This is the very point on which the differences have turned for several years between the Governors and the Assemblies of this Island.

On the 24th of October, a Committee of the House of Assembly was appointed " To inquire into the steps which have been taken in the Parliament of the United Kingdom, for an Abolition of the Slave Trade—into the measures adopted for equalizing the duties on sugar imported from the East Indies, and from the British Colonies; and the additional imposts which have been laid on our principal staples—to consider the effects which these measures have produced, and are likely to produce, on the agriculture and commerce of this colony; and to report the facts, with their opinion of the conduct which ought to be pursued by the House, in the distressed situation to which the Island is reduced."

It is worthy of remark, that all the papers subsequent to the 24th of October, are totally silent on the result of the very important subjects committed to the deliberation of the said Committee. Prudential motives probably induced the Assembly to enter upon these discussions with shut doors, and the total exclusion of all strangers. The Report has therefore not been published.

AMERICA.

Vice-Admiral Sir A. MITCHELL, *K.B.* HALIFAX.
Vice-Admiral Sir E. GOWER, *Knt.* NEWFOUNDLAND.

At a dinner given at New York to Mr. King, late American Ambassador to this Country, the following Patriotic Toast was drank, among many others:—THE COUNTRY OF OUR FATHERS! MAY ITS SPIRIT KEEP IT SAFE, AND ITS JUSTICE KEEP IT FREE!

The American Papers contain long details of the operations of the American Cruisers before Tripoli during last summer. In the two attacks which the Americans made upon that place, they lost a Gun-boat, which was blown up, with her Commander, Lieutenant Caldwell, and several of the Crew; and the Tripolines are stated to have lost several of their Boats. After these affairs, the Bashaw offered the Americans Peace for 150,000 dollars. It is said that 100,000 dollars were offered, but refused; in consequence of which another bombardment was expected to take place.

Washington, Nov. 8. From the Message of the President of the UNITED STATES, as delivered by Mr. Secretary Barwell, we have extracted the following Passages; illustrative of the Naval History of the Period:

" With the Nations of Europe in general our friendship and intercourse are undisturbed; and from the Governments of the Belligerent Powers especially, we continue to receive those friendly manifestations which are justly due to an honest neutrality, and to such good offices consistent with that as we have opportunities of rendering. The activity and success of the small force employed in the Mediterranean in the early part of the present year, the reinforcements sent into that Sea, and the energy of the Officers having command in the several Vessels, will,

I trust, by the sufferings of the War, reduce the Barbarians of Tripoli to the desire of Peace, on proper terms. Great injury, however, ensues to ourselves, as well as to others interested, from the distance to which prizes must be brought for adjudication, and from the impracticability of bringing hither such as are not Seaworthy. The Bey of Tunis having made requisitions unauthorized by our Treaty, their rejection has produced from him some expressions of discontent. But to those who expect us to calculate whether a compliance with unjust demands will not cost us less than a War, we must leave as a question of calculation for them also, whether to retire from unjust demands will not cost them less than a War? We can do to each other very sensible injuries by War. But the mutual advantages of Peace make that the best interest of both. Peace and intercourse with the other Powers on the same Coast continue on the footing on which they are established by Treaty."

" The Act of Congress of February 28, 1803, for building and employing a number of Gun-boats, is now in a course of execution to the extent there provided for. The advantage to Naval Enterprise, which Vessels of this construction offer to our Sea-port towns, their utility towards supporting, within our waters, the authority of the law; the promptness with which they will be manned by the Seamen and Militia of the place, in the moment they are wanting; the facility of their assembling, from different parts of the Coast, to any point where they are required in greater force than ordinary; the economy of their maintenance and preservation from decay, when not in actual service, and the competence of our finances to this defensive provision, without any new burthen; are considerations which will have due weight with Congress in deciding on the expediency of adding to their number from year to year, as experience shall testify their utility, until all our important Harbours, by these and auxiliary means, shall be secured against insult and opposition to the laws."

New York, Nov. 3. The British Privateer General Brevier, belonging to Nova Scotia, and mounting twelve 12-pounders, has been taken by a French Privateer, and carried into Point Petre. She was taken without any opposition, having been previously boarded by a British Frigate, which impressed her Men, leaving barely enough to navigate the Vessel.—A number of English Vessels have lately been sent into Point Petre.

Nov. 5. Extract of a letter from Commodore Preble to the Secretary of the Navy, dated June the 14th, 1804, on board the United States Frigate Constitution, of Tripoli:—" Yesterday I anchored off the Harbour, and sent Mr. O'Brien on Shore under a Flag of Truce to endeavour to ransom our unfortunate countrymen, and, if the Bashaw should desire it, to establish Peace. Mr. O'Brien did not succeed in his mission; he landed at noon, and returned on board at half-past two o'clock. You will see by the instructions how far he was authorized to go for the ransom. I presume, if the terms had been accepted, that our Government would have been satisfied; but they were refused, and we have no alternative but to oblige him to accept them or others more favourable for us."—Another letter from Commodore Preble, dated Messina, July 5, mentions, that he had taken on board there 700 Bomb-shells, and powder in proportion, for the purpose of bombarding Tripoli.

House of Representatives, New York, Nov. 20, 1804.

The engrossed Bill, making further appropriation for carrying into effect the Treaty of Amity, Commerce, and Navigation, between the United States and Great Britain, was read a third time, and passed in the House of Representatives.

House of Representatives, New York, Nov. 22.

Was read a first and second time, and ordered for reading on the 23d, " A Bill for the more effectual preservation of Peace in the Ports and Harbours of the United States, and in the Waters under their Jurisdiction."—Dr. Mitchell called the attention of the House for a few moments, whilst he explained a circumstance particularly interesting to the Sailors of the United States. The 8th Section of the Act, regulating the Merchant Service, &c. contained a regulation, " that Vessels of 150 tons, or upwards, whose Crews consist of ten Men, should be obliged to carry c Medicine Chest." But the most dangerous part of our Commerce to the health of Seamen, added Dr. Mitchell, was that to the West Indies, and it was well known that the Vessels engaged in that Trade were under 150 tons; of course the care of the health of such Seamen was entirely under the discretion of the Merchant and Captains; and, however distressing it might be, yet the fact was so, that we lost one tenth of our Sailors, nay I believe one eighth in that particular Trade . . . . While I would take effectual care of the health of the Seamen at Sea, I would submit it to consideration, whether the Medicine Chest ought to be at the expense of the Merchant, or Seaman? It may be recollected that Seamen pay twenty Cents a Voyage, Hospital Money, to form a fund for their assistance in sickness on Shore: I do not then understand why they should not contribute to their own safety at Sea; the Captain generally performing the part of the Physician in the latter place, as the Hospital Physicians do in the first mentioned.—I therefore move the Committee of Commerce and Manufacture to inquire into the propriety of altering the Law on this point."

COPY of ORDERS of the PREFECT of GUADALOUPE.
" To all American Captains:
" Orders of the Prefect of Guadaloupe.
" It is forbidden to all American Captains, under the penalty of 200 dollars, to introduce into this Colony any newspapers, gazettes, or proclamations, from any part of the world whatsoever: and if they have any on board, they may and must deposit them at the Captain of the Post's Office.—Done at Basseterre (G.) the 5th Vendemiaire, 5th year of the French Republic.
" G. ROBERT.
" SENORA, Interpreter."

Oct. 25. Arrived the armed Ship Leander, Captain Lewis, in 30 days from Port-au-Prince, with a valuable cargo of coffee.

The Leander left Port-au-Prince in company with the armed Brig Dolly, Richard, having been previously cautioned that one or two large French Privateers were expected to lay wait for them. On the third day after leaving Port a large armed Vessel hove in sight, which they expected was one of those Privateers, and bore down on the Leander. As it was near night-fall, and Capt. Lewis wished to ascertain whether she was friend or enemy before dark, he fired a gun and hoisted the American colours. No signal was given in reply, but the Vessel continued to approach, lighted her lamps, as it became dark, and the Crew of the Leander could distinctly hear the commands given with the trumpet, as the weather was remarkably serene, and she was now within a few fathoms' distance.

Her intention was supposed to board, and Captain Lewis thought it prudent to put her in confusion by commencing the attack. He accordingly poured a broadside of 18-pounders into her, which shattered her bow considerably, cut away her rigging, and killed one Man, the Captain of the main-top. Great confusion ensued, and she fell back; the Leander, aided by the Dolly, kept playing her with round shot, and occasionally with grape and langrage, which did great damage to her rigging.

The next morning she came up again, and proved to be the Fortunée British Frigate, Captain Vansittart, of 44 guns. Her guns, the preceding evening, had all been in the hold, in consequence of the late gale; and, as she had not expected an enemy, the Vessel was entirely unprepared for action.

The Captain at first threatened considerably, but Captain Lewis explained the circumstance, and stated to him that, had he shown his colours, the event would not have taken place. He impressed 26 Men from the Leander and Dolly, and obliged Captain Lewis to pay 500 dollars for the wife of the Man killed, and 1000 dollars to repair the damages; but his conduct was very gentleman-like, considering what had happened.

The Leander is a fine handsome Vessel, carries 12 eighteen-pound carronades, and two long brass twelves; the latter transferable. She has sixty Men.

Nov. 27.—The Brig America was captured from the Spaniards by an Indigene Privateer. The Crew were murdered, and the Vessel sent into Port de Paix, where she was condemned. The account published, says the Charleston Courier, on the 6th inst., respecting the infamous murder of Mr. Tate, Mate of the armed Ship Pilgrim, of Philadelphia, at Cape Francois, was in some respects incorrect. The following particulars are furnished by a Gentleman who was an eye-witness of the whole transaction :—It would seem that two unfortunate Frenchmen, together with two Mulattoes, had been introduced on board this Vessel (probably with the knowledge of the Officers), and securely stowed away under deck with the cargo. By some means information reached Christophe that they were concealed on board. Mr. Lynch, the Supercargo, and Captain Gibson, being on Shore, declared their ignorance of any person's being concealed on board. The Commander in Chief immediately dispatched a guard of Soldiers on board the Ship, who tore up the deck over the heads of the unfortunate fugitives, and, together with Mr. Tate, (he being the Commanding Officer then on board,) forced them on Shore. On their landing upon the Wharf, the unfortunate American saw but too plainly the fate which awaited him, and, addressing himself to his amazed Countrymen, he exclaimed—" Americans! will you see me thus dragged to execution like a dog, and no one step forward to assert my innocence?"—" Yes," said one (a Mr. Smith, Supercargo of a Vessel from Baltimore), " I will speak for you !" Instantly a Sentinel was ordered to run him through with his bayonet; but he escaped by springing into his Boat, and instantly pushing off. The Prisoners were then led to the public scales. Mr. Tate and the two Frenchmen had halters placed about their necks, mounted this temporary scaffold, and were precipitately launched into eternity ! The arms of the Frenchmen were pinioned, but those of Mr. Tate were left untied ; and in his struggles he repeatedly caught hold of the cord by which he was suspended, and entirely removed it from his throat, the cord passing round his chin and the back of his neck: in this manner he expired ! As he mounted the ladder, he said, " Americans ! Americans ! I die this ignominious death for duly executing my orders!" The feelings of the Americans on this occasion may be more readily felt than described.

Extract of a Letter from Washington, dated November 23.

" In the House of Representatives this day, the Committee, to which that part of the President's Speech which relates to the unauthorised arming of Merchant Ships was referred, brought in a Bill for regulating the Clearance of Armed Merchant Vessels. It was read twice, and ordered to be committed on Monday. This Bill enacts, that no armed Merchant Vessel, or Vessel of that description, having on board materials by which she might arm at Sea, shall be permitted to clear out from the Ports of the United States, until Bonds and Securities are given to the amount of the Cargo and Vessel, that no depredation or violence shall be committed on any Ships belonging to Nations with which we are at amity. An exception is made in favour of Vessels bound to the Mediterranean, or beyond the Cape of Good Hope. Vessels of this class, however, are restrained, under similar penalties, from committing depredations on the Citizens or Subjects of Nations at Peace with the United States."

Some of the Officers of the Revolutionnaire were on the 4th of December on Shore at Crumps Hill, near Hampton Roads, off which the French Frigate President was lying, and accidentally met M. la Brosse, the French Commander, with some of his People. Our Tars are said to have very politely invited him, in the name of their Ship's Crew, to put to Sea, and thus to save each party the mortifying inactivity of a blockade. M. la Brosse is stated to have replied, that when he had performed the Service with which he was immediately entrusted by his Government, he would seek the meeting to which he was invited. The British Officers smiled at the excuse, and took their leave. The two Frigates, at the date of the last accounts, lay near the Horse-shoe, within gun-shot of each other.

Extract of a Letter received at Philadelphia.

Dominique, Nov. 3.—" This Port was closed yesterday against all American Cargoes of every description ; this, I am informed, is to be the case in all the British Islands. The cause of this procedure is not known here—some suppose it owing to the application of Irish Merchants.

" The British Frigate Cambrian arrived at the Hook yesterday from Halifax. The Hon. Captain Beresford proceeds with her to Hampton Roads, to watch the motions of the French Frigate le President, and thus enable la Revolutionnaire to accomplish the object of her Voyage."

HOME REPORTS.

PORTSMOUTH.

The Medusa Frigate is appointed to carry out Marquis Cornwallis.

Jan. 15. Sailed the Merlin Sloop, Capt. Brenton, to join the Havre Squadron. The Medusa Frigate, Captain Gore, is taken into Dock. Arrived the Prince George, of 98 guns, Captain York; Plantagenet, of 74 guns, Captain Pender; and the Dragon, of 74 guns, Captain Griffith, from the Channel Fleet. The Plantagenet appears to have received damage by the late gales. Sailed the Speedwell Brig, Lieutenant Robertson, on a cruise.

17. It blew tremendously hard last night; yet so unequalled for safety is the anchorage at Spithead, that not an accident occurred to the Ships. The Decade Frigate, Captain Rutherford, was blown from her Station off Cherbourg, and anchored at St. Helen's. Arrived the Teazer Gun-vessel from off Havre. Came into Harbour the Ariadne, of 20 guns, Hon. Captain D. E. King, to be repaired. Sailed the Favourite Sloop, Captain Davie, to join the Havre Squadron.

20. Wind S. Arrived the Speedwell Brig of War from a cruise. Sailed the Raven Brig of War, with dispatches for the Mediterranean. The Avenger Sloop of War has made a Signal for a Convoy to the Mediterranean. A very heavy gale of Wind blew yesterday; several guns were fired, as signals, we fear, of some Ships in distress; it blows harder than we ever remember.

22. Arrived the Leopard, Trusty, Eagle, and Iris Men of War, Lily Sloop of War, Abundance Store Ship, Magicienne and Weymouth Frigates. The Lion Cutter, off Havre, fell in with a Vessel keel uppermost, and left the Isle of Wight Sloop in tow of her. Sailed the Clinker Gun Vessel, and l'Entreprenante Cutter, on a cruise.

25. Arrived from a cruise, the Autumn Sloop of War and Mægarie Fire-ship. Wind E.N.E. A Vessel from Southampton brought intelligence, that the Transports for Cavalry and Infantry are daily increasing: upwards of 50 Sail made a respectable appearance in that River. It is supposed that the Troops which are to embark in them are destined for Portugal. During the heavy gales, a Boat belonging to one of the Transports was unfortunately upset near the mouth of Itchen River; the whole of the Crew were saved except one Man, who had no idea of swimming, and consequently was drowned. A lad about fourteen, who, in sculling from the Quay to a Vessel in the Roads, fell over the starboard side of his Boat, was also drowned before any assistance could be given.

27. Rear-Admiral Louis, who has commanded the flying Squadron before Boulogne, since the vain threat of Invasion, is arrived here to shift his Flag from the Leopard to the Ambuscade Frigate, Captain Durban.

28. Sailed to St. Helen's, the Monarch, of 74 guns, Captain Searle, bound to the Downs, to receive Lord Keith's Flag.

Arrived the Mediator Frigate, from the eastward. Sailed the Pluto Sloop, Captain Janverin, with Bullocks for the Havre Squadron. Commissioner (now Admiral) Sterling arrived here this day, from Jamaica, having been succeeded by Captain Dilkes.

29. Arrived the Clinker Gun Vessel, from a cruise. Wind E.

30. Came into Harbour the Prince George, of 98 guns, Captain Losack, to refit; and the Sylph Sloop, Captain Goate, went out this morning. Sailed the Autumn Sloop, Captain Searle; and the Constant Gun Vessel, on a cruise off Dungeness; and the Speedy Sloop, Captain Giffard, on a cruise off Havre.

31. Sailed the Polyphemus, of 64 guns, Captain Lawford, to join Sir John Orde's Squadron. She will call off Plymouth to receive her Men from the Gertruyda Frigate, which she captured; the Eugenie Sloop, Captain Webb, with Mongo Park on board, for the Coast of Africa. Mr. Park is gone to complete his projected Travels into the interior of the Southern Part of Africa. The Ship was ordered purposely to take him.

Promotions and Appointments.

The gallant Earl of St. Vincent has signified his readiness to hoist his Flag, whenever his professional Services may be deemed necessary for the public Service.

We are informed that the necessary arrangements for increasing the pay of Surgeons of the Navy, has been confirmed by the Privy Council, and will immediately be put in force by the Admiralty. The accounts which are in circulation are far from being correct. The following may be depended upon as the rates of augmentation:—

	Per Diem.
	£. s. d.
Physicians of Naval Hospitals, after ten years' Service	2 2 0
Ditto - - - - - - - after three do.	1 11 6
Ditto - - - - - - - under do.	1 1 0
Surgeons of ditto - - - - after ten do.	1 0 0
Ditto - ditto - - - - under do.	0 15 0
Dispensers of ditto	0 10 0
Surgeons of his Majesty's Ships, on their first appointment after two years' Service, 5s. per day half pay	0 10 0
Ditto, half pay 6s. after six years' Service (three as Mate)	0 11 0
Ditto, ditto, after ten ditto (ditto)	0 14 0
Ditto, ditto, after twenty ditto (ditto)	0 18 0

Surgeons' Mates 6s. a day after two years' Service; 3s. half pay. Surgeons of Hospitals, Dock Yards, Marine Infirmaries, and Ships, after twenty years' Service, have the option of retiring from the Service on 6s. a day; and after thirty years' Service, on 15s. a day.

Captain Tyler is appointed to the Tonnant, vice Jervis; Captain Brown to the Atlas, vice Pym; Captain Ball to the Zealand, vice Renou; Captain Ellison to be a Supervisor of Greenwich Hospital, vice Sir Richard Pearson; Captain Oliver has resumed the command of the Melpomene, vice Laroche.

Sir T. Trowbridge, to the command of the Malabar Coast, in the East Indies; Captain Ekins, to the Amelia; Captain Mackenzie, to the Beaulieu; Captain Woolcombe, to the Carysfort; Captain Aldridge, to the Osprey; Captain M. Seymour, *pro tempore*, to the Illustrious; Captain Hatley, *pro tempore*, to the Leda; Lieutenant Hanchet, to command the Desperate Gun-Vessel; Mr. James Wilkes, to be Surgeon of the Sultan.

Captain Raggett is appointed to the Leopard, of 50 guns, at this Port, vice Austen, who is going to the Mediterranean with Admiral Louis.

Lieutenant Simpson is appointed by the Lords of the Admiralty to an armed Defence Ship.

Admiral Louis has quitted the Downs Station, and has hoisted his Flag on board the Ambuscade Frigate, to proceed to the Mediterranean.

Lieutenants Irwin, Skinner, and Down, of the Royal Yachts, are promoted to the rank of Commanders.

The Valorous, of 24 guns, which has been launched at Hull, is ordered into immediate Commission, and Captain Hardinge is appointed to the command.

Sir Thomas Livingstone is appointed to the command of the Renommée Frigate, at Woolwich; and Captain Seater to the Mediator, of 64 guns, in the room of Sir T. Livingstone.

Admiral Stanhope is appointed to superintend the fitting out of Ships at Deptford and Woolwich, in the room of Admiral Douglas.

Admiral Douglas is appointed to the command of the Ships on the Dungeness Station, in the room of Admiral Louis.

Captain Browell is appointed one of the Captains of Greenwich Hospital.

Vice-Admiral Sir John Colpoys, K. B., is appointed Treasurer of Greenwich Hospital, vice Captain Jervis, deceased.

Captain John Gore, of the Medusa Frigate, has had the honour of Knighthood conferred on him, and was afterwards introduced to the Queen.

Captain W. Hope has succeeded Sir J. Colpoys, as one of the Lords of the Admiralty.

Captain Bissell is appointed Sir T. Trowbridge's Captain; Captain Bedford, to the Hibernia; Captain Foster, to the Calypso; and Captain Prevost, to the Saracen, *vice* Beauchamp.

The Lords of the Admiralty have been pleased to promote Lieutenant Grant, who behaved so gallantly this War, (in a spirited action in an armed Vessel on the Coast of Holland, where he was dreadfully wounded and made prisoner,) to the rank of Commander. He was the Officer that made a Voyage of Discovery, from Botany Bay, in the Southern Pacific Ocean a few years since, and made several valuable Discoveries in those Seas, for the purposes of Navigation.

Letters from Jamaica, dated the 19th November last, state the gallant Captain Coghlan appointed to the Renard, of 24 guns, *vice* the Honourable L. Cathcart, deceased.

BIRTHS.

Feb. 4. The Lady of J. Barrow, Esq. Secretary to the Admiralty, of a Son.

13. At Portsea, the Hon. Mrs. Dashwood, Lady of Captain Dashwood, of the Navy, of a Son.

MARRIAGES.

Lately, at All Saints Church, North Street, York, by the Rev. George Brown, William Penrose, aged 74, late Boatswain of his Majesty's Royal Navy, to Miss Ann Webster, his Grand Niece, aged 21.

Lately, Mr. Rogers, of the Navy, to Miss S. Gray, Daughter of Mr. Gray, of the Cornish Arms, in Portsmouth.

Lately, Rear-Admiral Campbell, Brother to Lord Cawdor, to Miss E. Campbell.

Captain E. O'Bryen, of the Royal Navy, and Nephew to the Marquis of Thomond, to Miss Hotham, eldest Daughter of General Hotham, and Niece to Lord and Sir Beaumont Hotham.

OBITUARY.

(Additions to former Accounts.)

1. Lieutenant John Bellamy, of the Carysfort Frigate, whose death was noticed in our last Volume, page 432, was Son of the late Alderman Bellamy, of Leicester. This gallant young Man was with Lord Duncan when he defeated the Dutch Fleet off Camperdown and had been much engaged in perilous and severe Service.

2. On board his Vessel, Captain John Huddart, of the Townshend Revenue Cutter. The circumstances of this Gentleman's death are peculiarly distressing: He had been for a considerable time back in a very declining state of health, but from an extreme anxiety to do his duty, he resisted the remonstrances of his family, and all considerations of a personal nature; he combated with his infirmities to the last, and was in the act of conveying (by order of Admiral Lord Gardner) Captain Berry, of the Royal Navy, to Loughswilly, when he died. Thus did he close a faithful, loyal, and honourable Service of twenty-two years, the early part of which was distinguished at the Relief of Gibraltar, on which occasion he was Midshipman under the Hon. Captain (now Admiral) Pakenham. He was an affectionate and sincere friend, a fond husband and father; and in all the relations of life, the amiability of his manners and the integrity of his heart challenged the love and esteem of all who knew him. What remains to be told is the most melancholy. His own pains, his cares, and his sorrows, have died with him; but while he was expiring in the public Service, unaided by all the kind and soothing offices of domestic tenderness and love, he was leaving behind him, utterly unprovided for, a Wife and eight Children.

3. The late Sir F. Nightingale, Bart. of Kneesworth, Cambridgeshire, was the only Son of Captain Gamaliel Nightingale, of the Royal Navy, by Maria Daughter of Peter Clossen, Merchant at Hamburgh. Sir Edward proved his claim to the Title in 1797.

4. Mr. Uppington Brace, aged 71, who for forty-four years was a Surgeon in the Royal Navy.

5. Lieutenant Sir Samuel Hales, Bart. of Mundell, Lancashire.
6. *Dec.* 13. At Row Green, near Hatfield, Captain John Willes, one of the superannuated Commanders in the Royal Navy.
7. Lieutenant Richards, at Poole, in Dorsetshire, on the Impress Service, was found hanging in his bed-room. Some unfortunate attachment is supposed to have been the cause.

Lieutenant Mulcaster, who unfortunately fell in a late engagement with a French Privateer, was the Son of Major-General Mulcaster, of the Royal Engineers. This very promising young Man commenced his naval career under the protection and auspices of that great and ever to be lamented hero, Lord Howe, on board of whose Ship, in the memorable engagement of the 29th May and 1st June, 1794, he had the misfortune to lose his hearing in a certain degree, which he was never after able to recover. The death of his Admiral and gallant patron, and of Sir Andrew Snape Douglas, were lamentable misfortunes to this amiable Officer, who, had they lived longer, would have attained a higher and more important rank in that profession to which he was a real ornament. Lieutenant Mulcaster had the honour of being called after the *present* Lord Howe, who became his sponsor, and from whom (on account of the ancient intimacy between his Lordship and the late General Mulcaster) he experienced the most steady friendship. Mr. Mulcaster was made a Lieutenant in the Mediterranean by Lord Keith, and was subsequently appointed to the command of the Folkstone by Earl St. Vincent, who had always professed a strong and sincere desire and intention to promote this meritorious, but unfortunate young Man, who would, doubtless, have had additional rank conferred on him, had he survived the late engagement.

Sheerness, Jan. 18. This day a Seaman of the name of Edward Sullings, belonging to the Sophia Fire-ship, was found suffocated in his hammock, and another nearly so, having imprudently put a tarpaulin over the forecastle grating, where they slept, and not putting out the fire previous to their going to rest.

Extract of a Letter from an Officer now on board his Majesty's Ship the Galatea, off Antigua, dated November 23, 1804, *to his Mother in the City of Worcester.*

" I embrace the opportunity of this Packet, to prevent any uneasiness on your part, or any of our family, as to my death, which I understand is enclosed in the report of those Officers who died on board the Amelia while I belonged to her. We had the misfortune to lose, in the course of ten days, the Captain, fourteen other Officers, and about eighty Men, of a malignant fever; few of them lived thirty-six hours after the first attack. Among the Officers we lost a very promising young Man, a Son of C. Domville, Esq. of Stanbrook Hall, at Powick, near Worcester. I had a very severe attack, but, thank God, am now recovering."

The following melancholy accident occurred at Blyth on Wednesday afternoon, the 16th of January. About two o'clock a Ship wanting a Pilot to bring her into the Harbour, made the accustomed signal; upon which four Men put off to her in a Coble. As they approached the Ship, which was going very swiftly before the Wind, and the Sea very high, they were dashed with violence against her, and the Coble was overset; and, notwithstanding every possible assistance was given, they all unfortunately perished. They have all left Widows, and amongst them twenty-one small Children, to lament their loss.

The following are their names and families:—James Nicholson, seven Children, and his Wife pregnant; William Watt, four Children; John Hedley, three ditto; William Redpath, seven ditto.

Jan. 26. At Sandgate, B. F. Haddon, Esq. Lieutenant of his Majesty's Ship Stately, and Nephew to Mr. Alderman Combe.

It is with concern we state the melancholy death of Capt. Jervis, of his Majesty's Ship Tonnant, who was drowned a few days since off Brest, in going in his Gig (Boat) from the Tonnant to the San Joseph. The people who were in the Boat, except one Man, were saved. The Cockswain supported him till his strength was exhausted, and they both sunk; but the poor fellow being a good swimmer, ascended the surface and was picked up. Captain Campbell, of the Doris, who accompanied him, escaped only by sustaining himself upon an oar, until he was taken up by another Boat. This afflicting accident will be universally and sincerely regretted in the Navy: he was an Officer of the first talents, and of a disposition the most generous and urbane.

Captain Jervis succeeded Admiral J. W. Payne as Treasurer of Greenwich Hospital, and was also one of the Verdurers of the New Forest.

A private letter that has appeared, gives a different account. It begins with the loss of the Doris.

"I am sorry to relate the loss by Shipwreck, in a gale of Wind on the Coast of France near Isle Aix, of that fine Frigate the Doris, of 44 guns, Captain P. Campbell. The Captain, Officers, and Crew, are all saved, as far as at present can be learnt, by their own Boats and those of the Squadron off that Station. But every person must feelingly regret the loss of an excellent Officer, in performing the active duties of humanity, Captain Jervis (Nephew to Earl St. Vincent), of le Tonnant, of 84 guns, who, on the Doris's striking, and firing signals of distress, had his Barge hoisted out, with the other Boats of le Tonnant, and the Boats of the Squadron, to endeavour to save the Doris's Officers and Crew. He went in his own Boat, and it is supposed, from the surf over the rocks, the Boat he was in upset, by which means he was unfortunately drowned."

This gallant Gentleman was Nephew to the Earl of St. Vincent, whose illustrious name and titles, in the course of nature, he would have inherited. He was as amiable in private life as in his professional career he had shown himself valiant, skilful, and indefatigable. A braver Officer did not grace the Service, nor a milder character the circles of polished society. He will long be regretted wherever he was known, for his public and private worth.

Another account, and to which we attach the most credit, is as follows:— Captain Jervis had received some important information, and through his own energy for the Service, was extremely desirous of communicating it to Sir Charles Cotton, in the San Josef, then senior Admiral; but it having blown for several days a heavy gale, he took the opportunity, when it had abated, to get into a four-oared Boat, termed a Gig, and, with Captain Campbell, put off to make such communication to the Admiral, when a heavy Sea broke upon the bow of the Boat and upset her. Captain Jervis has left only two Daughters, so that his next Brother is presumptive heir to the family.

On Friday, the 18th ult., Mr. M'Donald, acting Lieutenant on board his Majesty's Ship Lapwing, and eldest Son of Thomas Macdonald, Esq. of Drayton Green, Middlesex.

Lately, in Quebec Street, London, R. Matson, Esq. Father of Captain Matson, of the Navy, and of Hambrook-house.

Lately, Captain A. Renou, of the Zealand Guard-ship, at the Nore.

Lately, of the fever at Gibraltar, Captain S. P. Mouat, of the Navy, Agent for Transports; also his two youngest Daughters; and Mr. Maxwell, the Husband of one of his Daughters, who was on business at Malaga, of the fever there.

Feb. 5. At Portsea, Mr. Simmonds, a Quarter Master in the Dock Yard.

6. At Newtown, near Portsmouth, Mr. Kirk, an old Surgeon in the Navy.

17. At Portsea, in the 73d year of her age, after a long and painful illness, Mrs. M. Wallis, Relict of the late P. Wallis, Esq. Master Shipwright of his Majesty's Yard, at Halifax, Nova Scotia.

Lately, at Alverstoke, Captain Saradine, of the Navy.

Lieutenant William C. C. Dalyell, of the Royal Navy, fifth Son of the late Sir Robert Dalyell, of Pinne, Bart. was killed in an action near Dieppe, on the 4th January.

On his passage from Jamaica, Mr. F. Stephens, Master of his Majesty's Ship Sagesse.

Lately, aged 72, Captain Geary, 24 years a Commander in the Navy.

On the 12th January, at Antigua, aged 17, Mr. J. S. Greig, of his Majesty's Ship Beaulieu.

Lately, Lieutenant Thurnham, of the Marines, in cutting out a Brig in the Boats of the Illustrious.

At Stone Castle, Kent, Miss S. E. Berkeley, second Daughter of Lieutenant-Colonel Berkeley, of the Royal Marines.

At Wherstead Lodge, near Ipswich, Dowager Lady Harland, Relict of Vice-Admiral Sir R. Harland.

Lloyd's Marine List

OF
SHIPS LOST, DESTROYED, CAPTURED, AND RECAPTURED, &c.
FROM SEPTEMBER 11, TO NOVEMBER 2, 1804.

A VESSEL, supposed to be the Pelican, Broad, from Smyrna to London, is taken by a Privateer, and carried into Sfax, near Tunis.

The Thomas, Vamanft, of Liverpool, was captured on the 9th May on the windward coast of Africa, by two French Privateers, after an engagement of an hour and a half, and carried into Cayenne, where the two Privateers arrived with her on the 15th June.

The Pelican, Broad, from Smyrna to London, was taken 18th June, within 18 leagues of Malta, by a French Privateer of 4 guns and 75 Men, and carried into Sfax, near Tunis.

A Convoy of 29 Sail, from Elsinore, put into Gothenburg 6th inst.

The American Ship Hopewell, Sciffon; and Brig Rockland, Aikin, from New York to St. Domingo, are taken, and sent for Guadaloupe.

An English Hermaphrodite Brig, from Philadelphia to Jamaica, was taken, and carried into Cuba, 14th July.

The American Ship Eugenia, from Bourdeaux, is taken off New York by the Leander Man of War, and sent to Halifax.

The Colombe, Day, from Virginia to Dunkirk, is detained by the Nautilus Sloop of War, and sent into Plymouth.

The Sophy, M'Lean, from St. Vincent's to Liverpool, is condemned at Tortola. Cargo arrived at Liverpool in the Sovereign.

The Mary, of Greenock, bound to Virginia ; and Two Sisters, of Dartmouth, from Newfoundland, are captured by the Uncle Thomas French Privateer, in lat 43. 30. long. 25. 10. Eleven of the People were taken on board the Pully, arrived at Penzance 3d September.

The Glamorgan, Molloy, bound to London, was left at Demerara 24th July, having struck on the Banks.

The Dart, Boland, from Liverpool to Africa, was totally lost at Cape Bajadore, 1st July. Crew saved.

The Teutonia, ———, from Surinam ; and the Ceres, ———, from River Plata, are detained, and sent into Portsmouth by his Majesty's Ship Agincourt.

The Hector, Marshall, from Antigua to Liverpool, is lost in Cardigan Bay. Crew saved.

The Mary, of Greenock, from Liverpool to Virginia, was retaken by the Illustrious Man of War, off Perrol, on the 8th September, and is arrived at Plymouth.

The Hope, Ellis, from Embden to Dieppe, is detained by the Zephyr Cutter, and sent into Portsmouth

The Wight, Ford, from Zant to London, arrived at Portsmouth, was taken near Zant by a Privateer, and retaken by his Majesty's Ship Thisbe, who captured the Privateer, and carried her into Corfu.

The Dutchess of York, Cornford, from London to Surinam, is captured on the Coast of Surinam, and carried into Guadaloupe.

The Rachael, Mellivil, from London to the West Indies, is taken by the Vengeur Privateer, and carried into Guadaloupe

The Esperance, Spanish Ship, bound to Dieppe; the Hoffnung, ———, and the Industry, ———, from Lisbon to Dieppe ; and the Fora, from Havre to Lisbon, are detained, and sent into Portsmouth.

The Diamond, Nesbitt, from Dublin to Limerick, was ashore on shore 14th September, near Strangford. Crew saved.

The Young Peggy, of Bristol, from Jersey, has been taken by a French Privateer, retaken by the Britannia Cutter, and arrived at Portsmouth.

The Brig Elizabeth and Mary, of Sunderland, Cowan, took fire on the 22d September, near Harwich, and burnt to the water's edge.

The Vandever, Franklin, from Narva to London, was on shore on the Barnard Sand, near Southwold, 21st September.

The Emanuel, Husler, from Jahde to Lisbon, is lost on the Coast of Holland.

The Malina, Faley, bound to Bourdeaux, is detained by the Railer Sloop, and sent into Portsmouth.

The Hibberts, of London, from Havanna to New York, is detained by the Leander Man of War, and sent to Halifax.

The Siemen, Brink, from St. Croix to Copenhagen, is lost on the Coast of Sweden.

The Boletta Johanna, Mouleus, from Bergen to Naples, is lost on the Goodwin Sands. Crew saved by the Deal Boats.

The Brig Eliza, David Seay, from Gothenburg to Cherbourg, with iron and deals, is lost on the Goodwin Sands. One of the Crew landed at Ramsgate.

The Althea, ———, from Bengal to London, is taken by the Belle Poule and Atalante French Frigates, and arrived at the Isles of France 7th of May. French Papers.

The Wanderer, Franklin, from Narva, which was on shore on the Barnard Sand, is got off without any material damage, and arrived in the River.

The Plymouth Packet, ———, from Dartmouth to Newfoundland, is captured.

The Marie Francoise, from Bourdeaux ; and the Desiree, ———, from Quimper, are taken by the Pickle Schooner, and arrived at Plymouth.

The Anker's Hope, Loss, from Dram to Falmouth, which was on shore near Yarmouth, is got off, and put into that Harbour.

The Purissima, ———, from Cadiz to Havre, is detained and sent into Portsmouth.

The Minerve Letter of Marque, out twenty days from Bourdeaux, pierced for 18 guns, mounting 14, and 111 men, laden with wine and brandy, bound to Martinique, was taken the 25th ult. in lat. 49. 30. long. 15. 30. by the Topaze Frigate, after a chase of 12 hours, and carried into Cork the 3d October.

The Elizabeth, French Schooner Privateer, of 6 guns, has been cut out of Guadaloupe by the Galatea Frigate, and carried into Dominica 3d August.

The Volante Brig, from Lisbon to Cherbourg, is detained by the Duke of Clarence Cutter, and arrived at Portsmouth.

The Young Nicholas, from Honduras to London, has been retaken, and carried to St. Kitt's.

The Kingster, Wells, from Jamaica to Honduras, was lost 1st June. Crew saved.

The Blanche Frigate has taken the Nymph Dutch Privateer. 4 guns, and carried her into Jamaica 26th July.

The Brig America, from Africa, has been taken by a French Privateer, retaken by the Hercule Man of War, and arrived at Jamaica 14th July.

The Mayflower, Watson, from Newcastle to Tonningen, foundered at Sea between 21st and 23d September ; crew saved. Captain Watson reports, that a Brig, coal laden, went down at the same time ; and that he saw another Vessel keel uppermost.

The Eagle, Barber, from New York to Jamaica, was taken 22d June, and carried into Cuba.

The Barbara, Leigh, is taken by a French Privateer and carried into Cuba.

The Gratitude, Scott, from Cardiff to London, was taken near Beachy Head, and carried into Boulogne on the 6th of July last.

The Sally, Burgess, from the Havana to Charleston, was detained and sent into Bermuda, 17th June, by the Furtunee Frigate.

The Bess, Grantham, from Jamaica to Dublin, foundered at Sea 1st September. The Crew and a small part of the Cargo saved by the Uranie Frigate.

The Sloop James, of and for Rochester, from Newcastle, was wrecked near Hull, on the Coast of Norfolk, on Tuesday night, the 9th October.

The West Indian, Richardson, from Jamaica to London, was taken about 8th of August, by a Privateer.

The Carleton, M'Whinney, from Jamaica to Liverpool, is on shore near Whitehaven ; great part of the cargo saved.

The Otter, Brown, from Wisbeach to Rye, with corn, foundered near the North Foreland. Crew landed at Ramfgate.

The Margaret and Eliza, of Liverpool, is carried into Porto Rico by a Privateer of 6 guns and 40 men.

LLOYD'S MARINE LIST OF SHIPS LOST, &c.

The Arthur Howe, ———, from Africa to the West Indies, is recaptured by the Elephant Man of War, and carried to Jamaica.

The Active, Razor, from Jamaica to London, taken 3d May off Cuba, by a Privateer, was carried into New Orleans the end of July, and detained by the Governor on suppofition of the Privateer being a Pirate.

The American Brig Richmond, laden with Naval Stores, bound to the Isles of France, has been detained and sent into St. Helena, from whence she arrived in the Downs 9th October.

The Two Sifters, White, from Newfoundland to England, is retaken and arrived at Ilfracombe.

The Countefs Northefk, Johnfon, from Arbroath to London, is loft near Yarmouth.

The Orange ———, Watfon, from Rhode Ifland to Jamaica, was taken by a Privateer off Cuba in August.

The Minerva, ———, from Jamaica to London, has been taken in the Gulf, retaken by the Cornwallis, of Bristol, and fent for Jamaica under Convoy of the Hound Sloop of War.

The Adventure, Penfep, from Newhaven to Jamaica, was taken in August off Port Morant, by a Privateer.

The Athea, Miller, from ———, engal to London, was taken 17th April in lat. 7. S. long. 92. E. by the Belle Poule and Atalante Frigates, and carried into the Mauritius 8th May.

The Swan, Prior, from Rotterdam to Boston, has been detained and fent into Halifax by the Driver Sloop of War.

The Ceres, ———, from River Plate, detained and fent into Portfmouth last month, by his Majesty's Brig Agincourt, is liberated, and failed for Embden.

The Sophia Dorothea, Schultz, failed from Hull for Lubeck 15 h November last, and has not since been heard of.

The Princefs of Wales, Campbell, from Jamaica to Greenock, is loft on Wicklow Lank, and only one man faved.

The San Francifco Xavier, Martinez, from Cadiz to Antwerp, is loft near Rye. A small part of the Cargo faved.

The Diligence, Butler, from Leith to Petersburg, is loft on a reef of rocks 10 miles N. E. of the Ifland of Hogland.

On the 5th October, off Cape St. Mary, the Indefatigable, Medufa, Lively, and Amphion Frigates, fell in with four Spanish Frigates, from Rio de la Plata, bound to Cadiz, under the command of a Rear-Admiral, and having a large quantity of treafure on board —The orders which Captain Moore, the fenior Officer, was under, to detain Spanish Veffels of this defcription, being refifted, an action enfued, in the event of which three of the Spanish Frigates furrendered to his Majesty's Ships, and the fourth blew up after firing one broadfide. The Lively arrived at Portfmouth, with la Fama, on Wednefday, and the Indefatigable, with la Medea and la Clara, are hourly expected.

The Spanifh Brig St. Jofeph, laden with linen and wine, and the Spanifh Ship Efperanzo (Cargo landed), were taken poffeffion of at Cowes yesterday, by order of the Admiral at Portfmouth.

The Peggy, of Scarbro', Captain Frankland, was taken 3d Sept. in lat. 50. 16. long. 16. 40. by the Braave French Privateer (late the King George Packet); and on the 7th the fame Privateer captured the Jamaica Planter, Feard. from St. Vincent's to London. Part of the Crew of the latter Veffel arrived at Cork 10th October in the Dryade Frigate, who took them out of the American Ship Nancy.

The Melcomb, Prowfe, of Weymouth, bound to Southampton, funk near the Shingles 16th October.

The Mary, ———, from Plymouth to Sunderland, is on fhore on Portland Beach. Crew faved

The Efperance French Privateer, of 10 guns, is taken by the Alcion Sloop of War, and carried into Gibraltar.

The Neptune, Guthrie, of Largo, was ftranded 23d Oct. in entering Pillau. People faved, and it is expected the Ship will be got off.

The Baltic, Peele, of Whitehaven, from Petersburg, went on fhore upon Gotland 27th September.

The Dolphin, Gillingham, from Swanage to London, was taken by a French Privateer off Brighton; retaken by the Rattler Lugger, and arrived at Portfmouth the 21ft October.

The Francis, of Sunderland, Bromley, in ballaft, has been taken, and is retaken by the Champion Frigate, and arrived at Lover.

The Juno, Guitzer, of Konigsburg, from Chatham, is wrecked near the Scaw.

The Anna Maria, Rabe, from Stettin to London, is loft on the Coaft of Jutland.

The St. Jofeph, Arrarte, from ——— to Bilboa, with linens, &c. detained at Cowes some days since, has been liberated, and failed for her destined Port.

The Einigheid, Poulfen, from Bergen to Naples, is on fhore on the Coaft of Holland, and it is feared will be loft.

The Nylpferd, Groning, from Liverpool to Rotterdam, is loft on the Coaft of Holland.

The Chriftian, Irvin, from Dublin to Memel, is loft near Memel.

The Neptune, Guthree, of Largo, in ballaft, was loft near Pillau 24th ult. Crew faved.

The Commerce, Alderfon, from London to Revel, is on Shore and full of water at Elfinore.

The Charotte Amelia, Jacks, from Sicily to Briftol, was loft near Kidwelley 18th inftant.

The Jamaica Planter, Feard, from Grenada to London; and the Peggy, Frankland, of Scarbro', laden with timber, captured by the Braave Privateer, are carried into Bourdeaux.

The William Pitt, Burgen, from Harwich to Embden, was totally loft 7th inftant, at the entrance of the Ems.

The Anna Maria, Haig, from Quebec to London, was captured 6th init. near Beachy, by two Lugger Privateers, and carried into Dieppe.

A Brig and a Sloop were taken off Beachy Head on the 22d October.

From the French Papers.—Le Sorcier Privateer of St. Maloes has taken and carried into Port an Englifh Sloop laden with Brandy, Gin, and Tobacco.—Le Profper Privateer, of Loulogne, has alfo taken and carried in an Englifh Sloop named London, laden with ftones, wood, and fome copper.

Le Wimereux Privateer captured on the 22d September, and carried into Boulogne, an Englifh Sloop laden with planks. The Crew confifted of four people.

The Swedifh Brigs, Hope de la Rofe, from Stockholm to Marfeilles; and Triden, Decher, from Stockholm to Spain, are detained and fent into Portfmouth. The former by the Pluto, and the latter by the Speedy Sloop.

The Polly, Cooper, of Dartmouth, was loft 26th October, t Plymouth.

The de Juffrow, Anderfon, from Dantzic; and the Young Peters, from Amfterdam, are detained, and fent into Portfmouth, by the Speedwell Sloop of War.

The Vrow Elizabeth, Lammefs, from Riga to Ferrol, and the Carlehendearg, Blichert, from Hull to Lilboa, are detained and fent into Yarmouth; the former by the Hawke Cutter, and the latter by the Vixen Gun Brig.

A Brig was captured off Haftings 27th October, by two Luggers, and was afterwards retaken by the Alert.

The Refolution, Syms, from Jamaica to London, was captured 2d October, by the Braave Privateer, retaken on the 9th by the Diamond Frigate, and is brought into Plymouth.

The St. Ifabel, alias Victoria, from Bourdeaux to Cadiz, is detained by the Felix Schooner, and arrived at Plymouth.

The Jupiter, Gibfon, from Memel to London, was deferted by the Crew near the Scaw, having nine feet water in her hold.

The Mercurius, from Amfterdam to Boston, is put into Weymouth, with lofs of rudder.

The John and Thomas, Cuming, from Gothenburg to Perth, foundered at Sea on the 5th October. Crew faved.

The Jane, Harrifon, from Stockholm to London, foundered at Sea 24th October. Crew faved.

Les Bons Enfans, Sundberg, from Dantzic to London, is totally loft off Yarmouth. Crew faved.

The Rebecca, ———, from St. Thomas's, bound to Tonningen, paffed Portfmouth 31ft October, after a paffage of 49 days. A paffenger addreffed from her, reports that a violent hurricane took place through the Iflands on the 3d and 4th of September, in which a great number of Veffels were loft, viz. at Antigua, 58 Sail and a Packet; at St. Bartolomew's, 50 fail; at Dominica, 26 out of 28, among them faid to be a Sloop of War; at St. Thomas's, 44 Sail, 5 of them Britifh.—Letters from Barbadoes of the 18th September, confirm the account of the hurricane, and add that fix Veffels were driven on Shore there, viz. Perfeverance, Hayes, from London; Sybil, from ditt, (retaken); Feffey, Moran, of Dublin; Schooner Friendfhip, both to pieces.—American Ship Thames, bilged; and Sloop En ——, ———.

A Veffel drove on Shore near Yarmouth 30th October, without any perfon on board, and is wrecked. The Boats are marked Ceres, of Sunderland.

[*To be continued.*]

Eng.d by Ridley from an Original Miniature

PRINCE of BOUILLON.

NOUS NE CHANGEONS JAMAIS

Pub. by I.Gold,103, Shoe Lane, March ,30 1805.

BIOGRAPHICAL MEMOIR OF
PHILIP D'AUVERGNE, DUKE OF BOUILLON,
COMMODORE IN HIS MAJESTY'S SERVICE, &c. &c.

" ONE COMMON ZEAL THE MANLY RACE INSPIRES,
ONE COMMON CAUSE EACH ARDENT BOSOM FIRES."
PYE.

IT is with much satisfaction that we undertake the present memoir; as, from the authenticity of its materials, it will tend to counteract certain improper and malevolent statements which have appeared; and as, from the interesting facts which it records, it cannot fail of imparting instruction, and of exciting emulation.

Philip d'Auvergne, now Duke of Bouillon, was born in Elizabeth Castle, in the Island of Jersey, on the 22d of November, 1754. Having shown an early predilection for the Naval Profession, he was, in the year 1770, borne on the books of one of the Royal Yachts, commanded by the late Vice-Admiral Campbell *, as was not unusual, at that period, to fill up the qualifying time for passing examination, while he continued to enjoy the advantages of a *private* education.

In the year 1772, under the patronage of the late Lord Howe, he joined the Flora Frigate, commanded by the late Sir George Collier. In the Flora he made several foreign Voyages, as a Midshipman, particularly to Cronstadt, when, together with all the Officers of that Ship, he had the honour of being presented,

---

* It was this gentleman, we believe, of whom the following humorous anecdote is related :—

After the total defeat of the Marquis de Conflans, in which he bore a conspicuous part, he was proceeding, in company with Lord Anson, to bear the news to the King. His Lordship said to Mr. Campbell, who was then only a Captain, " The King will knight you, if you think proper."—" Truth, my Lord," answered the Captain, who retained the Scottish dialect as long as he lived, " I ken nae use that will be to me."—" But your Lady may like it," replied his Lordship. " Weel then," rejoined the Captain, " his Majesty may knight her if he pleases."

by Lord Cathcart, the British Ambassador at Russia, to the Empress Catherine the IId, and her Court, at Peterhoff, near St. Petersburgh. On their return, they stopped at Copenhagen, where they met with the French Frigate la Flou, in which were embarked several members of the *Academy of Sciences*, of Paris, making observations on the time-keepers of Le Roy and Berthoud. The reciprocal communications which took place between the Officers of the two Frigates were frequent, and were the means of introducing Mr. d'Auvergne to an acquaintance with some of the " *sçavants*," that gave him a taste for, and an ardent wish to embark on similar expeditions. This circumstance may be regarded as one of those incidents which develope the tendency, and draw forth the exertions of genius. The youthful mind, when struck with any particular object, adheres to that object with avidity, and quits it but with pain and regret. So intent was Mr. d'Auvergne on qualifying himself for the pursuits alluded to, that, on the return of the Flora to England, when paid off, he prosecuted his studies of the mathematics, and the theory of his profession, under the most celebrated professors in London, until the Hon. Captain Phipps* having proposed a Voyage of observation to the northern hemisphere, he was presented to that Officer's protection by his patron Lord Howe, and performed the Voyage to Spitzbergen with him in the Racehorse.

We must here be permitted a short digression, in order to notice, that this Voyage was undertaken at the request of the Royal Society, with a view to discover how far navigation might be practicable towards the north pole, and to ascertain, whether there were a possibility of discovering a passage to the East Indies by those frozen regions. The Racehorse and Carcass Bombs, commanded by the Hon. Captain Phipps† and Captain Lutwidge, were accordingly equipped for this enterprise. On the 2d of June, 1773, they sailed from the Nore, and proceeded on their course to the north, without meeting with any quantity of ice to obstruct their passage. On the 31st of July they had

---

* The late Lord Mulgrave.
† *Vide* NAVAL CHRONICLE, Vol. VIII, page 92, *et seq*

reached the latitude of 81° 21' north, when both the Ships became suddenly enclosed within a large body of ice; and they were unavoidably driven, by a strong current, into a Bay, the entrance of which was immediately after closed up by the drifting ice. For four or five days the Crews laboured with indefatigable zeal and perseverance to force a passage, but their exertions were without effect. On the 6th of August their Commanders came to the resolution of hoisting the Boats out, and of endeavouring to save their lives by dragging them across the ice. Accordingly every man was furnished with a certain quantity of provision; they had actually quitted the Ships, and commenced this hazardous attempt; but on the following day the Wind blew from the eastward, and the Ships were observed to move forward. There now appearing some hopes of deliverance, they hastened back; and, on the 10th, the Wind blowing strong from the N.E. attended by a strong current, the ice gave way and began to drift. Every sail was set, and in the course of a few hours they were relieved from the prospect of that miserable and wretched fate which had befallen so many former adventurers. Finding it utterly impossible to penetrate farther to the north than the latitude of 81° 36, and that no practicable passage existed, Captain Phipps determined to return to England, where both Ships arrived in the month of October.

It is particularly worthy of remark, that Mr. d'Auvergne, and Admiral Lord Nelson[*], who embarked in the Carcass, were the only two exceptions of persons admitted on this expedition who were under age. The conduct of Mr. d'Auvergne was particularly noticed and approved by his Captain (Phipps), who, from that time to the day of his death, honoured him with the most distinguished patronage and cordial friendship. The engravings that elucidate the account of the Voyage to Spitzbergen, which was published by Captain Phipps in 1774, were all taken from original sketches made on the spot by Mr.

---

[*] *Vide* NAVAL CHRONICLE, Vol. III, page 160.

d'Auvergne, who was also charged with the Meteorological Registers*.

Still pursuing his profession, in the ensuing winter he embarked in the Asia, with the late Admiral Vandeput, then her Captain, and proceeded in her to Boston, where, during the following spring, he, with some other young Officers, narrowly escaped being detained prisoners by the Americans. This was on the day of the Lexington fight, (April 19, 1775,) when they had strolled as far as the village of Concord with the army†. A few days after this, Mr. d'Auvergne was appointed acting Lieutenant of the Kingsfisher Sloop, and had returned to the Preston, under Admiral S. Graves's Flag, a few days previously to the battle of Bunker's Hill, at which he attended in the Boats‡. He continued sharing in the several arduous services which the siege of Boston occasioned; was in the expedition against Falmouth, in Casco Bay, and was slightly wounded at the destruction of that

---

* The engravings which accompany Captain Phipps's Voyage are :—*A Chart showing the Track of his Majesty's Sloops Racehorse and Carcass, during the Expedition towards the North Pole; View of the Land from Cloven Cliff to Hackluit's Headland, taken July 18th, at 10 P.M.; View of the Land round the Bay where the Racehorse anchored July 4th, at 6 P.M.; View of the Racehorse and Carcass, July 31st; Five Views of the Land round the Seven Islands Bay, taken August the 6th, at 10 P.M.; View of the Racehorse and Carcass, August 7th; The Racehorse and Carcass forcing through the Ice, August 10th: View of an Iceberg; Plan of Fair Haven, with the Islands adjacent, on the North West Coast of Spitsbergen, from an actual Survey taken in 1773; Chart showing the different Courses steered by his Majesty's Sloop Racehorse, from July 3d to August 22d*; with some mathematical plates, and sketches from natural history.

† A detachment of the King's Troops and Marines, under the command of Lieutenant Colonel Smith and Major Pitcairn, having been sent to destroy some military stores, which the Americans had collected at Concord, were met and opposed at Lexington by a large body of the Militia, who obliged them to retire with considerable loss into the town of Boston.

‡ This took place on the 17th of June. The Americans having collected in great force under General Putnam, and thrown up some strong redoubts, General Gage, who commanded in Boston, ordered the Generals, Howe, Clinton, and Pigot, with about 2000 Troops, to attack the enemy's works, which, after an obstinate resistance, were carried at the point of the bayonet. The victory however was dearly bought; 226 of the British were slain, 19 of whom were commissioned Officers, and upwards of 800 wounded; while only 30 wounded Americans, and a few pieces of cannon, were taken.

town, on the 18th of October, 1775*, when his conduct obtained the full approbation of the Admiral. He then left the Preston, and joined the Chatham, of 50 guns, which had recently arrived, bearing the Flag of Admiral Shuldham, who had been appointed to a command on the American Station.

Early in the year 1776, on the evacuation of Boston by General Howe, Admiral Shuldham's Squadron convoyed that Officer, and the Troops under his command, to Halifax. In June the Fleet and Army sailed from Halifax, on an expedition to New York. In the course of the passage to the latter Port, Mr. d'Auvergne was made one of the acting Lieutenants of the Chatham. On the 3d of July the Fleet passed the Bar at Sandy Hook, and anchored off Staten Island, which was taken possession of by the Troops without opposition.

At the subsequent debarkation at Gravesend, on Long Island †, Mr. d'Auvergne commanded a division of Boats. He also attended the Army at the battle of Brooklyn ‡; was afterwards detached on the most active services of the campaign, occasionally on Shore with the Army, or attending it with divisions of Boats on the Rivers; was at the assault of Fort Washington, and at the almost daily skirmishes at New Rochelle, Kingsbridge, and on the White Plains.

In the beginning of December he went with Rear-Admiral Sir Peter Parker, in the Chatham, against Rhode Island ||, where, during the winter, he was selected to execute several

---

* The inhabitants of Falmouth having opposed with violence the loading of a Mast-ship, Admiral Graves directed one of his Captains to proceed thither with some Ships of War, and to demolish the town, unless they delivered up to him all their artillery and small arms. This demand being refused, the Ships opened a heavy cannonade, and in a short time destroyed a hundred and thirty houses, two hundred and seventy-eight store and warehouses, a large new church, the Court-house, and the public library. To complete the demolition of the town, a large body of Seamen and Marines were landed; but the Americans having by this time collected in great force, compelled them to retire to their Boats, with the loss of several Men.

† *Vide* the Biographical Memoir of Sir Peter Parker, Bart. NAVAL CHRONICLE, Vol. XII, page 177.

‡ NAVAL CHRONICLE, Vol. XII, page 178.

|| NAVAL CHRONICLE, Vol. XII, page 180.

commissions, from the Admiral and General, to the American Government at Providence. These he performed so much to their satisfaction, and to that of his patron Lord Howe, that, on the 2d of June, 1777, the latter sent him a commission, as Lieutenant, to command the Alarm, an armed Vessel (late the Mansfield East Indiaman, that had been cut down) fitted with considerable care and force for River service.

Lieutenant d'Auvergne commanded this Vessel on the Seaconnet River, until forced by a detachment of M. d'Estaing's Fleet to destroy it, on the 29th of July, 1778, with the other small naval force round Rhode Island, whose Crews were landed to do duty in the Batteries during the siege. On this occasion Mr. d'Auvergne was, early in August, appointed, by Major General Sir Robert Piggot, Brigade Major to the Brigade of Seamen and Artillery doing duty in that Garrison.

After M. d'Estaing's discomfiture and retreat to the southward, the Officers of the destroyed Vessels proceeded to New York, and severally accounted for the destruction of their respective commands. Having been discharged from farther responsibility, they returned to England, in the Leviathan, in the month of November.

A few days after his arrival, Lieutenant d'Auvergne was appointed First Lieutenant of the Arethusa Frigate, of 32 guns, commanded by Captain Charles Holmes Everitt. He continued in this Ship, on the Channel Station, till February, 1779, when she was wrecked near Ushant, after an action with the French Frigate l'Aigrette.

It was during the captivity which succeeded this disaster, that Mr. d'Auvergne was claimed and recognised by the then reigning Duke of Bouillon, as a member of a branch of his ancient house, long since emigrated*.—Some very tempting offers were made to him, by one of the French Ministers, for quitting the Service of his Country; but, with a becoming spirit, he resisted and resented the degrading proposal. In this conduct he was approved by his illustrious relation; and, on his return to

---

* In the thirteenth century.

England, he had the additional satisfaction of receiving the approbation of the Admiralty.

In the summer of 1780, Mr. d'Auvergne was appointed, as Lieutenant, to command the Lark, a large armed Cutter, which had been purchased to be converted into a Sloop of War. After having been one Voyage in her to the Baltic and the Coast of Scotland, with a Convoy, he was ordered, in January 1781, to fit for foreign Service: he accordingly sailed from Spithead, in the following March, under Commodore Johnstone's orders, for the memorable expedition against the Cape of Good Hope. The Squadron arrived at Porto Praya Road, in the Portuguese Island of St. Jago, after a short and successful passage. Lieutenant d'Auvergne, however, had been detached to Madeira, and consequently was absent on the day of the Praya fight, that strange scene of surprise and confusion. He joined shortly after, and preceded the expedition in the advanced Squadron under Captain Piggot. Early in July these detached Ships fell in with and captured a Dutch East Indiaman, called the Heldwoltemade, just out of Saldanha Bay, and bound to the Island of Ceylon, having on board stores and provisions, and 40,000l. sterling in money. From the Passengers of this Dutch Ship, Mr. d'Auvergne, by his knowledge of the language, drew a correct statement of the situation, number, and force, of the Shipping which they had left in the Bay, to the attack of which he subsequently had the honour to lead. The substance of the information received was, that M. de Suffrein, notwithstanding the damage which his Ships sustained in the Porto Praya fight, had safely arrived, with his whole force, in False Bay, on the 21st of June preceding, and that there were five Dutch East India Ships at anchor in Saldanha Bay, at some distance from the former*. Mr. d'Auvergne having rejoined the Fleet, and communicated his intelligence, it was clear to both the naval and military Commanders of the expedition, that their views on the Cape were entirely frustrated. Commodore Johnstone, however,

---

* *Vide* Commodore Johnstone's Gazette letter, announcing the capture of the Dutch East India Ships in Saldanha Bay.

determined to profit of what was yet within reach, by an attempt upon the Dutch Ships in the Bay of Saldanha. This scheme, by the assistance of Mr. d'Auvergne, was ably and successfully conducted. The Commodore having run in under the Shore, during the night, was enabled, by traverses, to turn into the Bay early in the morning. This was on the 21st of July. The movements of the English were so silent and rapid, that though the enemy were apprehensive of their danger, and had kept their fore-top-sails bent in preparation, they had scarcely time, from the discovery to the coming up of our Ships, to loose them, to cut their cables, and to run the Vessels on Shore. The Boats being instantly manned, our Seamen, with their usual alacrity, boarded the Ships, which were already set on fire by the enemy, and had the good fortune to extinguish the flames, and to save four large Ships, from 1000 to 1100 tons each; but the fire raged with such fury in the Middleburgh, of equal burthen, that all their efforts to save her were ineffectual, and she blew up in less than ten minutes after the Boats had abandoned her. Our Men, however, by a most extraordinary exertion of labour and courage, towed her out stern foremost, and thereby saved the other prizes from destruction.

To the timely arrival of the French Squadron and Troops in False Bay, Holland owed the preservation of the Cape and its dependent settlements; for neither their Troops nor their fortifications were at all capable of resisting the combined naval and land force under Commodore Johnstone and General Meadows. From a review of circumstances, it therefore appears extremely probable, that, had not the British Squadron suffered itself to be surprised in Porto Praya Bay, Suffrein could not have effected his escape; and that, consequently, the Cape must have fallen into our possession. As it was, however, the grand object of the expedition was frustrated, and Commodore Johnstone's enterprise was at an end. But we wish not to depart from the old and generous adage—*de mortuis nil nisi bonum*.

Excepting the Convoy which was detached to the East Indies, the remainder of Commodore Johnstone's Squadron had orders to rendezvous at St. Helena, where Mr. d'Auvergne arrived, in the Lark, on the 20th of August, 1781, after having experienced much distress off the Cape of Good Hope, round which, in company with the Jupiter, he had attended the division for India.

At St. Helena Mr. d'Auvergne received his Commission as Master and Commander, which had been filled up on the 21st of August. His attachment to his venerable patron, Lord Howe, rendered it unadvisable that he should return to England with the details of the late unfortunate expedition, in the Lark, which, by the interest of the Captain's friends, the Commodore had been directed to send with the results. He was therefore made to exchange with the Commander of the Rattlesnake (Clements), and was ordered for a Cruise under Captain Paisley, of the Jupiter, on the Coast of America, and to verify the position of Trinidad*, and to examine into its fitness for an establishment to refresh and recruit Shipping passing outward-bound in those Seas. On this island, since found to be unfit for such purposes, the Rattlesnake was wrecked, in a tornado, on the 2d of October, 1782. Notwithstanding the representation of such a fact, made to the Commodore † on his call there in the Diana Frigate, in the fervour of his enthusiasm, he affected to view it as " a jewel fit to adorn the British Crown ‡;" and gave orders to Captain d'Auvergne, and a few Men, to stay and maintain possession of it, until his Majesty's Ministers should determine, from his report, whether they should retain a possession that was disputed. For three long months the exiles remained there, subsisting upon wild sea-fowls only. They embarked for India on the 28th of December, 1782, on the Bristol, of 50 guns, and a Convoy of Indiamen, accidentally making the island on their outward-bound passage. On their

---

* For a descriptive account of the Island of Trinidad, see the NAVAL CHRONICLE, Vol. VII, page 332.

† Commodore Johnstone, who had removed his broad pendant into the Diana.

‡ The Commodore's own words.

arrival in India, the inquiry which was instituted on the loss of the Rattlesnake, produced to Captain d'Auvergne considerable credit for the temper and discretion with which, during so trying a situation, he had reconciled and inured the Men who were under his orders to the unusual and rigorous privations which they appeared to have been thus inconsiderately exposed to. His *passive* and *respectful deference* to the most extraordinary commands perhaps ever given by a superior Officer to a professional inferior, also obtained high commendation, and were afterwards remembered to his advantage by his gracious Sovereign, who granted him Post rank when he returned from India in January 1784.

Captain d'Auvergne brought with him Sir Edward Hughes's account of the cessation of hostilities in India, and was accompanied by the Hon. Colonel Cathcart, who was the bearer of General Stuart's dispatches to the same purport. On their way home, they called at the Cape of Good Hope; and, while they were at that place, the since notorious *Directeur*, Barras, arrived there from Europe. He was then a Subaltern in the provincial regiment *de Pondicherry*, and, even in that subordinate station, it clearly appeared that he was troublesome to his Colonel, General Comte Conway, who recently died Colonel of one of the Brigade Regiments in our Service.

On his return to England, Captain d'Auvergne found the Duke of Bouïllon waiting his arrival, he having then, through the learned persons whom he had employed in the research, traced to his entire satisfaction the filiation of his branch of the family, which he had been pursuing for many years.

His health having been much impaired during his stay at Trinidad, he was induced, by the advice of the Faculty, to seek a more genial climate. Accordingly, in the autumn of 1784, he passed over to the continent; and, while travelling in the pursuit of health, he endeavoured also to render it the source of mental improvement. In 1785, he was complimented with the honorary degree of LL.D. at one of the German Universities. He returned to pass the winter at the Duke of Bouïllon's seat.

in Normandy, that illustrious personage having, the preceding year, formally adopted him as his son and successor*.

In the course of the winter, he had an opportunity of seeing much of the Duke of Orleans, and of several of the characters who have since figured so conspicuously in the French Revolution. With their sentiments and principles, however, his were so widely different, as to preclude either respect, esteem, or intimacy.

Early in 1786, he came over to England, but left it again in the spring, on a tour through the western provinces of France, in the society of the present Lord Sidney. After having been presented at the Court of the late unfortunate and lamented Louis the XVIth at Fontainbleau, which they some time attended, they passed the principal part of the winter at that of Brussels, whence they returned to England, in February, 1787. In the course of the spring he had the honour of being elected and received a Fellow of the Royal Society. About the same time he also was appointed to the command of the Narcissus Frigate, on the Channel Station. In this Ship he had permission, in acquiring professional experience in the navigation of the Channel, to visit the Ports of Normandy and Bretagne, situated therein. Of this facility he availed himself to be present at the principal experiments made in the famous enterprise at Cherbourg; and, on this stupendous undertaking, he very early submitted an opinion to his patron, then First Lord of the Admiralty, which time has not given him any reason to alter†.

In January, 1790, his health obliged him again to relinquish

---

* Conformably to precedents established in the Dutchy, so far back as during the reign of the 1st Duke Godfrey, the celebrated Chief of the Crusade, and since repeated, and in the time of Louis the XIIIth of France, established the late reigning branch of the house d Auvergne.

† Early in the year 1788, the works which were carrying on at Cherbourg were almost entirely destroyed in a violent gale of Wind. The French Government abandoned the project of repairing them, from a representation of the principal engineers employed, who discovered that, on the rock on which the cones were sunk, were three or four feet of sand; of course, the weight of these enormous machines made the sand at different times give way, so that they could not keep their level. Nearly 200,000l. had been expended on this stupendous rock.

the command of his Ship; and the tottering appearance which all ancient institutions, near to or connected with France, presented at this time, called his attention to his private affairs. The Duke of Bouillon pressingly urging him to come to him, to settle them, he accordingly went, and staid privately in the country, with the Duke, till it was no longer safe for even a stranger, professing the loyal and moral sentiments which he always avowed, to remain. He left France some little time before the Duke of Dorset entered into the discussions which were followed by his return.

The Duke Godefroy of Bouillon died in December, 1793, and was succeeded by his only son, the hereditary Prince James Leopold, who was proclaimed reigning Duke of Bouillon; the oaths of fidelity and allegiance being taken, both to him and to the Prince Successor, the subject of this memoir, by the Governor General, the Administration, and the whole population of the Dutchy.

The Prince Successor of Bouillon had obtained the Royal License of our Gracious Sovereign, in February 1792, to accept the nomination to the succession and titles, to which he was called, on the specified conditions of taking the titles and armorial bearings, and continuing in the service of his country, which no personal motive could induce him to relinquish.

As a lover and patron of the liberal arts, his name was enrolled, as a perpetual member, on the books of the *Society of Arts*, established at the Adelphi; he was also one of the early associates of that which was instituted for the improvement of Naval Architecture, founded by the patriotic genius of the late Mr. Sewel; but, with many others, who saw it degenerate into a club of professional artificers, he ceased his attendance.

Early in 1793, introduced by his intimate friend, the Noble President of the Royal Society of Antiquarians, he was unanimously ballotted as member of that learned body.

In June 1794, our Officer was appointed Captain of the Nonsuch, and Commander of a Flotilla of Gun-boats, stationed for the cover of the Islands of Jersey and Guernsey, where they arrived in August. In the month of December following, he received the honourable commission to succeed Earl Balcarras, in the controul and direction of the bounties granted by Government to the French *lay* Emigrants in the islands of Jersey and Guernsey*; and, in January 1795, as Commandant of the Flotilla on the Station, he was vested with the supreme direction and inspection of the organization of the military *corps* of Officers raised from those refugees. The communication with the Royalist parties was also committed to his charge. His mode of administering the munificence of Government to those unfortunate victims to their faith and loyalty, exposed him to the envious calumny of a biographical libeller†; an attack which procured him an address, signed by all that were venerable and respectable among those noble victims, acknowledging, in the name of the whole, that the liberal delicacy which he exercised in the distribution of this munificence, was such as not to allow them to feel it as eleemosynary.

His direction of the emigrant *corps* became one of the ostensible causes for what he subsequently suffered at Paris, when he went thither to establish his claims of indemnities for his sequestrated property after the Peace of Amiens. The principles by which he directed these patriotic adherents to the ancient *regime*, may be seen in a *Confidential Address*, wherein he endeavoured to urge their loyalty to action. This, the indiscretion of some of them exposed, and it was afterwards published, as a State Paper, in one of the Annual Registers, during the late War.

A short time before the death of Earl Howe, feeling his situation with a Flotilla at Jersey too passive for an active disposition, he consulted his patron respecting a removal to such a situation in the Fleet as his seniority in the Service entitled him to. A very long and detailed letter from his noble and revered

---

* In the participation of these bounties the clergy were always administered by their Bishops, who, so far from deserving the calumnies pointed at them, received no greater portion than the meanest of their curates, and all under the directions of a committee of Government in London.

† We are in full possession of the name, character, &c. of the scribbler here alluded to; but we shall not drag him from that oblivion to which he has been long most justly consigned.

patron *dissuaded him from that* project; strongly inculcating, that it was not the rate of the Ship, or the evidence of the situation, that gave importance to the services of an Officer; and urging him to continue to exert his best abilities in the situation of confidence in which his Majesty's Ministers had placed him; as they were the best judges of who were to be passive, and who were to be defensive, in the public service.

In the year 1798, the Duke of Bouillon's professional services were honoured with the distinction of a Broad Pendant*, under which he continued to command the defensive Flotilla at Jersey till the Peace of Amiens.

This became an eventful period, a remarkable epoch in his life.

For restitution or indemnity for the alienated domains, for his feudal rights, and for his other property in the succession of the Dukes of Bouillon, Captain d'Auvergne, their legitimately designed successor, was counselled by some of our most distinguished lawyers, to apply to the Government of France. He was advised, also, by his friends, to assert rights which were the more important to him, as, after the preceding eight years of an uninterrupted service of his country, in a situation of trust, in which considerable sums of the public money had been administered, although not rich at his entrance upon that service, he was considerably poorer at its close. Accordingly, after the Definitive Treaty of Amiens had been ratified, he solicited, and obtained permission to go to Paris, to consult proper persons respecting the prosecution of his claims, and to endeavour to recover some of that property, the inheritance of which had been so solemnly entailed upon him. With these views, he provided himself with the usual passports from the Secretary of State for the Foreign Department, which, as a farther precaution, he procured to be countersigned by M. Otto, the *Chargé des Affaires* of the *(then)* Republic, here. Thus provided, with the addition

---

* This, for the expediency of service, was hoisted on board what his calumniator calls a Gun-boat; but which he should have informed himself, was a *rated Port Ship*, although of a construction particular for the services on which it was wanted.

of a letter of introduction to Mr. Merry, from Lord Hawkesbury's Office, he landed in Normandy, accompanied by a friend, Major Dumaresq, of the 31st regiment of the militia of Jersey, and two servants, and proceeded directly to Paris; acting with that circumspection, and having recommended the same to those with him, which prudence seemed more particularly to prescribe to an Officer, whose Services might perhaps not have escaped the notice of a Government from which he was about to claim justice with respect to his rights. He reached Paris on the 27th of August, 1802, and immediately occupied himself in putting his claims in a train to be submitted to the decision of the French Government. His leisure hours were employed in viewing the Louvre, and the rich collections which it had lately received. He visited the Thuilleries, to view the parade of *Quintidi* (the 2d of September) but declined presentation, from motives for which he conceived his friends would do him justice. Afterwards, however, he was given to understand, that visiting the Thuilleries, or indeed Paris, without the ceremonial of presentation, and humiliation before the Consul, was interpreted as a disrespect, which certainly was far from his intention. Having a leisure hour, he wished to satisfy himself respecting their much spoken of military exhibition, the parade of *Quintidi*; and he had been told from Mr. Merry, that he might innocently satisfy his curiosity, by presenting himself as an English Officer in his uniform, and retiring when he was gratified, which was all that he did. He was, however, on the morning of the 7th of September, about seven o'clock, surprised in his bed at the *Hotel de Rome (Fauxbourg St. Germain)*, where he lodged, by a number of ferocious looking men, whom, upon explanation, he found to be *sbires*, or persons of the Police, headed by a Commissary and two Exempts, who set about rifling his room, sedulously collecting every scrap of paper, and prying into the most private corners, rudely summoning him to attend them to the Minister of the Police, (the Ex-Priest Fouché,) who desired to see him immediately, scarcely allowing him to put on his clothes, or the horses to be put to the job carriage which he used. He, however, hurried himself, and after sending his servant to announce this unpleasant event to Mr. Merry, whose hotel was within two doors, he proceeded, with an Exempt of the Police in the carriage with him, and eight or ten *sbires*, or Officers, attending on foot, with the Commissary, who had made notes of the arrest, and who carried the private papers. Arrived at the *bureau de la Police General*, he was escorted up to the very top of the house, into a sort of anti-room, or garret, in which were five or six *employés*, or runners, of the vilest appearance, who kept going in and out every moment. About an hour after his first introduction to this place, he was shown into an office in another part of the building, where sat a M. Desmarets, Secretary to the Minister Fouché, who said he was charged by his principal to ask him a few questions; which were answered by asking a leading one, as, to what motive might be ascribed the violation of the laws of hospitality which he at that moment experienced, and had suffered at the hotel where he lodged?— The Secretary's reply was, that the Minister had a *" prevention"* (prejudice), a great *" prevention"* against him, for his services during the War; and sought to prevail upon him to avow, that Mr. Pitt had determined to wage a War of extermination in the bosom of France; that Mr. Windham had planned it; and that the Captain, by the influence of his name, as Duke of Bouillon, and his connexions in the Western Provinces, had directed its execution, to the utmost of his power, and the great detriment of the interests of the Republic. To this he replied, that he conceived that the Treaty of Amiens had terminated all discussions of the kind: he had no explanations to give of any part of his conduct antecedent to that epoch; and disdained to answer to such unqualified accusations, as were made with the most odious and insulting epithets against Messieurs Pitt and Windham, whose confidential agent they accused him of being. He professed his readiness to answer to facts, but declined combating *" preventions,"* which he could not think to be seriously the cause of the cruel insult which he experienced. After about an hour's discussion with this M. Desmarets, he was remanded to the same vile place which he had quitted, still more vilely attended than in the morning. He obtained leave to address a letter to

Mr. Merry, stating his then painful situation, which, notwithstanding M. Desmarets' promise, he afterwards found was never delivered. M. Desmarets informed him, that he would be called before the "*Magistrat de quartier*," to answer to these "*preventions*" of M. Fouché, for whom he patiently waited till two o'clock. When called before him, who was likewise an ex-priest, of the name of Faridel, he was ushered through the public hall of the building, where two *Emigrés*, who had been under his orders at Jersey, were waiting, to see and identify him, if necessary, as the person who had commanded the Naval department in that Island during the War, and had been the means of much mischief, as they pretended, to the Republic. To M. Faridel's questions, which he observed were written, and of the same tendency as those of M. Desmarets, he answered in monosyllables, conceiving it to be the only way that "*preventions*" should be treated. M. Faridel kept him nearly an hour, but suffered it to escape him, that he did not see the motive or "*but*" of his detention; and the Captain was conducted into the midst of the same vile assemblage that he had before been amongst. Here one, a little more decent than the rest, got a superior to come in, a sort of Commissary, who told him, that the Minister, Fouché, was going to *Malmaison*, to take the Consul's commands upon his detention; such importance did they affect to attach to what the Magistrate appeared not to comprehend. The tedious long day was drawing to a close, when Mr. Merry sent a message by a servant, desiring to be informed whither the prisoner was to be conveyed, if removed from his then situation; a circumstance which he had been in hopes that he would have been informed of by Mr. Merry; but, seeing no prospect of immediate release, he obtained, by means of his servant, who was allowed to wait without, a cup of coffee, the first refreshment which he had had that day. M. Fouché was in and out of the hotel several times in the course of the day, but did not deign to occupy himself an instant with the situation of Captain d'Auvergne.

An English Officer's liberty unjustly violated, was not of

sufficient moment to command a minute of the attention of an ex-monk, indulging in luxury and pride. He did not, as his Commissary, who perhaps was employed to deceive, had said, go to *Malmaison,* but went to dine with the Consul Cambaceres, and, at ten o'clock, the same person who had mentioned at first his going to the First Consul, came in and told the prisoner, that from Cambaceres' dinner the Minister had gone to the opera; he, therefore, must quietly go to the Temple for the night. The Captain offered to pay for a room in the Police till morning, which was refused him: and an *exempt* entered, who, with two *sbires,* conducted their prisoner down to the Courtyard, where a *fiacre* was waiting, into which they entered and proceeded to the Temple, within whose awful and blood-stained gate he was received about eleven o'clock, and ushered through three or four heavily-ironed wickets, to the *greffe.* Here his appearance was minutely detailed, and registered, after which he was conducted to the *keep,* or tower of the temple, through as many more iron doors as he had already passed, to the apartments which had been occupied by the late unfortunate Royal Family, in the anti-room of which he was shocked by the appearance of a rude ferocious half-naked figure, partly rolled in a blanket, and lying on a straw bag. It reared itself half up, as if disturbed by the grating of the iron doors on their hinges, and muttered, in a low and hollow tone of voice, " *Quoi donc, une autre victime! est-ce que cela ne finira jamais?*" The hideous aspect of this pale and wan figure excited horror, and may partly be conceived by those who have minutely examined the late Sir Joshua Reynolds's famous picture of Ugolini. The Captain hastened through this dismal dungeon to an inner room, to which he was shown, and which had been occupied by the beautiful and virtuous Princess Elizabeth. He stifled his complaints, which perhaps might have been just, as he was persuaded, that all that a prison could have of horrors, were found here; but the recollection of what virtue and grandeur these melancholy walls had within the few last fleeting years contained, silenced every selfish reflection. Here he was deposited by his rough guide, who requested him to pay for the candle which he left him, and proffered him his services. He bribed this *garçon* to procure him some *simple refreshment from without*. *Simple* he required it to be, for he had been cautioned, as he came down the stairs of the Police to proceed to the Temple, to be aware of what he ate and drank in the abode that he was going to; " *Le sage entend à demi mot.*"—" *On y debite des ragouts Italiens,*" was added, and it was understood as a friendly hint.

Tempted by the liberality of his new guest, the turnkey returned with bread and a cold fowl, with an uncorked bottle of wine, from without, which refreshment had become necessary to nature, now almost exhausted; and after significantly pointing to a straw bed and filthy prison blanket, added, " *Voila ou vous pouvez reposer,*" and was retiring, when, upon inquiry who the wretch apparently suffering in the anti-room was, he replied by shrugging his shoulders, and added, in a whisper, " *C'est un mouton, fermez bien votre porte,*" and left the prisoner to his reflections. Imagination soon presented him with the scenes, the melancholy scenes which those silent walls had encompassed: how, therefore, could he complain? He passed the night leaning upon a poele, or stove, which had been placed in the centre of the room, musing on the extraordinary cruelty of his situation, yet patiently and calmly waiting the official interference of his Majesty's Minister Plenipotentiary, who, he had no doubt, would, with the dignity becoming his Majesty's representative, claim and rescue from the jaws of despotic tyranny, an English Officer, who could not on any ground be accused of crime, unless that of being an Englishman were considered to be one. As he had not been ordered " *au secret,*" that is, under close confinement, he was in the morning permitted to take the air in a sort of court, called the garden, which surrounded the *keep*. In this walk he met a person whom he had some knowledge of before, M. Fauche, the celebrated bookseller of Neufchatel, who was confined for having been connected with a Bareuth correspondence, and who explained what was meant by a *mouton*, who is a villain disguised, put in the way of those who are detained upon slight pretexts, to endeavour, by exciting commise ration for apparent ill treatment, to betray the innocent into some unguarded expressions of indignation against the supposed authors of the cruelty, and thereby give a hold for farther persecution. This universal usage, in all the houses of detention, will convey an idea of the *equitable* practice of the late Consular Government. When Captain d'Auvergne expressed his indignation to the *concierge*, or keeper of the Temple, for this cruel illiberality, he ingenuously pleaded the obligations which he was under by his instructions; and, at the intervention of the confidential lawyer who had undertaken the care of his private concerns, the *mouton* was removed to another part of the *keep*; and, by the firmness of the same friend, decent bedding and refreshment were allowed to be brought in to the prisoner from without. He was also allowed, on the third day, to be attended by his servant, upon condition, however, of the latter being considered as a prisoner likewise.

At the moment, on the morning of the 9th of September, when the wickets were opened, he hoped for his release; but they were only unbolted for the admission of the friend who had accompanied him to Paris, and who came thither as ignorant as himself of even the probable cause of the detention of either of them. It appeared that Mr. Merry's representation and remonstrance to the Minister for Foreign Affairs, Citizen Talleyrand, remained without answer. This disrespect to the representative of his Master, and his Country, occasioned more pain to Captain d'Auvergne than even his own cruel situation did, as he was confident that that would be of but short duration, though he had not the satisfaction to obtain intimation of the cause of his confinement, farther than the idle pretext which had been suggested in M. Desmarets' conversation. This state of uncertainty continued until the 12th of September, in the morning, when the keeper of the Temple brought the glad tidings of liberation, with directions for the prisoners to call at the *bureau de la Police*, the next day at noon, for their papers. This they did, as prescribed, and had an interview with M. Desmarets, who much urged Captain d'Auvergne to write to the Minister, and state that Messieurs Pitt and Windham had engaged him to employ all unjustifiable means of destruction against the Republic;—in short, to avow all the infernal plots which their black minds presented to their troubled imaginations. This he indignantly spurned at, and absolutely declined entering into any sort of correspondence with M. Fouché. On the following day they were called, by a note from the *Prefect Dubois*, to the *bureau de la Prefecture Générale de la Police*, and had each a passport delivered to them, very equivocally worded, tending to expose them to every sort of embarrassment in their progress through the Country, which they were commanded to depart from, and to leave the territory of the Republic in twenty-four hours; which all who know Paris, the roads, and rate of posting, will readily admit to be a physical impossibility. On the day of their departure they were provided with proper passports from his Majesty's Minister Plenipotentiary, those of Lord Hawkesbury having been taken away. Those of Mr. Merry were countersigned by the Minister Talleyrand. The Captain, with great satisfaction, ordered post-horses, and left his interests and fortune to be pursued by agents, to whom he was obliged to confide them; having thus unjustifiably been expelled like an outcast, from a country which he had respected as at peace with his own, after the publication of the Treaty concluded at Amiens, under which he had conceived himself entitled to protection, in common with every other Englishman. Had pleasure, or idle curiosity, been the motive of his excursion to Paris, perhaps he would not have complained of the insult which he experienced; but, after having exhausted his very limited resources in the service of his Country, he had been driven to seek to recover some of that property which he confidently believed that the Treaty of Peace would restore and secure to him.

Captain d'Auvergne respectfully submitted his case to his Majesty's Ministers, and it became the subject of conversation in the House of Commons; but we believe no determination was formed, nor has any step been taken on the subject.

At the renewal of hostilities, however, our Officer's services were again called forth, in the situation which he formerly filled; and in September, 1803, the Severn, of 44 guns, fitted at Woolwich, was sent to him to receive his broad Pendant; the

States of Jersey having manifested their confidence in his exertions, by a liberal vote of bounties to such Seamen as would serve under his command, one hundred of whom were promptly raised in the Island.

Already a member, as Duke of Bouïllon, of two celebrated Equestrian Orders on the Continent, he was, in November 1803, at a Chapter General of the Capitulary Order of St. Joachim, elected a member of the Grand Cross of that Association of German Princes, whose device is order, and whose motto " *Dei Legi et Principi*.

Our readers are already in possession of the fate of the Severn*. The unusually heavy gales of Wind, which prevailed during last winter, were severely felt about Jersey and Guernsey: after breaking all her anchors, parting a Line of Battle Ship's mooring chain, and a 22-inch cable, she was cast ashore in the month of December last. Happily, however, she struck in such a situation, that, by the indefatigable exertions of the Officers and Men, no lives were lost; and though the Ship, from age and long service extremely weak, has been totally wrecked, her stores and materials have been saved, from amidst an impetuous tide, raging among a labyrinth of rocks and shoals.

At the period of writing the present memoir, we understand that the gallant Commodore is in daily expectation of being appointed to another Ship, on the same Station, his services in that quarter being considered of peculiar importance.

HERALDIC PARTICULARS.

The following particulars, the authenticity of which may be fully depended on, will inform the reader of the family connexions of the Duke of Bouïllon, and will farther tend to contradict the calumnious assertions of the anonymous libeller to whom we have before alluded.

Philip d'Auvergne was the fourth, and now the only surviving son of Charles d'Auvergne, Esq. and Miss Elizabeth Le Geyt, his first wife, daughter of Philip Le Geyt, Esq. Chief Civil Magistrate of the Royal Court, and President of the States of Jersey.

---

* *Vide* page 56.

Charles d'Auvergne, Esq. and his only brother, James d'Auvergne, Esq. both received commissions in the Army while at Greenwich Academy, where they were educated; one in the 7th Regiment of Foot, and the other in Frampton's *Corps.* Charles, the father of the Duke of Bouillon, quitted the Army for his health, but was in the expedition on the Coast of France, in 1758, with the Duke of Marlborough, and in his family; his Grace afterwards gave him a *nominal* appointment, on the Ordnance Establishment, merely to free him from personal services in the militia, to which every inhabitant of the Island is subject, unless attached to some part of the King's service.

It was on this expedition that he renewed his acquaintance with Lord Howe, which was afterwards of such advantage to his son, the subject of the above memoir. Neither of the brothers was concerned in trade, though they undoubtedly honoured the respectable character of the English Merchants; but James continued in the Army, was Equerry to the King in the early part of the present reign, and retired, as a Major-General, to Southampton, where he died, in December, 1799, universally regretted and respected, after having been Mayor of that ancient Corporation.

The Duke of Bouillon has two half brothers, by his father's second marriage to Miss Bandinel, daughter to the Seigneur de Meleschcs, and head of one of the most ancient families in the Island. This family is also connected, maternally, with the de Carteret and Lempriere families; and, by the former, has affinity with those of the English noble families, of kindred with, and descended from, the great Lord Granville, Viscount Thynne, of Spencer Llansdowne, Bath and Carteret, &c. Both the Duke's brothers are in his Majesty's service.

NAVAL ANECDOTES, COMMERCIAL HINTS, RECOLLECTIONS, &c.

NANTES IN GURGITE VASTO.

REMOVAL OF CONTAGION.

THE pre-eminence of the Navy of this country over every marine establishment of the world, whether military or commercial, is universally acknowledged; yet the permanence of this superiority must unfortunately depend, not only on the bravery of the British Tars, which we would fondly imagine to be essential in the soil of their nativity, but to the expedients that modern ingenuity has discovered. Pfaff, Professor of Chemistry at Kiel, has inserted in the Journal du Nord the following article, which will deserve the attention of the Board of Admiralty:—

" In the Danish Frigate Frederikstein, the Captain had directed frequent fumigation from the oxygenated muriatic acid, and the Crew enjoyed almost uninterrupted health, although the Ship was crowded with an uncommon number of Soldiers, destined to complete the Garrison of St. Croix. We all know the destructive effects on the ligneous material, from the decomposition of the metallic matter employed in Ship-building. On examining the Vessel we have named, after its return to Copenhagen, it has been found, that the ferruginous bolts and fastenings have not in the least degree been injured by the acid vapour. This circumstance, noticed by Mr. Schell on the authority of Holenberg, who has been placed both in the situation of a Captain and a Shipbuilder, gives to this mode of purification a decided preference over other means that have been employed. We will only mention one instance: we allude to the method of lining, or white-washing, which materially accelerates the destruction of the Ship, by preventing the aqueous evaporation."

At a period like the present, when a sort of general quarantine is adopted throughout Europe, the subsequent communication may be of some importance. It is given, on the authority of a learned foreign Professor, as a means of purifying a Ship, House, or Hospital, without removing the inhabitants.

To effect this, the operator may take a small portable chaffing dish, in which an earthen pipkin is placed, provided with some marine salt, or muriate of soda. Upon this should be gradually poured small quantities of the sulphuric acid, in order that the disengagement of the muriatic gas should not be precipitately effected. This apparatus may be conveyed, not only to the different apartments, but, for the greater security, to the corners of each of them, and it may be repeated, without any inconvenience, as frequently as the prudence of the practitioner shall deem necessary.

To augment the efficacy of these fumigations, to the quantity of marine salt required may be added two drachms of the black oxyde of manganese in fine powder. The same result may be obtained without the aid of fire, by introducing into a common flask, or other suitable vessel, the following active ingredients:

Muriatic acid, four ounces;

Black oxyde of manganese in powder, two drachms; Nitrous acid, half a drachm.

From this admixture will arise a volatile fluid, expanding in every direction, penetrating every crevice, and which may be stopped at pleasure, by a cork applied to the mouth of the flask from which it is emitted.

FLOATING MORTAR BATTERY.

A FLOATING Mortar Battery, for the bombardment of the enemy's Ports, has been invented by Mr. Congreve, son of General Congreve, of the Artillery, which is proof both against shells and red hot balls. It is said to be so contrived, that though provided both with masts and sails for any Voyage, yet they can be securely disposed of in less than a quarter of an hour, so that the Battery then presents nothing but a mere *hull*, with sloping sides, upon the water, which is rowed by forty Men under cover of the bomb-proofs, and may, by the peculiar construction of the masts and rigging, be brought under sail again as expeditiously as dismantled. The rudder and moorings are *entirely* under water, and protected by the bomb-proof, so that no disappointment as to them can possibly arise. The Battery is armed with four large mortars for bombardment, and four 42-pounder carronades for self-defence, though from being covered with plates and bars of iron, she can neither be set fire to, nor be carried by boarding. Four such Vessels, though they are not more than 250 tons burthen each, and draw less than 12 feet water, would throw upwards of 500 shells into any place in one tide, and with the greatest effect and precision; both because from their construction they have nothing to apprehend from approaching the enemy's Batteries, and because from the peculiar contrivance of the mortar-beds, the elevation of the mortars is not affected by the rolling or pitching of the Vessel. Several of our most eminent Naval Men have seen and approved of the contrivance, and it is said that Ministers have attended to this gentleman's plans, and have it in contemplation to institute, with all expedition, vigorous and regular bombardments of such of the enemy's Ports as contain any considerable accumulation of their Flotilla.

THE JAIL FEVER.

THE Jail Fever, according to a modern writer, is occasioned by two noxious airs combined. One of these airs is destroyed by lime water, and the other by the vapour of vinegar. Ninety-five Men of a Ship of the Line being infected with the Jail Fever, were sent to the Hospital, and the Captain, who had recovered from it, had lime water sprinkled over the deck, guns, and gun-carriages, which were then washed clean: the sides within, beams, &c. were also white-washed with lime mixed with size. Fires were lighted on shot placed on the bottoms of half tubs, and the shot, after being heated, were made cool with vinegar, which occasioned sufficient vapour. This last was repeated every day for a week, at the expiration of which time the Ship was free from contagion.

ENGLISH GRATITUDE.

A YOUNG Man, a Midshipman, whose father holds a situation in Covent Garden Theatre, was taken prisoner during the last Spanish War, and carried to Peru, in South America, where he remained on parole for some years. During this period an accident brought him acquainted with a lady, a near relation of a very high female personage in that kingdom of New Spain, whose influence at length procured his liberty; some time after which he returned to England. In the pursuit of his profession he had the fortune to have a birth on board the Ship, perhaps the most successful in capturing the Spanish prizes lately arrived in our Ports. It happened that this young man was detached with a party of Seamen, to take possession of a valuable prize just taken; when, upon boarding the Ship, he found, to his utter astonishment, the very lady to whose kind attentions he had been under so many obligations. It was now his singular fortune to have his case exactly reversed, and to enjoy the supreme felicity of being able to repay his obligations with a large interest. The circumstance was no sooner made known to his Shipmates, than with the generosity so characteristic of British Seamen, the Officers and Crew immediately agreed to restore her property to their illustrious captive. All her large and beautiful vessels of pure gold, an immense quantity of the most valuable jewels, all her costly furniture, and property of every description to an exceedingly large amount, with which she was returning to her native country, were restored to her: thus nobly proving, that humane and generous treatment of a British Seaman in misfortune, will never fail to be gratefully remembered by his gallant companions, when occasion shall present itself. The fortunate Midshipman (whose share of prize-money cannot be less than between 4 and 5000l.) has taken his illustrious friend under his protection during her stay in this country.

FORTITUDE AND HUMOUR OF A BRITISH TAR.

A SHORT time since, John Ryan, a Seaman of his Majesty's Ship Raisonable, after suffering a considerable time in the Royal Hospital at Haslar with a bad leg, was relieved by the amputation of it by Mr. Dodds, one of the Surgeons of the establishment. During the operation he neither uttered a sigh, or groan, or single syllable; but when carried back to his bed he requested one parting look at the limb, to which he then addressed the following serio-comic apostrophe:—" You d—d ungrateful rascal, who after helping me out of many scrapes, and into many prisons,.for the last two years have been a miserable torment to me; I thank God that in now losing you I am become comparatively at ease!"

SCALE OF EUROPEAN SHIPPING.

SIR Walter Raleigh made a very ingenious calculation of the maritime power of Europe in his time; and Sir William Petty, from better lights, gave another calculation, which was long considered as a correct standard. He thought that the Dutch had about 900,000 tons of Shipping; Great Britain 500,000; Sweden, Denmark, and the trading towns in Germany, 250,000; Portugal and Italy, 250,000; and France, about 100,000. Since that period, however, very great alterations have taken place.

About sixty years ago, on the supposition of the Shipping of Europe being divided into twenty parts, the following was given, as a scale of the proportions belonging to the respective Powers:—

Great Britain	*Six.*
The United Provinces	*Six.*
The Subjects of the Northern Crowns	*Two.*
The trading Cities of Germany and the Austrian Netherlands	*One.*
France	*Two.*
Spain and Portugal	*Two.*
Italy and the rest of Europe	*One.*

A calculation of this kind might be serviceable at the present day. Besides exhibiting the state of commerce, it might serve as a standard, by which to ascertain how far the respective nations rise and sink in that respect: for, as these proportions vary, it is evident that the general aspect of affairs must vary also. Thus, should France ever acquire as great a proportion of trade and naval force as Britain, it would be of far greater consequence to her than al the extension of territory which she has hitherto made.

CORRESPONDENCE.

MR. EDITOR,

AS your invaluable Work is the vehicle of every species of information which concerns or interests the Naval World; and as every particular which tends to the advancement of a science so important to Great Britain and the world in general, as that of Navigation, will, I am persuaded, be favourably received by you; I have reason to hope that you will admit into your excellent Miscellany the following brief description of a newly invented Sextant, for taking celestial observations; and of some essential improvements which have been recently made in the construction of the Mariner's Compass, particularly of the Azimuth Compass, which is used for determining the variation of the magnetic needle at Sea.

It would be superfluous for me to attempt a description of the great importance of these instruments to the Navigator. It would be equally so to describe the numerous defects to which they are subject, and the considerable errors in determining a Ship's place at Sea, which are experienced by the most expert and scientific observers, in consequence of the unknown errors of the Sextant, as well as of those which are found in the reckoning, in consequence of the defects of the Compass.

The methods of determining the longitude, the effect of the genius and labours of several distinguished Men, particularly of our own country, have been carried to a wonderful degree of accuracy; and the precepts which have been detailed with so much judgment, science, and clearness, by a MASKELYNE and a MACKAY, have been, in innumerable instances, carried into practice by careful observers, with instruments which had been improved by the mechanical skill of a RAMSDEN. But although the accuracy of the precept, the attention of the observer, and the ingenuity of the artist, have frequently been so combined as to promise the utmost precision in the determination, and to fix a result which should be considered as a standard; subsequent observations, made with equal care, by the same precepts, and even with the same instruments, have seldom been found to correspond therewith, while there have existed no means of ascertaining the truth or falsehood of any individual observation.

There is not the least reason to doubt, that these differences, which are generally very considerable, arise chiefly from the

Imperfection of the instruments in general use; and although means have been pointed out for reducing such inaccuracies, it does not appear that they have ever approached to perfection.

The new Sextant, which, from its figure, may be called a DOUBLE SEXTANT, (and as it answers the purpose for which two Sextants are generally taken to Sea,) is extremely simple in its' construction; and its size and weight are but very little greater than of those in common use. Its formation differs from the latter in having *two graduated arches* and *two indices*, by which it possesses the peculiar properties of *always exhibiting the index error*, (the most common error of the Sextant,) if any; the results of which will, of course, be obviated; and should there happen to exist, from any cause whatever, (that is to say, from the contraction or expansion of the metal, by cold or heat, in varying climates, &c.) the least degree of error, it may, at all times, be exactly determined and allowed for: so that in no case can any error, in a determination of latitude or of longitude, arise from this cause. For, in taking an observation, the two indices may be moved, almost at the same instant, in opposite directions, so as precisely to correct each other.

Another peculiar advantage is, that of allowing a *second observation to be taken without shifting the instrument* from the eye. Because no sooner shall an observation be taken by means of one arch, than, the index being clamped, a second observation may be instantly taken with the other arch, and equally correct. These are singular conveniences; especially as it frequently happens that, after taking one observation, before the angle on the arch can be read off, and the instrument adjusted for a second observation, the object becomes obscured. Observations are therefore made by the new instrument, with a saving of time and trouble, and with greater accuracy than heretofore.

Hence it will appear, that the principal errors of the Sextant hitherto in general use are obviated; that consequently determinations of latitude and longitude by celestial observations, and the angles taken in surveying, will be so much the more correct.— To the Navigator and Surveyor it will also prove the more acceptable, because they may vary their observations from different parts of the arch, even when the distance is from 90 to 100 degrees.

The divisions of the arches and the nonius divisions are executed with the utmost degree of precision, by the methods adopted and the identical engine used by the celebrated and much regretted *Ramsden;* and the telescopes are of a description very superior to those formerly used for the best Sextants, having a much larger field of view, and by which objects will appear much more distinct than usual.

The foregoing are the advantages of the new Sextant; an instrument which, more than any other, will be found to facilitate and determine, to perfection, the important problem of the longitude. The following observations on the Compass will show how much this valuable instrument has likewise been improved:—

It is well known among Mariners that the Compasses generally used have been liable to many and great defects : that it seldom happens that the centre of motion and centre of gravity are to be found in the same place; and that the card and needle have been subject to a great deal of unnecessary motion, arising from friction, &c. Nor are these and several other common, yet very gross defects, confined to the common Compasses alone; since they will be found in all the best azimuth and other Compasses of the superior description. An error in the construction of the centre point, or pin, is also common to most of them; as well as that, by the common mode of placing the gimbals, they are liable to a great deal of motion, arising from that of the Ship, which is completely avoided by the present mode of construction.

The graduated stop, or *nonius*, applied to Dr. Knight's and other azimuth Compasses, for taking the bearings more minutely, being placed vertically, is also the means, when used, *of pushing the card off its centre*, thereby injuring the centre point, and thus losing, in great measure, its utility.

In the new Compass these defects are obviated; perhaps to the highest degree of which the instrument is susceptible; as this is so formed that the centre of motion and centre of gravity will always be found in the same point. The gimbals act upon a very peculiar and improved principle, which precludes the motion that would otherwise be communicated by the rolling and pitching of the Ship. By the improper situation of the weight in the kettle of the Compass, it is likewise commonly subject to a great deal of motion in a rough Sea, which might be avoided, and is actually obviated in the new Compass, by its being so differently placed, that, however the instrument may be agitated, it will preserve its accustomed stability.—An azimuth may therefore be taken with correctness, although the Ship's motion be very considerable.

The card is fitted with an agate, and the point beneath is so constructed and so short as to have very little of that vibration to which the centre points of the common Compass are subject. The needle is of a new form, so fashioned as never to deviate, when placed without the attractive atmosphere of iron, in the slightest degree from the *real magnetic meridian*; and it is so tempered as to retain its magnetism for the longest period of time.

The graduated circle is equally correct with the divisions of the Sextant; and the nonius, which is *horizontal*, upon a new and original construction, is very peculiarly fitted to give the correct bearing with the utmost precision.

Added to all these, by another invention, no sooner is an azimuth or bearing taken, than the card is, in an instant, borne off the centre point, and *remains fixed at the observed bearing*, for any time, at the pleasure of the observer, until it again be suffered to act; whereby likewise *both the point and agate are effectually preserved when out of use.*

An apparatus, or sun-dial, for showing the exact variation of the needle, by inspection, whenever the sun is not obscured, is also occasionally fitted to the new Compass.

I need not enlarge farther upon the advantages of the new instruments.—By the Sextant it is presumed that the longitude will be astronomically ascertained with greater accuracy than heretofore; and by the Compass, that the dead-reckoning will be much more correct than usual; which must be of especial consequence in thick weather, or when observations for the longitude cannot, from that or any other circumstance, be made. For the purposes both of land and of maritime surveying, the advantages both of the Sextant and Compass may be experienced in the highest degree. The accuracy of every survey must depend upon correct bases; and the direction of these bases, unless a true meridian line can be determined astronomically, which is not always convenient, and sometimes not practicable, must be ascertained by the Compass. The angles may thence be most conveniently taken with the Sextant to a degree of perfection attainable with no other portable instrument.

I have the pleasure to add, that the principles of both instruments have received the unanimous approbation and sanction of many illustrious Naval and scientific Characters; among whom I have the honour to include the names of Sir Sidney Smith, Commodore Truxtan, of the American Marine, &c. &c. Dr. Mackay, &c. &c.

I am, Sir,
Your most obedient Servant,
E. HOPPE,

51, *Church Street*,   Manufacturer of the new Sextant and Compass.
Minories, February 16, 1805.

PLATE CLXXIV.

MR. EDITOR,

SHOULD the enclosed View of Marston Rock be worthy of being represented in your much admired Work, by giving it an early place you will greatly oblige

Yours,

AMOR.

P. S. I have taken the liberty of extracting the following description of Marston Rock from the five volumes of the Beauties of England and Wales:—

The Sea Shore between the North Pier of Sunderland Harbour and South Shields is bounded by lofty rocks, which in places assume a singular and grotesque appearance, particularly about one mile from the Suter Point, where an enormous craggy Mass, bearing the name of Marston Rock, has been detached from the Coast by the violence of the Sea, and at high water is fifty or sixty yards from land, though within memory it was so near as to have been reached by a plank. All the intermediate part has been washed away, and even a large aperture formed by the force of the waves in the body of the Rock, through which sailing Boats have frequently passed at convenient stages of the tide.

Vast numbers of sea-fowl used to build their nests in this Rock, and the quantity of manure they left was so great, that it was collected at the expiration of every five or seven years, and generally sold for eighty or a hundred pounds. To facilitate its conveyance to the summit of the Cliffs, a circular hole wa made in the roof of a recess or cavern in the Rocks, through which it was drawn in baskets.

Adjacent to Marston Rock are other large and irregular masses which have been separated from the land, and which rear their gigantic forms with considerable majesty.

Newcastle, Feb. 19, 1805.

Marsden Rock, Durham.

NAVAL LITERATURE.

The Narrative of a Voyage of Discovery, performed in his Majesty's Vessel the LADY NELSON, *of Sixty Tons Burthen, with Sliding Keels, in the Years* 1800, 1801, *and* 1802, *to New South Wales.* By JAMES GRANT, *Lieutenant in the Royal Navy. Including Remarks on the Cape de Verd Islands, Cape of Good Hope, the hitherto unknown Parts of New Holland, discovered by him in his Passage (the first ever attempted from Europe) through the Streight separating that Island from the Land discovered by* VAN DIEMAN : *together with various Details of his Interviews with the Natives of New South Wales; Observations on the Soil, Natural Productions,* &c. *not known or very slightly treated of by former Navigators; with his Voyage Home in the Brig Anna Josepha round Cape Horn; and an Account of the present State of Falkland Islands: to which is prefixed, an Account of the Origin of Sliding Keels, and the Advantages resulting from their Use; with an Appendix of Orders, Certificates, and Examinations, relative to the* TRIAL CUTTER. *The whole illustrated with Elegant Engravings.* 4to. pp. 221.

AS one of the objects of the Lady Nelson's Voyage was, to ascertain the utility of *Sliding Keels,* with which that Vessel was constructed, we shall commence our review of Lieutenant Grant's book by particularly noticing his experiments and remarks on that subject.

With the origin of sliding keels, most of our readers, we presume, are acquainted; they were invented by Captain John Schank, of the Royal Navy, formerly one of the Commissioners of the Transport Board. In the year 1774, that gentleman, while in America, in consequence of a hint from his Grace the Duke of Northumberland, first constructed a Boat with sliding keels, which is said to have answered the purpose in every respect. Since that period, several other successful experiment have been made, notwithstanding which the invention has never been received into general use. We have before had occasion to notice this innovation in Naval Architecture*. Among other objections which we then stated, it was our opinion, and this opinion we still hold, that two, or more, keels must be less compact and strong than one. We think also, and our supposition is strengthened by a circumstance which is related in the Narrative before us, that in certain instances sliding keels must be liable to be broken short off; and, consequently, that much trouble, expense, and danger, must be incurred. From the old law maxim, *audi alteram partem,* we shall not, however, swerve. Lieutenant Grant, profiting by Captain Schank's papers, considers with him, that the following advantages will be derived to Ships in general when constructed with sliding keels:—they will sail faster, steer more easily, and tack and wear quicker, and in less room; such Vessels will carry more freight, and draw less water; will ride more easily at anchor; will take the ground better; in case of Shipwreck, of springing a leak, or of fire, they are safer and more likely to be saved; they will answer better as Men of War, as Bombs, Fireships, Floating-batteries, Gun-boats, Gun-batteaux, and flat-bottomed Boats for landing Troops. Lieutenant Grant likewise considers, that Vessels thus constructed will answer better as Coasters of all kinds, and for the coal trade; that they would answer in canals above four or five feet deep; that they would be exceedingly convenient to carry corn, or mixed cargoes, part of which is required to be kept separate; that they have the advantage of all others in case of losing the rudder, and that they will last longer than those which are built according to the present mode.

For the respective reasonings, which are extremely ingenious and forcible, in support of these opinions, we must refer our readers to the volume which contains them. We shall conclude this part of our review with the following extracts from the Appendix, relative to the Trial Cutter alluded to in the title page:—

---

* *Vide* NAVAL CHRONICLE, Vol. VII, page 40.

In consequence of a request made to the Lords of the Admiralty by Captain SCHANK, *that the* TRIAL CUTTER *might be ordered into one of his Majesty's Ports, and there inspected, and the Officers examined touching her qualities, their Lordships were pleased to issue the following orders:—*

GENTLEMEN, *Admiralty-Office, April* 12, 1792.

WHEREAS Captain Schank hath, by his letter of the 7th ult., requested that his Majesty's armed Vessel built with Sliding Keels, of his invention, may be ordered into one of his Majesty's Ports, and taken into a Dock in order to examine whether the Keels are rubbed or worn, and whether the Vessel or the Wells are strained, and that the Officers may be examined touching the qualities of the Vessel in the trials that have been made of her: and whereas we have thought fit to order Lieutenant Malbon to proceed with the said Vessel to Woolwich for the purpose above mentioned, we send you herewith Captain Schank's said letter, and do hereby desire and direct you to cause the said Vessel, on her arrival at Woolwich, to be taken into a Dock, and fixed on blocks in such a manner as Captain Schank shall advise; and direct the Master Shipwrights of Deptford and Woolwich Yards with their Assistants, and also the Masters attendant of those Yards, carefully to inspect and report to you the state in which they find her to be; as also the different qualities of the Vessel, according to the best accounts they may be able to collect from her Officers in the various trials they have made of her; and you will also direct them to consider and report to you, whether the repairing of Vessels so constructed will be attended with great difficulty, and whether they will be more or less expensive than Vessels of the old construction: and when you have received and maturely considered the said reports, and received such explanation from Captain Schank as you may think necessary, you are to transmit to us copies thereof, with your opinion of the advantage that may be derived to his Majesty's Service from the invention above mentioned.

Navy Board.
We are
Your affectionate friends,
(Signed) CHATHAM,
HOOD,
J. M. TOWNSHEND.

In pursuance of this order the Trial Cutter was taken into Woolwich Dock-yard and there inspected, and the Officers belonging to her were distinctly and separately examined; after which the following Report was made to the Navy Board by the several Officers empowered to inspect the Vessel and examine the Officers.

HONOURABLE SIRS, *Woolwich Yard, April 26, 1792.*

In obedience to your orders of the 16th inst. we have taken his Majesty's armed Vessel into a Dock, on blocks five feet high, and have very carefully inspected the Vessel, Wells, and Sliding Keels, and cannot discover the least defect in either.

We are of opinion, Vessels so constructed will be a little more expensive than others, but may be repaired without any difficulty.

Enclosed you will receive the Questions put by us to the Lieutenant and Master separately, with their answers, and remain,

<blockquote>
Honourable Sirs,
Your most obedient Servants,
(Signed)   J. GILBERT,   M. WARE,
                J. DANN,   J. FRANKLAND,
Honourable Navy Board.   RICH. PROWSE,   WM. RULE.
                HENRY PEAKE,
</blockquote>

Questions put separately to Lieutenant MALBON, *and Mr.* WILLIAM MILNE, *Master, of the* TRIAL CUTTER, *with their Answers; being the Enclosure alluded to in the foregoing Letter.*

Quest. How long have you belonged to the Trial Cutter?——Ans. Lieut. Sixteen months.—*Master.* Sixteen months.

Quest. What kind of a Sea-boat do you find her to be?——Ans. Lieut. A very good Sea-boat.—*Master.* A very lively Vessel in a Sea.

Quest. Is she stiff in carrying sail?——*Ans. Lieut.* Very stiff—*Master.* Yes; very stiff.

Quest. What effect do you observe the Keels to have on her?——Ans. Lieut. When they are all up she does not hold so good a Wind.—*Master.* Keeping her to windward.

Quest. Does she steer well with the Keels all down?——*Ans. Lieut.* Very well.—*Master.* Very well.

Quest. Does she steer equally well with her Keels up?——Ans. Lieut. Not so well as with them down.—*Master.* She does not.

Quest. What effect has the fore Keel on her?——*Ans. Lieut.*

It brings her about with heaving the after Keel up.—*Master.* It brings her about with heaving the after Keel up.

Quest. What do you observe to be the effect of the after Keel?——*Ans. Lieut.* It makes her wear quick by heaving the fore Keel up.—*Master.* The same answer.

Quest. What effect has the main Keel?——*Ans. Lieut.* It keeps her to windward.—*Master.* The same answer.

Quest. You have frequently been in company with his Majesty's Ships and Cutters?——*Ans. Lieut.* Yes.—*Master.* Yes.

Quest. How do you think she sailed with respect to the said Ships and Cutters?——*Ans. Lieut.* Never was with any King's Cutter that beat her.—*Master.* None of the King's Cutters ever beat her.

Quest. What Ships and Cutters do you remember to have tried with?——*Ans. Lieut.* The Nimble, Sprightly, Spider, Ranger, and Resolution Cutters; the Salisbury, Nautilus, and Hyæna Ships.—*Master.* The Nimble, Sprightly, Spider, Ranger, and Resolution Cutters; the Salisbury, Nautilus, and Hyæna Ships, and King Fisher Brig.

Quest. Did you try with them upon a Wind?——*Ans. Lieut.* Yes, and was beat by none of them.—*Master.* Yes, and was beat by none of them, except the Ranger, which was not a fair trial.

Quest. What Vessels did you beat?——*Ans. Lieut.* The Resolution, Sprightly and Nimble Cutters, and all the above-mentioned Ships.—*Master.* All the above square-rigged Vessels; and the Resolution, Sprightly, and Nimble Cutters.

Quest. Do you find any difficulty in heaving up and down the Keels in different situations, such as a press of sail on a Wind?—— *Ans. Lieut.* Not any.—*Master.* Not any.

Quest. What strength does it require to heave up or down the Keels?——*Ans. Lieut.* One Man the fore and after Keel, and two the main.—*Master.* Two Men the main Keel, and one the fore or after.

Quest. Supposing a rope to break in heaving the Keels up or down, in what time can you replace it?——*Ans. Lieut.* In about three minutes, the fore or after Keel; and the main, nine or ten minutes.—*Master.* The fore or after Keel in five minutes; the main, ten or fifteen.

Question. Does she tack quick?—*Ans. Lieut.* Very quick.— *Master.* Very quick.

Quest. Does she wear quick?—*Ans. Lieut.* Very quick.—*Master.* Very quick.

Quest. Are the Keels of service in wearing and tacking?—*Ans. Lieut.* Yes.—*Master.* Yes.

Quest. What rate is your fastest sailing upon a Wind?—*Ans. Lieut.* Nine, and nine and a half knots.—*Master.* Nine knots.

Quest. What rate is your fastest sailing before a Wind?—*Ans. Lieut.* Ten knots.—*Master.* Ten knots.

Quest. Suppose a Vessel was to lose her Keels on a lee-shore, do you think you could work her off if she could carry sail?—*Ans. Lieut.* Yes.—*Master.* If she carries all her sails she will; but under a double-reefed main-sail she will only hold her own.

Quest. What quantity of iron or shingle ballast have you on board?—*Ans. Master.* Eighteen tons of iron, but no shingle.

(Signed)   J. GILBERT,   M. WARE,
           JOHN FRANKLAND,   JAMES DANN,
           WILLIAM RULE,   RICH. PROWSE.
           HENRY PEAKE.

[*To be continued.*]

NAVAL HISTORY OF THE PRESENT YEAR, 1805.
(*February—March.*)
RETROSPECTIVE AND MISCELLANEOUS.

THE pleasing hopes of a pacific disposition in our inveterate enemy, were prolonged only for a short period. The Beast of Prey crouches to ensnare its victim with more success. In the mean time preparations are continued for a Secret Expedition, but, as we learn, not on so extensive a scale as was at first projected. The French are playing a desperate stake, and as it seems their last, they give free vent to their irritation and malevolence. Their finances are by no means in the state which they represent—and the waggon loads of Spanish dollars which have found their way to the Bank, will be seriously missed in the treasury of the Corsican Despot. Captain Paget has been very successful in this respect; but having, as we understand, made an agreement to share his prize-money with Captain Elphinstone, the latter will derive nearly 50,000l. from the Endymion's capture.

According to an article in the ROTTERDAM MERCURY of the 12th of January— The Funds at Paris experienced on the 2d a great depression." The Pope, who continues a prisoner at large, when too late has endeavoured to restore the Jesuits. Had this order remained, the French Revolution would never have taken place.

The injurèd, yet independent spirit of the United Kingdom breathes throughout the remonstrance which our Ambassador at Portugal made to M. D. Aranjo d'Arevedo.—" No, Sir! we do not starve our prisoners to death! we do not force them to take up arms against their Country! If Spain mourns the fate of the unfortunate persons who perished at a moment when a measure of precaution dictated the necessity of detaining certain Ships of War belonging to that Nation, by the British Cruisers; do us, Sir, the justice to believe, that that Sorrow is as general and sincere in England; and that the mourning we wear is at the bottom of our hearts. No, Sir! our hands are not stained with innocent blood! and we would readily shed some of our own to restore to life the victims of a cruel chance, which we constantly deplore."

The Extract which has appeared in the Papers from the Tenth Report of the Commissioners of Naval Inquiry is of so much importance, that we have given it an immediate place on our Wrapper. It will probably be a considerable time before we can otherwise insert it.

Some months since a Ship of 90 guns was launched at l'Orient, and three others are in a state of forwardness, but there are no Seamen for them. There were about sixty Sail of Gun-boats, Praams, &c. there, the Crews of which are very sickly in consequence of the want of accommodation on board.

Persons employed by Government have been busily engaged in laying down buoys, and making other preparations, in Falmouth Harbour, for the accommodation of Ships of War. It is said to be determined that a Dock-yard and Arsenal shall be built in St. Just, near the Quarantine Pool, for the use of the Navy. Pilots, &c. are already appointed.

Feb. 19. Dispatches were received at the Secretary of State's Office from Governor King at New South Wales. They state the arrival of the Buffalo Store-ship, Capt. Kent, who, soon after his arrival, was sent on discoveries upon the Coast of New Caledonia, where he had found a most excellent Harbour on the N.W. side, which he called Port St. Vincent, in compliment to the Earl of St. Vincent.

A Cutter has been dispatched by Government to Sir Edward Pellew, to advise him of the escape of the French Fleet from Rochefort, and of the possibility of its being destined for the East Indies.

We are concerned to state the loss of his Majesty's hired armed Tender Constance, Lieutenant Menzies, Commander, at Roundstone Bay, in the County of Galway, on the morning of the 17th January. About three o'clock the first seabreak carried away her bowsprit, main boom, fore-top-mast, long Boat, and five Men, overboard: by the greatest exertions three of them were saved, the other two perished. The breakers and a heavy surf still continued, and carried off every article on deck. It being ebb tide, about five o'clock she struck on a rock, they hailed the Shore, when an immense number of country people collected, took possession of her, and plundered her stores, &c.

The Weymouth Frigate, Captain Draper, about which so many false reports have been circulated, and which, in fact, has never returned to Portsmouth since she left Spithead with her Convoy, is now pursuing her course to the East Indies,

The following Justification of Earl St. Vincent *appeared in Bell's Universal Advertiser for February* 16, *and we believe is a Copy of a Paper which was previously sent to the Members of both Houses of Parliament.*

LORD ST. VINCENT feels it due to a discriminating Public, to state the causes of so long a delay having taken place in bringing the Libellers of his public character to justice.

On the 17th December 1803, the following paragraph appeared in the True Briton and Sun Newspapers:—

" The detention of Linois's Squadron becomes daily more credited; indeed, from the variety of channels corroborative of one another, through which it has come, we think that little doubt ought to be entertained upon the fact. If such an event then has really taken place, how much is the country indebted to Admiral Rainier for the promptitude, spirit, and energy of his conduct! for it is a fact, which, if it were not well known would hardly be believed, that it was two months after the commencement of the War before any orders were dispatched from the Admiralty to the Naval Commandant in the Indian Seas. There is a boldness in taking upon himself so great a degree of responsibility, which those who know Admiral Rainier best are well informed is a distinguishing feature in his manly character, and the benefit which his country derives from his exertion of his spirit and judgment, must excite as much gratitude as that does admiration and applause. As the country has been saved by the voluntary spirit of the people, without any aid from the Executive Government, whose duty it is to lead and direct that spirit to its object, so our Officers abroad have been left pretty much to their own discretion, from the criminal negligence in certain public departments; but it is as glorious for the country as it is honourable for themselves, that their judgment leads them to actions at once splendid and beneficial."

Immediately on reading this paragraph, the Admiralty Board, at which his Lordship presided, directed it to be forwarded to their Counsel for his opinion, whether it did not amount to a libel, and as to the measures which were fit to be taken with regard to it. An answer was immediately returned, stating, that it was a gross and scandalous libel, and that as it affected a great and important department of the Executive Government, it ought to be submitted to the consideration of the Attorney General, in order that he might prosecute the offenders by a criminal information, *ex officio*; and the same day the Chancellor of the Exchequer happening to call on Lord St. Vincent, his Lordship showed him the paragraph, and the opinion of the Counsel to the Admiralty; and Mr. Addington not only entirely concurred in the latter, but advised that Mr. Erskine should be retained, which was readily acquiesced in by Lord St. Vincent, who had long been in habits of intimacy with that gentleman, and entertained the highest opinion of his abilities as an advocate. A case was accordingly prepared by the Solicitor to the Admiralty, for the opinion of his Majesty's Law Officers, by whom an opinion was soon given, that the publication was a libel, and, if it were to be prosecuted, that the only course to be taken was for an Information to be filed by the Attorney General against the proprietors of the above-mentioned Newspapers; at the same time that Officer observed, that " if the Board of Admiralty wished its prosecution, it would be very much against his inclination, as well as his duty, to withhold the prerogative process from such a prosecution, but that it was certainly matter well deserving the serious consideration of that department of his Majesty's Government, whether this libel (which, as he said, must probably be most authentically contradicted and refuted by the publication of the very first dispatch which might be received from Admiral Rainier,) was of such a size as to make it fit to be selected for prosecution?" It is scarcely necessary to observe, that the Board of Admiralty had felt, and did continue to feel, that a libel which imputed to them a criminal neglect of duty, amounting to treason against the country, was of sufficient magnitude to be selected for prosecution. It was not enough that they knew the imputation to be wholly false; that in point of fact they had not omitted to send the most timely, and even very frequent dispatches to Admiral Rainier, not only of the actual commencement, but of the prospect of an approaching war with France. There was a boldness in the assertion which demanded belief, and called for refutation, and there was a malignity in the libel which required that their refutation should not be unaccompanied with punishment; the Board, therefore, did not hesitate to direct that a criminal prosecution should be immediately commenced. Soon after which the Attorney General wrote to Lord St. Vincent as follows:—

" MY LORD, L. I. F. *7th April,* 1804.

" In obedience to the commands of your Lordship and the Board of Admiralty, I have caused an information to be prepared against Mr. Heriot and those concerned with him in the publication of his Newspaper, for the libel which he published in it against the Admiralty, in his remarks made upon the supposed detention of Linois's Squadron by Admiral Rainier; and I have the honour herewith to transmit the draft of it to your Lordship.

" I continue of the opinion which I expressed, together with the Solicitor General and the Counsel for the Admiralty, that the publication in question is a libel; but I still retain so strong a doubt upon the policy and expediency of the prosecution, I feel the principle of it to be so directly at variance with that which has influenced the forbearance of Government in prosecutions, not only during the present Administration, but for many years back, that I should not think I was doing right by the Board of Admiralty, or by the rest of his Majesty's Government, if I did not take the liberty of reque tingsthat your Lordship would have the goodness distinctly to submit to the Cabinet the propriety of taking this libel into Court. If it shall be the pleasure of your Lordship, and the rest of his Majesty's Ministers, that it should be proceeded in, it will be my duty undoubtedly to go forward with it; but I should be sorry to be instrumental in exposing the Government to many unpleasant observations, which I think may result from this single departure from the principle of moderation and forbearance upon these points, without distinctly submitting it to their consideration.

" I have marked in the margin the parts of the information which contain the libel, that your Lordship may have no trouble in referring to it, and I have the honour to be, &c.

" SP. PERCEVAL."

" I should be glad to receive the pleasure of his Majesty's Government on this subject by Monday the 16th instant, as the information, if filed, ought to be filed on the following day.

" *The Earl of St. Vincent, &c. &c. &c.*"

Lord St. Vincent lost no time in laying this letter before the Cabinet, and their sense of the transaction was made known to the Attorney General by the following letter:—

" SIR, *Admiralty,* 8th *April,* 1804.

" I have communicated to his Majesty's Ministers the repugnance that you have expressed upon the prosecution of the Publishers of the True Briton and

Sun Newspapers; and from all I have heard, they are of opinion with me, that no delay should take place in filing a bill against them.

"I have the honour to be, &c.

"ST. VINCENT."

"*The Hon. Spencer Perceval, &c. &c.*"

Various delays were nevertheless interposed by the Attorney General, till at last, to the astonishment of the Board of Admiralty, he refused to proceed without the direction of the Cabinet. Lord St. Vincent immediately communicated this extraordinary conduct to the Cabinet, and the Attorney General was positively ordered to proceed, and an information was accordingly filed; but before the trial could take place, a change in the Ministry was effected, and the Attorney General ordered the Solicitor of the Admiralty to stand fast; and, towards the close of the last Session of Parliament, told Mr. Addington, in the House of Commons, that he should not proceed in the prosecution without instructions from the present Ministers, which appeared to Lord St. Vincent tantamount to his having received instructions not to proceed—a very natural conclusion, when the libellers were believed to have acted under the auspices of persons who had recently been in opposition to his Majesty's Government, but who then held high official situations. Lord St. Vincent felt a considerable degree of surprise and indignation at this conduct; but wishing not to wound the feelings of the Attorney General, sought an expedient to make known to him his determined resolution to bring the offending parties before a Court and Jury, and his Lordship went on a long premeditated tour, in hopes his plan would succeed; he, however, failed in finding such an expedient, and the long vacation wearing away fast, he cut short his tour, returned to town, and directed his Solicitor to write the following letter to the Attorney General:—

"SIR,   *Swithen's Lane, Sept. 22, 1804.*

"Mr. Addington has acquainted Lord St. Vincent of your having informed him that you had been directed by his Majesty's present Ministers not to proceed in the informations which you had filed, under the direction of the late Administration, against the Printers and Publishers of the Sun and true Briton Newspapers, for a libel upon the late Board of Admiralty. Lord St. Vincent, still retaining the same sentiments which he ever entertained of the gross malignity of the libel, and the propriety of the prosecution, has directed me to request that you will have the goodness to acquaint me, whether it is your intention to proceed to trial upon these informations; and if not, that you will be pleased to enter a *nolle prosequi*, it being his Lordship's firm determination that the case shall be submitted to the consideration of a Court and Jury.

"I have the honour to be, &c. &c.

"JOSEPH KAYE."

"*His Majesty's Attorney General.*"

To which the Attorney General replied:—

"SIR,   *L. I. F. 24th Sept. 1804.*

"I yesterday received your letter of the 22d inst. wherein you state, that Mr. Addington had acquainted Lord St. Vincent of my having informed him, that I had been directed by his Majesty's present Ministers not to proceed in the information which I had filed, under the direction of the late Administration, against the Printers and Publishers of the Sun and True Briton Newspapers, for a libel upon the late Board of Admiralty; and you request, upon the direction of Lord St. Vincent, that I would acquaint you whether it is my intention to proceed to trial upon these informations, and if not, that I would be pleased to enter a *nolle*. *prosequi*, it being his Lordship's firm determination that the case should be submitted to the consideration of a Court and Jury.

"There must be some mistake with respect to Mr. Addington's communication with Lord St. Vincent, or I certainly must have explained myself very ill to Mr. Addington, if he understood me to have said that I had received any directions from the present Government to abandon the informations in question. I remember telling him, that I felt it my duty not to proceed in them, without obtaining the directions of Government: but any final directions, or any directions from Government, upon the subject, I could not have communicated to Mr. Addington, as I have not to this moment received them myself. The circumstance which decisively weighed with me, to countermand the notice of trial at the last Sittings, was the probability that the subject of the libel would become the subject of a debate and a motion in the House of Commons; notice having been given (if I recollect right, by Lord Porchester) of a motion upon that subject; and though this notice was put off from the time for which it was at first fixed, the postponement was accompanied with the intimation of an intention to renew it. And it appeared to me so advisable, that the result of the discussion in Parliament, especially if likely soon to take place, should be known before the trial, and so possible, nay so probable, that it would be thought proper to influence the determination, whether the trial should take place or not, that without waiting to receive the directions of his Majesty's Government, I directed the notice of trial for the last Sittings to be countermanded. The case being thus circumstanced, I have foreborne to press for directions upon the point, as, at all events, they would come sufficiently early for any purpose, if they were received in time to give the proper notice of trial for the Sittings after next Term. Your letter, however, furnishes me with a reason for wishing to have them earlier; I will endeavour to procure them, and you shall hear from me again when I have got them. I was desirous, however, not to delay answering your letter, especially as I am going out of town to-morrow for some little time, and shall hardly be able to get the information I want for you before my return.

"I have the honour to be, &c. &c.

"*Joseph Kaye, Esq.* "SP. PERCEVAL."

Some time having elapsed without receiving any further satisfaction, and Michaelmas Term approaching, Lord St. Vincent directed another letter to be written by his Solicitor to the Attorney General as follows:—

"SIR, *Swithen's Lane, 19th Oct. 1804.*

"I communicated to Lord St. Vincent the letter which I had the honour to receive from you on the 24th ultimo, and his Lordship has desired me to acquaint you, that he is anxious to obtain your determination on the subject. As the Term approaches, I hope you will excuse my entreating you to favour me therewith in the course of two or three days.

"I have the honour to be, &c. &c.

"JOSEPH KAYE."

(" *His Majesty's Attorney General.*

To which this answer was returned :—

"SIR, L. I. F. *20th Oct. 1804.*

"I am extremely concerned to find that you have not heard from me since the 24th ult. I imagined that you must have heard from me near three weeks since;

FOR HAVING, when in Northamptonshire, at the end of last month, RECEIVED DIRECTIONS FROM HIS MAJESTY'S GOVERNMENT TO PROCEED IN THE PROSECUTION AGAINST the True Briton, &c. for the libel upon Lord St. Vincent and the late Admiralty, I did, either in that month, or at the beginning of the present, write to you, informing you that I HAD RECEIVED SUCH DIRECTIONS, and that the prosecution would THEREFORE PROCEED. I know it so very rarely happens that any miscarriage of letters occurs by the post, that I hardly know how to suspect the fault to be there. I was at the time at Lord Northampton's, at C. Ashby. I suppose I did (for I have no distinct recollection of that circumstance) leave this letter where it is usual for letters to be left for the servant to come and take them to the post, and it is possible, certainly, that by some carelessness it might not have been put into the post. However, I beg you will acquaint Lord St. Vincent, with my respectful compliments, that I have received such directions, and that I feel much concerned at finding that he had not heard so before.

" I am, Sir, &c.

" Joseph Kaye, Esq. " SP. PERCEVAL."

When the trial came on, although the Defendants were ably defended by their Counsel, so far from difficulty, or any thing that should have deterred a public-spirited Government from proceeding in the prosecution, the publication was considered by Lord Ellenborough, who tried the information, as a most gross and injurious libel, imputing to Lord St. Vincent and the late Board of Admiralty the greatest crime that could be committed by men in a public situation—a traitorous neglect of duty, in omitting to send the information they were bound to communicate to our Naval Commander in India of an event, the ignorance of which in him would have hazarded the safety of that most important of our possessions;— a crime for which, if it had been committed, there was no punishment within the power of the law, or within the reach of legislative vengeance, which was or could be adequate.

The Jury, without the least hesitation, found the Defendants guilty.

MEDICAL ESTABLISHMENT

OF THE

ROYAL NAVY,

Office for Sick and Wounded Seamen, Jan. 28, 1805.

Particulars of such part of his Majesty's Order in Council of the 23d January, 1805, for improving the situation of the Medical Officers of the Royal Navy, as relates to the Hospital Department.

ALL Assistants of Hospitals, known at present under the denomination of " Visiting Assistants, Assistant Surgeons, and Assistant Dispensers," to be called in future " Hospital Mates," and to be allowed, without regard to the department of the Hospital in which they may serve, 6s. 6d. per day when employed at home, and 7s. 6d. per day when employed on foreign stations, with half-pay when reduced, at the rate of 2s. per day, provided they shall have served subsequent to the date of his Majesty's regulation, two years on full pay; and further, they are to be allowed lodging money at the rate of 10s. 6d. per week, when not accommodated within the Hospital.

Such Hospital Mates as may remove from one department of the Hospital to another, are nevertheless to be required to prove themselves qualified, by examination, for the department to which they may be about to remove; but they may be allowed, before joining the Hospital, to prove themselves qualified for every department, by the different necessary examinations.

The widows of such as shall have served as Hospital Mates abroad, and shall die on full pay, are to be allowed a pension of 16l. per annum; and the children of such Hospital Mates, and the widows and children of such as shall die on half-pay, are to have such allowances as the Lords Commissioners of the Admiralty, upon consideration of the circumstances of their case, shall think fit to grant.

All Dispensers of Hospitals are to receive, when employed, a full pay of 10s. per day, and when unemployed, a half pay of 5s. per day.

Dispensers, when a residence is not provided for them, shall be allowed 12s. per week lodging money.

Surgeons of Hospitals are to be selected from the List of Naval Surgeons, and to be allowed 15s. per day on their first appointment; and 20s. per day after having served ten years in Hospitals; their half-pay to depend on the length of their service, at the same rate as is directed in regard to Surgeons of Ships.

Surgeons of Hospitals, when not provided with a residence within the Hospital, to be allowed 15s. per week lodging money.

In all cases, time served by Surgeons or Assistant Surgeons of his Majesty's Navy in Hospitals, is to be added to and calculated with the time served on board Ship.

Surgeons of Naval Hospitals, of Dock Yards, and of Marine Infirmaries, being on the List of Naval Surgeons, are to derive the same advantage from completing the respective terms of twenty and thirty years' service, as those who shall have served on board Ship.

And whereas, at the present time, some of the Surgeons of Naval Hospitals may have served on board Ship, it is ordered that the advantage of this regulation shall extend only to those already appointed, and that their full pay, half-pay, and retirement, shall be regulated by the time they have served, as in the case of those who have been employed on board Ship.

No person is to be appointed Physician to a Fleet or an Hospital, who shall not have served as Surgeon at least five years. The daily pay of a Physician, on his first appointment, is to be one guinea; his half-pay half a guinea.

When a Physician shall have served three years as Physician to a Fleet or an Hospital, his full pay is to be one guinea and a half per day; his half-pay 15s. per day.

When a Physician shall have served in that capacity more than ten years, his full pay shall be two guineas per day; his half-pay one guinea per day.

Physicians, when a residence is not provided for them, are to be allowed one guinea per week lodging money.

The widows of Physicians and Surgeons are to be allowed such a pension as the Lords Commissioners of the Admiralty shall think it right to grant.

None of the Officers before mentioned, who shall retire from their respective employments without the approbation of the Commissioners for Sick and Wounded Seamen, or who shall refuse to serve when called on, if judged capable of service, shall be allowed to receive half-pay, nor shall their names remain on the Naval List. Their widows will not in consequence be entitled to any pension.

Office for Sick and Wounded Seamen, Jan. 28, 1805.

Particulars of such part of his Majesty's Order in Council, of the 23d January, 1805, for improving the Situation of the Medical Officers of the Navy, as relate to such Officers serving on board Ships.

It is ordered, that the number of Assistants, heretofore called "Surgeons Mates," to be allowed to the Surgeons of his Majesty's Ships, shall in future be regulated as follows:—

First Rate	3 Assistants.
Second Rate	3 ditto.
Third Rate	2 ditto.
Fourth Rate	2 ditto.
Hospital Ships	3 ditto.
And all other Ships entitled, according to the existing regulations, to bear Mates	1 ditto.

That no person shall, in future, be appointed to serve as an Assistant to the Surgeon of any of his Majesty's Ships, who shall not have been found qualified on examination to serve as Surgeon, or as First Assistant; that the pay of Assistants so qualified shall be 6s. 6d. a day, besides the Ship's provisions; with half-pay when reduced, at the rate of two shillings per day, provided they shall then have served two years subsequent to the date of this regulation, and three shillings per day, if they shall have served three years from that date. That such Assistants shall be required to furnish themselves with such surgical instruments as the Commissioners for Sick and Wounded Seamen shall direct; and that they shall be rated on the Ship's Books, where the complement admits of more than one, according to their seniority on the list to be kept by the Sick and Wounded Board.

Whereas there are many Surgeons' Mates now serving on board his Majesty's Ships who have not obtained, and who may not for some time have an opportunity of obtaining the qualification before required; it is directed, that such as serve as First or Second Mates or Assistants shall be allowed five shillings per day; and those rated Third Mates or Assistants, four shillings per day.

These three classes of Assistants shall not be required to provide instruments, nor shall they be allowed half-pay; but they shall, nevertheless, on proving themselves duly qualified, be placed on the same list with the other Assistants, from the date of the first appointment they may receive after such qualification, and commence the time to be reckoned for half-pay from such appointment.

All Surgeons of the Navy, who shall not have served in the whole six years, of which not more than three years time as Hospital Mate or Assistant Surgeon shall be allowed, shall receive, when employed, a full pay of ten shillings per day, and when not employed, a half-pay of five shillings per day.

Surgeons of Ships in active service, after having served six years, of which not more than three years time as Hospital Mate or Assistant Surgeon shall be allowed, shall be paid eleven shillings per day; their half-pay to be six shillings per day.

After having served ten years, allowing not more than three years as Hospital Mate or Surgeon, the Surgeon's full pay shall be augmented to fourteen shillings per day; his half-pay to remain at six shillings per day.

Surgeons of Receiving Ships, Slop Ships, Convalescent Ships, Prison Ships, and all other Ships, except Hospital Ships, employed only in harbour duty, shall be allowed full pay ten shillings per day, with half-pay according to the time of their service.

Surgeons appointed to Hospital Ships shall receive a full pay of fifteen shillings per day, unless in cases where, by the length of their service, they may become entitled to a superior rate of payment; their half pay to be regulated, as in the case of Surgeons of other Ships, by the length of their service.

Every Surgeon in the Navy, excepting Surgeons serving on board Receiving Ships, Slop Ships, Convalescent Ships, or any other Ships than Hospital Ships, employed only in harbour duty, shall, after twenty years' service on full pay, including not more than three years time as Hospital Mate or Assistant Surgeon, be allowed eighteen shillings per day; and, after such length of service, all Surgeons, in whatever Ships they may have served, shall have a claim to retire on a half pay of six shillings per day; but if the cause of retirement shall be ill health contracted in the Service, and it shall be so certified by the Commissioners for Sick and Wounded Seamen, the rate of half-pay on such retirement after twenty years' actual service, shall be ten shillings per day.

Every Surgeon in the Navy, after thirty years' service on full pay, including not more than three years as Hospital Mate or Assistant Surgeon, shall have an unqualified right to retire on half-pay, at the rate of fifteen shillings per day.

That medicines and utensils shall be provided for the service of his Majesty's Ships and Vessels, at the expense of Government, in such proportions as shall be arranged by the Commissioners for Sick and Wounded Seamen; but the Surgeons shall be required to provide, at their own expense, such surgical instruments as shall be judged necessary by the said Commissioners.

No person shall be appointed Physician to a Fleet or an Hospital, who shall not have served as Surgeon at least five years: the daily pay of a Physician, on his first appointment, to be one guinea; his half-pay half a guinea.

When he shall have served three years as Physician to a Fleet or an Hospital, his full pay shall be one guinea and a half per day; his half-pay fifteen shillings per day.

The full pay of a Physician who shall have served in that capacity more than ten years, shall be two guineas per day; his half-pay one guinea per day.

That Physicians, when a residence is not provided for them, shall be allowed one guinea per week lodging money.

To the widows of the Physicians and Surgeons such a pension shall be allowed as the Lords Commissioners of the Admiralty shall think it right to grant.

None of the Officers before mentioned, who shall retire from their respective employments without the approbation of the Commissioners for Sick and Wounded Seamen, or who shall refuse to serve when called on, if judged capable of Service, shall be allowed to receive half-pay, nor shall their names remain on the Naval List. Their widows will not in consequence be entitled to any pension.

No Officer, of whatever description, shall be entitled to any of the advantages arising from this regulation, who shall not have served during the present War, or until he shall have satisfied the Commissioners for Sick and Wounded Seamen, of his inability to serve; but such persons shall be permitted to remain on the same establishment on which they may now respectively happen to be.

Gazette Letters,

Copied verbatim from the LONDON GAZETTE.

ADMIRALTY-OFFICE, FEB. 23, 1805.

Copy of a Letter from Lieutenant Rose, commanding his Majesty's Gun-brig the Growler, to William Marsden, Esq.; dated the 15th February, 1805, Falmouth.

SIR,

I BEG leave to acquaint you, for the information of my Lords Commissioners of the Admiralty, with my arrival at this Port, with the French National Gun-brig No. 193, which I fell in with, and captured after a running action of one hour and a half. From what I can understand from the Captain, she was one of four of the same class, from Bayon bound to Brest, commanded by an Enseigne de Vaisseau, had on board fifteen Seamen, a Captain in the Army, and thirty-four Soldiers, mounts two long 24-pounders, and one 18-pounder, and four swivels, sixty-five feet on the keel, is quite new, and draws six feet water.

I should be negligent in my duty were I to omit saying, that Mr. Henry Ellis, Sub-Lieutenant, with the other Officers and Crew, did their duty much to my satisfaction. I am, &c.

JAMES ROSE, Lieutenant and Commander.

ADMIRALTY-OFFICE, MARCH 2, 1805.

Copy of a Letter from Admiral Lord Gardner, Commander in Chief of his Majesty's Ships and Vessels on the Coast of Ireland, to William Marsden, Esq.; dated at Cork, the 21st February, 1805.

SIR,

Enclosed I transmit to you, for the information of the Lords Commissioners of the Admiralty, a letter I have this day received from Captain Lake, of his Majesty's Ship Topaze, acquainting me of his having captured, on the 13th instant, in the latitude 48° 22' N., longitude 15° West, the French Privateer General Augereau, mounting fourteen 12-pounders, carronades, and eighty-eight Men, belonging to Bayonne, which Vessel had been cruising forty-seven days without making a capture. I am, &c.

GARDNER.

His Majesty's Ship Topaze, at Sea, February 13, 1805,
MY LORD, *lat. 48° 22'. long. 15°.*

I have the pleasure to acquaint your Lordship, that his Majesty's Ship under my command has this day captured the French Privateer General Augereau, ketch-rigged, mounting fourteen 12-pounder carronades, and eighty-eight Men on board. She is the same Vessel that has been so frequently heard of, and that boarded and carried the William Heathcote West Indiaman. This cruise she has been out forty-seven days without making a capture.

I have the honour to be, &c.
W. T. LAKE.

Right Hon. Lord Gardner, Admiral of the Blue,
&c. &c. &c.

Copy of a Letter from Sir John Orde, Bart. Vice-Admiral of the Red, &c. to William Marsden, Esq.; dated on board his Majesty's Ship Glory, off Cadiz, the 5th February, 1805.

SIR,

Enclosed I send for their Lordships' information, a copy of a letter received from the Honourable Captain Bouverie, Commander of his Majesty's Ship Mer cury, under my orders, acquainting me with the capture of el Fuerte de Gibraltar, a Spanish Gun-boat that had been driven from the land, in her passage from Cadiz to Algeziras, the evening before she was taken.

This Vessel, copper-bottomed, newly equipped, and completely stored, seems well calculated for the service of Gibraltar. I am, &c.

JOHN ORDE.

SIR, *His Majesty's Ship Mercury, at Sea, Feb.* 4, 1805.

I have the honour to inform you, that I this morning fell in with and captured el Fuerte de Gibraltar, a lateen-rigged Spanish Gun-vessel, which sailed yesterday morning from Cadiz bound to Algeziras; she is armed with two long 12-pounders, two 16-pound carronades, several swivels, and a large quantity of small arms and cutlasses, and commanded by Signior Don Ramon Eutate, Lieutenant de Frégate, and had on board fifty-nine Men.

I am, Sir, &c.

D. PLEYDELL BOUVERIE.

To Sir John Orde, Bart. Vice-Admiral of the Red,
Commander in Chief, &c. &c.

ADMIRALTY-OFFICE, MARCH 12, 1805.

Copy of a Letter from Vice-Admiral Sir John Thomas Duckworth, K.B. Commander in Chief of his Majesty's Ships and Vessels at Jamaica, to William Marsden, Esq.; dated at Port Royal the 19th of January 1805.

SIR,

You will herewith receive, for the information of my Lords Commissioners of the Admiralty, the copy of a letter from the Honourable F. F. Gardner, stating the capture of the French Brig Privateer Regulus, commanded by Jacque Mathieu. I am, &c.

J. T. DUCKWORTH.

SIR, *Princess Charlotte, December* 13, 1804.

I have the honour to inform you, that at ten A.M., Cape Antonio east four leagues, made all sail in chase of a Brig; and after a hard chase of seven hours, with a fresh breeze, came up with her in lat. 20° 50′ N. long. 85° 32′ W. having steered south the whole of the chase, and firing four or five shot at her, she struck, and proves to be the French Privateer Brig Regulus, from Guadaloupe, commanded by Citizen Jacque Mathieu, pierced for fourteen guns, but only eleven mounted, (having thrown two overboard, with her Boats and spars, in the chase,) and eighty-four Men. She is a very fine Vessel, sails remarkably well, is coppered, and is in my opinion perfectly adapted for his Majesty's service.

I have the honour to be, &c.

F. F. GARDNER.

Sir J. T. Duckworth, K. B. &c. &c. &c.

ADMIRALTY-OFFICE, MARCH 14, 1805.

Extract of a Letter from Peter Rainier, Esq. Vice-Admiral of the Red, and Commander in Chief of his Majesty's Ships and Vessels in the East Indies, to William Marsden, Esq.; dated on board his Majesty's Ship Trident, 18th October, 1804.

On the 17th Mons. Linois had seized on some Country Boats off Massulipatam Road, who gave him the intelligence of his Majesty's Ship Wilhelmina having left that Road a few days before for Vizagapatam Road, with the Princess Charlotte Indiaman in convoy, and accordingly he dashed into that Road in the forenoon of the 18th, and commenced a furious attack with the Marengo and Frigates on his Majesty's Ship the Centurion, of 50 guns, whom I had a few days before substituted for the Wilhelmina, having ordered the latter to proceed to Calcutta with the Bengal and Asia Indiamen, who had some treasure on board. For the particulars of what followed I beg leave to refer their Lordships to Captain James Lind's letter of the 19th, whom I had given an acting order to command that Ship in the absence of Captain J. S. Rainier, left dangerously ill at sick quarters.

The gallant and spirited conduct displayed by Captain Lind, his Officers and Crew, in the defence of his Majesty's Ship Centurion against so great a superiority of force, under every advantage on the part of the assailants, with the complete defeat given the French Admiral and Squadron in the conclusion, merits every encomium, and I trust will be honoured with their Lordships' fullest approbation For my own part I do not hesitate to rank this brilliant action with the most famous of the defensive kind recorded in the glorious Annals of the British Navy.

His Majesty's Ship Centurion, in Vizagapatam Road,
SIR, *19th September,* 1804.

Yesterday morning, whilst at anchor in this Roadstead, and waiting till the Indiaman, the Princess Charlotte, and the Country Ship the Barnaby, the two Ships you directed me to convoy to Madras, were loaded, three Ships were perceived under the land in the south west, coming down before the Wind, with all sail set. About half-past nine A.M. it was seen that the strange Ships were enemies, and were a Line of Battle Ship and two Frigates; the Line of Battle Ship hoisted, with her colours, a flag at the mizen-top-mast-head, and I believe was the Marengo, Admiral Linois, and I shall so call her in this letter. The Frigate appeared to be of thirty-six or forty guns. For the information of the Convoy the signal of an enemy being in sight was hoisted, and soon afterwards one for the Convoy, as they were best able, to put into a Port in view. This was done, that the two Ships that we had taken under convoy might get close in shore for protection, or, if necessary, to be run on it the Barnaby complied with this signal, she ran in shore, but unfortunately afterwards got into the Surf, and was totally lost.

About ten A.M. the headmost of the enemy's Ships, a Frigate, was about half a mile from the Centurion, without any colours flying. Several shot were fired at her. About the same time the cable was cut, and topsails sheeted home, which were already loose for the purpose; by this means the broadside was brought to bear upon the enemy, and prevented the Ship being boarded or raked; by this manœuvre likewise, a Frigate that was within a cable's length of the Centurion, and appeared to have an intention to board, got a close and well-directed broadside into her: the action soon became general; the three enemy's Ships directing their fire on the Centurion, their only object, for the Princess Charlotte Indiaman had very early struck her colours. The Centurion stood in Shore, the Marengo and one Frigate on the starboard quarter, the other Frigate on the larboard; they were all less than half a mile distant, and kept firing, which the Centurion returned. Her fire was chiefly directed against the Marengo. About a quarter before eleven the French Ships stood to Sea; and immediately after this I got on board, though with much difficulty and danger. I had been on Shore to expedite the sailing of the Convoy, and was not present in this early part of the action, for, till now, the Centurion had been under the direction of Lieutenant James Robert Philips, the First Lieutenant; and before I proceed any further in this account, permit me to notice the judicious conduct of this deserving and old Officer, and his gallant defence of the Ship against so superior a force as that of the enemy. I hope, Sir, his conduct will be thought worthy of a reward, and that he will be esteemed deserving of promotion.

On my coming on board I found the sails and rigging so very much cut as to render the Ship not in a state to be worked, and therefore anchored at the back of the Surf, about a mile and a half to the north east of the town; this situation was the best I had in my power to take, both for defence, and to prevent her falling into the possession of the enemy if overpowered.

A battery of three guns at the town, under the command of Colonel Campbell, of his Majesty's 74th Regiment, had kept a fire on the enemy whilst within reach in the Roadstead, but now we were too far distant to receive any support from it. I sent on Shore to request guns might be brought on the Beach nearer us; this was a thing, I have been since convinced of, totally impracticable, or it would have been done. We prepared again for action; and whilst thus employed the enemy in the Offing wore and stood towards us; the Marengo, after having repeatedly tried the range of her guns, came to an anchor abreast of us, and about a mile distant; clewed up her topsails, furled her courses, and commenced cannonading. This threatening appearance of being determined to persevere and to succeed only served to animate the Officers and Men of his Majesty's Ship to greater exertions of defence with the lower deck guns, the only ones that would reach the enemy, for she was too far distant for the carronades, but all the enemy's shot reached us. In the mean time one of the Frigates kept under sail on our quarter, and nearer than the Marengo, and annoyed us much by her fire; the other Frigate carried off the Indiaman from her anchorage in the Road.

At a quarter past one P.M., nearly two hours after this cannonading had commenced, and which had been kept up with vigour on both sides, the Marengo cut her cable, hoisted her jib, and stood to Sea. By some of her last shot our cable was cut, and we made some sail, and got further off Shore before we brought up with the sheet anchor. When the Marengo first made sail I supposed she intended to make a short stretch, tack, and renew the action nearer, and made all necessary preparations to receive her; but she, Frigates, and prize Indiaman, stood to Sea, and a little before sunset bore up to the north east, towards the bottom of the Bay.

What damage the enemy has sustained, or from what cause they declined further contest with us, I cannot tell.

After this full account of the transactions of the day, I feel it a duty incumbent on me not only to repeat the high sense I have of Lieutenant Philips' services, but likewise to inform you that the other Lieutenants of this Ship, Lieutenants David Pringle, Richard Coote, and William Fairbrother Carrol, displayed great gallantry and spirit on the occasion; the last mentioned, Lieutenant Carrol, though a young Officer, has seen much service, and as his commission of Lieutenant is not yet confirmed by my Lords Commissioners of the Admiralty, may I request that you will be pleased to represent his great merit, to induce their Lordships to do it. To the zeal and energy of Lieutenant Warring of the Marines I am much indebted.

To insert any thing in this letter in praise of the behaviour of the veteran and gallant Crew of his Majesty's Ship Centurion, must be needless to you, Sir, who are well acquainted with it; but I cannot refrain from saying that they displayed great experience, and cool courage, and the good discipline of the Ship was conspicuous, and does great credit to their proper Commander, Captain Rainier.

His Majesty's Ship has received considerable damage in her masts, yards, and rigging. The foremast, mizenmast, and mainyard, are badly wounded, as well as several smaller masts and yards; several shot remain in the bottom between Wind and water, one came through into the Gunner's store-room; but for your full information of particulars there accompanies this detailed reports of damages sustained in the Gunner's, Boatswain's, and Carpenter's departments, as far as they have been yet ascertained. It is with pleasure I acquaint you that very few Men, considering the long action, have suffered; none were killed, and only nine wounded, one of them is since dead, the others are not in apparent danger.

I have received all the assistance that this place could afford me from Colonel A. Campbell, of his Majesty's 74th Highland Regiment, commanding Officer of the district, and from all the Company's Servants, both Civil and Military, at this Settlement. I am, &c.

Peter Rainier, &c. &c. &c. JAMES LIND.

SIR, *Trident, Madras Road, Oct. 1, 1804.*

I am to acknowledge the receipt of your letter of the 19th ultimo, informing particulars of your proceeding in execution of my orders, and of the very noble defence you made in his Majesty's Ship Centurion, under your command, in Vizagapatam Road the preceding day, against the formidable attack of so superior a force of the enemy, as described in your letter, led on by the French Admiral Linois in the Marengo; the gallant and spirited conduct displayed on this occasion by yourself, Officers, and Crew, merits the highest applause, wherein you not only saved his Majesty's Ship under your command from falling into the enemy's hand, as well as from Shipwreck, by running her on Shore, as a very obvious resource that offered to prevent it, but gave the French Rear-Admiral a complete defeat.

I shall not fail to forward your letter to the Secretary of the Admiralty, for their Lordships' information, by the present opportunity, and have no doubt but their Lordships will bestow on you some honourable acknowledgment of their approbation of your gallant conduct. I remain, &c.

PETER RAINIER.

To James Lind, Esq. acting Captain of his
Majesty's Ship Centurion.

ADMIRALTY-OFFICE, MARCH 16, 1805.

The following letters and list, containing accounts of captures made from the enemy, have been transmitted to this Office by Vice-Admiral Rainier, Commander in Chief of his Majesty's Ships and Vessels in the East Indies:—

His Majesty's Ship la Dedaigneuse, off Cochin,
SIR, *December 14, 1803.*

I have the honour to acquaint you, that I captured this morning a small French Privateer, l'Espiegle, of four guns, some small arms, and thirty-six Men; and commanded by Francois Dubois.

She sailed from the Mauritius on the 8th of November, and had not made a capture. I have the honour to be, &c.

P. HEYWOOD.

To Peter Rainier, Esq. Vice-Admiral of the White,
and Commander in Chief, &c. &c.

His Majesty's Ship Caroline, Bay of Bengal,
Little Andaman, N. 79° 50', E. twenty
SIR, *leagues, Jan. 5, 1804.*

I have the pleasure to inform you, this morning at two o'clock we fell in with the French Privateer Brig, les Freres Unis, of 140 tons, pierced for sixteen, but with only eight guns on board, and 134 Men, fifteen of whom are Officers, and forty Soldiers from Bourdeaux, in July, and from Mauritius 11th November, on a cruise, but had taken nothing. It took us till near six A.M. to close with and capture this Vessel, who sails fast, and made every effort to get from us, firing all his guns into us, and as we hailed, but (thank God) without hurting any one. They had one Man shot by our musketry, and, with ourselves, received much injury to Boats, booms, rigging, &c. &c. I am, &c.

B. W. PAGE.

Vice-Admiral Rainier, &c. &c. &c.

His Majesty's Ship St. Fiorenzo, off Mount Dilly,
SIR, *14th January, 1804.*

I have great pleasure in acquainting you, that the French National Vessel Passe par Tont, (a Chasse Marée,) was this day at noon captured by the Boats of his Majesty's Ship under my command, without the loss of a single Man, after a most determined resistance, in which the enemy lost two Men killed, with the First and Second Captains, and three others very dangerously wounded, the Captain, I fear, mortally, having a ball through his body. About ten A.M. perceiving the chase to have got her sweeps out, and the Land Wind failing, I sent three Boats in pursuit; the Barge and small Cutter with Lieutenants Doyle and Beach (my First and Second Lieutenants,) being up first, most gallantly laid her on board in the face of a very heavy fire from two brass 6-pounders, several swivels, and repeated vollies of musketry, when in less than two minutes they laid down their arms. Great praise is due to my Officers and People employed on this occasion; and I have not the least doubt of their success, had the enemy been of a much greater force. One of the Bargemen is wounded on the back of his hand by a cutlass.

She proved to be the Passe par Tout, of two brass 6-pounders and six brass swivels, with twenty-five Men. I have the honour to be, &c.

Vice-Admiral Rainier. JOS. BINGHAM.

SIR, *His Majesty's Ship Caroline, between the Cocos and Preparis Islands, Feb. 4, 1804.*

I have the pleasure to inform you that his Majesty's Ship under my command has had the good fortune to capture the French Privateer Ship le General de Caen, of 360 tons, twenty-two guns, and 200 Men, this forenoon. This Ship fell to us by the superior sailing of the Caroline, both being under all possible sail, going large, our chase guns hulling her she struck. Came in from the Isle of France, last from Mergui, is stored and victualled for five months, and had not made a capture. I am, &c.

Vice-Admiral Rainier, Commander in Chief,   B. W. PAGE.
&c. &c. &c.

SIR, *His Majesty's Ship Sheerness, off Point de Galle, 6th May, 1804.*

Cruising here pursuant to your directions, for the protection of trade in general, and of the extra Indiaman the Glory in particular, I captured yesterday the French Privateer Brig l'Alfred; she was commanded by Captain Crevel, mounts fourteen guns, carries eighty Men; she left the Mauritius in December last, and the only prizes she has made are the Brigs Friendship, on the 27th March, and Endeavour, on the 16th April, both from Madras to Prince of Wales Island, and of little value; she sails well, and is a remarkable fine Vessel.

I have the honour to be, &c.
JAMES LIND.

Vice-Admiral Rainier, Commander in Chief of his Majesty's Ships and Vessels in the East Indies.

A List of the Enemy's Ships and Vessels taken, destroyed, and recaptured by his Majesty's Ships under the command of Vice-Admiral Rainier, in the East Indies, between the 21st of December, 1803, and the 1st of November, 1804:—

French Ship Clarisse, of 12 guns and 157 Men: taken by the Albion and Sceptre, December 21, 1803, in lat. 13° 18′ S., long. 95° 20′ E.

French Chasse Maree Passe par Tout, of two guns, 6 swivels, and 25 Men: taken by the St. Fiorenzo, January 14, 1804, off Mount Dilly.

French Brig l'Espiegle, of four guns, 4-pounders, and 36 Men: taken by la Dedaigneuse, December 14, 1803, off Cochin.

French Brig les Freres Unis, of eight guns (9 and 6 pounders, pierced for sixteen guns,) 134 Men, and 140 tons: taken by the Caroline, January 6, 1804, in the Bay of Bengal.

French Ship General de Caen, of 26 guns (9-pounders and heavy carronades,) 200 Men, and 360 tons: taken by the Caroline, February 4, 1804, between the Cows and Andaman Isles.

French Brig l'Alfred, of 14 guns (6 and 4 pounders), 75 Men, and 110 tons: taken by the Sheerness, May 5, 1804, off Point de Galle.

French Schooner Zephyr, of four Men and 90 tons, laden with 114 Slaves: taken by the Terpsichore, August 27, 1804, off Grande Port.

French Brig la Jeune Clementine, of 15 Men, laden with 180 Slaves: taken by the Sir Edward Hughes Indiaman, July 12, 1804, in lat. 4° 18′ S., long. 64° E.

PETER RAINIER.

Copy of a Letter from Mr. Thomas Musgrave, Commander of the Kitty private Ship of War, to William Marsden, Esq.; dated at Falmouth the 14th Instant.

SIR,

I have the honour to acquaint you, for the information of the Lords of the Admiralty, that on Sunday the 10th instant, in the latitude of 48° N., and longitude 10° 15′ W., we fell in with the Spanish private Ship of War Felicity, mounting 20 guns, and 170 Men, commanded by Jose Vincento de Cinza, out ten days from St. Andero, and after an engagement of one hour and a half, she struck to the Kitty, private Ship of War, of London, under my command. I am concerned to add, that we had one Man killed and two dangerously wounded. In justice to the Officers and Ship's Company, I must say their conduct deserves the approbation of their Lordships, when you take into consideration that not twenty of them ever saw a gun fired before, and not twice that number ever were at Sea before we left the Downs, on the 3d instant.

I have the honour to be, &c.

THOMAS MUSGRAVE.

ADMIRALTY-OFFICE, MARCH 23, 1805.

Copy of a Letter from the Honourable Rear-Admiral Cochrane, to William Marsden, Esq.; dated on board his Majesty's Ship Northumberland, off the Bar of Lisbon, March 5, 1805.

SIR,

I enclose a copy of a letter from Captain Rose, of his Majesty's Ship Circe, giving an account of his having captured a Spanish Privateer Schooner. She seems a remarkable fine Vessel; and as she proceeds with the Squadron, I shall soon be able to judge of her qualifications. I am, &c.

ALEX. COCHRANE.

SIR, Circe, at Sea, March 2, 1805.

I beg leave to acquaint you, that yesterday I captured off Oporto, la Fama, Spanish Schooner Privateer, mounting four brass guns, and sixty-two Men; out eight days from Vigo, but had made no captures.

I have the honour to be, &c.

Rear-Admiral Cochrane. JONAS ROSE.

Copy of a Letter from Captain Farquhar, late Commander of his Majesty's Bomb the Acheron, to William Marsden, Esq.; dated in Malaga Prison, the 12th of February, 1805.

SIR,

You will be pleased to lay before my Lords Commissioners of the Admiralty the enclosed copy of an account transmitted to Lord Nelson, of the capture and destruction of his Majesty's Sloop Arrow, Captain Vincent, and Acheron Bomb, under my command, acquainting their Lordships that, from the uncertain state I am in with respect to the safety of Captain Vincent, or to what Port he may have been carried, I have thought it my duty not to let an opportunity slip of giving his Lordship the earliest information, as well as the Commanding Officer at Gibraltar, that immediate assistance and protection might be afforded to the Convoy.   I have the honour to be, &c.

ART. FARQUHAR.

Proceedings of his Majesty's Bomb Vessel Acheron,
MY LORD, *Sunday, Feb. 3, 1805.*

At daylight two strange Sail were seen from the mast-head, bearing about E.S.E. of us; at eight A.M. they had considerably neared us; we were at this time in the rear of the Convoy. About half-past ten the Arrow asked, per telegraph, my opinion of Ships to the eastward; I immediately wore Ship and stood towards them; observed the headmost Ship to shorten sail, by hauling down the studding sails; made signal 642 to the Arrow, then hoisted the private signal, and continued upon a Wind standing to them; at a quarter past eleven made the signal for their being suspicious (they not having answered the private signal). I was now so near as to be able to observe they were Frigates, and at half-past eleven to discover that they had their spare anchors in their main chains, which immediately led me to suppose that they were French. At fifty minutes past eleven **more** Ship, and made all sail towards the Arrow, who had by this time quitted her tow, and made signal for Convoy to continue the same course, although Ships of War acted otherwise. At half-past twelve P.M. (Monday per log.) hoisted our colours and fired a gun, which they paid no attention to. Signals 360 and 322 were then made to the Arrow, who immediately made signal to the Convoy for an enemy, and to make all possible sail to the appointed rendezvous, which was repeated. The Frigates had by this time made all possible sail in chase of us, but the Wind being light and variable from the eastward we rather gained upon them. At half-past four P.M. having joined the Arrow, I went on board: Captain Vincent appeared satisfied they were enemy's Ships; they were now about five mnes from us; it was resolved to make sail, and keep in the rear of the Convoy, for their protection. It was calm until eleven P.M., when a breeze sprung up from the W.S.W., wore Ship, and stood towards the Arrow. At twelve she hailed, and desired we would keep in her wake in close order. At two A.M. saw two sail upon the lee bow; called the hands to quarters. At half-past came up with them, and discovered they were two of the Convoy. At a quarter past four A.M. saw two other Ships standing to us on he opposite tack. At forty-five minutes past four the Arrow hailed the headmost Ship, then passing under her lee; being in close order she soon came abreast of the Acheron. I saw she was a large Frigate prepared to engage. I hailed her, asking what Ship is that? she answered, What Ship are you? and immediately gave us her broadside of round and grape, which did us very considerable damage in rigging and sails, besides carrying away the slings of the main-yard, and main-top-gallant-yard in the slings, but did not kill or wound any one; we returned her fire, then hove about and gave her the guns from the other side, and kept up the fire while our shot would reach her. The Arrow bore up and raked her. At or about half-past five the second Frigate passed the Arrow (then laying to upon the starboard tack) without firing; a little afterwards she appeared as if intending to wear, and having her stern towards the Acheron, we gave her two rounds from the larboard guns. She then hauled her Wind and stood towards the other Frigate. The people were now employed in splicing the rigging and getting another top-gallant-yard and sail ready to send aloft. At daylight observed the enemy had French colours flying, and one of the Frigates bearing a Commodore's Pendant. They then wore and stood to us; answered our signal and repeated the annul to one of the Ships of the Convoy: bore up to close the Arrow; at seven she hailed us, and desired we would keep in her wake, in close order; made sail in the starboard tack, closing with the enemy: at twenty-five minutes past seven the headmost Frigate being abreast of the Arrow, and within half musket shot, fired her broadside at her, which was immediately returned: at thirty minutes past seven she was abreast of us, and gave us a broadside; we then commenced action with her, which we continued until the second Frigate, which was the Commodore's, came up to and fired into us (having engaged the Arrow in passing); we now turned our fire upon this Ship until we came close up with the Arrow, who had put her helm a-weather and was now raking her; we hauled our Wind to clear the Arrow, who appeared to be wearing; I hailed and asked if he meant to again come to the Wind on the starboard tack, but could not understand what he said: as soon as clear of the Arrow, we again directed our fire against the Commodore's Ship, which we continued until eight, when, with the greatest grief, I saw the Arrow obliged to strike, being no longer able to contend with the great superiority of force opposed to her. She had, I conceive, received much damage in the act of wearing; the Wind being light she lay a considerable time with her head to the enemy. The Acheron being now very much disabled in masts, sails, and rigging, and part of her sternpost carried away, I considered farther resistance on my part could answer no good, and, unwilling to sacrifice the lives of Men who had given me the highest proof of their courage, I determined to make what sail I could, with little hopes of saving the Ship, but with a view of prolonging the time of my being captured, to give the Convoy the better chance of escaping.

The superiority in sailing of the enemy's Ship rendered the chase but short; at three quarters past eight having in chase received one broadside and part of another, and the enemy now very near us, with the greatest mortification and sorrow I was obliged to surrender to the French Frigate l'Hortense, of forty-four guns, commanded by Monsieur de la Marre la Mellerie, who, finding her much disabled, as soon as the Officers and Ship's Company were removed, set her on fire.

ARTHUR FARQUHAR.

Imperial Parliament.

HOUSE OF LORDS, MONDAY, FEB. 11.

NAVAL DEBATES.

THE Earl of *Albemarle* said, that before proceeding to the business of the day, there was a motion with which he meant to trouble their Lordships, of which he had not deemed it necessary to give any notice, as he could not figure any objection which could be made to it. What he wished was a copy of the Commission granted by his Majesty to Sir Charles Middleton and others, for managing the Naval Concerns of the Country. Their Lordships were not ignorant that there was another Committee appointed for this purpose by Parliament, and it was but proper that it should be seen how far this Committee, appointed by his Majesty, was intended to supersede the Committee appointed by Parliament. He therefore moved, that an humble Address be presented to his Majesty, praying that he would be graciously pleased to order a Copy of the Commission to Sir Charles Middleton and others, to be laid before the House.—Ordered.

Earl *St. Vincent*, after apologizing for intruding himself on the House, said, that a Right Honourable Gentleman being now at the head of public affairs, who had in another place made his public conduct the subject of animadversion and complaint, he was desirous of knowing from the Noble Lord on the Ministerial Bench if it was the intention of Ministers now to bring his conduct forward to public inquiry, that he might be ready to meet the charge? He was happy to observe a Noble Lord present, whose entire approbation, he was happy to think, every step of his conduct while at the head of the Admiralty had experienced.

Lord *Hawkesbury* did not think that it was parliamentary to call on him to make an explanation in allusion to what had occurred in another place, and he was still the more unable to give any answer, as he did not know, farther than from report, the nature of the accusation alluded to. He thought, however, he could assure the Noble Earl, that he was not aware that there was any intention of making his conduct the subject of investigation.

Earl *St. Vincent* said, that on a subject such as the present he thought himself entitled to an explicit answer, nor would he sit down contented with any other.

Lord *Hawkesbury* said, that, as one of his Majesty's Ministers, he assured the Noble Lord it had never reached his ears, even that such an accusation had been surmised or hinted at.

The Earl of *Suffolk* said, that there had been some talk of a *Tenth* Report of the Board of Naval Inquiry. He was anxious that it should be before the House.

On the motion of the Duke of *Clarence*, it was ordered to be printed.

The House then went into the Order of the Day for considering the papers laid before them on the subject of the Spanish War.

13. Mr. *Williams* presented the Tenth Report of the Commissioners for Naval Inquiry.

On the motion of the Duke of Clarence it was ordered to be printed.

His Highness inquired in what degree of forwardness the Eleventh Report of this Committee was? He understood that the Tenth Report contained matter of high importance, and he intimated his determination to see it brought forward in the way which it was becoming that every paper of consequence laid on the table of that House should be attended to.

15. The Bills on the Table were forwarded.

The *Duke of Clarence* referred to what had passed some days ago respecting a Noble Earl (St. Vincent). He observed a Noble Viscount present who had been at the head of Administration while that Noble Earl managed the Marine Department of this Country. He could not, therefore, forbear from calling on the Noble Viscount for a declaration, now that he had joined with the present Ministers, of the sense in which he had formerly held, and still continued to hold, the conduct of that gallant Commander, while at the head of the Admiralty Board. His Royal Highness had known the Noble Earl for 26 years, and he felt himself called on to declare, both as a Peer of that House, and as a Naval Officer, that he had never seen cause to differ from the Noble Earl but once, and that was with respect to his ideas on the subject of the late Peace. Had the conduct of the Noble Earl in his Ministerial situation become the subject of discussion, it should unquestionably have met with his decided support. He expected, therefore, from the Noble Viscount a consistent declaration as to the impression which still remained on his mind of the conduct of that noble and respectable Naval Hero.

Lord Viscount *Sidmouth* said, that called on as he had been by the Royal Duke, he could not resist answering the question which he had condescended to put to him. He felt no hesitation, therefore, in declaring now, as he had uniformly hitherto done, that he highly approved of, and held in the most perfect respect, the conduct of the Noble Earl, both in his situation as a Naval Commander, and as the Head of the Marine of this Country. He would be guilty of gross inconsistency, and of a violation of his own firmly fixed sentiments on the subject did he not state so, and did he not declare that the Noble Earl was, in his opinion, entitled not to the thanks only, but to the warmest gratitude of the Country.

The Duke of *Clarence* felt pleasure in hearing the consistent declaration of the Noble Viscount. He should not therefore trouble their Lordships farther on the subject, the more particularly as there were other topics connected with the Naval Affairs of the Country to which he should at some future period, not at a great distance, feel himself called on to request the attention of their Lordships.

HOUSE OF COMMONS, Monday, Feb. 11.

Towards the close of the debate in the House of Commons, the following excellent Speech was delivered by the Advocate General *(Sir J. Nicholl,)* who entered at considerable length into a discussion of the merits of the case on the part of our Government, as their conduct appeared to him to be countenanced and authorized by the established usage or Law of Nations. All writers from Vattel to Martyn, who is one of the most modern on the subject, have agreed, that if an injury be received, or an injustice done, and that explanation is demanded on the one side, and refused on the other; if there is a notice given to the Power so refusing, that if such conduct is persisted in, it will be considered as a sufficient cause of War. If after this solemn warning, as the writers on this subject observe, that Power shall continue those acts which are deemed acts of aggression, and shall still withhold all explanation on the subject, hostilities against her will then be founded in the principles of justice. An Hon. Gentleman had compared this conduct beteen two Nations to similar conduct between man and man; this, however, was erroneous. An individual illegally threatened with a premeditated attack by another, would find protection and redress by appealing to the Tribunals of the Law. It was not so in national disputes; if one Country perceived that another had assumed a fighting attitude, and that her own destruction, or any serious injury to her was threatened, she then had no resource, but that of putting herself into a similar posture, and endeavouring to give the first blow instead of receiving it, as most probably would otherwise have been the case. Every publicist of eminence has declared, that we have a right to make use of the principle of fear to compel other Nations to accede to our just demands. If this has not the weight which we calculated it would have with them, there was no alternative but that of having recourse to Arms. That such a line of conduct should be adopted and acted upon pending a negociation, when all the other circumstances already mentioned were connected with it, was not without a precedent in the general conduct of civilized Nations. On the contrary, it would be found, that in almost every instance where it was thought necessary during the course of the last century, this was the general practice of this Country, and of all other Powers of Europe. In 1718, when Sir George Byng was sent to preserve the neutrality of Italy, a similar step was thought expedient, and was of course adopted. He did not want to conceal that an outcry was raised by Spain against the manner of proceeding, and that some persons in that House also protested against the measure. But the wisdom of the House over-ruled the objections, and the action was commended as a measure of necessary precaution. In 1726, Admiral Hosier was sent to cruise off Porto Bello, and an attack was made on Gibraltar, though War was not declared for six weeks after. In 1739, the Spaniards seized all British property, even though contrary to an express article, which they were apprehensive that we would otherwise inflict on them the first marked commencement of hostilities. In 1744, in 1755, in 1763, and down to the time of the dispute respecting Nootka Sound, it was to be observed, that there was hardly an instance of a maritime War being undertaken without a similar precautionary measure being adopted. He therefore most cordially supported the Address.

12. Mr. *Grey* moved for a copy of the Royal Warrant granting an additional Pension to Lord Melville, as Lord Privy Seal of Scotland.

13. The House went into a Committee of Supply, in which the following sums were voted for the expenses of the year :—

For Extraordinaries in the expenses of the Navy	£.1,404,000
Building, wear and tear of ditto	1,503,000
The Transport Service	975,000
Prisoners of War	575,000
St. John's	2,100
Cape Breton	2,100
Newfoundland	1,130
Bahama Islands	4,438
Bermudas	280
Dominica	680

Mr. *Alexander* brought up the Report of the Greenland Whale Fishery Bill, which was ordered to be engrossed.

14. The Greenland Whale Fishery Bill was read a third time, passed, and ordered to the Lords.

15. Mr. *Giles* wished to know whether it was the intention of Ministers to have the Act for appointing the Board of Naval Inquiry continued.

The *Chancellor of the Exchequer* replied, that there did not appear to him any possible ground for the continuance of that Act.

Mr. *Giles* then gave notice, that he would move on Monday se'nnight for the continuance of that Bill.

Mr. *Kinnaird* begged to observe, that he imagined some of the papers which he moved for on a former day, respecting the repairs of the Ships commanded by Sir Home Popham, might be laid on the table.

Mr. *William Dickenson* assured the Hon. Gentleman, that every possible exertion was making to procure all the papers moved for, in order to lay them before Parliament.

18. On the motion of Mr. *Creevey*, the Accounts presented in April last of the Duties on the Exports and Imports of the Isle of Man from 1798 to 1804, were ordered to be printed.

Mr. *W. Dickenson* presented the Letters and Papers relative to Sir Home Popham, moved for by Mr. Kinnaird, which were ordered to be printed.

The Report of the Quarantine Bill was brought up, several amendments were agreed to, and the further consideration postponed till to-morrow.

Sir *C. Pole* observed, that the Tenth Report from the Commissioners of the Naval Inquiry, which had been laid before the House, was unaccompanied by the proper signatures; he therefore moved that leave be given to withdraw it, in order to its being presented in a more accurate and authentic manner.—Leave was given.

Mr. *Brooke* gave notice, that to-morrow he would submit a motion to the House concerning the Passengers and private property detained in the Spanish Frigates.

The *Chancellor of the Exchequer* opened the budget in the following speech:—" Mr. Alexander, the first article of supply that has been voted, to which I shall call the attention of the Committee, is the Supply for the Naval Service; the total amount of what has been already voted, exclusive of the sum of 390,000l. for Ordnance Sea Service, is 14,645,630l., exceeding by 2,600,000l. the amount of what was voted last year for the same Service. The excess has arisen from the sum of 1,800,000l. for the expenses attending the 20,000 additional Seamen voted this year, and for the increase in the extraordinaries and Transport Service." But there is another article of Supply to which, though I shall not call upon the Committee to vote it at present, I shall still take the liberty of requesting the attention of the House. This article is one connected with a subject of the highest importance to the interests, not only of this country but of Europe. Gentlemen are aware that we have been engaged in a continental intercourse and correspondence, with a view to objects which we must all admit to be of the highest moment. Sir, I have felt the sincerest satisfaction at finding a general conviction on the part of this House, that the ultimate security of this country is materially and intimately connected with the security of the Continent. It must be the wish of every man who hears me, that the intercourse and correspondence should be so prosecuted as to restore Peace upon grounds calculated to produce and establish that ultimate security which is the object of all our wishes and all our efforts. But seeing what we do see, and knowing what we do know, it would indeed, Sir, be rash and presumptuous in us to entertain an expectation that that great object can be attained without further sacrifices on our part.

EXTRACT FROM THE SUPPLIES.

Navy, exclusive of 390,000l. Ordnance Sea Service, 14,645,630l.

EXTRACT FROM THE WAYS AND MEANS.

It appears by the disposition paper which has been laid before the House, that there is a surplus of 123,146l.—a sum of Navy Debt of upwards of 120,000l. There is also the sum of 931,000l. out of the vote of credit for the Naval Service, which is to be added to what was not called for by the end of December, 1804. But as the demands upon the Navy are paid in bills, and as bills increase with the Service, there is a larger sum of bills at the end of the year. The result therefore is, that there is a sum of upwards of 120,000l. not called for; 11,188,000l. was only called for, including the vote of credit of 931,000l. But still of course, though not called for, there is an increase of debt to that amount. But after all, there will remain a surplus of the Ways and Means of 1804, to the amount of 1,192,115l. It may here, Sir, be proper to say, that the amount of the Navy Debt is less than it was at many periods of the former War.

19. Mr. *Brook*, pursuant to the notice which he had given yesterday, moved, that there be laid before the House a return of the number of Spanish Prisoners now in England, describing distinctly what is the amount of the number of Officers, of Sailors, and of Passengers, and distinguishing those who had been taken previous to the declaration of War from those who have been since taken; and also an account of the amount of private property taken on board the Spanish Ships, together with the order or orders for the restitution of private property, if any such has been issued.---Ordered.

25. Lord *Dunlowe* moved for an account of the expenses of building his Majesty's Frigates Bombay, 1799, and Cornwallis, in 1800, both at Bombay.— Ordered.

27. Mr. *Grey* rose, and after alluding to a notice of an Honourable Friend of his (Mr. Kinnaird, then absent from town) respecting certain additional papers concerning Sir Home Popham, observed, that there were several other papers wanting. He therefore moved for

" An account of all Repairs, &c. of the Romney, when fitted out in September and October, 1800, and the expense attending the same."

After a few words from Mr. *W. Dickenson*, the motion was agreed to.

Mr. *Grey* then moved for

"An Account of all Repairs or Alterations of the masts and hull of the Romney, in the Months of October, November, and December, 1800, together with the expenses of the same."—Agreed to.

He next moved for

"The latest Report of the Survey or Examination of the Sensible, and the expense of the Repairs of 1800, with the Amount of the Stores furnished to the said Ship."—Agreed to.

Also, "An Account of all Repairs done to the Romney and Sensible, and other Ships under the command of Sir Home Popham, and of all Stores furnished to the said Ships, particularizing the separate expenses of each Ship, and Amount of Stores."—Agreed to.

Mr. *Grey* then moved for

"An Account of all Repairs done to the Romney, and the other Ships under command of Sir Home Popham, at the Cape of Good Hope, and of all Stores furnished at that Port, particularizing the quantity and expense for each Ship."—Agreed to.

Mr. *Grey* moved likewise for

"An Account of all Naval Stores bought in the Red Sea, &c. for the said Ships."—Agreed to.

Also, "For the Entries and Discharges, &c. to and from different Ships, with the Dates and the Names of the Ships, of Mr. D. E. Bartholomew."—Agreed to.

Also, "For a Copy of the Order of the Admiralty respecting the said D. E. Bartholomew."—Agreed to.

He then moved

"For an Account of the time of Service of the said D. E. Bartholomew, expressing any Broad R's. that might have been placed before his name previous to his being apprehended and restored to the Service."

Sir *W. Burroughs* objected to the word, "apprehended:" he thought it was too hurtful to the feelings, and should therefore prefer "taken up," or any other expression.

Admiral *Markham* contended, that as Bartholomew never was discharged from the Service at the time he left it, he could not be considered as a man impressed; he therefore must be of opinion that "apprehended" was the most proper word to be made use of in this instance. The orders sent to Sir Home Popham were to turn over all the Officers of the Romney. Why he did not do so, remained for him to show.

Mr. *Grey* said, he had no wish to make use of any word that might be unnecessarily hurtful to the feelings of any person; but the whole of the inquiry might be objected to on much the same grounds.

Mr. *Sturges Bourne* said, that some circumstances relating to Mr. Bartholomew made part of the defence of Sir Home Popham before the Admiralty and that House.

Mr. *Grey* observed, with respect to the objection to the word which he had used, that Bartholomew did actually belong to the Navy at the time he had absented himself from Service; that notwithstanding the order to Sir Home Popham, he was on Shore, and on this being heard and considered, the Lieutenant of the press-gang took him, and carried him back to the Service to which he belonged.

The *Chancellor of the Exchequer* said, there could be no doubt of the fact, that Bartholomew was taken by the press-gang: would it not therefore be the better way to use those words in describing a fact which came the nearest to the transaction itself? Why not say, "taken by a press-gang, and carried to the Nore?"

Sir *Home Popham* said, he would relate the transaction to the House as well as he could. It had been asserted by the gallant Admiral opposite, that he had orders to turn over all the Petty Officers; now, he believed, the order was to discharge the Crew. He had brought home with him a number of Officers, many of whom, on arriving here, went on Shore to their different connexions for their recreation. He believed the circumstance was mentioned at the time to Lord Keith; he was then under the eye of a Commander in Chief. They were all paid up their wages to the time of hauling down the Pendant. Mr. Bartholomew could not be a deserter, nor be considered as such, since he was afterwards made an acting Lieutenant in his Majesty's Ship Inflexible, of which the Commanding Officer was very well known to Lord St. Vincent; and surely would not have been, in that case, so treated, had he been for a moment considered in the light of a deserter.

Mr. *Grey* mentioned, that it appeared to be upon a consideration of the circumstances that the order was given.

Sir *Home Popham* said, that Mr. Bartholomew was treated just the same as the other Midshipmen, and had his money paid up. He was treated in common with all the other Officers, and the Crew were turned over to other Ships. He was himself under a Commander in Chief, when the Officers, many of whom were known to Members of that House, went to their different connexions.

Admiral *Markham* said, that according to the speech of the Baronet, it would be thought Mr. Bartholomew was some young gentleman known to many Members of that House, instead of what he appeared to be on entering the Service, a Landman, and afterwards becoming an able-bodied Seaman.

The *Speaker* spoke to order, and the motion was then put, amended according to the suggestions of the Chancellor of the Exchequer, and carried.

Mr. *Grey* was sorry to trespass further on the House, but he begged to present a petition from Captain Mitchell, complaining of the false representations made by Mr. Bartholomew, affecting the character of Captain Mitchell, the substance of which he had also transmitted to Mr. Marsden, and praying the House to grant him an opportunity of vindicating his character from the allegations he complained of, either by calling him to the Bar of the House, or by such other mode as to the wisdom of the House should seem fit. The Honourable Member concluded by moving, that the petition be laid on the Table.—Ordered.

Mr. *Grey* then moved

" For a Copy of the Affidavit and Letters referred to in the Petition he had presented from Captain Mitchell."—Ordered.

Mr. *W. Dickenson* moved

" For a Copy of the Certificate of Mr. Bartholomew's having passed his Examination for a Lieutenant."—Ordered.

Also, " For an Extract of the Muster of the Enterprize, relative to Mr. Bartholomew's being taken by the Press-gang."—Ordered.

Mr. *Canning* moved

" For Copies of Correspondence between the Admiralty and the Board of Naval Inquiry, on the Subject of the Papers of Sir Home Popham, with the Dates of the Returns of them to the Admiralty and Navy Boards, and Copies of the Examinations on that Subject before the Commission of Inquiry."

Mr. *Grey* said, he believed that the Papers had not been returned to the Admiralty and Navy Boards.

Mr. *C. Pole* said, the Papers remained with the Board of Inquiry till applied for by the Navy Board. They were then sent to the Admiralty, of which the Navy Board were apprised.—The motion was agreed to.

Admiral *Markham* said, that more Papers were still wanting. He then moved for

" An Account of all Bills drawn by the Naval Officer at Calcutta, in the years 1801 and 1802, on Account of the Romney, and other Ships, under Command of Sir H. Popham, specifying the Expense of the particular Ships, &c."—Agreed to.

Also, " For Copies of Letters from the Navy Board to the Secretary of the

Admiralty, relative to all Bills and Expenses incurred for Sir Home Popham, in the years 1801 and 1802."—Ordered.

He moved afterwards
" For Copies of all Letters directing the Navy Board to investigate the conduct of Sir Home Popham."—Carried.

Sir *W. Burroughs* gave notice of several other motions for Papers.

28. Sir *W. Burroughs* said, he rose in pursuance of a notice which he had given on the preceding day, for the purpose of moving for some additional papers relative to the question which had arisen respecting Sir Home Popham's papers, the production of which had been rendered necessary by those which were already laid upon the table. His object was to show, that the expense of this Squadron, under the command of Sir Home Popham, was less than the expense of the same Squadron, whilst it was commanded by Admiral Blanket, and that with respect to the Bills drawn, the rate of exchange was favourable to this country. He thought it unnecessary to say more upon the subject at present. He therefore moved for an account from the Sick and Hurt Offices of the rations for each man per diem, on board the Squadron in the Red Sea, under the command of Admiral Blanket, and afterwards of Sir Home Popham; and also an account of the rates of exchange at which Bills were drawn upon this country on account of the said Squadron. —Ordered.

MARCH 1. Mr. *Giles* rose, according to a notice formerly given, to move for a Bill to continue the powers of the Commissioners of Naval Inquiry. He had asked of that part of the present Ministry which had been in the former Ministry, Whether it was intended to continue those Commissioners? to which he had received no reply. The Act which he proposed to continue, was one to examine into the abuses of the Naval Department, and it enjoined the Commissioners to make such suggestions as appeared to them proper for remedying the abuses. The Bill had continued two years, and the Commissioners had discharged their duty with an ability and a zeal that exceeded all praise. There was still much to do; but the continuance of the Act was uncertain. The time appointed for the duration of the Act was two years, and from thence till the end of the next Session of Parliament. It had received the Royal Assent in December; and if the present Parliament had met before December, the Act would have been in force till the end of the next Session of Parliament. As it was, it would expire with the present Session, and the dissolution of Parliament for one day would put an end to its power. The Act was now, therefore, completely in the power of the Minister. At the time of passing the Act, it was in the contemplation of Parliament, he had no doubt, merely to give an opportunity for renewing it. It might be said, then, Why was this measure introduced so early? It was merely for the sake of security. It must be confessed that the present Ministry, though they had very little more vigour than the late Administration, held a great deal more boldness, and were apt to treat the House with much less respect. The intention of the late Ministry was to bring forward distinct motions on the Reports; but now a Royal Commission was appointed to supersede these motions; and even this was not communicated to the House. The Commissioners of Naval Inquiry had yet to examine into the state of the Commissioners of the Admiralty, the Commissioners of the Navy, the Victualling Office, the Office for the Sick and Wounded, and the Office of the Inspector General of Naval Works. Of the necessity of the Commission there was the evidence of notoriety, at least as much as there had been for the passing of the Habeas Corpus Act. He concluded by moving for leave to bring in a Bill to continue the powers of the Act for appointing Commissioners of Naval Inquiry.

The *Chancellor of the Exchequer* expressed his conviction that the Reports had brought to light many things, the knowledge of which might be attended with public advantage; and he had no difficulty in saying, that if the Commissioners could not complete their labour before the end of this Session, he would be ready to have the Act continued. But there was no proof that they might not finish their task in the time that yet remained. Even on the face of the enumeration that had been made, there was nothing of any essential importance, except the Victualling Office, and the Honourable Gentleman did not know whether the

Commissioners might not already have advanced a considerable way into that business. We therefore ought naturally to wait to see what the actual state of things might turn out to be. There was another circumstance to which he wished to advert. The Hon. Gentleman had said, that the appointment of the Royal Commission, without any communication with Parliament, was disrespectful to the House. But this Commission was appointed with a view to aid the Executive Government in acting upon the suggestions that appeared in the reports. Was it then any disrespect to Parliament to adopt a measure for carrying into execution those very plans which Parliament itself had approved? This surely could never be contended with any arguments that could weigh with the House. He would therefore move the order of the day.

Mr. *Martin* said, that the most infamous abuses existed in the Naval Department. He had the highest opinion of the Noble Lord who was lately at the head of the Admiralty. He had fought our battles with skill, vigour, and success. But the Country was not more obliged to him for his actions in a military than in a civil capacity. He had paved the way for the destruction of those vile abuses, that were equally disgraceful to the perpetrators and to those who had permitted them to exist for so long a time. He concluded with begging pardon of the House for troubling them thus long.

Sir *William Elford* was of opinion, that the powers of the Commissioners ought not to continue as they were at present. They were useful; but his objection to them was, that they had erected themselves into a criminal tribunal, upon principles inconsistent with the British Constitution. It appeared from the Reports, that they had taken *ex parte* evidence, and published it in these Reports, without allowing the other parties the power of defending themselves.

Here a question arose, Whether the Hon. Member was in order? It was agreed in the affirmative, when

The *Chancellor of the Exchequer* thought that this was not certainly the mode of proceeding to discuss these Reports with any prospect of advantage. The best plan would be to appoint a day for the purpose, and take them one by one.

Sir *William Elford* again rose, and proceeded to observe, that the case to which he was to advert was very serious. In the 8th Report, it appeared the Commissioners had questioned an Attorney respecting the failure of a Bill brought against a person accused of embezzlement before a Grand Jury. The Attorney gave it as his opinion that the Grand Jury had been tampered with. He was asked by whom, and he said he believed that it was by Mr. White, Sheriff of Exeter, who was connected with the person accused. Mr. White was a most honourable Gentleman; and this statement, if it had appeared any where else, would be considered as a foul and gross libel.

Mr. *Sheridan* observed, that the Hon. Baronet was not only in order, but this was the precise time at which he ought to make his objections. The Commissioners could not do their duty without their present powers. If they had abused them, they ought to be called to account, and it was incumbent on the Hon. Baronet to prove his allegations. The Report in question contained nothing improper. An *ex parte* statement was given of an opinion as the cause of a well known fact, which was, that a Grand Jury had refused to find a Bill against a person who had evidently been guilty of embezzlement.

Sir *William Elford* observed, that he had done nothing more than state what was in the 8th Report.

Mr. *Grey* said, that the question was, Whether what was contained in the 8th Report was a breach of duty? All parties, however, would have an opportunity of doing themselves justice before the House. He went on strongly to urge the necessity of continuing the powers of the Act, and appealed to an Hon. Baronet in the Commission, whether they would have time to finish their business in that Session.

Sir *Charles Pole* replied, that a great deal still remained to be done, and the difficulty of procuring Papers was increased by the War. He would say one word as to the Eighth Report. He was not surprised to hear the objection to it, considering the quarter from whence it came.

Sir *William Elford* declared, on his honour, that he had no connexion with the parties.

Sir *Charles Pole* said, that he did not mean to say that he had, but only that he came from a part of the country where this was the general talk.

Admiral *Markham* bore testimony to the necessity which existed for instituting the Board of Commissioners of Inquiry. He would take upon himself to assert, from his positive knowledge, that enormous abuses had existed in the Navy, and he really believed one-third of the entire expense of the Department of the Navy might be saved, if those abuses could be got rid of. Those abuses were not only in the Victualling Board, but in the Transport Board, and in that Board which he considered the most corrupt of all, the Sick and Hurt. He and almost every other Officer and Sailor felt themselves aggrieved for the want of a Bill to regulate the enormous abuses which had been pointed out in the Agency of Prizes. He hoped that the duration of the present Bill should be until all those abuses were thoroughly purged away. The Right Hon. Gentleman (Mr. Pitt) had himself agreed that the Commissioners had done a great deal of good, and he thought it was not quite fair for the Hon. Baronet (Sir W. Elford) to bring an accusation against them, as it were by a side-wind. It would have been more manly to bring a direct charge, if he had any means of substantiating it.

The *Chancellor of the Exchequer* said, the Hon. Gentleman was under a mistake in his observations on the Prize Agency question. An Hon. and Learned Gentleman had already given notice of a Motion for leave to bring in a Bill to regulate the subject.

Mr. *Creevey* thought that those Commissioners must be rather considered as acting under a Ministerial Commission, and therefore would not be very forward to direct their attention to any abuses but those which Ministers wished to be pointed out. About twenty years ago several abuses were discovered in the Department of the Navy, but no measures were adopted in consequence, and the only reason assigned for not taking measures was, that the Admiralty did not like it. There was one circumstance which appeared to him very extraordinary in the present Commission. He saw with astonishment among the names of those Reforming Commissioners, the name of Mr. John Fordyce, who had himself been a defaulter to the amount of 80,000l.; he would not pretend to say to what causes this might be owing, but that was the fact. The public had lost by him both the principal of the 80,000l. he had mentioned, and the interest of it for several years. He therefore considered the Hon. Baronet had been perfectly in order in the observations he had made. (*A loud cry of Question! Question!*)

Mr. *Fox* said he merely rose to state the question upon which the House was then going to divide. When the Bill was past, the presumption and general understanding certainly was, that Parliament would, according to its usual practice, have commenced the Session before the 29th of December, and, therefore, by the intention of those who brought in that Bill, it was to have a much longer duration than what it would now have unless expressly continued. The question then of continuing it for the duration that it was originally to have had, would come to this: Whether the House was disposed to abridge the period assigned for its Constitutional Inquiry into Ministerial abuses? The Honourable Gentleman (Mr. Pitt) had stated a possibility indeed of its not being necessary to continue the Bill, and of all the matters that the Commission was intended to investigate being thoroughly examined before the end of the Session. This however was but a bare possibility: on the other side there was every probability and positive proof. The Honourable Admiral who had brought in the Bill knew well the period that was intended for its duration. The other Honourable Admiral (Sir Charles Pole), who was the principal Commissioner under it, certainly did not appear in the least to imagine that the business would be so soon at an end as to give any reasonable prospect of the labours of the Commission being ended before the conclusion of the Session. He could not perceive that the Honourable Baronet (Sir William Elford) was at all out of order; on the contrary, it appeared to him that it was the most fair and manly course he could pursue, when the question was to continue the power of Commissioners that he disapproved of, to come forward at once and complain of the abuses he supposed existed from the conduct of the Commissioners themselves. The Hon. Baronet had once made a formal motion on the subject, but was not fortunate enough to find any Member to second him. This might be the case again, if he brought forward a formal charge, and therefore, perhaps, it was better for him to state his opinion in the manner he had done this night. He was not able to see all those who were at the other side of the House—he did not understand the new connexions that many of them appeared to have formed, but he called upon all of them, who were friends and supporters of the late Board of Admiralty, to come forward, and not content themselves with giving silent votes, but state to the House the reasons why they first supported this Bill, and why they now considered it necessary, or else why they had since changed their opinion. He hoped that the opposition to the motion of his Honourable and Learned Friend was not meant as an insidious method of preparing the minds of the House for letting the Bill drop in the course of the present Session.

Mr. *Canning* did not conceive that, by voting now for the Order of the Day, he pledged himself in any manner to oppose the further continuance of the Bill, if it should be judged necessary to continue it. The two Admirals who had already spoken, differed entirely in their opinions of the time when the Commission was originally intended to expire. The Admiral (Markham) who had brought in the Bill, stated the intention of the framers to be as stated by the Honourable Mover (Mr. Giles); but another gallant Admiral (Sir Charles Pole), who was first Commissioner under it, stated that he considered it in a different light. When such high authorities differed, he thought it was right to adjourn the consideration, which was all that was meant by the Order of the Day. There was a possibility, however, that the main task of the Commissioners might be finished within the year. There was a possibility, also, that the opinion of the Honourable Baronet might prevail; and in either case the House might be disinclined to renew it. Whatever might be his opinion of the importance of the charges suggested by the Honourable Baronet, he was convinced he was perfectly in order, and that he had a right to make such comment or observations as he thought right on the conduct of the Commissioners. He thought it was rather unfair to address him so tauntingly about having made a Motion which he could get nobody to second.

Mr. *Fox* denied any intention of addressing taunting expressions to the Hon. Baronet. If any taunt was meant, it was rather against his friends who did not support him.

Sir *Charles Pole* gave his opinion, that there were at present matters of the highest importance before the Commissioners, and that in all probability their labours could not be ended within the Session.

Mr. *Bragge* said, he conceived himself to be one of the persons called on by the Hon. Gentleman at the other side of the House (Mr. Fox), and he should therefore state his reasons. As to appealing to the opinion of the two Admirals about the meaning of the framers of the Bill, he disapproved of that manner of arguing. The intention of Parliament was what should be considered, and that intention was only to be known by the Act itself. As to the intention of the framers of the Bill, it could only be known by those who had confidential communication on the subject from all the Members of Administration, as such Bills as these are not brought forward merely on the opinion of any one Board. The intention of the Parliament was, that the Bill should remain in force until its objects were accomplished. The intention of the Honourable Gentleman (Mr. Pitt) appeared to be the same. Whatever might be said of constitutional jealousy of Ministers, yet the business of a Session would never get forward, if no confidence at all was to be placed in the positive assurance of an Honourable Member, that it was his intention to bring forward a certain measure. For his part, he felt a perfect confidence in the assurance that had been given, he therefore thought the present motion unnecessary, and should vote for the Order of the Day.

Lord *Henry Petty* could not see what great danger could befall the Country even if the case should happen, which was only stated as a possible one, that the business should be disposed of before the time had come for the expiration of the Commission. With respect to another case which affected the liberties of many millions of our countrymen, Parliament did not think it necessary to fix any very nice proportion between the time that these powers might be absolutely necessary, and that in which it would be dangerous to grant them. He had never thought of having recourse to those possible cases, when he agreed to continuing the Habeas Corpus Suspension Bill only for two months. He might as well have argued that it was very possible that perfect tranquillity would be restored in Ireland several months before this Bill would expire. That case would have been full as possible, and perhaps more probable, than that which had been supposed to-night, by way of argument, of the Commissioners having finished all their inquiries in the course of the present Session.

Mr. *Hawkins Browne*, although he placed a sufficient reliance on the assurance of the Right Hon. Gentleman, that he would move for continuing the Bill, if the time was not sufficient, yet as he thought there was sufficient evidence before the House, that the business could not be expected to be finished in the course of this Session, he supported the motion.

Mr. *Tierney* said, it appeared to be agreed by almost every one that the Commissioners had perfectly well discharged their duty. The principal doubt he had heard suggested was, Whether it was proper that they should be continued during a time of War? It would be recollected, however, that the principal part of their labours, which have been of such important benefit to the public, have been carried on in time of War. As the worthy Baronet (Sir C. Pole) had said distinctly that the length of the Session would not afford sufficient time to accomplish their task, he thought it was evident that the charge should be still entrusted in those hands who had hitherto so ably and faithfully executed it. There were many accounts which were to come from distant parts abroad, and would require considerable time before any Report could be made upon them. As to the intentions of the framers of the Bill, he could not speak positively of the intentions of others; he could answer, however, for his own. His intentions were to have thoroughly examined those abuses which he heard complained of. The difference between that time and the present was this: these abuses were only spoken of, but now they have been proved. He concluded by supporting the original motion.

The *Chancellor of the Exchequer*, in explanation, said, he would not wish to be understood as having considered all the Reports of those Commissioners as highly important; he had only said that they had suggested some very useful things.

Admirals *Markham* and *Pole* said a few words.

The question was then loudly called for, when the House divided—

    For the Order of the Day - - - - - - 92
    For the Original Motion - - - - - - 75
             Majority —17

Naval Trials.

COURT OF KING'S BENCH, Jan. 29, 1805.

J. JONES.

MR. GIBBS moved for a Writ of *Habeas Corpus*, to bring up the body of J. Jones, who had been subjected to the impress by an Officer of the Navy, not because he was a proper object of that Service, but because he had committed an offence which the Officer of the impress could not easily excuse. It appeared that the Deptford Tender was, to use the Sea phrase, thrown athwart the hawse of the Brig on board which Jones was the First Mate, and it seems this man did not exactly do what the conductor of the Deptford expected, to relieve him from this momentary difficulty; the Officer, therefore, took the law into his own hands, and subjected the offender to an engagement in his Majesty's Service, contrary to his wishes and interest, during the War. This person is noticed in an official letter from the Lieutenant, in which the latter says, " I thought by sending him to the Nore, it would be better known among the persons in the Merchants' Service how such Men ought to behave in regard to the Tenders."

Lord ELLENBOROUGH.—" Is he liable under the regulations of the Impress?"

Mr. *Gibbs*.—" I cannot say by law he is not liable, but I trust your Lordship will think the law is much better where it is, than if submitted to the controul of these Officers in the Impress Service."

Lord ELLENBOROUGH.—" This is an improper letter, and it may supply a ground for you to resort with success elsewhere; but here we have only to consider if he be a fit Man to be impressed? As far as I can discern, every part of the public Service is disposed to show great deference to what passes in the Courts; but in this case, in the point of law, we cannot interfere."

Mr. Justice LAWRENCE.—" I understand the instructions to the Officers of the Impress contain an exemption of the First Mates of Ships of above fifty tons burthen. This is a lenient regulation for the protection of trade, not by law required. This Man may be supposed to have misconducted himself so far as not to be entitled to such indulgence."—Rule refused.

JANUARY 31.

This was an application at the suit of Mr. Stowe, Collector of the Customs at the Port of Dover, and it was directed against a Lieutenant in the Navy, a Commander of one of his Majesty's hired Cutters.

Mr. *Garrow* said, he was instructed, at the instance of Mr. Stowe, who was Clerk of the Customs at Dover, to move for leave to file a criminal information against a Lieutenant in the Navy, who, at the time he committed the offence which was the foundation of the present application, was the Commander of one of his Majesty's hired Cutters. This was a case of considerable importance, for there was nothing an Advocate could have occasion to speak of in a Court of Justice, with regard to which the public were more concerned, than those laws respecting quarantine, on which depended the public health. The complaint arose out of a question of this sort, and the faithful discharge of those duties which were entrusted to Mr. Stowe. This mode of proceeding was the most lenient one that could be adopted towards the Defendant, and he trusted it would afford him an opportunity of preventing the necessity of the Court hearing further upon the subject, particularly as he was undoubtedly a very meritorious Officer. It was not necessary to go through all the preliminary circumstances of the transaction: it was sufficient to state that the Defendant brought his Vessel into Dover Harbour with the yellow flag flying, to denote that she was the object of the quarantine laws. This was exceedingly improper, as Dover Harbour was certainly one of the last places in which a Ship should perform quarantine. The Defendant informed Mr. Stowe, that he had been at the Downs—that he had boarded a Vessel near the French Coast, which had come from the Mediterranean—that he had examined her papers, and had, therefore, been obliged to perform quarantine. He added, that he had received some damage to his Ship's rudder, and hoped he should not be found fault with for coming into Dover Harbour; at the same time he said he would have no communication with the Shore. This apology was received, and it was only thought necessary, by Mr. Stowe, to put his Vessel under that controul which would prevent the intercourse of his Crew with the people on Shore. In the discharge of this duty, on the part of Mr. Stowe, it became requisite for him to order the Defendant to get out of the Harbour as soon as possible, which the other peremptorily refused to do, and this conversation took place:—" Sir, do you say you will not go?"—" No, I won't go."—" Then I shall be under the necessity of reporting your conduct; and I shall report, that, when I was here before, you did not perform your duty with regard to the quarantine laws." This threat doubtless referred to the favour that had been shown him. It was sworn positively by the Gentleman, on whose behalf the motion was made, that he had not used any provoking language which could possibly have given offence, but had been actuated solely by a sense of his duty. His remonstrance to the Defendant, however, produced the following letter:—" Sir, I have no hesitation in acquainting you, that from the indecorous language used by you on Tuesday last, you cannot possess the manners or principles of a Gentleman, and I recommend your using more becoming language in future, to secure you from that chastisement you merit." After this, the Collector of the Customs was walking on the Quays, when he perceived a Naval Officer pass him, who afterwards turned round, and called him by his name. Mr. Stowe stopped him, when the Defendant asked him if he had received his letter? Mr. Stowe replied, that he had received it, and had taken proper notice of it. The Officer then said, that if Mr. Stowe wished for the satisfaction of a Gentleman, he knew his address, and where he was always to be found. The learned Counsel remarked, it was not to be endured, that persons in the exercise of their duties should be exposed to the resentments of those with whom they necessarily had official communication. He repeated, that he hoped the Defendant would be sensible of the course which it became him to pursue upon this occasion, as it was far from the wish of the Prosecutor to press the matter against him, if he made a suitable apology.

Lord ELLENBOROUGH—" Take a rule to show cause."

THE KING AGAINST ——— HERRIOTT, ESQ. AND OTHERS.

THE *Attorney General* moved for the judgment of the Court against John Herriott, Esq. John Taylor, Esq. Richard Harris, and Richard Lathbury, for a libel reflecting on Earl St. Vincent and the Lords Commissioners of the Admiralty. The case we fully reported last term. It will be sufficient to remind our readers, that it was an information filed against Mr. Herriott and Mr. Taylor, as Proprietors of the True Briton Newspaper, and Messrs. Harris and Lathbury, as the Printer and Publisher of the same, for a paragraph, stating that Earl St. Vincent and the Admiralty Board had suffered two months to elapse after the renewal of the War with the French Republic, before an account of that event was transmitted to Admiral Rainier, the Commander in the Indian Seas.—The affidavit of Mr. Taylor stated, that he was only a quarter Proprietor of the Paper; that he had no controul in the conduct of it, and no concern, directly or indirectly, in its publication.—Richard Harris, by his affidavit, stated, that he was only a weekly servant to Mr. Herriott, and that the controul of the political part of the Paper was solely in that Gentleman.—Lathbury's affidavit was to the same effect.—Mr. Herriott did not offer any affidavit.

Mr. *Const* addressed the Court on behalf of Mr. Taylor, Richard Harris, and Richard Lathbury, and enforced the topics of exculpation urged by them in their affidavits.

Mr. *Morrice*, Counsel for Mr. Herriott, said, it would be highly unbecoming in him to offer any observations to the Court, which could possibly have a tendency to impeach the verdict; at the same time, he trusted he was in a condition to state that which would at least give a favourable inclination to the judgment of their Lordships. He had to urge, in extenuation of the libel, on the part of Mr. Herriott, his subsequent conduct, and the deep contrition he had expressed for having given offence to the Noble Earl. He held in his hand what would satisfy their Lordships.

The *Attorney General*, interrupting him, said, he hoped nothing would be advanced by the Learned Counsel as the foundation of the judgment of the Court, unless it was supported by the affidavit of the Defendant.

Mr. *Morrice* said, he only meant to submit a paragraph in the Sun Newspaper, inserted since the conviction.

The *Attorney General* was sorry to suppress any thing that was considered important. If, however, the Defendant was taken by surprise, by the opposition to the reading the subsequent paragraph, he had no objection to the matter standing over, in order that it might be introduced by an affidavit; but, at the same time, he wished also to be allowed to lay before the Court other papers, which would prove a continuance of the same spirit which had dictated the libel in question. He did not think he should be justified in bringing forward any matter of aggravation, unless the course adopted by the Defendant should render it necessary; on the contrary, he had controuled those who were desirous of doing so.

Lord *Ellenborough* observed, that the Attorney General was well warranted in his objection. If the Defendant thought that any conclusions could be drawn in his favour from his subsequent demeanour, the Court would afford him an opportunity.

Mr. *Morrice* declined offering the evidence to which he had alluded. He said, it was only necessary for him to state what was the impression on the mind of the Defendant. He repeated, that he felt the deepest contrition for his offence: he was anxious to avail himself of every means in his power to make atonement. The Learned Counsel said, he would not even indirectly attend to the channel through which the paragraph in question had got into the paper. He was satisfied Mr. Herriott would meet with all the indulgence to which he was entitled.

Mr. *Attorney General* began by saying, that it was not his habit to detain the Court on these occasions with many observations, because he was of opinion that when the Court were furnished with the materials which the record itself contained, they were possessed of every thing that was necessary. He agreed that the case before the Court was one in which their Lordships' judgment would lead them to discriminate. But with regard to Mr. Taylor, it was necessary to remark, that if a person thought fit to be a Proprietor of a Paper, he ought to take care to entrust the management of it to those who would not make it the vehicle of scandal and private slander.—With respect to Mr. Herriott, he had only to say, that it would have been as well if that Gentleman had condescended to state his contrition upon affidavit. As to the libel itself, it was not necessary to say much: it appeared to be directed against the late Admiralty Board, but it was obvious that Earl St. Vincent was the principal object of attack. Whatever difference of opinion there might be with regard to the Naval Administration of the Noble Earl, there could be but one sentiment in every British bosom as to his Services. From his zeal and patriotism in risking his life in his Country's Service, there was every reason to conclude he would have filled the high station to which he had been called with equal honour to himself and advantage to the Country; but perhaps from the circumstance of his being placed in a situation which was new to him, he might not, in the opinion of many persons, have conducted himself with those lights which others would have done. In whatever way the public opinion had decided on his merits, yet no doubt was entertained as to the most diligent exercise of such faculties as he was endowed with, combined as they were with an ardent desire to serve the public by the faithful discharge of his duties. What was the effect of this libel? Not that a man, who, having ably managed the Navies of the Country, was inadequate to preside over the Naval Administration, but it described him as totally ignorant of every thing that the nature of his high office required. It represented him to have been so completely criminal as not to have sent over to the East Indies an account of the commencement of hostilities with France till after a period of two months. For this libel no excuse had been attempted, except that it was one which could not possibly have had any effect. This was no excuse for the Defendant, who had done all in his power to induce its belief. This libel contained a charge, which, if true, would have called for the utmost severity of punishment upon the Noble Earl. The Defendant had published it as a fact well known. It was as gross a charge as had ever been made against a public character; and therefore those who had given it currency ought to be made responsible for their offence.

Mr. *Erskine* addressed the Court on the same side. He observed, that it was not more from attachment to the Noble Earl that he pressed for punishment than from considerations of the malignity and dangerous tendency of the libel. It was a very unpleasant thing to see such a person as Mr. Herriott standing in the situation he did. Doubtless he was a Gentleman who, for his general conduct, unconnected with this libel, deserved the estimation of his friends. The Learned Counsel admitted that it was the privilege, nay more, the duty of every man to examine strictly into the conduct of the different members of the Government of the Country; but that privilege never could authorize so gross a calumny on a man like

Earl St. Vincent, who had given those proofs of valour to which the Country was in a great measure indebted for the ability of commencing the present War with Spain with such superior advantage. He maintained there was not, nor ever had been, any difference of opinion in the public mind with regard to the character of Earl St. Vincent; or, if any such difference of opinion had ever existed, it had been excited by the newspaper in question, which had been devoted to the purposes of a party out of power; a party who, wishing to undermine the British Constitution, thought that the Admiralty, that British Bastion, was first to be beat down. It was not difficult to suppose, that in that garrison there were spies of the enemy, who furnished the artillery which was directed against it. If any thing could aggravate the libel against the Noble Earl, it was that it had been published at a time when the enemy threatened our Coasts with Invasion, and when every loyal man came forward to protect the Country. It was at a period like this we were told, that as the Country had been saved by the voluntary efforts of the people, so our Officers abroad had been left to themselves, and to their own exertions, without any aid from Government. We were represented to our enemies as sailing by our own spirit, without any chart or compass. If it had been the opinion of Mr. Herriott, from all he had read, heard, and seen, that the Admiralty Board had acted wrong, and he had fairly published that opinion, he should have been ashamed to have urged the Court to pronounce judgment against him; for he considered the liberty of the press as too sacred to be violated, where the exercise of it had been fair and dispassionate: but in this case, the Defendant, Mr. Herriott, had come forward as the volunteer of others in a perilous service. He had not thought proper to give up his author, and consequently he could not complain if he was made personally amenable for an offence which probably did not proceed from himself.

Lord ELLENBOROUGH.—Let the several Defendants be committed, and brought up for judgment on the last day of Term.

Naval Courts Martial.

PORTSMOUTH, FEBRUARY 21.

ON Thursday a Court Martial was held on board his Majesty's Ship Gladiator, on Captain Bennet, Commander of the Tribune Frigate, by order of the Right Honourable the Lords Commissioners of the Admiralty, for his conduct in returning from Gibraltar to England, without orders.

MEMBERS OF THE COURT.

Admiral Sir ISAAC COFFIN, Bart. President.

Captain LOSACK, Captain FRASER,
——— GRIFFITH, ——— OLIVER,
——— IRWIN, ——— BLAND,
——— OMMANNEY ——— ELPHINSTONE,
——— WOODRIFFE, ——— LORING,
——— WAINWRIGHT, ——— TAYLOR.

M. GREETHAM, Esq. Judge-Advocate of the Fleet.

After evidence had been examined on the part of the prosecution, and what Captain Bennet had to offer in his defence, the Court was cleared; and upon their deliberation, it was again opened, Captain Bennet and audience admitted, when the Judge-Advocate read the following sentence:—" That the Charge had been proved against Captain Bennet; but it appeared to the Court, that in deviating from their Lordships' order he was actuated solely by the *purest motives for the good of his Majesty's Service, did adjudge him to be acquitted.*"

HOME REPORTS.

PLYMOUTH.

THE Genereux, of 74 guns, is ordered to be prepared at Plymouth for the reception of Prisoners of War.

9. Came in the Spanish Ship, Santa Maria, from the Havana, detained by the Ajax and the Illustrious Men of War, (in sight of the Montague.) Sailed the Windsor Castle, of 98 guns, and the Plover Sloop of War, to the westward with dispatches.

10. The Spanish Vessel, mentioned in the letter of yesterday, was a Letter of Marque, of 14 guns, with a very valuable Cargo, consisting of 10,000 dollars, several hundred ounces of gold in dust and ingots; horn tips; 140 bales of cotton; 150 bales of fine wool; 1400 hides in the hair; 100 hogsheads of salted beef; 35 sheets of copper; and 100 quintals of cocoa. And the large Frigate seen off the Sound, in tow of an armed Ship, after beating off and on the whole day and last night, this morning the Wind springing up, made some progress. At 11 A.M. she stood in to the Sound, and fired a gun. On being boarded, on her anchoring between the Island and Marin, she proved to be a Spanish Frigate, of 40 guns, and 300 Men, mounting only 14 guns, from Peru and Mexico, for Corunna, deeply and richly laden on account of the King of Spain and Spanish Merchants. She was captured Dec. 8, 1804, off Cape St. Mary, by the Polyphemus, of 64 guns, Vice-Admiral Sir J. Orde, Capt. Lawford, but parted company in a violent gale of Wind on the 16th ult. since which she has experienced very bad weather, carried away her main-mast, and had her rudder choaked. She fell in with, a few days since, the Harriet armed defence Ship, of 18 guns, which took her in tow; and after beating about the Channel ever since, arrived safe this morning. She is called the Santa Gertruda, and has on board one million two hundred thousand dollars, registered on account of the Spanish King, besides cocoa, coffee, hides, platina, valuable drugs, cochineal, cotton, and several rich private ventures. The Spanish Captain of the Santa Gertruda speaks in the highest terms of the attention and politeness of Lieut. Gordon, of the Polyphemus, (put in as Prize Master,) and all the British Officers and Seamen on board the Santa Gertruda, particularly from their display of nautical skill, when she laboured so much in the gale of Wind on Christmas Day last, and carried away her main-mast, and had her rudder choaked. The Polyphemus has also taken four other Spanish Vessels, richly laden. Came in the Hind Cutter, with the Flying Fish, Smuggler, taken after a long chase, with 500 ankers of brandy on board. Also the Excise Cutter, Eagle, of 14 guns, Captain Adams, with a Raft grappled for and picked up off the Maystone last night, supposed to have been, from the cleanness of the anchors, very lately sunk.

12. Yesterday morning a great alarm was occasioned by blue lights having been thrown up at the signal posts from the westward, for an Enemy's Fleet being off the Coast; these were repeated here; and in the middle of the night, the Amphion, of 32 guns, Capt. Sutton, lying in the Sound, under orders for the Straits, was, with the Harriet, of 18 guns, sent by Admiral Young to the westward to discover the occasion of the alarm. The Santa Margaretta has the Blue Peter flying as a signal for Sea. Came in the Prince, of 98 guns, from the Western Squadron, with damage by the late gales; also the Spanish Ship St. Andero, laden with sugar, indigo, cochineal, and 100,000 dollars, captured on the 30th, by the Lucy hired Lugger, of 14 guns. Went into Barnpool to refit, l'Aigle, of 44 guns, Capt. Wolfe; she is to have her rigging overhauled.

13. Last evening (just before post), the Santa Maria, Spanish Prize, from the Havana, captured by the Illustrious, of 74 guns, moved from betwixt the Island and the Main, to go up Catwater for safety above Turn Chapel Rock. She had cleared the Gut of Mount Batten, and was endeavouring to wear Ship near Queen Anne's Battery, Teat's Hill; but the Wind flattening, and being a large Ship, she missed stays, and unfortunately before she could bring up, she sailed ashore, on the reef of rocks near the Victualling Office, Point Pier Head, where

she lay last night; but the tide flowing this morning, she swung off into deep water, without much damage.

14. Came in the Diamond, of 32 guns, Capt. Elphinstone, from a Cruise; and a valuable Spanish Merchantman, Pura Serpia Conception, Prize to the Repulse, of 64 guns, Hon. Capt. Legge, off Ferrol. The Santa Maria, Spanish Letter of Marque, which was ashore at Fisher's Nase, and was got off yesterday, went up Catwater this morning, above Turn Chapel Rock, where she is moored safe from gales of Wind, near Oreston Ouze Bank; she did not sustain any damage in either Hull or Cargo. The alarm last Friday, by the signal for an enemy off the Western Coast, was occasioned by the small Russian Squadron which sailed for the Streights, being seen off the Head Land, and not making the proper signal, were mistaken for an enemy. This same Russian Squadron had been chased by the light Frigates of Cornwallis's Fleet just after they made the Lizard. This morning there was the most extraordinary catch of gray mullet ever known in this Harbour; it is supposed they were driven in by the gales of Wind at E.S.E. and very nearly 30 Boat loads of prime fish were taken this morning outside and inside of the Pier Heads.

15. Passed up for Torbay, the Channel Fleet under Admiral Cornwallis, all well, having been during the late gales driven once or twice off their Station, which the persevering Admiral, in spite of Winds or weather, still endeavours to keep, and only bore up for Torbay to refit.

16 There were seen off the Western Islands, only sixteen days since, nearly forty Sail of Spanish Vessels, richly laden from the Havana, that were spoken with by a neutral Vessel, and had not the least idea of a War with this Country; no doubt several of them will find their way into the British Ports, by the activity of our Cruisers. The Charlotte hired armed Schooner, which sailed last night, is gone with dispatches to the West Indies. Sailed the Malta, of 84 guns, Captain Granger, with provisions for the Fleet at Torbay. Came in the Crescent, of 36 guns, and Amphion, of 36 guns, from a Cruise to the westward.

17. The Windsor Castle, of 98 guns, is gone to join Vice-Admiral Sir T. Graves's Squadron, off Rochefort. The following Ships bore up for Spithead, when Vice-Admiral Cornwallis's Fleet went into Torbay; Prince George, of 98 guns; Plantagenet, of 74 guns, much strained, and has her main-mast sprung; and the Dragon, of 74 guns. Came in the Crescent, of 36 guns, from the westward.

19. Came in this morning, with dispatches from Rear-Admiral Cochrane, dated off Ferrol last Sunday, the Minotaur, of 74 guns, Captain Mansfield; she experienced dreadful weather on her passage, and will be obliged to go into Dock to refit. Saded the Caroline, of 14 guns, Lieutenant Derby, on a Cruise to the southward and westward. The Amphion, of 36 guns, Captain Sutton, returned yesterday from a Cruise to the westward. Sailed the Santa Margaretta, of 36 guns, Captain Rathborne. on a Cruise to the westward. Yesterday being the birth-day of her Majesty, was observed with the utmost respect, loyalty, and affection. The bells rang the whole day; flags were displayed on board the Men of War, and at all the public offices; and the day ended with the utmost festivity and harmony. It blows now, three P.M., a violent gale of Wind at S.S.E. with a heavy Sea in the Sound.

20. Yesterday the Amphion, of 36 guns, Captain Sutton, lying in the Sound, was paid wages and prize-money, previous to her sailing for the Straits with dispatches. Went into the Sound, the Pretty Lass, of 14 guns; and from Barne Pool into Cawsand Bay, the Impetueux, of 84 guns, Captain Martin. Sailed for Guernsey, the Staunch, of 14 guns, to join the Squadron under Rear-Admiral Sir J. Saumarez, on that Station. In going up the Harbour to refit, the Diamond, of 36 guns, Captain Elphinstone, the tide running down very strong, tailed ashore on the Diamond Rock, off Devil's Point; but the tide flowing, she swung off without damage, and got to the lower moorings in safety.

21. Came in the Spanish Ship St. Anna Conformida, from Oronoko, captured eleven days ago by the Endymion, of 44 guns, in lat. 37º 17 , long. 156º 52 ; also the Spanish Ship Santa Thomas, laden with hides and tallow, captured on the 13th by the Ajax, of 74 guns, in sight of the Ferrol Squadron. Sailed for Guernsey, to take

official letter from the Lieutenant, in which the latter says, " I thought by sending him to the Nore, it would be better known among the persons in the Merchants' Service how such Men ought to behave in regard to the Tenders."

Lord ELLENBOROUGH.—" Is he liable under the regulations of the Impress?"

Mr. *Gibbs.*—" I cannot say by law he is not liable, but I trust your Lordship will think the law is much better where it is, than if submitted to the controul of these Officers in the Impress Service."

Lord ELLENBOROUGH.—" This is an improper letter, and it may supply a ground for you to resort with success elsewhere ; but here we have only to consider if he be a fit Man to be impressed ? As far as I can discern, every part of the public Service is disposed to show great deference to what passes in the Courts ; but in this case, in the point of law, we cannot interfere."

Mr. Justice LAWRENCE.—" I understand the instructions to the Officers of the Impress contain an exemption of the First Mates of Ships of above fifty tons burthen. This is a lenient regulation for the protection of trade, not by law required. This Man may be supposed to have misconducted himself so far as not to be entitled to such indulgence."—Rule refused.

JANUARY 31.

This was an application at the suit of Mr. Stowe, Collector of the Customs at the Port of Dover, and it was directed against a Lieutenant in the Navy, a Commander of one of his Majesty's hired Cutters.

Mr. *Garrow* said, he was instructed, at the instance of Mr. Stowe, who was Clerk of the Customs at Dover, to move for leave to file a criminal information against a Lieutenant in the Navy, who, at the time he committed the offence which was the foundation of the present application, was the Commander of one of his Majesty's hired Cutters. This was a case of considerable importance, for there was nothing an Advocate could have occasion to speak of in a Court of Justice, with regard to which the public were more concerned, than those laws respecting quarantine, on which depended the public health. The complaint arose out of a question of this sort, and the faithful discharge of those duties which were entrusted to Mr. Stowe. This mode of proceeding was the most lenient one that could be adopted towards the Defendant, and he trusted it would afford him an opportunity of preventing the necessity of the Court hearing further upon the subject, particularly as he was undoubtedly a very meritorious Officer. It was not necessary to go through all the preliminary circumstances of the transaction : it was sufficient to state that the Defendant brought his Vessel into Dover Harbour with the yellow flag flying, to denote that she was the object of the quarantine laws. This was exceedingly improper, as Dover Harbour was certainly one of the last places in which a Ship should perform quarantine. The Defendant informed Mr. Stowe, that he had been at the Downs—that he had boarded a Vessel near the French Coast, which had come from the Mediterranean—that he had examined her papers, and had, therefore, been obliged to perform quarantine. He added, that he had received some damage to his Ship's rudder, and hoped he should not be found fault with for coming into Dover Harbour ; at the same time he said he would have no communication with the Shore. This apology was received, and it was only thought necessary, by Mr. Stowe, to put his Vessel under that controul which would prevent the intercourse of his Crew with the people on Shore. In the discharge of this duty, on the part of Mr. Stowe, it became requisite for him to order the Defendant to get out of the Harbour as soon as possible, which the other peremptorily refused to do, and this conversation took place :—" Sir, do you say you will not go ?"—" No, I won't go."—" Then I shall be under the necessity of reporting your conduct ; and I shall report, that, when I was here before, you did not perform your duty with regard to the quarantine laws." This threat doubtless referred to the favour that had been shown him. It was sworn positively by the Gentleman, on whose behalf the motion was made, that he had not used any provoking language which could possibly have given offence, but had been actuated solely by a sense of his duty. His remonstrance to the Defendant, however, produced the following about at private houses almost every day. The Prince of the Peace, in his violent declamation against this Country, when he talks of the Spanish Sailors and Soldiers being forced into our Service, or on refusal confined in noisome dungeons, would have done well to have informed himself more accurately on the subject, before he ventured to commit himself in the eyes of all Europe: as the Spanish Soldiers and Sailors have been at perfect liberty, under the controul of their own Officers, to come ashore whenever they had leave of absence: of course, War being declared, they will in future, like other Prisoners of War, be placed in Prison Ships for security, with a daily and ample allowance of beef, biscuit, bread, and beer. Indeed, very much to the credit of the Spanish Officers, they are feelingly sensible of all the civilities they have received during their residence here for several months past. This day Captain Wolfe arrived from London, immediately hired a Trawl-boat, and sailed this afternoon to join his Frigate the Aigle, of 44 guns. This day the chests, containing one million and a half of dollars registered, part of the Cargo of the Santa Gertruyda, Captain Don J. Solyman, lying in Hamoaze, Prize to the Polyphemus, of 64 guns, Captain Lawford, were shipped on board Dock-yard Lighters, and landed at the Yard, previous to being put in a place of security before they are sent off to London, under a strong escort of the 2d Dragoon Guards and Royal Marines.

31. Came in this morning, with dispatches from Vice-Admiral Sir T. Graves, K.B. off Rochefort, the Felix, of 14 guns, (A. S.) Lieutenant Bourke; having on board part of the Crew of the Doris Frigate, Captain Campbell, which struck on a rock and was lost on the Coast of Spain, while in chase of one of the enemy's Brigs. The Officers and all the Crew were saved. The Felix also brings an account, that the Squadron of French Ships so long blocked up in Rochefort had, in the late gales of Wind, escaped and put to Sea. There may thus be a chance at last of seeing them conducted into this Port as Prizes. Letters received from Guernsey state, the Fame, of 32 guns, private Ship of War, Captain Hosier, (late la Blonde,) which sailed from hence for Guernsey last Friday, was found on Shore on some rocks in Guernsey Roads, and totally wrecked in a violent gale of Wind at E.N.E. Captain H. the Officers, and Crew, were all saved; but it is feared they will not save many of her Stores; she went to Guernsey to take in additional Stores and more Hands, and was to have sailed for the South Seas therefrom, as an annoyance to the French in that quarter. Her Shipwreck may be considered as a national loss, and a serious misfortune to her public-spirited owners, who had fitted her out at a great expense in the most complete stile as a private Ship of War.

Feb. 2. The Veteran, of 64 guns, which went into the Sound Thursday noon, was ordered to sail directly, and put to Sea at a moment's notice; destination at present unknown.

8. Sailed a large armed Transport (No. 391), with 450 of the Royal Irish, or 18th Regiment of Foot, Lieutenant-Colonel d'Espinasse, for Spithead, to join the expedition forming at the Isle of Wight. The Hound, of 18 guns, Captain Pakenham, which arrived from Jamaica, with dispatches for Government, is put under quarantine. She brings a confirmation of the loss of the Morne Fortunée, of 18 guns, on Crooked Island. The Officers and Crew were saved by the exertions of the Boats' Crews of the Penguin. This morning a melancholy accident happened in the Sound; as a Victualling Office Hoy, that had been with provisions to the Fleet in Cawsand Bay, was returning to load another Cargo, by a sudden squall the tiller struck the helmsman, a fine youth of 16, so violent a blow as to knock him off the larboard railing. The Moucheron, of 18 guns, Capt. Reed, which sailed on Wednesday with sealed orders, had them brought from town by an especial King's Messenger, who thought them of so much importance, that the Admiral sent him on board with them, and she sailed directly. Came in the Colpoys, of 14 guns, armed Ship, with a Spanish Prize, but the particulars are not yet known. The weather is now so foggy out, that it is impossible, from the Citadel, to see as far as the Sound.

14. Went into the Sound, the new Frigate Circe, of 32 guns, Captain Rose, quite equipped and ready for Sea; she is a beautiful Frigate of her class, and does credit to the Master Builder of the Dock-yard of J. Tucker, Esq.; she only waits for orders and proceeds to Sea directly. Went also into the Sound, the

Phœnix, of 44 guns, Capt. Baker; she sails the first spirt of Wind. Letters from the Conqueror, of 74 guns, Captain J. Pellew, dated off Barcelona, the 29th of December, state their being well on that Station, and that they had detained many Spanish Vessels, several richly laden. Letters received here from the Bacchante, of 24 guns, Capt. Dashwood, dated the 31st December last, at Sea, off Jamaica, state they are well and healthy, and the British Tars in that part of the world in high spirits at the then approaching Spanish War, and are overjoyed at the idea of making captures of Spanish Vessels laden with dollars. Remain in the Sound the Phœnix and Circe Frigates, with several Gun-brigs and Cutters. In Cawsand Bay, the Tonnant, St. George, Hero, and Illustrious, Men of War. In the evening a Cartel arrived from St. Maloes, with dispatches, which were ordered to be landed at Portsmouth; but the Ship could not make that Port, and was obliged to bear for Plymouth. The dispatches were immediately forwarded to London, and the Cartel sailed for St. Maloes on Saturday the 16th, escorted by one of the Lieutenants of el Salvador del Mundo, without Penlee Point, with her Cartel flag flying.

17. The Pallas, of 32 guns, Captain Lord Cochrane, which sailed for the Hon. Admiral Cochrane with dispatches, about fourteen days since, carried away, in a gale of Wind, her fore and main top-masts; but she joined the Fleet in safety, having rigged up two jury fore-top-masts. This accident happened from her being newly and slackly rigged, and often takes place in Ships the first time of going to Sea after being launched. Yesterday the Foudroyant, of 84 guns, was completely stripped, and went into Dock to be thoroughly examined, the gallant Admiral's Flag still flying at the mizen; and from the report of the Shipwrights, it is supposed her damages are not so great as was at first imagined. Several gangs are put upon her; and it is said she will, by the activity which at present prevails in the Dock-yard, be out of Dock in a day or two. The Ships and Vessels which dashed amongst the Flotilla of Gun-brigs, &c. a few days since on the Coast of France, were the Melampus, of 36 guns, Frisk Cutter, and a Lugger; the enemy were six Gun-brigs, six Luggers, and several small Craft. The Melampus succeeded, with the Frisk and the Lugger, to take and destroy six Sail, viz. two large Gun-brigs, two Gun-luggers, and two of the Gun-boats, with little loss on our side. Came in a neutral Ship, with Parpenburgh colours, supposed to have Spanish property, detained by the Naiad; and a Russian Brig, detained and sent in by the Colpoys. Yesterday the Hibernia, of 120 guns, took in her new guns from the Ordnance Wharf; and when she is down in the water, she will be a noble Man of War. Came in the Pluto Fire-ship from off Brest, to refit. Went into the Sound the Charlotte, armed Ship, of 10 guns, to wait for orders. The Eolus, of 32 guns, now in the Sound, is also ready for Sea, and waits for orders. This forenoon came in from the Fleet, the Britannia, of 110 guns, Rear-Admiral Earl Northesk; Temeraire, of 98 guns, and Mars, of 74 guns, to refit. They left the Channel Fleet all well the 15th instant at noon, on their old Station, and the enemy's Fleet in Brest Roads, as usual.

19. Sailed on a Cruise, with sealed orders, the Circe, of 38 guns, Captain Rose; yesterday she was paid wages and bounty-money, previous to her sailing. The Temeraire, of 98 guns, Captain Harvey, made a signal for going up the Harbour this afternoon; but as the Wind is scant, it is supposed she will wait the morning's tide. The Foudroyant, of 84 guns, Rear-Admiral Sir T. Graves, K.B., which went into Dock on Friday night, was repaired in her bottom, newly caulked and coppered, and hauled out again yesterday morning. So anxious was the gallant Admiral to get her ready for Sea, that the Shipwrights and Caulkers worked extra double tides in gangs of so many in each, being relieved alternately night and day till she was repaired and out of Dock. As soon as she was hauled out of Dock, and alongside the Jetty Head, the Thunderer, of 74 guns, was immediately taken in, to have her bottom examined. The greatest activity prevails in the Dock-yard, from the first Officer to the lowest oakum-boy, to get the Ships now in Port ready for Sea. Sailed to join the Channel Fleet, the Tonnant, of 84 guns, Captain Tytler. A Man fell from the Indefatigable, of 44 guns, when in the Sound, and fractured his skull so violently as to die just as he was brought to the Royal Hospital.

PORTSMOUTH.

The Spanish Ship Cors, of 400 tons, from the Havana, laden with cotton and sugar, Prize to the Tribune Frigate, is arrived at the Motherbank.

Feb. 1. The Warren Hastings ran foul of the Weymouth, yesterday afternoon, just as she was tripping her anchor, which prevented the Convoy from sailing; but this morning they got under weigh.

2. In consequence of the intelligence of the sailing of the Rochefort Squadron, Admiral Montague dispatched one of his Tenders, to order the Weymouth and East India Convoy, which sailed yesterday, to return to Spithead.

Sailed from St. Helen's the Speedy Sloop of War, Captain Gifford, for the Dungeness Station. The Monarch remains at St. Helen's, Wind bound.

5. Ten Troops of Horse, and 1000 Men, are ordered to be embarked on board of Transports lying at Spithead, which are to sail with the Magicienne Frigate, Captain M'Kenzie, for the West Indies. Between thirty and forty more Ships are to arrive from the Downs before the Convoy sails.

6. Sailed the Decade Frigate, from St. Helen's, on a Cruise; Rattler Sloop, on a Cruise off Dieppe; Sylph Sloop, for Guernsey; Furious Gun-vessel, on a Cruise; and the Sir Andrew Mitchell armed Ship, to land some Troops, which she brought from Cork, at Cowes. The Ant Schooner, which was dispatched by Admiral Montague to order the East India Fleet back to Spithead, is returned, not having fallen in with them.

13. Sailed the Magicienne, of 44 guns, Captain Mackenzie, with a Convoy for the West Indies.

18. The Blenheim, Captain Bland, has attempted these four days to go out of the Harbour. Sir T. Trowbridge is to hoist his flag on board of her for the East Indies.

20. Arrived the Greyhound Frigate from a Cruise. This day the Camilla Frigate was released from quarantine. Remain at Spithead:—

Ships.	Guns.	Commanders.
Prince George	98	Captain Losack.
Blenheim	74	———— Bland
Royal William	80	{ Admiral Montague. / Captain Wainwright.
Draton	74	———— Griffiths.
Plantagenet	74	———— Pender.
Puissant	74	———— Irwin.
Isis	50	———— Ommanney.
Calcutta	44	———— Woodriffe.
Medusa	44	———— Gore.
Aurora	28	———— Loring.
Experiment, armed en flute		———— Mackenzie.
Ariadne	24	———— King.
Ranger	18	———— Coote.
Sagesse	24	———— Shipley.
Gladiator	44	{ Rear-Admiral Sir I. Coffin, / Lieutenant Conelly.
Melpomene	44	Captain Oliver.
Pearl (Slop Ship)	44	
Camilla	24	———— Taylor.
Regulus	44	———— Boys.
Sir A. Mitchell (Cutter)		
Tribune	44	———— Bennet.
Serpent	18	———— Waller.
Hindostan	44	———— Fraser.
Boxer (Gun-brig)		
Dexterous (do.)		Lieutenant Tomlinson.

Promotions and Appointments.

(February—March.)

Sir Thomas Trowbridge is to have the command in the Indian Seas to the eastward of Point du Galle, in the Island of Ceylon; and Sir Edward Pellew to the westward of the same place.

Captain Bissell, who distinguished himself so gallantly in the West Indies, is chosen by Rear-Admiral Sir Thomas Trowbridge to be his Captain on board his Flag Ship the Blenheim.

Marshal Murat, lately created a Prince of the French Empire, is now appointed Grand Admiral. He took the oaths upon this promotion, after one of the usual monthly levees at the Thuilleries; and the next day the Senate congratulated him in an address, in which they mention a series of exploits, including " an honourable wound at the Victory of Aboukir!" and promise, that the French Navy will find it a glory to have him for its Chief.

Captain Forster is appointed to the command of the Calypso Sloop of War.

Sir Lawrence Parsons is to be appointed one of the Lords of the Admiralty.

Admiral Lord Gardner is appointed Commander in Chief of the Channel Fleet, in the room of the Hon. Admiral Cornwallis.

Captain Clement is appointed to command the Sea Fencibles at Berwick; and Captain Lock, in the Isle of Wight.

Captain Pearson is appointed to command the Fury Bomb; Hon. Captain Elliott, to the Combatant Frigate; Lieutenant Houston to be a Commander, and command the Investigator; and Captain Oldham, of the Nautilus Sloop, to be a Post Captain, and command the Argo.

Sir Isaac Coffin has shifted his Flag to the Royal William, as Commander in Chief, during the absence of Admiral Montagu. The Rev. H. Donne is appointed Sir Isaac's Chaplain.

Captain Walker is appointed to the Thalia Frigate; and E. Bromley, Esq. to be his Surgeon.

Sir Sidney Smith is appointed to a Command in India; Captain Byng, to the Belliqueux; Captain H. Hall, to the Malabar; Captain Brace, to the Iris; Capt. J. Baker, to the Castor; Captain Sykes, to the Nautilus; Captain Gascoyne, to the Hecla; Captain E. Hawker, of the Theseus, to the Tartar; Mr. G. Whitebread, to be Purser of the Rattlesnake, in the East Indies.

Major Home is appointed to the Portsmouth Division of Royal Marines, by the death of Major Cresswell.

Captain Halstead is appointed to the Namur; Captain Laroche, *pro tempore*, to the Ajax, *vice* Lord Garlies; Captain Snell, to the Avon Sloop; the Hon. Captain Bennet, of the Wolf, to be a Post Captain.

Lieutenant Phillips, who commanded the Centurion during the absence of Captain Lind, and so gallantly defended that Ship against the Marengo, is promoted to the rank of Commander.

BIRTH.

March 19. At Cambridge, the Lady of Colonel Desborough, of the Royal Marines, of a Daughter.

MARRIAGES.

Captain Stuvang, of the Aurora, and Captain D. Luckey, of the Lord Nelson, armed Ships, to the Daughters of Mr. Ollesson, of Deal.

March 11. The Hon. C. Paget, fourth Son to the Earl of Uxbridge, and Captain of his Majesty's Ship Endymion, to Miss E. A. Monk, second Daughter to H. Monk, Esq.

Captain Humphreys, of the Royal Navy, to Miss T. Morin, Daughter of J. T. Morin, Esq. of Hanover Square.

Captain Welsh, of the Royal Navy, to Miss Thompson, eldest Daughter to J. Thompson, Esq. of Southwold, Suffolk.

J. Cooper, Esq. of Lavender-hill, Surrey, to Miss A. Thomson, Ramsgate, Niece to Admiral Fox, of the same place.

At St. James's Church, Mr. G. Lackington, of Finsbury Square, to Miss Bullock, Daughter of Captain Bullock, of the Royal Navy.

OBITUARY.

M. Chappe, the Inventor of the Telegraph, died at Paris on the 3d January.

Lately, at his house on Ditton Common, Captain Thomas Geary, of the Royal Navy.

Captain Wilkinson, in the Greyhound Cutter (having diligently looked out for the bodies of the persons lost in the Abergavenny), took up, on the 14th of February, the corpse of Mr. Barwell, and three others unknown, who had his gold hunting watch, which stopped at ten minutes before ten. In his pocket was found twenty-three dollars, and his pocket-book, containing his Commission, dated 20th December, 1804, as a Cadet in the Company's Service, &c. and a ring on his finger, having a braid of hair set under a glass or crystal—all which Capt. W. has carefully preserved for the relations of the deceased, who now lies at an Undertaker's. Many bodies will, it is supposed, be now taken up daily.

Feb. 22. Last week, the bodies of two of the Crew of the Brig Blandford, wrecked lately on the Sussex Coast off Bishopstone, floated on Shore with the tide, near Newhaven Harbour. One of them, it is supposed, from the invoice being found in his pocket, was the Master. Their remains were interred in Newhaven Church-yard. During the course of the week a considerable quantity of the Cargo, consisting chiefly of bale goods, was recovered from the Sea, by means of drags, used in Boats, at the time of low water. Among other things that drifted on Shore, was a case, containing a marble tablet with the monumental inscription of a Nobleman engraven thereon.

23. The malignity of the yellow fever in the West Indies is represented by a Gentleman who arrived in the Sagesse to have so much increased, as to baffle every established method of treatment. Since the Diana Frigate, Captain Maling, left England, which is only a few months, every Officer of her Gun-room, except Mr. Christie, the Purser, has died: and amongst the number we are sorry to state Lieut. James Douglas, her First Lieutenant, a young Officer (25 years of age) whose merit was acknowledged, and whose death is lamented by his relations and a respectable circle of friends. The names of the Officers who have died, are —Lieutenant Furmidge, 2d Lieutenant; Mr. Kilbeck, Master; Mr. Harris, Surgeon; Mr. Cameron, Acting-Lieutenant; and several Midshipmen. Lieutenant Elliott, of the Marines, was killed in cutting out an American Ship.

At Plymouth, Captain F. Wooldridge, of the Navy, aged 64.

March 4. Montagu Hotham, Son of General Hotham, and Nephew to Admiral Lord Hotham. He was married about five weeks ago to Miss Bird, of Litchfield, and had just purchased an elegant house, splendid equipage, &c.

9. Major Cresswell, of the Portsmouth Division of Royal Marines. He was an Officer of considerable merit, and received a wound in the action of Lord Nelson at the Nile.

11. At Ryde, Isle of Wight, the infant Son of Captain Cumberlege, of the Surry East Indiaman.

13. At Bath, after a long and painful illness, which she bore with exemplary patience and resignation, Mrs. Bertie, Wife of Rear-Admiral Bertie, and Daughter of the late J. M. Heywood, Esq.

Lately, in London, S. Williams, Esq. Son of the late Captain Williams, of Herrinstone, Dorset. He was formerly Captain of an East Indiaman, but for some years past has held the honourable situation of being a Brother of the Trinity House, and an East India Director.

22. At Portsea, Mrs. Young, Wife of Colonel Young, of the Portsmouth Division of Royal Marines, and Sister to the late Major Cresswell.

Lately, in the East Indies, of a decline, Miss J. Hardyman, Sister of Captain Hardyman, of the Navy; an elegant and accomplished Lady.

Mrs. Clarke, Widow of the late Captain Peter Clarke, of his Majesty's Navy, and Niece to the celebrated Dr. Franklin.

Lloyd's Marine List

OF

SHIPS LOST, DESTROYED, CAPTURED, AND RECAPTURED, &c.

FROM NOVEMBER 2, TO DECEMBER 4, 1804.

THE Beckford, Dixon, bound to London with 320 hogsheads of sugar, and 86 pipes of wine; the William Pitt, Abercrombie, bound to London; the Aurora, Thompson, from Lancaster to St. Thomas's, with a cargo valued at 40,000l.; the Young Nicholas, from Honduras to London (retaken); the Nelson, Lennon, bound to London, and several small Craft, were driven on shore at St. Kitt's. Crews saved.

The Williamson, Clappisan, from Hull to Petersburg, was totally lost the 9th September about five miles from Arensburg. Great part of the cargo saved.

The N. S. del Carmen, ——, from Cadiz, is detained by the Argus Sloop, and arrived at Plymouth.

The Abeona, ——, from Falmouth to Quebec, is taken by the Uncle Thomas Privateer, of Rochelle, and carried into Vigo.

The Brig St. Jan, Badsen, from Cadiz to Embden, was totally lost off the Texel, 17th October. Crew saved.

The Speedwell, (of Southampton) Foot, from Cork, with butter, was lost 28th October, near Plymouth. The Crew and part of the Cargo saved.

The John, Towns, from Dantzic to London, was totally lost at Owthorne the 29th October. The Captain and Crew, except two Men, are floated on shore on part of the wreck. Some part of her cargo is expected to be saved.

The Spanish Ships N. S. del Carmen, from Montevedo; the Pomona, ——; and the Gusolinsa, ——, from the Havannah, are detained by his Majesty's Ships Narcissus and Maidstone, and arrived at Portsmouth from the Mediterranean.

The Piercer, M'Cain, from Shields to Portsmouth; and the Providence, de Gaur, from Newcastle to Guernsey, were taken 10th October off Beachy, and carried into France.

The Christopher, Walkers, from Newfoundland and Alicant to Carthagena, is taken by a French Privateer, and carried into Carthagena.

The Olive, Seager, from Hull, and the Exchange, Ely, with coals, are on shore near Yarmouth. The former is expected to be got off, and the cargo saved.

The Doncaster, ——, from the Humber to London, foundered in Ouseley Bay. Crew saved.

The Stranger, Carr, from Petersburg to Chatham, is on shore and bilged near Rochester.

The Union, Whitwell, from Dantzic, is on shore on Falsterbo Reef, and it is feared will be lost.

The George, Rippon, from Dantzic to London, is on shore near Yarmouth. The cargo is expected to be saved.

The Ship James, of Baltimore, of about 300 tons burthen, Wells, Master, supposed to be from Holland, went on shore on the 20th September last, in the Bay of Glenelg, on the West Coast of Scotland, and was sold.

The Hannah, Gavin, from Petersburgh, is put into Copenhagen to discharge and repair, having three feet water in her hold, in consequence of her being on shore.

The Albion, Caithness, from Petersburg for Dundee, is totally lost on Siska Rocks.

The Adder Sloop of War is on shore near Dungenness.

The John, Sedgwick, from Dantzig to London, is wrecked near Bridlington. Two people drowned.

The Justina Maria, Woller, from Liverpool to Tonningen, is on shore at Wicklow, with six feet water in her hold. Cargo landing.

The Grezzie, M'Kinley, from Liverpool to Tralee, is lost on Tuskar.

The Charlotte and Ann, M'Kirdy, from Liverpool to Galway, is lost in Tramore Bay.

The Ann, Oatler, from Dantzic to London, is on shore near Yarmouth, and it is feared will be lost.

The Union, Hurry, from Petersburg to London, is on shore near Grimsby.

The Dutchess of Bedford, Armed Defence Ship, was drove on shore near Sandown Castle 5th November.

The Anna Charlotta, Erick, from Bristol to Embden, is on shore near Lymington. Cargo landing.

The Charlotta, Vattison, from Tonningen to Seville, on shore near Broadstairs. Cargo landed.

The Betsey, of Rothesay, bound to Ballyshannon; and a Sloop belonging to Wexford, from Milford, with Culm, are stranded near Dublin.

The Active, Nicholas, from Swansea, was wrecked 27th October near Baldough, and all the Crew lost.

The Betty, Dawson, from Liverpool to Dublin, is put into Belfast.

The Sloop Auspicious, bound to Dundalk, is on the Rocks at Cranfield Point, near Dublin.

The Ann and Mary, from Glasgow to Quebec, is taken by the Brave Privateer, and carried into Passage about the 3d October.

The Nyfus, Sandland, of London; the Brigs Elizabeth and Concord, of Dublin, with 18 other Vessels, were drove on Shore at Dominica, in the hurricane of the 4th September, 14 of which went to pieces.

The Eurydice, Gebroelson, from Valentia to Embden, is on shore off Dungenness.

The Trowbridge, Smith, from Konigsberg to London, has foundered at Sea.

The Argo, Stafford, from Shields to Lynn, was wrecked 26th October on Tynemouth Bar.

The Mary, of Sunderland, Clover, Master, is on shore at Orfordness. Crew saved.

A Spanish Frigate, from Cadiz to the River Plata, is detained by the Medusa Frigate, and arrived at Portsmouth.

The Queen of Naples, Tennien, from Petersburg to London, was on shore near Elsinore, 30th October, but expected to be got off.

The Minerva, Reilly, from Jamaica to London, retaken, is arrived back at Jamaica.

The Betsey, Bamfield, from Poole to Hull, was run down 3d November, off the South Foreland, by the Bold Gun Brig. Crew saved.

The Flaxton, ——, from Memel to Hull, is on shore on the Herd Sand.

The Elizabeth and Margaret, ——, from Swansea to Waterford, is lost near Dungarven.

The Ranger, Tizard, from Weymouth to London, is on shore near Portland, and it is feared will be lost.

The Joseph and Mary Ann, Cornish, from Poole to Liverpool, is lost near Wexford.

The Two Sisters, Ontriedson, from Gottenburg to London, is on shore on the Norfolk Coast.

The John and Thomas, Evans, from Carmarthen to London, has been taken by a French Privateer, re-taken by the Falcon Sloop, and arrived at Portsmouth.

The Countess of Cork, ——, from Cork to Barbadoes, is taken, and carried into Guadaloupe.

The James, Hanscomb, from Boston to Rotterdam, was totally lost 5th November, on West Burrows Sand.

The Cecilia Margaretta, Wohler, from Liebau to Lisbon, foundered 5th November on the Holderness Coast.

The Tyne, Wright, from Southampton, is on shore near Newcastle.

The Martin, Bailey, from Selby to London, is lost. Crew saved.

The Industry, Cameron, of Perth, from Newcastle; and the Endeavour, Phillips, of Dysart, from Sunderland, both from Scotland, with Coals, were taken off Tynemouth Castle 7th Nov. in the evening, by a Lugger Privateer.

The Brig Enterprize, of New York, is totally lost near Surinam.

The Crawford, Jameson, from Clyde to Jamaica; and the Recovery, Hardcastle, from Cork to Barbadoes, are taken and carried into Guadaloupe.

The Mary, Coleman, from Liverpool to London, is left near Belfast. Several Vessels are said to be on shore in Dundrum Bay.

The Schooner Camaren, from Barcelona to ——, is lost at Sea. Three men saved by the Polly Transport, and arrived at Plymouth.

The Mercury, Valentine, from Miramichi to Newfoundland, is totally lost on the Island of Miquilon.

LLOYD'S MARINE LIST OF SHIPS LOST, &c.

The Anna Charlotta, Erick, from Briftol to Embden, that was on fhore near Lymington, is got off and proceeded to Cowes.

The Graces, ———, from Briftol to Dublin, is on fhore on the North Bull.

Journal du Commerce, 24th October.—La Racrocheufe Privateer captured on the 14th, and carried into Trepon, the Brig Elizabeth and Ann, laden with ftones and flates.

The Contre Amiral Magon Privateer, of 18 guns and 84 men, commanded by Blackman, is captured by the Cruifer Brig, and brought into Yarmouth. The Privateer had taken the Belifarius, of Newcaftle, from the Baitic; the Scipio, and the Content's Increafe, both with coals, the latter fince retaken.

The Endeavour, Philips, from Dyfart to Weymouth, has been retaken, and is on fhore near Yarmouth.

The Schooner Flora de Mondego, ———, from Peterfburg to Figueira, is carried into Lynn by the Pilots of that place.

The Harriet, Smith, from Demerara to New York, having loft her mafts, was deferted by the Crew in lat. 23. 30. long. 66.

The Brig John and Mary, of Aberdeen, Wales, Mafter, laden with deals and timber, is totally loft near Newark, in the Ifland of Sanday (Orkneys). Cargo will be faved.

The Elizabeth, of Archangel, from Riga to Morlaix, was burnt to the water's edge off Cromar, 6th November. Crew faved.

The Elizabeth, late Grant, from Dublin to Dominica, was driven on fhore on the 4th September, and totally loft, with part of her cargo.

The Salamander, from Africa, has been taken, retaken, and arrived at Barbadoes.

The Jefferfo, Croker, from Bourdeaux to New York, is carried into Halifax, and condemned.

The George, Finlay, from Africa to a Market, is on fhore at St. Thomas, but expected to be got off.

The Brig Neptune, with coals, John Wilfon, Mafter, bound to Cork, was wrecked in Courtmafherry Bay, Ireland, 4th November. Crew faved.

The Nyfus, Sandland, from London, is wrecked at Dominica. Great part of the cargo on board.

The Friends, Donald, from London, is loft at Nevis.

The Swift, Carey, from Guernfey to Trinidada, is taken in the Weft Indies.

The Catherina, Wickberg, from Stralfund to Peterfburg, is totally loft off Helingford.

The William and Mary, Robinfon, of South Shields, engaged a long Lugger Privateer the 8th November, for three hours, off the Tees, but was obliged to ftrike, and foon afterwards funk.

The Hannah, Captain Taylor, from Montreal to London, was captured by a Privateer of 14 guns, on the 7th October, about thirty leagues to the weftward of Scilly, and carried into Breft.

The Thetis, Rutherford, from Newry, is on fhore at Drontheim, and it is feared will be loft.

The William, Hunt, from Honduras to London, is captured. Part of the Crew arrived at Havannah.

The Accomplifhed Quaker, from Archangel to London, is loft near Drontheim. Crew faved.

The Lydia, Cumberland, of Baltimore, bound to Cape Francois, was taken 21ft Auguft by a French Privateer.

The Protector, ———, from New York and Bofton to Lima, is loft at Cape Cod.

The Ant, Rowles, from Briftol to Barbadoes, is reported to be taken by a Privateer of 6 guns in fight of Barbadoes.

The Brig Princefs Royal, from Barbadoes to Surinam, has been taken, retaken, and arrived at Barbadoes.

The Friendfhip, Gerrard, bound to Embden, and the Vrow Margaretta, Boles, bound to Amfterdam, which were detained and fent into Yarmouth, have been liberated, and failed for their deftinations 18th November.

The Three Sifters Tranfport, from Gibraltar, was totally wrecked 19th November, near Chichefter. Crew faved.

The Albion, King, from Newcaftle to London, is on fhore on the Home Sand, near Yarmouth, and is likely to be loft. Crew faved.

The Honduras Packet, ———; the Mary, of 118 tons; both from Portfmouth to Sunderland; and the Fox, of 50 tons, belonging to Sandgate, are ftated in French Papers to be taken.

The Duke of Clarence, from Petersburg to Guernfey;

the Phœnix, Bariles, from Dantzig to Barcelona; the Formafura da Silva, from Petersburg to Oporto; the Wil helmina, from Dantzig to Bilboa; the Atlas, ———, from Hambro to Cadiz, are ftated in French Papers to be loft near Calais.

The Venerable Man of War, of 74 guns, was loft on Paington Head, Torbay, 24th inftant. Three men loft.

The Difpatch, Harding, from New Orleans to Belfaft, was taken near Cuba 6th July, by a Schooner Privateer.

The Alliance French Privateer of 6 guns and 86 Men, is taken by the Racoon Sloop, and arrived at Jamaica.

The Hannah Maria of Bridgewater, laden with timber, is wrecked at Ruth, in Ireland. Cargo faved.

The Eleanor, Shaw, from Liverpool to Portland, has put into Cork in diftrefs, after being out 60 days.

The Scipio, with coals, taken by the Contre Amira Magon Privateer, is retaken and arrived at Yarmouth.

The Nelly, Cummings, from Teignmouth to Liverpool, is on fhore at Torbay.

The Mary and Jane, Crabtree, from Waterford to Hull, is taken and carried into Calais. French Papers.

The Maria, of Greenock, Bird, from New York to Jamaica, was taken on the 30th Auguft, by a French Ship of 24 guns and 150 Men. The Captain, Mate, and a Seaman, landed from an American at Tobago.

The Ontario, Weeks, for America, is returned to Liverpool with lofs of foremaft.

The Jenny, Mufgrove, from London to Weymouth, is driven on fhore near Deal Caftle, and it is feared will be loft. The Cargo is expected to be faved.

The Rumney Man of War, of 50 guns, was loft a few days ago near the Texel. Crew faved.

A large Brig went on fhore near the Spurn Lights, and is gone to pieces. It is feared all the Crew are loft; two handfpikes are come afhore, marked the Nile, of Aberdeen.

The Bruton, Maffham, from Archangel to Hull, foundered on the 8th October, on the Coaft of Lapland. The Mate and two Seamen arrived at Archangel in their Boat 26th October.

The Antwerp, Dickafon, from Falmouth to St. Michael's, is put into Helford with lofs of foremaft.

The Contre Amiral Magon, prize to the Cruifer Brig, is on fhore at Yarmouth.

The Fanny, Shimels, from London to Konigsburg, is on fhore near Pillan, and it is feared will be loft.

The Lady Hobart, Loughton, from Africa, is loft on Heneaga; moft of the peop e are expected to be faved.

The Expedition, Nell, of Hull, was taken the 6th November, by a French Privateer on the Yorkfhire Coaft.

The Start, Pittegrew, from Cardiff to London, was taken 10th inft. off Beachy, by le Profper French Privateer, and carried into Calais.

The Amphion, from New York to Amfterdam, ftruck upon the Hacks (Coaft of Holland), and is gone to pieces.

The Venus, Cunningham, from Baltimore to Amfterdam, ftruck upon the Hacks, and got off again.

The Ancient Briton, Davis, from Briftol to Milford, ftruck on an anchor at Milford 26th inft. and funk.

The Unanimity, Brinn, from Wyburg to Lynn, was taken 26th November by the Hirondelle French Privateer, of 16 guns, fince retaken by Cenfor Gun Brig, and arrived in the Humber. The Privateer had taken four other Veffels which were in fight.

The Agenoria, Wilkinfon, from Lynn to Plymouth, is on fhore near Grimsby.

Dublin, 27th Nov. 1804.—"The Triumph, Williams, of Waterford; the Eliza, Roach, of do. from Dublin; and a Sloop belonging to Whitehaven, in ballaft, were driven on fhore in the North Bay. Crews faved."

The Diamond, Innes, of Aberdeen, was taken off Tynem uth, about 20th November, by the Amiral Bruix Privateer, and carried into the Vlie with four other Veffels.

The Mary, Brade, from Naffau to Liverpool, failed 31ft Auguft laft, and has not fince been heard of.

The Fame, of Hull, Mennett, from Petersburg, was taken near the Humber 27th November, by a Lugger Privateer, of 16 guns, fince retaken.

The Grithorp, Young, from Dantzig to Newcaftle, is taken by the Amiral Bruix French Privateer.

The Squirrel, Nicholfon, from Stettin to London, is on fhore on Drago.

[*To be continued.*]

SIR RICHARD ONSLOW BART
Admiral of the White Squadron

Published 30 April 1805 by J Gold, 103 Shoe Lane, Fleet Street.

BIOGRAPHICAL MEMOIR OF
ADMIRAL SIR RICHARD ONSLOW, BART.

" LAUGHING AT TOIL, AND GAY IN DANGER'S FACE."
                                                    PYE

SIR Richard Onslow, Bart. is the second son of Richard, brother to Arthur Onslow, Esq. a gentleman of considerable celebrity in the annals of the British Parliament*. He in some measure may be considered as possessing an hereditary claim to consequence in his profession; for his mother was the daughter of Charles Walton †, Esq. and niece to the well-known Admiral Sir George Walton ‡.

---

* Arthur Onslow, Esq. was formerly one of the representatives in Parliament for the town of Guildford, in Surry; as he afterwards was for that County. He had also the honour of sitting, as Speaker of the House of Commons, for upwards of thirty-three years.

† Of Little Bursted, in the County of Essex.

‡ It was this gentleman who, after achieving a most gallant action, wrote the following celebrated laconic letter, to Sir George Byng, dated

" SIR,   Canterbury, off Syracuse, Aug. 16, 1718.
" We have taken and destroyed all the Spanish Ships and Vessels that were upon the Coast, the number as per margin. I am, &c.
                            " GEORGE WALTON."

And what is singular, as appears from the original now at the Admiralty, no names whatever were ever inserted in the margin, having through haste been omitted.

Sir George Walton, in 1692, was First Lieutenant of the Devonshire, of 80 guns; and, in 1695, held the same rank in the Restoration, of 70 guns, one of Sir Cloudesley Shovel's division in the main Fleet. In 1697 he was promoted to the command of the Seaford Frigate; and in 1699 he commanded the Seahorse, a small Frigate on the Mediterranean Station. At the end of 1701, Captain Walton having just before been promoted to the command of the Ruby, a Fourth Rate, of 48 guns, accompanied Admiral Benbow to the West Indies; and was one of those few brave Men to whose gallantry the Admiral was, in the memorable action with du Casse, indebted for his preservation from captivity. On his return from the West Indies, in 1704, he was promoted to the Canterbury, of 60 guns, and in the following year was sent to the Mediterranean, under Sir Cloudesley Shovel and the Earl of Peterborough. In October, 1705, he was dispatched for England before the Fleet, and brought the first confirmation of the surrender of Barcelona. He continued to command the Canterbury for several years; and

Mr. Onslow commenced his Naval Career at a very early period of life. His first appointment, as Lieutenant, bears the date of December 17, 1758. On the 11th of February, 1761, he was advanced to the rank of Commander in, we believe, the Martin Sloop; and on the 14th of April, 1762, he was made Post in the Humber, a forty-gun Ship.

Shortly after Captain Onslow's appointment to the Humber, he sailed in that Ship, to convoy the outward-bound Baltic Fleet. On his return to England, in the month of September, with a similar charge, the Humber unfortunately ran upon the south end of the Haysborough Sands, and was entirely lost. Several of the Convoy had the misfortune to ground also; but their Crews and Cargo were saved, as was the whole Crew of the Humber, one Man only excepted.

As a matter of course, Captain Onslow's conduct was regularly investigated before a Court Martial, which acquitted him in the most honourable manner.

Our Officer was next appointed to a Sixth Rate, in which we believe he continued to serve till the conclusion of the War.

In 1766 he was appointed to the Aquillon Frigate, of 28 guns, and ordered to the Coast of Guinea. In the following

---

in 1707 he was one of the Captains in Sir Thomas Hardy's Squadron at the time that that gentleman was sent to convoy the outward-bound Lisbon Fleet. For some time after this, Captain Walton is supposed to have been principally employed in the Mediterranean. In 1711 he commanded the Montague, of 60 guns, one of Sir Hovendon Walker's Squadron, employed on the unfortunate expedition against Quebec. In this service, though unable to acquire fame, he had the negative satisfaction of escaping censure. In 1718 he again commanded his old Ship, the Canterbury, and was sent, under the command of Sir George Byng, to the Mediterranean. After his memorable engagement with the Spanish Fleet off Sicily, he wrote the above-quoted laconic letter. It appears, that he captured four Spanish Ships of War, one of them mounting 60 guns, commanded by Rear-Admiral Mari himself, one of 54, one of 40, and one of 24 guns, with a Bomb-vessel, and a Ship laden with arms. He also burnt one Ship of War, mounting 54 guns, two of 40, one of 30, a Fire-ship, and a Bomb-ketch. This gallant achievement procured for him the honour of knighthood immediately on his return to England. In 1725 he was made Rear-Admiral of the Blue; and, passing through the regular gradations of rank, he became Admiral of the Blue in 1734. In the following year he retired from active service on a pension of 600*l.* per annum. He died some time in the year 1740, leaving behind him the character of a brave, an honourable, and an amiable Man.

year he was employed, in the same Ship, on the Mediterranean Station, where he remained till 1769, or 1770, and then returned to England.

In the early part of 1771, Sir George Rodney accepted the command on the Jamaica Station. Captain Onslow was, at the same period, appointed to the Diana Frigate, of 32 guns, in which he proceeded to Jamaica with Sir George.

Nothing particular occurred on that Station, where Captain Onslow remained for the usual period; but, after his return to England, we do not find that he held any farther command till the year 1777, when he was appointed to the St. Albans, one of the Ships which were ordered, in the course of that year, to North America. It was in the month of April that he sailed, having the Dispatch Sloop under his orders, as Convoy to a Fleet of Transports bound to New York. When a hundred and fifty leagues to the westward of that Port, the Fleet was in some degree dispersed; but it arrived in safety, as the St. Albans herself also did, early in June.

Captain Onslow was in the Squadron under the command of Lord Howe, at Sandy Hook, in July 1778, and accompanied that Officer on his expedition to Rhode Island, in August following, in quest of the French Fleet*.

Towards the close of 1778 he was dispatched to the West Indies, under the orders of Commodore Hotham, for the purpose of reinforcing Vice-Admiral Barrington, then commanding on that Station with a very slender Force, consisting of no more than two Ships of the Line, the Prince of Wales and the Boyne, with six or seven small Frigates and Sloops of War. Commodore Hotham's Squadron, consisting of his Majesty's Ships, Nonsuch, St. Albans, Preston, Centurion, Isis, and Carcass, with fifty-nine Transports, having on board 5000 Troops, under the command of Major-General Grant, joined Admiral Barrington on the 10th of December. The reduction of the Island of St. Lucia was now determined on. The Fleet immediately sailed from Barbadoes, and arrived off the Island on the 13th of

---

* *Vide* NAVAL CHRONICLE, Vol. I, page 16.

December, the same day that the Brigadiers General, Meadows and Prescot, landed in different parts of the Grand Cul de Sac with a considerable body of Troops, Brigadier General Sir Henry Calder protecting the landing place, to keep open a communication between the Fleet and Army. The British Forces had not been long in possession of this part of the Island, before the Comte d'Estaing made his appearance with twelve Sail of the Line, having on board 9000 Troops. Admiral Barrington, in the most judicious manner, ordered the Transports to be warped close in shore, and moored his comparatively small Squadron with so much skill and judgment, that he baffled the repeated assaults of the enemy. On the 15th, the Comte d'Estaing made two desperate attacks on the British Squadron; but the determined coolness, resolution, and bravery of its Commanders, supported by a steady and well-directed fire from the Batteries on Shore, compelled him to stand to Sea and relinquish all farther attempts. On the following day the French Fleet was seen plying to windward, and in the evening it anchored off Gros Islet. The French Troops which were landed made several attempts to carry the Batteries, in all of which they were repulsed with dreadful slaughter. Finding every effort to recover the Island ineffectual, they re-embarked, and left the Conquerors in quiet possession.

Captain Onslow appears to have been very actively employed in this expedition; for, in his official dispatch of December 23, Admiral Barrington says :—" More than half the Troops were landed the same morning (the 13th) under the direction of the Commodore, assisted by the Captains, Griffith, Braithwaite, and Onslow, and the remainder the next morning, when they immediately got possession of the careenage *."

Early in the summer of 1779 Captain Onslow returned to England with a Fleet of Merchant Ships under his Convoy, the St. Albans being unfit for farther service without first undergoing a thorough repair.

Soon after his arrival he was appointed to the Bellona, a

---

* Vide NAVAL CHRONICLE, VOL. IV, page 181.

Seventy-four gun Ship, and employed in the Channel Fleet, then under the command of Admiral Sir Charles Hardy. The latter Officer dying suddenly on the 19th of May, 1780, Admiral, afterwards Sir Francis Geary, succeeded to the chief command. In the following month Admiral Geary sailed from Spithead, with twenty-three Sail of the Line, among which was the Bellona, to cruise in Soundings, with a view to prevent the junction of the French and Spanish Fleets. Nothing material occurred till the morning of the 3d of July, when a Fleet of twenty Sail was descried. These were immediately concluded to be the enemy, of whom they were in search, and the utmost alacrity was used in getting up with them. They were at length, however, found to be nothing more than a Convoy from St. Domingo, under the protection of a single Ship, le Fier, of 50 guns. The chase was continued; and, had it not been for a fog, which suddenly came on, the whole of them would have been captured. Owing to this circumstance, le Fier, with eight Sail of the Convoy, escaped, the remaining twelve falling into the possession of the English. This achievement fell short of the expectations of the captors, but was notwithstanding of some consequence, the value of the Ships taken being estimated at 126,000l.

The Fleet continued at Sea for upwards of two months without meeting with any thing farther deserving of notice; after which, a number of the Seamen being ill, it returned to Spithead on the 18th of August.

Shortly after the arrival of the Fleet in Port, Admiral Geary being taken ill, the chief command devolved upon Vice-Admiral Darby. Captain Onslow still remained in the Bellona; and, in the month of December, being on a Cruise in the Channel, he had the good fortune to fall in with the Princess Caroline, a Dutch Ship of War, bound for Lisbon, from Amsterdam, mounting 54 guns, and carrying three hundred Men. A close action ensued, which lasted for half an hour; when, four of the Dutchmen having been killed, and twelve wounded, the Princess Caroline struck to the Bellona. Captain Onslow took possession of his Prize, and brought her safe into the Downs.

Great preparations having been made during the winter, to equip a formidable Fleet and Convoy for the relief of Gibraltar, it sailed from Portsmouth under the orders of Admiral Darby, on the 13th of March, 1781. This Fleet, to which the Bellona was attached, was equal in force to the magnitude of the object which it was sent to execute. It consisted of two Ships of 100 guns each, seven of 90, one of 80, eleven of 74, seven of 64, and one of 60, with eight large Frigates, a proportionate number of smaller Vessels, and a Convoy of upwards of two hundred Sail of Transports and Store-ships. The whole of them arrived off Gibraltar on the 13th of April, without experiencing the slightest interruption from the enemy, notwithstanding they had a Fleet ready for Sea in Cadiz considerably superior in force, amounting to thirty-three Ships of the Line. All the stores and reinforcements were put on Shore by the 20th of the month, and on that day the Fleet sailed on its return to England, having sustained no farther damage during the whole of so dangerous an expedition, than the loss of a mizen-mast in the Nonsuch, and a few Men wounded in some of the Frigates by the desultory attacks of the Spanish Gun-boats.

On the 13th of April, 1782, the Bellona sailed from Spithead on a Cruise to the westward, with the Squadron under the command of Vice-Admiral Barrington. On the 20th the Artois made the signal for having discovered an enemy's Fleet; and, on the following morning, the memorable action, which is described at length in our memoir of Earl St. Vincent*, between the Foudroyant and le Pegase, took place. The Fleet returned to Spithead on the 26th.

On the 3d of the following month Captain Onslow sailed with the unfortunate Admiral Kempenfelt on a fortnight's Cruise in the Soundings.

On the 11th of September, in the same year, Capt. Onslow, still in the Bellona, sailed from Spithead, with the Fleet under the command of Admiral Lord Howe, for the relief of Gibraltar. The British Fleet, with its Convoy, entered the Straits on the

---

* *Vide* NAVAL CHRONICLE, Vol. IV, page 9.

morning of the 11th of October, and, about five o'clock in the afternoon, arrived off the Bay. By the 18th, Lord Howe having effected the relief of the Garrison, the grand object of his commission, availed himself of the easterly Wind to repass the Straits. At day-break, on the morning of the 19th, the combined French and Spanish Fleets were seen at some distance in the N.E. Being then between Ceuta and Europa Points, and there not being sufficient room to form in order of battle, Lord Howe pursued his course, followed by the enemy, until he had got clear of the Straits. The next morning the Wind had shifted to the northward, so that the enemy still had the advantage of the Wind. The British Fleet, however, formed in order of battle, to leeward, to receive them. Captain Onslow was stationed in the Line, as second to Vice-Admiral Milbanke. It was sun-set before the enemy began to cannonade the British van and rear, which continued until ten at night, but at such a considerable distance as to produce very little effect. Owing to the partial approach of the enemy, the division in which Captain Onslow was stationed was but trivially engaged; the Bellona not having a single Man either killed or wounded. The fire was occasionally returned from those of our Ships whose shot might reach to make any impression; but the enemy soon hauled to the Wind, and the next day were seen standing off to the N.W. The whole loss sustained by the English amounted but to 68 killed and 208 wounded.

A few days after the action, the Bellona, with seven more Sail of the Line, was dispatched to the West Indies, under the orders of Sir Edward Hughes; but hostilities ceasing almost immediately after his reaching that Station, Captain Onslow returned to England early in the ensuing summer, without having met with the least opportunity of increasing either his fame or his fortune.

It does not appear that he held any command, subsequently to his return to Europe, until the year 1790, when he was appointed to the Magnificent, of 74 guns, one of the Fleet intended for Channel service, and equipped through the apprehension of a rupture with Spain relative to Nootka Sound. That alarm, however, having blown over, he quitted his command before the conclusion of the year, and, we believe, was never again employed as a private Captain.

On the 1st of February, 1793, he was advanced to be Rear-Admiral of the White; on the 12th of April, 1794, to be Rear-Admiral of the Red; on the 4th of July, in the same year, to be Vice-Admiral of the White; and on the 1st of June, 1795, to be Vice-Admiral of the Red.

On the 25th of November, in the latter year, Admiral Onslow had the misfortune to lose his eldest Son, who died at Sea, on board of the Barfleur, to which Ship he belonged, as Midshipman.

In 1796 our Officer was, for a short time, Port-Admiral at Plymouth, and was soon afterwards appointed second in command of the Fleet stationed in the North Sea, under the orders of Admiral Duncan, to watch the motions of the Dutch Fleet in the Texel. He accordingly hoisted his flag, first, we believe, in the Nassau, of 64 guns, and afterwards in the Monarch, of 74. No occurrence, however, sufficiently memorable to require particular mention, took place till the month of October, 1797, when he very conspicuously distinguished himself in the encounter with, and defeat of, the Dutch Fleet under Admiral de Winter.

Admiral Duncan's Fleet had blocked up the Texel during the whole summer; but early in October, being in want of some repairs, it put into Yarmouth Roads, leaving a small Squadron of observation under the command of Captain Trollope. The Dutch, availing themselves of this favourable opportunity, put to Sea. On the morning of the 9th of October this was intimated to Admiral Duncan, by a signal from a Vessel at the back of Yarmouth Sands; and in the course of the afternoon the whole British Fleet had got under weigh, and were out of sight. At nine in the morning of the 11th the Admiral got sight of Captain Trollope's Squadron, with signals flying for an enemy to leeward. Admiral Duncan immediately bore up, made the signal for a general chase, and in less than an hour came within sight of the enemy, who were forming in a line on the larboard tack to receive him*.

As Admiral Duncan approached near, he made the signal for the Fleet to shorten sail, and to form in close order. Soon after he saw the land between Camperdown and Egmont, about nine miles to leeward of the enemy; and finding that there was no time to be lost in making the attack, at half-past eleven he made the signal to bear up, break the enemy's line, and engage them to leeward, each Ship her opponent: by this decisive effort he got between them and the land, whither they were fast approaching. Admiral Duncan's signals were obeyed with great promptitude; and it is here requisite to notice, for the credit of Vice-Admiral Onslow, that the Monarch, on board of which his flag was flying, was the Ship that commenced the action, and that sustained greater injury than any one in the British Fleet, the Ardent excepted . The Monarch bore down in the most gallant manner on the enemy's rear, and was followed by the Vice-Admiral's whole division‡. About half past twelve he broke through the enemy's line, passed under the Dutch Vice-Admiral's stern, and engaged him to leeward.

---

* *Vide* NAVAL CHRONICLE, Vol. IV, page 109.

† The slaughter on board of the Ardent was very great, she having a Midshipman, and 34 Seamen, killed; 9 Officers, 79 Seamen, and 12 Marines, wounded.

‡ THE LARBOARD OR LEE DIVISION.

Ships.	Guns.	Men.	Commanders.	Killed.	Wounded.
Russel	74	590	Capt. Henry Trollope	0	0
Director	64	491	—— William Bligh	0	0
Montague	74	590	—— John Knight	0	0
Veteran	64	491	—— George Gregory	0	0
Monarch	74	599	Richard Onslow, Esq. Vice-Admiral of the Red Capt. Edward O'Brien	36	100
Powerful	74	590	—— W. O Br. Drury	10	78
Monmouth	64	491	—— James Walker	0	0
Agincourt	64	491	—— John Williamson	0	0

The Commander in Chief, in his official account of the action, pays the following very just tribute to our Officer's gallantry:—" My signals were obeyed with great promptitude; and Vice-Admiral Onslow, in the Monarch, bore down on the enemy's rear in the most gallant manner, his division following his example."

Admiral Duncan intended to engage the Dutch Commander in Chief, but was prevented by the States General, of 76 guns, bearing a blue flag at the mizen, shooting close up with him; the Admiral therefore ran under her stern, engaged her close, and soon compelled her to quit the line. The Venerable (Admiral Duncan's Ship) then fell alongside of the Dutch Admiral, who was for some time well supported, and kept up a very heavy fire. At one o'clock the action was pretty general, except by two or three van Ships of the enemy's line, which got off without the smallest apparent injury, and entered the Texel on the following day. The action continued with unabating fury for nearly two hours and a half, when all the masts of de Winter's Ship went by the board: she was defended for some time after in a very gallant manner; but at length finding all farther resistance vain, she struck her colours to the Venerable; the Dutch Admiral himself being, it is said, the only man left on the quarter-deck who was neither killed nor wounded.

About the same time that the Dutch Commander in Chief struck to Admiral Duncan, their Vice-Admiral * appeared dismasted, and surrendered to Vice-Admiral Onslow. The result of the action is well known. Seven Sail of the Line, two of 56 guns, and two large Frigates, were taken; the Delft, of 56 guns, foundered; one of the Frigates was afterwards lost, and the other was driven on the Coast of Holland and retaken.

From the crippled state of the Monarch, and the Wind blowing strong on the enemy's Coast, it was with some difficulty that Admiral Onslow could keep off from the land, and get over to the British Shore. He, however, with the rest of the Fleet, and its Prizes, arrived at the Nore on the 16th of October.

For his gallant conduct in this action, his Majesty was graciously pleased, on the 30th of the same month, to create Admiral Onslow a Baronet of Great Britain. He had also the honour of receiving the Thanks of both Houses of Parliament,

---

* Reintjies, of the Jupiter, of 74 guns, and 550 Men. He was severely wounded, and died soon after his arrival in England.

and was presented with the Freedom of the City of London, and a sword of a hundred guineas value.

Sir Richard Onslow retained his command in the North Sea Fleet, but without any farther opportunity of distinguishing himself, till the year 1799, when he resigned, and has not since hoisted his flag. On the 14th of February, 1799, he was promoted to be Admiral of the Blue Squadron; and on the 13th of April, 1804, he acquired the same rank in the White.

NAVAL ANECDOTES,
COMMERCIAL HINTS, RECOLLECTIONS, &c.

NANTES IN GURGITE VASTO.

SCARBOROUGH, FEB. 15, 1805.

THE following very affecting letter from a gallant youth of seventeen years of age, a Lieutenant of Marines, the son of Mr. Thurnham, of Scarborough, who fell in the service of his country, will evidence the delicate sense of honour and invincible courage which actuate our brave defenders in the most perilous enterprises, even under the strong presentiments of certain death.

His Majesty's Ship Illustrious, Jan. 9.

" HONOURED FATHER,—I think it my duty to write, as I am going this evening on a dangerous enterprise, to cut out a Spanish Sloop of War: if any disaster should happen to me, you must apply to Mr. Mackie for my clothes, to whom I have ordered them to be sent; but if they should not be sent, application must be made to Captain S., Royal Marines, of the Illustrious. Do not blame me for volunteering my services, as while the blood of the Thurnhams circulates in my veins, I could not bear to have it said that *he is a coward*. Give my love to my dear mother, my brother, and sister. I hope they will not regret what I have done.— If I escape, nothing will give me so much pleasure as to think that I have neither disgraced my commission nor my father, and to have it said that I am an honour to the family; if I die, I die an honourable death.—God bless you all! and may the next son you have die as honourably as I do!—I beseech you to remember me to my cousin, and to all my dear relatives.

" I remain your faithful son,
" D. THURNHAM."

[The above was accompanied by a letter of condolence from Captain S. announcing the instant death of the gallant youth in his bold exertion in the enterprise, by a mortal wound in the body.]

FRENCH NAVY.

THE following statement of the present Naval Force of France, is given by a gentleman who procured it from an Officer of one of the French Gun-boats which were lately brought into Falmouth:—

AT BREST.		Ships.	Guns.
Ships.	Guns.	Le Pheton,	74
Le Vengeur,	120	And one Frigate.	
Le Republicain,	110	L'ORIENT.	
L'Invincible,	110	L'Algeziras,	74
L'Alexandre,	80	Building.	
Le Foudroyant,	80	Le Regulus,	74
L'Impetueux,	74	Le Courageux,	74
Le Brutus,	74	L'Alcide,	74
Le Castor,	74	And one Frigate.	
Le Veteran,	74	AT ROCHEFORT.	
Le Pelago,	74	Le Majestueux,	120
Le Conquerant,	74	Le Magnanime,	80
L'Ulysse,	74	Le Suffrein,	74
Le Courville	74	Le Lion,	74
L'Eole,	74	Le Gemappe,	74
La Revolution,	74	Frigates.	
Le Dix d'Aout,	74	L'Armide,	18
La Constitution,	74	La Gloire,	18
L'Alliance,	74	L'Indefatigable,	24
Le Batave,	74	Building.	
Le Patriot,	74	La Ville de Paris,	120
Le Gauloire,	74	L'Achille,	74
AT TOULON.		L'Ajax,	74
Le Formidable,	80	AT NANTZ.	
L Indomptable,	80	Le President,	18
Le Neptune,	80	AT CADIZ.	
Le Bucentaure,	80	L'Aigle,	74
L Annibal,	74	IN INDIA.	
Swiftsure,	74	Le Marengo,	74
Berwick,	74	Frigates.	
L'Intrepide,	74	La Belle Poule,	
Le Monblanc	74	La Semmillante,	
Le Scipion,	74	&c. &c.	
L'Atlas.	74	IN AMERICA.	
Frigates.		La Sibelle,	
L Incompatible,	24	La Didon,	
La Cornelie,	18	La Milanaise.	
L'Horteuse,	18	AT FERROL.	
Le Rhin,	18	Le Heron,	74
La Musirou,	18	Le Duguay Trouin,	74
L'Uranie,	18	Le Redoubtable,	74
La Sirene,	12	Le Fougueux,	74
La Thamise,	12	L Argonaut,	74
Building.		Frigate.	
Le Borne.	74	La Guerriere,	42

SELF-TAUGHT NAVAL MECHANIC.

THERE is living not a hundred miles from Stonehaven, a man who has practised a greater variety of the mechanical arts, than any one person we remember to have heard of. He was originally bred a country Blacksmith, and is known to have attained considerable proficiency in that line. Self-taught, he soon became a professed clock and watch maker. He did not confine himself, however, to the movements only; for, as soon as it was completed, he formed the mahogany case; and this part of his workmanship would do credit to the regularly bred cabinet-maker. His genius next extended itself to musical instruments; in the evenings of one winter he made, for his amusement, six or eight violins. of which the workmanship and varnish were excellent, and the tones by no means despicable. One of them he constructed to play with eight strings, two of each kind; and the effect, especially in slow music, was very pleasant. He lately purchased a small Bark, which, with the assistance of his son, a boy, he now navigates in the coal trade. He was at Sea in this Bark during one of the last winter's Storms, and was supposed to have finished his career in *Davy's Locker;* but, after some time, he was found snug in the Harbour. About a month ago his Vessel encountered another Storm, in which several planks were stove, and her stern demolished. Here a new channel was opened for his multifarious ingenuity. He immediately set to work, and joining the old Blacksmith to the Ship-carpenter, forced bolts and shaped timber, and by the work of his own hands alone, has completed the necessary repairs. Had such a genius been under the direction of proper judgment, there is reason to believe that it would have conducted its possessor to not a little renown.

NEW LIFE BOAT.

OUR curiosity, says a letter from Dover, has long been raised by the knowledge that a Life-boat of a peculiar construction was building here by the Man who saved the Prize-master and Prisoners floating on the Wreck of the French Gun-boat that drifted past the Harbour in the winter. Sir Sidney Smith, who gave the plan of this Boat, came down from London yesterday, and tried it at Sea, with eighteen Men embarked on board, attended by Capt. Western, of the Sea Fencibles, in a Deal Boat. The Piers and Beach were crowded with spectators, who felt much anxiety at seeing her make her first plunge into the swell at the Harbour's mouth; she rose, however, at the top of every wave, and as soon as the mast was secured, the rigging of which appeared defective, the sails were set, and she moved with great rapidity through the breakers, which hid her from our sight. The Deal Boat, although a large Galley of above forty feet long, found the Sea too much for her, and put back into the Harbour. The Lifeboat, which is called the *Cancer* or *Crab*, from her manner of moving and taking the ground, landed on the Beach without the smallest inconvenience from the Surf, and was hauled above highwater mark by the spectators, who greeted the enterprising Crew, for whose safety they had been so anxious, with most heartfelt satisfaction.

ANECDOTE OF CAPTAIN NESHAM.

THIS gentleman, who has recently been appointed acting Captain of the Foudroyant, was in France during the fury of the Revolution, and while the popular rage was vented on the unfortunate bakers. Passing through one of the streets, he perceived a baker in the hands of the mob, who were hurrying him away *à la lanterne*. With all the inconsiderate bravery of a generous Tar, thoughtless of his own danger, he rushed among the sanguinary multitude, and throwing himself round the half-dead wretch, declared, that " if they destroyed one innocent man, they should the other." The extraordinary generosity of this heroic action was not lost on the surrounding multitude; and those very people, who but for him would have exulted in the destruction of their victim, now carried him and his deliverer before the National Convention. With loud shouts of applause he was welcomed, as having saved the life of a citizen; was presented with a National Sword, dedicated to such purposes, and a Civic Crown placed on his head.

ANECDOTE OF LORD HOWARD.

IN the reign of Queen Mary, Lord William Howard, first Baron of Effingham, and Lord High Admiral of England, put to Sea with twenty-eight Sail, to meet King Philip, the destined husband of his mistress. That Prince was escorted by one hundred and sixty Sail, and carried at his top-mast-head the Spanish flag. The English Admiral could not bear to see it flying in the British Channel, and without once considering that the Spaniards were almost six to one, without despairing of success, in case of an action, saluted the Prince with a shot, and made him take down his colours before he would pay any compliments to him.

REMARKABLE PRESERVATION.

DURING the passage of the Europe, East Indiaman, outward-bound to Madras, the following curious incident occurred, which is thus noticed by a Passenger:—

" June 29.—At 9 A.M. saw a small Sail on our lee-bow; at 10 hove-to, and sent a Boat on board with the second Officer; he found one Man only on board, whom he brought with him, and turned the Sail adrift, she being quite a Wreck. The Man gives the following very curious account of himself:—That he sailed from London as Second Mate of the Brig Thomas, of London, commanded by Captain Gardner, and belonging to Messrs. Broderick and Co. on the 4th of March, 1802, bound to the South Seas, on the whale fishery; that after touching at several places on their outward-bound Voyage, they arrived at Staten Land, where they remained six or seven months, and got about seven or eight hundred skins. In the course of that time they lengthened and decked their Long-boat, and converted her into a Shallop, of which they gave him the command, and put three Seamen on board, under him; at the same time giving him orders to accompany the Brig to the Island of Georgia, whither they were bound to procure seals and Sea elephants. They accordingly left Staten Island the latter end of January, 1803, in company with the Brig; and after eleven days' passage, arrived at the Island of Georgia, where they remained two months, and left it the beginning of April; the Brig, and another Brig, the John of Boston, in company, and stood off the Island of Tristan de Cunha.

" On the 14th of April they were parted from their Consorts in a heavy gale of Wind, in which he lost his three hands, who were washed over by a tremendous Sea, from which he narrowly escaped, having, *only the moment* before, gone below for a knife to cut away some part of the rigging. At that time he had on board only three pounds and a half of meat, three pounds of flour, six pounds of bread, and two hogsheads of water (all of which were much damaged by the Gale), some whale oil remaining in the bottoms of a few casks, a small quantity of salt, and some bark of trees. On this scanty pittance, and without any means of even dressing that, he had contrived to support existence for the surprising space of seventy-five days, for the last thirty of which his principal means of subsistence was tobacco, and the bark of trees soaked in whale oil. When we fell in with him he was shaping a course for the Cape of Good Hope, having missed Tristan de Cunha, where he first meant to proceed to rejoin his Consort; his debility was, however, so great, that two or three days more want of sustenance would have ended his earthly career. A subscription was immediately made for the poor invalid, which amounted to 110l."

FRENCH CRUELTY.

(From the Philadelphia True American.)

CAPTAIN Maley, of the Schooner Mount Vernon, informs, that his Vessel was captured on the 1st of October, near Tortuga, by a French Privateer, himself and Crew taken out, stripped of their all, the Vessel's papers destroyed or detained, and the Vessel sent into a bye Port near Barracoa, and there sold with her Cargo, without trial or delay. After being detained near a month on board the Privateer, Captain M., his Crew, and the Supercargo, Mr. John Caldwell, of this city, were put ashore about forty miles from St. Jago de Cuba, and after many difficulties reached that place, where all died except himself and Boy. He sailed from St. Jago on board the Brig Ceres, and left there the Ship Clarissa, of New York, discharging, and Schooner Lydia, of Norfolk. Eleven Privateers of and from three to seven guns each were fitting out, and many from different Ports in Cuba were cruising. Captain Maley saw a list of 97 Privateers out of that Island, several of them had received Spanish commissions since the capture of Spanish Vessels by the Hatyans.

THE DANISH NAVY.

THE following interesting account of the Danish Navy is extracted from the celebrated Travels of Kuttner through Denmark, Sweden, &c. which are now being translated into English.

" The whole Danish Navy lies in the Harbour of Copenhagen. Though this arrangement is in many respects very convenient, yet it is attended with great disadvantages, both on account of danger from fire and blockades, or surprises in time of War. The Harbour for Merchant Ships, and that for the Men of War, are separated only by wooden piles, or a kind of balustrade. Contiguous to the latter are several Islands, denominated Holms, upon which are Dock-yards, containing every thing necessary, not only for the building, but likewise the equipment, of Ships of War. The house in which the cables are made is said to be 900 feet in length, and I really think it the longest I ever saw. The thickest cables made there are 20 inches in circumference.

" We were conducted to the model-house, which is not usually shown in other Dock-yards; on this occasion it was observed, that no foreigner is permitted to see those at Portsmouth and Plymouth. A complete model of a Ship of the Line was shown us I never saw, even in England, any thing more perfect, or more exquisite workmanship, or better calculated to afford an idea of each individual part of a Ship. The whole can be taken into very small pieces, so that every thing may be seen in the most distinct manner. We were told that several Men had been employed nine years on this model.

Mr. Hohlenburgh has invented a new method of building Men of War, which consists in decreasing the width of the stern, so as to make it much narrower than across the middle, or than the Ships of War of any European nation usually are. This method is attended with the advantage, that the three aftermost guns on each side may be directed so as not only to fire straight forward, but likewise to the right and left. I saw a 24-gun Frigate of this construction nearly ready for launching. It likewise has this peculiarity, that all the knees are of iron. By the alteration a considerable space is gained in the Ship, and the movement of the guns greatly facilitated; for as the iron knee is much smaller than one of wood, and consequently requires less room, the guns may be pointed in a more oblique direction, either to the right or left. The English, however, are extremely hostile to this new method, and maintain that the knees must absolutely be of wood, because a Ship is so shaken by the firing of the guns, that every part must receive and yield to the shock: but if the knees are of iron, instead of yielding, they re-act upon the body of the Ship with greater violence, so that it is more liable to injury, and in the end will not last so long as those with wooden knees.—Time must decide who is right.

All Men of War, built at this place, are of oak. Fir, which the English occasionally employ, is absolutely rejected. The Seeland oak is held in the highest esteem.

Besides the above-mentioned Frigate, a 74-gun Ship was on the stocks, but not on Hohlenburgh's plan. I thought this Vessel very heavy in wood, when compared with an English Man of War of the same number of guns, but the Danes obstinately refused to admit the truth of this observation. I had before made the same remark on the Dutch Ships.

The whole Naval Force of Denmark consists at present of 24 Ships of the Line, the largest of which carries 84, and the smallest 64 guns. Only one, called Christian VII, carries 100 guns; but she is too heavy, and consequently draws too much water for these northern Seas, and is on that account never used. They could not or rather would not, tell me the number of Frigates and small Ships, but I know that it is inconsiderable. The heaviest cannon are thirty-six pounders; the largest English Ships carry forty-two pounders, but the Danish pound is ten per cent. heavier than the English.

To inspect the Holms, or Dock-yards, a special permission from the Court is required. Our names were transmitted to the Crown Prince, and this regulation extends to all foreigners. Particular precaution has been observed in this respect since the last conflagration.

DUTCH LIBERALITY.

THE following letter from Captain Colvill to the Dutch Admiral Kihkert, is published in the Dutch papers:—

Sir,—Before I quit this place, so different from the usual state of captivity and hardships we had to expect, I beg leave, as well on my own part as on that of my fellow Officers, who belonged to his Britannic Majesty's Ship the Romney, to return you our most sincere thanks, and to assure you, that the very humane attention which we unfortunate Men experienced from you, shall never be effaced from our memories.

We request you to assure Captain Verdooren, and the other Captains and Officers of the Ships under your orders, that we are sensible of the great friendship which has been shown to us. I will not intrude upon your occupations by a long letter; the remembrance of having shown every service of humanity and friendship to the unfortunate, is sufficient for Admiral Kihkert; yet we should have proved deficient in the respect that is due to him, if we had not, before our departure, assured him of our warmest gratitude.

Permit me, Admiral, to give you the assurance of my highest consideration and respect, with which I, personally, have the honour to be, Sir, your most obedient and most humble servant,

(Signed)   JOHN COLVILL,
Captain in his Britannic Majesty's Navy.

Letter from Admiral Russel *to Admiral* Kihkert.

His Britannic Majesty's Ship Eagle, North Seas,
sir,   Dec. 2, 1804, P.M.

I have this moment received your flag of truce, conveying to me the Hon. Captain Colville, late of his Britannic Majesty's Ship the Romney (wrecked upon your Coast), with eight of his Officers, which you have first humanely saved from impending destruction, and which your Government has, with its antient magnanimity, released and restored to their country and friends, on their paroles of honour.

They are all, Sir, sincerely affected with heartfelt gratitude to the Batavian Government for their emancipation from captivity, to Admiral Kihkert for their preservation from the jaws of death, and to all the Dutch Officers, and the inhabitants of the Texel, for their kindness and most humane attentions.

This, Sir, is nobly alleviating the rigours of War, as the Christian heroes of your country and mine were wont formerly to do in these Seas, before a considerable portion of European intellect was corrupted by false philosophy.

Captain Colville will communicate to the Right Honourable my Lords Commissioners of the Admiralty, your proposal for the exchange of Prisoners.

Accept, Sir, my sincerest thanks, and the assurance that I am with great respect,

Your most obedient humble servant,

(Signed) M. RUSSEL.

To his Excellency Rear-Admiral Kihkert,
Commander in Chief in the Texel.

PRIZES TAKEN AT THE BEGINNING OF A WAR,
FROM THE FIRST OF MARCH, 1744, TO THE FIRST OF APRIL, 1745.

In the Mediterranean.
46 French Turkey Ships, valued at £.276,000.
43 Spanish Xebeques, &c. .... 43,000.

From, and to the West Indies, &c.
173 French Ships, at 10,000l. each.. 1,730,000.

From, and to France, Newfoundland, &c.
124 French Ships, at 2,000l. each.... 248,000.

In, and near the Channel.
182 French Ships, at 3000l. each .... 546,000.
9 Spanish Register Ships.......... 1,300,000.
1 Acapulco, by Lord Anson...... 500,000.

On the Coast of Spain, and Portugal.
23 Spanish, at 3000l. each......... 69,000.

In Europe, and America.
59 French, at 2000l. each......... 118,000.
23 Spanish, at 2000l. each......... 46,000.
12 Neutral Ships, the Cargoes...... 48,000.

695 £.4,924,000.

286 of which taken by Privateers.

Also seven Neutrals, that were considered uncertain Prizes.

SPANISH GALLEYS.

IT is a custom in Spain, when a great person is shown the King's Galleys, to pay him the compliment of releasing whichsoever of the Slaves he thinks fit. It is related that the Duke of Ossuna being about to claim this privilege, asked many of them for what they had been condemned? All wanted to exculpate themselves, and persuade the Duke that they had been condemned unjustly—except one Man, who frankly confessed all his faults. *Here*, said the Duke, *turn out this villain from among these honest gentlemen, for fear he should debauch them*.

CORRESPONDENCE.

HINTS FOR IMPROVING THE NAVY.

Facts respecting the Royal Navy, and his Majesty's Dock-Yards, showing the Fallacy of the Assertion, that an efficient and powerful Navy may be kept up, even in Time of War, without having Recourse to the Merchants' Yards.

MR. EDITOR, *London, 30th March,* 1805.

IT appearing to be the opinion of several Members in each House of Parliament, as well as of many persons in private stations, who have no means of obtaining full and correct information on the subject, that it is unnecessary and imprudent to build or repair Ships for, or belonging to, the Navy, in the Merchants' Yards, even in time of War; it seems necessary, in some measure, to convince them how much they are mistaken, by laying before them a plain statement of such facts respecting his Majesty's Ships and Dock-yards, as cannot, it may be fairly presumed, fail of having the desired effect.

I begin with boldly asserting, that so far from its being practicable to maintain such a Navy as this Country has possessed for nearly the last fifty years, by means of the King's Yards only, both in War and Peace, and to keep an adequate number of the Ships in real good condition, it would be utterly impossible, without employing a considerably greater number of Shipwrights than are now in the Yards, or than ever have been employed in time of Peace; or unless the greatest number hitherto employed, at any time, were to work considerably more extra time than they have ever worked for a continuance, and throughout each year, in time of Peace, to keep up the Navy, as mentioned above, even during the most profound Peace, supposing (what will be very far indeed from being the case) that at the conclusion of the War one third of the Ships in the Navy should be nearly as good as new.

But as this will appear to many an ill-founded assertion, it will be necessary to adduce circumstances to establish the truth of it; and the Peace preceding the late War affords them in the fullest extent: for in the course of those ten years, 127 Ships of the Line were built or repaired, 29 of which were launched from the Merchants' Yards*; and yet so rapid is the decay of Ships, that at no one period of the before-mentioned Peace were there more than 98 of the Line on the list of those in good condition, and in commission. And in December, 1792, when we began to arm. the number was reduced to 77, and probably would not have exceeded 81, or 83, had there been no hinderances to the building and repairing of Ships, by the Armaments which took place in 1790 and 1791.—These circumstances, therefore, decidedly proved what had never before been rendered so certain; viz. that large Ships, after being built, or permanently repaired, and laid up in ordinary, will not continue in real good condition longer than ten years, if so long, taking one Ship with another; but that they will require in general, after that time, at least a small repair, as it is technically denominated, at an expense of several thousand pounds, to render them proper Ships to be fitted for permanent Service.—And let it be remarked, that the establishment of these facts arises from the history, not of a few Ships, (which from partial causes might have decayed faster than usual,) but from that of a great number of Ships.

It is mentioned above, that the period of the continuance of Ships in good condition was never so fully ascertained as in the Peace which commenced in 1783; and the reason partly is, that in no former period of only the same extent were so many large Ships built and repaired, and consequently never before was there so good an opportunity of judging of the time that Ships of the Line will continue in good condition, on a general average.

To those who are well acquainted with the civil history of the Navy, it is well known (and the sums voted for building and repairing Ships corroborate the fact) that exertions were never made for re-instating the Navy, after a War, in any degree equal to those made after the end of the American War, which were

---

* I believe that even the last of these 29 Ships were contracted for, or ordered to be contracted for, before the Earl of Sandwich left the Admiralty.

great indeed:—nearly 13 Line of Battle Ships having been annually built or repaired, throughout the Peace, as shown above, taking one year with another; whereas, from the 1st of January 1766, to 31st December, 1772, only seven were built or repaired, each year, on an average *.—The consequence of which slow proceedings in the latter period was, that, throughout the whole of it, nearly as fast as one Ship was built or repaired, one of those on the list of Ships in good condition was found to want repair; and when the Armament took place in the year 1770, more than half the Ships of the Line, nominally in good condition, that were intended to be put into Commission, were found not to be in a proper state to be fitted for Sea, to the great mortification and disappointment of the first Lord of the Admiralty, Sir Edward Hawke, and certainly to the great surprise and vexation of others, who were naturally supposed to be well acquainted with the state of the Ships lying up at the several Ports.

It is in vain to hope for impossibilities; and to expect to have a great number of efficient Ships, without constantly building and repairing the necessary number, must always end in disappointment, and may produce the most fatal consequences: for unless the state of the other maritime Powers shall become very different from what they have been ever since the year 1778, it is too evident that an immense Navy must be maintained, at whatever expense it may be attended with. And it is surely better that the public should know what great exertions must be made for that purpose, even in time of Peace, than that it should entertain fallacious notions on the subject, and be led to believe that Government ought to adopt a system which would terminate in consequences that cannot be thought of but with horror.

If then the great and unprecedented efforts to obtain and support a very powerful Navy, in the Peace preceding the late War, when the Ships, &c. in commission required only 18,000 Men to man them, (and when the wear and tear therefore of our Ships occasioned only a comparatively trifling interruption to the building and repairing of Ships,) proved insufficient for the latter purpose, at least to the extent originally intended, before the situation of affairs in France had occasioned a reduction to take place in our Naval expenditure; what must be the condition of a great majority of our Ships, after a War of more than nine years, during part

---

* In the Peace commencing in 1763, many Artificers were discharged, and very little extra was worked in the Dock-yards.—And the same practices prevailed in earlier periods.

of which, from 100 to 120,000 Seamen were employed*; a partial Peace (if Peace it may be called) of a year, in which no more could be done in building or repairing Ships, than in the height of the War; and after another War of two years' continuance already! And how can it be for a moment supposed, that the Service can now be carried on without very substantial aid from the Merchant Builders? Those who really entertain contrary ideas, either do not know, or have very little considered, what an immense number of the Ships and Vessels in commission require refitting in the course of every year, (many of them more than once,) at the several Dock-yards; how many Ships and Vessels are necessarily taken into the Service every year, in time of War, either by purchase, or in consequence of captures from the enemy; and how much work there is to be done to every one of those so taken into the Service, to fit them for Sea.

It certainly therefore was wisely determined not to postpone contracting for the building of 74-gun Ships:—and with regard to the high price per ton that is to be paid for the said Ships, which is undoubtedly a matter of some consequence, even in a national point of view, let it be observed, that from the advance which has taken place in workmen's wages, and in the price of timber; and above all, the increasing scarcity of that article, there was no certainty, and but little if any probability, that the Ships would have been built on cheaper terms, had the Contracts not been entered into until after the end of the War.—To those, therefore, who are aware of the difficulties in procuring large oak timber, at any price, in considerable quantities, the surprise was, not that the Builders should ask so high a price as 36l. per ton for the 74-gun Ships, and absolutely refuse to take less, but that persons could be met with to undertake to build so many as ten, on any terms, in the time allowed for building those in question.

The foregoing, it will be readily admitted, contains no symptoms of party spirit; nor is any thing more meant, than to prevent either the public at large, or any individuals, from being misled by those who speak or write under wrong impressions on this interesting subject, as I am neither directly nor indirectly interested therein, in a pecuniary way, or in any respect but as a member of the general community.

---

* The degree of interruption to the building and repairing of Ships in the King's Yards, must be nearly in proportion to the number of Seamen employed; except, that the casualties in War subject the Ships to a greater degree of wear and tear than in time of Peace,

From what is herein stated, and from a few concluding remarks, it will be seen, that whatever aid it may be advisable and practicable to draw from the Merchants' Yards during the War (agreeably to former practice, from the earliest period of our Naval History) or after the War, much more work must still be annually performed in the King's Yards, during the next Peace, than was performed in that which succeeded the American War, (much as was then done,) in order to obtain, or even to keep up, when obtained, (which it will take eight or ten years of Peace to accomplish,) as many large Ships in real good condition, as it seemed then to be intended to keep up, together with a proportionable number of smaller Ships and Frigates: as, in the first place, the tonnage of our Ships, of almost every class, is much increased of late years, as a great number of them are foreign Ships, and not so durable as our own:—secondly, as much timber and plank have for several years been used in a less seasoned state than in the before-mentioned Peace, owing to the scanty supplies that have been received at the Yards:—and, lastly, as from the time that very many of the Ships will have run without being repaired in a permanent manner, their repairs will in general require more labour than heretofore.—More artificers must therefore of necessity be employed, or they must be employed more extra time, according as may be thought most beneficial to the Service.

A WELL-WISHER TO THE BRITISH NAVY.

MR. EDITOR,

THE enclosed justification of a brave man's character by himself, deserves to be recorded in some more permanent publication than a Newspaper; it is therefore forwarded for insertion in your Naval Chronicle, by a well-wisher to that Work.

25th March, 1805. T———.

[From the Bristol Journal of March 16, 1805.]

ON our arrival at this Port, observing a paragraph in the London papers respecting a late action between the Buonaparte French Privateer, and the Ships Thetis, Ceres, and Penelope, off Barbadoes, which makes it appear to the public that the two latter did wonders, and the Thetis little or nothing; I now think it incumbent on me, and a duty I owe my Crew, as Commander of the Thetis, to state a few facts, and confute any reports that have been made of the action; which would have been passed over in silence by me, had they not resorted to the means they have of obtaining unmerited credit at the expense of others. The three Ships sailed in company from Cork, the Thetis to act as Commodore. Nothing material occurred till the 8th of November, when at seven A.M. the Man at our mast-head called out, a Sail! It soon appearing a suspicious one, I made a signal for an enemy, and to haul our Wind on the larboard tack to meet her; which was answered by our Consorts. At nine, the Privateer and the Thetis met; the other Ships not sailing so fast, were at this time about one mile a-stern in her wake: the Privateer hailed us in English twice, with English colours flying: the latter we answered with a broadside from our larboard guns. Seeing him determined to board us, we wore Ship and sailed large; in the act of doing which, she raked us twice, ran up alongside under a press of sail, and made herself fast to our mizen-chains. By this time the other Ships were nearly up; but instead of coming into action on the enemy's quarter, which ought to have been their station, bore up before they reached us, fired five or six guns (the contents of which we shared with the enemy); and during the whole time (upwards of one hour) we were lashed together they were sailing a-head of us at about half a mile distance, although the Crew of the Penelope went aft to their Commander, and told him it was a shame to see the Thetis so mauled and render no assistance: this was their report on board his Majesty's Ship Centaur. At the conclusion of the fight, a fortunate double-headed shot from our aftermost gun carried away the enemy's foremast, bowsprit, and main-top-gallant-mast; upon which he cut us adrift, when we hauled our Wind to the northward, with an intention to gain so far to windward as to get on his weather-side, where all the wreck was lying. On examining my Crew, I found two killed and seven wounded; our sails and rigging so much cut that the Ship was ungovernable: however, by uncommon exertions we got her wore on the other tack, but only fetched under the enemy's lee, when we passed almost shaving her, and gave her two broadsides, at the same time receiving one from her, which wounded two more Men and disabled four guns. I afterwards spoke the Ceres, whose Commander inquired into the state of our Ship and Men; he and his Passengers drank my health, and he expressed himself more than once (through his trumpet), that he was very sorry it was not in his power to give us any assistance. I then urged a wish to further annoy the enemy, as she would be an easy capture; his answer was, " It is impossible, she has too many Men." During this time, for about half an hour, the enemy was lying a complete log, while our Consorts had received no damage. However, at length all three of us made sail together for her again, and engaged her at a distance for about an hour. My wounded being in great agony, not having the assistance of a Surgeon on board, I shaped a course for Barbadoes, where we all arrived next evening.

When we anchored, I was visited by Captain Richardson, of his Majesty's Ship Centaur, who immediately sent for a Surgeon, Mr. Martin, who has my thanks for his particular attention to the wounded. Commodore Hood very handsomely gave me a protection for my Crew, and took the wounded into the Royal Hospital.

So little credit was given to the account of the action given by the Captains of the Ceres and Penelope, at Barbadoes, that they resorted to the means of obtaining the Captain of the Buonaparte's signature to a letter, in direct contradiction of his statement to a Naval Officer who captured him, which was in the fullest manner corroborated by the Surgeon who was stopped at Dominica on his way to Guadaloupe.

The action speaks for itself: neither of the Vessels, the Ceres or Penelope, was in the smallest degree injured, although one of them reported he expended *six barrels* of gunpowder. Double that quantity might have been expended with equal effect, as a large proportion of it was set fire to in the barrels. The Penelope, I understand, lost a Passenger by a chance shot, yet I believe was equally as fortunate as the Ceres in escaping without damage.

The steady behaviour of the Thetis's Officers and Crew in this action, and their conduct during the Voyage, demand my highest esteem, and will be for ever imprinted on my memory.

Bristol, 14*th March*, 1805. JOHN CHARNLEY.

While in the West Indies, Captain Charnley received a very handsome letter from a Committee of the Inhabitants of Dominica, in testimony of his conduct, of which the following is a copy:—

To JOHN CHARNLEY, Esq. *Commander of the Ship* THETIS, *of Lancaster, Letter of Marque, of* 16 *guns*, 45 *Men.*

SIR,—The inhabitants of this island, subscribers to a fund raised to reward the Crew of the Thetis, and to offer a Tribute to the bravery and good conduct of you, her Commander, for having so gallantly defeated the Buonaparte French Brig, of 20 guns, and 215 Men, to windward of Barbadoes, on the 8th of November last, thereby protecting two valuable Ships under your convoy; request of you, Sir, through us their Committee, to receive the sum of 250l. sterling, to be disposed of among the Crew as therein mentioned.

They further request your acceptance of a piece of plate, of the value of 60l. sterling, which they have ordered to be made in London, bearing an appropriate inscription, as a small tribute from this community, in testimony of their high sense of your exemplary and meritorious conduct on that occasion.

     (Signed) RD. HOOTON,
Roseau, Dominica,   J. P. LOCKHART, } Committee.
Dec. 5th, 1804.   WM. ANDERSON,

MR. EDITOR,

AFTER all that has been said respecting the Catamaran Expedition during last Autumn against the enemy, as it was termed in the House by Mr. Sheridan, the project was by no means entirely new. It neither originated with Lord Melville, nor Sir Home Popham, but was first attempted on a larger scale, by a Projector in the year 1693, whose name is lost. This will appear by the following account, extracted from the Gentleman's Magazine, for 1758, (Vol. XXVIII, page 253,) published soon after the Expedition against St. Maloes, under the Duke of Marlborough and Commodore Howe:—" On the 13th of November, 1693, seven years after the Revolution, King William sent out a Fleet of twelve Men of War, from 70 to 80 guns, four Bomb-vessels, ten or twelve Privateers, and several smaller Vessels, under the command of Captain Bembow, who was afterwards an Admiral. The contrivance to fire Mortars from Ships at Sea was then a new invention, having been first made about twelve years before, by one Renaud, a young Frenchman, who had never seen an action; and to increase the effect of the Bomb-vessels that were sent with this Fleet, a new Galliot, of about 300 tons burthen, was so contrived, as to be itself one great Bomb, capable of being discharged wherever she could float. In the hold of this Galliot, next the keel, were stowed 100 barrels of powder: and as the effect of powder is always in proportion to the resistance, this layer of powder was covered with a flooring of thick timber, which was perforated in several places to admit the train that was to communicate the fire: upon the top of this floor was laid 300 carcasses, consisting of grenades, cannon bullets, chain shot, great bars of iron, and an incredible variety of other combustible matter, which produced a fire that, according to the report of the French at that time, and of the author of a late Naval History, could not be quenched but by hot water: the Naval Historian adds, that besides the carcasses and combustibles already mentioned, 340 mortars were also put on board, loaded with small bombs and grenades; but it seems highly absurd to suppose that such a number of mortars should be put on board a Ship, that at one blast was to be destroyed, by an explosion, which would give of itself the utmost possible effect to all the bombs and balls which were on board.

"With this Machine, which from its office was called the INFERNAL, the Fleet set sail from Guernsey, the public being utterly ignorant of its destination. At four o'clock in the afternoon of the 16th of November, they anchored before one of the entrances into the Port of the City, called la Conchal, upon the front of which was an unfinished Fort, called Quince Fort: about eleven at night they came within cannon shot of the City, and bombarded it till four in the morning of the 17th, when they were obliged to warp, for fear of being aground.

"On the 17th and 18th the Vessels went in again, and the bombardment was renewed; being still obliged to return before the Tide was out. On the 19th some of the Sailors went on Shore in the Island of Cesamber, and burnt a Convent, and on the same day preparations were made for striking the great blow by playing off the INFERNAL. An Engineer being put on board carried her under full sail to the foot of the wall, where she was to be fixed, notwithstanding all the fire of the place against him; but it happened that the Wind suddenly veering, forced him off before the Vessel could be secured, and drove her upon a Rock within pistol shot of the place where she was to have been moored: all possible attempts were made to get clear of this Rock, but without effect; and the Engineer finding that the Vessel had received damage from the shock, and began to open, set fire to the train, and left her: the Sea water that broke in prevented some of her carcasses from taking fire, but the Vessel soon after blew up, with an explosion that shook the whole City like an Earthquake, uncovered about 300 houses, threw down the greatest part of the wall towards the Sea, and broke all the glass, china, and earthen ware for three leagues round.

"The consternation of the people was so great, that a small number of Troops might have taken possession of the place without resistance, but there was not a Soldier on board the Fleet; the Sailors however demolished Quince Fort, and having done considerable damage to the Town, the Fleet returned to England.

"S. S."

Mr. Editor,

DURING a walk through the beautiful Meadows that extend from Richmond, I lately visited the Churchyard of Petersham, that I might mark the spot where one of our latest Circumnavigators, Vancouver, was buried: and I must acknowledge my surprise, when, after some time spent in the search, I found only a plain common Grave, with this singular Inscription:—CAPTAIN GEORGE VANCOUVER DIED IN THE YEAR 1798. Neither the day of his death, nor his having been an Officer in his Majesty's Navy, are mentioned. This singular Tomb-stone appears on the south side of the Churchyard.

S.

Mr. Editor,

IN the year 1744, when the proud defiance of our enemies was not cast with so much virulence against us as in the present day, the following Act of Patriotism is recorded of the Members of WHITE's: may the recollection of it induce that and other fashionable Clubs to follow so glorious an example.—" The Gentlemen who use *White's Chocolate House* in St. James's Street, have raised money, by a voluntary subscription, to fit out a Privateer, to cruise against the French *."

A MEMBER.

P.S. The above reminds me of a somewhat similar letter respecting the Grave of Admiral Haddock, which appeared in the Gentleman's Magazine (Vol. XXX, page 623,) for 1760. And as I am unacquainted with the effects, if any, which that letter produced, I have sent it you.—" The Remains of the late Admiral Haddock lie interred in the Churchyard of Leigh in Essex; at the east end, next the highway, near those of his Ancestors, but in a distinct Vault, built by his order a little before his death; where his maiden Sister first, himself next, and afterwards his Brother the Comptroller, were deposited. Yet though his body has been buried about twelve years, no Tomb has been erected, as an honorary Monument to that brave Admiral; and as there is already no manifest difference between the place of his interment and the rest of the Churchyard, (the flat-sward growing thereon,) I hope, if any of his family remain, that they will speedily erect a Monument suitable to the memory of so brave and good a Man."

---

* Gentleman's Magazine, Vol. XIV, page 333.

MR. EDITOR,

I DO not recollect having ever seen any notice in your Chronicle, of a curious BOAT, made of Sheet Iron, that was launched on the 27th of May, 1777, on the River Foss in Yorkshire. She was twelve feet long; carried fifteen persons; and was so light that two Men might carry her. Perhaps a recollection of this may prove of service to some ingenious Ship-builder.

U.

MR. EDITOR,

TO preserve fresh water sweet at Sea, the following method has been long since adopted, and yet is not generally followed, so naturally careless are Sailors in any thing that relates to their own comfort. To every hundred gallons of fresh water put a quarter of a pound averdupois of fine white pearl ashes, and then stop the Cask. This is preferable to the filtering stone, since the water can be had in larger quantities for immediate use; and besides is not so flat.

C.

MR. EDITOR,

WHILST you render justice to recent merit, we must not forget the gallantry of former days, too much of which is omitted in the Histories that have appeared. The following particulars of a Naval Engagement are thus prefaced by a Letter in the Gentleman's Magazine for November, 1756.

C.

" I AM a Seaman, within one year of fourscore, who for many years past have been a constant reader of your Magazine, in this my last retreat at Greenwich, where I peep, as it were from behind the curtain, on the present stage of life, and employ my own simple judgment in approving or condemning the different behaviour of the actors.

" Among the many accounts you have, for several months past, given us of battles at Sea and Land, I have impatiently expected to find a more perfect relation of that engagement which his Majesty's Ships the Colchester and Lyme had in May last with two French Men of War, and which merits much more notice than has hitherto been taken of it. I enclose you an account, or rather journal, of the whole action, in which are evident marks of great bravery and seamanship, and which, I am well convinced, is penned with the utmost truth and exactness, by a warrant Officer of the Colchester, whom I know to be a Man of great veracity, and who, after much entreaty, sent it me since their late arrival at Spithead from the Mediterranean, and assures me he intended to have published it himself long ago, but was absolutely forbid the doing it by his Captain; telling him, it might as well be omitted, seeing that they had not been so fortunate as to take the Ship they engaged; and that it was now become common for the generality of mankind to measure the merit of an action in proportion only to the success that attended it. But I am not of that persuasion, and do therefore part with a copy of it, that others may be convinced of the just cause to commend the conduct and behaviour of Captain Obrian in the affair, who, as my friend also assures me, was rather pleased than otherways, at the appearance of the enemy's superior force, and gave this charge to the First Lieutenant: " You, Sir, as next to me in command, must take charge of the Ship if I should in the action be killed, or so wounded as to be obliged to quit the deck; but it is my directions, that you never strike our King's colours while there is a possibility of keeping the Ship above water."

" Capt. Obrian has often signalized himself, particularly in 1743, when he was Lieutenant of the Shrewsbury at Carthagena, in the attack of Boccha Chica Castle, which was taken, though with great loss. In the same Harbour, with Boats manned and armed, he took the Galicia Man of War, of 64 guns, first boarding her himself. In the time of the last rebellion he commanded the Sheerness, of 20 guns, and retook from the rebels, after a smart engagement, the Hazard, (by them called the Prince Charles,) crowded with Officers and Soldiers, with money, arms, and ammunition, to reinforce and supply the rebel Army then in Scotland*.

" It is but by public character that I am acquainted with the present Captain Obrian. His father, in the same honourable employ, I well knew, and served under his command in two of his Majesty's Ships, and in several engagements with him, and cannot but mention him as an Officer worthy the imitation of every gentleman in the Royal Navy, and am pleased to find the son so lively a copy of him. " Yours, &c.

" *Greenwich, Nov. 22.* " J. R."

---

* See Gentleman's Magazine, Vol. XV, April.

"*Colchester at Sea, June* 20, 1756.

"The Lyme, Captain Vernon, and we, the Colchester, Captain Obrian, were ordered by Admiral Boscawen from the Fleet, to cruise together on the Coast of Brittany, and scarce a day passed but we either burnt or sunk some French Vessel. On the 17th of May in the morning, took a French Snow laden with deals and rosin, and an Officer sent on board to burn her. While he was doing it, the Man at the mast-head called down, that he saw a Sail in the offing; upon which Captain Obrian hailed Captain Vernon, and desired him to make sail, and that he would follow, which we did with all the sail we could make, as soon as the Officer was returned from burning the Vessel, and our Boat hoisted in.—A second Sail was espied by the Man at mast-head, and at half-past nine A.M. we discovered they were enemies, and they the same of us, making all the sail they possibly could set to get from us, with top-gallant-royals, lower-top-mast, and top-gallant steering sails, keeping a good full. Seeing they could not weather us on the other tack, sometimes they bore away two or three points, then hauled their Wind; but finding we gained on them fast, and that it was impossible to escape us, they shortened sail by degrees, till they were under their three top-sails, hoisted their colours, and kept close together. We did the same; and as we neared them, saw plainly the name of each Ship wrote in their stern, the first called la Fidèle, of 32 guns; the other l'Aquilon, of 58, which we counted very distinctly, the latter having 11 guns below on a side, 12 on her upper deck, four on her quarter deck, and two on her forecastle, with a great number of Men at small arms in her tops, poop, quarter-deck, and forecastle. We had a clear Ship fore and aft, and every thing ready for action, with colours flying, and our people in great spirits gave three cheers, as did the Lyme's people also. The French indeed answered us, but it was very faintly. Our Captain's intention was to have gone between the two enemy's Ships, and to have given them each a broadside, but they kept too close for us to put that scheme in execution; we therefore took the first fire of the Fidele, reserving ours for the Aquilon, which was the headmost Ship, and at half an hour past five in the evening, being close upon her weather quarter, she gave us her whole broadside below and aloft, as did the Fidele also at the same time, which we immediately returned with our whole fire at the Aquilon, as did the Lyme at the other. The third broadside we received most unluckily broke our tiller rope, great part of the steering wheel, and lead trumpet, and directly our Ship came round too; upon which the Aquilon put her helm hard a-weather, and raked us fore and aft; and perceiving something extraordinary had happened on board us, let down their foresail and bore away, with design, as we supposed, to assist her comrade, then warmly engaged with the Lyme at some distance. But we soon got tackles upon our tiller below, shivered our after sails, put our helm a-port, and followed her, and got between the two enemy's Ships; and on the Aquilon's lee bow, and sheering from bow to bow, gave her five smart broadsides, most of which raked her fore and aft, and so near as to be almost on board each other, our yard-arms very near touching hers. We then exchanged hand grenades for some time from our tops, and one of hers falling on her forecastle, blew up a great number of musket cartridges, but happily did no great mischief. When we raked her she was silent, and for some time did not fire a gun; and her ensign being foul, our people gave three cheers, thinking she had struck; upon which the Aquilon put her helm a-lee, hauled up her foresail, (for we were then going large,) and began to fire again. At this time our braces, bowlings, &c. being most of them shot away, we got down our steering sails, tacks for braces, and hauled upon a Wind; but she got the weather gage of us, which we could never after recover. We now reeved a new tiller rope, but it proved too short, so that we were obliged to reeve the mizen sheet for a tiller rope, and put a luff tackle in lieu, and continued engaging about point blank musket shot, (the Lyme and Fidele also still engaged, but at a considerable distance from us.) The great quantity of bar-shot, pieces of old iron bars, &c. which the French fired in upon us, tore our sails and rigging all to shatters, our mizen top-sail down, the sheets, stoppers, and slings, entirely shot away, and the mizen all to pieces. In short, every thing so torn and cut to pieces, that we had not the Ship under the least command; and lucky for us it was fine weather and smooth water, or we must have lost all our masts, being all very much wounded, and scarce a whole shroud left to secure them. We saw before dark two of the Aquilon's ports beat into one, and about ten o'clock several great explosions on board her, and were so near, that the wads from each Ship fell on the decks on fire, and one from her guns came into an upper deck port of ours, beat a cartridge of powder out of the Man's hand that was going to put it into the gun, which set fire to some others, and blew up all the people near that gun in a terrible manner. Other wads set fire to our hammocks on the poop, but it was happily soon extinguished. Thus we continued to engage till about half-past twelve at night, when the Aquilon hauled on board her fore tack, set all the sail she could, kept close upon a Wind, and left us in such a situation as was impossible for us to follow her. The Lyme and Fidele had left off engaging about an hour and a half before us. Besides the shattered condition of our sails, masts, and rigging, we received several shot between Wind and Water, and were obliged to turn our people from the guns to pump Ship, for we made four feet water an hour, and heeled Ship to stop our leaks with plugs and tallow. All the remaining part of the night and next day we were employed in knotting, splicing, and reeving new rigging, and bending other sails.—Our Officers and Men behaved well, and in high spirits during the whole engagement; but our guns were very weakly manned, our people being obliged to help each other to run them out when loaded, and were all very much fatigued, having been up 35 hours. We had no more than four Men killed on the spot, and 35 wounded, several of whom are since dead of their wounds, and others not expected to recover. The Aquilon (by the account we have of a Danish Ship from France) had upwards of 60 Men killed, and a great number wounded, and went into Rochefort with great difficulty, being much shattered in her hull. The disproportion of the killed and wounded between us and the French may be easily accounted for, by considering, that it is their continual practice to fire at our masts and rigging, in order to disable our Ships that way; and that they have generally almost double our number of Men. In this action we fired upwards of 40 broadsides, which is at least four tons, 300 weight of powder, and all well expended, not a single gun fired but so near as to do execution on the enemy wherever it took place, and every thing conducted with as little noise and confusion as possible, during the whole engagement, which was full six hours and a half. After this it might be expected we should immediately have steered for some Port, (as we find the Lyme did,) but our Captain judged it more the duty of an Officer to do his utmost to rejoin his Admiral, which we did, and had the Carpenters from every Ship in the Fleet to fix our masts, yards, &c. and repair our hull; and with a fresh supply of stores and ammunition, I do suppose we shall make out the time first intended for our Cruise.

PLATE CLXXVI.
LORD HOOD'S ACTION WITH DE GRASSE, BASSETERRE ROAD, JAN. 25, 1782.

A View of the Action between the British Fleet of twenty-two Sail of the Line, under the Command of Rear-Admiral Sir SAMUEL HOOD, *and the French Fleet of twenty-eight Sail of the Line, commanded by the Comte de* GRASSE, *going into, and anchoring in Basseterre Road, St. Christopher's, January the 25th, 1782.*

EXTRACT.

ON the 25th of January, 1782, at daylight, the enemy were to leeward on the larboard tack, standing to the southward in a line a-head: soon after the signal was made for the British Fleet to form the line a-head on the starboard tack; variety of signals were occasionally made, and at half-past nine the Fleet brought to, at half-past ten the enemy tacked in succession, keeping close to the Wind, with a view to cut off our rear.

At two o'clock the signal was made to prepare to anchor: at 25 min. past two the enemy's van Ship was almost opposite our centre, and nearly within random shot, their centre and rear thronging to attack our rear, and they immediately began firing; about three o'clock the leading Ship anchored off Salt Pond Bay, the rest of the Fleet anchored in succession, the enemy veering as the British Ships anchored; the rear were still very warmly engaged, but not with that spirit as might have been expected from their great superiority in number and situation; at six the firing ceased on both sides, the British Fleet having all anchored, and the French Fleet standing to the southward.

This bold manœuvre, equally mortifying as astonishing to the enemy, was as happily conceived as executed.

The Plate which we here annex is from a Drawing of Mr. POCOCK's, taken from a Sketch made by a gentleman who happened at the time to be on a visit at a friend's, on a height between Basseterre and Old Road.

On the Fore Ground, horse taking fright at the noise of the cannon reverberating among the hills: the Buildings, part of the Works of the Sugar Estate, and the Circular Mound; a Cattle Mill unrigged; in the distance appears the Island of Nevis, with the Salt Ponds, down to Frigate Bay: the British Fleet partly come to anchor, the French engaging, and hauling to the southward in succession.

NAVAL HISTORY OF THE PRESENT YEAR, 1805.
(March—April.)
RETROSPECTIVE AND MISCELLANEOUS.

THE Naval Profession, and the Public at large, are so much occupied with the spirit that hath been shown in the House of Commons, that we have resolved to sacrifice the less important articles of our Chronicle, in order to give ample room to one of the most extraordinary and momentous Naval Debates that History has ever recorded. Our Readers may therefore rely on a full and impartial account.

The following requisition, preparatory to this debate, was presented to the Lord Mayor on the first of April, signed by several Liverymen; whom his Lordship informed that he should take their application into consideration, and give an answer:—

" My Lord,—We, the undersigned Liverymen, do request your Lordship to convene a Common Hall, upon an early day, to consider the flagrant abuses in the management and expenditure of the public money, brought to light by the Reports of the Commissioners appointed by Parliament to investigate the same; and to instruct our Representatives strenuously to promote and prosecute all inquiries into the said abuses; and also to vote for such motions as may have for their object the removal from his Majesty's Councils, or any place of trust or profit under the Government, all persons who may be implicated in the said abuses."

LORD MELVILLE'S LETTER TO THE COMMISSIONERS OF NAVAL INQUIRY.

" GENTLEMEN, *March* 28, 1805.

" Having read your Tenth Report, and observing particularly the following paragraph in the 141st page— However the apprehension of disclosing delicate and confidential transactions of Government might operate with Lord Melville, in withholding information respecting advances to other departments, we do not perceive how that apprehension can at all account for his refusing to state, whether he derived any profit or advantage from the use or employment of money issued for the services of the Navy. If his Lordship had received into his hands such monies, as were advanced by him to other departments, and had replaced them as they were repaid, he could not have derived any profit or advantage from such transactions, however repugnant they might be to the provisions of the Legislature, for the safe custody of public money.'

" I think it necessary to state the following observations, in order to place in their just view the grounds on which I declined answering your question, and which you appear not to have accurately understood.

" When you first called upon me for information, I stated to you that I had not materials on which I could frame such an account as you required me at that time to prepare; and in a communication with Mr. Trotter, before my examination on the 5th of November last, I learnt, for the first time, that in the Accounts he had kept respecting my private concerns, he had so blended his own private monies with what he had in his hands of public money, that it was impossible for him to ascertain with precision whether the advances he had occasion to make to me in the course of his running private account with me, were made from the one or from the other aggregate sums which constituted his balance with Messrs.

Coutts. This circumstance, which I understood Mr. Trotter had distinctly communicated to you, made it impossible for me to return any other answer than I did to the general question which you put to me 'Whether Mr. Trotter had applied any of the money issued for carrying on the current service of the Navy for my benefit or advantage?' and to this circumstance I uniformly referred in my answer to other questions respecting the manner in which Mr. Trotter applied the money in his hands.

"When you put the question to me, 'Whether I did direct or authorize Mr. Trotter to lay out or apply, or cause to be laid out or applied, any of the money issued for carrying on the current service of the Navy, to my benefit or advantage?' my answer was, 'To the best of my recollection I never did.'—That answer I now repeat. Had you proceeded to inquire, Whether I had ever any understanding expressed or implied with Mr. Trotter respecting any participation of advantage derived from the custody of the public money, or whether I at any time knowingly derived any advantages to myself from any advances of public money? I should have no hesitation in declaring, as I now declare, that there never was any such understanding, nor any thing like it, between Mr. Trotter and myself; that I never knowingly derived any such advantages; and that whatever emolument accrued to Mr. Trotter in the conduct of the pecuniary concerns of the office was, so far as I am informed, exclusively his own.

"With respect to any advances which Mr. Trotter might make on my private account, I considered myself as debtor to him alone, and as standing with regard to him in no other predicament than I should have done with any other man of business, who might be in occasional advance to me in the general management of my concerns entrusted to him. It is impossible for me to ascertain, from any documents or vouchers in my hands or now existing, what the extent of those advances might have been at any particular period. The accounts which you have inserted in your Report, I never saw till I saw them in the Report itself. They are no accounts of mine, nor am I party to them. They contain a variety of sums issued nominally to me, which never came into my hands, and they gave no credit for various sums received by Mr. Trotter on my private account from my salary as Treasurer of the Navy, and other sources of income, of which he was in the receipt, nor do they take any notice of the security of which he was in possession, for the re-payment of any balance at any time due to him from private funds.

"With respect to the sums of naval money advanced to me, and applied to other services, I do not feel it necessary to make any additional observations, except to declare, that all those sums were returned to the funds from which they were taken, having in no instance been withdrawn from it for any purpose of private emolument or advantage. Before I conclude, I wish to correct an inaccuracy which I observe in one part of the evidence in Appendix No. 7, page 192. The question is put to me, 'Did you derive any profit or advantage from the use or employment of money issued for carrying on the current service of the Navy, between the 19th August 1802, and 30th April 1803; or between the 1st February 1784, and 31st December 1785, during which periods you held the office of Treasurer of the Navy?' Which question I there answer by a reference to the answer given to a similar question put to me before. This answer is inaccurate, in so far as it contains a reference to Mr. Trotter's mode of blending his funds in his private account with Messrs. Coutts. Mr. Trotter was not Paymaster till the year 1786. This circumstance, therefore, relative to Mr. Trotter's account, which precluded my returning an answer to your former questions, do not apply to the periods specified in that mentioned; and I can therefore have no difficulty in declaring, that during those periods I did not derive any advantage from the use or employment of public money issued for carrying on the service of the Navy. Having stated these facts, it is almost unnecessary to add, that I am at any time ready to verify them upon my oath.

"I have the honour to be, Gentlemen,

"MELVILLE."

ANSWER OF THE COMMISSIONERS OF NAVAL INQUIRY TO LORD MELVILLE.

"*Office of Naval Inquiry, Great George Street,*
"MY LORD, *April 2, 1805.*

"WE have received your Lordship's Letter of the 28th of last month, by which you intimate that we appear not to have accurately understood the grounds on which you declined answering our questions, and submit to us some observations, in order to place those grounds in their just view, and also express a wish, before you conclude, to correct an inaccuracy in one part of your evidence, and a readiness to verify by your oath the facts stated in that letter.

"If it be the object of this communication, that we should again require your Lordship's attendance, for the purpose of being examined touching these matters, and that we should make a Supplemental Report upon the result of that examination, and such other examinations as we might thereupon judge necessary, there can be no disinclination on our parts (as far as we are concerned in the proceeding) to meeting your Lordship's wishes: But it appears to us that the inquiry, which is the subject of the Tenth Report, has attained that period, when it would not become us to adopt such a measure, merely upon the suggestion of any of the parties to whose conduct that Report relates.

We were occupied several months in investigating the mode of conducting the business of the office of Treasurer of the Navy. Those who were examined by us had the fullest opportunity of starting and explaining all things which related to the management of that department, or to the share which they respectively had in it; and of correcting at any time, during the progress of the inquiry, any mistakes which might inadvertently have been made. Our opinions and observations upon the irregularities and abuses which we discovered, were formed and drawn up with the utmost care and deliberation; and they are now submitted to the three branches of the Legislature, as the Act, by which we are appointed, requires. If it could be made to appear upon a representation to them, that any thing has been omitted on our part, that any misunderstanding or error had occurred, and that a further inquiry is advisable upon these, or any other grounds, it would be for them to direct such further inquiry, and to decide by whom, and in what manner, it should be prosecuted; but, in the present circumstances, it appears to us that we cannot with propriety resume it.

"We have the honour to be, my Lord,
"Your Lordship's most obedient humble Servants,

"CH. M. POLE,
EWAN LAW,
JOHN FORD,
H. NICHOLLS,
W. MACKWORTH PRAED."

A requisition to the Sheriffs of Middlesex, to call a meeting of the County on the subject of the Tenth Report of the Naval Commissioners, which was proposed by Major Cartwright, was signed by several of the Freeholders present.

Lord Melville's resignation was tendered to his Majesty at Windsor, March 31, by Mr. Pitt, and accepted.

KING'S LEVEE, March 21.

Sir Charles Pole, who attended the Drawing-room, was to have presented to his Majesty the Eleventh Report of the Commissioners of Naval Inquiry, elegantly bound and embellished; but as his Majesty was absent holding a Council at the Queen's House, the presentation of course did not take place. We have given a short extract on our Wrapper.

Orders have been issued from the Admiralty of Copenhagen, to place, as soon as the weather permits, the following beacons in the Categat:—

1. Two beacons, each 20 feet high, with brooms at the top, are to be placed, one on each side the Trindle, north of Lœssoe, in about 33 feet water.

2. Four ditto are to be placed along the edge of the reef, S. S. E. from the east point of the Lœssoe, the two nearest the Trindle somewhat lower than the other two—the one nearest the land in 24 feet water, and the other three in 30 feet, and distant half a Danish mile, or about two English miles from each other.

3. One ditto, of 20 feet high, will be placed on the point of the reef of the Knobben, east of Anholt, and Ships keeping east of the beacon are clear of the reefs.

Extract of a Letter from Penang, July 22.

"Public notice has been given here, that letters have been received from Mr. Drummond, Chief Supra-cargo at Canton, stating, that the Spanish Government at Manilla had fitted out a large Vessel of War, commanded by a Frenchman, to cruise off Cochin China and in the Chinese Seas. This information is given to all Masters of Vessels.

"Captain Lander, Commander of a fine Ship belonging to this Port, with his two European Officers, and many of his Crew, were murdered on their passage from the eastward by the Javemen of his Crew, who also scuttled the Ship; fortunately Captain Snowball, of a Brig bound to Bengal, fell in with her, stopped the holes the villains had made, and brought the Ship to anchor in these Roads."

The Dauntless, a new Frigate, which has been built at Hull, is arrived at Woolwich, for the purpose of being fitted for immediate service.

The Impregnable, of 98 guns, building at Chatham; and the Ocean, of 98 guns, building at Woolwich, are ordered to be finished for launching.

A very curious conversation passed, some time since, between Buonaparté and the Dutch Admiral Verheuil, in which the former displayed his usual intemperance and arrogance. He sent for Verheuil, to consult with him on the expediency of ordering the Expedition to sail from the French and Dutch Ports for the invasion of England, and to know his opinion on the probability of success. Verheuil said, that upon such a subject he found himself bound to give his opinion without reserve, even though it should offend. His opinion, he said, was, that if the Expedition sailed in its present state, the only result that he could anticipate would be defeat and disgrace. Buonaparté could not conceal his anger, and treated Verheuil with the greatest insolence. The latter behaved with great firmness on the occasion, and desired the Usurper to recollect that he was speaking to a Batavian Officer. After a few moments' reflection, Buonaparte recovered his temper, and made a slight apology to M. Verheuil.

Captain R. O. Vincent, the gallant Commander of the late Arrow Sloop, is the eldest son of Mr. Vincent, Banker, of Westbury.

Madrid, Feb. 20. To provide as much as possible for the extraordinary expenses which will be incurred by the fitting out of our Navy, recourse has been had to the commercial class. Cadiz and Madrid have each contributed a million of piasters; and an equal sum is expected from the other commercial cities. By means of these and other contributions, we shall be able to fit out 26 Ships of the Line. There is, however, a want of Sailors, as within the last two or three years more than 10,000 of them, falling victims to poverty and famine, have been obliged to enter into foreign service.

An Uniform sword and hat are to be immediately adopted by the Officers of the Navy.

A few months back a meeting took place, of the Gentlemen interested in the long standing claims of the mercantile interest of this country against the Spanish Government, when it was resolved to make application to Mr. Pitt for that redress, which in vain they had sought for from the Court of Madrid. The Minister gave all due attention to their case, and promised every assistance and relief which could fairly be extended to them; and he has now fulfilled his promise. A few days since it was officially made known to the claimants, that the treasure detained by the English Government in the Spanish plate Ships or otherwise, previous to the declaration of War, is to be appropriated in the first instance to the discharge of the claims above stated, with all possible expedition; for which purpose Commissioners are appointed, one by the claimants and another by Government. Some of the dollars are already safely lodged in the Bank, the remainder are coming up from Plymouth, and were insured by the claimants on Saturday. Some of the claims are very large—one house at Exeter demands 100,000*l*. We should suppose, however, that all the treasure detained before the declaration of War is not destined to the discharge of these claims. Part of it we imagine will be divided amongst the Crews of the Frigates by which the Spanish Ships were detained.

Captain Lind, in his letter to Admiral Rainier, giving an account of the defence of the Centurion, of 50 guns, against the attack of the Marengo, of 80 guns, and the two Frigates l'Atalante and la Semillante, of 36 guns each, mentions his getting on board the Centurion with great difficulty and danger. The circumstances were, that immediately after he was informed that there were suspicious Ships coming into the Roadstead, he hurried down to the Beach, and got into a Boat manned with natives: they proceeded some distance, ignorant of the cause of his hurry; but immediately the firing commenced, they wanted to return to the Shore; he prevented them doing so, but could not make them, either by threats or promises, put him on board during the firing. For some time the Boat was in the line of fire; and as he would not let the Boat be carried on Shore, the Boatmen were with great difficulty prevented by Captain Lind from jumping overboard, swimming to the Shore, and leaving him alone in the Boat. At last a favourable opportunity offered; the Boatmen embraced it quickly, then took the Boat to the nearest Port, and ran off into the country, as did many of the inhabitants of the town of Viccagapatnam.

Tuesday, March 5, the foundation stone of the East India Docks, now constructing at Blackwall, was laid by Captain Joseph Huddart (in the absence of the Chairman, Joseph Cotton, Esq. who was confined by illness), and John Woolmore, Esq. the Deputy Chairman, with some others of the Directors, amidst a numerous concourse of people, who testified their good wishes for the success of the undertaking, which is eminently calculated to promote the security of the East India Shipping, &c. by giving three cheers on the occasion. These Docks, though not so large in capacity as either the London or West India Docks, will be capable of admitting Ships of much larger burden, by having deeper water, and locks of larger dimensions. They consist of two Docks and an entrance Basin. That for discharging inwards will cover eighteen acres; that for outward-bound Vessels, nine acres; the entrance Basin will be about three acres; so that there will be in all thirty acres of water.

Extract of a Letter from Bombay, dated 7th June, 1804.

" While cruising on the Malabar Coast in his Majesty's Ship St. Fiorenzo, commanded by Captain Bingham, we took a Chasse Marce with two six-pound guns and six two-pound swivels. We first discovered her from the mast-head at day light in the morning, and chased her till about ten, when, being within about three miles of her, and the Wind dying quite away, we saw her get out her sweeps.— We had unfortunately some time before lost our Launch, but our Captain immediately sent the Barge and six-oared Cutter in chase with twenty-four Men, which proved to be exactly the same number as were on board the French Vessel. She got her guns on one side, and fired them and musketry at us at least fifteen times, as we were approaching her. Our fellows, however, rowed up in face of it, boarded her sword in hand exactly at twelve o'clock, and carried her in five minutes. It is scarcely credible, but it is an actual fact, that the first and second Captains were shot through their bodies, and appearing dead, were thrown overboard, but they were afterwards picked up again, and have since recovered, as have also three other Frenchmen who were badly wounded. Providence protected us, for we had only one Man slightly cut across the hand. Small as this Vessel was, her capture, which was a very gallant business, may be of more importance than at first sight appears to belong to it. She was in all respects a small Man of War, and had been fitted for the purpose of landing three French Officers to endeavour to stir up the Mahratta Chieftains to War. They had been put on Shore before we fell in with the Vessel, and she was on her return with dispatches, which were thrown overboard as we were rowing towards her. Our Captain, as soon as he found what business they had been upon, with his usual activity and zeal in the Service, sent off expresses in various directions, by which means the three Officers and their dispatches were caught at Poonah."

Imperial Parliament.

HOUSE OF COMMONS, Monday, April 8.

NAVAL DEBATES.

WE never recollect a fuller or more anxious attendance of Members. There were, so early as the time of the Speaker's taking the Chair, nearly 300 Members in the House; there were afterwards between 5 and 600; and at so late an hour as five in the morning 432 divided. The Prince of Wales and Duke of Clarence were under the gallery. Few of the Members left the House for any length of time during the course of the Debate, long and late as it was. The concourse of strangers too was very great. Some were in the avenues and passages so early as seven in the morning. Many came from distant parts of the

Country. By nine o'clock the staircases were crowded, and the gallery was filled and crammed within a few minutes after it was opened.

Sir *Charles Pole*, the President of the Board of Naval Inquiry, attended this important Debate; but, actuated by a sense of honourable feeling, retired before the division.

LORD MELVILLE.—TENTH REPORT.

Mr. *Whitbread* rose.—He said that it had originally been his intention to move, that the House should resolve itself into a Committee of the whole House, to consider of the variety of matter contained in the Tenth Report of the Commissioners of Naval Inquiry; but as this might have been productive of some difficulty, and as he was determined that the discussion of this important subject should not be allowed to evaporate in a dispute about the forms, but be solely confined to the substance of it; he had changed his purposed mode of proceeding, into certain propositions grounded upon that Report, which, before he concluded, he should have the honour to submit to the House. The Honourable Gentleman passed a high eulogium on the Commissioners of Naval Inquiry. Feeling every due respect for all preceding Commissions of a similar nature, he must be allowed to say, that the proceedings of none had been so honourable; that the labours of none had been so indefatigable; and that the result of the exertions of none had been so advantageous to the public, as those of the present. The House well knew that this Commission originated in the Board of Admiralty, over which a Noble Earl presided; who, after combating and defeating the open enemies of his Country upon the Ocean, returned to explode those mines of corruption, the existence of which rendered useless the most brilliant victories. The Commissioners had made various Reports, all of which contained matter highly deserving of investigation, but on none of these Reports had any proceedings been instituted. These Commissioners had experienced greater difficulty in the execution of their office than any of their predecessors, he sincerely believed; and their merit was therefore greater. In the course of their Inquiries they had met with rude rebuffs in the different Offices, through the corruption of which they waded; they had been violently opposed by the whole host of those whose depredations upon the Public they were unveiling; they had been taunted with the appellation of Inquisitors, and every possible means had been used, but in vain, to disgust them with the employment which they had so nobly and disinterestedly taken upon themselves; and he was as firmly persuaded, that the Public, whose interests had been so essentially served by their perseverance amidst all these obstacles, would not be found deficient in gratitude. They had dragged into day facts which had eluded the vigilance of all former Commissions; and it now only remained, to endeavour to bring to Justice the Delinquents whom their patriotic labours had so completely exposed to light. He was convinced that he need not descant on the importance of this subject. When any Person had been incontestably proved to have flagrantly violated the Law himself, and to have connived at the violation of it in others; when, in addition, he was exposed to the strongest suspicion of being an accomplice in the guilt, and a participator in the gains of such inferior culprits; if the House did their duty, they should at least arraign and censure him; and by so doing, confer the greatest benefit on their Country. In the present exhausted state of our Finances, it would show the People that the House of Commons were determined that the Revenues should be frugally administered; that they would keep a watchful eye over those entrusted with the disposal of them; and that no man, however high his rank, or however sanctified by the public confidence of many years, should be suffered to infringe the laws enacted for their regulation, with greater impunity than what would attend the meanest depredator in existence. Should the House, however, not come to a decision on the subject; or should they, in defiance of the clearest evidence that could possibly be adduced of the guilt of an individual, agree to find him not guilty, what would then be the opinion of the People on their conduct? Would they not say, and say justly, " it is for the emoluments of your situations that you contend for them, and for those alone; regardless of Justice, Honour, or Public Virtue, you wish for the Places of those who are accused before you, merely that you may reap the same iniquitous advantages: not from the laudable ambition of serving your Country, but for the base sordid expectations of Gain?" The Honourable Gentleman here entered upon a long and close investigation of the Tenth Report of the Commissioners. It contained matter in which Lord Melville, Mr. Trotter, Mr. Wilson, and Mr. Mark Sprott, were deeply implicated; some imputation of blame too attached to the Bank of England, who, according to the evidence given by one of their own Officers, had issued money on the draughts of Mr. Trotter in an illegal and unjustifiable manner. If he had not been very much misinformed, the Right Honourable Gentleman opposite came in for a share of the delinquency, for being privy to the practice of drawing the public money illegally out of the Bank of England, without having put a stop to it. With Mr. Trotter he should have little to do at present; at a future period he must become the object of a distinct charge. In bringing an accusation against Lord Melville, he was sensible he accused no mean person. The Noble Lord, during his whole life, had enjoyed a great share of the public confidence: for near thirty years he had almost constantly occupied Offices, for which his industry and his talents had been supposed peculiarly to qualify him. During that period he had possessed more extensive patronage than any Man in the Kingdom; and of course both in and out of Parliament he was surrounded by friends and connexions, who were, he apprehended, more willing than able to defend him in his present situation. When the origin of that Act of Parliament, for the violation of which the Noble Lord now stood accused, was considered, it would be found to be attended with circumstances of peculiar aggravation. At the close of the American War, when the Country was in the greatest distress, and when that distress was increased by the profusion which existed in all the Departments of public expenditure, petitions were presented to Parliament from all parts of the Kingdom, in consequence of which certain Resolutions were adopted by the House of Commons, on the motion of Lord George Cavendish. The Honourable Gentleman here read the Resolutions of the Committee of that period on this subject. They gave it as their opinion, that the *Paymaster General of the Army* and the *Treasurer of the Navy*, should not be allowed, directly or indirectly, to use the Public Money lying in their hands for their own advantage. They deprecated the leaving of large balances in the hands of the Treasurer of the Navy; and suggested, as essentially necessary, to remedy the grievances complained of, that for the future the Treasurer of the Navy should be merely an Accountant to the Public. Immediately after the Resolutions had passed, a reform took place in the *Navy Office*. The salary of the *Treasurer* was only two thousand pounds a year, but then he was permitted to enjoy the interest of the balances in his hands; the salary was augmented to four thousand pounds, and all fees, emoluments, and advantages derived from the use of the Public Money, were strictly forbidden. Mr. Barre, the then Treasurer, immediately paid all the balances in his possession into the Bank of England; and proved, that from that period neither he, nor any one of those under him, had received any emolument whatever of that description. To Mr. Barre succeeded Lord Melville in his first Treasurership. Whether he kept the Public Money in the Bank of England, in an iron chest, or at his private Banker's, it is impossible at this distance of time to say. In the extraordinary Letter which he sent the week before last to the Commissioners of Naval Inquiry, the Noble Lord declares he never derived any advantages from the use of it. Lord Blaney followed, and had made a similar declaration. On the 5th of January 1784, Lord Melville again became Treasurer of the Navy, which situation he retained until the 1st of June 1800, and it was to this period of sixteen years that the Honourable Gentleman intended to confine his animadversions. In 1785, the Right Honourable Gentleman opposite to him proposed a plan of public retrenchment, founded on the Report of the Committee before mentioned, in which he held out the most brilliant prospects to the Country; but unfortunately he was mistaken as to the character of the Persons whom he had selected to carry this plan into execution. The Noble Lord had been one of the Persons, and one too in whose praise the Right Hon. Gentleman had been most loud. As if he had been solicitous to place himself apparently in the van of reformers, that he might with more facility suppress all reform, the Noble Lord himself introduced the Bill for regulating the Office of Treasurer of the Navy. The Bill passed into a Law, the language of which was so clear and determinate, that he would defy the most dexterous Lawyer in the profession to torture the Letter of it into any construction foreign to the obvious one. The preamble of the Act stated it to be founded on the Report of the Committee, and intended to render the Treasurer of the Navy an Accountant instead of a Banker; by which means neither he, nor any of those under him, would incur the temptation of hazarding the Public Money in unsafe speculations. There was one Provision in the Act, the operation of which was to commence on the 1st of July, 1785, to which he wished particularly to call the attention of the House.—It was therein directed, that on that day all the Public Money in the possession of the Treasurer of the Navy should be deposited in the Bank of England, and that from that day no part of it should be issued from the Bank but on Drafts, specifying the service for which it was intended. Lord Melville, however, on his own sole authority postponed making this deposit until the 1st of January, 1786. Why? Because, forsooth, the arrangements in his Office could not be completed before the time! What, not in six months! The falsity of the cause thus assigned for this shameful delay was evident, and impelled us to search for the true one. On the 31st December 1784, the balance of the Public Money in Lord Melville's hands did not much exceed 70,000l. He was directed by Act of Parliament to transfer this Sum to the Bank of England on the 1st of July, 1785; but on the 31st of December, 1785, he had not done so, and the balance then amounted to above a hundred and thirteen thousand pounds, being an increase of about forty-three thousand pounds. No proof could be established; but the fair inference to be drawn from this delay undoubtedly was, that Lord Melville had withheld the Public Money from its proper destination for the purpose of his own private emolument. This transaction was comprehended in what he would call the first part of Lord Melville's second Treasuryship. In the second part arose the Facts which formed the basis of the charges against the Noble Lord. He would state them under three distinct heads.—The *first* was, that under his own authority, without the consent of Parliament, and even in direct violation of the Act of Parliament, he had diverted to other Public Services the Money appropriated by Law to the Naval Department. *Secondly*, that he had connived at a System of peculation in an individual, who will hereafter be responsible for his own conduct, but for whom Lord Melville is now responsible. To these two Charges he would confine the Propositions which he meant to submit to the House to-night; but, unless what had been said could be unsaid, and what had been done, undone; there existed but too clear a proof that Lord Melville had participated in the fraudulent profits of his Agent.—Should the House agree to his present motion, he pledged himself to prosecute this part of the Subject still further. To the honour of Men who have held high official situations in this Country, it must be said, that a charge of a similar nature has not been brought for many years. The last exhibited was by Lord Melville himself against a Gentleman who filled an important Office abroad, Sir T. Rumbold. In a case like the present he did not conceive that there existed any necessity for a precedent; but if there did, he should be unwilling to follow that just mentioned, as he thought too much severity had been shown in the proceedings. His intention was to move certain Resolutions, grounded on the Report of the Commissioners, and coupled with Resolutions of censure of the conduct of the Noble Lord. The House would afterwards have to consider in what way to proceed. It was highly material to consider the nature of the evidence that had been adduced. In the first place, the Commissioners discovered that, in direct contradiction to the Law, certain enormous deficiencies existed in the Department of Treasurer of the Navy, amounting at an average to about 43 or 44,000l. a year, (whether a little less or a little more was immaterial, it was not the sum, but the infraction of the Law that rendered the transaction culpable.) On that foundation the Commissioners raised their investigation. He should have frequent occasion to name Mr. Trotter in the course of his Speech: he would therefore observe here, that what applied to Mr. Trotter did not apply to him alone; Mr. Trotter and Lord Melville were one and the same. It was but too clear that Mr. Trotter, having such a principal as Lord Melville, his Lordship could not want such a second as Mr. Trotter. Having referred to, and read a part of the Report of the Commissioners, describing the nature of the Office of Treasurer of the Navy, he observed, that in order to show the situation of aggravated delinquency in which Lord Melville stood, it was necessary to state, that the Office of Treasurer of the Navy, subsequent to the Act of Parliament in 1785, was regulated by an Order of Council, on the motion of Lord Melville himself, drawn up by him, and presented to the King. This was on the 9th of August, 1786. The Honourable Member read the Order of Council, stating that the Treasurer of the Navy had submitted to his Majesty a Plan regulating the Office, and carrying the Act into effect, particularly with respect to the salary of the Paymaster; that his Majesty had taken the same into his Royal consideration, had been pleased to approve of it, and had given directions for carrying it into effect. There were two stages of aggravation in the conduction of the Noble Lord . first, his bringing in an Act of Parliament, which he had afterwards violated; and, secondly, submitting it as a mockery to the King; and from that time to the present moment, never attending to the Act of Parliament, or to the Order of Council, in any one way whatever. The first violation of the Act, and of the Order of Council, was by those deficiencies, the existence of which had been proved. Mr. Trotter, as Paymaster, had been called upon to explain why such deficiencies had been suffered to exist. On this part of the subject he desired to say a few words, as to the evidence given by Mr. Trotter and the other Persons mentioned in the Report: some of them had undoubtedly given very fair and honourable testimony, which, as far as it related to facts, they wished to conceal, was fatal to them; and as it related to facts extorted from them, was equally fatal, because it was given under circumstances which attached to it the strongest degree of credibility, and must be taken to be completely true. He had heard it said, that this Report was founded on *ex parte* evidence. He denied this assertion. If the Facts alledged were not true, could not the Persons examined have answered " No" to the questions put to them.—(*Hear! Hear!*)—Would they not have said, " No, upon my oath, no." They were examined to the Facts, and they sheltered themselves under the clause of the Act of Parliament, which he thought the Commissioners ought not to have allowed them to have availed themselves of; but their having screened themselves under the terms of such a Clause, formed the clearest evidence of their guilt.—Mr. Trotter had been called upon to account for his deficiencies: first, he had said he did not know to what cause to attribute them; then he admitted he did know, and that they arose out of the Public Money having been applied contrary to Act of Parliament. The Act of Parliament had been violated, by the Public Money having been taken out of the Bank, and lodged in the house of a private Banker, where Mr. Trotter insisted it became his private money, and he had arraigned the Commissioners for presuming to examine into his private accounts. This was not only foolish, but dangerous conduct; for he had committed himself by it, even more than his principal. On his first examination, he had denied knowing any thing of the deficiencies; but soon after he began to find them out, and that they arose from his having taken the money to his private Banker's, and advanced it to Lord Melville for other services; a circumstance which he pretended he did not know, till Mr. Long, an Honourable Member, had repaid him some of the Sums so advanced. He was really surprised Mr. Long had not been examined on the subject, and that the Commissioners had not called upon him for some information; but, though they had neglected to do so, it was afterwards confessed, in a Letter from Lord Melville, that the Public Money had been so improperly applied. A precept had been issued by the Commissioners, requiring his Lordship to account for the deficiency, and the application of the Money to other services. The answer was most extraordinary, but it was of a piece with another Letter written by his Lordship, at the conclusion of this business, and was certainly not of a nature to impress any man with an idea of the innocence of Lord Melville. Here the Honourable Member read the Letter from his Lordship, dated Wimbledon, June 30, 1804, stating, that it was impossible for his Lordship to furnish the Commissioners with the account they asked, as he had been in the habit of assorting his Papers, and destroying those that were useless. Now, a Man coming before the Public with such an assertion that because he had been in the habit of assorting his Papers, he had not any Document to make out the Account required of him, was altogether unworthy of belief. Could he not, even from his memory, have furnished an account of what he had advanced? It was impossible for a Man of his Lordship's talents, and so much in the habit of recollecting past circumstances, not to be able to give some account of his balance. But it was a serious charge against him, that he had destroyed his vouchers. He maintained they were the property of the Public, and it was consequently a high misdemeanour in the Noble Lord to destroy those Papers, for want of which the Public could not obtain the information that was necessary. He would ask, what had been the opinion of Commissioners in 1782, as to the consequence of destroying Papers?—Their endeavours in obtaining information had been frustrated. They stated in their Report, that it had been customary for the Paymaster to take his Accounts with him out of the Office—the Committee were of opinion, that they should be left for the use of Government and posterity; and therefore Lord Melville was highly reprehensible in suffering those Papers to be taken from the Navy Pay Office. But the Noble Lord had said further, that he could not give the Commissioners the Account they required, because, during a great part of the time he was Treasurer of the Navy, he held other very confidential situations under Government, and was intimately connected with others. Undoubtedly he was connected with others. He was at one time *Secretary at War, Secretary of State, President of the Board of Controul, and Treasurer of the Navy!* He observes, that several " delicate and confidential" transactions had occurred, which it was not consistent with his duty to reveal: his sense of duty should have restrained him, not from revealing these acts, but from committing them. The Noble Lord had held the situation of Treasurer of the Navy at a period most critical, when there were hardly sufficient means to pay the Fleet that was defending our Shores—yet had he, in contempt of the danger, ventured to turn the Money to other services. The next article of charge is, his having connived at the Public Money being drawn from the Bank of England for private emolument, and thus having allowed an infraction of the Law for which he is deeply responsible. Mr. *Trotter* confesses he did lodge large Sums of Money at *Coutts's*; because, he says, it was more convenient, and more secure; and, notwithstanding all the Acts of Parliament which expressly contradict his opinion, he thinks it was always intended that this should be permitted. That such a man as Mr. Trotter should make so weak, so absurd a defence, was not surprising; but that Lord *Melville* should imitate him, was really wonderful. After having himself introduced the Acts, and the regulation before alluded to, how was it possible that the Noble Lord could have the face to say, that in a private Banker's hands the Public Money was more convenient or more secure? It is much easier, he says, to give a Draft on a private Banker, than on the Bank of England. Why? Is not one as valid, and attended with as little difficulty as the other? As to security; it was a most extraordinary plan to seek security by going from a place where alone security could be found. If the Bank of England had failed, no responsibility would have been incurred by Lord Melville, because he was justified in placing the Public Money there; but the moment he went even to the most respectable private Bankers, his responsibility commenced. Events might happen, not possibly to be anticipated; the Money might be lost, and then Lord Melville and Mr. Trotter would be overwhelmed with destruction. After all, however, the Money had not been lying at *Coutts's*; it had been employed in discounting private Bills, and in speculating in the Funds. (*Hear! Hear! Hear!*) The House would be appalled when they reflected on the extent of the Trust reposed by Lord Melville in Mr. Trotter. In the course of Mr. Trotter's continuance in Office, Lord Melville states, that a hundred and thirty millions of the Public Money had passed through his hands. It had been proved, that, of this Sum, fifteen millions had at different times been placed at a Banker's.—That Lord Melville should have suffered this Man to go on in such manner, was of itself enough on which to rest his accusation. (*Hear! Hear!*) It was infamous that the pittance wrung from the necessities of the Poor, should be sported with in the hazardous game of Stock-jobbing. The only defence that Lord Melville could have set up (if any thing he could say on the subject deserved the name of a Defence), was, that he had inquired into the accounts and proceedings of Mr. Trotter, and was satisfied with their regularity; but no, he knew nothing, he had examined into nothing. The Sums with which Mr. Trotter speculated in the Funds were enormous, even by his own Book, which of course would not contain a tenth part of them. Mr. Mark Sprott, who, by-the-bye, ought to have been compelled to answer all the questions of the Commissioners, purchased for him in one day above 300,000l. Another Broker transferred above 35,000l. Was this for the sake of security? Lord Melville acknowledges in his evidence, that he knew all this; and yet when Mr. Trotter denied having made any use of the Public Money, he never came forward, as he ought to have done, and exposed the falsehood of his Paymaster; a falsehood, indeed, that might have remained undetected to this day, but for the praiseworthy vigilance of the Commissioners of Naval Inquiry. If there were any who yet doubted that the Treasurer and Paymaster shared in the spoil of the Public he would proceed to advance still more convincing proofs of their collusion. In the first place, the large Sums of Money paid to the account of Mr. Dundas, and which it would be difficult to explain in any other manner; and then that certain complexion which seemed to pervade the whole of the speculation. They were all lucky; this was a most suspicious circumstance, and indicated very strongly that an understanding existed between them to which Mr. Trotter was frequently indebted for secret intelligence. Not to mention again the private agency of Mr. Trotter, or the destruction of Lord Melville's Papers, it must be recollected, that in the course of a few years upwards of one hundred and six thousand pounds had been paid into Coutts's, in the names of the Right Hon. Henry Dundas, Henry Dundas, and Mr. Dundas: now, whether these were all one and the same Person, did not seem very doubtful. Allowing, therefore, that the whole amount of Lord Melville's Salary for that space of time had been paid into Coutts's, it would have borne but a small proportion to such a Sum as one hundred and six thousand pounds. Mr. Trotter was the most improper Person that Lord Melville could have selected in the whole Kingdom for his Agent. What! make his Paymaster his private Agent! receive Sums of Money from that Agent in advance, and then tell the Commissioners that he really did not know whether such advance was from the public or from a private fund. Let us inquire a little into the history of this Mr. Trotter. When Lord Melville first became Treasurer of the Navy, he was a Clerk in the Pay Office; he was a man of tolerably good connexions, but by no means rich.—Lord Melville makes him his Paymaster, and soon after (knowing his poverty) borrows considerable Sums of Money from him. Why, he must know that it was the Public Money from which these advances were made.—*(Hear! Hear!)*—Mr. Trotter had no other Money to lend. When Mr. Trotter is asked whether or not he ever derived any advantage from the use of the Public Money, he replies, " I won't tell you." What was Mr. Tierney's answer to a similar question?—" No." Mr. Bathurst's? —" No."—Lord Harrowby's?—" No." But when it came to Lord Melville, the same retort churlish is used, " I won't tell you."——Mr. Wilson too was equally taciturn; but he ought to have been compelled to speak. He had no doubt been influenced to silence by the threats and promises of his superiors. When Lord Melville gives his evidence to the Commissioners, one should have thought that he would have come fortified by the destruction of his papers, fortified by a previous knowledge of the questions that in all probability would be put to him. But when he is requested to account for the deficiencies, with the cause of which the Treasurer of the Navy ought certainly to be well acquainted, he gives a long equivocal answer, and refers them to Mr. Trotter for information on the subject. But did Mr. Trotter afford this information? O, no!—When he came to Lord Melville's affairs, he stopped short at once, and wisely held his tongue. Could there be a stronger proof than this of their participation in guilt? —And yet Lord Melville pretends that it was only in June last that he became acquainted with the way in which Mr. Trotter used the Public Money. Lord Melville was by no means remarkable for the weakness of his memory, perhaps rather the reverse: but when asked, if he had derived any advantage from the Public Money, he replies, " not to the best of my recollection." The Hon. Gentleman alluded to the case of Mr. Jellicoe, and contended, that it was an additional proof of Lord Melville's sharing in the spoil of the Public, as he had forborne to press the payment of Mr. Jellicoe's balance, apprehensive, no doubt, of making him an enemy. These suspicions were much confirmed by Ld. Melville's last letter to the Commissioners, an extraordinary production, and produced at an extraordinary period, four months after the delivery of his first statement, and on the eve of the present discussion. In the outset of this Letter he thinks it necessary to restate the grounds of his former answers, with which the Commissioners were sufficiently acquainted. He proceeds, and again complains of his want of recollection. He then asserts, that he never, " knowingly," derived any advantage from the Public Money, either directly or indirectly, through the medium of Mr. Trotter; that is, he borrowed money from a Man, who, when he first knew him, was worth nothing, and whose last dividend exceeded eleven thousand pounds, and yet did not " know" that such Loans must have come out of the public Purse. The destruction of Lord Melville's private Papers was a most suspicious circumstance, especially when corroborated by that of Mr. Trotter's Ledger, in which the Accounts of all his Employers and connexions must have shared the same fate. But when to these were added the loss of Mr. Jellicoe's writings, it was impossible not to feel complete conviction of Lord Melville's guilt. Having dwelt for some time on this topic, the Hon. Gentleman proceeded to comment on his Lordship's Letter, and contended that it left him precisely in the same situation in which he was placed by the Report. There were many points which he had left untouched, from an apprehension of exhausting the patience of the House. If, by the manner in which he had conducted himself on this occasion, he had departed from that moderation with which he proposed to regulate himself, it was matter of sincere regret to him. But he trusted the House would act in a manner consistent with its dignity in disposing of this question. Not only the character of Parliament, but of every individual Member of the House was concerned. It was due to the Country to prove, that no Man in power, no Person high in Office, or placed in a situation of trust or responsibility, could with impunity violate the Law, or prove unfaithful to their Duty. He had no wish to wound the feelings of any Gentleman, but he was confident he should obtain the support of every Member in the House, except the relatives of the Noble Lord, who could not be expected to vote for his propositions. He could not conceive it possible for any other description of Persons to oppose them. The Country Gentlemen, ever distinguished Guardians of the Public Money, could not lend their assistance to shelter from the vengeance of the House, any Persons guilty of great malversation in the management of the Public Money. Neither would those honourable and distinguished Officers of the Army and Navy, who were Members of that House, give any encouragement to transactions inconsistent with the noble sentiment of honour with which they were animated. They would be the first to stigmatise a flagrant violation of the Law. He called upon the House to recollect, before they should come to the vote, the circumstances under which the Offences he charged had been committed. He called upon them to contemplate the magnitude of the taxation with which the Country was burthened : he wished the House to consider the situation in which the Country now stood. From various circumstances of peculiar hardship, nay, the grievances that had already occurred, the more opulent were obliged to part with their superfluities in order to contribute to the support of the indigent and the poor, and to carry on the Wars in which we were engaged. Every class of the Community was struggling : the means of the poor Labourer were extorted; for at every meal he took he suffered from that most grievous system of taxation which now existed, every object being taxed which could afford a single farthing. We had been told that such exactions were absolutely necessary for the present circumstances of the Country; but what situation were we to be placed in, could we not prove that a proper use had been made of the Money so collected ? It was alone by the punishment of such Delinquents that the House could prove to the Public that they attended in every particular to their interests. The Honourable Member concluded with reading his Resolutions, in substance as follow :—

1. " That the House of Commons, in the year 1782, came to certain Regulations respecting the Treasurer of the Navy, prohibiting him from keeping any balances of Public Monies in his hands, and fixing a permanent and increased Salary in lieu of Fees and Emoluments. Likewise prohibiting any Paymaster or

Treasurer of the Navy from making use of the Public Money, or directly or indirectly applying the same to his own personal advantage or private emolument: and further, that the House was of opinion, that the Naval Commissioners had acted with honour to themselves, with benefit to the Community, and in a way calculated to ensure the prosperity of the Kingdom.

2. " That in the month of June 1782, the Salary of the Treasurer of the Navy was increased to 4000l. per annum.

3. " That the Resolutions above recited were strictly complied with by Mr. Barre, who, it appeared, had not derived any emolument or advantage from the Public Money; neither had Mr. Douglas, the Sub-Accountant.

4. " That on the 19th of August 1782, Mr. Henry Dundas succeeded to the Office of Treasurer of the Navy, with a fresh increase of Salary.

5. That he continued in Office till 1783, and that on being asked by the Naval Commissioners, Whether during that time he had made use of the Public Money for purposes of private emolument? he had declined to answer the question, but in a Letter subsequently written he had stated, that he did not derive any personal advantage from the Public Money.

6. " That Lord Bayning held the Office after that period, and did not apply the Public Money to private advantage.

7. " That on the 5th June, 1784, Mr. Henry Dundas again came into the Office of Treasurer of the Navy.

8. " That in 1785, an Act passed, regulating the Sums of Money placed at the disposal of the Treasurer of the Navy, that the same be lodged in the Bank of England, &c.

9. " That the execution of the said Act (the Act of 1785, for better regulating the Office of Treasurer of the Navy,) was postponed till the month of January 1786, and that from that time till the month of June 1800, when Lord Melville left the Office of Treasurer, contrary to the practice established in the Treasurership of the Right Honourable Isaac Barre, contrary to the Resolutions of the House of Commons of the 18th June, 1782, and in defiance of the above-mentioned Act of the 25th George III, chap. 31, large Sums of Money were, under pretence of Naval Services, and of a scandalous evasion of the Act, at various times drawn from the Bank and invested in Exchequer and Navy Bills, lent upon the security of Stock, employed in discounting private Bills, in purchasing Bank and East India Stock, and used in various ways for the purposes of private emolument.

10. " That Alexander Trotter, Esq. the Paymaster of the Navy, was the Person by whom, or in whose Name the Public Money was thus employed; and that in so doing he acted with the knowledge and consent of Lord Viscount Melville, to whom he was at the same time private Agent, and for whose use or benefit he occasionally laid out from 10 to 20,000l. without considering whether he was previously in advance to his Lordship, and whether such advances were made from his public or private balances.

11. " That the Right Honourable Lord Viscount Melville having been privy to, and connived at the withdrawing from the Bank of England, for purposes of private interest or emolument, Sums issued to him as Treasurer of the Navy, and placed to his account in the Bank, according to the provisions of the 25th George III, chap. 31, has been guilty of a gross violation of the Law, and a high breach of Duty.

12. " That it further appears, that subsequent to the appointment of Lord Melville as Treasurer of the Navy, in 1784, and during the time he held that Office, large Sums of Money issued for the Service of the Navy were applied to other Services; and that the said Lord Melville, in a Letter written in answer to Precept issued by the Commissioners of Naval Inquiry, requiring an Account of Money received by him, or any Person on his account, or by his order, from the Paymaster of the Navy; and also of the time when, and the Persons by whom the same were returned to the Bank, or Paymaster; has declared that he

has no materials by which he could make up such an Account; and that if he had materials, he could not do it without disclosing delicate and confidential transactions of Government, which his duty to the Public must have restrained him from revealing.

13. "That Lord Melville, in applying Monies issued for the Service of the Navy to other Services, stated to have been of so delicate and confidential a nature, that in his opinion no Account can, or ought to be given of them, has acted in a manner inconsistent with his duty, and incompatible with those Securities which the Legislature has provided for the proper application of the Public Money."

The *Chancellor of the Exchequer* employed every argument which his powerful eloquence could enforce to defend Lord Melville; and then concluded as follows :—For his own part, he was desirous that the House should look at the whole of the case in all its circumstances and bearings, and then do, without delay whatever the interest of the public, a just sense of their own duty, and the nature of the case may require. For this purpose, he thought the best course to pursue would be to refer the Report to a Select Committee, inasmuch as there were many points contained in it which required further explanation. The Hon. Member had dwelt with much earnestness on the application of certain sums for the accommodation of other branches of the public service; but in his own view of the question, the House was not in a situation to decide upon that transaction. Did the Hon. Gentleman mean to say, that in judging of this transaction, the House was not to take into its consideration the excuses, the motives, the circumstances, and the necessity of the transaction? Was the House, knowing only the bare fact, that the application of the money in such a manner was a violation of the law, to decide upon its merits without taking into consideration whether any loss had arisen from it, whether the motives were justifiable, wanton, or necessary; whether the circumstances were such as to warrant a departure from the letter of the law; and what the magnitude of the transaction? It would not be necessary for him to argue the propriety of permitting such a latitude with Englishmen, or with persons of liberal and enlightened minds; for he was confident that all such would agree with him, that cases might occur when the circumstances under which such a transaction might take place, would make it meritorious in the public officer to incur the heavy responsibility. This he stated, with a view to the stress that had been laid on the application of a particular sum to a different service from that for which it had been voted. There was an allegation in the report on this head, and the Hon. Gentleman had stated a particular sum as having been advanced in this way, and afterwards by his Hon. Friend (Mr. Long). He had himself been a party to that transaction, and he should be ashamed to address the House on the subject, if he could not explain the matter, as related to the share he had had in the business, to their entire satisfaction; so that however illegal the application might have been in the first instance, and he was ready to take that for granted, it would appear to have arisen from considerations of public interest, and to have been transferred from the service for which it had been voted only for a time, and, without any other inconvenience or loss, replaced afterwards. It was impossible to disclose the circumstances under which it had been applied; but if the House would consent to appoint the Committee, he should produce the most convincing statements, so far at least as he was concerned. The whole sum particularized amounted to 100,000l., out of which two different sums of 40,000l. each had been drawn with his privity, under circumstances which he could fully justify to the House; and as these sums made the much greater part of the whole sum specified, there was every reason to think that the whole had been applied in a manner equally justifiable. The Noble Lord had, at that time, other high official situations, and might have had occasion, and could, without his privity, have applied sums occasionally to a different service from that for which they had been voted, with a view to the public interest; and though he was not in possession of the circumstances, he had no doubt that the Noble Lord could satisfactorily account for the transaction. As to the other part of the Hon. Gentleman's charge, that Lord Melville had connived at the Paymaster of the Navy keeping the public money in his hands, and applying it to purposes of private profit, he confessed that this appeared to him a fit object of attention, when they should come to consider the question in the whole of its bearings. He was prepared to admit, that the conniving at such conduct in a Paymaster of the Navy was not justifiable, but thought, nevertheless, that much would depend on the circumstances, the extent, and the danger that had been incurred. He maintained that the Commissioners had not stated, that the issue had been greater than the service required; and he insisted, that from their Report it was evident that they believed that to be the case. It was also agreed to by them, that the public money had not been applied so as not to be ready to satisfy any demand or sudden emergency; and they had not even insinuated that any effect had been produced in the increase of expense, or the aggravation or augmentation of additional burthens; nor had they attempted to charge, that any demand of any individual had been a single moment retarded. As to this application of the money to private purposes of profit, it did not appear that Lord Melville had been aware of it; the Hon. Gentleman, however, had dwelt much on this circumstance, founding his observations on the intricate accounts of the Commissioners, by which it appeared that he had not considered the matter in detail. The Commissioners had stated, that various sums had come into the Bank of Messrs. Coutts, which had not been procured by draft on the Bank, and they had supposed that these consisted of sums for the services *in transitu,* applied in this way. One million had been particularly specified. But that million had been brought directly from the Bank to the house of Messrs. Coutts, by one of the forms of draft prescribed by the statute, and the whole of it had been issued thence in the course of a few days, to take up Navy bills then due. So that this was one instance of an error, on which they had rested much, and which being capable of being thus satisfactorily explained, proved the necessity of further investigation. The sums that had been vested in Messrs. Coutts had been neither lodged there for the benefit of the Treasurer of the Navy or of the Navy Paymaster, but in the course of office; and this was another error of the Report, for the same practice prevails at present of drawing in gross from the multiplicity of paying all the small Sums by drawing in detail. The Act of Parliament directed no such Drafts for small Sums, but for sufficient Sums to enable the Paymaster from day to day to issue the necessary Sums to the Sub-Accountants, so that the balances in hand appeared not to contravene the Law, but to be in direct conformity with it, and necessary for the management of the business of the Office. The question, therefore, was, Whether more had been issued than was necessary, whether an expense to the public had been the consequence, or an increase of issue? The House was aware that no money was issued to the Treasurer of the Navy, but on memorial from the different Boards, and that consequently the Treasurer would have no power of increasing the issues to him. (The Right Hon. Gentleman here described the operation by which the Treasurer of the Navy drew money from the Bank, and proved thence that it is not in his power on any occasion, or under any circumstances, to draw for more than the occasions of the different Boards require). In the next place, the Commissioners had divided the time during which Lord Melville had been in office into two periods, in making the average; instead of making the average for the whole of the time of his being in office. The first period they calculate up to 1796, the next to 1800; so that they had not given the average on the whole, nor distinctly in the separate periods. They calculated the balances on the first period at 45 average, and the last at 33, but they had taken the amount of the gross balances without deducting the assignments. When the Commissioners had stated ten days as the number that ought to be in advance in the Paymaster's hands, they calculated it exclusive of the out-posts; and if the money at the outposts were to be deducted, the balances would be in the first or the most favourable period, an average of seventeen days, and in the latter period an average of eight days; and on the whole period the average was but fourteen or fifteen, five only more than the Commissioners had thought necessary, and nearly the same number that the Clerk had stated in his examination. Now if it should turn out that this statement was correct, he could not admit a doubt that it would be sufficient to determine the House and the public to examine more narrowly and minutely into the matter and allegations of the Reports before they would ground upon it either censure or disapprobation. There were four different errors in this single statement, and these proved unanswerably the necessity of a fuller investigation. This could not be prosecuted in the whole House, nor with the Speaker in the chair, it could only be followed up with effect in a Select Committee. If the investigation should be proceeded with, he was convinced that many Sums stated to have been paid in the name of Lord Melville would appear to have been applied to official purposes: how far that was the case it was not for him to anticipate then, before the inquiry should be instituted. The House would determine for itself when the investigation should take place. Before they could judge whether any Sums of Public Money had been so advanced, they should see the credit account of Lord Melville, they should also see the different Sums paid in by Mr. Trotter, for Lord Melville, on account of his salary as Treasurer of the Navy, as also an account of his unappropriated Salary as Keeper of the Signet in Scotland, and for dividends in the Funds. Would Gentlemen under these circumstances give way to surmises? Would they think strange that Lord Melville, knowing that he had no contract with Mr. Trotter, no participation with, and knowing also the unfortunate way in which Mr. Trotter kept his accounts, had declined answering until he had ascertained the state of these accounts. And if it should appear even that a few thousands had been by inadvertence so advanced, could any Gentleman suppose that that would have been any object to a Noble Lord in a high and distinguished Office of trust and honour? He would not think it possible for a liberal and enlightened mind; for even common sense to entertain such an opinion. If so, then he contended, that the materials before the House were insufficient to form a final judgment, and that a further investigation was absolutely necessary, and that such investigation could not be conducted in the House, but in a Select Committee, which could be managed without much delay. With these sentiments, he felt it unnecessary and improper to say more on the subject. He should therefore move, as an amendment, that " the Tenth Report be referred to a Select Committee," &c.

Mr. Fox suggested the propriety of moving the previous question, rather than an amendment, in order that the previous Resolutions might be entered on the Journals.

The *Chancellor of the Exchequer* had no objection to the course proposed, as he should thereby obtain the substantial object of his motion; and understanding, however, that if the previous question should be agreed to, he should afterward move for the appointment of a Select Committee; he then moved the previous question. On the question being put,

Lord *Henry Petty*, at the same time that he acknowledged it was impossible for him to follow the Right Hon. Gentleman through the vast range he had taken in his view of the subject under discussion, was anxious to state the ground on which he supported the original motion. He had never felt greater surprise than when he heard the Right Hon. Gentleman alledge that his Hon. Friend (Mr. Whitbread) had travelled out of the record of the facts in the statement which he had laid before the House. This must be matter of surprise to the House also, when the whole of his Hon. Friend's charges, except the concluding ones, were merely matter of fact, and nothing but matter of fact. In truth, the whole of what had fallen from his Hon. Friend were either matter of fact, or plain and immediate deduction from fact. The Right Hon. Gentleman urged, with a view to induce the House to agree to the appointment of a Select Committee to inquire into this subject, that the attempt was made to influence the passions of the House, and that the subject involved a great deal of complicated details of figures. In considering this latter point it was necessary the House should recollect, that any confusion that existed in this way arose from the irregular manner in which Lord Melville and his Paymaster kept their accounts. It was obvious, however, from the plain matter of fact, that there had been a violation of the Act of Parliament. The Right Hon. Gentleman opposite was liable to a charge of having omitted facts in his statement. He had omitted the very material fact, that Lord Melville had allowed he had violated the Act of Parliament, by permitting his Paymaster to withdraw large sums from the Bank of England before they were actually wanted, and to keep them at his private Banker's. One part of the ground for proposing a Select Committee was, that part of the money voted for Navy Services had been applied to other public services; and the other ground was, the existence of complicated details of figures. Was this direct violation of the law included in either of these descriptions? He had no objection to a Select Committee in the proper time. On the contrary, he should be disposed to support the appointment of such a Committee, when the motion of his Hon. Friend should be agreed to, and the House should have come to a determination on the plain and obvious fact. Then a Committee would be proper to consider of the expediency, and the means of pushing the inquiry further, and he should be happy to contribute his small share to the institution of a Committee for so laudable an object. But first let the House consider what was before it, and let it consider that what Lord Melville admitted in one place, he could not deny in another; that he could not deny before a Committee of the House what he had avowed before the Commissioners of Inquiry; and let Gentlemen then ask themselves what necessity there was for delay. The House could at once pronounce on the breach of the Act of Parliament, and then it may examine more minutely in a Committee the circumstances of the transaction, and the precise amount of the criminality. The Right Hon. Gentleman argued that the public sustained no loss by these transactions, at the same time that he allowed this did not excuse the delinquency, though it extenuated the offence. He did not think it was any extenuation. He thought there was not only risk to the public, but positive loss. He distinguished between positive loss and precise loss; for though the precise amount could not be ascertained, the fact that there was a loss was beyond all question. The Right Hon. Gentleman had gone into great detail to show that the Paymaster did not draw the money from the Exchequer before it was wanted. But in this statement the Right Hon. Gentleman reduced himself to the following dilemma:—He stated that the money was not removed from the Exchequer before it was wanted for Naval Services; at the same time that he allowed large sums were given in accommodation from the Navy to other branches of the public service. How was it possible this accommodation could be given, unless larger sums were kept in the Paymaster's hands than were wanted in Navy Services, except indeed the Navy Service was distressed and defrauded to allow the advance? If the money were once allowed to be drawn, it may be allowed to private as well as to public purposes; and if the door were once opened, it was impossible to set limits to the abuse it may let in. The speculations of Mr. Trotter had not failed, but that was no excuse for putting the public money to so unwarrantable a risk. The success may besides be accounted for in another manner, by means of the connexion or combination that existed between the three individuals concerned. Mr. Mark Sprott touched the funds, and Lord Melville the secrets of State, and Mr. Trotter touched both these persons. Millions were thus managed in that nice and delicate machine of the public funds; though, at that time, combinations of another nature were much talked of; no Jacobin conspiracy that did exist, or could have existed, was calculated to do more than this conspiracy between these three persons. The Noble Lord had represented, that when the Committee of 1788, in prosecuting its inquiries as to the administration of the public offices, came to that of the Treasurer of the Navy, Lord Melville being called upon by the Committee represented the regulations for bringing up the arrear in that office, and preventing any future arrear, were in full effect. This statement was opposite to the fact; for at this very time the Accountant's branch, which had been instituted with a view to this object, having come up to that period when it was to take cognizance of Lord Melville's own administration, stopped suddenly short, and its labours were no more heard of. The account of Lord Melville's first Treasurership was not made out till last year, and the remaining part of the account at the time the Noble Lord was in office was still unprepared. The reason given for this was, that the clerks employed in this duty being borrowed from another department, and being withdrawn, the business could not proceed. It was evident from what Lord Melville had stated to the Committee, that the benefits of the acts then lately made were carried into full effect. This was, however, very remote from the fact. The Act of Parliament went to provide, that the public money was to be kept in the Bank, and that no public office was to be made a public treasury; and yet Lord Melville had, to all intents and purposes, made his office a public treasury. He dwelt on the systematic deviation from the law that had so many years prevailed in that office, and asked, Whether this was a case from which the House would turn away, referring the matter to a Select Committee without coming to a vote? As to whether the prominent act was right or wrong, or whether the Noble Lord was fit still to hold a high and confidential situation in the government, there was no difference between the situation in which the Noble Lord stood with respect to the House and the Country, and that in which any man may with his private agent. The House ought to consider for a moment what was the nature of this illegal combination between three persons, one of whom was touching the funds, and the other two the secrets of State. There was Mr. Mark Sprott, who enjoyed the confidence of Mr. Trotter; Mr. Trotter, who enjoyed the confidence of my Lord Melville; and my Lord Melville, who enjoyed, too long enjoyed, the confidence of the public. These enormous sums were therefore carried to the Stocks, and there employed in private point of view for individual emolument, and in a public point of view they were used to keep up the national credit. From such a combination, what dangerous consequences were likely to result! At the period when these combinations existed, there were also others existing of a different nature. There were combinations existing in this country, denominated Jacobinical; but he believed that never was there one of a more dangerous, insidious, and mischievous nature, than the one which was now discussing. (*Loud cry of Hear! Hear!*) There appeared to have been a systematic deception on the part of the Conspirators. His Lordship then read extracts from some letters by Lord Melville, to show his inconsistency. The principal intention of the Resolutions passed in 1786, was to regulate the disposal of the public money, and to prevent Public Offices from becoming Public Treasuries. Lord Melville must have known that these regulations were by him regularly and systematically violated for ten years preceding. If such a statement were true, Why should the House not come to a Resolution, declaring such persons unfit for any office of trust? He confessed he saw no reason why they should act otherwise than any private individual would do to his agent, who had been guilty of such gross malversation. Was Mr. Sprott to omit paying 10 or 12,000l. to Mr. Trotter; or, in other words, appropriate that sum to himself, by taking the use of it for his own emolument, would not Mr. Trotter immediately discontinue him as his agent? Mr. Mark Sprott might then say, I never meant to obtain any profit from that sum, it was only retained on account of the intricate manner in which we kept our accounts. What Broker in London would be allowed to keep his accounts in that state, that he could not ascertain whether he had a balance in his hands or not? The people of England, who pay these public servants most liberally, and in no instance more so than in the present one, have surely as good a right to expect that they be as justly and regularly served as any Broker on the Stock Exchange could serve his employer. If, from any part of Lord Melville's deposition—if from any part of that most extraordinary letter, written several months after his Lordship's examination (enemies only of the legality of Lord Melville), he could entertain any doubt as to the possibility of his being able to disprove his statement, he would vote for a Select Committee. But how was it possible to have any opinion in the smallest degree favourable to his Lordship from such a statement? What had the Right Hon. Gentleman said to do away the criminality? Acting as his Lordship had done, in violation of an Act of Parliament, he (Lord Melville) had put himself in that situation, that no man could lay his hand on his heart and pronounce him innocent. When he looked at his Lordship's letter, it recalled to his remembrance the celebrated Oration of Cicero against Piso, in which that Orator, breaking off from his argument, proving the guilt of Piso, says—" But who is more condemned, or more guilty, than you are, who dare not write, nor say, that you are innocent?"

" Quis te miserior qui nequis scribere rempublicam bene gestam, qui presens ne que dicere ausus es."

(*Loud and repeated bursts of applause from all quarters of the House.*) If the Noble Lord, on the passing of his Act for restraining this very evil, had been told that not a year would pass when that Act would be violated; when it would be violated by a Treasurer of the Navy, and that that Treasurer of the Navy would be himself, what would he have said? But if the prophecy had been carried

Further, and it had been said, that not only would the violation be made by a Treasurer of the Navy, but that after that violation had been for 14 years unnoticed till discovered by a Commission of Inquiry, and when at length the detection of it lay recorded on the table of the House, the House would be so culpable that it would be glad of getting rid of it by any means rather than pronounce upon it as it ought. He had too good an opinion of those of whom the House was composed, to think this business would be so passed over. It would indeed be fortunate if abuses were never detected, rather than that it should appear that when Ministers violated the most express and immediate laws for preventing abuses in their departments; that when the diligence of the Commissioners had brought forward this delinquency, Parliament should come in between law and its violator, and screen the delinquent from justice. This was the worst precedent that could be established in any country. A prompt declaration should be made on this subject. He therefore voted, in the first instance, for the motion of his Hon. Friend, with the intention, that after the primary resolution should be agreed to, inquiry should be instituted, and vigorously pursued.

The *Attorney General* said, if it were a necessary alternative that the supposed delinquency should be punished now, or that it should escape altogether, the propriety of coming to some resolution, at the present moment, may be more reasonably insisted upon. He doubted whether the Noble Lord would, on reflection, think it right to proceed to judgment, without the fullest investigation of the facts. It was agreed on all hands that inquiry should take place. The Noble Lord wished a separate decision on one point. Was any point so insulated as not to be still connected with the whole? While there were such important grounds of inquiry, the House should not be called upon to pronounce judgment when conviction was so remote, at the same time that further inquiry could have no ill effect.

Mr. *Tierney* complimented his Noble Friend. It was a matter of pride to any man to be allowed to call himself the friend of such rising talents and eloquence. He agreed with him, that nothing was more fit than to appoint a Committee after the first point should be agreed upon; a Committee in which all that related to Accounts and Calculations may be sifted and made clear. The transfer of money from one Service to another was also matter for a Committee, but what was to be done with the remainder of the Tenth Report? Did Lord Melville ask for any further delay, saying he had evidence sufficient for his acquittal? Did Mr. Trotter say any thing to that effect? But the people of England looked to this night for the opinion of their Representatives on this important case. He would ask the Right Hon. Gentleman how long it was since the expedient of a reference to a Committee occurred to him? The Right Hon. Gentleman had expressed his anxiety to have the letter of the Noble Lord before the House previously to their coming to any determination, as that letter, he had stated, would throw very considerable light on the subject; and now his anxiety was to have a Committee appointed for investigating the subject. But the question, he contended, was by no means complicated. There was not a single gentleman present, he apprehended, who could from his heart avow it as his opinion, that any proof could be brought to show that money had not been diverted from the public service, and removed from the Bank in opposition to the most express and positive declaration of Parliament. What occasion then was there for an inquiry? Would Mr. Sprott, who was silent when examined upon oath, speak more plainly when not upon oath, before a Committee of the House? or ought they to give more credit to his evidence in the one case than in the other? No evidence which they could take from the parties not on oath, could invalidate that which had been taken before the Commissioners on oath. For what purpose besides should Parliament appoint Commissioners for this express purpose, if their conclusions were not to be relied on without repeating the inquiry. They had been employed six weeks in this investigation, and had heard all that Lord Melville had to say in his defence, before they published their Report; and what was curious, not one of his Lordship's friends had yet dared to say that he was innocent. All they pleaded for was time. But the examination of the Accounts could afford no ground for this plea, for this examination might be necessary only to determine the sum to be refunded, but not at all for criminating the parties. In regard to the transfer of money from the Bank of England, the Noble Lord did not deny his knowledge of this practice, nor was it at all natural to believe that he would have allowed it for a period of twelve years, without participating in the profits; and it would have been more generous in his Lordship, he thought, instead of evading the question to the prejudice of Mr. Trotter, to have at once frankly avowed that the practice had been continued by his authority, as well as with his knowledge. The Right Hon. Gentleman concluded by observing, that the documents laid before the Commissioners had been afforded by themselves, and that therefore if it could b called *ex parte* evidence, it was because it was all on the side of the accused. He commended the conduct of the Commissioners, and was proud to have been one of an Administration that had virtue enough to appoint them. The question put to them by the motion of the Right Hon. Gentleman, in short was, Whether they should have confidence in those who had detected, or those who had profited by the frauds that were the object of the inquiry?

Mr. *Canning* wished to offer some reasons that induced him to second the motion of his Right Hon. Friend.

Mr. *George Ponsonby* was decidedly in favour of Mr. Whitbread's Resolutions. He observed, that it was a monstrous proposition to maintain there had been no criminality, because there was no loss. The Right Hon. Gentleman opposite to him had acknowledged, that Sums of Money had been taken contrary to law, and applied to a particular purpose. Why was not that circumstance mentioned at the time in the House of Commons, and a Bill of Indemnity applied for? It was said, that attempts had been made to inflame the public mind against Lord Melville, by the circulation of libellous hand-bills. Then it was the business of the Attorney-General to prosecute the authors of them; but it was no reason that the House should stop short in its present inquiry, because there were libellers in the country who circulated offensive hand-bills. He insisted that Lord Melville and Mr. Trotter ought not to be suffered to walk quietly about the streets, without an account being taken of their property, in order that they might be compelled to refund what they had taken from the public; and bills ought to be brought into Parliament, to disable them from disposing of their property while the present question was agitated. There never was a period in the History of the Country in which the character of the House of Commons was so involved as the present. He hoped that those Members of the House who represented the same part of the kingdom with himself would consider the peculiar situation they were now placed in—that they would now give the People of England a proof of their spirit and independence, by voting for the motion that night, and in so doing, they would remove the unfavourable impression which the easy surrender of their own Parliament had made on the public mind. He felt more than common anxiety on the subject. It was generally supposed that the accession of one hundred Irish Members to that House, was giving an accession of so much strength to the Minister, who could always command their votes. He was grieved to think this idea had gone abroad. And, as an Irish Member, he should be ashamed to walk the streets if he did not think that his countrymen in that House were as free from corrupt influence as any of those Gentlemen who represented England.

The *Master of the Rolls* disapproved of the manner in which the business was taken up by Gentlemen on the other side; it tended to make the House enter upon a judicial proceeding. They were eager to bring the accused person to punishment, but he was at a loss to see how they were to be punished before the exact nature and extent of their offence was ascertained.

Mr. *Fox* began by stating, that he should be extremely unwilling to suffer this question to be put, without expressing his sentiments upon it. For if unhappily the vote of the House should be opposite to that which he hoped and wished, he should feel very uneasy indeed that his name should partake in the universal odium that must attach to any decision tending to second such notorious delinquency as the Report on the Table declared. Before he would proceed to the merits of the Charges under consideration, he thought it proper to notice the arguments of the Gentlemen upon the other side; not because he considered those arguments possessed of any intrinsic force; but lest from the authority of the persons from whom they proceeded, they might have the effect of leading the House to a decision, which, if it should correspond with the wishes of those by whom such arguments were used, must destroy its character with the country and with all Europe. The first Gentleman with whom he would begin was the last who spoke. That learned Gentleman directed the whole of his observations to show that the House should go into a Committee in order to ascertain whether the breach of the Act of Parliament, not of which Lord Melville stood charged, but of which he confessed himself guilty, proceeded from corrupt motives. If corruption consisted merely in a man putting money into his own pocket, according to the vulgar conception, perhaps some of the deductions of the Learned Gent. would be right. But he would contend that nothing could be more corrupt, in his opinion, than to permit a man's own agent to convert the money of others to his own private emolument. This was the amount of Lord Melville's confession; and although it might be possible, from a further examination, to prove the Noble Lord more guilty, it did appear to him utterly impossible to prove him less so. For the most conclusive evidence of the Noble Lord's corruption, he would only refer to that paragraph in the 119th page of the Report, in which the Noble Lord stated, that "although he knew his agent Trotter was applying the Public Money to other purposes, than that for which it was legally intended, that he did not prohibit him from doing so." What was that, he would ask, but complete corruption, even taking he case *simpliciter?* but combining it with other circumstances, could any man entertain a doubt upon the subject of his guilt? What greater aggravation of his delinquency in tolerating the breach of his own Act of Parliament could be imagined, than allowing his agent to misapply the Public Money, for the safe custody of which that Act was intended? But it is pretended that no loss had accrued to the Public from this malversation; and a very singular argument was advanced, that as there was no loss there was no risk. Now (said Mr. Fox) it happened in certain parts of my life, which I do not quote with a view to recommend my example to others, that I was in the habits of engaging in speculations which are commonly called gaming *(a laugh)*. If a man should, in that kind of speculation, win a large sum of money, I am sure that an argument would not thence arise that he had made no risk. I rather think the natural inference would be, that his risk was considerable. Probably however, in this case, Lord Melville did not care that Mr. Trotter should not lose any money. Mr. Trotter was the confidential agent of Lord Melville, and Lord Melville was the confidential agent of the State. Therefore, in this sort of speculations in which Trotter engaged, Lord Melville could guard against much risk. If two men play cards together, and that a third person stands behind one of them and throws hints to the other, he that receives the hints is tolerably sure of winning. Just so in this business; Lord Melville knew when the Navy Bills were likely to be funded, and Mr. Trotter could act upon the information he might receive. Will any one say then, that from such acting upon such information, no loss would accrue to the public? On the contrary, I maintain, that the public would suffer a loss of 1 per cent. upon the discount of such bills. But then, observed the Honourable Member, the Learned Gentleman desired the House to go into an inquiry, in order to obtain farther evidence. He would appeal to the judgment of the House, Whether any farther evidence could be necessary to enable it to come to a decided opinion upon the breach of law, which the Noble Lord himself confessed? That opinion the House was called on to declare. The Public had a right to demand it from them. It was said, that the House ought not to think of acting judicially, of inflicting punishment without the fullest examination into the merits of the accusation, and affording the accused the fullest opportunity of vindicating himself. And so far as the confession of Lord Melville went, he had been already tried. He would, however, defy those Gentlemen who rested their objection so very much upon the question of punishment, to show that it was at all times in the power of that House to inflict any punishment on such delinquents as Lord Melville and Trotter. But if the House should determine on prosecution in any way with a view to punishment; whether by directing the Attorney General to prosecute, whether by moving an Impeachment, or preparing a Bill of Pains and Penalties, which perhaps would be a more proper mode of proceeding, he would maintain that the confession of the Party accused would be evidence to proceed upon, and that the House was now called on to act, as it must in every similar case, as a Grand Jury, to pronounce upon the guilt of the accused. It was strange to hear it asserted that the accused was not guilty, because no loss accrued from this scandalous transaction. To those to whom the loss of honour was nothing, perhaps it might be said that no loss had arisen. But what was the loss of honour to that Government which, after such a palpable instance of delinquency, should preserve its connexion with the delinquent? and what is the loss of character and honour to that House, should it attempt by its vote to screen such a delinquent? infinitely more than any sum of money could possibly amount to. Whatever the Learned Gentleman to whom he had already adverted might assert, he could not see that any farther inquiry could be necessary to enable the House to decide that a great Public Officer, who allowed his servants to make illicit profit from the Public Money, in the teeth of an Act of Parliament, was guilty of a most serious offence. The guilt consisted in the violation of the law, and it never could be pretended that any such violation could be innocent. There were, indeed, many cases in which the most severe punishments attached to offences to which the charge of moral turpitude did not apply, but which were criminal in consequence of the precept of the law. Such were many of the offences against our revenue laws. Not two years ago an act was passed declaring a man guilty of felony, without benefit of clergy, if paper of a certain sort should be found in his possession, this sort of paper being used for the manufacture of Bank-notes. Now the reason of this statute was this, that a man could not be presumed to have such paper in his possession but with a criminal intention. Therefore the breach of the Act was proof against him. And the Act of the 25th of the King, which applied to the case under consideration, was drawn up upon a similar principle, and the breach of it was to be deemed the proof of the criminal intention. Upon this proof, those which arose out of the reason of the law, he had no hesitation in pronouncing the Noble Lord Guilty. The Noble Lord, it would be recollected, retained the office of Treasurer for nine years after he was appointed to that of Secretary of State. [This was denied by the Chancellor of the Exchequer across the table] No matter, resumed Mr. Fox, as to the precise time. The Noble Lord retained the office for several years; and when in that House allusion was made to the circumstance of his holding the two offices, the answer from the other side of the House was, that although he held those offices, he only received the salary of Secretary of State, and nothing from that of Treasurer of the Navy. Ay, that is nothing of the legal salary. Did not this justify something more than suspicion? Why should the Noble Lord so fondly cling to this office of his Friend, Mr. Trotter? There were many other persons among even his own relations would have been glad to occupy this situation. But no, Lord Melville seemed particularly attached to it; and would common sense, in considering a thing of this kind, make no inference from that attachment. Another objection arose against the proposed Committee, from this consideration, that he did not see that any of the difficulties which some Gentlemen complained of, could be removed—that any of the obscure accounts could be explained. Those accounts were indeed of such a nature, that the Parties themselves could not understand them, and how then could it be possible for a Committee of that House to make any thing of them.

It had been said that the House should proceed with the utmost deliberation in deciding upon character. But upon whose character were they to decide on this occasion? Not certainly upon that of Lord Melville, for his character was entirely gone, (a loud cry of Hear! Hear!) but upon the character of the House and the Government, which must depend upon the vote of this night. As to the character of Lord Melville, it was so completely destroyed in public estimation for ever, that he would venture to say, that were the vote of the House unanimous in his favour, it would not have the slightest effect in wiping away the stigma that was universally affixed to his name. What then must the World think of retaining such a Man at the head of the glory of the Country? It was dreadful to reflect that the most honourable claims (honourable professions) should be placed at the disposal of a Man with whose name dishonour was inseparably associated—who had confessed himself guilty of an act of corrupt illegality. The

Honourable Gentleman took notice of an ingenious and forcible argument advanced by a Noble Friend behind him, (Lord Henry Petty,) whose speech he considered, and he was sure the House felt it to be, the best that had been delivered in the course of the Debate. He recollected, that when the Right Hon. Gentleman on the other side (Mr. Pitt) made his *entrée* in that House, his first essay was in favour of reform and against corruption. With what pleasure did the House listen to him upon that occasion!—but how soon was the promise of his early years abandoned!—

" Quantum mutatis ab illo."

Let the Speech which the Right Honourable Gentleman delivered on that occasion be contrasted with that of this evening, and the change would be glaring? There was something also in the dying legacy of *Trotter* to the Navy Office, that was particularly deserving of a remark. It amounted to this, that Trotter said to his Successors, " Now, as I am leaving the Paymaster's Office, I shall provide that not one of you shall ever make a shilling by the same means that I have done."—But this he left as a bequest after the death of his own power. He did not even offer it while living—*(a laugh.)* An Honourable Gentleman had expressed a hope that some measure would be adopted to prevent the recurrence of such a practice as the Report on the Table disclosed. But there was no measure in the shape of an Act of Parliament could be efficient, if this precedent were to be established, that an Act of Parliament was to be violated with impunity. For his part, when he read over the Evidence, he was rather filled with disgust than indignation. He was ashamed of having any connexion, even hostilely, with a Person who had so degraded himself. Indeed it made him ashamed of being of the same class. What does the Evidence exhibit? A Man of such power and elevated situation as the Noble Lord shrinking from answering the questions put to him, on the ground that he was not to criminate himself; and again saying, when the question was repeated, that he did not recollect how far he might have benefitted by Mr. Trotter's Money transactions.—Recollect! Does a man apply to his recollection on such occasions and respecting such circumstances! A man, when asked whether he was ever in company with John Noakes, for example, may very well say, ' To the best of my recollection I never have.' But, were it inquired whether he had not been kicked out of company by the same Person for attempting to pick his pocket, what would he have thought of him if his answer was, ' To the best of my recollection I was not?' Besides, the Noble Lord never thought of attempting any explanation of his evidence till the Report had been nearly two months before the House. He knew nothing of it till it was printed.——What! the Report was so long before the House of which the Noble Lord is a Member, and, though it so nearly concerned himself, he never had the curiosity to look into it until it was printed. Who can believe it? Or did the Noble Lord only begin to be alarmed when he found the effect which the printed Report had made on the Public? Then he writes a letter, which he had much better have left unwritten. It was a vain attempt to do away the damnation. He still remains involved by Mr. Trotter's Evidence. Was it not wrong in Mr. Trotter thus to commit his Principal? Yet no anger is betrayed against him—no indignation manifested by the Noble Lord at the slur thus cast upon his character. But how could he blame Mr. Trotter? He must have known the whole transaction. The Honourable Gentleman after again adverting to the situation to which the Right Honourable Gentleman (Mr. Pitt) was reduced by his Noble Friend, could not help asking how it came to pass that, although notice had been given a fortnight ago of the motion brought forward this night by his Hon. Friend, yet the Right Honourable Gentleman never then alluded once to the letter he was afterwards to produce; nor, when he produced it, did he make any mention of the necessity of a further inquiry. How did this happen? If he was to believe the Reports of the day, the idea was suggested to him from a quarter which he did not choose to disoblige; though that quarter was not generally supposed to be in possession of power. From whatever intimation the measure arose, no good could be expected from a Committee of Inquiry. When it was known and seen how low was sunk the man, who holds so splendid a situation in the State, what would be thought of the Government? in what light could it be beheld, either abroad or at home? The bravest Generals, the most gallant Admirals, the ablest Statesmen, have abstained from the discharge of office while under an accusation, though conscious of their innocence, and certain to come forth more spotless than before. Could the Noble Lord continue the administration of his high department while his character was thus exposed? The House no doubt would feel the necessity of speedily deciding on that point, and of showing, that to innocence they would afford protection, in defiance of influence or power. With respect to the Noble Lord's offer to swear positively that he did not profit from the misappropriation of the Public Money, it was remarkable that this offer was confined to the period in which Sir Andrew Douglas, who was now dead, was Paymaster of the Navy, but did not at all extend to the Paymastership of Mr. Trotter. What was the conclusion then to be drawn from this? Why, that he was ready to make oath as to the Paymastership of Douglas, because he was dead; but did not think proper to swear as to Trotter, because he was alive. The Honourable Gentleman made an appeal to the pride and feelings of the House, and particularly to that of Mr. Pitt, advising him not to risk the little of reputation that remained to him upon this occasion—not to take this card for his last. He concluded with expressing a hope, that the facts exposed in the Tenth and Eleventh Reports would provoke an inquiry into, and a reform of, the several departments of the public expenditure. He trusted that there were men around him who would promote an investigation so desirable for the cause of justice and the interests of the Country.

Mr. *Wilberforce* expressed himself in decisive terms in favour of the Motion. Though it was not fully evident to the House that Lord Melville had any direct gain from the transactions which were alluded to, yet he could not say that his Lordship had not received accommodation from them. It was, however, very clearly in evidence, that Mr. Trotter had acted on a very large and extensive scale. If the House was once to suffer a Minister to say, that he had connived at the breach of a law, by his deputy, a confidential deputy, a confidential servant, constantly for a number of years, and that the superior was to be allowed to pass uncensured, because no personal corruption had been proved against himself; if that was once to be admitted as a principle by which the conduct of the House of Commons was to be directed, there was no security remaining for the faithful discharge of any Public Trust.—Such was the opinion which he entertained of the consequences of the loss of confidence and honour, that it was beyond the value of any thing else which could be set in balance against it. Much as the People of England disliked the conduct of Charles I, in levying Ship Money without the consent of Parliament, they thought it ten times worse that the Judges gave their opinion in favour of the measure. When the Body that they looked to for protection had declared against them, they saw no resource to which they could then lawfully turn, and the consequences were too well known for him to think it necessary to repeat them. The House was now applied to as the Constitutional Guardians of the People's Rights, and he should discharge his duty to the People to the best of his judgment as an upright Member of that House, and as a conscientious Man, in giving his vote this night. He thought that the case was broad, plain, and palpable before them, and gave the Motion his most sincere support.

Sir *C. Price* observed, that as a Magistrate and a Man, he felt himself most fully justified in declaring, that if Lord Melville had been entirely free from any criminality, he would have answered more fully and unequivocally than he had done. He therefore supported the original Motion.

Lord *Archibald Hamilton* rose, he said, at that late hour, only to remark, that no one Scots Member had spoken against the nefarious proceedings of the two Scotsmen, whose conduct had been the subject of the Debate. He rose, therefore, to declare, that he should vote for the original Motion.

The House then divided on the Original Motion.

Ayes 216—Noes 216.

The numbers being thus even, the Honourable Speaker gave the casting vote. AYE, ONE; which made 217 for the original Question.

The other Motions were then put *seriatim*, and carried in the affirmative, without interruption, till they came to the 11th, containing the censure on Lord Melville.

Mr. *Pitt* here moved an amendment to leave out the last words, " gross violation of the Law, and a high breach of duty ;" and to insert the words, " contrary to the intention of the Law."

On this a Debate took place.

Mr. *Grey* said, that it would be a scandalous dereliction of their own duty, to say, that the connivance of Lord Melville in the conduct of Mr. Trotter was not a gross violation of Law, and a high breach of duty.

Mr. *Pitt* said, he would withdraw that amendment, and only move to insert after the words " for purposes of private interest or emolument," the words " to Mr. Trotter," because he said there was no proof or confession that he connived at the drawing out of the Money for his own interest or emolument. Nay, he had in his Letter denied it.

Sir *William Pulteney* said, he thought this would be reasonable, provided the words " as acknowledged by Lord Melville," were inserted.

Mr. *Whitbread* said, he had no particular objection to this amendment. The words in his Motion had been left general, because it was confessed that the Sums were drawn out for private interest and emolument, but not specified directly whether for Lord Melville as well as Mr. Trotter.

In this way the Motion was read by the Chair. It then stood thus :—
" That the Right Honourable Lord Viscount Melville having been privy to and connived at the withdrawing from the Bank of England (as acknowledged by Lord Melville) for purposes of private interest or emolument, to Mr. Trotter, Sums issued, &c."

Mr. *Windham* contended, that after the clear elucidation of the case, the Treasurer of the Navy could answer whether or not he had derived advantage from the Public Money ; and till then the words in the Resolutions ought to be left ambiguous.

Mr. *Fox* said, that the attempt to screen Lord Melville from the result of the previous Resolutions by so trifling an amendment, would do the Noble Lord no good, but would put that House in a very awkward point of view.

Mr. *Wilberforce* said, that not to brand the transaction by the epithets of gross violation of the Law, and a high breach of Duty, after the confession of Lord Melville, would be ignominious to the House.

Mr. *Sheridan* said, that the amendment made the Motion almost nonsense. To say, in the first instance, that Lord Melville connived for sixteen years, and then to fritter away the conclusion, was a most extraordinary way of acquitting his Colleague.

Mr. *Bastard* said it was impossible for any Gentleman to support such an amendment.

Mr. *T. Grenville* spoke to the same effect.

Mr. *Pitt* persisting in his declaration that he would take the sense of the House, the Gallery was cleared ; but on the question being put on the Motion as it originally stood, the Speaker declared that the Ayes had it, and Mr. Pitt did not divide.

The two other Motions were then put and carried.

Mr. *Whitbread* said, he had of course a Motion necessarily to make in consequence of the Resolutions of the House that day, but it was then too late.

Mr. *Pitt* moved, that the House should adjourn to Wednesday.

Mr. *Fox* submitted to the good sense of the House, whether in so critical a moment they should adjourn over a single day. They would recollect, that the Country was now in the hands of a disgraced Ministry.

Mr. *Pitt* pleaded for an adjournment, and hinted, that it might be necessary in the present circumstances.

The House accordingly adjourned to Wednesday.

APRIL 10.

Sir *William Scott* moved the order of the day for the second reading of the Prize Courts Bill.

Sir *Charles Pole* expressed a wish that this measure should not be hurried through the House, but that the Hon. Member would consent to have it printed, and that sufficient time should be allowed to the Parties concerned, to consider the several clauses which it contained.

Sir *W. Scott* proposed to have the Bill read a second time this day, and committed *pro forma* to-morrow, after which he should move to have it printed, and after the holidays recommitted, when as much time as the Hon. Gentleman should deem necessary should be allowed.

The Bill was read a second time and ordered to be committed to-morrow.

Mr. *Giles* desired to be informed, whether it was the intention of his Majesty's Ministers to bring forward a Bill for continuing for a further period the Commission of Naval Inquiry; as if not, he should feel it his duty to submit a Motion to the House on that subject, at an early day after the holidays.

LORD MELVILLE.

The *Chancellor of the Exchequer*, the moment he entered the House, rose to state, that in consequence of the decision of the House on a former evening, Lord Melville had tendered his resignation of the Office of First Lord of the Admiralty, which resignation his Majesty had been graciously pleased to accept.

Mr. *Whitbread* moved, that the resolution which the House had come to respecting Lord Melville, on Monday night, be read, which being read,

The Hon. Member rose, and spoke to the following effect:—I rise, Sir, in pursuance of the notice I gave on a former evening, to submit a proposition which is the natural consequence of the resolutions that have just been read. This proposition is of such a nature as I cannot be induced to abandon by the notification that the Right Hon. Gentleman has made to the House; for the event to which that notification refers, by no means answers the object of my Motion. I feel that much more is due to the vote of this House, and to the feelings of the Public. The demand of Public Justice is not yet satisfied. If the Issue of the debate of Monday evening were merely of a personal or party nature, if our object only was to injure the feelings of Lord Melville, we might be satisfied with his removal from the responsibility, dignity, and emolument, attached to the high Office that has been mentioned. As far as the principle of Individual humiliation can extend, the triumph is complete indeed. But I trust it cannot be imagined that any Gentlemen who act with me on this important occasion, are actuated by any private or party feelings. No; the Cause in which we are engaged is of the highest nature. It is the Cause of Public Justice. It is that which we shall not abandon, but still continue to urge from the fairest motives, until complete satisfaction shall be obtained. I am fully assured of the pure and exalted views of those by whom I have the honour to be supported; and for myself I can say, that if I know my own heart and feelings, I am completely free from the slightest influence of a vindictive spirit.—Impelled by a sense of duty to my Country to bring forward this Accusation, my opinion of the grounds upon which it rested has been justified by your concurrence. I have appealed to you, and you have given me your verdict—*that Lord Melville has been guilty of grossly improper conduct, and that he, of course, deserves punishment.* Thus stigmatized by the vote of this House, and aware that he must, in consequence, be dismissed, Lord Melville has done nothing more than that which would naturally suggest itself to any man's feelings—he had tendered his resignation. But although that resignation has been accepted—although Lord Melville has been removed from a high Office, what security have we, what security has the Country, that he may not be restored to-morrow to the same Office; or placed in some other high and confidential situation? Is it fit that any ground for even the apprehension of such a circumstance should exist? Is it fit that a possibility of its occurring should not be guarded against? It is necessary to the dignity of the Country—to the satisfaction of the people—to the consistency of this House, that the return of

Lord Melville to power should be rendered impossible. *(A cry of Hear! Hear!)* In reflecting upon the event of a former night's debate, I cannot but feel that it was a proud day for this Country, and I am persuaded that such is the general feeling. Can any one who looks abroad for a moment doubt the approving testimony which the people so gladly bear? The assembly of Members was, on that occasion, unusually numerous. The point came to the balance, and it rested with the Chair, that seat of impartiality, to determine upon what side it should turn.—It remained for you, Sir, without wounding any party spirit, to decide which Party was right, and your decision was founded in Justice. That decision, Sir, was consistent with the dignity of your station and character, and has secured you the gratitude of your Country. No where has it produced dissatisfaction, but in the breast of the criminal. All that are honest, independent, and just, rejoice and thank us. Such, indeed, is the exultation abroad, such is the pleasure that is visible in the looks of the people, that one might say that our history may be read in a nation's eyes. After having done so much, after having obtained so much gratitude for our conduct, shall we not take another step to complete our work? Shall we not render it impossible that Lord Melville shall ever again pollute the Councils or Presence of his Majesty? *(A cry of Hear! Hear!)* At the same time that I express my feelings thus warmly, with respect to the Delinquent who is the object of my Motion, let it be understood, that it is my particular wish to speak with the utmost deference to this Assembly, which has conducted itself with so much honour. Let me assure you, that if I did not think the Motion which I am about to submit essentially necessary, with respect to the Individual whom you have so much stigmatized by your Vote, I should not press it upon your attention. From all that I have collected among my own friends, who belong to the Party with which I have the honour to act, (and to act with such a Party I shall certainly always feel my Pride and Honour,) as well as what I can understand from the Gentlemen who generally oppose, but who happened on this occasion to concur with that Party; it appears to be the generally prevailing Sentiment, that farther and more effectual proceedings should be taken against Lord *Melville*. Other proceedings will undoubtedly be had; but upon this occasion it is my intention to submit a Motion, the object of which will be to deprive that Noble Lord of every civil office he holds, during the pleasure of the Crown, and to dismiss him from his Majesty's Councils and Presence for ever. I ask of the Right Hon. Gentleman opposite (Mr. Pitt), Whether he is prepared to make a pledge to that effect? I also ask, Whether the Vote of this House has been treated with a due deference in another quarter? Whether *Trotter* has been dismissed? (Mr. Canning answered, *Yes.*) Has *Wilson* also been dismissed? (Mr. Canning answered, *No.*) Then I say that all this was necessary, in respect to the decision of this House. There may, however, be particular reasons why *Wilson* should not be dismissed for a few days. Some arrangements may be previously necessary. But is it not the intention to dismiss him? (Mr. Whitbread paused for an answer; but none was given, and he resumed.) Whether or not it be the intention of the Right Honourable Gentleman to dismiss *Wilson*, sure I am that he ought to be dismissed, and that, from his conduct before the Commissioners, he is unfit to hold any Public Office. He was evidently the accomplice of Lord *Melville* and *Trotter*; and as those Delinquents have been dismissed, *Wilson* ought certainly to meet the same fate. With respect to the course of proceeding I mean hereafter to follow against Lord *Melville* and *Trotter*, I shall avail myself of this opportunity to give notice, that it is my intention, immediately after the Holidays, to move, that the Attorney General shall be directed to take measures to compel those Delinquents to give an account of the Monies they have had, and to refund the Profits obtained through the misappropriation of the Public Money. As to the way in which this should be done, that must be left to the judgment of the Right Honourable Gentleman himself. There are other proceedings also which it will be necessary to take. There are many dark and mysterious points connected with the Tenth Report, and other subjects which must be brought to light. It is my purpose to move an Inquiry into those several topics. It is stated in the Tenth Report that Sums of Money had been transferred from the Treasury of the Navy to other Services In the illegality of such conduct the Right Hon. Gentleman over against me (Mr. Pitt) has confessed that he was a Party to a certain extent. The purpose for which transfers were made might be meritorious; but still it must be recollected, that the transfer was a violation of the Law. This violation is admitted; and whether the purpose to which the money was applied, was, or was not meritorious, yet remains to be seen. To inquire into this, and various other transactions, I shall, after the Holidays, move for the appointment of a Select Committee. Give me leave here to observe, that nothing can be of more importance than that the Public Money should not be disposed of by any other authority than the Vote of Parliament; and here is a direct, avowed assumption of that authority. Whatever the pretence, or however meritorious the object, I feel that this withdrawing of Money from one Service to supply the purposes of another at the mere will of a Minister, calls for the most serious examination. It is rather remarkable, that this practice of misappropriating the Money belonging to the Treasury of the Navy, appears to have taken place only while Lord Melville was in office. No transfer, or even negotiation for such a transfer, seems to have occurred during the time of any of those who preceded or succeeded the Noble Lord in that Office. The reason of this singular difference, and whether any, and what justification can be produced for that part of the Noble Lord's conduct, may be ascertained in the Committee, as I must suppose that papers are in existence to account for such transactions—that some records of the cause of such things is preserved—that all the documents respecting these particulars also are not burned. *(A cry of Hear! Hear!)* Several other parts of the Tenth Report, upon which I shall not now dwell, and many subjects besides, which are not included in that Report, but which call for examination, may be referred to the consideration of the Committee. I touched slightly the other night on the conduct of the Bank of England in the course of this transaction. It appears that the Cashier had not sufficient Vouchers, according to the Act, for the Money advanced to Mr. Trotter. I am, however, given to understand, that there was a slip or mistake in the evidence of the Cashier before the Commissioners, but that the conduct of the Bank was correct. If this be the case, the imputation should not be suffered to remain; a farther examination should be instituted, and may arise before the Committee. Before that Committee also the Right Honourable Gentleman opposite (Mr. Pitt) may have his conduct inquired into. That Right Honourable Gentleman, according to what I have heard in the course of conversation, and indeed it is the general rumour, was for years apprised of the irregular manner in which the Public Money was drawn from the Bank by *Trotter*, and that he never attempted to put a stop to that practice. This is a serious Charge against the Right Hon. Gentleman, and may be referred to the consideration of the Committee, before whom he will have an opportunity for explanation. Unless the Right Hon. Gentleman shall exculpate himself from the guilt of such connivance, serious proceedings must be taken against him also. What! that the Finance Minister of the Country should be acquainted with such proceedings, as I have every reason to believe that he was, and not take measures to prevent their continuance? Is not this matter deserving of inquiry? and, if the rumour be well founded, of serious animadversion? The Case of *Jellicoe* also I would propose to refer to the Committee. That certainly forms a serious Charge, not merely against Lord *Melville*, but against other persons. If I am rightly informed, the Commissioners of the Treasury were implicated in the Guilt of this Case, and are responsible for the loss arising from the debt which Jellicoe's property owed to the public. We have been speaking so much in the course of this discussion of Millions, that perhaps the 24,000l. due from the property of Jellicoe may not appear of much consequence. Indeed, such talk about Millions has had the effect of making even the Right Honourable Gentleman on the other side (Mr. Pitt) forget his arithmetic, and confound 134 Millions with 136 Millions. But the Case of Jellicoe appears to me, notwithstanding the comparatively smaller amount of the Sum, to be peculiarly entitled to attention. It affords an opportunity of estimating the conduct of the Commissioners of the Treasury, who will be found, I am justified in believing, to have granted Lord Melville a release from this debt most improperly, and to have acted on very false grounds. This may be brought to light before the Committee. Perhaps, also, evidence may be found by this Committee, to ascertain that important question, Whether Lord Melville had any participation, and to what amount, of the profits resulting from the use which Trotter made of the Public Money? This is a most material point to establish; and if it be possible to get at the facts of this part of the subject, I have no doubt that the Committee will be able to accomplish it. The principal cause of the suspicion impressed upon my mind that Lord Melville did participate with Trotter in his illicit gains, arises, as I before mentioned, from the fond attachment with which the Noble Lord so long, and under the various changes of circumstances, clung to the Office of Treasurer of the Navy; and it is remarkable, that not one of his friends has attempted to account for this attachment, or to remove the impression it is naturally calculated to produce. This omission must serve to strengthen the impression in the mind of any man, that the motive of such attachment was suspicious. Adam Smith observes, that two and two in the Customs don't always make four. Lord Melville, although so frequently heard in this House to complain of the great fatigue he had to encounter in the discharge of his official duty, and the quantity of business he had to perform; yet thought proper to add to the Presidentship of the Board of Controul, and Treasurership of the Navy, &c. that of Minister of War. I am not now about to argue, that the Office of Treasurer of the Navy is unnecessary, although it appears, that in that Office Lord Melville had no business to perform. Then he found it convenient to accept the place of Secretary of State; the Salary of which he declined, retaining the Salary of the Treasurer of the Navy, although the one was as good as the other; the Salary of each being 4000l. a year. It is curious to think what could have been the reason of this preference. These are the circumstances which have urged me to suspect Lord *Melville* of a participation in the fraudulent profits of *Trotter*. But whether he has been guilty of this participation or not, he stands convicted of the most odious thing imputed to him; that of sanctioning the misapplication of the Public Money. This is the principal Article of Charge against him, and this Charge he has acknowledged. After this acknowledgment from his own mouth, and the Vote of this House upon it, it would be inconsistent with the dignity of the Country to allow such a man as Lord *Melville* to remain in any Office under the Crown, from which he can be removed. The removal of Lord *Melville* from an Office of such high rank and honour as the Presidency of the Admiralty, is no doubt a great humiliation; but yet that is not sufficient to satisfy the ends of Public Justice, one hair's breadth beyond which I do not wish to proceed. When these ends are attained, the duty I have undertaken will have been discharged. But, until then, I should not wish it to go forth, that this House should even manifest a disposition to stop short. If punishment only were our object, it might perhaps be said, that Lord Melville has had enough of that in his degradation, and what his feelings must in consequence suffer. But it will be recollected, that punishment is not our only object. Example is the great end we should have in view, and that end we shall not have reached until the criminal shall have suffered all the consequences that should justly attach to his Crime If Lord *Melville* should escape those consequences, we shall not have done our duty. Independent of the Offices and Emoluments held by Lord *Melville*, I understand that since his last accession to Administration, even within the last year, he has had 1500l. a year conferred on him for life, in addition to the Revenue of a Patent Office he holds in Scotland. This Noble Lord had, it seems, retired from public affairs, as it was said, for life. But the circumstances, not of the Country, but of the peculiar wish and necessity of the Right Honourable Gentleman on the other side (Mr. Pitt), drew the Noble Lord from his retirement, and he became a Member of the Administration formed by the Right Honourable Gentleman. The Noble Lord was appointed to an Office, the first in rank, power, and patronage, in the Country, with the exception of that only which is held by the Right Honourable Gentleman (Mr. Pitt). But yet that was not sufficient to content Lord *Melville*. No, he must be induced to accept it by the grant I have already alluded to of 1500l. a year for life. Previous to this addition, a grant was made to Lady Melville out of the Public Money. The merits of Lady Melville are quite out of the question. All this liberality must be considered as a compliment to the services and character of Lord Melville. But there is something very mysterious about this grant. It was made in a very clandestine manner. In point of fact, under such circumstances, that there is good reason to believe those who fixed their names to the grant were not aware of the nature of it. It was indeed one of those grants that, I fancy, it never was expected that any investigation would take place respecting, or perhaps that it would ever be noticed. I have reason to entertain strong doubts that the grant of 1500l. a year, as an addition to Lord Melville's salary as Lord Privy Seal of Scotland, is not valid. If revocable, it certainly ought to be revoked under the Motion I mean to submit. This Motion, which, under all the circumstances of the case, I have thought it my duty to bring forward, will, I trust, meet the approbation of the House. Gentlemen who honoured me with their support to the resolutions on the table, cannot consistently refuse to concur in this proposition, which is the natural result of those resolutions. Even many of the Gentlemen who differed with me on a former evening, from a wish for a further inquiry, will, I hope, seeing that such decisive resolutions have been adopted, support the consistency of the House, by voting with me on this occasion, should the Gentlemen on the other side press this question to a division. The Honourable Member, after repeating the opinion, that he had good grounds for believing that a decisive majority concurred with him as to the necessity of this measure, concluded with moving "That an humble Address should be presented to his Majesty, praying that he would be graciously pleased to dismiss Lord Melville from all Offices held by him during pleasure, and also from his Councils and Presence for ever."

Mr. *Canning* rose to oppose the arguments of Mr. Whitbread. However desirous the Hon. Gentleman might have been of disclaiming any other motives for the course he pursued, than what proceeded from a wish to establish an example, he could not help hinking, and he was sure many more were of the same opinion, from the topics which the Hon. Gentleman had introduced, and the time he had adopted, that he had been actuated by something more than by the motives he had alledged. The Hon. Gentleman had given a specimen of the spirit by which he was actuated when he set out, with asserting that what Lord Melville had done in obedience to the resolutions and wish of the House, which he was himself by no means disposed to find fault with, now that it had become the act of the House, was imputable to him as an aggravation of his guilt. What would have been the feelings and the animadversions of the Honourable Gentleman, what his expressions of indignation and resentment, if the House had met this day, Lord Melville, instead of bowing to its decision, still continuing to hold the Office of First Lord of the Admiralty? (*A cry of Hear! Hear! from the Opposition Benches.*) Would he not have made that the ground of further and increased invective? (*Still a loud cry of Hear!*) He was sure the Hon. Gentleman opposite (Mr. George Ponsonby), who had urged his suffering Mr. Trotter to continue in Office, an accusation of his conduct, would, in the present instance, if he possessed any of the character or spirit of a British Lawyer, confess that his accusation was unfair, unfounded, tyrannical, and despotic. (*A loud cry of Hear! Hear!*) With regard to Mr. Wilson, he still continued in the same Office which he before held. The Honourable Gentleman had asked, Whether he too had been dismissed? The Right Hon. Member, as far as he could discover, had no reason to think that Mr. Wilson had been in any way implicated. Mr. Wilson had been one of those who had been reported by the Commissioners as having given reluctant testimony. He was convinced that a more conscientious Officer did not exist. If the decision of the House should be declared against continuing Mr. Wilson in Office, he should deem it his duty to obey. The Honourable Gentleman had, in adverting to the Resolutions adopted by the House on the former night, dwelt with exultation on the virtue that had been displayed. The Honourable Gentleman might have adverted to many instances of equal virtue, not only in the best periods of the most distinguished times of our history, but he might also have found a similar instance of patriotic conduct in 1795, when two Noble Lords (Lords Grey and St. Vincent) were on their trial before the House under similar circumstances. These Noble Lords had been then defended by their political enemies; and the Noble Lord, the object of the Motion of this night, had fought in that House many obstinate battles in their defence. This Noble Lord, who had acted so generously on that occasion, so far from experiencing equal generosity, was now persecuted and hunted down; and by whom? by the friends of Lord Grey and Earl St. Vincent. He congratulated the Gentlemen on their sense, true spirit, and virtue, and prayed God Almighty to forbid that he should ever imitate their example.

Mr. *Grey* and Mr. *C. Ponsonby* rose at the same time.—Mr. Ponsonby having with some difficulty given way,

Mr. *Grey* said it was impossible for him on the sort of appeal made by the Hon. Gentleman who spoke last, an appeal which could have no advantageous effect whatsoever for persons whose characters were under consideration, not to offer himself for a few moments to the House. The Honourable Gentleman congratulated him, and those about him, on what he was pleased to term more than Spartan virtue, of being insensible to the support which those who were most dear to them had formerly received from the person now under accusation; and the Hon. Gentleman at the same time represented that this person had, on that occasion, fought the most difficult battle ever remembered in that House. He begged the Hon. Gentleman and the House to recollect the circumstances of that transaction, and on the strength of that recollection he disclaimed and denied the difficulty so broadly stated. The noble persons alluded to had, in that instance, received support from those who had recommended them to the Crown, and among the few solid glories of the last War, he hoped to be allowed to rank the services they had performed. He hoped to be allowed also to claim credit for their conduct in not flying from inquiry, in not seeking shelter in delay and subterfuge, but boldly and candidly appealing to the justice of the House, and desiring the strictest investigation. Under these circumstances, he disclaimed the idea that any benefit had been conferred on them. The Defence afforded on that occasion, was no more than was due in justice to the Country, and what those who had recommended the Officers whose conduct was under discussion owed to themselves. This was the sentiment of the Honourable Gentleman who moved the amendment at the time, being of opinion, that the original resolutions did not express fairly the sense that ought to be entertained of the conduct of these Noblemen. These noble persons had been recommended to the Crown to conduct an arduous enterprize, and they had succeeded; they afterwards encountered difficulties; and the House was of opinion, on full consideration of the case, that no blame was to be imputed to them. No benefit was therefore conferred; and if any person conceived it was a favour, that person must have a different view of the case from what he had. With respect to the merit assumed for recommending without partiality persons of all Parties for the public service of the Army and Navy, he begged the House to recollect, that if, instead of employing those meritorious Officers who were best qualified to serve the Country, private pique and narrow considerations were to prevail, to the exclusion of those meritorious Officers, and to the employment of others less capable of promoting the national glory, the person who would act on such a system would be guilty of a gross dereliction of public duty. The persons best qualified to attain the objects the Country looked for, were in these instances above all others to be called upon by those at the head of affairs, without any consideration of political animosity. As to the difficulty of the battle fought in the House for the noble persons whose conduct was then under discussion; the Honourable Gentleman was then a Member of the House, though he did not take a part in the debate, he might therefore have recollected that the Minority, on that occasion, amounted only to sixteen, the odd sixteen of the other night. Where then was the difficulty that the Hon. Gent. had represented, and the extraordinary merit and exertion of the person whose conduct was now under consideration, to obtain the decision then made. It was not agreeable to him to enter into these particulars, but he could not sit silent under the unprovoked and ill-judged allusion of the Hon. Gentleman—ill-judged, for the Character and the Cause which the Hon. Gent. was supporting. For himself, however warmly he felt at times, no one was generally less liable to excess of warmth—it was not in his nature; the Hon. Gentleman did not know him; but those who did know him, knew that he was incapable of holding permanent resentment against any man; it was impossible he could have any against the Noble Lord whose conduct was now the subject of debate. He would bear testimony for his Hon. Friend who had made the Motion, that he was as little likely to be actuated by such feelings, and the House would go with him in the understanding, that the only motive was a sense of duty, which they had sanctioned.—He was of opinion, that if any blame lay, it was for not being sufficiently severe. The Honourable Gentleman said, this attack was pursued with bitterness. That it was maintained with strength he was ready to allow; but that there was no rancour in pressing the House to a declaration of its just sense on delinquency so clearly established, was what he maintained, and he was sure the House would go with him. If it were the general sentiment of the House that the present Motion should not be now pressed, he should not be for, pressing it; but till some better reason could be offered on the other side than those urged by the Hon. Gentleman, he thought the House having come to the resolution that the Noble Lord was guilty of a gross violation of the Law, and culpable neglect of his duty, the House would not sustain its character if such a resolution was suffered to remain on the Journals without being followed up. Nothing like argument had been blended with the appeal made to the passions of the House, from the other side. His Hon. Friend had been misrepresented when he was stated to have said, that what the Hon. Gentleman had called an act of humiliation and deference to the sense of the House, was an aggravation of his guilt. What his Majesty's Minister, the friend of the Noble Lord, had stated, that the Noble Lord had tendered his resignation, and that it had been accepted, would, in other circumstances, be sufficient. As to the question put by the Honourable Gentleman, of an adjournment for the day in the express expectation that his Majesty's Ministers would do their duty by dismissing Lord Melville, not with the intention that it should be left a matter of choice to Lord Melville, as it was the sense of the House that the Noble Lord should be removed from his Majesty's Councils for ever.—With a resolution of this kind on the Journals of that House, he conceived it impossible Lord Melville could hold any situation of trust or confidence.—(Conceiving some surprise to be expressed by Mr. Pitt at this idea.) If the Right Honourable Gentleman meant to intimate that there was any danger of such an event, it was particularly fit to guard against it: but he still continued to say, that after such a resolution, there was no danger of the Noble Lord's being appointed to any Office of trust. Still, however, the Noble Lord was a Member of his Majesty's Privy Council, and he ought to be so no longer. In Scotland the Offices which the Noble Lord held were chiefly for life; but he held others during pleasure, and he ought to be removed from them, if the Justice of the House, or of the Country, was to be satisfied. If Lord Melville had had an increase of his salary as Keeper of the Privy Seal of Scotland, on his coming into the Office of First Lord of the Admiralty, he hoped, if it was intended on his retiring from the Admiralty, that he should retain that and all his other honours and emoluments, the good sense of the House would put a negative on that intention. Till, therefore, some better arguments were adduced than the appeal to the feelings and delicacy of the House, he should persevere in supporting the Motion. He adverted to the Charge so unwarrantably made on his Honourable and Learned Friend behind him (Mr. Ponsonby), who was accused of conduct inconsistent with British Law and British Justice, with tyrannical and despotic principles in pressing the punishment of this delinquency. He had been called up by the personal allusion that had been made by the Hon. Gentleman; but being up, he thought it right to state thus far his reasons for supporting the Motion; and he saw nothing in all the Hon. Gentleman had uttered with so much rant and fury, to induce him to alter his opinion. The Motion was a necessary consequence of the resolution of the former night, and ought to be supported by every friend to the honour of the House, to the Justice of the Country, and the Character of Administration.

Mr. *Ponsonby* was sure, that after this very marked personal allusion which the Hon. Gentleman who spoke on the other side had made in so very broad a manner to him, there was not a Member in the House who would not excuse him for so immediately pressing himself upon its attention. He owed this to that value he had always had for the good opinion of the House since he had the honour to be a Member of it; but that good opinion was doubly due to him since the

Vote of the last night of meeting. The good opinion of an Assembly so raised, so exalted, so justly established in the admiration and gratitude of the Country, and so honourably entitled to the applause and approbation of the World, could not but be matter of increasing value to every man who could claim the happiness to enjoy any portion of it. The Honourable Gentleman said, if he had imbibed the principles of British Law, he would not have advanced the tyrannical, despotic, and arbitrary doctrines he had maintained. He was extremely unfortunate if he had advanced such doctrines. But he was not aware that he had. It was in his recollection that he had been followed in that debate by an Honourable and Learned Gentleman, not less high in authority for legal knowledge, than he was in legal station, (the Master of the Rolls). That Honourable and Learned Gentleman had done him the honour to notice some part of what had fallen from him; and if he had been guilty of uttering those arbitrary, tyrannical, and despotic sentiments, which the Honourable Gentleman charged on him, he was sure they would not have escaped his animadversion. When the Honourable Gentleman supposed him deficient in the principles of British Law, he conveyed an idea of distinction of countries. He was not ashamed of his country! and he trusted his country would never have occasion to be ashamed of him. But if the Honourable Gentleman placed a value on British blood and British connexion, he could boast, that as good British blood flowed in his veins, and his British connexions were as honourable as those of the Hon. Gentleman; and though he could not boast of those talents, which at so early a period of life raised the Honourable Gentleman to that high station, which others could attain only at a late period of life, by constant and toilsome exertion; though he who had but slowly and gradually, and at a mature age, attained the moderate elevation on which he stood, could not boast of such talents or such fortune, it was some consolation to him, that he had never before been charged with being the advocate of arbitrary power. He wished the Hon. Gentleman, therefore, in future, if he should do him the honour to notice what should fall from him, to confine himself to what he had said. Being forced up by the personal allusion made to him, he should take the opportunity to say a few words to the question before the House. The Right Honourable Gentleman opposite had notified that Lord Melville's resignation had been tendered and accepted, but the Right Hon. Gentleman had not at the same time notified that this was to be the conclusion of Lord Melville's political life. The resignation was but an act of obedience due to the sense of the House; but if it was to be understood that this obedience was to conclude the Noble Lord's political career, he had so little personal hostility to him, so little disposition to press on his feelings, or to aggravate his fall, that he would be disposed to acquiesce. But it remained now matter of consideration, Whether, having ceased to be First Lord of the Admiralty, he should still be suffered to hold his other Offices of trust and emolument? He was a Member of the Privy Council; and when persons had been struck off the list of that Council for what they conceived their duty dictated, and without any vote or resolution of the House of Commons, was it not natural that the House having passed such a resolution, should expect such a respect for it? He would put a case: Supposing the personal friends of Lord Melville, in credit and power in his Majesty's Councils, and suppose their creatures continually representing Lord Melville as an injured individual, hunted down by unjust persecution; if the Public, during a Vacation, should be continually impressed with the innocence of this injured Minister, by the venal advocates that could be so easily mustered in his cause, he saw no reasons why he may not before the next Session be restored to his former situation in the Cabinet. If the Right Hon. Gentleman gave reason to understand that this was to be the end and issue of the Noble Lord's public life, he was not averse to the lenity of stopping the censure; but now there was nothing to prevent his return if his Majesty's Ministers thought proper to advise his Majesty to employ him. There was no security at present against the re-employment of Lord Melville or any other person in like circumstances. As to the other parts of the business, he could not consent to let them merge into oblivion. When the Public Money got into the hands of agents, or any other hands into which it ought not to have got, it was the duty of Parliament to have it accounted for and restored to the Public. He would also adhere inflexibly to the other points, that the person at the head of the Treasury, as presiding over the whole administration of the Public Money, had been guilty of culpable negligence in overlooking their transactions. He was not disposed to impute any improper motives to the Right Honourable Gentleman, or to make the charge lightly; but it appeared in the Report that his superintendance was lax, and as a Representative of the People it was his duty to call him to account; for though he was not a British Lawyer, or a British Representative, nor of British birth, he would here claim it as a privilege due to that portion of British blood that belonged to him, to consider himself the Representative of the People at large, and to assume a right to investigate the Administration of the Empire in all its parts.

Mr. S. *Thornton* rose, in consequence of the allusions made this night and on a preceding one to the evidence of an experienced and meritorious Officer of the Bank before the Commissioners of Naval Inquiry. That Officer (Mr. Newland) had there intimated that the drafts passed by the Treasurer of the Navy had not always expressed the service on which they were drawn, conformably to the provisions of the Act of Parliament. If this were the case, the Bank was certainly to blame, as he held in his hand a copy of the power under which the Paymaster had passed his drafts from the year 1786 until the resignation of Lord Melville. This power stated in express words, " that he should be particularly careful to specify in each and every draft the service for which the money was drawn." The fact was, that Mr. Newland, though at the head of the Cashier's department of the Bank, was not the Officer under whose inspection the detail of this branch of business was carried on, and therefore had only delivered a matter of opinion. The Officer who paid the drafts from the Navy had assured the Honourable Member, that after every research in his power, and to the best of his recollection, no draft had ever been paid without specifying the service.— Since August 1803, the mode of conducting the business had been varied, and sums were written off at once by the Bank from the Treasurer's account to that of the Sub-paymasters of the Navy, which accounts were kept also with that Corporation. He had long considered Lord Melville an active, zealous, and meritorious servant of the public, and the movers must excuse him if he could not at once go the length of thinking with them, that he was deserving of such severe degradation and punishment as the motion before the House went to inflict.

Mr. *Barham* entered his protest against the introduction into the debate of the personal allusion to the case of two Noble Characters, relative to whom he had formerly felt himself called upon to take an active part. Nothing could be more injudicious than this reference. He contended no obligation had been imposed on them, no benefit conferred by Ministers joining in their defence.

Mr. *Bankes*, though he was certain he was in no way entitled to offer his advice to the Hon. Gentleman from whom the Motion came, with whom he had neither personal acquaintance, nor any political connexion, would yet take the liberty of recommending to that Hon. Gentleman not to persevere in this Motion. If it should be persevered in at present, the same sense of duty which induced him to vote with the Hon. Gentleman the last night would oblige him to vote against him on this. He understood the sense of the adjournment on the former night to be, to allow an opportunity for his Majesty, from his own royal motive to remove Lord Melville; or for Lord Melville, feeling that he could be no longer an useful servant to his Majesty under the stigma that had been cast upon him, to tender his resignation. Gentlemen seemed disposed to cavil with that resignation, but he maintained that such an act preceding any step taken by his Majesty in consequence of the resolution of the House, could not be imputed to any other motive than the Noble Lord's deference to the sense of the House, and his determination to conform to it as quickly as possible. It was to be considered also, that the resolutions that had been agreed to were but part of Lord Melville's case, and that they remained to be followed up with other proceedings. Could there be a better reason than this for abstaining for the present from the resolution now proposed? It was impossible to foresee what may come out in the inquiry which was agreed to on all sides. Could any one undertake to say that there may not be matter sufficient to call for an impeachment.—Was it then right to proceed further, when the grounds of the ultimate determination and proceedings which the House should adopt were so imperfectly made out? The precedents on the Journals were, so far as he could make out, against voting an Address, such as that proposed. He instanced the cases of Sir R. Walpole, Lord Ranelagh, and Lord Halifax. There was no instance of an Address to remove a person not in Office. Such an Address, and indeed an Address under such circumstances, would be absurd on the face of it. He did not think there could be any intention or any possibility of reinstating the Noble Lord in Office in the interval between the present time and the period when this subject would be again under the cognizance of the House. It was possible too, that circumstances of extenuation may come out in the further investigation, which would induce the House to content itself altogether with what it had done. He believed such circumstances may exist, and he would see them with more pleasure than the circumstances of delinquency and malversation, which induced him to vote against the Noble Lord the last night. There being no precedent, no necessity, and no probability of his returning to power, he would vote against the Motion.

The *Chancellor of the Exchequer* rather hoped and expected that the express understanding which had been given, and which he had no difficulty to confirm, would have prevented further argument, and put a stop to any ulterior resolution. The House, he was sure, would be disposed to spare those who were nearly connected with the Noble Lord, as well as those who could not help feeling the tenderest friendship for him ; a feeling which he was sure the House would not be disposed to censure. It was impossible while the vote of the former night was entered on the Journals, that the House could apprehend any danger of seeing the Noble Lord again in Office, unless the vote itself were at an end. As to the extension of the inquiry, if any thing should come out in consequence of that to change the opinion of the House, he was sure Gentlemen would allow that the Resolution should be changed with the opinion. But in no other case than the House being convinced that the Resolution was founded in error, and rescinding it on that ground, could the Crown be advised by its Ministers to re-employ the Noble Lord. He had been misconceived by the Hon. Gentleman opposite (Mr. Grey) in the expression of surprise he had uttered : it was surprise, not that the Hon. Gentleman should imagine there was no danger of his return, but that he should not, in the confidence that it could not take place with the Resolution on the Journals, think it unnecessary to press this Motion, which went only to attain the same end, though by a different mode. This understanding, while it was conformable to the liberality of the House, would not take from its firmness the means of enforcing its Resolution.

Mr. *Fox* rose to reply ; and after some introductory observations, proceeded in substance as follows :—The Right Hon. Gentleman who spoke second in the debate, has delivered himself in a manner so extraordinary and injudicious, that it is really hardly worth while to take notice of his observations. The Resolutions of the House on Monday night seem so completely to have irritated the Right Hon. Gentleman, and so fully to have overpowered his mind, that he has this evening taken an opportunity of throwing forth his indignation without providing himself with any grounds on which to exercise it. He has chosen to attack, without the slightest appearance of truth, my Learned and Honourable Friend (Mr. G. Ponsonby) as the author of arbitrary and despotic doctrines ; and on this I shall not long detain the House, after what my Learned and Honourable Friend has said in so satisfactory a manner. The Right Hon. Gentleman accuses my Honourable and Learned Friend of arbitrary doctrines, because he says that a person proved by evidence to have been guilty of a most corrupt use of the Public Money, should at least be suspended from his Office till the Charges against him be fully investigated. Now all that I have to say on this is simply, that if such doctrine be arbitrary, the most eminent lawyers in the kingdom have never been backward to promulgate it. It is a doctrine universally acknowledged and acted on in all the relations of life. When we hear or read of a Servant, or a Steward suspected of peculation or any other breach of trust ; and not merely suspected, but actually confessing guilt; we of course order them to quit the Office where the grounds of suspicion arose, conceiving that persons so situated are utterly unworthy of trust. But perhaps the Right Hon. Gentleman meant to take up the business of the Tenth Report, and was therefore unwilling to incur the charge of prejudice by the discharge of Mr. Trotter before the Trial took place. Under what circumstances is it that the Right Hon. Gentleman determines to retain Mr. Trotter in the important office of Paymaster of the Navy? He had heard that before the Commissioners he refused in some cases to answer questions at all, and in others had given equivocating replies. He had heard that he not only refused to answer questions to which, supposing him innocent, the reply was quite obvious—but he had known T. to have used every effort to retard the investigation of the Commissioners; and after all this previous knowledge, the Right Hon. Gentleman retains him in his employment as Paymaster. What, then, is the reason for this most extraordinary conduct? It is, Sir, that Trotter's case was *sub jure*, and the Right Hon. Gentleman does not wish to prejudge him on his Trial. The Right Honourable Gentleman has this evening declared that Trotter is dismissed, when he is as much *sub jure* as he has been at any period since the Commissioners finished their examination. Trotter has not been formally condemned by the House, for we have found him guilty only collaterally, our Resolutions on Monday evening being exclusively directed against Lord Melville. Perhaps, Sir, the Right Hon. Gentleman was alarmed by the impression made by our proceedings, (and they were calculated to make an impression on persons like the Right Hon. Gentleman,) and, by a sudden impulse of feeling, thought it most prudent to discharge Trotter without further delay. I cannot impute this decision to any other principle; for all the reasons that operated for retaining Trotter for several months back, still continue in force. The next feature in the very extraordinary speech of the Right Hon. Gentleman was the arguments he used for the lenient application of our Resolutions against Lord Melville, and the circumstances on which this lenity is to be founded. Perhaps, in what I am now about to say, the Right Hon. Gentleman may think me bitter and rancorous; but in spite of this, I feel myself called on to say, that I shall never sit in this House, and patiently hear these extravagant panegyrics on Lord Melville's public conduct. I am at a loss where to find what are the circumstances which are to incline us so powerfully to mercy. What particular claims does he possess to induce the House to pass over his aggravated offence with a comparatively trifling punishment? Is this motive to lenity to be found in the eagerness which his Lordship has ever shown to heap up emoluments, and to systematize corruption? Is it in the gift of the Chamberlainship of Fife granted to his wife, with arrears to a vast amount, procured under false pretences? Is it in procuring a year ago fifteen hundred a year in addition, not, Sir, to the salary of First Lord of the Admiralty, for I know that is very inadequately paid, but in addition to his salary as Lord Privy Seal for Scotland? But, Sir, the Right Hon. Gentleman lays great stress on his discovering no political or party partialities in the appointment of Officers either for the Naval or Military Service. I deny, Sir, that there is the least merit in this supposed impartiality. It is what every Minister, whatever he is, is obliged to preserve an appearance of, as an open dereliction of it would be attended with instant disgrace. I need not remind the house that Lord North sent Sir Charles Saunders and Admiral Keppel to Faulkland Islands, though that expedition unfortunately failed. Indeed, Party distinctions were almost always, from necessity, overlooked. But, Sir, I cannot hear the Right Hon. Gentleman stating that the Noble Lord was free from Party violence, without reminding the House of one or two circumstances, which demonstrate existence of Party spirit in all its most intolerant and disgusting features. I shall mention one, Sir, which fell within my own knowledge, and which will fully illustrate my position. At a period of the late War, when the danger of Invasion was supposed to be at the height, when offers of voluntary service were eagerly accepted, a numerous and loyal body of men in Tavistock made a tender of their services. The tender was refused by this self same moderate Lord Melville, on the sole ground, for no other could be alledged, that the Corps, when raised, was to be commanded by the late Duke of Bedford. It may perhaps be imagined, that my feelings at the recolfection of the deceased are so strong as to hurry me into some degree of exaggeration; but I solemnly protest that I am stating the matter precisely as it happened. And yet, Sir, we are to hear of Lord Melville's moderation and perfect freedom from all party spirit. There is another circumstance, which also pretty strongly illustrates his Lordship's forbearance and superiority to any of the workings of the angry passions. It is well known that the Dean of the Faculty of Advocates in Edinburgh is generally the most eminent person in the Profession, and that it is seldom customary to interfere with him from any political considerations. Yet this mild and moderate Lord Melville actually did interfere, and by employing all the influence of Government against the Hon. Henry Erskine, a Gentleman confessedly the most eminent at the Scotch Bar, he was actually dispossessed of a situation which he had many years held with the greatest honour and credit. So much, Sir, for the boasted liberality of the Noble Lord, which we were called on to look to for a motive to influence our decision. As to the favour bestowed on two Noble Lords, on which the Right Hon. Gentleman rested so much stress, I entirely agree with my Hon. Friend near me (Mr. Grey,) in every one of his observations. The Right Hon. Gentleman says, that my two Hon. Friends must possess Spartan virtue to be able to follow that line of accusation against the Noble Lord which they had pursued. If extraordinary exertions in virtue were required, I don't know any Men in whom they would be more readily found than in my Honourable Friends. But I must beg leave to say, that they are under no obligations to the Noble Lord for the defence he made of those relations, to whom they were naturally so strongly attached. Sir Charles Grey and Sir John Jervis were selected for a very difficult service in the West Indies, which they performed with gallantry. Some misunderstanding, however, arising, they returned, and a Charge was preferred against them in this House. If I recollect right, there were three divisions on the subject, when the Minority were successively thirteen, fourteen, and seventeen, and this was the formidable phalanx which the Noble Lord had so much merit in combating. I take it for granted, that he believed the Charge to be false ; and if he did believe it to be unfounded, what merit had he in defending the gallant Officers ? It was no more than indispensable duty to those whom he had employed on a difficult Service, which they executed with promptitude, vigour, and success. If this be merit, it is impossible to say, Sir, how far the line of obligation may be extended. An Honourable Gentleman under the Gallery (Mr. S. Thornton,) has given a curious reason for voting for the Resolutions on Monday night, on which it is impossible for me not to make a few observations.—He says, that he voted for the Motion, conceiving the Noble Lord guilty of a certain degree of negligence and inattention. I confess I am utterly astonished at such a declaration, after attending to the language of our Resolution, that the Noble Lord had been guilty of a gross violation of an Act of Parliament, and a high breach of Duty. Surely, Sir, this heavy Charge is not to be confounded with inattention and negligence. How the Honourable Member could have misunderstood them, is to me incomprehensible, as they were particularly objected to on the other side of the House. With respect to the Resolutions, it appears to me that they complete the criminal part of the Charge against the Noble Lord, and I am not at present for pressing any further proceedings in that way. If the Attorney General is to proceed against him for refunding the Money derived from the profits of Money misapplied, this will be by civil, and not by criminal action ; for recovery of Money is always ranked among the civil actions. The same observation will apply to any action for recovering grants obtained under false pretences. I have the less objection to press the Motion in the mean time, on the grounds of the pledge which the Hon. Gentleman has this night so distinctly given to the House. I find, Sir, after a careful examination, that during his Majesty's long reign, now a period of nearly forty-five years, only the Duke of Norfolk and myself have been dismissed his Majesty's Councils ; and I assure you, Sir, we want no such person as the Noble Lord to be our associate. I had almost forgotten Mr. Grattan, who had the like fortune in Ireland. None of us could, however, be proud of any connexion with such a Man as Lord Melville has shown himself to be throughout his whole career of life. I have said, Sir, that I would not now press the Motion to a discussion, in consequence of the Right Honourable Gentleman's pledge; but I should be grieved indeed to see the Resolutions passed without being followed by some lasting result. Such a work as that which we on Monday accomplished, must not be suffered to pass away unimproved. From one end of the Empire to the other the People will rejoice in the hope that a better system is about to be adopted. and we must not let their just expectations be disappointed. It is necessary for us, by making Lord Melville a signal mark of the vengeance of this House, to show the Country that we are indeed their Representatives—that we are determined equally to watch over their Property and their Liberties. The Public have received our work with the purest gratitude; but is there no part of this great work to belong to the Government? Is his Majesty to have no opportunity of manifesting his paternal interests on the subject? In what situation do we leave our Sovereign? The People applaud us in the warmest terms. They say the House of Commons have taken up our Cause against the whole host of Contractors and Peculators. The House of Lords may do the same; and shall not our beneficent Sovereign have an opportunity of expressing the warm interest he takes in every plan for alleviating the burdens, and improving the condition of his People? I admire this House as the corner stone of the Constitution—as the source of all reforms and improvements—as the balance by which the Constitution is kept in purity and vigour. But I do not wish to exclude the Monarchy from its proper share in every beneficent work. I think our Resolutions ought to be presented to the Throne. Like us his Majesty has read the Report, but he has not hitherto had an opportunity of expressing his feelings on the subject. I strongly impress this subject on the minds of Ministers. They are bound to carry the Resolutions to the Throne. They owe it as a sacred duty to the King whom they serve. After a few more observations, Mr. Fox consented to withdraw the Motion now, on an understanding that the whole matter should hereafter be fully investigated.

Mr. *Wilberforce* repeated the opinion which he expressed on Monday evening, as to the importance of the subject, and the necessity of searching into abuses, the existence of which was pregnant with danger to the Constitution and the Country. It was by no means his wish to shelter public Offenders from that punishment which the House were imperiously called upon by their duty to inflict on them; but he certainly thought that the circumstances of the present case were considerably changed by the resignation of the Noble Lord, and he therefore confessed, that he wished the Honourable Gentleman would withdraw his Motion; at the same time, if the Honourable Gentleman pressed it to a division, he by no means meant to say that he should vote against its adoption. In the execution of their Public Duties, Public Men ought not to be governed by any motives but those of Public utility. He did not like the system of adhering to a Party for the sake of that Party alone. What had been said by an Honourable Gentleman that evening showed the danger of acting on such a system, although he could not but admit that Lord Melville had at least acted liberally in employing the two Noble Lords alluded to. Mr. Wilberforce concluded with trusting, that the determination of that House to reform the abuses in the Public Departments, would not be a transient one; and that the Hon. Gentleman would not hazard lessening the effect of the Vote of the House on Monday, by persisting in his present Motion, when it was evident that many Members were unfavourable to the latter, who were warm in their approbation of the former proceeding.

Mr. *Kinnaird* would only trouble the House with one word on the observation made by the Hon. Gentleman in the Gallery, founded on the remarks of the Right Honourable Gentleman opposite, who had said, that no one ever accused the Noble Lord of being a bitter political enemy. Had that Right Honourable Gentleman been in Scotland, he would have heard the reverse: he would have heard that the Dean of Faculty, a most learned, able, and beloved Man, had been turned out of his situation solely at Lord Melville's instigation, without any offence having been alledged against him, but a difference of opinion on political subjects. This was as gross an instance of bitter party spirit as he had ever heard of.

The *Secretary at War* had meant cautiously to abstain from uttering a word on the subject which was under the consideration of the House, had he not felt himself loudly called upon by the statements of the Honourable Gentleman who had just sat down. He wished to ask that Honourable Gentleman at what period he had discovered that Lord Melville was a bitter political enemy? Was it during the days and weeks of social friendship which he had passed with the Noble Lord? and did he now in the hour of his need, show his gratitude by introducing extraneous accusatory matter at the close of a Debate, when the question did not demand it, and when those who had proposed the Motion to which the discussion of to-night owed its origin, had intimated their intention of withdrawing it? He trusted that in the breasts of Englishmen there existed feelings which wouldrevolt at such conduct. With respect to the history of the expulsion of the Dean of Faculty from his situation, he would briefly state the facts. At a time whendemocratic principles were but too prevalent, a meeting had been called of thoe who were named "Friends of the People." At this meeting the Dean inadvertently, or rather injudiciously, attended, and by his attendance gave a sanction to the proceedings. Without the slightest interference on the part of Lord Melville, who had nothing whatever to do with the business, the Faculty, indignant at such conduct, brought forward a Motion to deprive the Dean of his situation; a step in which he repeated that they were entirely uninfluenced by the Noble Lord alluded to.

Mr. *Fox* remarked, that although it perhaps would have been as delicate, had the observations of his Honourable Friend been suppressed, yet it should be recollected that he had been provoked to make them by the assertions of the Right Honourable Gentleman opposite, and of the Honourable Gentleman in the Gallery.

Mr. *Kinnaird* declared, with considerable warmth, that were he not convinced the House must be aware of the futility of the charge that had been exhibited against him by the Honourable Gentleman, he should consider himself bound to call upon him for further explanation. Was it decent to expect, that because he had lived on terms of good neighbourhood with Lord Melville, whose private character he highly esteemed, he should therefore withhold his opinion in the House on his public conduct?

Mr. *Elliston* said a few words.

Mr. *Whitbread* observed, that he had been arraigned for the great bitterness which it was said he had evinced in his Speech at the commencement of this evening's Debate; and on a former night he had been accused of introducing more of passion than became him in the observations with which he prefaced the Motion that he had the honour of submitting to the House. To prove the existence of the bitterness, and this passion, his observations had been industriously misrepresented. He had never blamed Lord Melville for having tendered his resignation to his Majesty; on the contrary, he thought it was a step highly incumbent on him, and the omission of which would grossly have aggravated his misconduct. But this he had said, that Ministers were deeply culpable for not having anticipated his resignation by a dismissal. The two Delinquents were equally guilty, yet Mr. Trotter was dismissed with disgrace, Lord Melville was allowed quietly to resign. He should say little on the Charge that had been brought against him, of having ungratefully attacked a Man, who in 1795 defended two Noble Lords, to one of whom he had the honour of being related, as the subject had been so ably handled by his Honourable Friend. He was far from thinking that these Noble Lords were under the slightest obligation to Lord Melville for what he had said on that occasion. Did the Right Honourable Gentleman mean to assert that Lord Melville had done a job for his Noble Friends in that instance, and therefore that he was bound now to do a job for Lord Melville in return? Lord Melville had spoken favourably of the conduct of the Noble Lords; if he did not think favourably of it, he had certainly acted wrong; and if he did think favourably of it, his expressing that opinion was merely justice. It appeared from what had fallen from every quarter of the House, that the general sentiment was, that it was highly improper that Lord Melville should ever hold a situation of trust in his Majesty's Government. A kind promise had been given by the Right Honourable Gentleman opposite, that he never should hold such a situation. On this promise he was inclined to rely; it might be good as long as that Right Honourable Gentleman himself continued in Office: but might not his Majesty change his advisers, and might not Lord Melville be then again admitted into his Councils? What means had the King of knowing what was done in that House? Had the Right Honourable Gentleman communicated their Resolutions to his Majesty? That could not be, else he must have been dismissed, and would not have been allowed to resign.— The Honourable Member felt anxious that the House should stand high in the public opinion—he felt doubly so, after the proceedings of last night, lest it should be again let down. He begged to be allowed to state the way in which matters stood on the morning when they last adjourned. Many Members were anxious that the concluding Motion should then be made. He intimated his intention of bringing it forward that very night. Nothing fell from him indicative of any intention to relinquish his Motion; he only wished to postpone the moving it for a few hours on account of the exhausted state of the House. The Right Honourable Gentleman, without assigning any reason for the additional delay, proposed an adjournment for thirty-six hours. This was objected to by his Right Honourable Friend (Mr. Fox), unless it was understood that in the interval no public business should take place; and the Right Honourable Gentleman, with a countenance which he (Mr. W.) should not easily forget, said, in any view of the case it would be better to adjourn. Could it, however, be in the contemplation of the House, that this delay was for the purpose of allowing Lord Melville time to *resign?* If any Member, however, found himself taken by surprise, he should withdraw his Motion; but at the same time he knew that was not a thing calculated to satisfy the Public. He said so, not in any spirit of resentment against Lord Melville, as if this Resolution were necessary to make him feel his situation. If he had any feelings, and the Honourable Member entertained no doubt he had, nothing could wring them more than the Resolutions already passed by that House. He was conscious the sense of the House went with him, that it was necessary Lord Melville should never again hold any Office of Trust. All, therefore, that he desired, was to find out some way of entering this opinion on the Journals of the House, and that the Motion had on that account been withdrawn. The parallels which had been set up as to the Motions against Ministers being allowed to drop on their resignation, did not at all apply. They were made on the ground of incapacity; this was founded on a delinquency. He knew that in common cases to be expunged from the List of the Privy Council was no disgrace. It had occurred to his Hon. Friend (Mr. Fox). The Right Honourable Gentleman then, in the plenitude of his power, had recommended it as a measure proper for his Majesty's adoption. He had, however, since retracted that opinion, and had recommended to his Majesty not only to restore him to that honour, but to promote him to his highest confidence. He had asked pardon for his offence before God and Man. But could ever such a recommendation avail in favour of Lord Melville, after the Resolutions adopted by that House? He was happy to understand that the Bank was not so much to blame as he had supposed. And also, to learn by what fell from the Right Hon. Gentleman (Mr. Canning), that the mode of conducting business in that Office was entirely changed; such would always happen when Principals began to do their duty.—But why, he must ask, was Trotter dismissed and Wilson not? The Right Honourable Gentleman had said, Wilson was a deserving Officer.—With all respect for the assertion of the Hon. Gentleman, he however, could not help having also a high respect for the authority and opinion of the Commissioners of Naval Inquiry: they said, and the Honourable Member said too, that Wilson was an improper Person to continue in his present or any other situation of Public Trust. The Honourable Member could not, after what had fallen from Hon. Friends of his, and from other Honourable Gentlemen, whose support he was anxious to procure, refuse in the meantime to withdraw his Motion. He was anxious, however, lest the Public should suppose that in passing their former Resolutions, they had only adopted in a heat what they were unwilling to follow up; he, therefore, had to suggest what he hoped would meet the opinion of every Gentleman present;—That a Copy of the Resolutions of that House, of the former night, be laid before his Majesty without any comment. Thus it would be impossible that Lord Melville should ever after be admitted to his Majesty's Councils, and at the same time the Resolutions of that House would be consistent.

It was then put and unanimously agreed to—" That the said Resolutions be laid before his Majesty."

Mr. *Whitbread* then moved that the said Resolutions be carried up by the WHOLE HOUSE.

Mr. *Pitt* submitted, that as the Resolutions were to be laid before his Majesty without comment, this formality ought to be dispensed with.

Mr. *Whitbread* said, that when he said without *comment*, he did not say without *form*. In so important a business, every species of ceremony ought to be adopted.

It was then ordered that the Resolutions be carried up by the WHOLE HOUSE.

Mr. *Pitt* asked on what day it was Mr. Whitbread's intention to bring forward the Motions he had alluded to, and in what order he was to bring them forward?

Mr. *Whitbread* answered, that he would take the first open day after the Holidays. That he should move first, That instructions be given to the Attorney General, to commence a prosecution against Lord Melville and Mr. Trotter, calling them to account for their improper intromission with the Public Money. And secondly, for a Select Committee to investigate the other points to which he had alluded. In imitation too of a measure adopted by Lord Melville himself, he should feel it his duty immediately to bring in a Bill for restraining Lord Melville and Mr. Trotter from alienating their property.

Mr. *Sheridan* expressed a hope that a General Committee to consider all the Reports would be moved for, and that the adjournment of the House should not take place till it was known what time his Majesty had appointed to receive the Resolutions of the House.

After a conversation between Mr. Pitt and Mr. Grey, it was understood that the House would adjourn to-morrow till to-morrow fortnight; and then Mr. Whitbread should bring forward his Motion on that day, Mr. Pitt having declared that, as far as he was concerned, he wished the earliest possible day to be fixed.

Mr. Serjeant *Best* gave notice of his intention, after the Holidays, to submit to the House a Motion on the subject of the Eleventh Report.

The other Orders of the Day were deferred, and the House adjourned at ten o'clock.

FOREIGN REPORTS.

WEST INDIES.

THE Rochefort Squadron sailed from France on the 11th of February, consisting of six Sail of the Line, and some Frigates, with 600 Troops on board. The West Indies are at this time, generally, very healthy.—Governor Bentinck of St. Vincent is recalled, and Major-General George Beckwith, formerly Governor of the Bermuda Islands, is to succeed him. The Rochefort Squadron anchored at Port Royal, Martinique.

March 11. A Mail from Jamaica arrived, brought by the Augusta Packet, which left Jamaica on the 28th of January, under convoy of the Bacchante. The island is perfectly tranquil. On the 28th, the John Bull Cutter, of 14 guns, arrived at Port Royal, in 38 days, from Plymouth, with dispatches for the Governor and Admiral. The order for detaining Spanish Ships was known at Jamaica:

but no intelligence of the War with Spain had yet been received. On her passage to Jamaica the John Bull spoke the Acasto, off Madeira, and learned that she had parted company with the outward-bound Jamaica Fleet, in a gale of Wind, and intended cruising in that latitude for a day or two, in hopes of falling in with them. Ten of the Fleet arrived at Barbadoes before the Cutter left that island, and the remainder were supposed to be with the Hyæna Frigate. The Augusta Packet saw, about sun-set the day after she left Port Royal, many Sail to windward, which she thought were the Fleet under the Acasto. On the 30th she saw a French Prize steering for Port Royal. On the 12th February she landed the Mails at Crooked Island, and parted company with the Bacchante on the 13th. A Spanish Corvette, of 12 guns, from Old Spain, bound to the Havana, with Naval Stores, detained by la Surveillante Frigate, and the Spanish Brig el Destino, from Cadiz, bound to Carthagena, with wine and dry goods, detained by the Diana Frigate, arrived at Port Royal on the 12th. The Princess Charlotte Frigate has sent into Port Royal a Spanish Ship from Carthagena to Barcelona, with 35,000 dollars. The Mermaid Frigate, Captain Holles, was at the Havana on the 15th November, and had given invitations to all the principal Spanish Officers at the Havana to a ball and supper that evening on board the Mermaid; when a Brig sent by Admiral Duckworth arrived; Captain Holmes instantly weighed, and stood out to Sea, and the whole of the British Merchant Ships in Harbour followed, and were preserved from falling into the hands of the Spaniards, 300 British Seamen from Guadaloupe have been landed from the Comet Cartel at Barbadoes. The Spanish Brig St. Sebastian, with French property, and a Spanish Ship with four guns and 50 Men, laden with Naval and Military Stores, a Spanish General and a Colonel, with their families, are sent into Barbadoes, by l'Heureux, Captain Younghusband. The Spanish Brig Isabella, with wine and brandy, is sent into Barbadoes by the Amelia Frigate.

LETTER FROM GENERAL PREVOST.

SIR,

"*Head Quarters, Prince Rupert, Dominica,*
24th February, 1805.

" You will inform the Commander in Chief of his Majesty's Naval and Land Forces, that a Force from France, consisting of one Three-decker and two 74's, Frigates, &c. with Troops on board, invested the Island on the 20th, and made good their landing on the following day (the 21st); they were most successfully resisted by the Troops under my command, and repeatedly driven back.

" The Ships of the Line in vain attempted to silence the Batteries; but unfortunately the Town being on fire, and the Militia on the right, notwithstanding their spirited conduct, were compelled to fall back.

" I deemed it prudent to allow the Council to capitulate for the Town of Roseau and its dependencies, whilst I attempted, by forced marches, to get into Prince Rupert with such force as I could collect, in which I have succeeded, and wait their attack on this Post, with a well-grounded expectation that his Majesty's Regulars and Militia Forces will again distinguish themselves. I retreated from Roseau on the 21st, at 4 P.M., and understand the terms I prescribed are acceded to. I ordered none to be accepted that were not honourable, and desired the French Commander not to allow his Troops to disgrace themselves by plundering, or any act of wantonness. You are hereby to sail immediately, and make the first Island you can. If Privateers in the Guadaloupe Channel prevent your turning to windward, make Monserrat or Antigua.

" I have the honour to be, Sir,

" Your most obedient Servant,

" *To the Master of the Sloop Endeavour.*   " GEORGE PREVOST."

April 3. Lieutenant Lancaster arrived at the Admiralty, charged with dispatches from Commodore Hood, containing the confirmation of the landing of the French Troops in Dominica, and the surrender of Roseau.

The following is a list of the Ships of War at Jamaica, under the Command of Sir J. T. Duckworth:—

Ships.	Guns.		Guns.
L'Hercule	74	La Blanche	36
Theseus	74	Tartar	32
Vanguard	74	Unicorn	32
Acasta	44	La Magicienne	32
Diana	38	Princess Charlotte	
Franchise	36	Jason (sailed with the last Convoy	
La Desiree	36	from Cork)	32
La Pique	36	Mermaid	22
La Surveillante	36	La Bacchante	20
La Seine	36	And several smaller Vessels.	

The Ships of War in the Leeward Islands, under the Orders of Sir Samuel Hood, are—

Ships.	Guns.		Guns.
Centaur	74	Carysfort	28
Beaulieu	38	L'Heureux	24
Amelia	36	Hyæna	24
La Fortunee	36	Proselyte (sailed with the last Con-	
Amsterdam	32	voy but one from Cork)	24
Galatea	32	Besides small Vessels.	

HOME REPORTS.

NARROW SEAS.

(WE are obliged to those Correspondents who enable us by their communications to give novelty and additional interest to these Reports. All Letters on this subject, addressed to Mr. Gold, No. 103, Shoe Lane, Fleet Street, will be thankfully received.)

The Diana Packet, on the 18th of December, shipped a very heavy Sea, which threw the Vessel on her beam-ends, in which situation she remained three minutes before she righted. The great pressure of water swept away nearly all the starboard bulwarks, boarding nettings, stantions, &c. and washed over the midship a twelve-pound carronade; and on the 19th a very heavy Sea struck her on the quarter, which broached her to the Wind, threw the starboard side wholly under water, the Sea making a breach over her, which carried away every moveable off the deck, forced the small Boat over the stern on the bumkins, and stove her to pieces, and carried away the sprit-sail yard. The Prince of Wales Packet also was struck abaft on the 19th of December, by an uncommonly high Sea, which forced her head under water to such a depth, that the foresail floated upon the surface. The water rushed abaft, tore the fore hatchway to pieces, stove the Boat under the booms, and did other considerable damage.

Since the formation of new Harbours and other improvements which have been made by the enemy on their coast, from Calais to Boulogne, it has become an object of importance that our opposite Coast should be rendered equally defensive. With this view, the Canal through Romney Marsh, from Shorncliffe to Rye, has been projected, and is executing with unexampled activity, at various places along the line; and great numbers of labourers lately employed at the Docks and public works of the metropolis, and at other places, are arrived to assist in effecting it. The expense of cutting is estimated at 150,000l. In addition to this line of defence, Martello towers are to be constructed on the edge of the Sea, three of them equidistant between Hythe and Romney; those near Dymchurch will be placed immediately behind the wall.

Torbay, Jan. 10. The brave Brixham Pilots who so nobly saved the Blonde Crew, have, with the assistance of two Sloops, swept for and weighed (as no buoys watched) the four anchors and six cables of that Ship, and brought them on Shore. Arrived and sailed again immediately, the Lord Nelson hired Schooner, having sent to Portsmouth a Prize supposed of 10,000l. value.

Brixham Quay, Jan. 19. Last night his Majesty's Frigate Blonde, Captain Faulkner, with the assistance and exertions of Captain Somerville of the Nemesis, and her Crew, was got off with very little damage, having knocked away her gripe, and part of her keel aft.

Torbay, Jan. 21. Yesterday afternoon Admiral Cornwallis sailed in the Ville de Paris, for Portsmouth.

Falmouth, Jan. 23. Blows hard. Arrived a Spanish Ship, the Agila Corodora, Prize to the Malta, of 84 guns, taken on the 18th. She is of 500 tons burthen, laden with cotton, logwood, and a large quantity of dollars.

Torbay, Jan. 29. By a Sloop which arrived here last night from Guernsey, I have learnt the sad effects of the tremendous gale last Thursday there, in which a number of Vessels suffered, but most particularly that beautiful Ship Privateer Fame (late Blonde), of 38 guns, and 240 Men, Captain Hosier, belonging to H. C. Blewett, Esq. of Plymouth, and which sailed from thence last Monday. She parted one cable in the gale, and dragged the other two anchors, till she went ashore against the Castle, and is become a mere wreck. She had previously cut her mizen-mast away, to ease the Ship, but it availed nothing. She had her commission, and was to have sailed the next day.

Feb. 18. The Melampus Frigate, and Rhoda and Frisk hired armed Cutters, fell in with, on the 10th, a Squadron of the enemy's Gun-vessels off the Saints, endeavouring to get into Brest coastwise from Ambolette. The Wind being off Shore the enemy were not able to keep close in Land, and our Ships dashed in among them, and captured eight Sail; another was afterwards taken by the Growler Gun-brig. Two of these Gun-vessels arrived in Mount's Bay on Thursday last; and three more of them were brought into Falmouth on Friday. They are Nos. 193, 286, and 430; the first has two 18-pounders and one 24-pounder; the others have one 24-pounder each. No. 480 had a Commodore on board; during the chase the Growler's mainmast-head was shot away, and the Frenchmen lost their bowsprit; no lives were lost in the contest, but five Frenchmen were drowned in exchanging Prisoners. On board the Luggers were 30 Men, amongst whom there was only one Seaman, the rest Soldiers; they are the most miserable Craft that can be conceived; no other accommodation for Officer or Men, than straw to lie on.

It is now determined that the Channel Fleet shall in future rendezvous at Falmouth; and moorings (which are preparing with all possible expedition at Plymouth) are to be laid down immediately in Carrick Roads for fifteen Sail of the Line. We are assured that Plymouth Dock-yard, capacious as it is, is become unequal to the docking and repair of our numerous Ships of War, with that expedition which the nature of the Service requires; and that, in addition to this evil, which is peculiar to a state of War, in time of Peace Hamoaze is barely sufficient to receive the numerous Ships required to lay there in ordinary.

Penzance, March 23. A French Privateer, which has for some time frequented this Coast, has this morning captured three English Brigs off the Land's End. An express is just arrived here from the Signal-house, for a Ship of War to go in quest of her, but there is no armed Vessel of any kind in the Bay.

PLYMOUTH.

Twelve Ships of the Line are getting ready at this Port with all possible dispatch. They are old Ships, and are to be cased over with Oak Planks about two inches thick. This is a new expedient, and the Shipwrights are employed Night and Day in completing the Work.

Feb. 24. Came in the Caroline, from the Havanah, with sugar and logwood, captured the 12th Instant off the Coast of Spain, by the Pallas, of 32 guns, Captain Lord Cochrane; she had also taken another, name as yet unknown, with sugar, logwood, specie, &c. very valuable, part of a Fleet bound from the Havana to Old Spain, with valuable cargoes, hourly expected, and in pursuit of which the Pallas had shaped her course; his Lordship declaring if it ever was in his power he would fulfil his public advertisement (stuck up here) for entering Seamen, of filling their pockets with Spanish *pewter* and *cobs*, nick names given by Sailors to silver ingots and Spanish dollars.

March 2. This afternoon, pursuant to Signal from the Port Admiral, that beautiful Ship the Hibernia, of 120 guns, Captain Bedford, unmoored from her moorings off the North Jetty Head, and was seen under weigh; she went down the Harbour piloted by the King's Pilots, in a very grand and magnificent style into Cawsand Bay; the Wind was leading and fine at N. N. W. and weather moderate. She came to in Cawsand Bay about three o'clock, and is in truth a model of a Ship. She will be ready to join the Channel Fleet in about ten days.

7. Came in a rich Spanish Prize, from Rio de la Plata, with some diamonds, ingots of gold and silver, dollars, and a valuable cargo, taken by the Pallas, of 32 guns, Captain Lord Cochrane. Another Spanish Ship, Fortunee, from Vera Cruz, laden with mahogany, logwood, and 432,000 dollars, captured by the Pallas, is not arrived.

16. Came in the Urania, of 44 guns, Hon. Captain Herbert, from a Cruise, with a very valuable Spaniard, her Prize, captured on the Coast of Portugal a few days since, valued at 70,000l. sterling.

17. Came in the Topaze, of 38 guns, from Cork, having Admiral Lord Gardner on board, with his Flag flying at the main: she came-to off Cawsand Bay, and was saluted by the Men of War now there; and the Hibernia, his Lordship's future Ship, was manned in compliment to him. He will shift his Flag to-day, or to-morrow forenoon.

18. Arrived the Roebuck Privateer, with a very valuable Spanish Prize; she has also captured another.

19. Yesterday the Right Hon. Lord Gardner struck his Flag at the main of the Topaze, of 38 guns, in Cawsand Bay, and, accompanied by Lady Gardner and his Suite, he landed at Dock and set off directly for London in his travelling post chariot and four, to receive his final instructions before he relieves the Hon. Admiral Cornwallis in the Command of the Channel Fleet.

23. Came in, and went up the Harbour, a most beautiful Spanish Letter of Marque, of 14 guns, said to be very rich and valuable, Prize to the Pallas, of 32 guns, Captain Lord Cochrane.

24. The keel, stem, and stern of the Caledonia, of 120 guns, are all laid down, and it is said that she will have several gangs upon her very soon, to get her ribs up for seasoning.

30. Accounts were received at this Port, that the Brest Fleet, consisting of 22 Sail of the Line had come out of the Harbour, and were at anchor in Camaret Bay, under protection of the Batteries.

31. All was bustle and hurry at this Port last night. The Crew of the Naiad, of 38 guns, worked all night to warp her out into the Sound. Lord Gardner hoisted his Flag on board the Hibernia, of 120 guns, amidst three cheers from all the Ships.

April 1. Admiral Lord Gardner took the first opportunity of a spirit of Wind in his favour, and sailed in the Hibernia, of 110 guns, with the Ajax, of 74 guns, to the Command of the Western Squadron off Brest.

PORTSMOUTH.

Feb. 25. A Court Martial was held on board the Fleet at Torbay, on Captain Bligh, of the Warrior, of 74 guns, on charges of tyranny preferred against him by one of his Lieutenants, (who was tried some time since for disobedience of orders and acquitted.) After a trial, which lasted the whole of the day, Captain B was reprimanded, with an admonition from the President in the Court, and restored to the Command of the Warrior.

This morning Sir T. Trowbridge hoisted his Flag on board the Blenheim, of 74 guns, Captain Bissett, on which the Admiral (Montagu) saluted from the Royal William. Sir A. Hammond and Sir W. Rule are arrived here to inspect the state of the Ships lying in ordinary at this Port. They were afloat yesterday from nine o'clock till five in the afternoon. The Lieutenants of the Endymion, by the four Spanish Captures, which arrived on Saturday, will share 12,000l. each. The Galleon is worth a million and a half.

28. Arrived a Danish Galliott, detained off Havre by the Favourite Sloop, Captain Davie. The Master of her has died since her arrival. Sir A. Hammond and Sir W. Rule completed their inquiries into the condition of the Ships in Ordinary at this Port; and this morning, at nine o'clock, they went for London. Several Ships of the Line are to be repaired for Commission immediately: the Artificers are to work all the extra time it will be possible. One hundred and twenty Men began to work on the Zealous this morning.

March 3. The comprehensive Address of the Comptroller of the Navy (Sir A. Hammond) to the Officers of the Dock-Yard, upon the following Ships being selected for immediate repair, " that he should hope to see the sterns of all of them pass the platform before July," will stimulate the exertions to be made in completing them. They are to be doubled (that is three inch planks to the lower deck ports), which will much accelerate the works. The Gibraltar, of 80 guns, San Antonio, Triumph, Zealous, Canada, Orion, Bellerophon, Brunswick, Saturn, and Robust, of 74 guns each.

4. The Ships of the Line ordered for repair, will require an additional number of Men to be entered into the Dock-yard: 200 Shipwrights, 50 House Carpenters, 50 Labourers, and 8 pair of Sawyers, are now wanted. The Men were yesterday (Sunday) taken off the Alexandria, a new Frigate, to work upon the Prince George. Arrived the Helena Sloop, Captain Losack, from a Cruise; also a Dutch Galliott, from Bilboa, bound to Embden, laden with Spanish wool, Prize to the Cockatrice Sloop. Sailed the Tribune Frigate, Captain Bennet, on a Cruise. Came into Harbour the Endymion, of 44 guns, Hon. Captain Paget. This morning D. Campbell, a Seaman of the Tribune, received 150 lashes round the Ships at Spithead, for desertion: it is honourable to the Crew of the Tribune, that they generously gave him a dollar each, and the Midshipmen five dollars each, a part of their prize money, which he forfeited by the charge against his name on the Ship's Books.

16. The preparations for the intended Expedition are now nearly mature. Fourteen Ordnance Transports have come into Harbour from Southampton, to have their Stores more judiciously stowed.

22. A Court Martial was held here, on Arch. Duff, Commander of the Megæra Sloop, for using unofficer-like language, and rating Officers not qualified; upon which charges he was sentenced to be admonished to be more circumspect in his conduct for the future.—Sir Isaac Coffin, Bart. President, Thomas Greetham, Esq. Judge Advocate of the Fleet.

NORTH SEA.

Admiral Lord KEITH, K.B.
Vice-Admiral J. HOLLOWAY, *Downs.*
Rear-Admiral B. S. ROWLEY, *Sheerness.*
Rear-Admiral T. M. RUSSEL, *Yarmouth Roads.*
Rear-Admiral T. LOUIS, *Downs.*

(*We are sorry that this interesting Report has unavoidably, from the great press of other important Naval State Papers, been delayed. We shall now endeavour to complete it from (December—March.)*

Deal, Dec. 18. Wind N.E. Blows hard, weather squally. The Floating Light, which was placed on the Galloper Sand, parted from her moorings, and yesterday afternoon passed through the Downs; a Deal Boat put two Men on board to assist her to Dover Pier. Sailed to Portsmouth, the Eugene Sloop of War.

Margate, Dec. 20. His Majesty's Ship Tartarus, Captain Withers, was lost off this place on the dangerous Sands in the Roads, from which no Ship was ever known to be saved.

Hull, Dec. 24. On Saturday se'nnight the Jane, of Sunderland, Captain Hallowel, being off Whitby, sprung a leak, and immediately sunk. The whole of the Crew, except a Boy (who was sick in his hammock below), were saved.

Deal, Dec. 24. Wind E. Arrived l'Immortalite Frigate, from a Cruise off the French Coast; l'Immortalite took off seven Men from the Wreck of a Swedish Vessel in Boulogne Bay; one of the Swedish Seamen was drowned, and one was also lost from l'Immortalite, who parted two cables.

A Court Martial was assembled at Sheerness on the 31st of December, on board his Majesty's Ship Africaine, to inquire into the circumstances relative to the loss of his Majesty's late Ship the Romney, on the Sand called the South Haaks, off the Texel, on the 19th of November, and to try the Hon. Captain Colvill, his Officers, and Crew, for the same.

PRESENT,

F. PICKMORE, Esq. Captain of his Majesty's Ship RAMILIES, and Second Officer in the Command of his Majesty's Ships, &c. in the Medway, and at the Buoy of the Nore, President.

Captain A. Fraser
—— J. Draper
—— J. W. Spranger
—— W. R. Broughton
—— A. Renou
—— A. J. Griffiths

Captain H. Inman
—— Geo. Dundas
—— James Colnett
—— A. M'Kenzie
—— Sir T. Livingstone, Bart.

J. RICHARDS, Esq. Deputy Judge Advocate.

After a very full investigation of all the circumstances relative thereto, it appeared to the Court, that the loss of the Ship was occasioned by the thickness of the fog, and the ignorance of the Pilots in regard to the tides, &c. they having undertaken a charge, to which it appeared they were wholly incompetent. The sentence of the Court was, that the Pilots shall be mulcted of all their pay for the Romney, and rendered incapable of taking charge of any of his Majesty's Ships and Vessels of War in future, and to be imprisoned in the Marshalsea, one for the space of six, and the other for twelve calendar months. The Captain, Officers, and Crew, were most justly and honourably acquitted of all blame, it appearing to the Court that the utmost exertions were used by them to save the Ship after she had struck, and to prevent the Ship's Company from becoming prisoners to the enemy; and the Court expressed, by the President, the high satisfaction which they felt at their conduct under the very trying circumstances attendant upon that melancholy occasion.

Jan. 1. This afternoon Admiral Lord Keith shifted his flag from his Majesty's Ship Monarch to the Ardent. The Monarch sailed to Portsmouth.

The Contre Amiral Magon Privateer, commanded by the noted Blackman, is ordered to be surveyed at Sheerness, and if found proper for his Majesty's Service, she is to be purchased.

Sheerness, Jan. 3, 1805. Notwithstanding the recent severe and foggy weather, several Ships have been paid wages and advance. Yesterday, after much difficulty and some danger, the Gentlemen of the Pay-Office succeeded in getting to the Great Nore, and paid the Elk Brig.

Deal, Jan. 8. Wind S.S.W. Last night a Gun-vessel, the Tickler, arrived in the Downs with a French Officer on board, who was taken out of a fishing Vessel which came out of Boulogne Harbour, bearing a flag of truce. He had a dispatch from Talleyrand to Lord Harrowby, which was sent express from Paris to

Boulogne, with orders that it should be forwarded without a moment's delay to some of the British Cruisers, and that the Officer should accompany it.

Yarmouth, Jan. 8. Wind S. W. Admiral Russel this morning shifted his flag from the Eagle, of 74 guns, to the Monmouth, Capt. Hart.

On Wednesday morning, Jan. 9, between eight and nine, being off Flamborough Head, a French Brig Privateer came close upon her stern, through a Fleet of Colliers, and was within pistol-shot, before Captain White knew she was an enemy, and saw them loading their guns. The Frenchmen called out repeatedly to Haul to! and Captain White, ordering down his square sail, immediately cleared his deck to engage. In the mean time the Frenchman hauled up his colours halfway up his mainsail, and fired a broadside, with a volley of musketry; but being opposed, with as much precision and regularity as the suddenness of the alarm admitted of, with round and grape shot from the Snack's 12-pound carronades, he, after a short time, thought proper to sheer off to a safer distance, keeping up his fire, but happily without doing any injury. After some time an English armed Ship came down upon the Privateer, and hastened her retreat. She kept hovering about, however, all day, and, it is feared, may have taken several Vessels in the evening. Captain White fought with the greatest resolution; and, we are happy to say, neither Ship nor Crew sustained any damage. The Swift Packet, Captain Orr, was in company. As this short Engagement was quite close to Flamborough Head, it is much regretted there was not a Battery upon it, as a few guns might not only protect a whole Fleet, but have sunk this Privateer. She was a blacksided Brig, mounting apparently 14 guns, full of Men; carrying a white-bottomed Boat over her stern.

Deal, Jan. 10. Wind E. N. E. Sailed this morning, on a Cruise to the French Coast, the Castor Frigate; the Vesuvius Bomb to Sheerness; the Jackall Gun-brig, Lieutenant Stewart, having on board Mr. Kercaldie, Pilot, to replace the Floating Light on the Galloper Sand.

15. Wind W. Arrived from Dungeness His Majesty's Ship Leopard, Rear Admiral Louis, with Castor Frigate, Captain Brace; and Bonetta Sloop of War, Captain Savage.

18. On Friday se'nnight, eleven Vessels within Scarborough Piers broke from their moorings and were some of them stranded; the others totally wrecked upon the beach and rocks, to the south of the Harbour. The Liberty, of Shields, was driven out to Sea, and forced on Shore near a mile from Spaw, where she was entirely lost; the Crew were taken out by the Life-boat. One Brig drove out of the Harbour with only two boys on board; they were with difficulty saved by the Life-boat: the mainmast went away, she drove upon the rocks and became a total Wreck: a Sloop, name unknown, had entered the Harbour to assist in mooring her; two Midshipmen and nine Seamen, part of the Crew of the Romney Man of War, who were lately landed out of a Cartel from Holland, went on board. This Vessel likewise drove out to Sea again, and being forced upon the rocks, about two miles to the Southward of Scarborough, became a total Wreck; and we are sorry to add that every soul on board perished.

20. Wind S. S E. It blew so hard during the greater part of yesterday, that no Supplies could be sent off; and in the course of the night it was almost an Hurricane. A Swedish Vessel drove on Shore during the gales, but there are hopes of her being got off without much damage, should the weather moderate. To-day it continues to blow most violently, and a signal was in consequence hoisted by the Port Admiral for no Boats from the Men of War to venture on Shore; notwithstanding which several have attempted it:—A Boat belonging to the Ardent, of 64 guns, in sailing for the Beach, upset, and a fine young Man, a Midshipman, of the name of Gilbert, was unfortunately drowned. The Crew were saved by the intrepidity of the Deal Boatmen, who, fearless of danger, rushed through a tremendous Surf to their assistance, and brought the exhausted Mariners on Shore, who were immediately sent to the Naval Hospital, to receive such comforts as the nature of their situation demanded.

Sheerness, Jan. 21. The Adder Gun-vessel, Lieutenant Wood, is reported so bad, that she is ordered to be paid off.

25. Arrived the Galgo Sloop of War from Hull, with three new Praams under Convoy, built at that place, to be fitted out here.

Yarmouth, Jan. 29. This morning arrived His Majesty's ship Hindostan, of 50 guns, to join the N. S. Squadron; and from a Cruise, the Scout Gun-brig. The Russian and English Messengers which have been detained here by contrary Winds, embarked this morning on board the Griffin Cutter, and are accompanied by the Hawke Cutter, for Gottenburgh. Wind S. E.

Extract of a Letter from Balmborough, Jan. 29.—" On Sunday night, the 20th ult. in a gale, the Brig Dispatch, of Yarmouth, laden with barley, for Alloa, in Scotland, was driven on Shore near Newton. Some Soldiers were on board going on a furlough; one of them, a Serjeant, aided the whole Company in getting on land; but when returning on board for the last Man, (one of his Comrades,) he found great difficulty to accomplish his wish, by reason of the Man's incapability, and the boisterous Sea breaking over them : it was thought by those who had got to land, that both were lost in the waves, and therefore they made the best of their way to some houses: but the next morning the Serjeant and his Comrade were found lying behind some bushes in a field by a shepherd. The Serjeant was able to speak, but the other was speechless, and near dead. Some hope was entertained of the Serjeant's recovery; but I am since informed that he is dead likewise. About the same time a Brig, the John, of Sunderland, the Cargo belonging to Mr. Appleby, of Alemouth, laden with wheat, broke from her moorings, in the Harbour of Beadnell, and drifted ashore on the outside of the Harbour. The Cargo is pretty safe, and the Vessel is expected to be got off with little damage."

Deal, Feb. 3. The Monarch has this day returned to the Downs from Portsmouth, where she has been for a payment of Prize-money. To-morrow Lord Keith again hoists his flag on board her.

10. Wind. S. W. Rear-Admiral Douglas arrived here this morning and hoisted his Flag on board the Leopard Man of War, in the Downs.

Dungeness, Feb. 24. On Friday last his Majesty's Brig Harpy captured French Lugger Privateer, of 10 guns, from Boulogne, and sent her for the Downs The same day a French Privateer, full of Soldiers, was so bold as to come within two miles of the Shore to the West of Dungeness. In the evening she fired into the Stag Cutter, and wounded one Man; he was carried on board the Leopard, and had his arm amputated; he is now in a fair way of recovery.

Deal, March 10. His Majesty's Gun-brig the Locust, commanded by that gallant Officer Lieutenant Lake, is just arrived in the Downs, almost a complete Wreck, being towed in by the Pincher Gun-brig. The Locust is attached to the Boulogne Squadron, under the orders of Capt. Owen; and on Friday last was ordered, per signal from l'Immortalite, to run close in under the Batteries of Ambleteuse, to destroy or drive on Shore a number of the enemy's small Craft, coming from the eastward to the grand rendezvous. This service Lieutenant Lake completely performed, although exposed to a most tremendous fire of eleven Batteries and a number of field pieces, at about pistol shot distance. One of the enemy's superior Vessels had struck to the Locust, and the gallant Commander was in the act of lowering the Jolly-boat to take possession of a cutter-rigged Vessel, when a 42-pound shot struck the foremast of the Locust, which went immediately over the side, and prevented the Commander from executing his intended purpose. The Frenchman taking the advantage of the disabled state of his opponent, immediately re-hoisted his colours, and made all sail for the Shore, where he got under the protection of the Batteries. Notwithstanding Lieutenant Lake was exposed, within pistol shot, to such a tremendous fire, he had not a Man hurt, which can only be attributed to the judicious management of the Vessel under his command. The Locust is going to Sheerness to repair, being much damaged in her hull and rigging.

28. The Imperial Boulogne Flotilla have again began to display their manœuvres. Yesterday about 150 of their Gun-boats, and several large Praams, made

their appearance in the outer road, practising their usual gasconading feats, but with the most especial care to be under the protection of their numerous Batteries. There appear to be nearly 2000 Vessels of different descriptions in the inner Basons and Harbour of Boulogne. L'Immortalité quitted her Station lately at midnight, with sealed orders, and which orders were so sudden, that Captain Owen was called out of bed, and the Ships on the Station ordered to supply him from their own stores with four months' provision, and every other necessary. So much good speed was used on this occasion, that l'Immortalite sailed at daybreak. The generally received opinion here is, that this Frigate is ordered to cruise in the track of the homeward-bound Spanish Galleons.

Yarmouth, March 28. Arrived from the Texel the Boadicea Frigate with 250 Men, the remaining part of the Crew of the Romney, that was wrecked. The Prisoners speak in high terms of the hospitable treatment they received. The Dutch Transports, stated to be ready for Sea, have all gone up to Amsterdam to be paid off.

Promotions and Appointments.

His Majesty has been pleased to confer on Sir Charles Middleton, Bart. Admiral of the White, and his Heirs Male, the dignity of a Baron of the United Kingdom, by the title of Baron Barham, of Barham Court and Teston, Kent; and in default of Male Issue, the title of Baronness to his Daughter, the Wife of G. N. Noel, of Exton Park, Rutland, Esquire, and of a Baron to her Heirs Male. The King has also been pleased to appoint Lord Barham to be First Lord of the Admiralty, in the room of the Right Honourable Lord Viscount Melville, resigned.

Captain Pender is appointed to command the Queen, of 98 guns.

Captain Mackenzie, of the Experiment Guard-Ship at Lymington, is appointed to the Command of the Wolf Sloop, at Portsmouth.

Lieutenant Baker is appointed to command the Winchelsea Recruiting Ship at Sheerness, in the room of Lieutenant Pope, deceased.

Captain Bradley is appointed to command the Plantagenet, of 74 guns, at Portsmouth.

The Achille, of 74 guns, which has been thoroughly repaired at Portsmouth, is ordered into Commission, and Captain King appointed to the Command.

Previous to the death of Ad. Bruix on the 19th of March, the following was the state of Appointments in the French Naval Department. The new created upstart Prince Murat had resigned that Office, and the French Fleets for the future were to be commanded by twelve Vice, and eight Rear Admirals. The latter were the Minister of Marine Decres; Gantheaume, who has the Chief Command of the Brest Fleet: Villeneuve, who commands the Toulon Fleet; Bruix, late Commander in Chief of the Channel Flotillas; Villaret Joyeuse, Captain General of Martinico; the Maritime Prefects, Thevenau, with Admirals Rosilly and Trouguet. Among the twelve Vice-Admirals are also Linois, Magon, Lacrosse, Bouvettee, Mississi, Liques, and others.

Captain Hanwell is appointed to the Majestic; Captain Loring, to the Salvador del Mundo; Captain J. Cooke, to the Bellerophon; Captain Pigot, to the Dauntless Frigate.

Rear-Admiral Thornborough to be Captain of the Channel Fleet, of which Lord Gardner has taken the Command; Captain Bradley, to the Plantagenet; Captain Pender, to the Queen, on board of which Ship Rear-Admiral Knight has hoisted his Flag, to go to Gibraltar, as Port Admiral. Captain Mackenzie, of the Experiment Troop Ship, to the Wolf Sloop.

Captain Moorsom is appointed to the Revenge, a new 74; Captain Parker, to the Stately; Captain Short, to the Porpoise, which is bound to New South Wales;

Lieutenant Sir George Keith, to command the Protector Fire Vessel; Lieutenant Dobbin, to the Royal Hospital at Haslar, in the room of Lieutenant Williams, who is appointed to Greenwich Hospital.

Dr. Charles Ker, Inspector of Hospitals, by his late appointment, takes his passage to Barbadoes.

BIRTHS.

March 25. At Southampton, the Lady of Captain Seward, of the Navy, of a Daughter.

April 26. At Yarmouth, the Lady of Lieutenant Champion, of the Royal Navy, of a Daughter.

At his house in York-place, the Lady of Sir Home Popham, of a Son.

MARRIAGES.

March 28. At Sandwich, Kent, Captain Thomas Harvey, of the Royal Navy, second Son of Admiral Sir Henry Harvey, K. B., to Miss Sarah Harvey, Daughter of the late Captain John Harvey, who so gloriously fell in the ever memorable Action of the 1st June.

At Lymington, Hants, James Monro, Esq. to Miss Samber, only Daughter of James Samber, Esq. Captain in the Royal Navy.

At St. George's, Hanover Square, Augustus Hamilton, Esq. Son of Vice-Admiral Hamilton, to Miss Hyde, Daughter of the late Judge Hyde.

Captain Croft, of the Navy, to Miss Plumer, of Bilton.

April 4. At St. George's Church, Hanover Square, Captain Henry Waring, of the Royal Navy, and late Commander of his Majesty's Ship Serapis, at the capture of Surinam, to Miss Margaret Franks, only Daughter of John Henry Franks, Esq. of Misleton, in the County of Leicester.

OBITUARY.

Sept. 17. At Prince of Wales's Island, Captain Delafons, of the Dasher.

March 15. At Bath, Mrs. Bertie, Wife of Rear-Admiral Bertie.

19. At his house in Paris, Admiral Bruix, late Commander of the Boulogne Flotilla.

Of a wound he received from a cannon-ball, in cutting a French Prize out of Harbour in the East Indies, Mr. Z. Betty, Son to the late Mr. Z. Betty, Apothecary-General to his Majesty's Forces in the West Indies, and Nephew to Mr. H. W. Betty, Father of the Young Roscius.

A letter from Weymouth, of March 21, says, "The body of poor Captain Wordsworth, of the Abergavenny, was last night taken up here; and, on being identified, sent to Wyke to be buried. The hull of the Vessel is not yet broken up; but nine bodies have just floated ashore on the beach above the turnpike, where they lie till means can be taken for their interment, which will be tonight.

We are concerned to state the following melancholy event:—Lieutenant J. E. Baker, who had lately been appointed to the Winchelsea at the Nore, endeavouring to join his Ship from New South End, Essex, was unfortunately upset in a Jollyboat belonging to the Terror, (Repeating Signal Ship,) when himself, Mr. Day, Gunner; Edward Hughes, Robert Oakyey, R. M. Mr. Grikand, Thomas Ralph, Seamen, all belonging to the Terror, and a person supposed to be Lieutenant Baker's Servant, were drowned. Lieutenant Baker was an Officer very highly respected, and had lost a leg in the service of his Country.

Homeward-bound, Lieutenant John Ashlington, of his Majesty's Ship Serapis.

A short time since, at Barbadoes, Captain Paul, of the Pheasant Sloop; a young Officer who several times proved himself a spirited and good Officer

Lloyd's Marine List

OF

SHIPS LOST, DESTROYED, CAPTURED, AND RECAPTURED, &c.

FROM DECEMBER 4, TO DECEMBER 21, 1804.

THE Hambro Packet, Steadman; and the General Wayne, Conklin, were on shore in the Eyder, 28th November, but expected to be got off.

The Supply, Ham, of and from Sunderland, bound to London with coals, was run down in Sea Reach 30th November. Crew saved.

The Nile, of Aberdeen, Wilson, from Dantzig to London, is supposed to be lost off the Humber, and all the Crew.

The Anna Cat'arina, Sczwetz; and the Johannes der Tauffer, Borcherding, both from Riga to Varel, are lost; the former upon Schelling, and the latter on Heligoland. Crews saved.

The Union, Harrow, from Petersburg to London, that was on shore near Grimsby, is got off and gone to Hull to be repaired.

The George, Dunn, from Sunderland to London, is on shore near Grim by, but expected to be got off.

The Olive, Barnes, from Ipswich to Exeter, sailed from Harwich the 2d November, and has not since been heard of.

The Morning Star, ———, is sunk at the North Bull, in going into Dublin Harbour. Crew saved by the Life Boat.

The George, Mearn, from London to Leith, was captured 20th November by a French Privateer.

The Fame, Minnett, from Peterburg to Hull, retaken, is arrived at Burntisland, near Leith.

The Mary Ann, Wardropper, from Wyburg to Liverpool, is wrecked in the Orkneys. Crew saved.

The Amphion, Blanchard, from Dort to Cadiz, is detained by the Pluto Sloop, and sent into Cowe.

The Sir Edward Hughe, being leaky, sailed from Madras the 19th June for Bombay, to be docked.

The Pelican, Broad, from Smyrna to London, taken and carried into Sfax, near Tunis, has been retaken on a voyage from thence to Constantinople, and sent for Malta.

The Samuel and Jane, Blackburn, from Quebec, arrived in the Downs, sailed with the Fleet 28th October, and parted in the Gulf.

The Express, ———, from Belfast to Bristol, was taken off the Saltees 26th ult. by a French Privateer, which also captured three other Brigs.

The Sibella, Barton, from London to Barbadoes, put into Cork the 3d instant rather leaky.

The Morning Star, Hudson, which sunk on the North Bull, Dublin, is got off.

The Onderneeming, Jansen, from Bilboa, was wrecked near Helvoet 22d ult.

The Adler, Hanson, from Norway to Galway, is on shore near Limerick, but expected to be got off with damage.

The Robert and Sarah, Fairfoot, from Riga, was lost on Dumness 24th October. Cargo expected to be saved.

The George, Simpson, of and from Greenock, from New York, is taken by a French Privateer, and carried into Guadaloupe.

The Annowan, Briggs, from Liverpool to Philadelphia, is put into New York with much damage.

The Fortune, Mone, from Embden to Philadelphia, upset in the Delaware.

The Germani, ———, from Cadiz, is detained by the Phoenix Frigate, and arrived at Plymouth.

The Spanish Ship Echo, from Petersburg; and the Hoffnung, from Bourdeaux, are detained and sent into Plymouth.

The Juno, Baxton, from London to Antigua, is taken by a Privateer off St. Kitt's.

The Jane, Davis, from Cardiff to London, is put into Dartmouth, with damage, and will be obliged to unload.

The Thomas, Scott, from the Havana; and the Sparrow, Wheatley, from New Orleans, both bound to Liverpool, are put into Charleston, leaky.

The Friendship, Simkin, from St. Kitt's to London, foundered at Sea. People saved, and arrived at St. Ive's, in the Gute Hanna, from Antigua.

The James, Lutter, from Jamaica to Bristol; the Benjamin and Elizabeth, Gibbs, and the Flora, of Whitehaven, from Jamaica to London, were taken in August by the Flubister Privateer. The former is carried into Guadaloupe, and the latter are sent for that Island.

The Hannah, Bartlett, from Boston to Rotterdam, is put back with damage.

The British Ship General Bowman, from Nova Scotia to the West Indies; and the Nancy, from Cork, are taken and carried into Guadaloupe.

The Industry, Dalton, of Whitby, was lost near the Humber 3d inst. Crew saved.

The Martha, Russell, from Oporto to Waterford, put into Lisbon 22d ult.

The Anna Bella, from Jamaica, is on shore near Liverpool, and has seven feet water in the hold.

A French Lugger Privateer, belonging to Calais, of 16 guns and 77 men, is taken by the Favorite Sloop of War, and arrived at Dover.

The Alert, Salter, from the Current Islands to London, is put into Malta with damage, and must unload to repair.

The William and Henry, Burn, from Stockholm to London, has put into Swederland with loss of anchors and cables, and masts and rigging cut away.

The Ant, Rowles, from Bristol to Barbadoes, is taken and carried into Guadaloupe.

A Privateer, formerly the Duke of Kent Packet, is captured by the Barbadoes, and carried into Barbadoes.

The John, Metchinson, from Stockholm to Hull, was taken by a Privateer off the Dogger Bank, 2d December, and carried into Helvoet the next day.

The Brig Rover, from Jamaica to Halifax, was taken off Cape Antonio 11th October by two Privateers.

The Dædalus, ———, from Hull to Konigsburg, is stranded near Konigsburg.

The Ranger, Orton, from London, is on shore on the Swine Bottoms.

The Henrietta, Ross; and the Roweliffe, Aubden, from Honduras to London, were spoken with in the Gulf, by the Active, arrived at Halifax from Jamaica.

The Isabella, Livingston, from Wilmington to Greenock, was totally lost on 14th October near Cape Fear. Crew saved.

The Rover Transport, of Hull, was lost at Plymouth in the night of the 12th instant. Three of the Crew drowned.

The Elizabeth, Glofs, of Aberdeen, was totally lost on Memel Bar 12th ult. Crew saved.

The Catherine, Williamson, from Dantzig, foundered 23d ult. off Bornholm. Crew saved.

The Flora, Beldoem, is lost at St. Michael's.

The Ann, Williams; and the Adriana, Seddon, from Africa to the West Indies; are taken and carried into Guadaloupe.

The Defiance, Mudge, bound to Oporto, is stranded near Quebec.

The Nelly, Stewart, from Yarmouth to Gibraltar, drove on shore on the North Sand Head, Downs, yesterday, and overset. Crew saved.

The Brothers, Jones, from Drogheda to Liverpool, is sunk near Beaumaris.

The Portuguese Ship Ceylām, de Faren, from Lisbon to New York, having sprung a leak, was deserted by the Crew on the 27th October.—They were taken up by the Sloop Sea Horse, from New Bedford, and arrived at New York 9th November.

The New Concord, Light Collier, of Sunderland, has been taken, retaken, and arrived at Dover 13th Dec.

An embargo was laid yesterday on Vessels of every description bound to Spanish Ports.

The Two Brothers, Anderson, from Liverpool to Pictow, is lost near Cape Breton. Crew saved.

[*To be continued.*]

Engraved by RIDLEY from a drawing by T. MAYNARD
From an Original Picture Painted in Malta

SIR RICHARD BICKERTON BAR.^T

Rear Admiral of the White

Pub.^d by I Gold 103 Shoe Lane June 1 1805

BIOGRAPHICAL MEMOIR OF
SIR RICHARD BICKERTON, Bart. and K.C.
REAR-ADMIRAL OF THE RED SQUADRON.

" Hereditary worth adorns his brow."
Anon.

SIR Richard Bickerton, the Father of the Gentleman whose professional life we are about to trace, was an Officer of distinguished merit in the British Navy At a future period, we indulge the hope of being enabled to present a detailed account of his services; but, for the present, we shall content ourselves with exhibiting a brief sketch, by way of introducing the Naval Career of his Son to public notice.

Mr. Bickerton, the late Admiral, having been educated at Westminster School, entered into the Royal Navy, and received his Commission as Lieutenant in the month of February, 1745-6. In 1759 he was rated Post in the Culloden, and immediately afterwards sailed for the West Indies, in the Glasgow, of 20 guns. Having displayed much activity and gallantry in that quarter, he returned to Europe in 1761, and served for some time on the Home Station. In 1767 he again proceeded to the West Indies, in the Renown, a Fifth Rate; but quitting that Ship before the conclusion of the following year, he remained unemployed till the end of the year 1770, when, on the apprehended rupture with Spain, he was appointed to the Marlborough, of 74 guns, in which he remained for three years.

When the King reviewed the Fleet at Portsmouth, in 1773, Captain Bickerton had the honour of steering His Majesty's Barge, on which occasion he received the honour of Knighthood on board of the Barfleur.

On quitting the Marlborough, Sir Richard was appointed to the Augusta Yacht, in which he continued till the year 1777; when, the dispute with America having commenced, he was nominated to the Terrible, of 74 guns, in which Ship he was present at the encounter which took place with le Comte d'Orvilliers, off Ushant, on the 27th of July. In the May preceding, when the second Naval Review took place, Sir Richard was raised to the dignity of a Baronet of Great Britain. In the month of April, 1778, having been ordered on a Cruise in the Bay, in company with the Ramillies, he fell in with a French Convoy of thirty Sail of Merchantmen, of which eight or more became their Prize; and the rest were so completely dispersed, that several of them were afterwards picked up by different Cruisers and Privateers.

Sir Richard continued in the Terrible till the end of the year; when, that Ship being under orders for the West Indies, he quitted her, and was appointed to the Fortitude, of the same force, in the Channel Fleet. In the Spring of 1781, he accompanied Vice-Admiral Darby on his Expedition for the Relief of Gibraltar. On his return to England, the Fortitude having been nominated as the Flag-ship of Vice-Admiral Hyde Parker, Sir Richard left her; and in the month of August following, in consequence of His Majesty's intention to visit the North Sea Squadron at the Nore, he was re-appointed to the Augusta. Before the end of the year he hoisted his Broad Pendant, as an established Commodore, on board of the Gibraltar, of 80 guns. In February, 1782, he sailed with the Convoy for India, with a considerable Force, and joined Sir Edward Hughes there, just in time to share in the Encounter which took place with Suffrein on the 20th of June 1783. In the year 1784 he returned to England, and early in 1786 was appointed Commodore on the Leeward Island Station, where he hoisted his Broad Pendant on board of the Jupiter; but on account of bad health resigned, when Commodore Parker succeeded him. In September 1787, he was promoted to be Rear-Admiral of the Blue. At the time of the Armament against Spain, in 1790, he hoisted his Flag on board of the Impregnable, in the Channel Fleet; and, after that threatening Storm had blown over, he was appointed Port Admiral at Plymouth; in consequence of which he removed his Flag into the St. George. Unfortunately he did not long enjoy this Command, as, to the deep regret of his Family and Friends, he was unexpectedly carried off by an apoplectic fit, on the 28th of February, 1792*.

We have thus, without comment, exhibited a rapid sketch of the late Sir Richard Bickerton's Professional Career, in which he repeatedly distinguished himself in a very eminent manner, nobly earning the honours which his Sovereign as liberally bestowed on him, and which he has transmitted, unsullied, to his Son.

In the year 1758 the late Sir Richard Bickerton married Miss Hussey, the Daughter of Mr. Thomas Hussey, of Wrexham; by whom he had four Sons and two Daughters; the eldest of whom, and only surviving Son, the present Admiral, has succeeded to his Title and Estates.

It is not surprising that, with so splendid an example before him, an aspiring Youth should fix upon the Navy for his Profession, as the path to glory and honour. The Subject of this Memoir made an early choice; and in the year 1774, he entered into the Service of his Country, on board of the Medway, bearing the Flag of Vice-Admiral Man, who was at that period appointed to command in the Mediterranean. He continued in the Medway two years †; at the expiration of which, Admiral Man removed him to the Enterprise Frigate, of 28 guns ‡, in

---

* At the period of his decease he held the rank of Vice-Admiral of the Blue Squadron, and was Representative in Parliament for the City of Rochester.

† The routine of his employment on this Station must, we conceive, have been rather of a monotonous nature. It was in the time of Peace; and the Force which was under the Command of Admiral Man was, as is usual at such a period, extremely insignificant. That Officer, however, had sufficient address to render himself highly respected, as well by the Spaniards as by the different Barbary States, notwithstanding two or three little disputes occurred, which required a considerable share of firmness and management on his part, to enable him to maintain his proper consequence.

‡ Commanded by Sir Thomas Rich. Of this Gentleman the following anecdote records an instance of very spirited conduct, which does him great credit:—On the 25th of July, 1776, being in the Bay of Biscay, he fell in with a French Squadron, consisting of two Ships of the Line, and several Frigates, under the Command of the Duke de Chartres. The Enterprise stood on her course, and passed within hail of the French Admiral, who hailed, and desired the Commodore of the British Frigate to bring to, and come on board. Sir Thomas Rich replied, that if the Admiral had any thing to communicate, he might send on board the Enterprise. The French Admiral, enraged at this refusal, declared, that unless his orders were obeyed he would fire into the Frigate. This threat had no effect on Sir Thomas Rich, who continued firm in his resolution, and told him,

order that he might see, and be accustomed to, more active service. He there acted as Mate; and his conduct was so highly approved by his Captain, that he recommended him for Promotion, and sent him home in the Invincible, Captain Parker *, who made him acting Lieutenant.

It may perhaps appear somewhat extraordinary, that the first intelligence of hostility, on the part of the French, in the year 1776, should be communicated by a Youth : this however was the fact, Mr. Bickerton being the bearer thereof; a circumstance which his Father thought proper to communicate to the First Lord of the Admiralty †. Sir Thomas Rich's dispatches did not arrive until some weeks after.

In December, 1777, Mr. Bickerton was made Lieutenant, and appointed to the Prince George, Captain Middleton ‡, who afterwards took the Command of the Jupiter, of 50 guns. When that Officer resigned the latter Ship, on being made Comptroller of the Navy, he exerted his interest in favour of Mr. Bickerton being made First Lieutenant of her, under Captain Reynolds , who succeeded him in the Command. The subsequent Engagement of the Jupiter with the Triton, a French Line-of-Battle Ship, is yet fresh in the memory of many of our Readers, and will ever be considered as a brilliant Naval Action.

It was on the 20th of October, 1778, that the Jupiter, being on a Cruise in the Bay, in company with the Medea Frigate, Captain Montagu, fell in with the Triton. At five P.M. the Jupiter brought her to close Action, in which she was joined by

---

that he obeyed no orders but those which came from his own Admiral. The spirited conduct of the British Commander so pleased the Duke de Chartres, that he changed his demand into a request; upon which all animosity ceased, and the First Lieutenant of the Enterprise was sent on board, where he was received by the French Admiral, and all his Officers, with much respect.

* The late unfortunate Sir Hyde Parker, who, in October 1782, sailed in the Cato for the East Indies, but was never heard of after he had passed the Cape of Hood Hope.

† The Earl of Sandwich.

‡ Afterwards Sir Charles Middleton, and now Lord Barham, First Lord of the Admiralty.

ǁ Afterwards Lord Ducie.

the Medea; but, unfortunately at the commencement of the Engagement, a thirty-six pound shot entered the bow of the latter, under water, and compelled her to bring to, for the purpose of stopping the leak. The Medea was unable to take any farther share in the Conflict, and was ultimately under the necessity of bearing away for Lisbon. Captain Reynolds, however, continued the Engagement with great bravery till eight o'clock, when the Triton made sail and bore away for Ferrol; where it was reported that she arrived, with the loss of her Captain, and two hundred Men killed and wounded. The gallantry of Captain Reynolds and his Officers was greatly enhanced by the circumstance of the Frigate having been totally prevented from affording him any assistance*. After the Action, the Jupiter put into Lisbon to refit.

On the return of Captain Reynolds to England, he made a point of recommending all his Officers, and obtained the rank of Master and Commander for his First Lieutenant; a sufficient proof of the able and proper manner in which that Gentleman had conducted himself.

On the 19th of March, 1779, Captain Bickerton was accordingly appointed to the Swallow Sloop, and stationed in the Channel, where his chief employment was that of convoying the trade to the Downs.

This was the memorable year, in which, by some unaccountable event, the combined Fleets, consisting of sixty-six Sail of the Line, escaped the notice of the British Fleet, then cruising in the Soundings, entered the Channel, and paraded during two or three days before Plymouth. Captain Bickerton, however, was so fortunate as to elude this hostile Force; and, by dispersing his Charge, they all reached their destined Ports.

During the time that he was employed on this Station, the

---

* Considerable fears were for some time entertained in England for the safety of the Jupiter. Many fictitious letters, said to have been written by persons belonging to her, were inserted in many of the prints of the time, stating, among other falsehoods, that Captain Reynolds had surrendered, and was carried into Brest. Calumny at length met with its refutation.

Swallow, in company with another Sloop, commanded by Captain Inglefield, captured the Black Prince, a large American Privateer, which had committed great devastations upon our trade. The eagerness of our young Officer to engage led him so near the enemy, that they could use only small arms and cold shot. Captain Bickerton's ardour, however, had nearly cost him dear; for the Captain of the Privateer aimed a pistol at him, which, had it not been perceived by Mr. (afterwards Captain) Arden, a Midshipman, would in all probability have terminated his existence. That Gentleman fired, and, wounding the American, averted the intended shot. The Ship afterwards struck.

At the close of the year, Commodore Fielding, with a Squadron under his Command, put to Sea from St. Helens, for the purpose of intercepting a Dutch Merchant Fleet, and its Convoy, reported to be laden with Naval Stores, bound to some of the enemy's Ports. The Commodore employed Captain Bickerton to assist him in detaining such Dutch Ships as might fall in his way, and expressed himself highly pleased with his vigilance in the Service*.

Towards the end of the year 1780, the Swallow was ordered to proceed, under Sir Samuel (afterwards Lord) Hood, to the West †

---

* On the second of January, 1780, Commodore Fielding's Squadron fell in with the Dutch Convoy, a little to the westward of the Isle of Wight, escorted by two Sail of the Line and two Frigates, commanded by Admiral Count Byland. The Commodore desired that he might be allowed to examine the Merchant Vessels, which the Dutch Admiral persisted in refusing, and fired at the Boats which had been sent to board them; to resent which insult the Commodore ordered a shot to be directed a-head of the Admiral, who instantly discharged a broadside into the Namur (the Commodore's Ship), and upon her returning it, struck his Colours. Seven of the Merchant Vessels, laden with Naval Stores, were detained; and Count Byland was given to understand, that he was at liberty to hoist his Colours and prosecute his Voyage with the remainder of his Convoy. The Dutch Admiral accepted the former part of the proposal, and saluted the British Flag, but declined proceeding without the whole of his Charge, and sailed into Spithead. From the darkness of the night, many of the Transports with Stores escaped and got safe into Brest.

† On the 2d of December, 1780, Rear-Admiral Sir Samuel Hood sailed from Spithead, with a Squadron of Ships of War, for the Relief of Sir George Rodney, having under his Convoy the Trade bound to the West Indies. Not long after the Fleet was overtaken by a violent gale of Wind, which scattered the Convoy, and disabled both Ships of War and Merchantmen.

Indies; and, in the Spring of 1781, Captain Bickerton was at the taking of St. Eustatius.*

Sir George Rodney made Captain Bickerton Post in the Gibraltar, of 80 guns, but afterwards gave him the Invincible, of 74. In the latter Ship he was in the Action off Martinico, under Sir Samuel Hood, on the 29th of April, 1781†. The result of the Action is well known. It was a drawn Battle, between the British and French Fleets, notwithstanding the great disparity of Force on the part of the former‡. The Invincible had two Men killed and four wounded: the total Loss, on the part of the English, was forty-one killed and a hundred and thirty wounded.

Sir Samuel Hood's opinion of this Engagement, and of the conduct of his Officers and Men, may be well collected from the following concluding passage of his official account of the transaction :—

" I think it very much my duty to say, that the zeal and exertion of Rear-Admiral Drake, and of the Captains, Officers, and Men I had the honour to command, were such, that if Monsieur de Grasse had thought fit to have brought His Majesty's Squadron to close Action, and it should have pleased God to have given him the Victory, I trust he would not have found it an easy one, great as the superiority of the enemy was against us."

Captain Bickerton afterwards commanded the Russel, and the Terrible, both 74's; but, finding the latter unfit for service, he exchanged into the Amazon, and was ordered Home. The Amazon was paid off in the month of February, 1782.

---

* *Vide* NAVAL CHRONICLE, Vol. I, p. 384. The Mars, a fine Dutch Frigate, of 38 guns and 300 Men, commanded by Count Byland, and five other Vessels of War, from 14 to 26 guns, all ready for Sea, were taken in the Road, together with upwards of 180 Sail of Merchantmen, many of them richly laden.

† *Vide* NAVAL CHRONICLE, Vol. II, p. 8.

‡ The total number of Ships, Guns, and Men, of the respective Fleets, was as follows :—

	Ships.	Guns.	Men.
British	18	1320	10680
French	26	1784	16850
	8	464	6170 Superiority on the part of the French.

In September following he was appointed to the Brune Frigate, which, in consequence of the Peace, was, in 1783, put out of Commission.

For the first time since he had entered the Service, Captain Bickerton now enjoyed a period of relaxation from the fatigues of duty. He was not called upon again till the month of January, 1787, when he was appointed to the Sybil Frigate, and ordered to the West Indies. On that Station he remained until the year 1790, when he brought Home the West India Fleet; but, as a general Peace then prevailed throughout Europe, he was not concerned in any transaction immediately deserving of record.

In 1793 War having commenced between Great Britain and France, Sir Richard Bickerton* commanded the Ruby, of 64 guns, on detached service; and in 1794 he was appointed to the Ramillies, of 74 guns, which, on the 3d of September, sailed with Lord Howe's Squadron, to cruise in the Bay. On that Station the Squadron remained during the whole of the Winter, returning occasionally to Spithead, Torbay, and Plymouth, to refit and water.

In 1795 the Ramillies carried General Sir John Vaughan to the West Indies. Sir Richard then went down to Jamaica with a Convoy, thence proceeded to Newfoundland, and returned Home in 1796, when he joined the Channel Fleet under Lord Bridport. In 1797 he was appointed to the Terrible, the Command of which he resigned in the month of February, 1799, on being promoted to the rank of Rear-Admiral of the Blue †.

During the time, however, that Sir Richard commanded the Terrible, that Ship had a chase of fifty hours of the French Ships which formed part of the Squadron that was taken by Sir John Borlase Warren. When just up with them, her Commander had the mortification to witness the springing of her mast; and when she reached Portsmouth she was almost a Wreck.

---

* His Father, the late Sir Richard Bickerton, as we have before stated, died on the 25th of February, in the preceding year.

† This Promotion took place on the 14th of the month.

In the month of September, 1799, Admiral Bickerton was made Second in Command, as Port Admiral at Portsmouth; and such was his vigilance while in this situation, that to him must be ascribed the speedy Equipment of a number of Troop-ships which were then fitting for a Secret Expedition.

On the 13th of May following, Sir Richard went out in the Seahorse *, to the Swiftsure, under Lord Keith, in the Mediterranean.

Lord Keith's Fleet was, at this period, exceedingly numerous and powerful. Sir Richard joined him in the month of June; and soon after was sent by his Lordship to command the Blockade of Cadiz, with the following detached Squadron:—

Ships.	Guns.	Commanders.
Swiftsure	74	Rear-Admiral Sir R. Bickerton, Bart. Captain B. Hallowell.
Kent	74	—— W. Hope.
Dragon	74	—— George Campbell.
Hector	74	—— John Elphinstone.
Phœnix	36	—— L. W. Halsted.
Emerald	36	—— T. M. Waller.

Shortly after his arrival off Cadiz, he found it requisite to send a Notice to the Consuls of Neutral Nations residing in that City, apprising them of the instructions which he had received to enforce the Blockade with the greatest rigour †.

It having been determined, in the course of the Summer, that a grand Attack should be made upon Cadiz, about the middle of September Lord Keith collected his Fleet at Gibraltar, accompanied by several Transports, having on board upwards of 10,000 Troops commanded by General Sir Ralph Abercrombie. At Gibraltar this Armament was joined by other Transports with Troops, under Sir James Pulteney, the whole amounting to between 18,000 and 20,000 Men.

The Fleet and Transports, having sailed from Gibraltar, anchored between Tetuan and Ceuta; and on the 3d of Octo-

---

* Commanded by Captain Edward James Foote, and taking out General Sir Ralph Abercrombie, Major-Generals Hutchinson and Moore, and the Honourable Colonel Hope.

† See NAVAL CHRONICLE, Vol. IV, page 244.

ber got under sail and passed the Straits. On the 4th they entered the Bay of Cadiz, and anchored between it and St. Pietri, in Force as follows:—

Ships.	Guns.	Commanders.
Foudroyant	80	{ Vice-Admiral Lord Keith. { Captain Thomas Stevenson.
Ajax	80	—— Hon. A. Cochrane.
Gibraltar	80	—— W. H. Kelly.
Swiftsure	74	{ Rear-Admiral Sir R. Bickerton. { Captain B. Hallowell.
Kent	74	—— W. Hope.
Audacious	74	—— D. Gould.
Hector	74	—— J. Elphinstone.

In addition to the above were several Frigates, Sloops, armed Transports, and other small Vessels of force.

Arrangements were immediately made for the landing of the Troops, in order to proceed to the Attack of the Town of Cadiz, and the Forts in its vicinity.

A violent epidemic disease at this time raging in Cadiz, the Governor represented the miserable situation of its Inhabitants to the General and Admiral, which was communicated to them by a Flag of Truce*.

It is probable that, had the attempt been made at an earlier period, the Capture of Cadiz would have been effected; but, had such a Service been performed now, when a dreadful contagion was ravaging the City, the consequences to the Captors might have been more dreadful than their Victory could be important. In consequence, therefore, of the above correspondence, it was considered proper, by the Admiral and General, that the Expedition should be relinquished. The Troops, which were already in the Boats, were ordered back to their respective Transports, and the Fleet sailed for Gibraltar; where, on the 16th of October, it experienced a heavy gale of Wind, but fortunately without sustaining any other mischief than the loss of a few anchors and cables, top-masts, &c.

Having blockaded the Port of Cadiz for five months, Sir Richard Bickerton now proceeded with Lord Keith to Alex-

---

* See NAVAL CHRONICLE, Vol. IV, pages 426, 427.

andria, which Port he continued to blockade until it surrendered to the British Arms.

The following is a List of the English Fleet at Alexandria in the Spring of 1801:—

Ships.	Guns.	Commanders.
Foudroyant	80	Admiral Lord Keith. 1st Captain, J. E. Elphinstone. 2d Captain, J. C. Searle.
Ajax	80	Captain Hon. A. Cochrane.
Tigre	80	—— Sir W. S. Smith.
Swiftsure	74	Rear-Adm. Sir R. Bickerton, Bart. Captain B. Hallowell.
Kent	74	—— W. Hope.
Minotaur	74	—— T. Louis.
Northumberland	74	—— George Martin.
Flora	36	—— B. G. Middleton.

SHIPS ARMED EN FLUTE.

Dictator	64	Captain J. Hardy.
Stately	64	—— George Scott.
Europa	50	—— J. Stevenson.
Trusty	50	—— A. Wilson.
Expedition	44	—— T. Wilson.
Charon	44	—— Richard Bridges.
Dolphin	44	—— J. Dalrymple.
Regulus	44	—— T. Pressland.
Renommée	44	—— P. M'Kellar.
Thetis	38	—— H. E. R. Baker.
Hebe	38	—— George Reynolds.
Inconstant	36	—— J. Ayscough.
Romulus	36	—— J. Culverhouse.
Iphigenia	32	—— H. Stackpole.
Astrea	32	—— R. Ribolieu.
Eurus	32	—— D. O. Guion.
Heroine	32	—— J. Hill.
Dido	28	—— D. Colby.
Alligator	28	—— G. Bowen.
Cyclops	28	—— J. Fyffe.
Resource	28	—— J. Crisps.
Thisbe	28	—— J. Morrison
Vesta	28	—— V. Collard.

In the month of June Sir Richard Bickerton shifted his Flag into the Kent.

Subsequent to the Action which took place after the Surrender of Aboukir, in which the brave Abercrombie was mortally wounded, the Reduction of Alexandria became the grand object. Accordingly, the Town was closely blockaded by Admiral Bickerton, whilst the Army under General Hutchinson cut off all communication on the land side.

The position of the enemy's Flotilla on the side of the Lake Mareotis having been examined by Lord Keith, who was of opinion that it could easily be subdued, and that a debarkation could be effected without much difficulty, General Hutchinson determined to carry the measure into immediate effect. To secure the landing from interruption, Captain Stevenson, of the Europa, who commanded the British Flotilla, was directed to take a Station in front of the Enemy's gun and armed Boats, which were drawn up in a line, under the protection of the Batteries that had been thrown up for their defence, and to keep them in check until they could be seized or destroyed.

On the night of the 16th of August, a strong Body of Troops, under the Command of Major-General Coote, was embarked, and landed the next morning without opposition, under the superintendance of Captain Elphinstone. Whilst the landing was effecting, Sir Sidney Smith was directed to make a demonstration of attack upon the Town of Alexandria, with some Sloops of War and armed Boats. The enemy, seeing no prospect left of saving their Flotilla, set fire to them; and with the exception of two or three which were taken, blew them up. In the mean time, two spirited Attacks were successfully made on the east side of the Town, by Detachments from the Army under the Major-Generals Craddock and Moore.

On the evening of the 21st, the small fortified Town of Morabout, which protected the Harbour of Alexandria on the western side, at the distance of seven or eight miles, surrendered to Major-General Coote, who was very ably supported on this Service by the armed Launches from Sir Richard Bickerton's Squadron*.

---

* In performing this Service, Mr. Hill, Midshipman, and one Seaman of the Ajax, were killed; and two Seamen of the Northumberland were wounded.

On the same afternoon, Sir Richard ordered four Sloops of War*, with three Turkish Corvettes, to proceed into the Harbour, under the direction of the Hon. Captain Cochrane, of the Ajax, (a Channel having been previously surveyed with great industry and precision, by Lieutenant Withers, of the Kent); and on the morning of the 22d, Major-General Coote's Detachment moved forward four or five Miles on the narrow Isthmus leading to the Town, formed by the Mareotis, or Inundation on the south side, and the Harbour on the north; Capt. Stevenson, with the Gun-vessels, on the Lake, covering the right flank; and Captain Cochrane, with the Sloops of War and armed Boats, the left.

On the approach of the British Ships the Enemy sunk several Vessels between them and their own Ships, with the view of obstructing their farther progress to the eastward, and moved their Frigates and Corvettes close up to the Town. Major-General Coote, with his Detachment, marched on with the greatest success, carrying all the strong Posts of the Enemy, who retreated in the greatest confusion, leaving behind them their cannon and wounded Comrades. By the 26th, the Town was completely invested. On the morning of that day four Batteries were opened on each side of the Town against the Enemy's entrenched Camp, which soon silenced their fire, and induced them to withdraw their guns.

On the morning of the 27th, General Menou sent an *Aid-de-camp* to General Hutchinson, to request an Armistice for three days, in order to give time to prepare a Capitulation, which was granted, and that instrument was signed on the 2d of September †.

Thus terminated an Expedition, which reflected the highest honour on our Naval and Military Prowess; and which afforded

---

* The Cynthia, Port Mahon, Victorieuse, and Bonne Citoyenne; which were afterwards joined by la Diane.

† For the official details, relative to the Attack and Surrender of Alexandria, vide NAVAL CHRONICLE, Vol. VI, pages 323, 405, and 409.

another illustrious proof, that no climate, howsoever uncongenial to their frames, could repress the daring ardour and collected courage of Britons.

Lord Keith and Lieutenant-General Hutchinson, in their Public Dispatches, speak in the most honourable terms of the vigilance, activity, and judicious conduct, of all the Sea Officers who were employed to co-operate with the Army on this Expedition; and Lord Keith, in his Letter to the Admiralty of the 2d of September, bears the following liberal testimony to the merits of Admiral Bickerton, and the Officers who were immediately under his Command:—" The Captains and Commanders of the Ships appointed for guarding the Port, have executed that tedious and anxious duty with diligence and success. During my absence from the Squadron, the Blockade has been conducted much to my satisfaction by Rear-Admiral Sir Richard Bickerton."

The Nation was not unmindful of the gallant Exploits of its Heroes; for, on the 12th of November, the Thanks of both Houses of Parliament were voted to the respective Commanders, and to the Officers and Men who acted under them.

On the news of Peace arriving in Egypt, Lord Keith returned to England, leaving Sir Richard Bickerton at Alexandria as Commander in Chief. He consequently had the care of superintending the Embarkation of the French Army; and the celerity with which that business was conducted obtained for him the acknowledgments of General Menou, accompanied by the flattering compliment from that Officer, that *the vigilance of his Squadron had accelerated the Reduction of Alexandria, as it cut them off from all supply.*

During the Admiral's stay in Egypt, he had the honour of being invested, by the Captain Pacha, with the Imperial Ottoman Order of the Crescent*.

---

* This took place on the 8th of October, on the spot where the Battle of the 21st of August, which decided the fate of Egypt, was fought. For a full Account of the Ceremony, *vide* NAVAL CHRONICLE, Vol. VII, page 353.

The Peace, or, as it has more aptly been termed by some, *the hollow armed Truce*, which succeeded the last long-protracted Contest, scarcely allowed our Officer a breathing time from the toils of Service, as he has again been called to exercise the duties of his Profession.

On the 23d of April, 1804, Sir Richard Bickerton was made Rear-Admiral of the Red Squadron, and, we believe, about the same time he hoisted his Flag on board of the Royal Sovereign, as Second in Command in the Mediterranean.

On this Station he has remained ever since, without any opportunity of particularly distinguishing himself; but, from the present aspect of affairs in that quarter, it is not likely that he will be much longer without adding a Wreath of new Laurels to those which he has already so industriously won.

HERALDIC PARTICULARS.

ARMS.—Sable on a Chevron Erminois three Pheons azure; on a plain Canton *Or*, another embattled of the third charged with a Star of eight Points within an Increscent *argent*, in allusion to the Badge of the Ottoman Order of the Crescent.

CREST.—A Dexter Arm in Armour embowed, the Hand grasping a Sword Proper from the Wrist, a Shield pendant by a Tawney Ribbon charged with the honourable augmentation as on the Canton in the Arms.

SUPPORTERS.—On the Dexter Side a Sailor habited and armed with a Cutlass Proper, the Exterior Hand supporting a Staff, thereon hoisted a blue Flag charged with a Pheon, and thereunder the word EGYPT *Or*,

And on the Sinister a Female Figure representing Egypt habited in a Robe flowing to the Feet, and superverted with a Tunick *argent*, the latter inscribed with hieroglyphicks: her Mantle *vert* suspended by a Band over the Right Shoulder across the Breast *Or*: upon her Head an Elevation representing three Pyramids; and in her Exterior Hand a Sistrum Gold, at her Side an Ibis Proper.

MOTTO.—PRO DEO ET REGE.

NAVAL ANECDOTES,
COMMERCIAL HINTS, RECOLLECTIONS, &c.

NANTES IN GURGITE VASTO.

FRENCH ACCOUNT OF CAPT. FRANCIS MASON'S ACTION.

THE Moniteur contains the following Official Account of the late unsuccessful Attack made at St. Valleri by the Boats of His Majesty's Ships Rattler and Folkstone, on the French Ship of War le Vimereux. We learn from the Gazette of the 22d of January, that this fine Vessel has since been captured by one of our Cruisers.

Ministry of Marine, Paris, Jan. 9.

On the 4th of the present month, the Boulogne Privateer, le Vimereux, Captain Paulet, being at anchor in the Road of St. Valleri-en-Caux, an English Vessel of War, lugger-rigged, took possession in the evening of a Fishing-boat. At midnight, this Boat, manned with twenty Men, and commanded by the Captain of the Enemy's Vessel, proceeded with two armed Launches against the Privateer, and boarded her fore and on both sides. The Crew of the Privateer were on their guard, prepared to receive them, and the deck was soon cleared of all the English that boarded. The whole Party were either killed or drowned, except eight, who remained Prisoners; amongst these are the Lieutenants of the Sloops Rattler and Folkstone, which latter had joined in the Expedition, both dangerously wounded. It is impossible to ascertain the number of the English that have perished, inasmuch as they were thrown into the Sea in the dark, according as they came aboard, or were slain. The Vimereux has but two Men killed and twelve wounded in this Action. The more roughly the Crew of the Vimereux treated the Enemy during the Engagement, the more generously they conducted themselves in their attention to the wounded after the Battle.

MERCANTILE MARINE.

WE are happy to record another gallant instance of bravery in our Mercantile Marine.

Extract of a Letter from Captain JOHN SCOTT, *of the Ship Scarborough, of London.*

Barbadoes, Jan. 27.—I am happy to inform you of the arrival of the Scarborough this morning. We were separated from the Fleet on the 25th December, the day after we sailed from the

Motherbank, the Fleet being much dispersed. The next day we fell in with His Majesty's Ship Swift, one of the Convoy, and kept with her and ten more Ships till the 5th of January, when we were all separated in a heavy gale of Wind from the W.S.W., and afterwards joined by the Dorset, Captain Newton; and King George, Captain Cotter. We all agreed to keep company to Barbadoes, and give each other mutual support. On the 26th of January (yesterday,) we fell in with a French Privateer, of 16 guns, full of Men, (by the information I have received since my arrival, not less than two hundred,) mostly people of colour, from Guadaloupe, which has done a great deal of mischief, having captured several Vessels. The only means I saw for the protection of the three Ships were to get some people from the Dorset and King George on board the Scarborough, and bring her to action, which their Commanders very handsomely complied with. I had seven Men from the Dorset and five from the King George, who all volunteered their services in a very handsome manner. At four o'clock the enemy came alongside the Scarborough, and opened a most tremendous fire of musketry and grape shot, and attempted once to board, but was repulsed, and compelled to sheer off, with a great loss of Men; I may boldly affirm, not less than seventy. I am sorry to inform you, that my first Officer, Mr. Peacock, is dangerously wounded, and I am almost afraid mortally; one of my Boys shot dead, and our hull, sails, and rigging, much cut. The Scarborough, notwithstanding, will be ready to proceed by to-morrow. I am much indebted to Mr. Joseph Wilson, of the 60th Regiment, who volunteered his service on board the Scarborough, and fought most gallantly. My people behaved well. The Action lasted for upwards of an hour. The Scarborough mounts 13 guns, and had on board 27 Men and Boys, including those from the Dorset and King George."

GALLANT ENTERPRISE.

ON Wednesday, April 3d, arrived at Whitehaven, the Shannon, of Workington, which had been captured the 24th ult. about 65 leagues to the westward of Gorée, by a Lugger Privateer, fitted out at Flushing, carrying 14 guns and 150 Men.

From the examination of Westray Curwen, the Mate of the said Ship, taken on Wednesday, the 3d of April, before the Magistrates, James Steel, Esq., and the Rev. William Harrison, Clerk, it appears that the Shannon, Thomas Osborne, Master, belonging to Workington, took in a freight at Liverpool, from which Port she sailed on the 15th of February last, for Baltimore, in Maryland; that on the 23d of the same month she was by stress of weather put into Lochindol, in Ireland; at which place she remained till the 22d of March, when she left it, and pursued her Voyage; but on the 24th she fell in with, and was captured by, a Dutch Lugger Privateer, from Flushing, called the Admiral Brisque, (more probably the Admiral Bruix,) Captain Sieves. Captain Osborne, and three of his Crew, were put on board the Privateer; and the remainder of the Crew, seven in number, were left on board the Shannon, under the Prize Master and nine Seamen, who had orders to navigate her to a Port in Holland. Of these, eight were Dutch, and two Frenchmen. The next day the Shannon's people, which consisted of the Mate, five Men, one of whom has a wooden leg, and a Boy about eleven years of age, rose upon the ten Foreigners, whom they confined in the cabin, and took possession of the deck of the Vessel, which they kept till the 29th; when, being almost exhausted through want of provisions, they made a proposal to the Frenchmen, that if they would quit the Vessel, they should be accommodated with the Yawl, to carry them on Shore in Donegal Bay, Ireland, near to which they then were. After some parleying, the eight Dutchmen consented to this offer, and accordingly, and as stipulated, passed singly through the cabin window into the Boat, and steered towards the Shore. The two Frenchmen remained on board the Shannon, which, after encountering many Storms and Dangers, arrived in Whitehaven Harbour on the 3d of April, as already mentioned. The two Frenchmen are both young Men; one aged 21, born at Ostend, and has his discharge from the Army; the other aged 23, born at Rennes, and by trade a Tailor. It might not be proper to mention the means employed by the English to recover the Vessel. Their situation altogether was a very extraordinary one. They confined the enemy, who were well armed and had plenty of provisions, in the cabin, whilst, it may be said, they themselves were *confined* to the deck, with scarcely any thing to subsist on, for so many days!

FILTERING MACHINE.

PROFESSOR PERROTT, of Paris, has invented a Filtering Machine, which purifies water by descent and ascent. It consists chiefly of a curved tube, one of whose legs is longer than the other. The tube is to be filled to a certain height with fine pure sand: the water to be purified is to be put into the longer leg; and it will of course flow out of the shorter; and in its passage through the sand the impurities will be left behind.

SINGULAR PRESERVATION.

Extract of a Letter from Dover, April 2.

THE Princess Royal Smack, laden with potatoes, arrived here this morning: on Sunday last, about three P.M., they discovered something floating on the water, and on their nearer approach found it to be a kind of flat box, something like a washing shawl, with a young Lad about fifteen years of age in it; they hoisted out their Boat and took him in, off the Spanyard Buoy: he and another Lad had got into the box at Sheerness, and the Tide had drifted them out of the Harbour; the other Lad jumped overboard, and endeavoured to swim on Shore; the one which came in here continued drifting until picked up by the above Vessel: he had been two days and two nights without any thing to eat or drink, and the box he was in was only six feet long, two feet nine inches wide, and twelve inches deep. Great praise is due to the Master of the Smack, who took every care, by administering food, &c. to him in small quantities at first, to recover him; and the Lad is now well, but uncertain of the fate of his companion.

JEAN DE ST. FAUST.

A MORNING Paper has published the following intelligence, which was communicated to the Editor in a Letter written by a Gentleman at Yarmouth, and dated the 13th April:—

Jean de St. Faust, who commanded, and was taken on board l'Honneur Schooner, by His Majesty's Sloop of War the Scorpion, Carteret, (see London Gazette, 16th April,) is the celebrated de St. Faust, who, about twelve months since, attacked His Majesty's Ship the Amethyst, and for which gallant action Buonaparté declared him a Member of the Legion of Honour. He is considered by Buonaparté as one of the most brave, able, and enterprising Officers in the French or Dutch Service. He was going to Curacoa, there to assume the Command of a Dutch Naval Force, and from thence to attack, by a *coup-de-main*, some of our possessions in the West Indies. He was also charged with very important Dispatches, which, at the time he struck, were thrown overboard, but not in time to be out of reach: they were secured, and are in the possession of Government. He attempted to disguise himself, but in vain. He quitted Paris at the beginning of the present month, and on his arrival at Delfzyel, immediately embarked, and had only left that place one day, before he fell into our hands.

SHOAL NEAR DUNGENESS.

THE subjoined account of a Survey lately taken on a dangerous Shoal near Dungeness, is inserted for the information of the Commercial Interest:—

The Floating Beacon is placed by Captain Johnstone, of His Majesty's Sloop Alert, nearly on the middle of the shoalest part of the Ridge, and the most distinct objects on the English and French Coasts have the following bearings from it by Compass; viz.

FRENCH COAST.	Deg. Min.
Mount Lambert, or Telegraph Hill, over Boulogne	S. 36 30 E.
The Signal House on Cape Griz-Nez	S. 72 00 E.
Blanc-Nez	S. 83 00 E.

ENGLISH COAST.	
South Foreland Light-House	N. 31 00 E.
Dover Castle	N. 25 00 E.
Folkstone Church	N. 3 30 E.
Dungeness Light-House	N. 52 30 W.
The West Buoy, distant 2 miles	S. 48 00 W.

The Beacon is placed in three fathoms, at low water, and about a cable and half distant from the north side of the Bank, whereon there is only 12 feet water; this small depth is on the very north brink of the Shoal; from thence to the northward the depth suddenly increases to 5, 10, and 17 fathoms.

The depth from 14 to 16 feet on the north edge of the Bank, extends about a mile and a half to the N.E. of the Beacon, and nearly the same distance to the S.W.; from thence to the termination of each end of the Shoal is from $3\frac{1}{2}$ to 7 fathoms, very irregular.

The West Buoy lays close to four fathoms; and the east end has the depth of $3\frac{1}{2}$ fathoms; but within those extremities there is more water. The length of the ridge is 9 miles, and its greatest breadth about half a mile.

The depths above mentioned were taken at low water the last Spring Tides.

AMERICAN NAVY.

THE American Squadron in the Mediterranean is reported to be very sickly; it comprised, at the date of the last accounts, five Frigates, three Brigs, two Schooners, four Bombs, and twenty Gun-boats, for another Expedition against Tripoli. Several American Sailors, taken in the Philadelphia Frigate, have turned Mussulmans, and have in consequence been released from slavery, and sent on board the Tripolitan Gun-vessels.

So rapidly do the Anglo-Americans spread over the American Continent, that in a Settlement upon the Ohio, seven hundred and forty leagues from the Sea, where, in the year 1787, only one hundred Colonists could be found, six thousand seven hundred are now established, and Docks have been formed, from which, last year, eleven Merchant Vessels were launched.

The thanks of the Congress has been decreed to Commodore Preble, for his gallant and meritorious service against Tripoli, by which the Naval Character of the American People has, says the decree, in the infancy of their national existence, acquired a respect and rank among the Nations of the Earth highly honourable and exalted. A gold medal is ordered to be struck, and it is to be presented to him by the President of the United States, in such a manner as he shall judge the most honourable. Suitable rewards are likewise ordered for the Officers and Men under his command.

SHIPS BUILDING AT ROCHFORT.

THE following Ships of the Line are building at Rochfort:— La Ville de Paris, of 120 guns; l'Achille and l'Ajax, of 74 guns; and at l'Orient, le Regulus, le Courageux, and l'Alcibe, of 74 guns: a Frigate, l'Algeziras, was lying there, on the 3d instant, ready for Sea.

PRESS GANG.

A WHIMSICAL circumstance happened lately off Gravesend. A West Indiaman arrived at that place, and was soon boarded by a Press-gang. The Crew of the West Indiaman were brought upon deck, and while the Lieutenant was examining them, a Health-boat arrived. As no clean bill of health was found on board the West Indiaman, or at least none that was deemed satisfactory, the Crew of the West Indiaman, the Lieutenant of the Man of War, and all his Gang, were ordered to Stangate Creek to perform quarantine for forty days, which they will no doubt pass in perfect harmony and good fellowship with each other.

CAPTAIN LORD COCHRANE.

THE following is another instance of the generosity of our Naval Officers and Seamen, exemplified in the recent conduct of Captain Lord Cochrane, his Officers, and Ship's Company, of the Pallas, to the Spanish Captain and Supercargo of la Fortuna, one of the rich Prizes captured among others by the Pallas in her late Cruise; which deserves to be recorded, to the honour and credit of the Royal Navy of Old England :—

The Pallas, Captain Lord Cochrane, on his late Cruise off the Coast of Spain and Portugal, fell in with and took la Fortuna, a Spanish Ship, from Rio de la Plata, to Corunna, richly laden with Specie, (Gold and Silver,) to the amount of 150,000l., and about the same sum in valuable Goods and Merchandise, in all near 300,000 dollars value. When the Spanish Captain came on board with the Supercargo, who was a Merchant and Passenger from New Spain, they appeared much dejected, as their private property on board was lost, which amounted to 30,000 dollars each person, in Specie and Goods. The Papers and Manifest of the Cargo of la Fortuna being examined, the Spaniards told Lord Cochrane that they had Families in Old Spain, and had now lost all their property, the hard earnings by commerce in the burning clime of South America, the savings of nearly 20 years, and were returning to their native Country to enjoy the fruits of their commercial speculations. The Captain in particular stated he had lost, in the War of 1779, a similar fortune, by being taken in a British Cruiser, and was forced to begin the world again. Both the Spaniards appeared to feel their forlorn situation so much, that Lord Cochrane felt for them; and with that generosity ever attendant on true bravery, consulted his Officers as to the propriety of returning each of these two Gentlemen to the value of 5000 dollars of their property, in specie, which was immediately agreed to be done, according to their respective proportions. On this his Lordship ordered the Boatswain to pipe all hands on deck, and addressed the Seamen and Royal Marines with much feeling, and in a plain seamanlike way stated the above facts.—On this the gallant Fellows, with one voice, sung out, "Aye, aye, my Lord, with all our hearts!" and gave three cheers. The Spaniards were overcome with this noble instance of the generosity of British Seamen, and actually shed tears of joy, at the prospect of once more being placed in a state of independence; they of course returned their thanks to the Captain, Lord Cochrane, his Officers and Ship's Company, for their unprecedented munificence on this occasion.

ABSTRACT OF A BILL

(AS AMENDED BY THE COMMITTEE)

For the more effectual Prevention of Smuggling.

THE Preamble of the Bill sets forth, that, in defiance of the Laws, great quantities of goods are illegally imported into the United Kingdom, as well by clandestine means as by open force, and by Gangs of daring and dissolute persons, armed and assembling to carry into execution their evil and pernicious purposes, to the great detriment of the Revenue, and the subversion of all civil authority.—It is the object of the Bill to provide some further remedy for these evils. It is therefore proposed to be enacted,

1. That any Vessel of the burthen of 200 tons, or under, belonging wholly or in part to His Majesty's Subjects, or any Vessel whereof the Master or one-third of the Crew are British Subjects, found in any part of the British or Irish Channels, or North Seas, or within 100 leagues of the Coasts of Great Britain and Ireland, having on board spirits in casks containing less than 60 gallons, or any Salt, exceeding in quantity one bushel to each Seaman (unless under certificate for curing Fish, or for exportation); or any Tea, exceeding six pounds in the whole; or any Tobacco or Snuff, in any cask or package containing less than 425lb. weight, shall be forfeited with the said Goods. Exceptions are made of articles for the use of the Crew, as Spirits at the rate of two gallons for each Seaman, and Tobacco at the rate of 5lb. for each Seaman; Tea and manufactured Tobacco, duly shipped for exportation, are also excepted.—2. That no foreign Spirits, Wine, or Tobacco, shall be imported or exported from Guernsey, Jersey, Alderney, or Sark, in Ships, Vessels, Casks, Packages, &c. of the dimensions above described, (with the before-mentioned exceptions,) under pain of forfeiture of the Vessels and Goods.—3. That any Vessel having on board Spirits, Tobacco, &c. in quantities declared illegal by the preceding clauses, and found at anchor or hovering within two leagues of the Coast of Guernsey, Jersey, or Sark, or within two miles of Alderney, (unless in case of distress of weather, illness of the Master, &c..) shall be forfeited, with her Cargo.—4. That persons on board Vessels liable to forfeiture, or assisting in unloading or concealing the Cargoes of such Vessels, shall each forfeit either 100l., or treble the value of the Goods attempted to be concealed: one half of the forfeiture to go to the Informer, or persons discovering Offenders. The Offenders to be carried before a Justice of the Peace, who must hold them to bail; but if they choose to enter into His Majesty's Service as Seamen or Marines, they may be carried before the proper Officers for that purpose.—5. That the powers of Excise and Custom-House Officers to examine Vessels under former Acts, shall be extended to all Vessels liable to forfeiture by this Act.—6. That persons assaulting or obstructing Officers of Excise, &c. shall be adjudged Felons, and be liable to transportation for seven years, or imprisonment in the House of Correction; and that persons firing at any Boat belonging to the Navy, Customs, or Excise, and persons shooting at, maiming, or

wounding any Officer of the Navy, Customs, or Excise, shall be adjudged guilty of felony, and suffer death, without benefit of Clergy.—7. That offenders under this Act may be tried in any County in England.—8. That all Spirits seized to the southward of the Frith of Forth shall be brought to London, and lodged in the King's Warehouses; that all seized on the Coasts of Scotland, or adjacent Islands, shall be carried to any Port in Scotland appointed by the Lords of the Treasury; and that the strength of the Spirits deposited shall be taken, and an account kept of the quantity.—9. That the Lords of the Treasury shall have power to order the Spirits seized to be redistilled; to deliver what quantities they think proper to the Victualling Office; and to settle the rewards to be given to the Officers or others, by whom such Spirits were seized.—10. That protections from actions and powers granted by other Acts to Custom and Excise Officers shall be extended to Officers of the Navy and Army.

These are all the enacting clauses; but it is besides provided that the Act shall not extend to French Wines imported in bottles packed in cases, or exported under bond and certificate: it is also provided, that the Commissioners of the Customs and Excise shall give rewards to Informers, Officers, &c., in cases where there is no forfeiture, in consequence of the persons liable having entered into His Majesty's Service.

MR. TROTTER.

IN 1791, by the accounts of Messrs. Coutts, set forth in the Tenth Report, the whole of the Dividends on Mr. Trotter's property in the public Funds appear to have amounted to 80l. per annum; in 1792 to 200l.; in 1793 to 457l. 10s.; 1794 to 556l. 8s.; in 1796 to have increased to 2006l. 3s.; in 1797 to 4062l. 17s.; in 1801 those dividends farther increased to 6816l. 13s. 3d., and in 1802 amounted to the sum of 11,308l. 1s.

Mr. Trotter's Funded Property, at the close of the account, appears to have consisted of

£.53,221 13 4 Consols.
17,858 7 0 India Stock.
2.142 17 2 Bank Stock.

£. 44,000 Red. 3 per Cents.
130,005 Four per Cents.
1,500 per ann. 1m. An.

SIR NATHANIEL DANCE.

WE insert with great pleasure a very handsome and splendid testimony of the commercial gratitude of Bombay, for the Services of Sir Nathaniel Dance, in the protection of the India Fleet, of which he was Commodore, in the Action with the French National Fleet under Admiral Linois, in the Marengo, off Paulo-Auor.

The liberality of the Gentlemen of Bombay, and, indeed, every part of the correspondence, on the occasion, does much honour to " him that gives and him that takes."

To DAVID SCOTT, *Esq.*, M.P., JOHN FORBES, *Esq.*, *and* PATRICK CRAUFURD BRUCE, *Esq.*, M.P., *London.*

GENTLEMEN, *Bombay, August* 1, 1804.

WE have the honour to transmit to you the enclosed Copy of certain Resolutions of a General Meeting of the Bombay Insurance Society, which was also numerously attended by Commercial People of all descriptions, held at the Office on the 13th March last, and in conformity to the unanimous wish of all concerned, to solicit your acceptance of the charge of carrying them into effect in England.

It appeared to the Meeting, that, from the well-known interest you continue to hold for the commercial prosperity of this Settlement, so long the scene of your own mercantile operations, you will prove a peculiarly appropriate and desirable medium of conveying the honorary and remunerative testimonies which the able and gallant conduct of Commodore Dance and his associate Captains has called forth from a grateful and applauding Community.

It is unnecessary to dwell on the particulars of an Exploit so glorious in itself, so honourable to those who shared in it, and so important and advantageous in its consequences, as that of so powerful a Squadron of French Men of War attacked, beaten off, and pursued in their flight, by a Fleet of British Merchant Ships: but while we have the pleasure of addressing you on a subject of such deserved exultation, we hope it may be permitted us to congratulate you on the effect which the communication of this brilliant Victory had upon the minds of those here interested in its result, and on its having produced so conspicuous and creditable a proof of their gratitude and admiration.

This Government, as a mark of their approbation of the proceeding in question, have granted a Bill on the Hon. the Court of Directors for the amount which was subscribed at the Meeting, rupees 45,500, at the favourable exchange of two shillings and sixpence per rupee, and payable nine months after date, which we have the honour to enclose for five thousand six hundred and eighty-seven pounds ten shillings, in your favour.

We are sensible that unforeseen circumstances may occur to render nugatory any minute and specific appropriation of the fund now remitted to your management, and are therefore solicitous only of expressing the wish which has unanimously prevailed here, and leaving it to your judgment and discretion to make such other arrangement as may appear eligible, in the event of the one now offered to your consideration being impracticable or inexpedient.

The distribution proposed is, that five thousand pounds be presented to Commodore Dance, in token of the gratitude and approbation of the Mercantile Community of Bombay for the zealous and successful protection he afforded the very valuable Ships belonging to this Port entrusted to his care. That an elegant Sword, of the value of one hundred guineas, be presented to Commodore Dance, and to each of the Captains under his orders, whose Ships shared in the Action off Paulo-Anor, as marks of the esteem and admiration with which the minds of all commercial people at this place are impressed by the skill and gallantry they displayed on that occasion, and in thankfulness for the effectual support and assistance they afforded to the Commodore; and that one hundred pounds be distributed among the Men who were wounded in the Engagement, or to their Families.

We enclose a Copy of the Resolutions above referred to, and a List of the Subscriptions which were then made, and have the honour to remain, with much esteem and regard, Gentlemen,

Your most obedient humble Servants,

ALEX. ADAMSON, JAMES KINLOCK,
CHARLES FORBES, WILLIAM CRAWFORD.
JAMES LAW,

Committee of the Bombay Insurance Society.

SUBSCRIPTION for the purpose of bestowing a handsome Public Remuneration, in Testimony of the Gratitude of the PROPRIETORS OF THE BOMBAY INSURANCE OFFICE, the MERCHANTS, SHIP OWNERS, and UNDERWRITERS of BOMBAY, to Commodore DANCE, for his gallant and judicious Conduct in protecting the China Ships belonging to this Port from a very superior French Squadron, which he engaged and defeated on the 14th of February, 1804.

The Bombay Insurance Society, by Patrick Hadow, Secretary 20,000	Nasserwanjee Monackjee Cursetjee and Jauger Ardaseer 300
Bruce, Fawcett, and Co., and Pestonjee Bomanjee - - - 5,000	Paul Shewcraft - - - - - 600
Forbes and Co. and Hormarjee Bomanjee - - - - 5,000	N. D. Lima de Souza, per Sir Miguel de Souza, Mr. Quadros and Self - - - - - - 500
Alexander Adamson and Ardashir Dady - - - - 9,000	W. Whitaker - - - - - 200
	John Leckie - - - - - 300
Wm. Kennedy - - - - 500	Muncherjee Nourojee - - - 200
J. Cumberledge - - - - 500	Nassuwaujee Cawasjee - - 200
Francis Warden - - - - 300	Nemehund Amuhund - - - 400
Edward Atkins - - - - 300	Luckmuhund Poonzraz - - 200
Edward Popham - - - - 300	Eduljee Bomanjee - - - 100
T. A. Grant - - - - - 500	Bywsrjee and Muncherjee - 100
Sorabjee Muncherjee - - 3,000	Dorabjee Byramjee - - - 100
Dorabjee Rustomjee Patett - 700	
Robert Kitson - - - - - 400	Rupees 45,500
L. Philips - - - - - - 300	

TO SIR NATHANIEL DANCE.

SIR, *London, March 24, 1805.*

WE have the honour to enclose a Copy of the Resolutions passed by a numerous and most respectabe Meeting, which was held at Bombay, on the 31st March, 1804, for the purpose of considering of the manner in which the Bombay Insurance Society, the Ship Owners, the Merchants, and Underwriters of that Settlement, could best testify their high sense of the great and important services rendered by yourself, and the Fleet of Indiamen under your Command, by the brilliant Victory which you gained over a powerful Squadron of French Men of War, on the 14th February, 1804. A list of the subscriptions which have been made with this view, we have likewise the honour to enclose; and the copy of a letter, by which, with sentiments of the highest gratification, we find ourselves deputed, on this occasion, as the medium for conveying to you the tribute of gratitude and admiration called forth by your gallantry, and tendered by a Community whose dearest interests you have more immediately protected.

Hereafter, when the Bill on the Court of Directors falls due, we shall, conformably to the directions given to us, have the pleasure of sending the 5000l. we are directed to present to you, together with a Sword of the value of 100 guineas; and we shall likewise request, through you, to present Swords of the value of 100 guineas to Captain Timmins, of the Ship Royal George; to Capt. Moffatt, Commander of the Ship Ganges; and to Captain Wilson, Commander of the Ship Warley.

In fulfilling so grateful a duty, we might, perhaps, be allowed to dwell with minuteness on the Glory which has been achieved for yourself; the Fame which results to the Country, and the incalculable advantages which have arisen to its vital interests, by an Exploit so splendid and important; but it is superfluous for us to enter on this extensive field, and we content ourselves merely in offering our tribute of congratulation, proud in the opportunity afforded us of expressing our sentiments on an Action which adds lustre to the Annals of the Empire. We have the honour to remain, with sentiments of the highest respect, Sir, your very faithful and most obedient humble Servants,

(Signed) DAVID SCOTT,
JOHN FORBES,
P. CRAUFURD BRUCE

To DAVID SCOTT, *Esq.*, M.P., JOHN FORBES, *Esq.*, *and* PATRICK CRAUFURD BRUCE, *Esq.*, M.P.

GENTLEMEN, *Pall Mall, 29th March,* 1805.

I HAVE been favoured with your letter of the 24th inst. and its enclosures, communicating to me the proceedings of the Insurance Society of Bombay, in conjunction with various other Gentlemen resident at that Presidency, at a meeting held on the 31st of March, 1801.

I shall not attempt to express by words those feelings of gratitude, to which no force of language could do justice, but with which I am impressed by an act of approval so unexpected, and marked by such substantial and splendid liberality, as that which your communication announces.

Placed by the adventitious circumstances of seniority of service, and absence of Convoy, in the chief Command of the Fleet entrusted to my care, it has been my good fortune to have been enabled, by the firmness of those by whom I was supported, to perform my trust not only with fidelity, but without loss to my Employers.

Public opinion and public rewards have already far outrun my deserts; and I cannot but be sensible, that the liberal spirit of my generous Countrymen has measured what they are pleased to term their grateful sense of my conduct, rather by the particular utility of the Exploit, than by any individual merit I can claim.

Allow me, Gentlemen, through you, to offer to those whom you represent, my sincere and fervent thanks for the unexampled proof which they have been pleased to give me of their good opinion, and at the same time to express not my hope only, but my conviction, that their liberality, boundless as it seems to be, will hereafter find its noblest reward in the new motive it gives to emulation and exertion; qualities which, though when the occasion calls, they have never been wanting to the British character, have yet, in all ages and all countries, flourished with most effect when fostered by honourable applause, and have ever acquired fresh strength from every varied mode of encouragement.

To you, Gentlemen, I beg also to express my particular thanks for the very handsome and flattering terms in which you have been pleased to communicate your own, and the sentiments of those whom you represent on this occasion.

I have the honour to be, Gentlemen,
Most respectfully,
Your very obedient humble Servant,
(Signed) NATHANIEL DANCE.

STATE OF THE EFFICIENT FORCE OF THE BRITISH NAVY, APRIL 15, 1805;

Comprising the Line of Battle Ships, and those of 50 guns, now actually in Commission, and ready, or fitting for Service.

(To be continued occasionally.)

CHANNEL FLEET.

Guns.		
100	Britannia	Rear-Admiral Earl of Northesk.—Capt. Bullen.
98	Barfleur	Capt. George Martin.
74	Bellerophon	—— John Loring.
74	Colossus	—— J. N. Morris.
74	Courageux	—— Charles Boyles.
74	Defiance	—— P. C. Durham.
110	Hibernia	Ad. Lord Gardner, Commander in Chief. 1st Captain, Rear-Admiral E. Thornborough. 2d Captain, William Bedford.
74	Hero	Capt. Honourable A. H. Gardner.
80	Impetueux	—— J. E. Douglas.
74	Illustrious	—— Michael Seymour (Acting).
74	Mars	—— George Duff.
74	Minotaur	—— C. J. M. Mansfield.
98	Neptune	—— Sir Thomas Williams, Knight.
98	Prince	—— R. Grindall.
74	Ramillies	—— F. Pickmore.
110	San Josef	Vice-Admiral Sir Charles Cotton, Bart. Capt. T. R. Ricketts.
80	Tonnant	—— Charles Tyler.
98	Windsor Castle	—— D. Gould.
74	Warrior	—— William Bligh.

To which add the following, now in Port under Repair, but could join in 24 hours' notice, viz.

110	Ville de Paris	Capt. J. Whitby.
98	Prince George	—— G. Losack.
98	Princess Royal	—— R. C. Reynolds. { Belonging to the Irish Station.
80	Foudroyant	Rear-Admiral Sir Thomas Graves, K.B. Capt. Peter Paget.
64	Diadem	—— Sir Home Popham.
50	Calcutta	—— D. Woodroffe.
50	Malabar	—— Robert Hall.

Making in the whole 24 Sail of the Line, (of which 10 are of three decks), and two 50 gun Ships, to oppose the Brest Fleet of 21 Sail, 3 of which only are Three-deckers ; viz.

Vengeur, 120 guns; Republicaine and Invincible, 110; Alexander and Foudroyant, 80, Impetueux, Brutus, Castor, Veteran, Pelage, Conquerant, Ulysse, Tourville, Eole, Revolution, Dix d'Août, Constitution, Alliance, Batave, Patriot, and Gauliore, of 74. Total 21!

DOWNS AND NORTH SEA FLEET.

Guns.			Guns.			
74	Monarch	{ Admiral Lord Keith. Captain J. C. Searle.	64	Inflexible	Rear-Adm. Russel.	Yarmouth Roads.
64	Utretcht	Vice-Admiral Holloway.	74	Majestic	Capt. Hanwell.	
50	Diomede	Capt. Downman.	64	Monmouth	—— Hart.	
50	Isis	—— Ommanney.	64	Ardent	—— Winthorp.	
50	Trusty	—— G. Argles.	50	Adamant	—— Burlton.	
			50	Antelope	—— Plampin.	

Guns. **OFF BOULOGNE AND DUNGENESS.**
50 Leopard   Rear-Admiral Douglas.—Captain R. Raggett.

The above Force is kept to look after six Sail of Dutch Line of Battle Ships in the Texel, and the French Flotilla at Boulogne; the present Station of the Diomede and Isis is *temporary*, they being the Flag-ships of the Guernsey and Newfoundland Stations.

COAST OF SPAIN.

Guns.	OFF CADIZ.		Guns.		
64	Agamemnon	Capt. Harvey.	74	Montague	Capt. Otway.
74	Defence	—— Hope.	74	Repulse	{ —— Hon. A. K. Legge.
98	Glory	{ Vice-Admiral Sir J. Orde, Bart. Capt. C. Craven.	98	Dreadnought	{ Vice-Admiral Collingwood. Capt. E. Rotherham.
64	Polyphemus	—— Lawford.			
64	Ruby	—— C. Rowley.			
74	Swiftsure	—— M. Robinson.	98	Temeraire	Capt. Kelly.
	OFF FERROL AND CORUNNA.		80	Malta	{ —— Buller (*In Port.*)
98	Prince of Wales	{ Vice-Admiral Sir R. Calder.	74	Terrible	{ Capt. Lord H. Paulett.
80	Ajax	{ Capt. la Roche (Acting).			

Total, 14 Sail of the Line, of which there are four of three decks, to watch about 16 French and Spanish Ships, (the Dutch being stripped of their Men and dismantled,) and of which number not above 10 or 12 are ready; of which the five following French Ships, of 74 guns each, make a part:—Le Heuron, Guay Trouin, Redoubtable, Fougueux, and Argonaut.

Guns.   **IRISH STATION.**
74 Goliath   -   -   -   Capt. C. Brisbane.
74 Princess of Orange { Rear-Admiral William O'Brien Drury.
                        { Capt. Thomas Rogers.
64 Raisonable   -   -   —— Robert Barton.

N.B. The Princess Royal and Thunderer belong to this Squadron, but are at present at Ports repairing.

WEST INDIES.

Guns.	JAMAICA.		Guns.	LEEWARD ISLANDS.	
74	Hercule	Capt. R. D. Dunn.	74	Vanguard	Capt. A. F. Evans.
74	Theseus	{ Rear-Admiral Dacres. Capt. ——	74	Centaur	{ Commodore Sir S. Hood. Captain Richardson.

To which add the

74	Atlas	- -	Capt. Brown.	74	Eagle	- -	Capt. Colby.
74	Northumberland		{ Rear-Admiral Cochrane. Capt. Tobin.	98	St. George		—— de Courcy.
				74	Spartiate	-	—— Sir F. Laforey.
				64	Veteran	-	—— J. N. Newman.

Making 10 Ships of the Line, carrying 754 guns, to oppose le Majestueux, of 120, Magnanime, 80, Lion, Suffrein, and Jemappe, of 74 each; or a total of 422. What can we dread!

AMERICA.

Guns.   HALIFAX.
50 Leander { Vice-Admiral Sir A. Mitchell, K.B.
            { Capt. Lyall.

NEWFOUNDLAND.
The Squadron on this Station is not yet returned.

MEDITERRANEAN.

Guns.			Guns.		
74	Belleisle	Capt. Hargood.	100	Royal Sovereign	{ Rear-Adm. Sir R. Bickerton, Bart. Capt. Stuart.
80	Canopus	{ Rear-Admiral Louis. Capt. F. W. Austen.	74	Spencer	Capt. R. Stopford.
74	Conqueror	——— ———.	80	Tigre - -	——— B. Hallowell.
100	Victory	{ Vice-Adm. Lord Nelson. 1st Capt. Rear-Admiral G. Murray. 2d Capt. T. M. Hardy.	74	Superbe -	——— R. G. Keats.
74	Excellent	Capt. Southeron.		*To which add*	
80	Donnegal	——— Sir R. Strachan.	98	Queen -	{ Rear-Adm. Knight. Capt. Francis Pender.
74	Leviathan	——— Baynton.	74	Dragon -	——— E. Griffiths.
74	Renown	——— P. Malcolm.		Under Orders for that Station.	

EAST INDIES.

Guns.			Guns.		
74	Albion	Capt. Ferrier.	50	Hindostan	*(On her passage.)*
74	Russel	——— R. Williams.	74	Sceptre -	Capt. Bingham.
64	Trident	Vice-Admiral Rainier.	74	Culloden	Rear-Ad. Sir E. Pellew.
64	Lancaster	Capt. Fothergill.	64	Athenienne	Capt Fayerman.
50	Grampus	——— Caulfield.	74	Tremendous	——— Osborne.

To which add, (under Orders for that Station,)

74	Blenheim	{ Rear-Admiral Sir T. Trowbridge. Capt. Bissel.	74	Plantagenet	Capt. Bradley.

To oppose which the Enemy have only the Marengo, of 80 guns, Admiral Linois, and four Dutch Ships of the Line, (badly conditioned,) under the Batavian Admiral Hartsinck !!

The following Ships are in Commission, but *not* ready for IMMEDIATE Service; the two last are to be paid off, the other five have just been repaired.

Guns.	AT PLYMOUTH.		Guns.		
74	Achille - -	Capt. Richard King.	64	Belliqueux - -	Capt. G. Byng
	AT CHATHAM.		74	Elephant - -	——— G. Dundas.
74	Namur - -	Capt L. Halstead.	50	Centurion - -	——— J. Lind.
64	Agincourt -	——— T. Briggs.			

STATIONARY GUARD SHIPS OF THE LINE.

64	Zealand - -	Rear-Adm. B. S. Rowley.—Capt. H. L. Ball. At the Nore.
80	Royal William	Admiral G. Montague. ——— Wainwright. Portsmouth.
112	Salvador del Mundi	Vice-Admiral Young. ——— J. Cooke. Plymouth.
64	St. Albans (Floating Battery) - - Capt. J. Temple. Yarmouth Roads.
50	Tromp - - - - - - - ——— J. A. Norway. Falmouth.
64	Texel - Rear-Admiral J. Vashon. ——— D. Campbell. Leith, Scotland.

The foregoing making a grand total of 104 Ships, (without the Thunderer,) may fairly be presumed to be fully equal to the Navies of France, Spain, and Holland ; and are exclusive of the *Hospital, Prison,* and *Receiving Ships* in the different Ports, amounting to upwards of twenty ; but as they are unarmed, dismantled, and altogether unfit for Service, (though necessarily commissioned,) they are omitted in this Abstract.—Of the *Ships building,* some may be expected to be launched in the course of the Year : of one (the Revenge, of 74 guns, at Chatham,) notice has been given that she will be off the stocks this month. Of the Ships NOW ACTUALLY UNDER REPAIR, I subjoin the succeeding List, which may all reasonably be expected to be commissioned, fitted, and ready for Sea, before the end of the year, *one third* of which will be more than equal to replace those it may be found necessary to *pay off !!* At Portsmouth, the Gibraltar, of 80 guns ; the Alexander, Bellona, Brunswick, Ganges, Orion, Robust, Saturn, San Antonio, Triumph, and Zealous, of 74 each :—At Plymouth, the Cæsa , of 80 ; the Carnatic and Thun derer, of 74 each :—At Chatham, Edgar, of 74 :—In the King's minor Yards, and in private Dock Yards ; the Powerful, of 74 guns ; Africa, Dictator, Intrepid, Lion, Standard, Stately, and the Danish Ship Holstein, of 64 guns each :—being twenty-three now repairing for Service !!!

F. F.

Upper Clapton, 15*th April,* 1805

CORRESPONDENCE.

MR. EDITOR,

YOU are requested to insert the following Copy of a Letter from Mr. TUCKER, late one of the Commissioners of the Navy, to Mr. MARSDEN, Secretary to the Admiralty, in reply to a Letter from the Navy Board respecting the Accounts of the Romney, &c.—Ordered to be laid before the House of Commons, April 25, 1805.

SIR, *Lisbon Green, 24th April, 1805.*

THE Copy of a Letter from the Commissioners of the Navy, to the Lords Commissioners of the Admiralty, dated the 1st instant, having, together with other Papers relating to the Repair of His Majesty's Ship Romney, &c. been presented to the House of Commons, in explanation of some statements contained in a former Report made by that Board to their Lordships, respecting the expenses incurred for that Ship at Calcutta, I must request liberty to observe upon the evident tendency of that letter to produce the most improper effect, not only on the minds of their Lordships, but on the Votes of the House, on an approaching discussion; and I entreat that their Lordships will patiently listen to what I have to advance in reply to the aspersions which the Navy Board have endeavoured to throw on my conduct.

I beg leave to premise what I have to offer, by observing, that it is not in my intention, nor within my power, having no access to the Papers in the Navy Office, either to sustain or abandon any part of the Report which was drawn up by me, as a Member of the Committee of Stores; and I trust their Lordships will recollect, that I was not a Member of the Navy Board at the time that Report was decided on, having been removed to the Admiralty at least a month previous to its date; consequently, I have not to reproach myself, or to account to their Lordships, to the Country, or to the Parties interested, for having signed a Report of such a nature as to have required any change, recall, or explanation.

Having no knowledge whatever of any or either of the Parties concerned in the statement alluded to, I most solemnly declare, that I had no other object or consideration, in the discharge of a very disagreeable part of my duty, than to make such inquiries, and to bring forward such circumstances, as would enable the Board to make a full, fair, and honest Report on the expenditure of an immense sum of money, into which their Lordships had directed a minute investigation; and now, in proceeding to my own vindication, I shall abstain from making any comments or observations on the merits of the case, further than may be absolutely necessary to enable their Lordships to form a just decision between the Navy Board and myself.

However painful it is to be compelled, in self-defence, to declare, and prove, that statements, authenticated by a Public Board, which has been considered of much respectability, can have been made with no other view than to mislead their Lordships, I do most distinctly and solemnly deny, that the examination of the Romney's Accounts was undertaken by me, upon the principle stated by the Navy Board, which it has been endeavoured to connect with my removal from the Committee of Correspondence to that of Stores; or in consequence of any thing which had passed between their Lordships and that Board, on the subject of allotting to each Member the superintendance of a particular branch of the business of the Department; nor does their Lordships' order of the 11th August, 1803, which is quoted *in part* by the Navy Board, contain any direction for that purpose, but merely orders the Board " to take into their serious consideration the duties of their respective branches of the Office, under the superintendance and direction of the several Committees, and to make such division thereof, as shall allot to each Member of the Committees, a proportionate and proper part of the duties to be placed under his immediate superintendence and responsibility, as suggested by the Commissioners of Naval Inquiry in the 188th page of their Third Report; *and to transmit the same to you, for their Lordships' information*, with as little delay as possible, and as the importance and nature of making such arrangements will admit." In obedience to this direction, the Navy Board, on the 20th October, 1803, replied in the following words:—" In compliance with their .Lordships' directions, we have accordingly considered in what manner the several duties of this Office can be divided, agreeably to the suggestion of the Commissioners of Inquiry; and the enclosed Papers contain our *proposals* for the same, which we desire you will please to lay before their Lordships." These *proposals* were immediately sent by their Lordships to the Commissioners of Inquiry, that they might be considered when the duties of the Navy Board should be investigated; but no direction whatever was given for their being adopted. I defy the Navy Board to prove, that the regulation for the allotment of a particular duty to each Commissioner, which they have ventured to say applied to me, was ever considered as the regulation of the Office, or adhered to, or acted upon, by any one Member, whilst I sat at the Board. I defy the Board to infer, by the most overstrained construction that can be given to any thing which passed on the subject, that their Lordships ever signified the most distant approbation of the arrangements which had been *proposed* to them, much less directed that they should be carried into effect! I shall offer no comment on this attempt to confound and substitute their own *proposals*, to which their Lordships never replied, for *positive directions* from the Board of Admiralty; but I must call their Lordships' attention to page 198 of the Sixth Report of the Commissioners of Inquiry, where the Comptroller, on the 6th January, 1804, deposes, " that the Committees of the Navy Board have distinct and separate duties, but that their proceedings are laid before the Board for its approval, before put into execution; and that the Committees have *no particular instructions for their guidance more* than is directed by the Order in Council," dated the 17th August, 1796:—and on a reference to page 153 of the Eleventh Report, their Lordships will see, that *on the 8th November*, 1804, Mr. Nelson, the Secretary to the Navy Board, deposed as follows:—*Q.* " Have any, and what regulations been established, since that period, (17th August, 1796,) for regulating the official duties of the Navy Board, *or of any particular Member thereof?" A. "* NONE."— The truth is, Sir, that their Lordships' order, pressing for the Report on the Romney's Accounts, &c. is dated 29th July, 1803, and that I was not removed to the Committee of Stores till September following, at which period little having been done towards the investigation of the Accounts, and the particular attention of some one Member being necessary, to follow up the inquiries, I did (in the same manner as one of my colleagues, Sir W. Rule, had, for years, taken under his controul the conversion or appropriation of Stores; and the other, Mr. Harmood, the management of the Slop Office,) undertake to make the inquiries necessary to enable the Committee to submit a Report to the Board on the receipt and expenditure of Stores on board the Romney: but, in making these inquiries, I affirm, that in no instance did I cause a letter to be written, or reference to be made, to the Dock-yards, for information on the subject, without the consent and concurrence of my Colleagues or Colleague, Sir W. Rule having been for a great part of the time absent on duty: and it must be in the recollection of every Member of the Navy Board, that when the

Comptroller demanded to know why the Boatswain's expense and the log-book had been sent for examination to Portsmouth, instead of Deptford, as was usual in all such cases, that he was instantly answered by *Mr. Harmood*, (my senior in the Committee,) Sir W. Rule being absent, and *not by me*, that the Committee had thought it right, as it was a matter of much importance, and extraordinary complexion, that they should be sent to Portsmouth, where, there being three Masters attendant, they could be more fully and carefully examined than they could be at Deptford, where there was only one, who, besides the general investigation of similar references, had *all* the duties of the situation to attend, both on Shore and afloat.

When I first took the account in hand, I requested of Mr. Derrick, the Secretary to the Committee of Stores, that particular attention might be paid to every statement and calculation, as it was of the greatest importance they should be made as correct as possible, and he gave the examination thereof to Mr. Rolt, the senior and most intelligent Clerk in the Office of Stores, who assured me, on my interrogating him on the subject, " that the calculations had been gone over *twice* by him, and had been chequed by Mr. Moss;" and, with these precautions, I feel that the Committee of Stores was justified in submitting them to the Board, for their final consideration and approval.

As I have no longer any of the documents before me, it is impossible for me to follow the Navy Board through the inaccuracies, which it is said have been *discovered* in the Report drawn up in the Committee of Stores, or to point out all the fallacies in their present statements; nevertheless, I cannot help observing, that if, on the subsequent examination, any difference had appeared, which threw a doubt on what had been before submitted to the Board, the explanation, so far as I could have given it, was always at hand, had it suited the views of the Board to have asked for it; and I trust I should not have found the smallest difficulty in satisfying even the Navy Board, that none of my calculations were wilfully incorrect. Indeed, when I left the Board, the investigation respecting the Stores could not be considered as *complete*, as it had not been made to appear, by any of the Documents which I had seen, whether or not any of the cables, rigging, or sails, of either the Romney or Sensible, had been surveyed previous to their being sent on Shore; nor does that appear, by the Navy Board's subsequent letter, to have been ascertained: and, notwithstanding it is advanced by that Board, by way of apology for the Report having been sent without their investigation, (as they now affirm,) " that it was not practicable with respect to the facts alledged in the Report, without an entire revision of it, which would have taken up as many months as had already been employed upon it ;" I must, in reply, beg to observe, that the great length of time during which the account had been in hand, was occasioned by the correspondence with the Dock-yards, Captains of Ships, and others, in order to gain information, touching several matters, which on the face of the account were inexplicable ; and after this information had been collected, *the revision of it could not have taken up much time*. In proof thereof we see, that on the 1st of April the Navy Board sent the result of their revision, and of various consequent inquiries, in *thirty-two days* after they received the letter which occasioned it ; and it is well known to their Lordships, that the First Report was not made till *thirty-one days after I had quitted that Board*. In addition to which, I beg to call their Lordships' attention to that part of the Navy Board's letter, wherein they say, " that when the Report, as it came out of my hands, was presented to them" (for consideration), " it did appear to them of an extraordinary nature ; but *as it was framed under their Lordships' order*, and they had no reason to doubt of the facts which it stated, they did no more than soften the asperities of expression which pervaded it." In reply to which, I beg leave to observe, that their Lordships' order (10th September, 1802) directed the Navy Board " minutely to investigate the Accounts, and to report *their* opinion on the several charges ;" consequently, if the statement from the Committee of Stores appeared of *an extraordinary nature*, and as I was not present to give explanations as to the grounds or documents upon which it had been framed, it was their bounden duty, *with this doubt on their minds*, not to have suffered it to have passed the Board, without having minutely investigated it, that they might have been able to report *their* opinion ; for *mine*, at that time, was totally out of the question, not being a Member of the Board. But if they did not investigate the several points, (a pretence which I believe their Lordships, on inquiry, will find to be utterly without foundation,) on what ground did they soften any of the asperities, without knowing whether or not they had been called for by the facts which had appeared, or were, or were not inherent, and inseparable from the opinion, it was their duty to form and to transmit ? Independent of all which, how, Sir, will the Navy Board reconcile their late declarations on this subject with the assertions contained in their letter to Sir Evan Nepean, (382d page of the Romney's Papers,) dated 28th October, 1802, nearly twelve months *before* I was removed to the Committee of Stores, wherein they say, " *we have exercised the utmost attention in investigating* the several Accounts;" and again, in the same letter, " taking into due consideration the result *of our own inspection* of the Accounts?" &c. &c.

In detailing the inaccuracies in the former Report, the Navy Board say, " that though by the Boatswain's stated account there appears to be a deficiency of one bower anchor, yet it is accounted for by the Ship's log, under date the 10th June, 1801, as had been pointed out by Sir Home; and the official statement which was transmitted to him, with their before-mentioned letter, showed, that allowing the Boatswain credit for this anchor, the account of the bower anchor is completely balanced." I must now pray their Lordships' attention to that part of the Navy Board's letter to Sir Home Popham, of the 15th of February last, (page 392,) which relates to this anchor, wherein they say, " that though, by the Boatswain's stated account, there appears to be a deficiency of one bower anchor, yet it is accounted for by the Ship's log-book, under date of the 10th June, 1801, with *the omission only of the mention of the weight of the anchor,* the flukes of which were on that day carried away in weighing it in Cossier Roads, and THE OMISSION LIKEWISE BY THE BOATSWAIN, TO PRODUCE THE RING, AND PART OF THE SHANK, AT THE YARD WHERE SHE WAS PAID OFF."—Sir, I shall make no farther comment on this apology for the Boatswain, made by the Navy Board, whose duty I had conceived it was to watch over the interests of the Public, than to challenge them to produce one instance where, before now, a Boatswain has been cleared of his charge of an anchor, from the loss of the flukes, WHO HAD NOT PRODUCED THE RING AND SHANK!

I cannot pass over what the Board have said on the subject of the bitts, without observing, that notwithstanding the answers which were received to the various inquiries which had been made to gain information respecting them, appear *now* to be so very satisfactory to the Board, they were not sufficiently so, in my eye, to elucidate the consequences, which were stated to have followed the accident, alledged to have happened to them, which was the difference in the statements of the expenditure of a bower cable, which in the log-book was stated to have been *cut in the splice,* and in the Boatswain's expense book to have *parted;* the latter of which, of the two, appeared to me the most *probable,* as it was declared by the Boatswain, that sixty Lascars had been employed to pick the *remains* into ochum, and, in that case, it was natural to suppose, that the cable was bitted when the accident happened; and, notwithstanding the Navy Board gravely observe, *in order to remove every doubt upon the subject*, that there is a charge *actually made* both for *iron work* and *Sissoo timber*, for repairing the bitts, yet, if in making this second investigation, which was *intended to throw so much discredit on their own former Report*, they had taken the trouble to inspect the Merchant Builders' statement of the particulars of the work done to the Ship, (page 83,) they would have seen, that the bitts, for which this timber and iron-work were charged, were the mizen topsail-sheet bitts, and two new bitts on the quarter-deck, and that the cable bitts were never once mentioned! Does it not, Sir, appear somewhat more than extraordinary, that the Navy Board should, a second time, have solemnly reported on a subject of so much importance, without having minutely investigated every account; the more especially, as the last Report is offered in extenuation of their negligence, in not having examined the former one?

On the subject of the expenses particularized in the First Report, the Navy Board say, they do not know on what ground I determined that they were enormous and extraordinary, as it does not appear to what the epithets allude. Whether these characteristics were suggested by me, or any other person, I have, at this period, no recollection; but as the Board have thought proper to disclaim them, and affect not to comprehend to what part of the expenses they apply, I have not the smallest objection to their being considered as having originated with me; and I request their Lordships' attention to that part of the First Report referred to, (page 5,) which says, " nevertheless, if *the whole* of *these* enormous and extraordinary *expenses are* allowed, there will remain," &c., which evidently includes, as completely as any words can describe, *all* the expenses before enumerated. And will it be credited, that the Navy Board, to whose care, superintendence, and final checque and controul, is confided the immense expenditure of Stores for the Navy, feel a repugnance to describe as *enormous* and *extraordinary*, the expenses alluded to? Sir, I am certain their Lordships will think, with me, that the expenditure of 3,600 fathoms of rope, for tailing and strapping, in fourteen months, on board a 50 gun Ship, which had been completely fitted with new rigging at a King's Yard, and had only made a passage to India, without having been once in action, was both *enormous* and *extraordinary.* Can the records of the Navy Office produce one single instance of a similar expense, to justify that Board's present observation?—Does not the repeatedly blowing away of studding sails, when the Ship appears to have been on a Wind—the expenditure of a complete set of top-gallant-masts, (with top-gallant and royal yards,) which were particularly stated to have been got down on the booms—and the expenditure of 50 fathoms of a nine-inch hawser in towing the Sensible, although the weather during the $17\frac{1}{2}$ hours she was in tow, was so fine, that the Ships never exceeded three miles an hour, and which both the log-book and journals state to have been *cast off,* appear *enormous* and *extraordinary?*—and was not the sending nearly all the sails, rigging, and cables of the Ship, on Shore to an Acting Naval Officer, whose profits depended on the amount of his purchases, and, so far as I am informed, without any Reports having been produced to show whether the whole, or any part, had been surveyed and found unfit for their proper services, *enormous* and *extraordinary?*

Sir, it appears by the Vote of Supply, that no less a sum than FOUR MILLIONS SIX HUNDRED AND EIGHTY THOUSAND POUNDS has been consigned to the Navy Board, for the wear and tear of the Fleet for the current year, (independent of wages and provisions); and are not their Lordships astonished, to see that Navy Board palliating, and doubting, and hesitating, and disclaiming the epithets *enormous* and *extraordinary*, as applied to the expenses before described—more especially when they were immediately followed by the purchasing of articles of the same sort and description? What! Sir, is it not *enormous*, that nearly all the sails in the Ship should have been sent on Shore, and sold at less than one penny per yard, and at the same time *old canvass* demanded, and purchased, at sixteen-pence per yard! as well as new canvass for awnings, bags for colours, hammock-covers, screens for cabins, wind-sails, Boats' covers, bags for sand, cushions, and smoke-sails, when there was a Sailmaker and Sailmaker's Mate belonging to the Ship? Is it not *enormous*, that the rigging and cables of the Ship (not nine months from England) should have been sent on Shore and sold, and at the same time points and robins purchased, as well as junk, at nearly 200 per cent. advance on the price, for which the Public has credit for the cables? And if the identical sails and cables which had been sent on Shore, were not again sent off, under the appellation of old canvass and junk, it appears to me to be morally impossible, that any other could be procured one half so good; it being notorious that Ships in the Merchant Service do not condemn and cut up their sails and cables for old canvass and junk, before they have been worn bare, and to the last thread!— No change of Ministers, or of situation—no variation in the political compass, shall deter me, Sir, from declaring, that I did regard these expenses as *enormous* and *extraordinary*, in the *highest degree;* and, in the discharge of my duty to the Public, I have no doubt but I expressed that feeling, in the Paper which I drew up for the consideration of the Board.—If the Members of the Navy Board, who signed the letter of the 1st of April, (for I observe that an honourable Member, Mr. Markham, who did sign the Report, has not subscribed that letter,) do not think them *enormous*, it is most likely that I shall for ever differ in opinion with them; and if indeed they do not regard them as *extraordinary*, I can only lament *that* force of habit, and *that* familiarity, which have divested accounts *like these* of their characters of strangeness, and their power to surprise.—I cannot, however, quit this topic without again referring their Lordships to the Navy Board's Letter, (page 383,) dated 18th October, 1802, wherein they say, " we, however, apprehend, that if there were sufficient time for the exercise of this œconomy, the condemned cables and sails might have been converted to answer the supply of part of the junk, spun-yarn, hammock-covers, and awnings purchased." *If there were sufficient time for the exercise of this œconomy?* Why, Sir, in the preceding paragraph but one of the same letter, they expressly state to their Lordships, " that the making good the defects of the hull, masts, and yards of the Ship, *necessarily occupied considerable time!!*" In any event, did the Navy Board mean to tell their Lordships, that it required *less time* to demand, purchase, and send off from the Shore, junk and old canvass, than it would to convert the cables and sails then on the Ships' decks? Or what time can, *in their minds*, ever arrive for conversion and œconomy, if it is not when a Ship is to be repaired and refitted at a Merchant's Yard in India, where they state (page 401) the advance on the price of Stores to be 175 per cent?

The Navy Board are pleased to observe, that in pursuing the investigation, it appeared as if I had been anxious to avoid explanation; an assertion as extraordinary, as it is totally void of foundation and justice. In support of that assertion, they, however, quote a minute written by me, directing the Clerk of the Survey at Chatham, " to proceed in making the statement of the Boatswain's accounts," (notwithstanding he had been written to,) "without waiting for his explanation, as the Ship was on Foreign Service." But, Sir, they have omitted to say, whether there was any reason to suppose that I knew that he was then the Boatswain of the Zealand, the contrary of which is most distinctly implied by the observation, *as the Ship was on Foreign Service;* and they knew that the repeated directions received from the Admiralty, to hasten the Report, would not admit of the delay, till an answer could be received from a Ship which had but just sailed to run down the Coast of Africa, and then to proceed to the West Indies. The truth, however, is, Sir, although the Navy Board have thought proper to conceal it from their Lordships, that the Clerk of the Survey perceived the error under which the person was who had dictated that letter; and in reply thereto, on the following day, acquainted the Board, that the Boatswain was not in the Romney, but on board the Zealand, and that he was coming to the Yard to give all the explanation he could respecting the deficit of Stores; and it was then, and not before, first known that he was at the Nore. I leave to their Lordships' feelings, what ought to be the opinion, and what epithets are applicable to persons capable of perverting so plain a fact to the crimination of one of their Colleagues. I would rather their Lordships should name them than I.

In reply to the observation respecting the manner in which the Boatswain was debited for the deficiency of Stores, I have no hesitation to avow, that it was my express direction, that they should be charged to him at the highest rate which they had cost the Public; and if, indeed, that is a " *novel mode* " at the Navy Board, I can only lament that the interests of the Public have been so long misunderstood there. This " *novel mode* " appears to me fair and just, on every principle of equity; and I am confirmed in that opinion, by the uniform practice of the Victualling Board. In the first place it should be considered, that if the Stores had been fairly and faithfully expended, no debt whatever could arise; and if they had not been fairly and faithfully expended, it appears to me but just, that the whole expense to which the public had been put for them, should be reimbursed, as it matters not, (provided any articles of the sort had been purchased,) whether the Stores on charge, which did not appear when the Ship was paid off, were supplied from the King's Yards, before she sailed, or had been purchased after her arrival at Calcutta; for the embezzlement or improper expenditure of the former, would occasion the purchase of the latter, and the Public suffered to the whole amount of the highest price. If the English price only has heretofore been charged for the deficiency of Stores, where purchases have been made abroad, what an abominable temptation to traffic with the King's Stores has been held out to the Warrant Officers! for the Navy Board, in the very next paragraph of their letter, state, that the advance upon the price of Stores in India is no less than 175 per cent.

If the observations made by the Navy Board, respecting the vouchers of the Boatswain's Accounts, are meant to insinuate that I took, or conveyed away the papers in question, I do most solemnly declare, that they are totally destitute of truth. It is well known to Mr. Rolt and to Mr. Moss, and I believe to every Clerk in the Office of Stores, that the papers relating to the accounts under my investigation, were kept in a place locked up, the key of which was in the custody of one of the Gentlemen above named; and it must be in the recollection of all the Clerks in that Office, that frequently I have not been able to have access to them, when the Gentleman who had the key happened not to be in the Office. I have most carefully looked over all my papers, and send herewith every item and rough memorandum which I brought from the Navy Office, relating to these accounts; for being, personally, indifferent as to the result of the Report, I left every paper and calculation, that was of the smallest consequence, in the Office, nor have I even a copy of one of them.

With respect to the smoke-sail, whether it cost 73*l.* or *only* 7*l.* 6*s.* 8*d.*, is no longer in my power to demonstrate, not now having the original vouchers to refer to; but if there was not, in any of the accounts produced to me, a smoke-sail charged at 73*l.*; I must confess it is most extraordinary how that sum should have been assigned, and passed all the checques mentioned in the former part of my letter. Is it, Sir, reasonable or probable, that a fabricated statement (for such it is insinuated to be) of such a singular nature, would have been so particularized, as if for the express purpose of inviting curiosity to investigate and detect it? And is it not extraordinary that it did not rouse the curiosity, *at least*, of some one Member of the Board to inspect the correctness of such an item, during a whole month, between my leaving the Board and their making the Report? Among the rough memorandums enclosed, their Lordships will perceive one, stating the quantities of canvass purchased for various sails for the Sensible, with the prices set against each article, in the hand-writing of Mr. Rolt; and by that memorandum. which proves to be correct by the statement in page 18, it appears that 90 yards of canvass were purchased to make her smoke-sail, at 3s. 4d. per yard, and 's charged accordingly at 15l. Now, Sir, as every sail for a 50 gun Ship necessarily requires to be made of much larger dimensions than for a Frigate of 32 guns, I do not know how to reconcile this quantity, which I have the means of proving to have been purchased for the Sensible, with the 7l. 6s. 8d. which the Navy Board state to have been all that the smoke-sail for the Romney cost, which is only the price of 44 yards of canvass; and the Navy Board cannot be ignorant, that, even in the King's Yards, a much larger quantity of canvass is allowed to make the smoke-sail of a 50 gun Ship. But, Sir, whether it cost 73l. or only 7l. 6s. 8d., is, comparatively, of little consequence: it was the purchasing a smoke-sail at all, as well as the other articles mentioned at the same time, to which it was my duty to draw the attention of the Navy Board: and I feel, Sir, that as a Commissioner of the Navy, who had been 26 years employed in the Naval Service, (and let it not be forgotten that four of the Members who signed the letter of the 1st of April, viz. Sir A. Hammond, Mr. Duncan, Mr. Harmood, and Sir F. Hartwell, were brought up in the Navy, and have commanded Ships of War,) I should not have discharged my duty to the Public, if I had not drawn the particular attention of the Board and of their Lordships to such purchases, when so many thousand yards of canvass were sent on Shore to be sold, a great part of which, having brought the Ship to Calcutta, would at least have answered the purpose of wind-sails, sand-bags, cushions, and smoke-sails!

I cannot regard the insinuation, in the early part of the Navy Board's Letter, that I had been removed by an Admiralty order from the Committee of Correspondence to that of Stores, for the purpose of making the Report on the Romney's Accounts, in any other light than as a malignant attempt to calumniate an illustrious Character, for having developed, and endeavoured to correct, the enormous abuses which have pervaded the Civil Departments of the Navy: but how, let me ask, is the Navy Board borne out in that insinuation, by the concluding part of their letter, wherein they say, that on the 24th of February, 1804, at which time I was one of the Secretaries to the Admiralty, " their Lordships directed them to employ *the same persons* to investigate the subsequent account of the Romney, as had been employed on the former one!" Need I request their Lordships' particular attention to these opposite and irreconcilable statements and inferences?

It is difficult to guess, what could have led the Navy Board to give their Lordships that laboured account of the reasons which had induced them to proceed in the manner they had done, with respect to the examination of these accounts, unless it is meant as an apology for the last paragraph in their former Report, wherein they say, " it had been formed from documents in Office, without having called on the Captain, agreeably to their usual mode, for an explanation of any of the circumstances referred to therein, conceiving it to have been their Lordships' intention that they should have proceeded in that manner."—In truth, Sir, much apology is due for these assertions; for, in the first place, it is notorious to every Clerk in the Office, and to every Navy Agent in this town, that the usual, I believe I may say the invariable practice of the Office, is a direct contradiction to their assertion, namely, to report and lay imprests on the wages of Captains, for alleged irregularities in their accounts, without calling on them for any explanation whatever; and in the next place, I never saw or heard of any intimation from the Admiralty, (it is very certain there is no order, or they would have produced it,) which conveyed what they term their Lordships' intentions. But, admitting that such had been conveyed, what can possibly be so unworthy of a Public Board, as to depart from an established rule of office, to the prejudice of an Officer of rank, in order to gratify what they might conceive to be the intentions or wishes of the Admiralty? Do not their Lordships spurn at such a declaration? and does it not evidently convey, that their last letter has been written upon the same conception of supposed intentions in their Lordships, and, consequently, that we may now expect a third Report, or even a fourth, should there be another First Lord of the Admiralty before this case is decided on?

Having, I trust, fully vindicated every part of my conduct through the whole of this investigation, I think it my duty to their Lordships, to the Country, and to the House of Commons in particular, to call their attention to one of the papers which has been laid by the Navy Board before the House of Commons, dated 19th February, 1805, (page 301,) purporting to be " An Account of the Expenses of the Romney, from the 25th November, 1800, to 2d June, 1803, as nearly as can be ascertained at the Navy Office," in order that their Lordships may judge, whether that paper could have possibly been drawn up with any other view, than to deceive and mislead the judgment of Parliament. That account is declared to be framed, so as to bring under one point of view " how much she exceeded the proportion of the vote of Parliament allowed for wear and tear, or came within that sum." Sir, in that statement there are omissions of the most extraordinary nature and magnitude; and I must take the liberty to add, in the language of the Navy Board, that I scarcely think there ever were such extraordinary means resorted to, to produce a particular effect!—Will the Navy Board pretend that they have not examined that account before they signed it, and that their confidence has been a second time misplaced, and upon whom will they charge it? Or, Sir, will they continue to vouch for the fairness and truth of that paper? Sir, in that paper they have omitted, by what *accident* they best know, all her repairs, and the Stores supplied to her, between December 1801, and June 1803! They have suppressed all knowledge of the Stores purchased in the Red Sea, and of those supplied at Madras, as well as of her repair and refit when she was docked at Bombay, in the months of October and November 1802; notwithstanding they have, in that very paper, given credit for *eight months'* Stores which were brought home in her, and must of necessity have been received at one of these places; and that it appears, (page 114,) " a Frigate could not have come out of Dock at Chatham, by two Tides, had it not been for the Romney's *Sea store of copper!*" They cannot plead ignorance of these transactions; the purchases in the Red Sea have been reported on by the Navy Board to their Lordships, (page 378,) and the repairs at Bombay were proved on oath, (page 99,) by the Carpenter of the Ship at Chatham, before the Junior Surveyor of the Navy!! These facts, Sir, speak too plain to require any comment from me, or to be susceptible of satisfactory explanation any where, but at their Lordships' Table, or at the Bar of the House of Commons.

I have the honour to be, Sir,
Your very obedient humble Servant,

To William Marsden, Esq.   B. TUCKER.

Extract of a Letter from an Officer on board His Majesty's Ship Arrow, dated Carthagena, Feb. 26, 1805.

YOU will, no doubt, be not a little surprised, when you read from whence this is dated, and on what occasion we are here. Know then, on the 4th of January we sailed from Malta, in company with His Majesty's Bomb Acheron, and a Convoy of 34 Sail for England, and had a fine fair Wind, which carried us within a few days' sail of Gibraltar, when the Wind shifted, and blew exceedingly hard for ten days. Sunday, February 3, it being a very fine day, we observed two strange Frigates on our weather quarter, with all sail set—made the private Signal to them, which was not answered—tacked with the Bomb, and stood towards them. At two, could perceive they were two large Frigates—cleared Ship for Action. It now fell calm—at sun-set sprang up a breeze, nearing the Enemy very fast—every body at quarters all night. At four in the morning the Frigates came close alongside, when several shot were exchanged without any damage on either side; they then stood off again, and ran to leeward—we were not positive of what nation they were, whether French, Spanish, or Algerines. The long wished for day at length appeared, when we saw the French Colours flying on board the Frigates—at six they tacked, and stood towards us and our Consort the Bomb—at seven the Action began with great spirit on both sides, which lasted till half-past eight; when, from our disabled state, and being overpowered by so superior a Force, we were under the necessity of striking the Colours:—the Bomb seeing our condition, made sail, but was afterwards taken and burnt by the other Frigate. I leave you to judge, if we gave up the Arrow with disgrace. The Frigate which took possession of us was called the Incorruptible, mounting 44 eighteen-pounders, and carried upwards of 600 Men. The other Ship was called l'Hortense, mounting about 50 guns, and the same number of Men. The Arrow mounted 28 thirty-two-pounders, (carronades,) and 134 Men; and the Acheron only 8 guns. During the Action, we had 13 Men killed, and 27 wounded—masts, yards, sails, ropes, and rigging cut all to pieces, so that the Ship was a most complete Wreck, floating like a log on the water for the last ten minutes of the Action: four guns out of six at my quarters were disabled. About three hours after they took possession of us, the Frenchmen found she was sinking fast, as we had upwards of thirty shot-holes under water. Every body now began to look out for himself, and I was one of the last of the Prisoners on board; was obliged to take a leap overboard, to get into one of the Frigates' Boats; and after a cooling swim, was taken on board the Boat by one of our Men; but in spite of all the efforts made by the French and Englishmen, she sunk about one o'clock in the afternoon, with three unfortunate wounded Englishmen on board, who could not possibly be taken out. To aggravate our misfortunes, not a stitch of clothes did we save, but what we had on our backs: every thing I had in the world went to the bottom in the poor little Arrow. We could not learn exactly what damage we did the Enemy, as the Ship we engaged most parted company in chase of the Bomb, and did not join again. They behaved very well to us on board the Frenchman. While we remained on board the Frigate, she took and burnt two of the Convoy, a Transport, and a Merchant Brig. We have not been able to learn what damages the other Frigate did the Convoy—we hope not much; but had we not engaged them so long, a great many must have fallen into their hands. We are in great hopes Captain Vincent will be made Post, for his gallant resistance against so superior a Force. The French themselves own they never dreamt of our engaging them. They brought us here on Thursday the 7th Feb. and landed us on the Tuesday following. The Spaniards have given the Officers their parole of honour: they allow us about four shillings a-day each for our subsistance. We have formed a Mess of 12.—Captain Vincent, two Ladies, Passengers, four Soldier Officers taken in the Transports, and five of the Officers of the Arrow, and we live as comfortable as our situation will permit, in daily expectation of hearing of our exchange. We all think ourselves very fortunate in not having more Officers killed; the Boatswain and Captain's Clerk were the only Officers killed; two of the wounded Men have died in the Hospital, but the rest are in a fair way of recovery. After we are exchanged and tried for the loss of the Ship, all the Officers will be sent home; perhaps we may be sent home to take our trial—I hope the latter may take place—I hope, at farthest, to be in England in six months. Tell Dick, when you write, of my being in limbo, as also a friend of his, a Captain Green, formerly of the 35th Regiment, but now of the 24th: he was going home from Malta to join his Regiment:—he desires to be remembered to him.

The English Commissary for Prisoners of War at Madrid, gives us great hopes of a speedy exchange.

Yours, &c. &c. &c.

MR. EDITOR,

HAVING arrived in England from Demerara only a few days ago, I have not been afforded an earlier opportunity of noticing the unjust, unprovoked, and absurd misrepresentations of the Master of the Ship Thetis, of Lancaster, which have been published, respecting the Action of the 8th of November last, off Barbadoes, with the Buonaparté Privateer, and the Ceres, Thetis, and Penelope, which, in justice to the Commanders and Crews of the other two Ships, require to be refuted. I am happy in having brought with me a letter from Barbadoes, which I received from the Commander of the Buonaparte Privateer, which was afterwards captured and carried into Barbadoes.

Those persons who take any interest in this affair, are requested to compare the following letter of Captain Painpeny, with the partial and pompous account of the Action, inserted on the authority of Mr. Charnley, in the Public Papers.

I am, Sir, yours, &c.
DANIEL BOUSFIELD.

Lloyd's Coffee-House, April 27.   Commander of the Ship Ceres.

Translation from the Barbadoes Mercury, of December 8, 1804, with the Editor's Comment thereon.

AS there appears to have been some misrepresentation of the late Action of the Ships Thetis, Ceres, and Penelope, with the French Privateer Brig Buonaparté, the following letter will remove whatever unfavourable impression may have been made towards the Masters of the Ceres and Penelope, who, it is now established, equally shared with the Master of the Thetis in the honour of the contest with the Enemy; and evinces, on the part of the Captain of the Buonaparté, a liberal, brave, and generous mind:—

Captain PAINPENY, *late Commander of the French Brig the Buonaparté, to Captain* DANIEL BOUSFIELD, *Commander of the English Ship the Ceres.*

SIR,   *Bridge Town, Barbadoes, Dec. 5, 1804.*

I HAVE been astonished at the account given against you, of the Engagement we had together: the manner in which you conducted yourself obliges me, upon my honour, to inform the Public of the fact. On my arrival here, I was surprised to find that the Captain of the Thetis took to himself all the merit of having fought with me. It is true that, during the heat of the Action, he was the nearest Ship to me, but that was from necessity, as it was him that I attacked first, and which I did because I saw that he was the best armed of the three: he commenced the fire, which was soon followed up by you and the other Letter of Marque. The courage you have all three shown, cannot be too much admired. Your manœuvres convince me that they were the result of reflection and experience; and the national character which you have manifested, certainly merits the eulogium of the Public.

Your fire was tremendous for me; and I can with truth affirm, that it was you who did me most damage, and who dismasted my Vessel, which was the reason that I was unable to capture the

Second View of Torbay.

Thetis. A single Ship then has not all the honour of the fight, but certainly all three. In short, Sir, I thank the accident that has procured me the pleasure of your acquaintance, and to express the satisfaction that I feel in my heart on writing this letter. I leave you full liberty to make it public among your Countrymen. In proving my particular esteem for your person, it will no doubt, at the same time, ensure you the public approbation, and preserve you from those malicious tongues who shall dare attack your respectable character.

I have the honour to be, with consideration and esteem, Sir, your obedient Servant,

(Signed) PAINPENY.

PLATE CLXXVIII.

THIS Plate is intended to represent the Western Squadron entering Torbay, and is engraved by Medland, from a Drawing of Anderson's.

CORRECT RELATION OF SHIPWRECKS.

[Continued from page 129.]

No. X.

Again the dismal prospect opens round,
The wreck, the shore, the dying, and the drown'd.
—— FALCONER.

LOSS OF THE RAVEN BRIG.

The following Letter from an Officer who belonged to the RAVEN *Brig, contains a more particular Account of the Loss of that Vessel than any yet published:—*

> In Prison, Fort St. Mary's, in the Province of Andalusia,
> February 6, 1804.

IT is my great misfortune to address you as a Prisoner in Spain, but I am happy in being saved, after having, with my Shipmates, suffered all the horrors and perils of Shipwreck on an Enemy's Coast.

I can only mention to you the outlines of our case; to describe it would be as impossible as for you to conceive it. We had left England just a week, and expected, in the course of another, with the same favourable weather as had till then attended us, to reach the place of our destination. We had arrived within 25 miles of Cadiz on Monday evening, January 28, as we imagined, but were unfortunately mistaken, for before twelve that night we found ourselves drifted into an Enemy's Harbour, among Rocks and Shoals, the recollection of which makes me shudder. Our situation, just before daylight on the 29th, was most truly distressing—a tremendous Sea and Shoals on either hand, presented each moment as our last. At daylight we found ourselves among the Enemy's Ships, and within the Batteries, but it was determined the Raven should not be tamely surrendered, and till nine o'clock there was a hope that we should get clear off; but this hope was transient. At ten the Gale increased, and we anchored, expecting every moment to be driven on the Rocks by the violence of the Wind and the Sea. In this awful state of suspence and despair we remained till eight at night, at which time the Vessel broke from her cables, and at nine we felt the awful shock—she struck! To describe the same would baffle the efforts of the ablest pen. The groans, shrieks, and cries of Men threatened with instant destruction; no hope of saving life; blowing, raining, and dreadfully dark; Sea after Sea dashing over us; the crashing of the falling masts; and the shocks which the Vessel received in striking the ground, presented nothing short of instant dissolution. Thus circumstanced, we remained on the Wreck from nine at night till daylight; when we were made Prisoners by the Spanish Soldiers. After getting on Shore, how shall I speak of that Providence which saved our lives, as only two were lost, one a Messmate of mine, and the other a Marine! Bateman got no hurt, is well, and with me: we expected soon an exchange of Prisoners. The Spanish Government have behaved in the most handsome manner—and as they had an opportunity of witnessing our exertions on Tuesday morning, they have, from a sense of admiration and honour, allowed us more indulgence than has been before known to be given. We have the liberty of going where we please, within 20 miles, (I mean the Officers,) and they seem anxious to render our situation as comfortable as possible. I was attacked with my old disorder, and had it very severely for about eight days, owing to the wet, cold, and fatigue; but am now much better. I shall lose about 250*l.*, but my life is spared, which gives the balance in my favour. When exchanged, I know not whether we shall be sent to England, or to Lord Nelson.

LOSS OF THE
EARL OF ABERGAVENNY, EAST INDIAMAN.

THE following additional Facts relative to the Loss of the Abergavenny, East Indiaman, appeared in a Letter sent to the Gentleman's Magazine for March :—

ON the awful night of the 5th of February, about nine o'clock, the Passengers were apprised of their perilous situation; on which every one was endeavouring to gain an imagined place of safety. Mr. Gramshaw, and two more of the Cadets, after hearing these terrific words, *We must all go down with the Ship!* went into the cabin; where they continued some time looking at each other, without uttering a word. At last one of them said, *Let us return upon deck!* and two of them did so. Mr. Gramshaw remained behind. He then opened his writing desk, and took out his Commission, his letters of introduction, and some cash; after which he went upon deck, but did not see either of his Companions. He then bent his eyes forward; when, at that moment, the Ship went down head foremost! The Sea in an immense column traversed along the deck to where he then was; endeavouring to ascend the steps leading to the poop—when he was launched into the deep! The night dark, cold; the Sea in its utmost rage! The Wind blowing very vehemently! Not knowing how to swim; and encumbered with a great coat and boots, he supposed, that when the stern of the Ship went down, he must have been drawn round it by the vortex occasioned by her sinking, as he found himself on the contrary side of the Ship from whence he had been precipitated.

Whilst he was endeavouring to keep himself from sinking, something dashed against the back of his hand two or three times; which he caught hold of, and found it to be a rope hanging from the mizen shrouds. This fortunate circumstance re-animated his drooping spirits. He endeavoured, and did climb up it several feet; but, what with the boots, and great coat, and other clothes, now in every part saturated with water, he slipped down into the Sea! His spirits now failed him, having made his utmost effort to preserve life: when at this fearful moment, resigning himself to the will of his Creator, the Ship gave a lurch, by which he was canted into the mizen shrouds! He then fixed himself as well as he could, by grasping the rattlings. In this situation he remained a length of time, shivering and benumbed with cold.

Mr. Gilpin, the fourth Mate, a Man possessing an heart of the most inestimable texture, had, with about twenty others, gained the mizen top. Impelled by the dictates of humanity, he descended the shrouds; with a view, no doubt, to render assistance to any that might be in want thereof; when he discovered Mr. Gramshaw, whom he lifted into the mizen top, and placed him with the others already there. During their stay in the mizen top, viz. from the hour of eleven at night to seven in the morning, he at various times continued cheering his Companions in distress, and requesting them to keep up their spirits.

SUFFERINGS AT SEA.

THE following Account of the Sufferings of some Deserters, from St. Helena, is extracted from the Supplement to the Calcutta Gazette, of the date of July 8, 1802 :—

Letters lately received from St. Helena give a most singular and affecting Narrative of six Deserters from the Artillery of that Island. Their extraordinary adventures produced a kind of inquiry on the 12th of December last, when John Brown, one of the Survivors, delivered the following account upon oath before Captain Desfontain, President, Lieutenant B. Hodson, and Ensign Young :—

" In June 1799 I belonged to the First Company of Artillery, in the Service of this Garrison ; and on the 10th of that month, about half an hour before parade time, M'Kinnon, Gunner and Orderly of the Second Company, asked me if I was willing to go with him on board of an American Ship called the Columbia, Captain Henry Letor, the only Ship then in the Roads. After some conversation I agreed, and met him about seven o'clock at the Play-house, where I found one M'Quinn, of Major Seate's Company—another Man called Brighouse—another called Parr—and the sixth, Matthew Conway.

" Parr was a good Seaman, and said he would take us to the Island of Ascension, or lay off the Harbour till the Columbia could weigh anchor and come out. We went down about eight o'clock to the West Rocks, where the American Boat was waiting for us, manned with three American Seamen, which took us alongside the Columbia. We went on board—Parr went down into the Cabin ; and we changed our clothes after having been on board half an hour.

" Brighouse and Conway proposed to cut a Whale-boat from out of the Harbour, to prevent the Columbia from being suspected; which they effected—having therein a coil of rope and five oars, with a large stone, she was moored by. This happened about eleven at night.

" We observed lanterns passing on the line towards the Sea-Gate, and hearing a great noise, thought we were missed, and searched for. We immediately embarked in the Whale-boat, with twenty-five pounds of bread in a bag, and a small keg of water, supposed to contain about thirteen gallons, one compass, and one quadrant, given to us by the Commanding Officer of the Columbia; but in our hurry the quadrant was either left behind, or dropped overboard.

"We then left the Ship, pulling with two Oars only, to get a-head of her. The Boat was half full of water, and nothing to bail her out. In this condition we rowed out to Sea, and lay off the Island a great distance, expecting the American Ship hourly.

"About 12 o'clock, the second day, no Ship appearing, by Parr's advice we bore away, steering N. by W., and then N.N.W., for the Island of Ascension, using our handkerchiefs for sails. We met with a light Wind, which continued two days. The weather then became very fine, and we supposed we had run about ten miles an hour. M'Kinnon kept a reckoning with pen, ink, and paper, supplied by the Columbia, as also Charts and Maps.

"We continued our course till about the 18th in the morning, when we saw a number of Birds, but no Land. About twelve on that day, Parr said he was sure we must be past the Island, accounting it to be eight hundred miles from St. Helena. We then each of us took our shirt, and with them made a small sprit-sail, and laced our jackets and trowsers together, at the waistband, to keep us warm; and then altered our course to W. by N., thinking to make Rio de Janeiro, on the American Coast. Provisions running very short, we allowed ourselves only *one ounce of bread* for *twenty four hours*, and *two mouthfuls of water*.

"We continued until the 26th, *when all our provisions were expended*. On the 27th M'Quinn took a piece of Bamboo in his mouth to chew, and we all followed his example. On that night, it being my turn to steer the Boat, and remembering to have read of persons in our situation eating their shoes, I cut a piece off one of mine; but it being soaked with salt water, I was obliged to spit it out, and take the inside sole, which I ate part of, and distributed to the rest, but found no benefit from it.

"On the 1st of July Parr caught a Dolphin, with a Gaff that had been left in the Boat. *We all fell on our knees, and thanked God for his goodness to us.* We tore up the Fish, and hung it to dry: about four we ate part of it, which agreed with us pretty well. On this Fish we subsisted till the 4th, about eleven o'clock, when, finding the whole expended, bones and all, Parr, myself, Brighouse, and Conway, proposed to *scuttle* the Boat, and let her go down, to put us out of our misery. The other two objected, observing, that God, who had made Man, always found him something to eat.

On the 5th, about eleven, M'Kinnon proposed, *that it would be better to cast lots for one of us to die, in order to save the rest;* to which we consented. The lots were made—William Parr, being sick two days before with the spotted fever, was excluded. He wrote the numbers out, and put them in a hat, which we drew out blindfolded, and put them in our pockets. Parr then asked whose lot it was to die—none of us knowing what number we had in our pockets—each one praying that it might be his lot. It was agreed that No. 5 should die; and the lots being unfolded, M'Kinnon's was No. 5.

" We had agreed, that he whose lot it was should *bleed himself to death;* for which purpose we had provided ourselves with nails sharpened, which we got from the Boat. M'Kinnon, with one of them, cut himself in three places in the foot, hand, and wrist, and praying God to forgive him, died in about a quarter of an hour.

" Before he was quite cold, Brighouse, with one of those nails, cut a piece of flesh off the thigh, and hung it up, leaving his body in the Boat. About three hours after, we all ate of it—only a very small bit. This piece lasted us until the 7th. We dipped the body every two hours in the Sea, to preserve it. Parr having found a piece of slate in the bottom of the Boat, he sharpened it on the other large stone, and with it cut another piece off the thigh, which lasted us until the 8th; when, it being my watch, and observing the water about break of day to change colour, I called the rest, thinking we were near Shore; but saw no Land, it not being quite day-light.

" As soon as day appeared, we discovered land right a-head, and steered towards it. About eight in the morning we were close to the Shore. There being a heavy surf, we endeavoured to turn the Boat's head to it; but being very weak, we were unable. Soon after the *Boat upset!* Myself, Conway, and Parr, got on Shore. M'Quinn and Brighouse were drowned.

" We discovered a small Hut on the Beach, in which were an Indian and his Mother, who spoke Portuguese; and I, understanding that language, learnt that there was a Village, about three miles distance, called Belmont. This Indian went to the Village, and gave information that the French had landed; and in about two hours, the Governor of the Village, (a Clergyman,) with several armed Men, took Conway and Parr Prisoners, tying them by their hands and feet, and slinging them on a bamboo stick; and in this manner took them to the Village. I, being very weak, remained in the Hut some time, but was afterwards taken.

" On our telling them we were English, we were immediately released, and three hammocks provided. We were taken in them to the Governor's House, who let us lie on his own bed, and gave us milk and rice to eat; but not having eaten any thing for a considerable time, we were lock-jawed, and continued so till the 23d; during which time the Governor wrote to the Governor of St. Salvador, who sent a small Schooner to a place called Porto Seguro, to take us to St. Salvador. We were conducted to Porto Seguro on horse-back, passing through Santa Croix, where we remained about ten days. Afterwards we embarked; and, on our arrival at St. Salvador, Parr, on being questioned by the Governor, answered, ' that our Ship had foundered at Sea, and we had saved ourselves in the Boat; that the Ship's name was the Sally, of Liverpool, and belonged to his Father, and was last from Cape-Corfe Castle, on the Coast of Africa, to touch at Ascension for Turtle, and then bound for Jamaica.' Parr said he was the Captain.

" We continued at St. Salvador about thirteen days, during which time the Inhabitants made up a subscription of 200*l.* each Man! We then embarked in the Maria, a Portuguese Ship, for Lisbon; Parr, as Mate; Conway, Boatswain's Mate; myself, being sickly, as Passenger. In fourteen days we arrived at Rio de Janeiro. Parr and Conway sailed for Lisbon, and I was left in the Hospital. In about three months Captain Elphinstone, of the Diomede, pressed me into His Majesty's Service, giving me the choice of remaining on that Station, or to proceed to the Admiral at the Cape. I chose the latter, and was put with seven suspected Deserters, on board the Ann, a Botany Bay Ship, in irons, with the Convicts. When I arrived at the Cape, I was put on board the Lancaster, of sixty-four guns. I never entered. I at length received my discharge; since which I engaged in the Duke of Clarence as a Seaman. I was determined to give myself up the first opportunity, in order to relate my sufferings to the Men of this Garrison, to deter them from attempting so mad a scheme again."

Naval Poetry.

Bright-ey'd Fancy hovering o'er,
Scatters from her pictured Urn
Thoughts that breathe, and words that burn!

DIBDIN'S CHARMING KITTY;
OR, THE TAR'S DANCING SHOES LENGTHENED AND FITTED OUT AGAINST BUONAPARTE.

IN a Vessel of my own I have oft ta'en a trip,
    And I christen'd her the Charming Kitty;
Tho' not quite so big as a three-mast Ship,
    Yet she looks, when at Sea, quite as pretty;
Copper is her bottom, and her planks all sound,
    And then not a Sloop,
    From the head to the poop,
Is so timber'd, berigg'd, caulk'd, and pointed all round:
  Her canvass and cordage are all in their places,
  Her anchors and grapnels, and lanyards and braces,
  Her mainsail and foresail, and topsail and cluelines,
  Her shrouds and her yards, and her block and her bowlines,
  Her rattlings, her steerage, her capstan and cable,
  With Lads who to work are both willing and able:
    Anchor heave—taking leave—
    Off we go—yo ho!
Full sail—catch the gale—nothing dread—heave the lead,
    Till in Port—that's your sort—
  Then again in the Ocean—d'ye see I've a notion—
  No Seaman to own how she trips will refuse,
  Like a Tar upon Shore in his dancing shoes.

When War added Storms to the Storms of the Waves,
    I ventur'd to Sea bold and hearty,
Determin'd for Britain and Ireland to brave
    Death, the Devil, and great Buonaparté.
When Peace was in fashion, and Commerce afloat,
    Not a Brig nor a Hoy
    Could you better employ,
For passage and freightage, than my little Boat:
  Her guns were ashore, and instead of such lading,
  In broadcloth and hardware, and silks she was trading;
  In hides and in coaches, in pinknies and ponies,
  In buckles and buttons for French macaronies.

To change for tobacco, and rice, and molasses,
Cheese, butter, and cambric, and large looking-glasses,
    Indian canes—British grains—
    Burton ale—fresh or stale—
Spanish blades, pallisades, sugar-candy, gin and brandy—
    Bottle port—that's your sort:
And while no embargo was laid on my Cargo,
I was rich in my trade among Christians and Jews,
As a Tar upon Shore in his dancing shoes.

Since the great Buonaparté has taken Hanover,
    And threatens to spoil all our trading,
His Army of England he means to bring over,
    To teach us the mode of invading;
But could we once see them embark'd and afloat,
    Not a Ship in the Fleet,
    But would give them a treat,
From a Ship of the Line down to my little Boat:
We'll give them a test of our old British thunder,
Shall spoil all their stomachs for carnage and plunder:
Our bombs and our balls from our mortars and cannon,
Shall make Ocean ring from the Seine to the Shannon;
Whole broadsides at once we'll incessantly send them,
Shall cripple and tear them, and hole them, and rend them:
    Point your guns—Freedom's Sons—
    Fire away—that's your play—
Britons cheering—Frenchmen fearing, burning, flying, sinking, dying—
    All their decks—floating Wrecks—
Having sunk Buonaparté, our Sailors quite hearty,
Send the few whom they sav'd back to France with the news,
And on Shore at the Nore take their dancing shoes.

THE BELLS OF OSTEND.

BEAUTIFUL MORNING AFTER A STORM.
BY THE REV. W LISLE BOWLES.

(From his recent Publication called "The Spirit of Discovery.")

NO, I never, till life and its shadows shall end,
    Can forget the sweet sound of the Bells of Ostend!
The day set in darkness, the Wind it blew loud,
And rung as it pass'd through each murm'ring shroud*;

---

* Shrouds are the ropes of the mast.

My forehead was wet with the spume of the spray,
My heart sigh'd in secret for those far away;
When slowly the morning advanc'd from the East,
The toil and the noise of the tempest was ceas'd;
The peal, from a land I ne'er saw, seem'd to say,
" Let the Stranger forget every sorrow to-day;"
And I never, till life and its shadows shall end,
Can forget the sweet sound of the Bells of Ostend.
Yet the short-liv'd emotion was mingled with pain—
I thought of those eyes I should ne'er see again;
I thought of the kiss, the last kiss which I gave,
And a tear of regret fell unseen on the wave.
I thought of the schemes fond affection had plann'd,
Of the trees, of the towers, of my own native land—
* * * * * * * * *
But still the sweet sounds, as they swell'd to the air,
Seem'd tidings of pleasure, though mournful to bear;
And I never, till life and its shadows shall end,
Can forget the sweet sound of the BELLS of OSTEND!

BALLAD,
BY DIBDIN.

I.

TOM TACKLE was noble, was true to his word,
If merit bought titles, Tom might be a Lord;
How gaily his Bark through Life's Ocean would sail,
Truth furnish'd the rigging, and Honour the gale.
Yet Tom had a failing, if ever Man had,
That, good as he was, made him all that was bad;
He was paltry and pitiful, scurvy and mean,
And the snivlingest scoundrel that ever was seen:
For so said the Girls, and his Landlord's long score—
Would you know what that fault was—Tom Tackle was poor!

II.

'Twas once on a time when we took a Galloon,
And the Crew touch'd the Agent for cash to some tune,
Tom a trip took to jail, an old Messmate to free,
And four thankful Pratlers soon sat on his knee.
Then Tom was an angel, down right from heav'n sent!
While they'd hands, he his goodness should never repent.
Return'd from next Voyage, he bemoan'd his sad case,
To find his dear friend shut the door in his face!

Why d'ye wonder, cried one, you're serv'd right to be sure,
Once Tom Tackle was rich—now—Tom Tackle is poor!

III.

I ben't you see vers'd in high maxims and sitch,
But don't this same Honour concern poor and rich?
If it don't come from good hearts, I can't see where from,
And damme if e'er Tar had a good heart 'twas Tom.
Yet, somehow or 'nother, Tom never did right;
None knew better the time when to spare, or to fight;
He, by finding a leak, once preserv'd Crew and Ship,
Sav'd the Commodore's life—then he made such rare flip!
And yet, for all this, no one Tom could endure;
I fancy as how 'twas——because he was poor.

IV.

At last an old Shipmate, that Tom might hail Land,
Who saw that his heart sail'd too fast for his hand,
In the riding of comfort a mooring to find,
Reef'd the sails of Tom's fortune, that shook in the Wind:
He gave him enough through Life's Ocean to steer,
Be the breeze what it might, steady, thus, or no near.
His pittance is daily, and yet Tom imparts
What he can to his friends——and may all honest hearts,
Like Tom Tackle have what keeps the wolf from the door,
Just enough to be generous——too much to be poor.

TO THE RIVER WYE.

BY DR. H. KETT.

O WYE! romantic Stream! thy winding way
    Invites my lonely steps, what time the night
Smiles with the radiance of the Moon's pale light,
That loves upon the quivering Flood to play.
O'er thy steep banks the Rocks fantastic tower,
    And fling their deepening shadow cross the stream;
To Fancy's eye worn battlements they seem,
    Which on some beetling cliff tremendous lower.
Hark! Echo speaks, and from her mazy Cave
    Sportive returns the Sailor's frequent cry;
Ah! how unlike the old Bard's minstrelsy,
    Warbled in wild notes to the haunted Wave!
Warlike as seems the Hurricane's rude sweep,
    To the light Breeze that lulls thy placid deep.

SONNET

BY CHARLOTTE SMITH.

(Written in the Churchyard at Middleton in Sussex.)

PRESS'D by the Moon, mute Arbitress of Tides,
  While the loud Equinox its power combines,
  The Sea no more its swelling Surge confines,
But o'er the shrinking Land sublimely rides.
The wild Blast, rising from the western Cave,
  Drives the huge Billows from their heaving bed;
  Tears from their grassy tombs the Village dead,
And breaks the silent Sabbath of the Grave!
With shells and sea-weed mingled, on the Shore
  Lo! their bones whiten in the frequent Wave;
  But vain to them the Winds and Waters rave;
They hear the warring Elements no more:
While I am drown'd—by life's long Storm opprest,
To gaze with envy on their gloomy rest.

MARINE DESIGNS, NAVAL PORTRAITS, &c.

IN THE

EXHIBITION AT THE ROYAL ACADEMY,

MDCCCV.

THE THIRTY-SEVENTH.

Nutrix Artis emulatio est.
    VELLEIUS PATERCULUS, SUB FINEM, LIB. 1.

The Numbers refer to their Place in the Exhibition. R.A. *Royal Academician.* A. *Associate.* H. *Honorary.*

5	PORTRAIT of Captain Gooch —	*A. W. Devis.*
7	Morning — —	*J. Opie,* R.A.
15	A Sea Storm — —	*N. Pocock.*
47	View of Brighthelmstone, with the towing a Boat on Shore — —	*Sir F. Bourgeois,* R.A.
48	Admiral Lord Keith — —	*W. Owen,* A.
52	View of the Reculvers, near Margate	*W. Pickett.*
77	The Deluge — —	*B. West,* R.A.
80	His Majesty's Frigates the Medusa, Indefatigable, Amphion, and Lively, chasing a Squadron	

of Spanish Frigates; the Medusa, Sir John Gore, coming up with the Spanish Commodore — — — *T. Whitcombe.*

92 His Majesty's Frigates the Medusa, Indefatigable, Amphion, and Lively, engaging four Spanish Frigates; the Mercedes a-stern; the Spanish Admiral blowing up — *Ditto.*

111 Boarding an Enemy — — *S. Drummond.*

118 View in lat. 44° 30″ on the desolate Coast of Patagonia — — *A. W. Devis.*

138 A Storm: Shipping embayed on a rocky Shore. *N. Pocock.*

140 Prospero and Miranda — *H. Thomson,* R.A.
MIR.—" If by your art, my dearest father, you have put the wild waters in this roar, allay them."—TEMPEST, Act 1, Sc. 1.

163 Landing of the British Troops in the Bay of Aboukir, in the face of an expecting and prepared Enemy, on the 8th of March, 1801.
P. J. de Loutherbourgh, R.A.

184 Earl of St. Vincent — *Sir W. Beechey,* R.A.

196 View of Dublin and Harbour, from Mount Minion, the Seat of Lord Viscount Fitzwilliam *W. Ashford.*

224 Scene at the Back of the Isle of Wight — *J. J. Chalon.*

233 Truth directing History to record the Actions of the Heroes presented by Britannia — *J. Nixon,* A.

ANTI-ROOM.

281 His Majesty's Frigate the Endymion, commanded by Sir T. Williams, attacking a Dutch Admiral's Ship of 74 guns, a Brig, and two Schooners, Gun-vessels, as they lay at anchor off Flushing; the three latter cut their cables, and made their escape over the Shoals, as did also the 74, (by lightening her in the Night,) the evening of the Victory off Camperdown, 11th October, 1799 — *N. Pocock.*

COUNCIL ROOM.

315 Ships at anchor — — *S. Atkins.*

326 An easterly View of Corfu, (ancient Corcyra,) the principal of the Seven Islands, taken in the Year 1803 — — *W. Walker.*

329 View in the Isle of Thanet — *W. Pickett.*

MINIATURES.

361 A Frame, containing Mr. P. Barker, R.N., and other Portraits — — *B. Pym.*
408 Portrait of Captain Skene, R.N. — *A. Robertson.*
429 Lord Viscount Nelson, after J. Hoppner, R.A., Enamel — — — *H. Bone,* A.
430 Earl St. Vincent, after Sir W. Beechey, R.A., Enamel — — — *Ditto.*
442 A Fisherman's Wife watching the Return of her Husband's Boat during a Storm — *R Westall,* R.A.
444 River Liffey, Dublin; showing the Four Courts, and Ruins of the Coal-quay Bridge *T. S. Roberts.*
473 A Wreck — — *J. E. Robinson.*
498 A Frigate and the Convoy bearing away in a Gale of Wind — — *J. T. Schetky.*
499 View of the Bay of Pines, New South Wales, long. 150° 30″, lat. 22° 20″, discovered by Captain M. Flinders, in His Majesty's Ship Investigator, Feb. 1802 — *W. Westall.*
524 View near Blackwall — — *A Gentleman,* H.

ANTIQUE ACADEMY.

558 His Majesty's Ship Centurion, 50 guns, Captain Lind, beating off the Marengo Flag-ship, Admiral Linois, and two French Frigates of 36 guns each, in Vizagapatam Road, on the 19th September, 1804 — — *F. Sartorius.*
562 View on the River Mersey, near Liverpool *D. Cox.*
647 Our Saviour walking on the Sea — *H. Richter.*

" He cried, saying, Lord, save me! And immediately Jesus stretched forth his hand, and caught him; and said unto him, O thou of little faith, wherefore didst thou doubt?"

MATTHEW, chap. xiv.

MODEL ROOM.

711 A Design of a Monument intended for Westminster Abbey, to the Memory of two Naval Officers — — *J. Nollekins,* R.A.
749 Design for a Naval Mausoleum — *G. Moore.*
788 Ocean receiving a lost Mariner: Design for a Monument — — *C. Houvsll.*

NAVAL HISTORY OF THE PRESENT YEAR, 1805.

(April—May.)

RETROSPECTIVE AND MISCELLANEOUS.

ALTHOUGH the public Mind has been on the rack for a considerable time respecting the destination of the combined Fleets, no authentic documents had appeared on this Subject, when this Sheet went to Press. We only learnt, and that from no common source, that these Fleets had certainly sailed for the West Indies, and had been seen under a Press of Sail, standing in that direction. Our attention will therefore be principally given at present to the important proceedings of the British Senate. When Party runs so high, and so much bitter animosity prevails, we shall merely give with accuracy and impartiality a view of those Naval Debates, which are almost without a parallel in the History of our Country. We trust that the adage of an old Politician and Courtier will not hold true in this instance :

Quicquid delerunt Reges plectuntur Achivi!

It was the Fisgard, of 48 guns, Captain Lord M. Kerr, cruising without the Gut of Gibraltar, that discovered the French Squadron having passed the Gut, and, with his usual vigilance, sent advice of this important circumstance immediately to Vice-Admiral Sir John Orde, Bart., cruising off Cape St. Mary's, who dispatched the Felix Schooner to England.

Yarmouth, April 27.—The Red Breast, a very fine Gun-brig, of 14 guns, for His Majesty's Service, was launched this morning from the Dock Yard of Mr. John Preston, of this place; and on Thursday next will be launched from the same Yard, another Gun-brig, intended to be called the Exertion. Within the space of twelve months, Mr. Preston will then have launched one Sloop of War, called the Helena; the Musquito Brig, and two Gun-brigs. The Musquito is now on this Station, and allowed to be the swiftest sailing Vessel of her description in the North Sea; and he has now building two more, one of which is in a very forward state.

On Monday, April 22, James Douglas, a Petty Officer belonging to the Cruiser Sloop of War, was flogged round the Fleet, for beating and ill-treating a Prisoner on board of a Prize, in which Ship he was placed as Prize-Master.

One of the numerous Vessels which have lately carried German and Flemish Refugees to America, the Sarah, from Antwerp to New York, with 250 Passengers, was met at Sea by a Schooner from Portland for Barbadoes, nearly sinking, having five and a half feet water in her hold, with the loss of rudder and mizenmast, and destitute of Provisions, having been 170 days at Sea. The Schooner took on board all the People except thirty, who, in consequence of a gale, were necessarily left to perish, having neither food nor water. The Stores of the Schooner were however soon exhausted, notwithstanding they allowed only a gill of water and a raw potatoe to each Person daily ; and forty Persons were starved to death before the Vessel reached Barbadoes.

The following extraordinary circumstance, we learn by a Letter from Husum, lately occurred at Tonningen :—The Master of an English Vessel lying there, was ordered by the Captain of the Guard-ship to slack his cable, which he did, till he could slack no more; he was then ordered to cut, which he refused to do, saying, he would, or could not, if the King himself was there. In consequence of this reply, the Danish Captain sent a Party of Men on board of the English Vessel, who brought the Master on board the Danish Ship, and he was there flogged severely, by order of their Captain. The Dane, in vindication of his conduct, says, the Master of the English Vessel damned the King of Denmark. This charge has, however, been refuted by a number of witnesses who were present when the altercation took place. A petition, praying for redress, signed by about fifty English Masters of Vessels, has been sent to our Ambassador at Copenhagen.

Deal, April 25. Eight French Schuyts, each having on board from twenty to twenty-five Soldiers, besides Seamen, and carrying two 18-pounders, were last night and this morning towed into the Downs by His Majesty's Ship Railleur, Captain Collard. The Locust and Starling Gun-brigs appear to have sustained the brunt of the Action, being within pistol-shot of a range of French Batteries. The Starling arrived yesterday much damaged; and last night, at eleven o'clock, the Locust, commanded by that meritorious Officer, Lieutenant John Lake, also arrived in the Downs, in order to repair the damages sustained in this gallant Action.—A considerable number of the Enemy's Flotilla were manœuvring close in under the Rocks of Cape Griznes. The Locust, in company with the Squadron under Captain Honeyman, was ordered to the Attack, and immediately ran one of the Flotilla alongside; and notwithstanding a most tremendous fire was opened from the Batteries, and a spirited defence made by the Commander of the French Vessel, the Locust succeeded in cutting off her opponent, and bringing her out; the Prize was then ordered by the Admiral to receive the Prisoners from the other captured Vessels, which are arrived safely in the Downs. The Locust, in running so close in Shore, received three shot from the Batteries in her hull: one at the water-line, going through the starboard side, cut the cables between the decks, and forcing her planks quite open in the bends on the opposite side, occasioned her making so much water, that she was obliged to bear away for the Downs. Notwithstanding the severity of this Engagement, within pistol-shot, Lieutenant Lake had not a Man killed or wounded. It was mentioned yesterday, that the Starling had three Men killed; but from all the information I can get to-day, am in hopes it is not the fact.

On Wednesday morning, May 15, at nine o'clock, the Signal was made on board the Nemesis Frigate, at Spithead, for the Ships lying at that Port to send a Boat, manned and armed, to attend the execution of N. Lincoln, a Seaman of that Ship, who had been sentenced to die for desertion. The summons was obeyed, and a Man from each Boat was ordered on the deck, where the unfortunate Criminal was in prayer, in the presence of the Ship's Company, attended by a Catholic Priest. The scaffolding had been erected; the Marines were under arms; the rope was rove; and every preparation made for the awful moment. He requested leave to address the Men, and said he was prepared to die —A few minutes before the time of execution, Captain Somerville read to him the Sentence, which included a declaration of *free pardon* : he seized the paper, fell prostrate on the deck, and kissed it, expressing the feelings of a penitent, pardoned Criminal, whose hope of mercy, as he said, had forsaken him. Captain Somerville then seriously admonished him; and he retired from the deck, with the Priest, with whom he continued afterwards nearly an hour in prayer.—The next day he was sent on board the Triumph; the Men of the Nemesis (greatly to their credit) having previously made a liberal subscription for him, from a twelve-month's pay, which they had just received.

Official Letters,

Copied verbatim from the LONDON GAZETTE,
[Continued from page 223.]

ADMIRALTY-OFFICE, APRIL 6, 1805.

Copy of a Letter from Captain William Selby, Commander of His Majesty's Ship Cerberus, to William Marsden, Esq.; dated at Sea, April 2, 1805.

SIR,

I BEG to acquaint you, for the information of my Lords Commissioners of the Admiralty, that I this morning, at daylight, discovered a Sail to the Southward, which after a chase of six hours I captured. She proves to be le Bonheur Private Brig of War, mounting 14 guns, commanded by Francis Folliott, one hundred and thirty tons burthen, and forty-six Men; sailed from Cherbourg thirteen days since, and had made only one Capture.

I have the honour to be, &c.

W. SELBY.

Copy of a Letter from Admiral Lord Keith, K.B., Commander in Chief of His Majesty's Ships and Vessels in the North Sea, to William Marsden, Esq.; dated Monarch, off Ramsgate, April 4, 1805.

SIR,

I herewith enclose, for their Lordships' information, copies of a letter which I have received from Captain Owen, of His Majesty's Ship Immortalité, and of the one from him to Captain Oliver, to which the former refers, reporting the Capture of the Spanish Privateer Brig el Intrepede Corune, alias la Maria, Petricio Fasto, Commander. I have the honour to be, &c.

KEITH.

His Majesty's Ship Immortalité, March 17, 1805, lat. 36° 46' N., long. 7° 41' W.

MY LORD,

I enclose, for your information, a copy of a letter I have written to Captain Oliver, who tacked after a large Ship, which was detained by the Privateer, and is a Dane from Dartmouth. I shall stand to the westward for the night, in hope of rejoining the Melpomene, who, by the shift of Wind, is now to windward, and in the morning continue my course to the rendezvous.

I have the honour to be, &c.

Admiral Lord Keith, K.B., &c. &c. &c. E. W. C. R. OWEN.

His Majesty's Ship Immortalité, at Sea, March 7, 1805, lat. 36° 46' N., long. 7° 41' W.

SIR,

After parting with you this morning I continued in chase till three P.M., when we came up with and took the Spanish Privateer Brig el Intrepede Corune, alias la Maria, out twenty-two days from Corunna without making any Capture, carrying fourteen guns and sixty-six Men. I am, &c.

E. W. C. R. OWEN.

On further inquiry, I find she had detained a Portuguese Schooner and the Danish Ship Isaac this morning. The Commander's name is Petricio Fasto.

R. D. Oliver, Esq., Captain of his Majesty's Ship Melpomene. (A Copy) KEITH.

Copy of a Letter from Vice-Admiral Sir John Thomas Duckworth, K.B., to William Marsden, Esq.; dated on board the Shark, Port Royal, Jamaica, the 9th February, 1805.

SIR,

The accompanying recital of the destruction of a French Felucca Privateer, by His Majesty's Sloop Peterell, I send for the information of the Lords Commissioners of the Admiralty. And I am, &c.

J. T. DUCKWORTH.

His Majesty's Ship Peterell, off Cape Antonio,
SIR,   *24th January,* 1805.

I have the honour to acquaint you, that on the 23d instant, in passing Cape Cerientes, we discovered a French Felucca in Sand Bay, who weighed immediately on seeing us: on finding we were coming up with her, they ran her on Shore, upon which I anchored the Ship, and sent the Boats to burn her, which I had the satisfaction of seeing completely effected before we got under weigh. She mounted one four-pounder, a swivel, and had a number of small arms, and twenty-seven Men, who made their escape on Shore, except one Man. She had lately captured an American Brig, that was carried into the Havana, and sold.

I have the honour to be, &c.

To Sir J. T. *Duckworth, K.B., Commander*   J. LAMBORN.
  in Chief, &c. &c. &c.

Copy of a Letter from Commodore Sir Samuel Hood, K.B., Commander in Chief of His Majesty's Ships and Vessels at the Leeward Islands, to William Marsden, Esq.; dated in Carlisle Bay, Barbadoes, February 16, 1805.

SIR,

I have the honour to transmit to you the copy of a letter from Captain Bettesworth, Commander of His Majesty's Sloop Curieux, detailing an account of the Capture of the Madame Ernouf Privateer, after a very sharp Action, in which the Captain of the Privateer displayed an extraordinary degree of obstinacy, and by it lost the lives of many Men. The coolness and bravery of Captain Bettesworth, his Officers and Men, early manifested its superiority. Indeed I want words to express the gallantry and spirit of this Officer, who so lately received three wounds in capturing the Sloop he now commands, has again a severe wound by a musket-ball in the head; and, I trust, will merit the notice of the Lords Commissioners of the Admiralty, as an emulative and promising Officer, that has gained every step by his zeal and courage. I am, &c.

SAM. HOOD.

SIR,   *Curieux, at Sea, February* 8, 1805.

I have to inform you, that this morning, at break of day, Barbadoes bearing west about twenty leagues, I perceived a large Brig on our lee bow, who immediately bore up and made all sail away; and after a chase of twelve hours, during which time she tried every point of sailing to escape us, we arrived within point-blank shot of her, when she took in her studding sails, and brought to on the starboard tack, hoisted French Colours, and commenced a very brisk and heavy fire of great guns and small arms; on our arriving within pistol-shot, and ranging upon her weather quarter, we discharged our guns, and the Action continued with great obstinacy on both sides for about forty minutes, when the Enemy getting on our weather quarter, I conceived, from their having in great measure left their guns, and giving three cheers, that they intended to board us; she was then steering for our leeward quarter, when we put our helm to starboard, and caught his jib-boom between our after fore-shroud and fore-mast. In this situation she remained until her decks were completely cleared, when, at the moment we were going to take possession, the Vessel parted, and her fore-top-mast went overboard; she continued a short time firing musketry, and then hauled down her Colours, and proved to be la Dame Ernouf, of sixteen long French sixes, and 120 Men, out twenty days from Guadaloupe, and had taken one Merchant Ship (since retaken by His Majesty's Sloop Nimrod); sails very fast, coppered, and remarkably well found: but although she carries the same number of guns, and of the same calibre as the Curieux, she is not near so large.

I can attribute her fighting so long and obstinately to nothing but the Captain being part owner; her having run, since the commencement of the War, with so much success; and her being so well manned.

His Majesty's Brig had five killed, and three wounded, besides myself: of the former, I have to regret the loss of a valuable Officer, Mr. Maddocks, the Purser, who (on account of Mr. Boss, First Lieutenant, having been left behind, on leave, from the hurry of our sailing,) volunteered his services, and was killed gallantly fighting at the head of the small arm Men. I cannot help stating, as a tribute to the memory of so worthy a young Man, that to the Service he is the loss of a very good Officer, and to every body that knew him, a valuable friend and companion.

Lieutenant Boss having been left behind, deprived me of the services of an able and gallant Officer, but Lieutenant Donaldson so well supplied his place, not only by exertion at the guns, but putting the orders that were given in execution, although the only Officer I had on board, but Mr. Caddy, Master's Mate, and Mr. Templeton, Boatswain, that I did not, by their great assistance, feel the want of an individual.

The enemy had thirty killed, and forty-one wounded; and in justice to his gallantry, I must say, he never struck whilst there was a Man on his decks.

I have the honour to be, &c.

Commodore Sir Samuel Hood, K.B.,   G. E. B. BETTESWORTH.
&c. &c. &c.

Copy of another Letter from Commodore Sir Samuel Hood, to William Marsden, Esq., dated as above.

SIR,

Enclosed I have the honour to send, for the information of the Lords Commissioners of the Admiralty, a List of Vessels captured and detained by the Squadron under my Command since the last return. I am, &c.

SAM. HOOD.

List of Vessels captured, recaptured, and detained by the Squadron under the Command of Commodore Sir Samuel Hood, K.B., since the last Return.

English Brig Albion, laden with Coals, &c.: recaptured by the Curieux, June, 1804.

English Ship Elizabeth, laden with Slaves: recaptured by the Centaur, July, 1804.

French Schooner Privateer Elizabeth, of six guns: captured by ditto, same date.

French Schooner Betsey, in ballast: captured by ditto, same date.

French Schooner Bellona, laden with Provisions: captured by the Netley, August, 1804.

English Ship Young Nicholas, laden with Mahogany, &c.: recaptured by the Hippomenes, August, 1804.

French Schooner Three Brothers, laden with Nails, Whips, &c.: captured by the Cyane, same date.

French Sloop Try Again, laden with Provisions: captured by Eclair, same date.

Leghorn Ship Augusta, laden with Merchandize: captured by the Emerald, same date.

English Brig Swift, in ballast: recaptured by ditto same date.

English Brig Princess Royal, laden with Government Stores: recaptured by the Curieux, September, 1804.

English Ship Salamander, (a Guineaman:) recaptured by the Heureux, same date.

A French Sloop, laden with Sugar: captured by the Kingfisher, September, 1804.

French Privateer Ship Napoleon, of 18 guns, and 150 Men: captured by the Barbadoes, October, 1804.

French Sloop Privateer Heureux, of 10 guns and 80 Men: captured by ditto, November, 1804.

Danish Brig Hoff, laden with Slaves: recaptured from a French Privateer by the Alligator, same date.

French Brig Privateer Buonaparté, of 18 guns and 150 Men: captured by the Cyane, same date.

A French Sloop, in ballast: captured by the Imogen, December, 1804.

English Ship Lord Nelson, laden with Slaves: recaptured by the Amsterdam, same date.

English Ship Admiral Peckenham, laden with Provisions: recaptured by the Centaur, same date.

French Schooner Privateer Deux Amis, of 6 guns and 40 Men: captured by the Kingfisher, January, 1805.

English Sloop Experiment, laden with Wood: recaptured by the Mosambique, same date.

English Ship Queen Charlotte, laden with Coals, &c.: recaptured by the Carysfort, same date.

An American Ship, from St. Domingo, laden with Coffee: captured by the Curieux from a French Privateer, same date.

An English Brig, laden with Sundries: recaptured by ditto, same date.

American Ship Ardent, laden with Coffee and Logwood: captured by the Nimrod from a French Privateer, same date.

An English Guineaman, laden with Slaves, &c.: recaptured by the Barbadoes, same date.

English Brig Peggy, laden with Dry Goods: recaptured by the Beaulieu, same date.

French Brig Privateer Dame Ernouf, of 16 guns and 130 Men: captured by the Curieux, same date.

English Sloop Hero, in Ballast: recaptured by the Grenada, same date.

Spanish Brig Francis Paula, in Ballast: captured by the Centaur, December, 1804.

Spanish Brig St. Sebastian, laden with Wine, &c.: captured by the Heureux, same date.

Spanish Ship St. Sebastian, laden with Merchandize and Military Stores: captured by ditto, same date.

A Spanish Ship, laden with Silks, Merchandize, &c.: captured by the Centaur, same date.

Spanish Brig Isabella, laden with Wine and Brandy: captured by the Amelia, same date.

Spanish Ship Conception, laden with Wine and Brandy: captured by ditto, same date.

Spanish Ship Commerce of Havana, laden with Cotton, &c.: captured by ditto, same date.

Spanish Brig Jesu Maria, in Ballast: captured by the Centaur, same date.

Spanish Ship Jesu Maria, laden with Wine, &c.: captured by ditto, same date.

Spanish Brig Esa, laden with Tallow, &c.: captured by the Carysfort, January, 1805.

Spanish Brig Esta, laden with Tallow, &c.: captured by the Barbadoes, same date.

Spanish Ship Lady Montanio, laden with Dry Goods: captured by the Kingfisher, same date.

A Spanish Sloop, laden with 2200 Dollars, &c.: captured by the Guachapin, same date.

A Spanish Schooner, laden with Dry Goods: captured by ditto, same date.

A Spanish Schooner, laden with Fish: captured by ditto, same date.

A Spanish Schooner, laden with Flour: captured by ditto, same date.

SAM. HOOD.

Copy of another Letter from Commodore Sir Samuel Hood, K.B., to W. Marsden, Esq.; dated as above.

SIR,

I beg leave to enclose you, for the information of the Lords Commissioners of the Admiralty, copy of a letter from Captain Cribb, Commander of His Majesty's Sloop Kingfisher, giving an account of the Capture of the Deux Amis French Privateer, in company with His Majesty's armed Schooner Grenada.

I have the honour to be, &c.

SAM. HOOD.

Grenada, E.N.E. 11 leagues, His Majesty's Sloop Kingfisher, Dec. 29, 1804.

SIR,

A chase of six hours S.W. to this situation, enabled the Sloop I command to capture les Deux Amis French Schooner Privateer, pierced for eight guns, only two on board as captured, the remainder thrown overboard; her Crew thirty-nine Men, commanded by Francis Dutrique, ten days from Guadaloupe, her first and unsuccessful Cruise. I should be doing great injustice to His Majesty's Schooner Grenada, were I not to give her the credit, on chasing the Enemy to my view, and when her Commander saw that I had every chance of success, he judiciously chased, and recaptured the Sloop Hero. I am, &c.

Commodore Sir S. Hood, &c. &c. &c. R. W. CRIBB.

APRIL 16, 1805.

Copy of a Letter from the Right Honourable Lord Gardner, Admiral of the Blue, &c., to William Marsden, Esq.; dated on board the Hibernia, off Ushant, April 10, 1805.

SIR,

I herewith transmit to you, for their Lordships' information, copy of a letter, dated the 25th ultimo, from Captain Prowse, of the Sirius, (addressed to the Honourable Admiral Cornwallis,) which I received this morning, enclosing a letter of the same date, which he had received from Lieutenant James Rose, of the Growler Gun-brig, (copy of which is also enclosed,) giving an account of his having captured two of the Enemy's Gun-brigs between the Bec du Raz and the Penmarks. I have the honour to be, &c.

GARDNER.

His Majesty's Ship Sirius, off the Penmarks,
SIR, *March 25, 1805.*

Enclosed is a letter from Lieutenant Rose, commanding His Majesty's Gun-brig Growler, of his having captured two French Gun-boats, of the third class, close in with the Penmarks; one, No. 443, being so bad a Vessel, I did not think her trust-worthy to cross the Channel, and ordered the long brass nine-pounder, two small carronades, &c. to be taken out, and to destroy her. I am, &c.

Honourable William Cornwallis. W. PROWSE.

His Majesty's Gun-brig Growler, off the Penmarks,
SIR, *March 25, 1805.*

I beg leave to inform you, that this morning, between eleven and twelve, as I was standing in Shore, between the Passage du Raz and the Penmarks, I observed fifteen Sail of the Enemy's Gun-boats standing in Shore; I made sail in chase of the headmost, but not finding it practicable to cut her off, I bore up and made sail for the Leewardmost, and succeeded in capturing two of them; they proved to be No. 443, with fifteen Men, and No. 450, with twelve Men on board; the remaining thirteen having anchored under the Penmarks preventing me from capturing any more. I have the honour to be, &c.

William Prowse, Esq., Captain of JAMES ROSE.
His Majesty's Ship Sirius.

Copy of a Letter from Rear-Admiral Russell to William Marsden, Esq.; dated on board His Majesty's Ship the Monmouth, in Yarmouth Roads, the 14th Instant.

SIR,

Enclosed herewith you will receive the copy of a letter from Captain Carteret, of the Scorpion, informing me of his having, in company with the Providence armed Ship, captured the Schooner l'Honneur, Captain Antoine Doudet.

I have the honour to be, &c.

T. M. RUSSELL.

His Majesty's Sloop Scorpion, Yarmouth Roads,
SIR, *April 13. 1805.*

By Captain Rye's letter, of His Majesty's hired armed Brig the Providence, their Lordships are already apprised, I believe, of the Capture of a Dutch Schooner, under National Colours, on the 11th instant, off Scheiling; she had quitted Delfzyel on the preceding day; was chased on the ensuing morning for a considerable time by the Providence, as well as by His Majesty's armed Sloop the Thomas, and was finally taken possession of by this Sloop.

The Vessel proved to be the Honneur, of 12 guns, having 1000 stand of arms on board, a complete set of cloathing for that number of Men, and a considerable quantity of warlike Stores; she has besides two field-pieces, twelve-pounders, and two mortars, besides tents, &c. for Troops: Jean Saint Faust, so noted for his successful depradations on the British Commerce in these Seas, is a Passenger on board of her. I have the honour to be, &c.

To T. M. Russell, Esq., &c. &c. &c. PHILIP CARTERET.

Copy of another Letter from Rear-Admiral Russell to William Marsden, Esq.; dated on board the Monmouth, Yarmouth Roads, the 14th Instant.

SIR,

I enclose a letter from Captain Burlton, of the Adamant, transmitting one from Captain Bayley, of the Inflexible, respecting the Capture of l'Alert French Privateer, on the 12th instant, and the Recapture of the Brig Mary of Lynn. The latter arrived here this morning. I am, &c.

T. M. RUSSELL.

SIR, *Adamant, at Sea, April 13, 1805.*

In consequence of information I received of an Enemy's Lugger Privateer being to the S.W. of the Inflexible and Adamant, I directed a course to be steered in hopes of meeting with her, and have the honour to inform you we succceded in capturing the said Lugger, named l'Alert, (as you will perceive by Captain Bayley's letter:) we also recaptured the Brig Mary of Lynn, and it is probable we may be able to stop the Schooner. I have the honour to be, &c.

Rear-Admiral Russell, &c. &c. &c. GEORGE BURLTON.

SIR, *His Majesty's Ship Inflexible, at Sea, April 12, 1805.*

I have the pleasure to inform you, that the Boats of His Majesty's Ship I command this day captured, after a chase of between three and four hours, l'Alert French Lugger Privateer, of four small carriage guns, and small arms, Egide Colbert, Commander, having thirty-two Men, ten of whom he had put on board an English Schooner and Brig, named in the margin*, captured close off the Spurn on the 8th instant.

The Capture of this Vessel is very fortunate, as she sails remarkably well, and has done much damage to our Trade. I am, &c.

George Burlton, Esq., Captain of His T. BAYLEY.
Majesty's Ship Adamant.

N.B. I have the pleasure to inform you, that we this morning recaptured the Brig named in the margin.

April 13, 1805. T. BAYLEY.

APRIL 23, 1805.

Copy of a Letter from Vice-Admiral Sir Andrew Mitchell, K.B., Commander in Chief of His Majesty's Ships and Vessels at Halifax, to William Marsden, Esq.; dated Bermuda, 24th of March, 1805.

SIR,

I have the honour to enclose, for the information of the Lords Commissioners of the Admiralty, three letters relative to the Capture of His Majesty's Ship Cleopatra, on the 17th of February last, by the French Frigate la Ville de Milan, after a very severe Action.

Their Lordships will with pleasure observe how fortunate the Leander has been in falling in with both Ships, taking la Ville de Milan, and retaking the Cleopatra.

No language of mine can do sufficient justice to the perseverance in the chase, and gallant conduct of Sir Robert Lawrie, Bart., his Officers, and young Ship's Company, in the Action with the Enemy, which will ever reflect the highest honour on them, when their Lordships consider the superiority of the Ships and Men.

---

* Nimble Schooner of Aberdeen, Brig Mary of Lynn.

I cannot omit, at the same time, to give full credit to the zeal shown by the Leander's Ship's Company, and with what alacrity and anxious wish (Captain Talbot reports to me) they showed to engage both the Frigates, then in the Haze, and under French Colours, when the Leander bore up to place herself between them to bring them to Action. From the high opinion I have of the Officers, and the uniform good and steady conduct and discipline of the Men, I trust they would have given a good account of them.

The Cleopatra sailed for Halifax the 18th instant, under the charge of Captain Sir Robert Lawrie, for the purpose of being valued and refitted as soon as possible.

La Ville de Milan I shall take to Halifax with the Squadron. She is a very fine Frigate, of the largest class, only one year old the day of the Action, and completely fitted for His Majesty's Service in every respect, except the damage she received in her masts, yards, &c. in the Action, having also a great quantity of spare Stores on board. I therefore trust their Lordships will give the necessary orders for her being purchased into His Majesty's Service. I shall take upon me to direct Commissioner Inglefield to cause the proper Officers of His Majesty's Dock-yard to value her hull, stores, &c., agreeable to their Lordships' instructions on that head. I have the honour to be, &c.

A. MITCHELL.

His Majesty's Ship Leander, off St. David's Head, Bermuda,
SIR, *Wednesday, 6th March, 1805, at ten A.M.*

I have the honour to inform you, that I proceeded to Sea, and cruised in His Majesty's Ship under my Command, according to your orders, dated the 13th of last month.

On Saturday the 23d of February, at twelve o'clock at noon, a Sail was seen from the mast-head, bearing south of us; the weather at this time was hazy, with squalls of Wind and Rain from the northward. All sail was immediately made in chase; the weather becoming still more hazy, in a few moments we lost sight of the chase; at half-past two o'clock it cleared away a little to the southward, and we again got sight of her. I found we had considerably neared the chase, and that it was a large Ship under jury masts, standing to the south-east. At three o'clock we saw another Ship a short distance from the chase, steering the same course, also under jury masts, in appearance a much larger Vessel. As we closed them very fast, we soon clearly saw they were both Frigates; on their making us out to be a Man of War, they closed to support each other, fired a gun to leeward, and hoisted French Ensigns from their main-stays; at four o'clock we were within gun-shot of them, they separated, the Frigate nearest to us put before the Wind, the other steered with it, on her larboard quarter. By half-past four o'clock we got within musket-shot of the smallest Frigate, gave her one of the main-deck guns; when, after a few minutes' hesitation, she hauled down her Colours, and hove to.

On my hailing this Frigate, I am sorry to tell you, Sir, that I was informed by them she was His Majesty's Ship Cleopatra, of 32 guns, lately commanded by Sir Robert Lawrie, Bart. She was taken on Sunday the 17th of February, after having brought to and sustained a most severe and gallant Action for the space of three hours and a quarter, by a French Frigate nearly double her force, in size, complement of Men, and weight of metal.

Observing that the part of the Crew left on board her belonging to His Majesty's Ship Cleopatra, had come on deck, and taken possession of her on the Ship striking to us, I hailed, ordered them to make sail, and steer after His Majesty's Ship Leander. Again made sail in chase, and in about an hour's time got alongside the French Frigate; she hauled down her Colours, and struck to us without a gun being fired on either side.

On hailing the French Frigate, you, Sir, may easily judge how happy I must have felt, on hearing I was answered by my friend Sir Robert Lawrie, who told me he was well, and that the Ship was la Ville de Milan, nineteen days from the Island of Martinique, bound to France.

La Ville de Milan is a remarkably fine and handsome Frigate, about one year old, 1200 tons burthen, mounting fourteen long nine-pounders on her quarter deck, six long nine-pounders on the forecastle, fifteen ports of a side on the maindeck: when she sailed from France, had twenty-eight eighteen-pounders mounted on it—now twenty-six; two were landed from her at Martinique.

When the Action commenced between la Ville de Milan and His Majesty's Ship Cleopatra, she was commanded by Mons. Reynaud, Capitaine de Vaisseau, had on board 360 Men as her complement, besides a number of Officers and Soldiers of the French Army, going Passengers to Europe.

The Officers of la Ville de Milan agree in saying, that having dispatches on board for France, with orders not to speak any thing during their passage, every thing was done in their power to avoid being brought to Action by the Cleopatra.

Mons. Reynaud was killed by the last shot fired from the Cleopatra; he was esteemed an experienced and active Officer, and had served in the late King of France's Service as an Auxiliary Officer. He sailed in la Ville de Milan from l'Orient, the 1st of last August, as Commodore of six of their largest Frigates, with Troops embarked on board them, to be landed on the Island of Martinique: after having performed this service, he was ordered, as the French Officers express it, to make a *Sweep* through the Islands.

Mons. Guillet, Capitaine de Fregate, and Second Captain of la Ville de Milan, commanded when she struck to us; and Mons. Carron, her Second Lieutenant, had the Command of the Cleopatra.

It is not possible for Officers to speak in stronger terms than the French Officers do in praise of Sir Robert Lawrie's perseverance in so long a chase, except it is in the praise they bestow on him, his Officers, Seamen, and Marines, for their gallant conduct during so long and severe an Action.

It is a very painful part of my duty to be obliged to inform you, Sir, that your eldest Son, who was doing duty as an acting Lieutenant, is included among the number badly wounded on board the Cleopatra: as soon as the weather admitted of his being removed, I had him brought on board this Ship, and I have great pleasure in telling you he is much recovered; and from the experience, great care and attention of Mr. Clifford, Surgeon of the Leander, I have every reason to believe that you will, in a short space of time, have the satisfaction of finding him once more gallantly exerting himself for the honour, and in the defence of his King and Country. Sir Robert Lawrie speaks in the highest terms of his conduct, and, indeed, of that of all the Officers, Seamen, and Marines, of His Majesty's Ship Cleopatra.

Sir Robert has, at my request, been so kind as to take charge of the Cleopatra till she arrives in Port. I have given Mr. Nairne, First Lieutenant of his Majesty's Ship Leander, charge of la Ville de Milan: the length of time he has had the honour to serve under your Flag would make it superfluous in me to attempt to point out to you, Sir, his meritorious services and abilities as an Officer; the only comment I can make on his conduct on this occasion is, that nothing can exceed the exertions he has made in putting la Ville de Milan in a sea-worthy state.

The alacrity of the Officers, Seamen, and Marines, of His Majesty's Ship under my Command during the chase, and their steadiness on going down to attack the two Frigates, who had closed, in appearance with a determination to make a formidable resistance, convinced me, Sir, that had they waited to make the resistance they seemed disposed to do, the Leander would not have *sullied* her good name. I have the honour to be, &c.

To Vice-Admiral Sir A. Mitchell, K.B., JOHN TALBOT, Post Captain.
&c. &c. &c.

SIR, *His Majesty's Ship Leander, Murray's Anchorage,*
  Bermuda, March 7, 1805.

I have the honour to send you enclosed a letter I this day received from Sir Robert Lawrie, Bart. From the statement made therein, you will find, Sir, that the credit of the British Flag has seldom been more honourably and gallantly supported than on the present occasion; and the French Officers, whom I have Prisoners on board this Ship, cannot themselves avoid to acknowledge, that had not the Cleopatra unfortunately forged a-head of la Ville de Milan the latter part of the Action, la Ville de Milan must have surrendered to the Cleopatra.

I have the honour to be, &c.

Vice-Admiral Sir A. Mitchell, K.B. J. TALBOT.
&c. &c. &c.

SIR,
His Majesty's Ship *Cleopatra*, at Sea,
February 25, 1805.

I have to request that you will be pleased to acquaint the Commander in Chief, that on Saturday the 16th instant, in lat. 28° N., long. 67° W., at ten A.M., saw a Ship in the S.E. standing to the E.N.E., the Wind at N.W.; made sail towards her; at eleven perceived the chase to be a large Frigate, with fifteen ports of a side on the main deck; cleared Ship for Action, and hoisted American Colours to induce him to bring to for us; but instead of which he made more sail; the weather squally; made and shortened sail occasionally; carried away several studding-sail-yards, and the fore-top-mast studding-sail-boom, shifted over the starboard one, and set the reefed lower studding sail; a good deal of swell; the chase apparently steering so as to keep the studding-sails drawing full: and that at day-light on the 17th, was about four miles a-head; fresh breezes and swell as before. At half-past ten he took in his studding-sails, and hauled more up; when we got within about three quarters of a mile, took in ours also. At half-past eleven he hauled his main-sail up, and kept more to the Wind; upon our steering so close with him upon his quarter he again set it and stay-sails, trying to gain the Wind of us (upon which point of sailing he had the advantage); we made all sail, the chase having some time before hoisted French Colours, and we ours.

On his seeming to draw a-head from us, at the distance of about half gun-shot, fired our bow chasers, which he returned occasionally from his stern.

His guns appearing so well directed, and of heavy metal, and to prevent being raked by them, I was obliged to steer so as to keep on his quarter, though prolonging the chase. Latitude, at noon, 29° 24' N., long. 64° 20' W. At half-past two P.M. having got within about a cable's length from the Enemy, he luffed close to the Wind, and gave us two broadsides, which, when at less than half a cable's distance, we returned, and a warm Action commenced, both Ships trimming sails, steering sometimes close to the Wind, and at others about three points free, during which we had considerably the advantage. About five, having shot away his main-top-sail-yard, we forged a-head, although the mizen-top-sail was squared, and both jib, stay, and haulyards gone, finding neither fore nor main clue-garnets left to haul the courses up, our running rigging cut to pieces, so as to render it impossible to either shorten or back a sail, and both main and spring stays were shot away, the main-mast only supported by the storm-stay-sail-stay, I was induced to cross his bow, and, by hauling up, to have raked him, in preference to exposing our stern to the fire of twenty-five pieces of cannon from his broadside; but in the act of which an unfortunate shot struck the wheel, the broken spokes were jammed against the deck, so as to render it immovable, as well as the rudder, which, at the same time, was choaked in the end by splinters, pistols, &c. placed near it. Our opponent, availing himself of our ungovernable situation, with the Wind upon his quarter, gave us the stern, running his head and bowsprit over our quarter deck, just abaft the main rigging; and, under the cover of a very heavy fire from muskets and musketoons, attempted to board us, but was drove back; we exchanged a few musketry with them; but their great advantage in height and superiority of numbers, as well as by their musketoons from their tops, cleared our decks, and in at our ports. The only two guns we could bring to bear, being fired from within board, did them little injury, the shot passing through their lower deck. Most of our sails laying a-shiver, or partly a-back, and bore down by so heavy a Ship, (having been intended for a 74,) going almost before the Wind, and much Sea running, appearing to cut us asunder at every send, I saw no prospect of saving this Ship, or the lives of the numerous wounded that then were below. On the suggestion of the First Lieutenant we attempted to hoist the fore-top-mast-stay-sail; and I directed the sprit-sail top-sail to be set also; but, in the execution of which orders, every Man was knocked down by their musketry and other small shot, as they made their appearance. At a quarter past five they succeeded in boarding, and I was compelled to surrender to the French Frigate la Ville de Milan, of 46 guns, French eighteen-pounders on the main-deck, and eights on the quarter-deck and forecastle; 350 Men, besides several Officers and Passengers: commanded by Mons. Reynaud, Capitaine de Vaisseau, and Mons. Gillet, Capitaine de Fregate; the former was killed, and the latter badly wounded in the Action, and immediately afterwards the Cleopatra became a perfect Wreck, not a spar standing but the mizen-mast, the bowsprit and other masts gone by the board, and I fully expected she would have foundered before both Ships could get clear of each other.

I trust it will be found that every exertion was made to bring a Ship of so superior force into Action, and in maintaining of it. La Ville de Milan is nearly double our size and force, being a new Ship of about 1200 tons burthen, and having almost twice our number of Men on board, as we only mustered at quarters one hundred and ninety-nine, being ten short of complement, and that from the strength of the Ship's Company in able Seamen, and there were several in the sick list.

From Lieutenant Balfour I received every assistance, as from a good and zealous Officer; as also from Lieutenants Kinsman and Crooke, and Lieutenant Bowen of the Bermuda, who kept up a well-directed fire from the main-deck, and Mr. Mitchell, Midshipman and acting Lieutenant, from the quarter-deck, at which Lieutenant Appleton of the Marines assisted, having no Men to spare for small arms, but was wounded early.

The steady and cool conduct of Mr. Bett (the Master) confirmed what I had always expected from him: to go further in particularizing individuals would be too tedious; but I think it my duty to mention Mr. M'Carthy's (the Boatswain) conduct, who is badly wounded, was highly spirited and active; and more gallantry and bravery could not have been displayed than by both Officers and Men of so young a Ship's Company, many being under twenty years of age, and only three Marines, who had joined that corps more than two weeks before they were embarked.

I have no hesitation in saying, that had not the above unlucky accident occurred, she must have struck to us, as the next morning her foremast and bowsprit were the only masts standing, much cut in the hull, and I counted eleven shot in the wreck of her main-mast; that our twelve-pounders could not do that justice too from its size, nor the thickness of her sides, that was so well intended.

I beg most earnestly to solicit Sir Andrew Mitchell's patronage in favor of Messrs. Howes and Ridgeway, (Master's-Mates,) as two very meritorious and promising young Men, having considerably more than served their time, and passed for Lieutenants: their conduct on this occasion, as well as for several years before with me, has been much to my satisfaction, and in my humble opinion, to entitle them to promotion, as well as for Mr. Balfour the First Lieutenant; as you, Sir, must be the best judge of the Situation we have reduced the French Ship to, so as to render her chance of escape from our numerous Cruisers almost an absolute impossibility. I have the honour to be, &c.

To Captain John Talbot, His Majesty's Ship Leander.   ROB. LAWRIE.

A return of Killed and Wounded on board His Majesty's Ship Cleopatra, in Action with the French Frigate la Ville de Milan.

Killed.

George Trepass, Boatswain's Mate; William Lewis and Matthew Shawe, Quarter-Masters; James Hammond, Caulker; William Danney (1st), William Danney (2d), James Pierce, Joseph Hyams, Richard King, Henry Fenlayson, Henry Betson, Uriah Hudsbal, Jeremiah Murphy, John Cargell, William Farley, and —— Sabday, Seamen; John Pearce, a Boy; Frederick Miller, Serjeant of Marines; James Ridley and John Smith, Privates of Marines.

Since dead of wounds.

William Hull, Corporal of Marines; Edward Witley, Private of Marines.

Dangerously wounded.

Mr. Mitchell, (Midshipman,) Acting Lieutenant; Mr. Bett, Master; Mr. M'Carthy, Boatswain; 1 Quarter-Master; 1 Captain's Coxswain; 8 Seamen; 1 Corporal of Marines; 4 Privates of Marines.

Slightly wounded.

Mr. Balfour and Mr. Crooke, Lieutenants; Mr. Bowen, Lieutenant of His

Majesty's Ship Bermuda; Mr. Appleton, Lieutenant of Marines; Mr. Standly, Midshipman; 1 Boatswain's Mate; 12 Seamen.

Total.—20 killed, 2 since dead of wounds, 18 dangerously wounded, and 18 slightly wounded.

ROB. LAWRIE.

Copy of a Letter from Captain Langford, Commander of His Majesty's Sloop Lark, to William Marsden, Esq.; dated Port Praya, Island of St. Jago, February 8, 1805.

SIR,

I have the honor to inform you, that in consequence of information of a Spanish Merchant Schooner being at anchor off the Bay of Senegal, I proceeded immediately in quest of her, and had the good fortune to meet with her at that Anchorage. She proves the Spanish Schooner the Carmerara, pierced for sixteen guns, having only two on board, laden with wine, formerly in possession of the French, employed as a Privateer by Victor Hughes at Cayenne, has done considerable mischief to the British Trade on this Coast, was now intended to have been presented by the Governor of Senegal to Victor Hughes as a further Annoyance to our Trade on this Part of the Coast. I have the honour to be, &c.

FREDERICK LANGFORD.

APRIL 27.

Copy of a Letter from the Right Honourable Lord Keith, K.B., Admiral of the Blue, &c., to William Marsden, Esq., dated on board His Majesty's Ship Monarch, off Ramsgate, 25th April, 1805.

SIR,

You will be pleased to acquaint their Lordships, that I understand that seven Dutch Schuyts, part of a Convoy passing towards Boulogne from the eastward, were yesterday cut off by some of the Boulogne Squadron; the particulars of which, however, have not yet reached me: but I enclose a copy of a Letter from Lieutenant Shirley, of the Gallant Gun-brig, to Vice-Admiral Holloway, reporting the particulars of the discovery and first attack upon this Convoy.

I have the honour to be, &c.

KEITH.

SIR, *His Majesty's Gun-vessel Gallant, Downs, 24th April, 1805.*

I have the honour to state to you, for the information of the Commander in Chief, while sailing Guard off Ambleteuse this day, at six A. M., Rear-Admiral Douglas made the Watchful and Gallant's Signals to chase N.E.; on which bearing I discovered a number of the Enemy's Schuyts under Dutch Colours, endeavouring to round Cape Grisnez, from the eastward. I made all possible Sail, in company with the Watchful Gun-brig, standing well in to cut them off. About eight o'clock I closed in with the Enemy, and commenced a well-directed fire with round and grape, which threw them into great confusion; but, unfortunately, having received four shot between wind and water from heavy Batteries, I was obliged to haul to the Wind on the starboard tack in order to stop the leaks, which were gaining very fast. Under these circumstances I was prevented from capturing the chief part of this Flotilla. One of them I perceived struck to the Watchful; and I have the satisfaction of adding, that the inner Shore Squadron was in pursuit of the remainder. I am happy to say the Gallant has not a Man hurt, although she was engaged within musket-shot of the Batteries for nearly an hour. The Officers and Crew under my Command conducted themselves with great bravery. Mr. Joseph Derby, my Sub-Lieutenant, I beg leave strongly to recommend to my Lords Commissioners of the Admiralty, for his meritorious conduct in attending so well to my orders.

I have the honour to be, &c.

Vice-Admiral Holloway,   THO. SHIRLEY.
&c. &c. &c.

Copy of another Letter from Admiral Lord Keith, to William Marsden, Esq., dated Monarch, off Ramsgate, 25th April, 1805.

SIR,

I transmit, for their Lordships' information, copies of a Letter from Captain Honeyman, of His Majesty's Ship the Leda, to Rear-Admiral Douglas, and of the list to which it refers, reporting the Capture of seven Vessels of the Enemy's Flotilla, part of a Division yesterday attacked on their Passage from the eastward, towards Boulogne.

I have the honour to be, &c.

KEITH.

SIR, *Leda, off Boulogne, April 24, 1805.*

I have the honour of informing you, about six o'clock this morning, twenty-six of the Enemy's Vessels were discovered coming round Cape Grisnez : I immediately made the Signal for the detached Squadron to get under weigh, which consisted of the Vessels named in the Margin * ; and have great pleasure in acquainting you, that after engaging them about two hours, we succeeded in cutting off seven Schuyts, a list of which I enclose. I am happy to acquaint you, there was only one slightly wounded on board the Archer, and that both Officers and Men who were employed on this Service, performed it to my satisfaction.

The Gallant having received some damage in her hull, bore up for the Downs, which prevented my getting her Report. I am, &c.

Rear-Admiral Douglas, ROB. HONEYMAN.

&c. &c. &c.

A Report of the Capture of the Enemy's Flotilla off Cape Grisnez, April 24, 1805.

Schuyt No. 52, Loriol, Sub-Lieutenant of Infantry, Commander, of 3 twenty-four pounders and small arms, 25 tons burthen, from Dunkirk bound to Ambleteuse, and had 18 Soldiers, 15 Seamen, 1 Cannonier, and 1 Pilot on board.

Schuyt, No. 48. A. Joron, of 51st Infantry, Commander, of 2 six-pounders, 1 twenty-four pounder, and 1 brass howitzer, 26 tons burthen, from Dunkirk bound to Ambleteuse, and had 21 Soldiers and 4 Seamen on board.

Schuyt No. 57. Loriol, Lieutenant of 51st Infantry, Commander, of 2 six-pounders and 1 twenty-four pounder, 25 tons burthen, from Dunkirk bound to Ambleteuse, and had 18 Soldiers, 5 Seamen, 1 Cannonier, and 1 Pilot on board.

Schuyt No. 45. Litner, Sub-Lieutenant of 51st Infantry, Commander, of 1 twenty-four pounder, 1 twelve-pounder, and 1 six-pounder, 28 tons burthen, from Dunkirk bound to Ambleteuse, and had 20 Soldiers, 5 Seamen, and 1 Cannonier on board.

Schuyt No. 3. Mr. Calder, Senior, Commander, left her before taken possession of, from Dunkirk bound to Ambleteuse, and had 4 Seamen and 1 Pilot on board.

Schuyt No. 54. Bragur, Sub-Lieutenant of 51st Infantry, Commander, of 1 twenty-four-pounder, and 2 six-pounders, 28 tons burthen, from Dunkirk bound to Ambleteuse, and had 20 Soldiers, 5 Seamen, and 1 Cannonier on board.

Schuyt No. 43. Billa, Sub-Lieutenant of 51st Infantry, Commander, of 1 twenty-four pounder and two six-pounders, from Dunkirk bound to Ambleteuse, and had 20 Soldiers, 5 Seamen, and 1 Pilot on board.

B. DOUGLAS.

Copy of another Letter from Admiral Lord Keith to William Marsden, Esq.; dated Monarch, off Ramsgate, 26th April 1805.

SIR,

Be pleased to acquaint their Lordships, that two more of the Enemy's armed Schuyts have been sent into the Downs this morning, by the Archer Gun-brig; and that Rear-Admiral Douglas reports very favourably to me upon the conduct of Lieutenant Price, her Commander.

I herewith enclose a copy of Lieutenant Price's Letter to the Rear-Admiral on the occasion, and have the honour to be, &c.

KEITH.

---

* Leda, Fury, Harpy, Railleur, Bruiser, Gallant, Archer, Locust, Tickler, Watchful, Monkey, Firm.

His Majesty's Gun-brig Archer, off Cape Grisnez,
SIR,   *25th April, 1805.*

In obedience to your Signal on the evening of the 24th, to look out, during the night, off Cape Grisnez, I proceeded with His Majesty's Gun-brig Archer under my Command. At daylight on the 25th, I perceived two of the Enemy's Gun-boats had drifted off the Land, which I immediately gave chase to, and at six o'clock took possession of them. No. 44, twenty-six Men, 1 twenty-four pounder, and 2 twelve-pounders; and No. 58, twenty-seven Men, 1 twenty-four pounder and 2 twelve-pounders, part of the Flotilla from Dunkirk.
I have the honour to be, &c.
W. PRICE,
Rear-Admiral Douglas, &c. &c. &c.   Lieut. and Commander.

MAY 21.

Copy of a Letter from the Right Honourable Lord Keith, K.B., Admiral of the Blue, &c., to William Marsden, Esq., dated off Ramsgate, the 19th Instant.

SIR,
I transmit for their Lordships' information, a Letter which I have received from Captain Jackson, of His Majesty's Sloop the Musquito, acquainting me with the Capture of two of the Enemy's small Privateers.
I have the honour to be, &c. KEITH.

His Majesty's Sloop Musquito, North Yarmouth
MY LORD,   *Roads, April 14, 1805.*
I beg leave to acquaint you, for the information of the Lords Commissioners of the Admiralty, that on the 12th Instant, Scarbro' West thirteen miles, three Sail were discovered in the Offing, two of them firing guns apparently to bring-to the third. I immediately made Sail in chase of them. The first I came up with was a Sloop from Guernsey, with a cargo of contraband goods, who informed me that the other two were French Privateers: no time was lost in making all Sail after them; and though night was setting in, I am happy to say we succeeded in capturing the first about twelve o'clock, and the other shortly after day-light the next morning. They proved to be the Orestes and Pylades, Dutch-built Koffs, fitted out as a deception, with a French Commission, but generally under Prussian Colours, commanded by Citizens Wepperman and Cavin, each armed with a twenty-four pound Carronade, six Swivels, a considerable number of small Arms, and manned with 33 Men; this is their first Cruise; they have been at Sea three weeks, but owing to the bad weather have made no Captures. By their Charts I find their views were directed chiefly against the Trade on the Coast of Scotland, and might have done a great deal of mischief, as no one would have suspected them of being Privateers.   I have the honour to be, &c.
S. JACKSON.
Admiral Lord Keith, K.B., &c. &c. &c.

Copy of a Letter from the Honourable Rear-Admiral Cochrane, Commander in Chief of His Majesty's Ships and Vessels at the Leeward Islands, to William Marsden, Esq., dated at Barbadoes, the 5th April, 1805.

SIR,
I herewith enclose you, for the information of the Lords Commissioners of the Admiralty, a copy of a Letter I have received from Captain Colby, of His Majesty's Ship Eagle, of his having captured l'Empereur French Privateer. She is a remarkable fast-sailing Vessel, and appears well calculated to cruise in these Seas against the Enemy's Privateers, which are very numerous.
I am, &c.   ALEX. COCHRANE.

SIR,   *His Majesty's Ship Eagle, Carlisle Bay, April 3, 1805.*
I have the honour to inform you, that the Schooner I parted Company from the Squadron by Signal last evening, I came up and captured at midnight; she proved to be l'Empereur Privateer, belonging to Guadaloupe; she is a very

fine Vessel of her description, coppered and sails well, is one hundred and sixty tons, mounts fourteen six-pounders, and had on board eighty-two Men; has been forty-six days at Sea, but made no Captures.

I have the honour to be, &c.

DAVID COLBY.

To the Honourable Alexander Cochrane,
Rear-Admiral of the Blue, &c. &c.

MAY 23.

Copy of a Letter from Rear-Admiral Dacres, Commander in Chief of his Majesty's Ships and Vessels at Jamaica, to William Marsden, Esq.; dated at Port Royal, March 15, 1805.

SIR,

I enclose you, for their Lordships' information, a copy of a letter this day received, (under cover of one from Captain Atkins, of the Seine,) acquainting me of the Rein Deer having captured a Spanish Privateer. I am, &c.

J. R. DACRES.

His Majesty's Sloop Rein Deer, off Montego Bay,
SIR,   *7th March, 1805.*

I have the pleasure to inform you, that after a chase of five hours and a half, in company with His Majesty's Sloop Hunter, I have captured the Spanish Schooner Privateer Santa Rosalia Galundrina, commanded by Francisco de Naras, having on board 57 Men.

Previous to our falling in with her she appears to have mounted three guns, which were thrown overboard during the chase, (one of eight and a half, and two of four pounds calibre,) and has on board musketry for the whole of her Crew.

She sails remarkably fast; is victualled for fourteen days; left Caliodam, in Cuba, yesterday, but belongs to St. Jago; has taken nothing during her Cruise.

The Privateer I have sent into Port Royal, under the protection of His Majesty's Sloop Hunter, with the greatest part of her Crew, having only fifteen remaining on board the Rein Deer. I have the honour to be, &c.

David Atkins, Esq., commanding His Majesty's   J. FYFFE.
Ship Seine.

MAY 25.

Copy of a Letter from Commodore Sir Samuel Hood, K.B., Commander in Chief of His Majesty's Ships and Vessels at the Leeward Islands, to William Marsden, Esq.; dated on board the Centaur, at Sea, the 26th March, 1805.

SIR,

The enclosed copy of a letter from Captain Impey, of His Majesty's Sloop Epervier, which I send for the information of the Lords Commissioners of the Admiralty, gives an account of the Capture of a small French Privateer.

I have the honour to be, &c.

SAM. HOOD.

SIR,   *Epervier, Tortola, Jan. 31, 1805.*

I have the honour to acquaint you, that on the 26th instant, Crab Island bearing north two leagues, I saw a suspicious Sail to the southward, and after a chase of five hours in His Majesty's Sloop under my Command, came up with, and captured l'Elizabeth French Schooner Privateer, belonging to Mariagalante, mounting four carriage guns, with muskets, pistols, cutlasses, &c., and manned with 34 Men, one of whom was killed by their obstinate attempt to escape. The Schooner had previously taken a Sloop, belonging to Tortola, and sent her into St. Thomas.   I have the honour to be, &c.

Sir Samuel Hood, K.B., Commander in Chief,   JOHN IMPEY.
           &c. &c. &c.

Imperial Parliament.

HOUSE OF LORDS, May 6.
NAVAL DEBATES.

THE Committee of Privileges appointed to search for precedents relative to the Message sent from the House of Commons, requesting the attendance of Lord Viscount Melville before the Committee of the House, respecting the Tenth Report of the Commissioners of Naval Inquiry, sat for some time, but no strangers were admitted.

May 16. Sir *J. Stewart*, and several other Members of the House of Commons, brought up a Message, desiring their Lordships would permit the Earl of St. Vincent to attend the Select Committee of that House, respecting Sir Home Popham. They were informed, the House would send an answer by Messengers of its own.

HOUSE OF COMMONS, April 29.

MR. *Williams*, from the Office of the Commissioners of Naval Inquiry, presented the Correspondence of the Treasurer of the Navy with the Commissioners, of the 10th and 17th July, 1804.—Ordered to be printed.

Sir *A. Hammond* moved for the Papers he had given notice of on Thursday, relative to the Eleventh Report of the Commissioners of Naval Inquiry. Upon this a conversation of some detail took place between Sir A. Hammond, Mr. Tierney, and Mr. Grey, in which the latter expressed a wish for the expunging of Sir A. H.'s Motion.

Mr. *Pitt* said, The Motion, Sir, is for a copy of a letter from the Comptroller of the Navy to the Commissioners of the Admiralty, together with its enclosures. Now, when we know that the Papers moved for refer to the conduct of the Comptroller of the Navy in his official capacity, and when in a printed Report of a Commission of this House the strongest language is employed respecting such conduct, will any Man deny that the Hon. Baronet ought to have an opportunity given him to vindicate himself to the utmost he is able?

Sir *A. Hammond* again rose. It was impossible, when the Comptroller of the Navy was particularly reflected on by the Commissioners of Naval Inquiry, for him to pass over a great part of the Eleventh Report: Either the noble Lord or myself will stand, after the investigation of the evidence therein given, and after the perusal of the documents moved for, in a situation in which no Man of honour could wish to be.—Sir Andrew proceeded : The Papers I wish to be laid before the House consist of my own letters to the Commissioners, their answers, and those various documents, which I deem necessary to my defence.—Upon a question asked by Mr. Creevy,

Mr. *Pitt* said, that Sir C. Middleton (now Lord Barham) had been appointed First Lord of the Admiralty. Upon Sir A. Hammond's Motion being carried, the papers were presented.

Mr. *Grey* made some objections to some deficiency of arrangement in them. In a conversation of some warmth, which followed,

Mr. *Tierney* explained upon the expenses of the Stone Expedition, which was conducted by other Persons not Officers in his Majesty's Navy. No Man could deny that Lord St. Vincent must have known that such an Expedition was going forward; but then it was evident, from the letter of Earl St. Vincent to Sir A. Hamond, that he could not possibly have any knowledge of the application of public money for that purpose, as it was there expressly stated the whole expense was to be paid by the Treasury. He could not possibly have more completely washed his hands of the business than he there did. He knew nothing of the depositing of 14,000l. in Messrs. Hammersleys' Bank. As a Seaman, he had given his opinion of the practicability of choaking up one of the Enemy's Harbours; but as an honourable Man, he had taken care that the public money voted for the services of the Navy should not be applied to a purpose that was not in the least connected with that service. He now thanked the Hon. Bart. for having brought before Parliament, and before the Public, a Paper which had so completely removed all doubt upon that subject.

Admiral *Markham* said, that he would not state what were the opinions of Earl St. Vincent or of Sir T. Trowbridge; but he would mention what he had said himself on the subject of the Stone Expedition; and that was, that he never did approve of it, and that it was such a Secret Expedition, that nothing else was talked of from one end of the River to the other. After a few other observations from different honourable Members, the question was put, that these Papers be printed, which was carried unanimously. After Mr. Pitt's Motion, for leave to bring in a Bill to continue the powers granted to the Naval Commissioners, had been agreed to, together with a second Motion for leave to bring in a Bill for appointing Commissioners to inquire into the military expenditure of the country, to correct any abuses that may prevail therein, and to report upon such remedies as may appear to be expedient,

Mr. *Fox* said, that however anxious he might be to see Bills introduced for the cure and prevention of abuses, he could not bring his mind to approve of any Bill of the kind brought in at the present moment, under the auspices of the Rt. Hon. Gentleman. Considering every thing which had been lately brought to light against the dear Friend and Colleague of the Rt. Hon. Gentleman, the House was called on the present proceeding with a considerable degree of doubt and suspicion.

Lord *Castlereagh* asked if there was, in the political annals of the country, a long political life more marked for its purity than that of Mr. Pitt? or if there was at that moment a person in that House so much entitled to public confidence? (*A laugh.*) Leave was then given to bring in the Bill, and Mr. Pitt and the Attorney and Solicitor General was allowed to prepare and bring in the same.

Mr. *S. Stanhope* moved, " That the Attorney General be instructed to pursue the most effectual means of ascertaining and recovering, in the due course of law, any sum of public money applicable to Naval Services used by Lord Melville or Mr. Trotter, subsequently to the 1st of January 1786."

Mr. *Banks* moved, as an Amendment, " That a criminal prosecution should be instituted against Lord Melville and Mr. Trotter." This gave rise to a long Debate, in which Dr. Lawrence, Messrs. Windham, Fox, Sheridan, and T. Grenville, took part.

Mr. Serjeant *Best* contended, that a prosecution by civil suit could answer no good purpose, but a criminal proceeding might secure the punishment of the Offenders, who he denied were yet punished.

The House then divided,

For the original Motion for a Civil Suit 223
For Mr. Banks's Amendment - - - 128
Majority —95.

A division also took place on a Motion of Mr. Grey, that the House should adjourn,

Noes - - - - - - - - - - 240
Ayes - - - - - - - - - - - 98
Majority —142

Some further conversation took place on the Report of the Scrutineers. On the List of the Select Committee being brought up,

Mr. *Grey* objected to several names, beginning with Lord Castlereagh, and the Debate thereon adjourned till to-morrow. The List is as follows: Lord Castlereagh, Mr. Whitbread, Master of the Rolls, Mr. W. Windham, Sir W. Scott, Mr. T. Grenville, Mr. Ryder, Lord G. Cavendish, Lord Dunlo, Lord W. Russell, Mr. Leycester, Mr. St. John, Mr. Foster, Mr. H. Lascelles, Sir H. Mildmay, Mr. S. Thornton, Mr. J. Fane, Lord Boyle, Mr. Cartwright, Mr. H. Browne, and Mr. Gunning. Adjourned.

MAY 3. The *Chancellor of the Exchequer* presented a Bill for continuing the

Act of the 34th of His Majesty, appointing a Commission to inquire into the Naval Abuses, and the better conducting the business of Prize Agents.

6. The *Speaker* informed the House he had received a letter from the Commissioners of Naval Inquiry; it was dated from the Office of Naval Inquiry, Great George Street, 4th May, and was to this effect:—" Sir, We have had the honour of receiving your letter of the 3d instant, transmitting to us the Resolutions of the House of Commons of the 2d. It is most gratifying to us to learn that our conduct has been considered deserving a vote of approbation by that Honourable House—a testimony which is one of the highest honours that can be conferred on Persons employed for the Public. We receive it with gratitude, respect, and thankfulness, and beg you will communicate to the House our sentiments. We also return you our thanks for the obliging manner in which you have conveyed the Resolution of the House."

LORD MELVILLE.

Mr. *Whitbread* being called upon by the Speaker, spoke to the following effect:—Whatever motives may be attributed to my conduct during the course of the business which I have undertaken, there are none, I trust, who will not suppose that I have been impressed with feelings of anxiety; but those feelings were not to be compared with what I now experience. There are two points open before us: the one leads to immortal honour; and the other, if we are guided by mistake, will lead to the dishonour of the House, and the detriment of the public interest. If it had been proposed that the Resolutions of the 8th of April should have been immediately followed up by an Address to His Majesty to dismiss Lord Melville from the places he holds, and from his Councils and Presence for ever, I apprehend there would not have been a dissentient voice.

The *Chancellor of the Exchequer* called Mr. Whitbread to order, and said, that the communication he had to make to the House would anticipate what the Hon. Gentleman might have to propose.

Mr. *Whitbread*:—Whatever communication the Rt. Hon. Gentleman may have to make, will come with more propriety after the Motion which I shall submit to the House. I do persist, that if Mr. Dundas had been a Member of the House of Commons, and there had been a motion made for his expulsion, there would not have been a dissentient voice. If I possess accuracy sufficient to distinguish between the Resolutions that have passed, and the Measure I now propose, if the latter be not carried, I contend he is not punished at all. If he is sensible of remorse, and possesses a broken heart and a contrite spirit, he is punished, in one sense, superior to any punishment that can be inflicted by this House, inasmuch as it is inflicted by a higher Hand; but it behoves us to inflict some punishment, to serve as an example to others. We must take care that no Man in his situation treads in his steps. There were three parliamentary methods of pursuing Delinquents of this description:—1st, Impeachment; 2dly, A Bill of Pains and Penalties; 3dly, A Removal from all situations of honour and profit, in consequence of an Address from that House. What I propose is lighter than these. After the order of the day for taking into consideration His Majesty's answer is disposed of, I shall move—" That an humble address be presented to His Majesty, praying that Lord Viscount Melville may be removed from all Offices of trust and emolument which he holds during the pleasure of the Crown, and from His Majesty's Presence and Councils for ever."

The *Chancellor of the Exchequer* conceived that the Hon. Gentleman would have confined himself, as is usual in such cases, simply to moving the order of the day in the first instance. He should have then stated a communication from His Majesty, which, perhaps, in his own judgment, as well as that of the House, would have made his Motion unnecessary. The communication is this: *That His Majesty has been advised that the name of Lord Melville should be struck out of the list of the Privy Council, and that accordingly it would be erased on the first day that a Council shall be held.* As soon as the prevailing sense of the House was for removing Lord Melville from the Privy Council, he felt it his duty to advise His Majesty accordingly. He could not dissemble, that he felt a deep and bitter pang at being the

Person to whose lot it fell to execute such a painful duty, as that of doing any thing to add to the punishment of the Noble Lord.—It was a feeling of which he was not ashamed—a feeling he could not separate from his bosom. He could only separate it from his conduct, when he thought he was acting on principles of public duty—a conformity to the sense of the House, and with a view to avoid a discussion, which, if unnecessary, could not be less congenial to the feelings of every Man in the House, than it would be painful to his own. He had reluctantly given his advice, and he was authorised to state, that His Majesty had determined to act upon it. [*During the latter part of these observations, the Rt. Hon. Gentleman appeared extremely affected.*]

Mr. *Fox* congratulated the House and the Country upon what had fallen from the Rt. Hon. Gentleman. The cause of justice, he said, had completely triumphed; still he could have wished that the erasure of my Lord Melville's name from the list of Privy Counsellors had been done in a different manner; and instead of the Rt. Hon. Gentleman collecting the necessity of such a measure from the sense of the House by canvassing individual Members, he wished he had collected it from the Resolutions of the 10th of April. Some conversation ensued between Mr. Fox, Mr. Pitt, &c. Mr. Whitbread then withdrew his Motion.

Mr. *Grey*, in the absence of Lord H. Petty, gave notice, that his Noble Friend would bring forward his Motion to-morrow week, respecting the grants made to Lord Melville. On the Motion for the second reading of the Stipendiary Curates' Bill,

Mr. *Western* wished that it should be postponed for some time, in order that it might be further considered. This produced a short conversation, after which Mr. W. withdrew his Amendment. The Bill was read a first time, and ordered to be committed to a Committee of the whole House to-morrow. The House then adjourned.

NAVY BOARD.

7. Sir *A. S. Hammond* presented a Petition from the Commissioners of the Navy, expressing a most anxious wish to vindicate their honour, and praying that two letters of theirs to the Admiralty, dated the 4th of May, 1805, written with that view, be taken into consideration. The Hon. Member then moved, that these letters be laid before the House.

Mr. *Kinnaird* was apprehensive that the production of papers so recently written by the Navy Board, might be connected with the question of which he had given notice for to-morrow, respecting the repairs of the Romney and la Sensible; and suggested, whether it would not be more proper to withhold the papers for the present.

Sir *A. S. Hammond* said, that Sir H. Popham had written to the Admiralty in his own exculpation; his letter was on the table; and, as these letters were very short, he should suppose that Members might very easily read them to-morrow. The Navy Board had certainly as fair a right to the indulgence of that House as any individual.

The *Chancellor of the Exchequer* was of opinion, that the question had now become a great and constitutional one, involving not only the character of Sir H. Popham, whom he had a right to suppose an honourable Officer, but also involving the character and conduct of many other most respectable individuals. The letters were at length presented, and ordered to lie on the table.

LORD ST. VINCENT.

Mr. *Jeffery* (of Poole) rose to bring forward his promised Motion, for the production of several Papers relating to the Naval Department, during the Administration of Earl St. Vincent : and though, he said, they were certainly voluminous, there was not one among them idle, trivolous, or unimportant ; but such as would not fail to make a strong impression on the mind of the House, and fully to account for the depressed and degraded state to which the British Navy was at this moment reduced ; and which, had Lord St. Vincent continued at the head of our Navy Affairs to this day, would have sunk to a state still lower, and less competent to meet the formidable Enemy with whom we have to contend. He then proceeded to detail to the House a series of eighteen motions for Returns of the State of the Navy, from the year 1793 to the present time, with a view of comparing the state of our Navy during the Administration of Earl St. Vincent, and those which preceded his Lordship's appointment, and immediately followed his resignation.

The *Chancellor of the Exchequer* said, that as to the first Motion of those proposed by the Hon. Member, he had no great objection; but he was by no means prepared to judge of the propriety of agreeing, at the moment, to so long a string of Motions, involving such a variety of subjects, many of which, upon mature deliberation, it might be utterly improper to comply with. He hoped the Hon. Member would not urge his Motions.

Admiral *Markham* assured the House, that nothing could possibly give to the Noble Lord, whose conduct was the avowed object of the Motions just proposed, higher pleasure than the production of every document, and the fullest investigation of every circumstance that in any degree concerned his character or conduct. With respect to the Motion, generally, he presumed the Hon. Gentleman was not aware of the extent and tendency they would go, not merely to the conduct of Earl St. Vincent, but of the whole British Navy, since 1793 to the present time. He was ready to admit our Navy was not altogether in quite so good a state as could be wished; where the blame rested he did not wish to say, but certainly it was not with the Noble Lord, upon the whole of whose conduct, so far was he from deprecating inquiry, that he anxiously desired and courted it.

Mr. *Grey* said, the production of the papers required, might render it necessary to move for others quite as voluminous, both must be printed: and what time could then remain of the Session to read, to consider, and to discuss them? If the Hon. Member had any charge to make against the Noble Earl let him bring it forward. It was an inquiry desirable to the House, and to the Country, and to none more so than to the Noble Lord.

Mr. *Jeffery* replied, he did not bring forward those motions lightly. It was no light charge for him to state, that the degraded state of our Navy was entirely owing at this moment to the negligence of the Noble Lord. He wished, however, to bring no charge until the papers were before the House, out of which that charge was to arise. With respect to the Laurels acquired by the British Navy under the Noble Lord's Administration, they were attributable not to his direction, but to the eminent state of perfection in which he found that Navy on his succession to its direction. He asked, was the boasted superiority and perfection it maintained gained under the auspices of the Noble Earl, who never contracted for more than the building of two Ships of the Line? He avowed the purity of his motives in bringing forward the Motion, which, however, he had no objection to postpone to a more distant day, if the House wished. After some further conversation, in which Mr. G. Ponsonby, Mr. Tierney, Mr. Pitt, Admiral Markham, Sir R. Buxton, and Mr. Jeffery, bore a part, Mr. Jeffery agreed to defer his Motion until Thursday.

SIR HOME POPHAM.

Mr. *Kinnaird*, pursuant to his notice, rose to make his Motion on the subject of the Papers before the House, relative to the conduct of this Hon. Officer. As he understood that there was no intention to oppose his Motion, he should not make any prefatory observations, but move, "that a Commitee be appointed to consider of the matter contained in the Papers before the House, relative to the Repairs of the Romney and la Sensible, whilst under the Orders of Sir Home Popham in the Red Sea."

Sir *Home Popham* said, that if the House was perfectly satisfied that no stigma as yet rested upon his conduct, he should have no objection to a Committee being appointed, otherwise he should oppose it. He would say a few words respecting the charge which had been brought against him, and which he felt himself able to refute. It had been said on a former night, that he had been treated as all Officers in his situation were; and the testimonies of Sir R. King, Sir R. Bickerton, and Sir Andrew Mitchell, had been brought forward to support it. He had a Letter which he had received from Sir R. King, to contradict it. (The Hon. Baronet read it to the House). He had been refused an interview; the Navy Board had departed from their usual practice, and had singled him out to be the Victim of their vengeance. The Hon. Gentleman had a Document in his possession, which was that scurrilous Pamphlet, wherein the charges against him were brought forward; but whether it was not with a view to twist and torture his conduct, let the House judge. His reasons for putting his Ships in the most respectable state, was in consequence of an Order from the Marquis of Wellesley, stating the propriety of attacking either the Mauritius or Batavia. It was a desire to comply with this Order, and his wish to have a sufficient Force immediately, that induced him to apply to the Merchant Yards. He held it necessary to state, that from the very first time he received notice of the Accusations tgainst him, he had pressed to be heard in his defence, but was refused: never did an Officer pass through such an ordeal. He contended that a Court Martial was the properest way to proceed against him, being a mode of trial to which every British Officer was entitled. In such a Service as that he was engaged in, there might be many irregularities in his conduct, but he persisted there was nothing criminal. He felt great pride in considering what was likely to be the result of an investigation.

The *Chancellor of the Exchequer* observed, that the Papers were so numerous, complicated, and detailed, that they could not be advantageously discussed but in a Committee, when it would be proper also to consider other collateral matters. There were various points respecting the Admiralty and Navy Boards, and the short examination of one single witness to which their attention might be directed. There was likewise the circumstance of the publication of the Report from one Board to another. The loss of the Vouchers was a matter fit for inquiry, as well as the singular manner in which an English Subject, an Officer of the Navy, had been impressed. He was apprehensive, as the Motion was worded, that it would not embrace all these objects. It was at present confined to the repairs of the Romney and Sensible. He should therefore propose an Amendment to this effect: "That the Commissioners should examine the matters of the repairs of the Romney and Sensible, and the proceedings of the Admiralty and Navy Boards, and Commission of Naval Inquiry thereon; and also to inquire into the circumstances of the unauthorized publication of February 20, 1804; the loss of the Vouchers; and the circumstances of impressing Mr. David Evan Bartholomew; and report to the House, with such observations as arise to them from the consideration of the whole.

Admiral *Markham* said, that the Pamphlet alluded to was not manufactured by Lord St. Vincent and the late Board of Admiralty. The Hon. Officer seemed to forget a Pamphlet that he had circulated before. At the end of that Pamphlet there was a most extraordinary opinion, purporting to be a legal opinion. When Lord St. Vincent came to the Admiralty, it required all his care and attention to bring things to their original, at least to their proper state. He met with numerous difficulties, but he persevered against a host of enemies of every description.

Mr. *W. Dickinson* thought this business should have been referred to a Committee before now; but why had not the Admiralty brought the gallant Officer before a Court Martial, or ordered a criminal prosecution?

Admiral *Markham* explained. He never thought it a fit subject for a Court Martial, because it was too complicated. The amended Motion being carried without a division,

The *Chancellor of the Exchequer* moved, "That the number of the Committee be twenty-one; and that they be chosen by ballot;" both of which Motions, after some Debate, were agreed to.—Adjourned.

10. Mr. *Jeffry*, of Poole, moved the following Resolutions:—

1st. " That there be laid before the House an Account, showing the number of Line of Battle Ships and Frigates built between the 1st of January, 1783, and 31st of December, 1792, distinguishing the number of Ships launched from the Merchants' Yards, and from the King's Yards.

2d and 3d. " Accounts of Line of Battle Ships and Frigates at each Port, from 1st of January 1793, to 1st of January 1794, including Ships for Harbour Service.

4th, 5th, 6th, and 7th. " Accounts of the number of Ships launched at different periods, including Harbour Service, and distinguishing those launched from the King's Yards and Merchants' Yards.

8th. " An account of building Slips, and how occupied, at the different Yards, 15th May, 1804.

9th. " Account of Ships now in the King's Yards and Merchants' Yards, including those taken from the Enemy.

10th and 11th. " Accounts of correspondence between the Navy Board and Admiralty.—Withdrawn at the instance of Mr. Pitt.

12th. " An account of Ships contracted for in the Merchants' Yards, &c.

13th. " Copies of Letters from the Navy Board to the Dock Yards, concerning the quantity of timber in store.

14th. " Relating to the quality of the timber in the Dock-yards.

15th. " An account of the principal articles of Naval Stores in the several Dock Yards at different periods.

16th. " An account of Naval Stores ordered to be provided between May, 1804, and May, 1805."

Mr. Dent rose, pursuant to his notice on Wednesday, to move for some other Papers, not included in the Hon. Gentleman's Motions.

1st. " An account of the Returns of all Lieutenants promoted to the rank of Masters and Commanders; and of all Masters and Commanders promoted to the rank of Post Captains, from 1795 to 1804; and from 1st January to 18th March 1804.

2d. " An account of all Ships in Commission commanded by Post Captains, for the same period."

17. Mr. *Alexander* brought up the Report of the Committee on the Naval Inquiry Bill. On the suggestion of Admiral Markham, the Bill was recommitted, with a view to comprehend Greenwich Hospital in the range of the Inquiry. It was stated by this Bill also, those who are concerned in applying to profitable purposes the money of Persons in public situations connected with the Navy, or Persons acting in trust for them, are required to answer questions, when there may be reason to think such Money or any part of it may be Public Money. This provision was made to apply to Persons in the situation of Mr. Mark Sprott. The Report was brought up, and the Bill ordered to be read a third time on Tuesday.

ELEVENTH REPORT.

21. Mr. *Serjeant Best* rose, pursuant to his notice, to call to the most serious consideration of the House, the facts which were disclosed in the Eleventh Report of the Commissioners of Naval Inquiry. It was the first duty of that House to watch over the Constitution of the Country, and take care that no inroad should be made upon it. It was, however, impossible for any Man, who should look at those transactions, not to see that the most fundamental principles of the Constitution had been violated, and every law broken, by those whose peculiar duty it was to administer the affairs of the Country according to the laws; it was clear that it was most unconstitutional to raise money, even for the public services except by the consent of Parliament. If no money could be constitutionally raised by Exchequer Bills, without the vote of that House, still less could it be raised by Navy Bills, which were expressly intended for another purpose.—(The Learned Serjeant then read an Act passed the 7th of January, 1680, a few years before the Revolution, stating, that whoever, by loan or otherwise, raised money for the public service, without the consent of Parliament, should be responsible for the same in Parliament.)—Not only in the law which he had just read, but in all their laws, and the whole practice of Parliament, it was evident, that this was the

sense of our Ancestors, and the spirit of the Constitution. He thought he had already said enough to prove that such a practice was altogether illegal; he should therefore now come to the fact of the present case. From the latter end of the year 1800, to the month of March 1802, no less than the sum of 4,300,000l. was raised by loan on Navy Bills.—As to the first sum of 500,000l. it was issued on the 10th of November, 1800, and Parliament sat the very day after, and yet no communication was made. If a powerful State necessity had existed, he should not have charged the act as criminal; but then it behoved those who rested their defence on that ground, to prove the existence of the absolute necessity. There was also a positive law, that the Secret Service Money of the Navy should only be laid out under the directions of the First Lord of the Admiralty; yet, in a remarkable instance, *no less than* 100,000l. *had been issued out of the Secret Service Money of the Navy, by the directions of the Lords of the Treasury to the Comptroller of the Navy; and, as he understood, without the sanction of the First Lord of the Admiralty*—(*A loud cry of Hear! Hear! from the Ministerial Bench.*) The case he alluded to was the Stone Expedition. This was the business which Government said was so extrememy delicate, that the Commissioners of the Navy Board even were not to be trusted with the secret. It was a secret, however, which was known to every Waterman on the Thames, at the same time that it was not to be trusted to the Navy Board. After dwelling for some time on the pernicious consequence that would result from suffering such practices to be continued, he concluded by moving, " That the Eleventh Report of the Commissioners of Naval Inquiry be referred to a Select Committee of the House to examine and report thereon."

The *Chancellor of the Exchequer* rose, and observed, that he would not oppose the Motion generally, because he was anxious, after what had fallen from the Hon. and Learned Gentleman, that the matter should be investigated. But he would not consent, however, to the Motion in the exact shape in which it was proposed. There was one part of the Report of so secret a nature, that it could not be entrusted to any but a Secret Committee. At the same time he had no objection that the Report, with the exception of that part which related to the 100,000l. for Secret Service, should be referred to a Select Committee, and that the part excepted should be at the same time referred to a Secret Committee. With regard to the 100,000l. Secret Service money, he could give no public explanation; but he pledged himself that the Secret Committee would be satisfied. He stated, that the First Lord of the Admiralty was fully aware of the expenditure of the 100,100l. and of the Stone Expedition, to which the 100,000l. had no reference. He was glad that this Committee was proposed, and only begged leave to add a few words to except the 100,000l. Secret Service Money. The Motion was then put as amended.

Mr. *Fox* assented to the Amendment moved by the Rt. Hon. Gentleman, and justified his Hon. and Learned Friend, who brought forward the original Motion, in having so much insisted upon the law, that no money should be raised without the consent of Parliament.

Sir *A. S. Hammond* admitted, that if he had done any thing against the directions of the First Lord of the Admiralty, he should have been guilty of a great misdemeanour; but he did not :—the fact was, that he was not in the habit of seeing the First Lord of the Admiralty. My Lord St. Vincent was in the country for months together. When he had a letter from my Lord Hobart, signifying the King's pleasure that he should undertake a certain service, he was desirous of communicating that to my Lord St. Vincent, and said so to my Lord Hobart, who said he thought he had better not, for that he, my Lord Hobart, would write, which he did, and received Lord St. Vincent's approbation of that service. He (Sir A. Hammond) afterwards wrote to Lord St. Vincent, and the House was in possession of the answer; there was no reflection on him for not pursuing directions. The question was then put on Mr. Pitt's Amendment, and carried. The number of the Committee was fixed at 21, and it was agreed that it be chosen by ballot.—Adjourned.

7

Promotions and Appointments.

(April—May.)

Captain E. D. King is appointed to the Command, *pro tempore*, of the Endymion, *vice* Hon. C. Paget.

THE HAGUE.—M. H. Van Royen is provisionally charged with the Navy Department.

At the Court at St. James's, the 1st of May 1805, Present, the King's Most Excellent Majesty in Council.—This day the Right Hon. Charles Lord Barham was, by His Majesty's Command, sworn of His Majesty's Most Honourable Privy Council, and took his place at the Board accordingly.

His Majesty has been pleased to confer the honour of Knighthood on Captain Yorke, of the Royal Navy.

Captain S. H. Linzee is appointed to the Warrior, *vice* Captain W. Bligh, who is appointed Governor of New South Wales. Captain Lee, to the Courageux; Captain C. Boyles, to the Windsor Castle; Captain Curry, *pro tempore*, to the Tribune, *vice* Bennett, M.P. Lieutenant Talbot, to the Swan Cutter; Captain Paget, who has been so often stated to be the Agent for Prisoners of War, is re-appointed to the Foudroyant. Captain Kelly to the Cæsar.

Mr. Thompson is appointed private Secretary to Lord Barham.

His Majesty has been pleased to confer the honour of Knighthood on Captain James Lind, of the Royal Navy, for his late gallant Action in the Centurion, with the Marengo, (Admiral Linois,) and two Frigates.

Captain Freemantle is appointed to the Neptune, *vice* Sir T. Williams; and Mr. Neagle is to be Surgeon of the same Ship. Captain Grant to the Diadem, *vice* Sir Home Popham; Captain Bland, to the Flora; Captain Brown, to the Ajax; Mr. Harris is made a Lieutenant, and appointed to the Zebra.

Captain T. White (of Portsea,) is appointed to la Fleche, *vice* Digby, promoted; Captain Barton, of the Raisonable, to the Goliath; Lieutenant Packwood, of the Glory, to the Acting Command of the Wasp; Sub-Lieutenant G. F. Somerville, Son of Captain Somerville, of the Nemesis, to be a Lieutenant of that Ship; Captain Rodd, to the Cæsar; Mr. Banes, to be Surgeon of the Puissant; Captain Hunt to the Raisonable; Captain J. O. Hardy, to the Zealous; and Captain Dundas, to the Elephant.

Captains Sawyer, Hunter, and Lumsdaine, are appointed to superintend the payment of Ships at Portsmouth, Plymouth, and Sheerness.

Mr. Thomas Simpson, Surgeon of the Goliath, is appointed to the Arethusa Frigate, fitting in the River Thames.

BIRTHS.

April 25. The Lady of Captain Buckle, of the Sea Fencibles, in the Portsmouth District, of a Son.

29. The Lady of Captain Sir Joseph Sydney Yorke, of the Navy, of a Son. At Portsea, the Lady of Captain G. Losack, of the Navy, of a Daughter.

May 15. At Lower Tooting, Surrey, the Lady of Captain Curry, of the Navy, of a Daughter.

16. The Lady of Captain Towry, of the Navy, of a Daughter.

MARRIAGES.

Captain Ferris, of the East-India Service, to Miss P. Haynes. Captain F. has settled 16,000*l*. per annum on his Bride.

Lately, at Sidmouth, Devon, Lieutenant J. C. Stone, of the Royal Navy, to Miss H. S. Salmon, both of that place.

Lieutenant Morris, Commander of the Insolent Gun-brig, to Miss Mary Soady, third Daughter of Mr. W. Soady, of Plymouth Dock.

OBITUARY.

Lately, (was drowned) at Jamaica, Capt. Templer, of His Majesty's Ship Gælan. A few days since, at Sea, Mr. Heron, Purser of His Majesty's Ship Hibernia.

Lloyd's Marine List

OF
SHIPS LOST, DESTROYED, CAPTURED, AND RECAPTURED, &c.
FROM DECEMBER 21, 1804, TO JANUARY 4, 1805.

THE Pigard Frigate (on the Mediterranean Station) has detained thirteen Sail of Spanish Vessels: two of them are arrived at Penzance, viz. Ship Dido, from River Plate, and Schooner la'Linda, from Caraccas.

The Anna Maria, Leydon, from Bristol and St. Thomas's, to Honduras, is captured by le Voltigeur Privateer, and carried into Guadaloupe.

The Grace, Williamson, from Limerick to Liverpool, is lost at Lochindahl.

The Enterprize, Hall, from Konigsburg to Hull, is taken and carried into Rotterdam.

A Vessel belonging to Barbadoes, from Newfoundland, was taken off Barbadoes about the end of October or early in November.

The Harmony, Wickham, from Sumatra, is on shore on Deal Beach, and it is feared will be lost.

The Hinde, Darby, from Surinam, is towed into Penzance by a Sloop of War, being much damaged.

"Hamburgh, Dec. 4, 1804.—A Privateer, said to be fitted out from Norway, was captured a few days since in the mouth of our River by the blockading Frigate."

The Twee Gebroeders, Hendrichs, from London to Tonningen, is put into Harlingen with damage.

The Endeavour, Comben, was driven on shore on Wednesday night near Weymouth, and is full of water.

The Active, Hansen, from London, has been seen at the mouth of the Eyder, but not being able to get up for the ice, bore away towards Heligoland.

The Ranger, Orton, from London, is got off the Swinebottoms, and gone to Copenhagen to refit.

The Fame, Anderson, from London to Tonningen, is returned to Sheerness, having lost an anchor and cable, and being three days in the ice near the Eyder.

The Industry, Hardie, from Grangemouth to London, is lost near Hartlepool. People saved.

The Skene, ———, from Shields to London, with coals, is on shore near Saltfleet, after being on the inner Dowsings.

The Diligence, Carler; the Lydia, Johnson; and the Friendship, Lotie, laden with stones, are taken by le Vimereux French Privateer. Journal du Commerce, 18 December.

The Brig Industry, of 100 tons and 24 Men, from Newfoundland to Guernsey, is taken by le Bonheur Privateer, of Calais, of 14 guns and 80 Men, and carried into Port. Journal du Commerce, 30 Nov.

The Mary, Denham, from Demerara to London, was stranded on the Oester, Coast of Holland, the 15th instant. Crew saved.

The Neptune, Neil, from Quebec for Clyde, is on shore near Ayr, and bilged. Part of the Cargo saved.

Penzance, Dec. 21.—Several Vessels have lost anchors and cables here in the hard gales.

The Triton, Hudson, for Tonningen, is returned to Hull, having lost her foremast, bowsprit, anchors, and cables.

The Harmony, Wickham, from Sumatra, that was on shore on Deal Beach, is wrecked. A small part of the Cargo saved.

The Jenny, ———, of Sunderland, coal loaded, has sunk off Staith, on the Coast of Yorkshire. One Boy drowned.

The Carolina, Carrode, from Halifax to Newfoundland, was lost 21st October, near Cape Canso.

Da Purification de Nostro, from Barcelona, detained by the Squadron under Command of Lord Nelson, is put into Ramsgate, with loss of windlas, anchors, and cables.

The Speedwell, Findlay, from Zant to London, is arrived at Malta. She sprung a leak on the 20th October in a violent gale of wind, and will be obliged to unload to repair.

A Sloop, with Groceries, supposed to be the Endeavour, Hooper, from Exeter to Falmouth, is wrecked to the westward of Falmouth. Crew lost.

The Blonde Frigate was lost near Torbay 20th December. People saved.

The Triton, Drewit, is returned to Stettin, much damaged.

The William and Henry, Burn, is put into Lutherorn, in the Baltic, with loss of mast, anchor, and cables.

The Malvina, Bell, of North Shields, in ballast, from London, is on shore near Sneerness, and it is feared will be lost.

The August Wilhelm, Anderson, for Embden, is returned to Hull.

The Aurora Remende, a Spanish Vessel with dollars, and a valuable cargo, has been detained by the Neptune, of Greenock, and carried into Ballyrain, in Ireland, by the Brilliant Frigate.

The Antelope, Corran, from Virginia to Dunkirk, upset off Calais; Crew saved. Cargo expected to be saved.

The Admiral Nelson, Irvin, from Copenhagen to London, is lost upon the Coast of Norfolk.

The Francis, M'Kennan, sailed from Grenada, for Newfoundland, about the end of March, and has not been heard of since.

The Brig Padstow, from Cardiff to London, is wrecked at Scilly.

The Ship Active, Morgan, in ballast, from Plymouth, is lost at Scilly. Crew saved.

The Rochdale, Davey, from London to Selby, is on shore near Lowestoffe, but expected to be got off.

The Minerva, Oxley, from Petersburg to Teneriffe, is detained in the Humber.

The Severn Frigate was driven on shore 21st inst. at Jersey. People saved.

A Spanish Ship, laden with coals, is detained at Portsmouth.

The Starling Gun-brig run on shore near Calais, 25th instant, in a fog, and was burnt. Crew saved and arrived at Deal.

The Catharine, of Ringsend, with coals, was wrecked near Howth, in Ireland, 20th inst. All the Crew drowned.

The Reliance, Gordon, from Bristol, is lost in Gamba River.

Journal du Commerce, 10th Dec.—"An English Vessel of 100 tons, laden with butter and provisions, Prize to the Sorciere Privateer, is arrived at Conquet."

A Swedish and a Danish Vessel, bound to Spain, are detained and sent into Grimsby.

The Familian, Holm, from Longsound to Hull, is on shore on Stoney Binks. Crew and Cargo saved.

The Brig Union, Williams, from Bangor to London, has been driven out of Scilly, and since wrecked going into Cork.

The Nelson, Larmour, from Demerara to Liverpool, is on shore near Kinsale. Part of the Cargo saved, and the Ship is expected to be got off.

Three English Vessels laden with Fish, were seized at Malaga 24th Nov. The Success, Green; and Abeona, ———, were in the Road the 14th.

The Polly and Mary, Llewellyn, from Glasgow to Liverpool, was sunk in Rofskove Bay, near Wexford, 21st December. Crew saved.

A ship from Wales to Cork is on shore near Kinsale.

The Pitt, Newcombe, bound to New Providence, has been run foul of, and is returned to Blackwall with considerable damage.

Th. Marianas, a Spanish Vessel, with an English cargo, from Trieste, was seized at Malaga 24th November. And the Li tie Aspy, of Poole, Lander, from Newfoundland, was embargoed there the same day.

The Wata Orden, Hierta, from Stockholm to Dublin, is on shore near Harwich, after having been deserted by the Master and Crew.

The Thunderer M. W. is on shore in Bantry Bay.

The Neptune, le Gresley; the Mercury, Valpy; and the Boston, Huelin, belonging to Jersey, were embargoed at Valencia on the 20th November; but on the 26th they cut their cables, and made their escape; the former having about 45 pipes of brandy on board, and the two latter in ballast, having unloaded their Cargoes previous to the embargo.

[To be continued.]

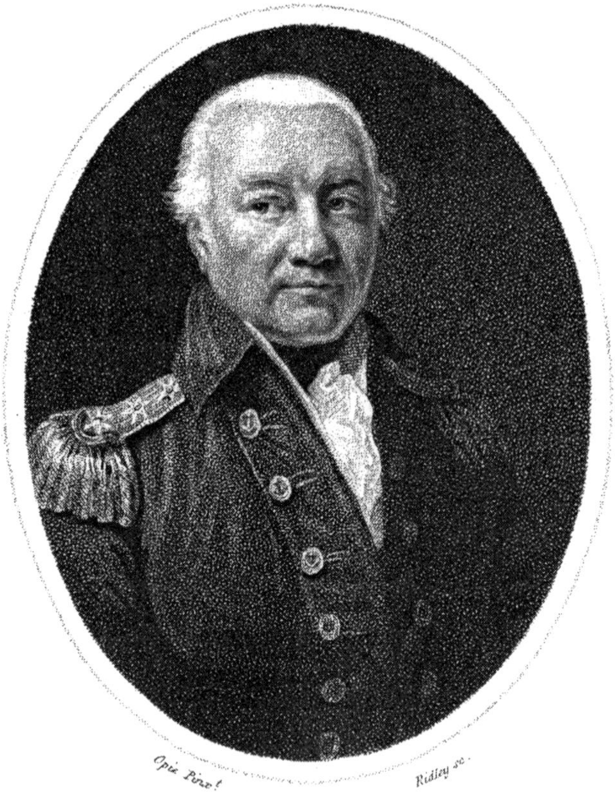

Opie Pinx[t] Ridley sc.

RICH[D]. RODNEY BLIGH ESQ[R].

Admiral of the Blue Squadron.

Pub. by I. Gold, 103, Shoe Lane, 1 July 1805.

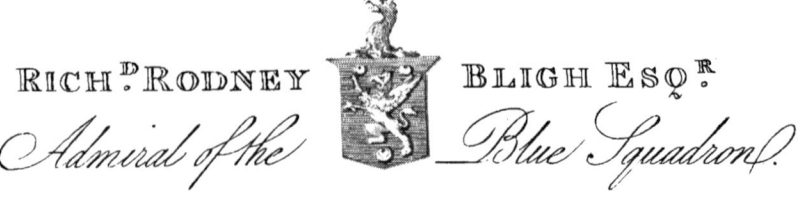

BIOGRAPHICAL MEMOIR OF
RICHARD RODNEY BLIGH, Esq,
ADMIRAL OF THE BLUE SQUADRON.

"FOR ALL THE TOILS THAT RACK HIS MANLY FRAME,
VIRTUE REQUIRES NO OTHER MEED THAN FAME."
                                                CAREY.

FIRED by example, the generous bosom pants for glory, and emulates the most illustrious models of heroism. In contemplating the gallant Exploits of Rodney, we cannot wonder that from the school of so distinguished an Officer some of the fairest ornaments of the British Navy should have risen;—Men eminently conspicuous for their modesty, their bravery, and their general worth. Admiral Richard Rodney Bligh, whose Naval Career we are now about to trace, is fully entitled, by the general tenor of his conduct, to rank with such Men. This Gentleman, who is descended from an ancient and respectable Family in Cornwall, was born in the year 1737. Having been destined to the Naval Service of his Country, he received an appropriate education; and, in 1750, he commenced his professional progress under the immediate auspices of his Godfather, the late Lord Rodney; who, in the preceding year, had been made Governor and Commander in Chief of the Island of Newfoundland*.

Of the manner in which Mr. Bligh passed the immediately succeeding years, we are not accurately informed; but we believe that he continued under the protection of his Patron, employed in various service; and in the year 1757 he received a Lieutenant's Commission.

Soon after the taking of Martinique†, at which he was present, he was, in 1762, appointed a Commander in the Virgin Sloop of War, and was actively employed in cruising against the Enemy's Privateers, of which he captured several that had greatly annoyed our Commerce in those Seas.

---

* *Vide* NAVAL CHRONICLE, Vol. I, page 356.   † *Ibid.* Vol. page 363, *et seq.*

During the long Peace which succeeded, Captain Bligh was occasionally on service; and in the year 1777 he was made a Post Captain*; with which rank he served during the whole of the American War, in the Channel, the Mediterranean, and the West Indies.

At the commencement of the last War, Captain Bligh received a Commission for the Excellent, of 74 guns; and in the early part of 1794, was removed to the Alexander, of the same force. In this Ship, as he was returning on the 6th of November, to England, from Cape St. Vincent, whither he had escorted a Convoy, in company with the Canada, he fell in with a French Squadron, consisting of five Ships of the Line, three Frigates, and a Brig, commanded by Rear-Admiral Neuilly, having under him a *Chef d'Escadre*. By superior sailing, the Canada effected her escape, and the Alexander was left alone to combat this disproportionate Force, which she most gallantly did for three hours, during the last of which she was attacked at once by every Ship of the Enemy. Yet, under these circumstances, she did not strike until great slaughter had been made among her Crew, her masts and sails being utterly disabled, having eight feet water in her hold, and being dangerously on fire.

Captain Bligh's account of this desperate conflict, which was so bravely supported on his part, exhibits such an interesting specimen of British courage, accompanied by the most unassuming modesty, that we should deem ourselves guilty of injustice to his professional character, were we to withhold it from the readers of the NAVAL CHRONICLE.—The following is his official letter, as it appeared in the Gazette, addressed to Mr. (now Sir Philip) Stephens:—

SIR, *On board the Marat, Brest, Nov.* 25, 1794.

THE arrival of the Canada must long since have informed their Lordships of my misfortune, in losing His Majesty's Ship Alexander, late under my Command, having been taken by a Squadron of French Ships of War, consisting of five of 74 guns, three large Frigates, and an armed Brig, commanded by Rear-Admiral Neuilly. Farther particulars and details I herewith transmit you for their

---

In, we believe, the Wasp, of 18 guns.

Lordships' information. We discovered this Squadron on our weather bow, about half-past two o'clock, or near three, in the morning of the 6th instant, being then in lat. 48° 25′ north; 7° 53′ west, the Wind then at west, and we steering north-east; on which I immediately hauled our Wind, with the larboard tacks on board, and without Signal, the Canada being close to us. We passed the strange Ships a little before four, the nearest of whom at about half a mile distant, but could not discover what they were. Shortly after we bore more up, let the reefs out of the top-sails, and set steering-sails. About five, perceiving by my night-glass the strange Ships stand after us, we crowded all the sail we could possibly set, as did the Canada, and hauled more to the eastward. About day-break the Canada passed us, and steering more to the northward than we did, brought her on her larboard bow. Two Ships of the Line and two Frigates pursued; and three of the Line and one Frigate chased the Alexander. About half-past seven the French Ships hoisted English Colours. About a quarter past eight we hoisted our Colours, upon which the French Ships hauled down the English and hoisted theirs; and drawing up within gun-shot, we began firing our stern chases at them, and received their bow chases. About nine, or shortly after, observing the Ships in pursuit of the Canada drawing up with her, and firing at each other their bow and stern chases, I made the Canada's Signal to form a-head for our mutual support, being determined to defend the Ships to the last extremity; which Signal she instantly answered, and endeavoured to put it into execution, by steering towards us; but the Ships in chase of her, seeing her intentions, hauled more to the starboard to cut her off, and which obliged her to steer the course she had done before. We continued firing our stern chases at the Ships pursuing us till near eleven, when three Ships of the Line came up, and brought us to close Action, which we sustained for upwards of two hours, when the Ship was a complete Wreck; the main-yard, spanker-boom, and three top-gallant-yards shot away; all the lower masts shot through in many places, and expected every minute to go over the side; all the other masts and yards were also wounded, more or less; nearly the whole of the standing and running rigging cut to pieces, the sails torn into ribbands, and her hull much shattered, and making a great deal of water, and with difficulty she floated into Brest. At this time the Ships that had chased the Canada had quitted her, and were coming fast up to us, the shot of one of them at the time passing over us. Thus situated, and cut off from all resources, I judged it advisable to consult my Officers, and accordingly assembled them all on the quarter deck; when, upon surveying and examining the state of the Ship, (engaged as I have already described,) they deemed any farther resistance would be ineffectual, as every possible exertion had already been used in vain to save her, and therefore they were unanimously of opinion, that to resign her would be the means of saving the lives of a number of brave Men. Then, and not till then, (painful to relate,) I ordered the Colours to be struck; a measure which, on a full investigation, I hope and trust their Lordships will not disapprove. Hitherto I have not been able to collect an exact list of the killed and wounded, as many of the former were thrown overboard during the Action, and, when taken possession of, the people were divided and sent on board the different Ships, but I do not believe they exceed forty, or thereabout. No Officer above the rank of Boatswain's Mate was killed. Lieutenant Fitzgerald, of the Marines, Messrs. Burns, Boatswain, and M'Curdy, Pilot, were wounded, but in a fair way of doing well. The cool, steady, and gallant behaviour of all my Officers and Ship's Company, Marines as well as Seamen, throughout the whole of the Action, merits the highest applauses; and I should feel myself deficient of my duty, as well as in what I owe to those brave Men, were I to omit requesting you will be pleased to recommend them in the strongest manner to their Lordships' favour and protection; particularly Lieutenants Godenech, Epworth, Carter, West, and Daracott; Major Trench, Lieutenants Fitzgerald and Brown, of the Marines; Mr. Robinson, the Master, together with the warrant and petty Officers, whose bravery and good conduct I shall ever hold in the highest estimation. I have hitherto been treated with great kindness and humanity, and have not a doubt but that I shall meet with the same treatment during my Captivity. I am, with great respect, &c.

R. R. BLIGH.

The damage sustained by the French in the above Action, was not less in proportion. They found both their Prize and their own Ships so shattered and unmanageable, that they were compelled to return immediately to Brest; and their departure from their cruising ground probably was the means of saving some very valuable English Convoys from becoming their prey; for, at that moment, the Mediterranean Trade under Admiral Cosby, and the Lisbon and Oporto Trade under Captain Rodney, were within a distance of little more than twenty leagues from the scene of Action; and Lord Hood, in the Victory alone, was returning from Corsica, and believed to be very near; of all which circumstances the Enemy were apprised.

Fourteen days before the Capture of the Alexander, Captain Bligh had been appointed a Rear-Admiral of the Blue, the Promotion closing with him; but it was not until a considerable time after he had become a Prisoner, that he was acquainted with such an event having taken place.

The Admiral was exchanged, and returned to his native Country, in the month of May, 1795, when he was tried, agreeably to the custom of service, for the surrender of the Alexander, Admiral Cornwallis being President of the Court Martial, whose sentence " MOST HONOURABLY" acquitted him; and, in less than two months after, he hoisted his Flag under Sir Peter Parker, at Portsmouth.

In the following year, 1796, Admiral Bligh was appointed Second in Command , under Sir Henry Hervey, in the Windward Islands; but, on his arrival at Martinique, in the month of September, he was directed by Sir Hyde Parker to proceed to Jamaica, and assume the Command of that Station, until he himself should arrive there, which he did in about a month after.

Our Officer remained at Jamaica, actively employed in the protection of our Commerce, until the Summer of 1799; when, having been promoted to the rank of Vice-Admiral in the preceding February, he returned to England, and struck his Flag.

Towards the end of the year 1803, the Vice-Admiral was appointed to the Command of His Majesty's Naval Force in Scotland, under the general orders of Lord Keith, where he remained until a farther accession of rank, by his being made an Admiral of the Blue, rendered his longer serving on that Station incompatible with our Naval regulations. He accordingly struck his Flag, by direction of the Admiralty, in April 1804; and, ever since, has resided in London.

In the Brunswick, of 74 guns.

The Gentleman who has furnished us with this short epitome of a Life, which has been passed in active, honourable, and distinguished pursuits, in the service of our beloved Country, has had the honour of serving under Admiral Bligh; and has seen him, calm and serene amidst danger, brave and animated in battle, the Friend of his Officers, and the Protector of his Men.

Admiral Bligh's defence of the Alexander has never been surpassed in our Naval Annals; and, had it been his good fortune to have had with him, in that unequal conflict, such a Force as might have attacked the French Squadron with any fair estimate of success, the result will not be questioned by any one who is conversant with the superiority of British nautical skill and courage.

NAVAL ANECDOTES, COMMERCIAL HINTS, RECOLLECTIONS, &c.

NANTES IN GURGITE VASTO.

INVASION.

WE have here collected every instance of a Descent upon the English Coast from the year 1066; because it has been asserted in some French publications, most falsely and insidiously, that out of these forty-eight examples of the violation of British ground, forty-one have been crowned with success, and twelve have hurled our Monarchs from their thrones. It will have been seen by the historical reader, that the Invasion under Duke William alone was triumphant, unless the English were themselves concerned in facilitating the object of the enterprise; and with respect to the event under the Norman Bastard, it was not a Conquest effected by Frenchmen, but by Northern Emigrants, who had taken possession of one of the most productive and beautiful Provinces of France.

Catalogue of all the Descents, or Attempts, for the Purpose of Invasion on the Coasts of the United Kingdom, from the Time of HAROLD *to the ineffectual Experiment in the Bay of Donnegal.*

1066. Successful Invasion under William Duke of Normandy.

1069. The Sons of Harold, from Ireland, plunder the Vicinity of Exeter.

1069. Sueno, King of Denmark, enters the Humber with two hundred Ships.

1101. Duke Robert, the Brother of Rufus, lands at Portsmouth.

1139. The Empress Maude lands at Portsmouth.

1142. Henry, the Son of Maude, lands at Wareham.

1152. Henry again enters England.

1171. Henry the Second invades Ireland.

1216. Lewis of France lands on the Isle of Thanet.

1296. The Duke of Montmorenci lands at Dover.

1326. Isabella, Daughter of Philip the Fair, landed at Orwell with three thousand Men.

1339. The French engaged and worsted the English Fleet and sacked Portsmouth.

1340. The French lay waste the English Coasts, burn Plymouth and several Ships at Hastings, and reduce the greater part of Southampton to ashes.

1377. The French take the Isle of Wight, and do much mischief at Portsmouth, Plymouth, Dartmouth, and Hastings.

1380. The French and Spaniards land at Winchelsea.

1386. Twelve hundred Ships, with sixty thousand Men on board, were equipped under Charles the Fifth to invade England, and were dispersed by a Storm. *On board the Ships were planks of wood nicely joined, intended for the construction of barracks, wherein the Army might be sheltered immediately upon its disembarkation.*

1398. The Duke of Lancaster embarked at Vannes, and landed on the Coast of Yorkshire.

1403. The Count de St. Pol landed in the Isle of Wight; and the same year Plymouth was reduced to ashes.

1404. Another Descent on the Isle of Wight.

1405. The French, with twelve thousand Men, land at Milford Haven, take Carmarthen, and several other Towns.

1457. The French surprise Sandwich.

1460. Several Descents under the Earl of Warwick.

1470. The same Nobleman lands at Dartmouth.

1471. The deposed Edward lands in Yorkshire. The French land at Weymouth under Queen Margaret.

1485. The Earl of Richmond lands at Milford Haven, with two thousand Men.

1487. Lambert Simnel, a Baker's Son, who was crowned at Dublin lands in Lancashire.

1495. Perkin Warbeck, a converted Flemish Jew, landed at Deal.

1498. The same Adventurer landed in Cornwall.

1513. Commodore Pregent landed on the Coast of Sussex.

1514. The same Commander burnt Brighton.

1545. One hundred and fifty large Ships, sixty smaller ones, and twenty-five Gallies, pass the English Fleet cruising in the Roads, when Ennibault landed on the Isle of Wight, and on the Coast of Sussex.

1588. The famous Expedition of the Armada.

1594. The Spaniards landed at Mount's Bay, in Cornwall, burned Penzance, and several other places.

1601. Don Juan d'Aguilar, with forty-eight Ships and two thousand Soldiers, landed at Kinsale, and took the Town.

1667. The Dutch Commander de Ruyter lays waste the English Coast with a prodigious Navy. On the 18th of June he entered the Thames, and sent up the River seventeen Sail and some Fire-ships. The Magazines of Sheerness were burnt, and three Ships at the entrance of the Medway, &c.

1685. The Earl of Argyle landed in Scotland.—The Duke of Monmouth landed in Dorsetshire.

1688. The Prince of Orange landed at Torbay.

1689. James having embarked at Brest, with twenty-three Ships of War and numerous Transports, landed at Dublin.

1690. Tourville, with twenty-two Ships of War, met the English and Dutch Fleets, when the latter were overcome. They arrived in Torbay with forty-eight Shallops and some Gallies, carrying 1800 chosen Men. *This kind of Vessel was made choice of, because, being lower than the others, they were less exposed to the fire of the Enemy.*

1691. Tyrconnel landed in Ireland. A reinforcement was sent the same year with nineteen pieces of artillery.

1745. Prince Charles Edward Stuart landed at Moiratt, in Scotland. The fruitless Descents of the Father of Prince Charles in 1708, 1717, and 1719, scarcely deserve notice.

1760. Thurot landed at Carrickfergus. *His instructions were, to make occasional Descents upon the Coast of Ireland, and divide and distract the attention of the Government of that Kingdom.*

1796. The recent attempt in Bantry Bay from Brest with seventeen Ships of the Line and several Frigates, carrying 1800 Men, which were lost in the passage of the Raz.

1797. The landing of 1200 Men near Fishguard.

1798. The French landed in Ireland, on the Shores of Sligo Bay, under General Humbert, 1500 strong, with a considerable quantity of arms, and sixteen pieces of cannon.

General Rey, with Napper Tandy, and the Crew from a single Ship, landed at Raghlin, Ireland.

Unsuccessful attempt at Donnegal Bay, with one Ship of 80 guns, eight Frigates, and a Schooner, having on board 3600 Men under General Hardie, with great quantities of arms and warlike Stores. Of this Force only one Boat with 60 Men ventured to land, who were repulsed by a body of Yeomaury under Captain Montgomery.

RUSSIAN VOYAGE OF DISCOVERY.

THE most satisfactory accounts have been received concerning the Russian Expedition for circumnavigating the Globe. They are contained in a letter transmitted by the Commander, M. Krusenstern, to M. Schubert, a Member of the Academy, and dated August 8, 1804, from Kamtschatka, where the Voyagers arrived, without any accident of importance, on the 14th of the preceding month, about five weeks after quitting the Coast of Brazil. They touched, on their passage, at the Marquesa Islands, on one of which M. Krusenstern found a Frenchman and an Englishman, whom he intends to bring with him to Europe. The latter had completely forgotten his native language; and the Frenchman, who had not spoken his for seven years, with some difficulty gave the Russians to understand, that he had been wrecked in an American Ship near the Coast of the Island. Both of them having learned the language of the Islanders, and adopted their manners, will probably furnish many curious particulars relative to those Islands, which are but little known. M. Krusenstern was preparing to sail for Japan, to convey thither M. de Rasannoff, who is to reside there in the quality of Ambassador Extraordinary of the Emperor of Russia.

JOHN DEAN, OF THE SUSSEX INDIAMAN.

IN the year 1738, the Sussex Indiaman sprung a leak off the east of the Cape of Good Hope. The Captain and Officers, and part of the Crew, plundered and deserted her, and went on board the Winchester, her Consort, leaving John Dean and fifteen brave Men in the Sussex, who resolved to stay with the Ship and bring her into Port, conceiving she ought not to have been abandoned and deserted. They repaired her leak, and carried her into Madagascar; but, on going from thence to Mosambique, she afterwards unfortunately struck on a Rock, on the Bassas de India, lat. 23°, long. 41°, lost her rudder, and was finally lost.

In this state, John Dean, with eight Men, resolved to try their fate in the Pinnace, while the remainder determined to continue on board and share the fate of the Ship. The Pinnace got stove, and three of the Men out of the eight were drowned; the remainder drifted into shoal water, as did a part of the Pinnace, which the survivors converted into a Raft. The next day the Ship also parted, and drifted nearer Shore. John Dean and four Men then committed themselves to Sea on their little Raft, and were *seventeen* days getting on Shore to Madagascar.

Their stock consisted of a piece of pork, part of a butt of water, and three small crabs found afloat at Sea. The Men duly returned thanks to God for their miraculous escape. They resided for many months in different parts of Madagascar, when three of them died. John Dean found his way in an English Ship bound to Bengal, and came from thence to England; when he sent his narrative to the East India Company, who granted him a pension, and had his picture taken, which is now hanging up in one of the Committee rooms at the India House. He died on the 17th of December, 1747.

LA PEYROUSE.

IN the NAVAL CHRONICLE (Vol. XI, page 101,) we presented an interesting article, from an American Paper, relative to the fate of the unfortunate and lamented Peyrouse. The following letter, dated Oct. 1, 1801, and written by this Navigator, with the subjoined reflections, appeared some months ago on the Continent; and it is scarcely necessary to observe, that at Paris it excited considerable sensation.

In les Nouvelles à la Main, of Nivose, year XII, No. III, it is said, that the French Government has received from America some of the journals, letters, &c. of la Peyrouse, and of his unfortunate Comrades; and that the copy of the following letter is circulated in the Consular Circles, and is signed by this Officer in his name and that of his fellow-sufferers.

To His Majesty LOUIS XVI, *King of France and Navarre.*

" SIR,—Should this letter be presented to your Majesty, with the Journals, Memoirs, and Remarks, on our long, distant, and disastrous Voyage, your Majesty's heart will do justice to our labours, in considering our efforts, and forgiving their issue; which, from circumstances fully explained, we most humbly hope will not be ascribed either to neglect or temerity.

" Isolated from the universe, uncertain whether we ever again shall see the civilized world; and doubtful whether even these sincere effusions of our loyalty will reach the best of Kings; nay, whether even posterity will not continue without any information concerning our cruel fate, as well as our contemporaries, our parents, our relatives, and our friends, who, no doubt, have often lamented the ignorance of our destiny, and bewailed our death, whilst we endured a life worse than destruction, in existing upon a remote and unfrequented Shore, more inhospitable, more to be dreaded than the grave itself; it is for us, however, a great consolation, and the sole consolation we have, that the most virtuous of Sovereigns, and most beloved of Kings, must enjoy upon the throne of his Ancestors, surrounded by a brilliant Offspring, the same respectful love from his faithful subjects, as from his Queen, Children, Brothers, and Royal Relations; and that his generous, humane mind distributes among Frenchmen, and amongst all other people, the blissful tranquillity of his own bosom, makes Europe happy in an uninterrupted Peace, and receives in return the well-merited blessings of mankind.

" Happy Countrymen! thousand times happy Frenchmen! You enjoy, from the benevolence and patriotism of your lawful Prince, that liberty of which most Republics only know the name; which has cost Holland and America so much blood, and which makes them yet agitated; whilst, as dutiful subjects, your portion of freedom is only surpassed by your uninterrupted prosperity.

" May your Majesty, for the welfare of the universe, long continue in health and felicity to occupy your glorious throne, and to rule over France, as your Majesty reigns from gratitude and affection in the hearts of all Frenchmen!" &c.

When M. de la Peyrouse wrote this letter (continues the French writer,) he had only been absent from France fourteen years; and his King and Queen had already been murdered eight years; France a republic nine years; in revolution twelve years; and in continual anarchy and agitation for the same period. The *faithful* subjects of Louis XVI, after butchering their good and innocent Sovereign, had been butchering and proscribing each other, by turns victims or executioners; plundered or plunderers; and at all times slaves since they were called *free* citizens of a commonwealth

Of the King's Family, one Dauphin had been fortunate enough to die before the *dutiful* French subjects were become regicides: the other was poisoned by them in the Temple, in the same prison from which he had seen his Father, Mother, and Aunt, dragged to the scaffold. All the other Bourbons were proscribed; none existed in France. Of Frenchmen, two millions had perished in civil Wars, by drowning, shooting, or by the guillotine; one million had died in the Hospitals, or in combating for different Kings of factions against foreign foes; twenty millions had been beggared; and one million enriched, but dishonoured. After passing through rivers of blood, and fighting only for the choice of Tyrants, the *happy*, *loyal*, and *quiet* French Citizens, had at last picked up an obscure but fortunate Corsican, who, when M. de la Peyrouse left France, was a charity Scholar in one of the King's Colleges; but who, at the date of this letter, was seated upon the Throne of Henry IV and of Louis XVI, upon the republican Throne of modern France; who had extended its territory *per fas et nefas*, defeated and humiliated the House of Austria, insulted England, enslaved the Continent, and, *in facto*, was the Sovereign Usurper of the Sovereign Power, not only of Europe, but of the World.

Had M. de la Peyrouse been absent the fourteen preceding centuries, instead of the last fourteen years, in returning to life and to France, he would not have met with more unaccountable, more surprising, and, for the happiness and tranquillity of mankind, more wretched changes.

What numerous meditations! what painful reflections may not be made upon this subject! Perhaps M. de la Peyrouse and his Companions are yet innocently praying, *Domine, salvum fac Regem!* whilst we are treacherously repeating, *Domine, salvos fac Consules!!!*

DESCRIPTION OF THE TOWN AND HARBOUR OF TRIEST.

(From Kuttner's Travels.)

TRIEST cannot be called a handsome Town, though it contains a great number of good, well-built, stone houses. Most of the streets are wide; indeed they are so spacious that the houses at first seem to be lower than they actually are, till you observe that most of them are three or four stories high. The streets are all paved with broad flag-stones, many of which are seven, eight, and even ten feet long, by three, four, and five, broad.

The number of stationary Inhabitants of this Town is computed at from 28 to 30,000 persons; and that of the Seafaring People and Strangers, who are continually coming and going, is stated at several thousands more. This statement was given me by a person in an official situation in this place, and I think is likely to be correct: but the English Consul, who has resided several years at Triest, asserts, that the population exceeds 36,000 souls; and that, including the Mariners and Strangers, it cannot be less than 40,000. The increasing population is a cause of general complaint among the oldest Inhabitants, who find it difficult to accustom themselves to the advancing price of every commodity. In fact, Triest is a very extensive place, and every thing is dearer than at Vienna.

I was surprised to observe the number of Ships lying in the Harbour, which appears to be equally secure and commodious. Two large Canals run out of it a considerable distance into the Town, and afford a place for the reception of a large number of Vessels. These Canals were the labour of an early period. for they are not calculated for the kind of Commerce in which of late years this Town has been engaged. The Harbour is a scene of constant bustle and activity, and I am much mistaken if it be not more lively than that of Leghorn. It is a free Port in the most extensive sense of the word.

Triest contains a great number of carriages, many of which are very elegant. I was astonished to find so many coaches in a Seaport, and surrounded by such a mountainous country; but was informed, that almost every Tradesman who does any business keeps his carriage, and at no very great expense. The Coffee-houses are likewise numerous at Triest, and a considerable part of the company by which they are frequented sit before the door: for this purpose a large linen cloth is spread upon poles, so as to form a kind of Tent.

Triest has for many years been increasing in wealth and consequence, at the expense of her neighbour Venice. Büsching says, that in 1770 it contained thirty great mercantile houses; it now has above one hundred. The magnificent Mole was constructed by the directions of Maria Theresa. It extends about fifteen hundred feet into the Sea, and forms an excellent Road: upon it there is room for fifty pieces of cannon, though not more than thirty are mounted; but all these are in good order; and among them I saw eighteen and twenty-four pounders. The Mole includes the old Lazaretto, or place of quarantine, which is now used only as Barracks for Soldiers. Opposite the Mole, and consequently on the contrary side of the Town, is the new Lazaretto, with a distinct Harbour, which is likewise enclosed by a Mole, and which must not be confounded with that belonging to the Town. The Castle stands on an eminence considerably higher than the Town, and must once have been pretty strong. It is now scarcely used but as a place of confinement for Prisoners; but the view from the Platform is such as amply to repay the trouble of going to see it. The great Imperial Flag is kept flying on this Edifice, and below it are a few pieces of cannon, with which the Salutes fired by Ships of War on their arrival are returned.

MR. EDITOR,

THE ready attention you pay in inserting my occasional Communications, merits my warmest thanks, and encourages me to offer you a fresh Anecdote of another *true British Game Cock;* the veracity of which you may depend on, as it was well known to most of the Fleet under the late renowned Rodney, in whose Ship this gallant affair took place, during the Engagement between his Lordship and Mons. de Guichen in the West Indies.

I remain, Sir, yours truly,

Great Queen Street, Lincoln's-inn-fields,   CHANTICLEER.
April 10, 1805.

ANECDOTE OF A TRUE BRITISH GAME COCK.

A SHORT time after the Engagement between Sir George Bridges Rodney and Mons. de Guichen in the West Indies, a Game Cock, that had been principally fed upon the main deck, and was much caressed by the Sailors, immediately after the firing began flew upon the quarter deck and took his station near Sir George and General Vaughan. The feathered Hero seemed not only to enjoy the conflict, but endeavoured by every means in his power to inspire all within hearing of him with the love of glory; for every five or six minutes he was sure to set up a loud crow, and continued to strut the deck, and conduct himself in this manner during the whole of the Engagement. Sir George pointing to the Phænomenon, called out to the General in the heat of the Battle— " Look at that fellow, Vaughan! by G—d he is an honour to his Country!"—Chanticleer had the good fortune to escape unhurt during the conflict, and was ordered to be taken particular care of by the Commander in Chief, and that deservedly.

AS the GAZETTE LETTERS of ADMIRAL SAUNDERS were not inserted in our Biographical Memoir of that Officer, (Vol. VIII, page 1,) we have now given them among our *Naval Recollections,* to illustrate the Account given by LIEUTENANT HUNTER in his preceding Memoir.

(First Letter.)

SIR, *Stirling Castle, off Point Levi, September 5, 1759.*

IN my letter of the 6th June, I acquainted you that I was then off Scatari, standing for the River St. Laurence. On the 26th I had got up, with the first division of the Fleet and Transports, as far as the middle of the Isle of Orleans, where I immediately prepared to land the Troops; which I did next morning. The same day the second and third Division came up; and the Troops from them were landed likewise. I got thus far without any loss or accident whatever; but directly after landing the Troops a very hard gale of Wind came on, by which many anchors and small Boats were lost, and much damage received amongst the Transports by driving on board each other. The Ships that lost most anchors I supplied from the Men of War, as far as I was able; and in all other respects gave them the best assistance in my power. On the 28th, at midnight, the Enemy sent down from Quebec seven Fire-ships; and though our Ships and Transports were so numerous, and necessarily spread so great a part of the Channel, we towed them all clear and aground, without receiving the least damage from them. The next night General Monkton crossed the River, and landed with his Brigade on the South Shore, and took Post at Point Levi: and General Wolfe took his on the westernmost Point of the Isle of Orleans.

On the 1st of July I moved up between the Points of Orleans and Levi; and it being resolved to land on the North Shore, below the Falls of Montmorenci, I placed, on the 8th instant, the Porcupine Sloop, and the Boscawen armed Vessel, in the Channel between Orleans and the North Shore, to cover the Landing, which took place that night. On the 17th, I ordered Captain Rous, of the Sutherland, to proceed, with the first fair Wind and night-tide, above Quebec; and to take the Diana and Squirrel, with two armed Sloops and two Cats, armed and loaded with provisions. On the 18th, at night, they all got up, except the Diana, and gave General Wolfe an opportunity of reconnoitring above the Town; those Ships having carried some Troops with them for that purpose. The Diana ran ashore upon the Rocks of Point Levi, and received so much damage, that I have sent her to Boston, with twenty-seven Sail of American Transports, (those which received most damage in the Gale of the 27th of June,) where they are to be discharged; and the Diana having repaired her damage, is to proceed to England, taking with her the mast Ships, and what Trade may be ready to accompany her.

On the 28th, at midnight, the Enemy sent down a raft of Fire-stages, of near a hundred radeaux, which succeeded no better than the Fire-ships. On the 31st General Wolfe determined to land a number of Troops above the Falls of Montmorenci, in order to attack the Enemy's lines; to cover which, I placed the Centurion in the Channel, between the Isle of Orleans and the Falls, and ran on Shore, at high Water, two Cats which I had armed for that purpose, against two small Batteries and two Redoubts, where our Troops were to land. At six in the evening they landed; but the General not thinking it proper to persevere in the Attack, part of them soon after re-embarked, and the rest crossed the Falls with General Wolfe: upon which, to prevent the two Cats from falling into the Enemy's hands, (they being then dry on Shore,) I gave orders to take the Men out, and set them on fire, which was accordingly done. On the 5th of August, in the night, I sent 20 flat-bottomed Boats up the River to the Sutherland, to embark 1260 of the Troops with Brigadier-General Murray, from a Post we had taken on the South Shore. I sent Admiral Holmes up to the Sutherland, to act in concert with him, and give him all the assistance the Ships and Boats could afford; at the same time I directed Admiral Holmes to use his best endeavours to get at, and destroy the Enemy's Ships above the Town; and to that purpose I ordered the Lowestoffe, and Hunter Sloop, with two armed Sloops and two Cats with provisions, to pass Quebec, and join the Sutherland; but the Wind holding westerly, it was the 27th of August before they got up, which was the fourth attempt they had made to gain their passage.

On the 25th, at night, Admiral Holmes and General Murray, with part of the Troops, returned. They had met with and destroyed a Magazine of the Enemy's cloathing, some gunpowder, and other things; and Admiral Holmes had been ten or twelve leagues above the Town, but found it impracticable at that time to get further up.

General Wolfe being resolved to quit the Camp at Montmorenci, and go above the Town, in hopes of getting between the

Enemy and their provisions, (supposed to be in the Ships there,) and by that means force them to an Action, I sent up on the 29th, at night, the Sea Horse and two armed Sloops, with two Cats laden with provisions, to join the rest above Quebec: and having taken off all the artillery from the Camp of Montmorenci on the 3d instant, in the forenoon, the Troops embarked from thence and landed at Point Levi. The 4th, at night, I sent all the flat-bottomed Boats up, and this night a part of the Troops will march up the South Shore above the Town, to be embarked in the Ships and Vessels there, and to-morrow night the rest will follow. Admiral Holmes is also gone up again to assist in their future operations, and to try if, with the assistance of the Troops it is practicable to get at the Enemy's Ships. As General Wolfe writes by this opportunity, he will give you an account of his part of the operations, and his thoughts what further may be done for His Majesty's Service. The Enemy appear numerous, and seem to be strongly posted; but let the event be what it will, we shall remain here as long as the season of the year will permit, in order to prevent their detaching Troops from hence against General Amherst; and I shall leave Cruisers at the mouth of the River, to cut off any supplies that may be sent them, with strict orders to keep that Station as long as possible. The Town of Quebec is not habitable, being almost entirely burnt and destroyed.

Twenty of the Victuallers that sailed from England with the Echo, are arrived here; one unloaded at Louisbourg, having received damage in her passage out, and another I have heard nothing of. No Ships of the Enemy have come this way, that I have had any intelligence of since my arrival in the River, except one laden with flour and brandy, which Captain Drake, of the Lizard, took. Before Admiral Durell got into the River, three Frigates, and seventeen Sail, with Provisions, Stores, and a few Recruits, got up, and are those we are, if possible, so anxious to destroy.

Yesterday I received a letter from General Amherst, (to whom I have had no opportunity of writing since I have been in the River,) dated Camp, at Crown Point, August 7, wherein he only desires I would send Transports and a Convoy to New York, to carry to England 607 Prisoners taken at Niagura. I shall very soon send home the great Ships; and have the honour to be, with the greatest respect, Sir,

Your most obedient and most humble Servant,

CHARLES SAUNDERS.

(Second Letter.)

From Vice-Admiral *Saunders* to the Right Honourable Mr. Secretary Pitt.

SIR, September 20, 1759.

I HAVE the greatest pleasure in informing you that the Town and Citadel of Quebec surrendered on the 18th instant, and that I enclose you a copy of the Articles of Capitulation. The Army took possession of the gates on the land side the same evening, and sent safe-guards into the Town to preserve order, and to prevent any thing being destroyed; and Captain Palliser, with a body of Seamen, landed in the lower Town and did the same. The next day our Army marched in, and near a thousand French Officers, Soldiers, and Seamen, were embarked on board some English Cats, who shall soon proceed for France, agreeable to the Capitulation. I had the honour to write to you the 5th instant, by the Rodney Cutter; the Troops mentioned in that letter, embarked on board the Ships and Vessels above the Town, in the night of the 6th instant, and at four in the morning of the 13th began to land on the North Shore, about a mile and a half above the Town. General Montcalm, with his whole Army, left their Camps at Beauport, and marched to meet him. A little before ten both Armies were formed, and the Enemy began the Attack. Our Troops received their fire, and reserved their own, advancing till they were so near as to run in upon them and push them with their bayonets; by which in a very little time the French gave way, and fled to the Town in the utmost disorder, and with great loss; for our Troops pursued them quite to the walls, and killed many of them upon the glacis, and in the ditch; and if the Town had been farther off, the whole French Army must have been destroyed. About 250 French Prisoners were taken that day, amongst whom are ten Captains, and six Subaltern Officers, all of whom will go in the great Ships to England.

I am sorry to acquaint you that General Wolfe was killed in the Action, and General Monckton shot through the body; but he is now supposed to be out of danger. General Montcalm and the three next French Officers in Command were killed; but I must refer you to General Townshend (who writes by this opportunity) for the particulars of this Action, the state of the Garrison, and the measures he has taken to secure the possession. I am now beginning to send on Shore the Stores they will want, and provisions for 5000 Men, of which I can furnish them with a sufficient quantity. The night of the landing, Admiral Holmes, with the

Ships and Troops, was about three leagues above the intended landing place. General Wolfe, with about half his Troops, set off in Boats, and dropped down with the Tide, and were by that means less liable to be discovered by the French Sentinels, posted all along the Coast. The Ships followed them about three quarters of an hour afterwards, and got to the landing place just in the time that had been concerted to cover their landing; and considering the darkness of the night, and the rapidity of the Current, this was a very critical operation, and very properly and successfully conducted. When General Wolfe and the Troops with him had landed, the difficulty of gaining the top of the hill is scarce credible. It was very steep in its ascent, and high, and had no path where two could go abreast; but they were obliged to pull themselves up by the stumps and boughs of trees that covered the declivity.

Immediately after our Victory over their Troops I sent up all the Boats in the Fleet with Artillery and Ammunition; and on the 17th, went up with the Men of War, in a disposition to attack the lower Town as soon as General Townshend should be ready to attack the upper; but in the evening they sent out to the Camp, and offered terms of Capitulation. I have the further pleasure of acquainting you, that during this tedious Campaign there has continued a perfect good understanding between the Army and Navy. I have received great assistance from Admiral Durell and Holmes, and from all the Captains: indeed every body has exerted themselves in the execution of their duty; even the Transports have willingly assisted me with Boats and people on the landing of the Troops, and many other services.

I have the honour to be, Sir, &c.

CHARLES SAUNDERS.

THE LADY'S ROCK.

THE following Historical Anecdote is extracted from the Hon. Mrs. Murray's *Companion and Guide to the Highlands of Scotland:—*

At the south end of the Island of Lismore we sailed near a small Rocky Isle, over which the Sea rolls at high Tides; at other times it raises its rough head somewhat above the surface of the water. It is called the Lady's Rock, for the following reason:

In former times, one of the M'Leans, of Duart, whose Castle (now in ruins) stands on a promontory in Mull, in nearly an opposite direction to the Lady's Rock, married a Sister of Argyle. The Lady was handsome and amiable, but unhappily she was barren. In those times it was a high crime in the eye of a Husband when his Wife bore him no Children. Duart hated his hapless Lady for that cause, and determined on her destruction. To accomplish it with ease, and as he imagined safe from detection, he ordered Ruffians to convey her secretly to the bare Rock near Lismore, and there leave her to perish at high Tide. The deed was executed to Duart's wish, and the Lady left on the Rock, watching the rolling Tide rising to overwhelm her. When she had given herself up for a lost being, and expected in a very short time to be washed from the Rock by the waves, she fortunately perceived a Vessel sailing down the Sound of Mull, in the direction of the Rock on which she was sitting. Every effort in her power was exerted, and every Signal in her possession was displayed, to attract the notice of the people in the Vessel. At length they perceived her, and drew near the Rock. She made herself known, and related that it was by the order of her barbarous Husband she was left on the Rock, and thus reduced to the wretched state in which they found her. The Mariners, ever a generous race, took compassion on her, received her on board their Vessel, and conveyed her safely to her Brother at Inverary.

M'Lean Duart made a grand mock funeral for his much loved, much lamented Lady, whom he announced to have died suddenly. He wrote disconsolate letters to her relations, particularly to Argyle, and after a decent time went to Inverary in deep mourning; where, with the greatest show of grief, he lamented to his brother-in-law the irreparable loss he had sustained. Argyle said little, but sent for his Sister, whose unexpected appearance in life and health proved an electric shock to her tender Husband. Argyle was a mild and amiable Man, and took no other revenge on M'Lean but commanding him to depart instantly, at the same time advising him to be cautious not to meet his brother Donald, who would certainly take away his life for having intended to destroy that of his Sister. Sir Donald Campbell did meet him many years afterwards in a street at Edinburgh, and there stabbed him for his crime towards his Sister, when M'Lean was eighty years of age.

CORRECT RELATION OF SHIPWRECKS.
[Continued from page 391.]

№ XI.

Again the dismal prospect opens round,
The wreck, the shore, the dying, and the drown'd.

FALCONER.

NARRATIVE

Of the Singular Adventures of Four Russian Sailors, who were cast away on the Desert Island of East Spitzbergen.

[From the Original of M. P. L. le Roy.]

IN the year 1743, one Jeremiah Okladmkoff, a Merchant of Mesen, in the government of Archangel, fitted out a Vessel, carrying fourteen Men, destined for Spitzbergen, to be employed in the Whale or Seal fishery. For eight successive days after they had sailed, the Wind was fair; but on the 9th it changed, so that instead of getting to the west of Spitzbergen, the usual place of rendezvous, they were driven eastward of those Islands; and after some days, they found themselves at a small distance from one of them, called East-Spitzbergen. Having approached this Island within about two English miles, their Vessel was suddenly surrounded by ice, and they found themselves in an extremely dangerous situation.

In this alarming state a Council was held; when the Mate, Alexis Himkof, informed them, that he recollected to have heard, that some of the people of Mesen, some time before, having formed a resolution of wintering upon this Island, had accordingly carried from that City timber proper for building a hut, and had actually erected one at some distance from the Shore.

This information induced the whole Company to resolve on wintering there, if the hut, as they hoped, still existed. They dispatched therefore four of their Crew in search of it. These were Alexis Himkof, the Mate; Iwan Himkof, his Godson; Stephen Scharapof, and Feoder Wercgin.

Having maturely considered the nature of their undertaking, they provided themselves with a musket, a powder-horn containing twelve charges of powder, with as many balls, an axe, a small kettle, a bag with about twenty pounds of flour, a knife, a tinder-box and tinder, a bladder filled with tobacco, and every Man his wooden pipe. Thus accoutred, these four Sailors quickly arrived on the Island.

They began with exploring the country; and soon discovered the hut they were in search of, about a mile and a half from the Shore. It was thirty-six feet in length, eighteen feet in height, and as many in breadth. It contained a small anti-chamber, about twelve feet broad, which had two doors, the one to shut it up from the outer air, the other to form a communication with the inner room: this contributed greatly to keep the larger room warm, when once heated. In the large room was an earthen stove constructed in the Russian manner; that is, a kind of oven without a chimney, which serves occasionally either for baking, for heating the room, or, as is customary amongst the Russian Peasants, in very cold weather, for a place to sleep upon.

They rejoiced greatly at having discovered the hut, which had suffered much from the weather: our Adventurers, however, contrived to pass the night in it. Early next morning they hastened to the Shore, impatient to inform their Comrades of their success.

I leave my readers to figure to themselves the astonishment and agony of mind these poor people must have felt, when, on reaching the place of their landing, they saw nothing but an open Sea, free from the ice, which but a day before had covered the Ocean. Whatever accident had befallen the Ship, they saw her no more; and as no tidings were ever afterwards received of her, it is most probable she sunk, and that all on board perished.

This melancholy event deprived the unhappy wretches of all hope of ever being able to quit the Island: they returned to the hut whence they had come, full of horror and despair.

Their first attention was employed in devising means of providing subsistence, and for repairing their hut. The twelve charges of powder which they had brought with them, soon procured them as many rein-deer; the Island, fortunately for them, abounding in those animals.

I have before observed, that the hut which the Sailors were so fortunate as to find, had sustained some damage, and it was this: there were cracks in many places between the boards of the building, which freely admitted the air. This inconvenience was however easily remedied: as they had an axe, and the beams were still sound, it was easy to make the boards join again very tolerably: besides, moss growing in great abundance all over the Island, there was more than sufficient to stop up the crevices, which wooden houses must always be liable to. Without fire, however, it was impossible to resist the rigour of the climate; and without wood, how was that fire to be produced, or supported? But Providence has so ordered it, that in this particular the Sea supplies the defects of the Land. In wandering along the Beach, they collected plenty of wood, which had been driven ashore by the waves; and which at first consisted of the wrecks of Ships, and afterwards of whole trees with their roots, the produce of some more hospitable, but to them unknown climates.

Nothing proved of more essential service to these unfortunate Men, during the first year of their exile, than some boards they found upon the Beach, having a long iron hook, some nails of about five or six inches long, and proportionably thick, and other bits of iron fixed in them; the melancholy relics of some Vessels cast away in those remote parts. These were thrown ashore by the waves, at a time when the want of powder gave our Men reason to apprehend that they must fall a prey to hunger, as they had nearly consumed those rein-deer they had killed. This lucky circumstance was attended with another, equally fortunate: they found on the Shore the root of a fir tree, which nearly approached to the figure of a bow.

As necessity has ever been the mother of invention, so they soon fashioned this root to a good bow, by the help of a knife; but still they wanted a string and arrows. Not knowing how to procure these at present, they resolved upon making a couple of lances, to defend themselves against the white bears, by far the most ferocious animal of their kind, whose attacks they had great reason to dread.

Finding they could neither make the heads of their lances, nor of their arrows, without the help of a hammer, they contrived to form the large iron hook mentioned above into one, by beating it, and widening a hole it happened to have about its middle, with the help of one of their largest nails. This received the handle, and a round button at one end of the hook served for the face of the hammer. A large pebble supplied the place of an anvil; and a couple of rein-deer horns made the tongs. By the means of such tools, they made two heads of spears; and after polishing and sharpening them on stones, they tied them as fast as possible with thongs made of rein-deer skins, to sticks about the thickness of a man's arm, which they got from some branches of trees that had been cast on Shore.

Thus equipped with spears, they resolved to attack a white bear; and after a most dangerous encounter, they killed the formidable creature, and thereby made a new supply of provisions. The flesh of this animal they relished exceedingly, as they thought it much rese nbled beef in taste and flavour. The tendons, they saw with much pleasure, could with little or no trouble be divided into filaments, of what fineness they thought fit. This perhaps was the most fortunat discovery these Men could have made; for, besides other advantages, they were hereby furnished with strings for their bow.

The success of our unfortunate Islanders in making the spears, encouraged them to proceed, and to forge some pieces of iron into heads of arrows of the same shape, though somewhat smaller in size than the spears above mentioned. Having ground and sharpened these like the former, they tied them with the sinews of the white bears, to pieces of fir; to which, by the help of fine threads of the same, they fastened feathers of Sea-fowl; and thus became possessed of a complete bow and arrows. Their ingenuity in this respect was crowned with success far beyond their expectation; for, during the time of their continuance upon the Island, with these arrows they killed no less than two hundred and fifty rein-deer, besides a great number of blue and white foxes. The flesh of these animals served them also for food, and their skins for cloathing, and other necessary preservations against the intense coldness of a climate so near the Pole.

They killed however but ten white bears in all, and that not without the greatest danger; for these animals being prodigiously strong, defended themselves with astonishing vigour and fury. The first our Men attacked designedly; the other nine they slew in defending themselves from their assaults; for some of these creatures even ventured to enter the outer room of the hut, in order to devour them.

To remedy in some degree the hardship of eating their meat half raw, they bethought themselves of drying some of their provisions, during the summer, in the open air, and afterwards of hanging it up in the upper part of the hut, which was continually filled with smoke down to the windows: it was thus dried thoroughly by the help of that smoke. This meat, so prepared, they used for bread, and it made them relish their other flesh the better, as they could only half dress it. Water they had in summer from small rivulets that fell from the Rocks; and in winter from the snow and ice thawed. This was of course their only beverage; and their small kettle was the only vessel they could make use of for this and other purposes. Our Mariners seeing themselves quite destitute of every means of cure, in case they should be attacked with the scurvy, judged it expedient not to neglect any regimen generally adopted as a preservative against this impending evil. Iwan Himkof, who had several times wintered on the Coast of West Spitzbergen, advised his unfortunate Companions to swallow raw and frozen meat, broken into small bits; to drink the blood of rein-deer warm as it flowed from their veins immediately after killing them; to use as much exercise as possible; and lastly, to eat scurvy grass, which grows on the Island, though not in great plenty. Three of the Sailors who pursued the above method, continued totally free from all taint of the disease. The fourth, Feodor Weregin, on the contrary, who was naturally indolent, averse to drinking the reindeer blood, and unwilling to leave the hut when he could possibly avoid it, was, soon after his arrival on the Island, seized with the scurvy, which afterwards became so bad, that he passed almost six years under the greatest sufferings. In the latter part of that time he became so weak that he could no longer sit erect, nor even raise his hand to his mouth; so that his humane Companions were obliged to feed and tend him like a new-born infant, to the hour of his death.

I have mentioned above that our Sailors brought a small bag of flour with them to the Island. Of this they had consumed one half with their meat; the remainder they employed in a different manner, equally useful. They soon saw the necessity of keeping up a continual fire in so cold a climate, and found that if it should unfortunately go out, they had no means of lighting it again; for though they had a steel and flints, yet they wanted both matches and tinder.

In their excursion through the Island they had met with a slimy loam, or kind of clay, nearly in the middle of it. Out of this they found means to form an utensil which might serve for a lamp; and they proposed keeping it constantly burning, with the fat of the animals they should kill. Having therefore fashioned a kind of lamp, they filled it with rein-deer fat, and stuck in it some twisted linen, shaped into a wick. But they had the mortification to find, that as soon as the fat melted, it not only soaked into the clay, but fairly run through it on all sides. The thing therefore was to devise some means for preventing this inconveniency, not arising from cracks, but from the substance of which the lamp was made being too porous. They made therefore a new one, dried it thoroughly in the air, then heated it red hot, and afterwards quenched it in their kettle, wherein they had boiled a quantity of flour down to the consistence of thin starch. The lamp being thus

BIOGRAPHICAL MEMOIR OF
RICHARD RODNEY BLIGH, Esq.
ADMIRAL OF THE BLUE SQUADRON.

"FOR ALL THE TOILS THAT RACK HIS MANLY FRAME,
VIRTUE REQUIRES NO OTHER MEED THAN FAME."
CAREY.

FIRED by example, the generous bosom pants for glory, and emulates the most illustrious models of heroism. In contemplating the gallant Exploits of Rodney, we cannot wonder that from the school of so distinguished an Officer some of the fairest ornaments of the British Navy should have risen;—Men eminently conspicuous for their modesty, their bravery, and their general worth. Admiral Richard Rodney Bligh, whose Naval Career we are now about to trace, is fully entitled, by the general tenor of his conduct, to rank with such Men. This Gentleman, who is descended from an ancient and respectable Family in Cornwall, was born in the year 1737. Having been destined to the Naval Service of his Country, he received an appropriate education; and, in 1750, he commenced his professional progress under the immediate auspices of his Godfather, the late Lord Rodney; who, in the preceding year, had been made Governor and Commander in Chief of the Island of Newfoundland*.

Of the manner in which Mr. Bligh passed the immediately succeeding years, we are not accurately informed; but we believe that he continued under the protection of his Patron, employed in various service; and in the year 1757 he received a Lieutenant's Commission.

Soon after the taking of Martinique†, at which he was present, he was, in 1762, appointed a Commander in the Virgin Sloop of War, and was actively employed in cruising against the Enemy's Privateers, of which he captured several that had greatly annoyed our Commerce in those Seas.

---

* *Vide* NAVAL CHRONICLE, Vol. I, page 356. † *Ibid.* Vol. page 363, *et seq.*

died, after having in the latter part of his life suffered most excruciating pains. Though they were thus freed from the trouble of attending him, and the grief of being witnesses to his misery, without being able to afford him any relief, yet his death affected them not a little. They saw their number lessened, and every one wished to be the first that should follow him. As he died in winter, they dug a grave in the snow as deep as they could, in which they laid the corpse, and then covered it to the best of their power, that the white bears might not get at it.

Now, at the time when the melancholy reflections occasioned by the death of their Comrade were fresh in their minds, and when each expected to pay this last duty to the remaining Companions of his misfortunes, or to receive it from them, they unexpectedly got sight of a Russian Ship: this happened on the fifteenth of August, 1749.

The Vessel belonging to a Trader, who had come with it to Archangel, he proposed it should winter in Nova Zembla; but fortunately for our poor Exiles, Mr. Vernezobre proposed to the Merchant to let his Vessel winter at West Spitzbergen, which he at last, after many objections, agreed to.

The contrary Winds they met with on their Passage made it impossible for them to reach the place of their destination. The Vessel was driven towards East Spitzbergen, directly opposite to the residence of our Mariners, who, as soon as they perceived her, hastened to light fires upon the hills nearest their habitation, and then ran to the beach, waving a Flag made of a rein-deer's hide fastened to a pole. The People on board seeing these Signals, concluded that there were on the Island some persons who implored their assistance, and therefore came to an anchor near the Shore.

It would be vain to attempt describing the joy of these poor People, at seeing the moment of their deliverance so near. They soon agreed with the Master of the Ship to work for him on the Voyage, and to pay him eighty rubles on their arrival, for taking them on board with all their riches; which consisted of fifty pud, or two thousand pound weight of rein-deer fat; in many hides of these animals, and skins of the blue and white foxes, together with those of the ten white bears they had killed. They took care not to forget their bows and arrows, their spears, their knife and axe, which were almost worn out, their awls, and their needles, which they kept carefully in a bone-box, very ingeniously made with their knife only; and, in short, every thing they were possessed of.

Our adventurers arrived in safety at Archangel on the twenty-eighth of September, 1749, having spent six years and three months in their ruefu solitude.

The moment of their landing was nearly proving fatal to the loving and beloved Wife of Alexis Himkof, who, being present when the Vessel came into Port, immediately knew her Husband, and ran with so much eagerness to his embraces, that she slipped into the water, and very narrowly escaped being drowned.

All three on their arrival were strong and healthy; but having lived so long without bread, they could not reconcile themselves to the use of it, and complained that it filled them with wind. Nor could they drink any spirituous liquors, and therefore drank nothing but water.

Before I conclude, I cannot help subjoining a reflection of Mr. Vernezobre, with which he concludes one of his letters.——" I make no doubt but some of your Readers will consider the adventures of these Sailors in the same light as they do the English history of Robinson Crusoe. But however ingenious that composition is, a comparison with this Narrative will prove much in your favour; as the former is all fiction, whereas your subject consists of facts sufficiently authenticated. And Crusoe is represented as having almost lost what knowledge he had of Christianity; but our Sailors carefully retained their religious principles; and, as they assured me, never wholly departed from their confidence in the goodness of God, to be exerted in their behalf, even in this world."

Naval Reform.
FIFTH REPORT OF THE COMMISSIONERS OF NAVAL INQUIRY.

[Continued from Vol. XII, page 379.]

IT is stated by Mr. Eve*, that in the last year the Commissioners have not assembled once; that the Receiver and the Accoun-

* See Mr. Eves's Examination.

By what authority does the Receiver of the Sixpenny Duty collect the wages of the Run Men in the African Trade?—We have always considered ourselves authorized by the Act of 30 Geo. III, although no particular specification of the Sixpenny Office is made in that Act.

tant have met at the Office in that period about seven or eight times; and that the Comptroller has been there, within the year, about six times; but then only for the purpose of signing Papers.

By what authority has the allowance of twelve and a half per cent. been made to the Receivers at the Out-Ports for the collection of the Run Men's wages?—There is no particular authority; but it is an allowance similar to that made for the collection of the Sixpenny Duty.

Do the Commissioners of the Sixpenny Office appoint Deputy Receivers at the Out-Ports for receiving the Run Men's wages, and by what authority?—The Deputy Receivers are appointed to collect all the monies payable to Greenwich Hospital at the Out-Ports.

Does the Receiver of the Sixpenny Duty receive the whole amount of the wages of Run Men in the African Trade, or only the moiety forfeited to Greenwich Hospital?—Under the authority of the Sixpenny Office only, the moiety forfeited to Greenwich Hospital; but I believe some of the Receivers collect the other moiety for the Merchant Seamen's Hospitals.

Do you know what allowance the Merchant Hospitals make on the collection?—I do not.

How is the money received on account of Run Men's wages carried to the account of Greenwich Hospital?—It is paid into Greenwich Hospital under the Head of " Sixpenny Duty collected from Seamen in the Merchants' Service."

Why is it not stated in the accounts furnished to Greenwich Hospital as the amount of Run Men's wages, and paid as such?—It has not been customary so to do.

Can the Directors of Greenwich Hospital, from the accounts furnished to them by the Sixpenny Office, have any knowledge whatever that the revenue of the Hospital is increased by the moiety of Run Men's wages in the African Trade?—They can not.

What commission is allowed to the Receivers at the Out-Ports for the collection of the wages of Men dying in the West India Trade, made payable to the Sixpenny Office by the Act of the 37th of His present Majesty, cap. 73?—The Receivers at all the Out-Ports were originally allowed 12½ per cent.; but on account of the magnitude of the receipts at Liverpool and Bristol, the commission to the Receivers there was reduced to five per cent. on the receipts of the first quarterly accounts.

By what authority was the commission first established at 12½ per cent., and afterwards reduced to five at Liverpool and Bristol?—No provision being made in the Act for the expense of carrying it into execution, the Commissioners of the Sixpenny Office applied to the Lords of the Admiralty to get the Act revised, or to give them directions for their guidance; and the Admiralty approved of their allowing the Receivers at the Out-Ports 12½ per cent.; and the Commissioners themselves thought it right to reduce the commission at Liverpool and Bristol to five per cent.

Out of what monies has the commission on Dead Men's wages been paid?—Out of the revenue of Greenwich Hospital arising from the Sixpenny Duty, and the moiety of Run Men's wages, by the authority of the Lords of the Admiralty at the time of passing the Act.

What sum has been advanced out of the Sixpenny Duty on that account?—One thousand nine hundred and eighty-eight pounds and ninepence.

By virtue of the Statutes of the 10th of Queen Anne, and the 2d of George the Second, the Commissioners appoint Deputy Receivers at the several Out-Ports of Great Britain and Ireland, and

What part thereof has been repaid to the Hospital?—Five hundred and fifty-one pounds and ninepence; and Greenwich Hospital, until some other provision be made, must always be in advance the commission for three years on the receipt of Dead Men's wages.

Out of what money has that sum been repaid to Greenwich Hospital?—Out of the unclaimed wages of Men dying in the West India Trade, which are forfeited at the end of three years, and directed by the Act to be paid to the Merchant Seamen's Hospitals, or to the Magistrates of the County, to be distributed among the old and disabled Seamen of the Port where the Ship on board which the Men died may belong. Previous to distribution, the whole amount of the Commission for the year is deducted, there being no other way of repaying Greenwich Hospital, although the Act contains no direction for that purpose.

Has Greenwich Hospital in any instance benefited by the penalties, or in any other way, by the provisions of the Act respecting the appropriation of the wages of Men dying in the West India Trade?—The sum of seventy-four pounds eleven shillings and twopence has been received on account of the penalties directed by that Act; but the salaries of the Clerks of the Sixpenny Office were in February 1798 increased £.50 per annum, on account of the additional duty imposed on them by the Act, so that Greenwich Hospital has been a loser.

It appearing by an account rendered to us, that the sum of one hundred and nine pounds seventeen shillings and tenpence has been collected on account of Men dying on board Ships belonging to Ports in America and the West Indies, and is stated to remain in the Office unappropriated, does it appear to you, on reading attentively the seventh and eighth clauses of the Act, that such monies were authorized to be collected?—It does not appear to me that it ought to have been collected.

Has not the amount of wages of Men dying in the West India Trade been frequently very small?—Frequently not exceeding one pound; and although the Act directs the money to be paid to the Executors and Administrators, the Receiver has allowed sums, not exceeding ten pounds, to be paid upon proofs of next of kin, conceiving the Merchant would have so paid such sums had the Act not been passed.

What has been the greatest annual amount of the commission allowed by the Sixpenny Office to any of the Receivers at the Out-Ports on the collection of the Sixpenny Duty, the Run Men's wages, and the Dead Men's wages?—In 1800, the commission to the Receiver at Liverpool amounted to one thousand and eighty-one pounds sixteen shillings and tenpence.

What has been the average amount of the commission to the Receiver at Liverpool for the last three years?—Nine hundred and seventy-seven pounds fourteen shillings and ninepence.

Does the commission at any of the other Ports amount to any thing near that sum?—No; it does not. In 1802 the largest amount of commission, next to the Port of Liverpool, was Newcastle, being one hundred and sixty-two pounds fifteen shillings and twopence halfpenny.

in His Majesty's Colonies, Islands, and Dominions in America, who are selected from the Officers of the Customs; and upon the

Do you apprehend that the Receivers at the Out-Ports are put to any expense on account of the duties performed by them under the Sixpenny Office?—I should think at some of the principal Ports they may make some additional allowance to a Clerk, particularly at the Ports of Liverpool, Newcastle, Bristol, and Sunderland.

Was the first Commissioner and Receiver of the Sixpenny Duty, whose salary is only £.300 per annum, aware that the emoluments of the Deputy Receiver at Liverpool amounted to upwards of one thousand pounds per annum, and he had it in contemplation to reduce the commission?—Mr. Rashleigh was aware of it, and he had it in contemplation to propose a reduction of the commission to the Lords of the Admiralty.

In the accounts furnished to Greenwich Hospital, has there been any specification made of the amount of the commission allowed to the Receivers at the Out-Ports, on the receipt of Dead Men's wages out of the Sixpenny Duty, or of the sums that have been repaid to the Hospital on that account?—No.

Why have those transactions been kept from the knowledge of the Directors of Greenwich Hospital?—It has been customary to make all the payments to Greenwich Hospital of the monies received by the Sixpenny Office, under the head of " Sixpenny Duty;" and the Commissioners, being authorized by the Admiralty to make this allowance out of the Sixpenny Duty, the balance has always been paid in under that head; and I never had any directions from the Commissioners to make a detail of it.

How has the number of Seamen paying the Sixpenny Duty to Greenwich Hospital (an account of which the Commissioners have furnished the Admiralty with annually) been ascertained?—It has been calculated from the gross amount of money received.

In making such calculation, has not the amount of the moiety of Run Men's wages in the African Trade been included, and must not the account be therefore fallacious?—It has been included, and the number is thereby over-rated.

Has the Sixpenny Office sued for any penalties during the forty-three years you have belonged to it?—No.

CHARLES EVE.

Chs. M. Pole.
J. Ford.
Henry Nicholls.

Mr. Eves's Examination; continued 27th July, 1803.

Why are the accounts of the Deputy Receivers in England made up to different periods?—The time for their accounting is generally reckoned from the time of their appointment.

Would it not be better that the accounts of all the Receivers should be made up to a given period?—Yes.

You have said in a former part of your evidence, that the Deputy Receivers make their remittances yearly, half yearly, and quarterly, according to the amount of the sums collected by them; but we observe that the receipts of some of the Ports from which remittances are made annually, exceed the receipts of those where the remittances are made quarterly; how long is it since a revision conduct of those abroad a considerable check has been established, by the Board of Customs withholding the payment of their sala-

of the time of the Deputy Receivers making their remittances took place?—About the year 1766 or 1767.

Why have the Deputy Receivers in Ireland been permitted to be so much in arrear, particularly the Receiver for Galway, whose average collection is stated to amount to fifteen pounds per annum, and who does not appear to have made any remittance since the 25th March, 1790?—Repeated applications have been made to Mr. Kinsey, the present principal Deputy Receiver, and the Honourable Sackville Hamilton, the former Receiver, but they have not been properly attended to.

Have any and what steps been taken by the Commissioners to enforce the payment and remittance of the Sixpenny Duty from Ireland?—None, but the applications I have before stated.

Has it appeared to the Commissioners that the principal Deputy Receivers for Ireland have done their utmost to enforce the collection of the duty, and that they have made their remittances as regular as circumstances would allow?—I do not think it has been properly attended to by the principal Deputy Receivers for Ireland.

CHARLES EVE.

Chs. M. Pole.
John Ford.
Henry Nicholls.

The further Examination of Mr. Charles Eve; taken upon Oath the 9th of August, 1803.

What was the amount of the collection of the Sixpenny Duty for the Port of Beaumaris for the year 1802?

The net collection at the following places, which are Member Ports of the Port of Beaumaris, was as follows:—

	£.	s.	d.
Conway	6	0	11
Caernarvon	6	9	4
Pulhelly	0	8	9
Holyhead	21	7	0
	34	6	0
The Collector at Beaumaris has an allowance of 5 per cent. for collecting the money from the Member Ports, which amounted to	1	14	3¼
Making the collection in the Member Ports	36	0	3¼
The net collection for the Port of Beaumaris was	22	18	6
	58	18	9¼
The 12½ per cent. commission on the collection of this money, amounted to	8	8	4¾
Making the gross amount of the collection for the Port of Beaumaris	£.67	7	2¼

ries, unless they produce a certificate from the Commissioners of the Sixpenny Office, that they have regularly accounted to them for the monies received.

The allowance made to the Deputy Receivers for their trouble in the collection is twelve and a half per cent.—The Commissioners have no authority for making this allowance, but it is reasonable to suppose it was contained in their original instructions, which have been lost; as, by the records of the Office, the commission does not appear to have been altered since the first institution.

The receipt of the Deputy Receivers in the West Indies and America are checked by the Plantation Clerk in the Custom House in London, for which an allowance is made to him of ten per cent. upon the net amount of the collection; and the Secretary to the Commander in Chief at Newfoundland is employed to receive the Sixpenny Duty collected by the Deputies there, upon which he has an allowance of seven and a half per cent.

The commission of twelve and a half per cent. upon a small receipt, may not be more than adequate to the trouble; but at the principal Ports, where the collection is large, it amounts to a sum very much beyond what we consider to be a reasonable compensation.

The following Ports appear, by the account annually laid before Parliament for the year 1801, to require the number of Men expressed against the name of each to navigate the tonnage belonging to them; how has it happened that there has been no money paid to Greenwich Hospital from those Ports, on account of the Sixpenny Duty?

Port	Men
Cardiffe	81
Carlisle	76
Chichester	167
Gweek	30
Looe	91
Maldon	462
Penryn	27
Preston	77
Scilly	27
Stockton	205
Woodbridge	123

There never has been any Receiver appointed at Cardiffe, Carlisle, Scilly, nor Gweek. There are Receivers at the other Ports, but no remittances were made by them to the Sixpenny Office in the year 1802.

CHARLES EVE.

Chs. M. Pole.
Ewan Law.
John Ford.
Henry Nicholls.

The emolument derived by the Deputy Receiver at Liverpool from the percentage allowances on the monies collected under the direction of the Sixpenny Office, amounted in the year 1800 to the sum of one thousand and eighty-one pounds sixteen shillings and tenpence; and on an average of the last three years, to nine hundred and seventy-seven pounds fourteen shillings and ninepence: and as the commission on the receipt of the wages of Men dying in the West India Trade, soon after the passing of the Act in 1797, for the forfeiture of the same to the use of the Merchant Seamen's Hospital, was reduced at the Ports of Liverpool and Bristol from twelve and a half to five per cent., on account of the largeness of the emolument, we can see no good reason why the commission on the receipt of monies payable to Greenwich Hospital should have been continued at twelve and a half per cent., particularly at Liverpool.

We therefore recommend, (as no permanent percentage allowance can be fixed, owing to the variation in the receipt of the different Ports,) that the rate of commission allowed the Deputy Receivers be revised annually by the Commissioners, and such alterations as they may judge necessary, submitted to the Lords of the Admiralty for their directions. The percentage allowance so granted, we think, ought not to exceed the sum of five hundred pounds per annum to any one Receiver; and this, we trust, will be deemed a fair and adequate compensation, especially when it is considered, that this allowance is in addition to the emoluments derived from appointments under the Board of Customs.

The Statutes of the 8th and 9th of William the Third, 10th of Queen Anne, and 2d of George the Second, direct, That all and every Master, Commander, or Owner of Merchants' Vessels, liable to the duty of Sixpence per month payable to Greenwich Hospital, shall be examined upon oath as to the Number, Rates, Salaries, Wages, and times of Service, of all and every Person and Persons belonging to or serving in such Ships or Vessels; and sufficient power is given by the Act to the Receiver or Receivers, or their Deputies, to administer the same.

Although the Commissioners, in their instructions to the Deputy Receivers, direct this regulation to be adhered to, and furnish them with a form, in which the accounts of the Crews shall be rendered by the Masters, of which the following is a copy; viz.

MEN's NAMES.	Quality.	Time of		Number of		Money due.
		Entry.	Discharge.	Months	Days.	
Thos. Edwards	Master	15th May, 1774	20th Dec. 1774	7	5	
Robert Jones	Mate	20th do.	16th do.	6	26	
Wm. Atkinson	Able	19th June	15th September	2	27	
Chas. Lawrence	Ord.	2d July	20th Dec.	5	18	
John Cook	Boats[n]	4th August	2d do.	3	28	
						£. s. d.
				26	104 which are 3 months and 14 days.	0 13 3

Yet this very proper and necessary regulation has been very much neglected at the Office in London, though under the immediate inspection of the Commissioners; and the Masters have generally been required to state only the number of Men for which they were willing to pay the duty, to the truth of which an affidavit has seldom been administered. Mr. Stanbridge states*, that where there has

---

* *The Examination of Mr. Charles Stanbridge, Senior, Clerk to the Accountant of the Sixpenny Office; taken upon Oath the 28th July, 1803.*

What is your present situation in the Sixpenny Office? and what are its duties?—I am Clerk to the Accountant or Second Commissioner, and the duties of my situation are to receive and examine the accounts of the Deputy Receivers, and compare them with the remittances. Upon payment of the Sixpenny Duty by the Masters of Vessels, they leave the last receipts with the Receivers, which are transmitted to the Office with their accounts; and when collected for the year, the accounts are examined by the receipts, to see that the several Receivers have debited themselves with the sums for which they have given acquittances. I keep a ledger account against the Deputy Receivers of the Sixpenny Duty, Run Men's wages, and penalties, which is compared at the end of the year with the account kept by the Receiver. I receive all sums paid by Masters of Ships and others, on account of the wages of Men dying in the West India Trade, and make the payments to the Representatives; and I assist in the general business of the Office.

Have you performed such duties in person?—Yes.

What security is given by the several Deputy Receivers on account of the receipt of wages of Men dying in the West India Trade?—At Liverpool, one thousand pounds; at Bristol, two hundred and fifty pounds; at Newcastle and Lancaster, one hundred pounds; at Sunderland, Hull, Falmouth, Whitehaven, Leith, and Greenock, fifty pounds each.

What sums are the Deputy Receivers at the several Ports allowed to keep in

been an appearance of fraud, the Masters have been asked by the Clerks if they could make oath to their accounts; but an oath has never been administered, as the Clerks have no authority for that purpose.

---

their hands of the monies they receive on account of Dead Men's wages?—At Liverpool, about five hundred pounds; at Bristol, about one hundred pounds; and the other Ports hold all they collect until the distribution of the unclaimed wages.

To whom are the remittances to the Sixpenny Office from the Deputy Receivers on account of Dead Men's wages made?—To the First Commissioner, being the Receiver.

Have the other Commissioners any cognizance of, or controul over, the receipts and payments of the wages of Men dying in the West India Trade?— None.

Have the payments of Dead Men's wages, since Mr. Rashleigh's death, been continued to be made to the Representatives?—Yes: at the time of Mr. Rashleigh's death I had in my hands from four to five hundred pounds, out of which I have made the payments.

What duties have been performed by the several Commissioners of the Sixpenny Office?—The late First Commissioner, Mr. Rashleigh, was resident at the Office, and when he was capable, used to perform the duties required of him; but during the last twelve months he was incapable of performing any duty, from illness, and he died on the 17th of May last. The Second Commissioner or Accountant, and the Third Commissioner or Comptroller, used to attend to sign the quarterly and general accounts, and for no other purpose that I know of.

By whom has the business of the Office been principally conducted?—By Mr. Charles Eve, the Receiver's First Clerk.

Do you consider the appointments of the Commissioners to be sinecures?— From the duty that has been done by them they are little otherwise.

Who has performed the particular duties of the several Commissioners?— Mr. Charles Eve has performed the duty of the First Commissioner, as First Clerk to him. I have done the duty of Accountant or Second Commissioner; and the duty of the Comptroller has been performed by Mr. Eve and myself jointly.

What Clerks have been actually employed in the Office for the last four years?—Mr. Charles Eve, myself, and my Son, Mr. Charles Stanbridge, jun.

Have the duties of any of the Clerks been performed by Deputy?—The duty of the Comptroller's Clerk, Mr. John Bryan, has been performed by Mr. Charles Eve and myself.

How has Mr. Bryan's salary been appropriated?—Mr. Eve received it, and made me an allowance out of it of twenty-five pounds a year.

Who signed the receipts as vouchers for the payment of such salary?—Mr. Eve signed the receipts for Mr. Bryan, I think, and I used to witness them.

Was the salary of Mr. Bryan so appropriated with the knowledge of the Commissioners?—It was by the knowledge of the First Commissioner.

What extra duties did you perform for the part you received?—It is the duty of the Comptroller's Clerk to take an account of the receipts of the Port of London, and to keep a set of books to check the Receiver. I kept the day-

Having required of the Commissioners a detailed account of the establishment of the Office, with the amount of the annual receipt of each individual, by salaries, fees, perquisites, and emoluments, a statement was delivered to us, similar to that presented to the Committee of Finance in 1797. In the column for fees was written " No established Fees;" and in the column of " Total Receipt of each Individual," the amount of the Salaries only was placed against each name, which would appear to have been intended to convey an idea that no fees were taken; but on our

book of the receipts of the Port of London, and the bill-book of the remittances from the Out-Ports; and Mr. Eve performed the remainder of the duty.

What accounts have been usually presented by Masters of Merchants' Vessels and others, when they come to pay the Sixpenny Duty?—The Masters of Vessels in the West India Trade generally bring an account of the Men, with the times of their entries and discharges; the Masters of Merchants' Vessels in other Trades state the number of hands only, and the time for which they mean to pay the duty.

Have such accounts been usually sworn to?—No: if there should be an appearance of fraud, they are asked if they can make oath to their accounts; but the oath has never been administered, as the Clerks have no authority for that purpose.

By whom have the receipts for the Sixpenny Duty, and other monies payable to Greenwich Hospital, been usually signed?—In the absence of Mr. Rashleigh, Mr. Charles Eve signed them for him, and he likewise signed them for the Comptroller. Blank receipts have lately been signed by the Receiver and Comptroller, and left with Mr. Eve to fill up as occasion required.

What check has there been upon the receipts of the Receiver of the Sixpenny Duty for the Port of London?—The established check should have been the Comptroller; but his duty having been performed by Mr. Eve and myself, there has been no actual check: the accounts have, however, been examined annually by us, with the assistance of the Receiver's Second Clerk.

Have the payments, as they were made, been regularly entered in the Comptroller's book, and by whom?—They have by me generally; but I have sometimes entered them from the Receiver's book.

Have any, and what fees, been received by any person or persons belonging to the Sixpenny Office?—No fees for the Hospital Duty have been received by any person but the Receiver's First Clerk, which are as follow:—East Indiamen one guinea; West Indiamen three shillings and sixpence to five shillings; other Merchantmen generally two shillings; but some do not give any thing. The fees arising from the receipts and payments of Dead Men's wages have been divided between Mr. Eve and myself; and are generally, upon payments to the Office by the Masters, two shillings and sixpence for their discharge; and the Executors and Administrators generally give two shillings and sixpence on receiving the money due to them, but in some cases more. The general average of the fees I have received has been about thirty pounds a year. Upon the whole, I have not received from my situation in the Sixpenny Office above one hundred and thirty or forty pounds a year. Upon the distribution of the unclaimed wages, inquiring whether any fees, though not established, were received, we discovered that certain fees were taken by the First Clerk from Masters of Vessels paying the Sixpenny Duty, upon the plea of dispatching their business, and also gratuities on the payment of wages to the Representatives of Men dying in the West India Trade, as well as for those forfeited to the Merchant Seamen's Hospitals; which, on an average of the last four years, have amounted in the whole to about three hundred and ninety pounds per annum.

---

a compliment was made to Mr. Eve by the Merchants' Hospital at London, of ten guineas; and at Liverpool I believe the same.

Is there any examination made of the accounts furnished to Greenwich Hospital by the Receiver of the monies collected at the different Ports, previous to the account being certified by the Accountant and Comptroller?—The accounts were in the first instance examined by Mr. Eve and myself, and afterwards by Mr. Rashleigh and Mr. Eve, and then the Accountant and Comptroller used to sign them.

Are the deductions made from the Sixpenny Duty on account of the charge of collection, stated in the accounts rendered to Greenwich Hospital?—No.

Under what head is the money received at the Out-Ports, on account of the moiety of Run Men's wages in the African Trade, paid into Greenwich Hospital?—Under the head of the "Sixpenny Duty."

Why has it not been paid in as arising from the moiety of Run Men's wages in the African Trade?—I cannot say.

From what head of receipt is the commission on the collection of the wages of Men dying in the West India Trade defrayed?—From the receipt of the Sixpenny Duty and the Run Men's wages.

How are such monies repaid to Greenwich Hospital?—They are deducted from the unclaimed wages of Men dying in the West India Trade, previous to the distribution to the Merchants' Hospitals.

Is there any specification in the accounts furnished to Greenwich Hospital of the expense or the repayment of this money?—No, I believe not.

From what head of receipt are the salaries and incidental expenses of the Sixpenny Office deducted?—They are deducted from the receipt of the Out-Ports, I believe, to make the receipt of the Port of London appear more important.

Can the Directors of Greenwich Hospital, by the accounts furnished them, have any knowledge whatever of the increased revenue to the Hospital, arising from the moiety of Run Men's wages in the African Trade collected at the Out-Ports, or of the diminution of the revenue occasioned by the payment of the commission on Dead Men's wages out of the monies that ought to be paid to the Hospital?—They can not.

CHARLES STANBRIDGE.

Chs. M. Pole.
John Ford.
Henry Nicholls.

NAVAL LITERATURE.

A Tour in Zealand in the Year 1803: *with an Historical Sketch of the Battle of Copenhagen. By* a NATIVE of DENMARK. 8vo.

THOUGH we have not hitherto been able to attend, as we could wish, to this department of our Chronicle, we hope now to have an opportunity of returning to it, and more particularly in our next Volume. The following extract from *a Tour in Zealand,* as it gives an account of *the Battle of Copenhagen by a Dane,* cannot fail of being interesting to our Readers; and may induce some of them to peruse the whole of the above-mentioned amusing Work.

On the morning of March the 30th, about seven o'clock, the thundering peals of Cronburg put an end to suspense. Very shortly after, we could discern the Fleet, which approached rapidly. The tremendous cannonading from the Fort gave us an idea of what it might effect, if it could reach its object. His Majesty of Sweden (who observed the passage of the Fleet from Helsingborg,) appeared sensible of this; and after the cannonading had ceased, dispatched an Officer to compliment the Governor of Cronburg.

As the Gale was blowing fresh, the British soon advanced within seven or eight miles of the City, where they came to an anchor. A Frigate, a Lugger, and a Brig, got rather nearer; but the Battery of the three Crowns, and the fire from the Block Ships, compelled them to retire. The magnificence of this Spectacle naturally left various impressions on our minds; but whether favourable or unfavourable, they were soon forgotten in the enthusiasm and unanimity which prevailed among all Classes. The question was not, *Who is the Enemy?* but, *Where is the Enemy?* It was a moment of impending Danger; the duty we owed our Country, therefore, inspired us with only one sentiment. The noble spirit displayed by the Students at the Siege in 1658-60, was equally conspicuous in their Successors; who, with one hand and one heart, associated themselves into a Corps of twelve hundred; while those Sons of the Muses, whom age and infirmity prevented from rallying round the Standard of Patriotism, did all in their power to encourage and confirm so laudable an effort. Chamberlain Lindenkrone sent a thousand dollars to the aid of those Students whose private means were unequal to the expense of their public duties.

The first and second days passed quietly over; but on the morning of April 1st, we could perceive an unusual bustle among the English Shipping. Some Frigates and lighter Vessels got under weigh, and were employed in Sounding. Towards evening, twelve Sail of the Line, all the Frigates, and most of the smaller Vessels, weighed; and with a northern breeze passed through the Hollander Deep. Admiral Parker, with eight Sail of the Line, and two small Vessels, preserved his Station; while Admiral Nelson anchored, with his Division, beyond the fire of our outermost Ships.

Conjecture was now at an end. A change of Wind to the southward would enable Lord Nelson to bear down with his Division; and we anxiously awaited the awful moment. Our Ships were moored with four anchors, and manned, indiscriminately, by people of all descriptions, hastily collected for the present emergency: they had been constantly on the alert during the former two nights, a third was now added to their fatigue; and when it is considered, that these people were unacquainted with the exercise of great guns; that they were all day employed in practising, and all night in watching; the compliment paid them by Mr. Bardenfleth, First Lieutenant on board the Charlotte Amelia, in his professional account of the Battle, will not be deemed superfluous.

He says, " The spirit which animated all hands on board, and not their real strength, enabled them to perform what they did."

The morning of April 2d dawned, and the Wind blowing southerly, our Commodore made a Signal for the whole Line to lay their broadside to the Enemy.

Between nine and ten, both Divisions of the British weighed; and our Commodore hoisted the Flag of Defiance from the Danbrog. Admiral Parker, with the zeal that is characteristic of a British Seaman, beat up against Wind and Current, towards the Battery of the Three Crowns, proposing to awe our Ships in the inner Roads, while the Hero of the Nile bore right down upon our Line.

The Edgar led the British Van, advancing in a most gallant style against the Proevesteen, 58 guns, which opened her fire on the former, five minutes after ten. The Vagrien, 50 guns, then poured in a broadside, just as the Edgar was upon the tack to take her Station; a second broadside was discharged from the Proevesteen, when the whole of the British Line gained rapidly on ours: in a few minutes two-third parts of our Ships were in Action. As our Line was not broken, only one half of the Force on either side was consequently engaged.

Our foremost Ship, the Proevesteen, was exposed, during the whole of the Action, to the fire of the Polyphemus, of 64 guns, the Russel, and the Bellona, which two latter Ships run aground at the commencement of the Battle; but this misfortune, (as Lord Nelson observed,) did not impede their Service. The Proevesteen was, at the same time, raked by la Desirée, of 40 guns, and a Gun-brig.

Great as was the distinction which Commodore Fischer, in his report, conferred on the Proevesteen and her gallant Captain Lassen, " notwithstanding my high sense of Danish bravery, it was heightened by the conduct of the Proevesteen, which continued to fight till all her guns were dismounted," the compliment of Lord Nelson is in my opinion * greater.

" Captain Rüsbrigh stood, on this occasion, as undaunted upon the quarter-deck of the Vagrien, as when a Lieutenant on board the Formidable, under the gallant Rodney, on the 12th April, 1782. For England he assisted to acquire glory and success; for Denmark he obtained only the former."

Soon after eleven o'clock the Danbrog, 64 guns, Captain Braun, took fire, which compelled Commodore Fischer to shift his broad Pendant to the Holstein; but Braun continued to fight her till he lost his right hand. Captain Lemning succeeded in the Command; and although the flames blazed around them, threatening immediate destruction, the Danbrog maintained her fire, till the close of the Engagement, against her powerful adversary the Glatton; which latter mounted 68 pound carronades on her lower deck.

When Commodore Fischer, famed for the coolness and perspicuity of his judgment in the hour of trial, left the Danbrog, the Battle raged with the utmost fury. The British finding that our foremost Ships were far from slackening their fire, now extended their Line, and at noon all our Ships, as well as the Battery, were strenuously engaged in the awful Contest.

---

* Nos. 1, 2, 3, and 4, being subdued, which is expected to happen at an early period, the Isis and Agamemnon are to cut their cables, and immediately make Sail, and take their station ahead of the Polyphemus in order to support that part of the Line.

Captain Thura, of the Infoedsretten, 64 guns, fell at the beginning of the Action; and all the Subaltern Officers were either killed or wounded, except a Lieutenant and a Marine Officer. In this state of confusion, the Colours were, by accident, struck. The British, however, made no attempt to board the Infoedsretten, she being rather dangerously moored athwart our Battery. A Boat was dispatched from the Ship to carry the tidings of her Commander's death to the Prince Royal, who had from the dawn of day taken his station upon a Battery. Here, amid showers of shells and cannon balls, Frederick, the wise, the good, and the brave, superintended, calmly and actively, for the assistance of the Ships engaged. By showing how a Prince ought to meet danger, he taught others to despise it.

When the Prince received the message from the Infoedsretten, he turned round, and with an air that gave confidence to all about him, said, *" Gentlemen, Thura is killed; who of you will take the Command?"*—" I will," replied Mr. Schroedersee, in a feeble voice, and hastened eagerly on board. This Gentleman had been a Captain in the Navy; but on account of ill health had lately resigned. The hour of necessity seemed to invigorate his wasted form, and in hopes to serve his Country, he forgot his want of strength.

The Crew seeing a new Commander coming alongside, hoisted their Colours and fired a broadside. When he came on deck he found great numbers killed and wounded; and therefore instantly called to those that had rowed him to get quickly on board. It was his last effort; a ball struck him, and Schroedersee was no more! Mr. Nissen, a Lieutenant in the Navy, who attended this gallant Tar to his noble fate, next took the Command, and continued to fight the Ship for the remainder of the day.

The Engagement had now lasted upwards of three hours, without any glimpse of Victory on either side. A determined perseverance appeared to inflame both Parties. Our Line steadfastly preserved its original position, and every Ship maintained its station except the Rendsbrog Prame, which drove ashore, her cables having been shot away at the commencement of the Attack; and the Elven, a Repeating Sloop of War, which had sheered off a little after twelve, her masts being very materially damaged.

When the British Fleet first bore down upon us, the eleven Gunboats retired.

About two o'clock the fire from the respective Fleets abated considerably, and our Ships appeared very much disabled. The damage sustained by the British was apparently trivial, from our Ships having constantly directed their fire at the Enemy's hulls. This was undoubtedly the slowest method of disabling an adversary; yet it was the surest; and certainly is, at all events, preferable to chance.

Considering the exposed situation of our Men on board, it was a matter of real surprise, that so few, comparatively, suffered from the immense quantity of shot which had been poured in upon them.

Had every ball that struck our masts wounded our hulls, there would, in all probability, have been no Prisoners of War.

At two o'clock the Nyeborg Prame having her main, mizenmasts, bowsprit, and foretop-mast shot away, and the Captain perceiving her almost ready to sink, ordered the cables to be cut, and the foresail to be set, that they might steer for the inner Roads. As he passed the Line he descried the Aggershuus, a Vessel of the same description as his own, in the most miserable plight; her masts having all gone by the board, and the hull on the eve of sinking. Captain Rothe showed himself a true Seaman, who not only meets his own danger, but also cheerfully shares in that of others. Having made fast a cable from his stern to the stern of the Aggershuus, he towed her off; and thus obtained as glorious a triumph as if he had come in with an Enemy's Ship.

Soon after two o'clock, Commodore Fischer removed his broad Pendant from the Holstein to the Battery of the Three Crowns, whence he commanded during the latter part of the Engagement.

At this moment Lieutenant Lillienskiold finding his Ship, the Hielperen, surrounded by a superior force, cut his cables, and brought her safe into the inner Roads. Mr. Lillienskiold was no stranger to the business of the day; he had, in the year 1799, fought in the West Indies with a Privateer; and both contended so obstinately, that they were obliged to separate for want of powder.

Last, though not least, is Mr. Villemoes, a Second Lieutenant, who commanded the floating Battery, No. 1. Much has been said about his skill in manœuvring his Raft, which consisted merely of a number of beams nailed together: on them a flooring was laid to support the guns. It was square with breast work, full of port holes, and without masts. I shall not take upon myself to argue how far it were possible to manage such a log; but merely say, the manner in which Villemoes manœuvred his guns, and ultimately saved his Raft, attracted the notice of Lord Nelson, whose Ship lay for some time opposite the floating Battery. That Admiral is said, in the handsomest manner, to have noticed to the Prince

Royal, how much the Country, on future occasions, might fairly expect from the abilities of young Villemoes. This trait of his Lordship I consider as a never failing flower in the wreath which military talents and success have twined around his brows.

At half past two our fire had nearly subsided; but the Rutland, the last Ship that returned the Enemy's shot, was still engaged, as was the Proevesteen. However, the Three Crowns had just opened its Batteries with a dreadful effect, when the white Flag was unfurled from Lord Nelson's main-top.

An English Boat, with a Flag of Truce, came alongside the Elephant; the Captain of which sent an Officer in his Boat to accompany it on Shore. The Battery, in the mean time, kept up a heavy cannonade, as did the Elephant. As the Wind had been south south-west, south, and south-east, the whole day, with a strong Current, Admiral Parker's Division advanced but very little; insomuch, that a broadside from the Ramillies, a 74, (his foremost Ship,) fell very short of the Battery.

The Flag of Truce having delivered a dispatch to the Prince Royal, returned; and soon afterwards orders were sent to the Commander of the Battery to cease firing; their guns had, in the interval, been pointed with the utmost effect on the Monarch and Ganges, which Ships were awkwardly situated on the Shoal of the Battery.

Two Flags were then dispatched from Shore, to Admirals Parker and Nelson; while the British took possession of eleven of our Ships.

In the course of the forenoon Admiral Nelson came in his Barge into the inner Roads, and went on board of the Denmark, where he partook of some refreshment, and then proceeded ashore. On his landing he was received by the people neither with acclamations nor with murmurs; they did not degrade themselves with the former, nor disgrace themselves with the latter. The Admiral was received as one brave Enemy ever ought to receive another— he was received with respect. A carriage was provided for his Lordship, which he however declined, and walked amidst an immense crowd of persons anxious to catch a glimpse of the British Hero, to the Palace of the Prince Royal. After dinner the Admiral was introduced to the Prince, and the negociation commenced. The next day his Lordship came again on Shore, and dined with the Prince Royal, as he did frequently till the ninth of April, when the Armistice was finally concluded.

On one of his visits to Copenhagen, Lord Nelson inspected our Naval Academy; to which he, in a manner highly honourable to himself and to us, presented some gold medals of value, to be distributed among the most skilful of the Midshipmen.

The Narrative of a Voyage of Discovery, performed in His Majesty's Vessel the LADY NELSON, *of Sixty Tons Burthen, with Sliding Keels, in the Years* 1800, 1801, *and* 1802, *to New South Wales. By* JAMES GRANT, *Lieutenant in the Royal Navy, &c.*

[Continued from page 206.]

FROM the smallness of the Lady Nelson, the general appellation which she received in the River was that of His Majesty's *Tinder Box;* and, from the circumstance of this little Vessel being destined for so long a Voyage, Mr. Grant had frequently the pain of hearing unpleasant remarks, and was at times subjected to more serious inconveniences. In January 1800, however, His Majesty's Tinder Box sailed from the Thames; and in the month of July following she arrived safely at the Cape of Good Hope.

On the 18th of June, about six weeks after sailing from St. Jago, a circumstance occurred, which Mr. Grant thus relates:—

On the 18th we had a very heavy Sea, with the Wind as yesterday. By observation at noon, we were in lat. 31° 13 S., long. per account, 11° 48 W. We were often obliged this day to throw the Vessel before the Sea, as it followed us, and rose more perpendicular than I had observed before. About five P.M. my attention was excited by a more than ordinary motion of the Vessel. On my reaching the deck, I found no more Wind than we had all day, but the Sea was running very hollow, and breaking at times. On asking the Mate, who had the watch, how long it was since the Sea had got up? He answered, about ten minutes, when it rose and broke about half a cable length from the Vessel on the starboard bow. It appeared to me so much like a break, that I believed the bottom could be at no great depth. Both of us were so much surprised, that, without speaking a word, I went and took the sails in to heave the Vessel to, and put the deep Sea-lead over, but had no soundings with one hundred and twenty fathoms line out. I saw the Sea break twice as we passed it, one Sea following the other; but as we were going six knots, and the Sea very high, I could only observe it rise, while the Vessel was rounding to, higher on that spot than the place we were on. From the different form of the Sea, together with the manner in which it broke, I think there must be some ground at no great depth in this spot; for it did not gradually rise into a heavy long swell, and break at top, as it had done all day, but was lifted suddenly up perpendicular, throwing itself forward, and doubling over as it fell into an immense column of water, breaking in a very heavy surge. There is little doubt, if we had been in it, that it would have overwhelmed us as it fell; so that more owing to chance than good management we escaped. The Sea we had been going through all day, when in the hollow of it, was much higher than our mast head, so that we had no great scope in view; but no inconveniency was felt, as it was long, regular, and heavy, admitting the Vessel to remain on the top of it some time before it rolled from under her: but these breakers were of a very different nature. I observed before, that it was the sudden motion of the Vessel which brought me on deck; but as soon as she was hove to, we found ourselves in the state we had been in all day. After laying to about an hour, we bore up. In the chart prefixed to the East India Directory, some breakers seen by Captain Smith are laid down in the same latitude we were in at noon this day; but judging myself to the east of them, and having a powerful swell from the N. W., with a strong W. S. W. Gale, steering S. E. half S. with the addition of sometimes being obliged to throw the Vessel farther off to the E. to avoid the break at the top of the Sea at times, I did not apprehend falling in with them, as laid down by him in 13° W. Whether these be the same or not, or whether there is any ground, (though I have no doubt there is,) yet it will be some satisfaction to Seamen to know, that they may guard against them. The latitude so nearly corresponds, that I have every reason to believe them the same. On my arrival at the Cape of Good Hope, I seized the first opportunity to transmit an account of them to Europe, with my opinion. I before remarked the latitude and longitude at noon; from which, until we fell in with these breakers, we had run thirty-two miles S. E., half S. by compass. On the 16th the variation was observed to be 11° 30′ W., and on the 20th 11° W. I allowed the variation to be about 12? 15 W. when we saw those breakers.

The Lady Nelson sailed from the Cape of Good Hope in October; and in December she arrived at New South Wales.

The Harbour of Port Jackson, and Paramatta, are thus described by Mr. Grant:—

To the stranger the Harbour of Port Jackson appears pleasing and picturesque, as he advances up it to the Town. A small Island with a house on it, named Garden Island, (which afterwards became my residence,) enriches the view. On the main is Walmoola, so named by the Natives; a rural situation, where Mr. Palmer, the Commissary, has built a large and commodious house, and bestowed much labour in cultivating the land round it. Such a house in so young a Colony excites a degree of surprise in a new comer. The Town of Sidney is much larger and more respectable than can be imagined, considering the time it has been built. The streets are by order made broad and strait; each house is generally separated from the adjoining ones, (an excellent regulation in case of fire); few or any are without gardens, and many of the houses are large and commodious. When I landed I found that the heavy rain, which I had experienced some days before, had been equally felt here. The Hawkesbury River had been swelled almost instantaneously, to the great annoyance of the Settlers on its Banks. Various were the causes assigned for the rapid increase of water: some supposed it owing to the bursting of a cloud in the mountains, which hurried the water down the level Country; others to the overflowing of a lake or morass, which augmented the currents of all the neighbouring Rivers, for that of Paramatta had also overflown its banks to a very great height, as I afterwards was shown by Dr. Thompson, now a Resident Colonial Surgeon, as almost to be supposed impassable.

Paramatta, which is the name given by the Natives to what was at first called Rose Hill, is a very pretty Village; and from what I can judge, much preferable in point of soil to Sidney. The Government House stands at the end of a street, nearly an English mile in length, making a very fine appearance. There is an excellent garden adjoining to it, well stocked with vegetables and fruit trees; amongst which the peach and fig were large and fine. All the houses had gardens to them well cultivated, the soil of which is good. The Rev. Mr. Marsden, Clergyman to the Colony, has his residence here. That Gentleman, while I was here, was indefatigable in superintending the building of a small neat church. The first that was erected was at Sidney, but it was unfortunately burnt down; Divine Service was therefore obliged to be performed in a Store cleared out for the purpose in that Town; but as from its excellent Harbour and increase of houses and population it will always remain the seat of Government, the Church will, no doubt, be rebuilt in a durable manner.

The houses of the Convicts in general are constructed with wattles, covered with shingles, and plaistered inside and out with clay, over which they put a coat of lime, burnt from shells, giving them a very neat and clean appearance. It is seldom that two families inhabit one dwelling, therefore every Man becomes absolutely Master of his house, and when he can afford it he weatherboards and paints it. In the smallest dwellings I entered I never saw less than two apartments. Many houses are constructed with bricks, and as well finished to the eye as European buildings: in such the apartments are numerous. In short; from the very comfortable manner these people are lodged, (much more so than the poorer sort in England,) I cannot avoid remarking, that it no doubt has a tendency to promote the great degree of health and flow of spirits I observed them possessed of, and readily accounts for many wishing to remain, whose years of banishment have expired.

The principal object of the Lady Nelson's Voyage was to sail through and make a survey of the Straits, deservedly called Bass's Straits, after Mr. George Bass, late Surgeon to His Majesty's Ship Reliance, that Gentleman having first entered them in a Whale-boat to the eastward, and discovered a Harbour to the westward of Wilsons Promontory, which he named, from its relative situation, Western Port. Mr. Grant was completely successful in his undertaking, as it appears to have been reserved for the Lady Nelson most accurately to ascertain the extent of the Straits, she sailing along the land nearly four degrees to the westward of Western Port, discovering various Islands and Rocks in her passage.

As Lieutenant Grant remained at New South Wales for some months, employed in surveying the Coast, &c., he had frequent opportunities of seeing and conversing with the Natives; of one of whom he gives the following account:—

On the 23d of May, 1801, Mr. Barreillier and the Second Mate went on Shore, and in the woods met with a Native, whom they conducted on board the Vessel. He was an elderly Man, of the class termed here Bush Natives, who are considered as an inferior tribe by the inhabitants of the Sea Coast. This Man's legs and arms bore no proportion in length to the rest of his body, and the manner of ascending the Ship's ladder was remarkable, and plainly proved he was much accustomed to climbing. His method was to stretch out his arms as far as he could reach, and then bring his feet to the same place with a jerk. His language was unintelligible to all on board, and the sounds he uttered strangely dissonant and uncouth, having however something plaintive, but without the least similitude of speech. He had the whole of his front teeth perfect, contrary to the usage of the other Natives of New Holland, who cause one of the *incisors* of the upper jaw to be eradicated at an early period of their lives. Of this custom Mr. Collins has given a particular account in his work relating to the manners and customs of the New Hollanders. This Man could by no means be persuaded to eat or drink with us. I offered him sugar, supposing, as the Bush Natives live much on wild honey, it might prove acceptable. I was on the point of putting him on Shore, as he seemed so averse to partake of our food, and was otherwise so far from docility, when he espied a crow of the carrion species, which one of my people had shot: this he seemed to express a longing desire for, and on its being presented to him, he went with it to the galley fire, and heating it a little, devoured it greedily, entrails and all. On his going on Shore, Colonel Paterson gave him a tomahawk, which he took, and appeared to know readily how to use it: however, he did not seem to have any name to give it, which was what we endeavoured to make him express; but placing it under his arm, went off with it. The Crew of the Boat in which we were conveyed on Shore, willing to have a proof of his dexterity in the use of his new acquisition, pointed at a tree, as if they wished to see him climb it. He readily understood them, and making a notch in the tree with his instrument, placed his foot into it, continuing the same practice; thus he very nimbly ascended to the top, though the tree was of a great thickness, and without branches that could assist him in the ascent, to the height of forty feet. From this tree he removed to another, by which he descended, and passing hastily through the bushes, was soon out of their sight. The Natives have hatchets of their own, formed with sharp stones, and which they use for the same purpose; and I have indeed remarked, that many of their trees are notched. Colonel Paterson, whose long residence in New Holland, and curiosity of observation, have enabled him to decide upon questions of this nature, declared that he never met a Native who differed so widely from the rest of the New Hollanders. It will probably appear to my readers that we have as yet but an imperfect knowledge of the natural productions of the neighbourhood of Sidney, and of its aboriginal inhabitants. This Man appeared in a state of perfect nakedness, and was without the mark of the ornament described by Colonel Collins, of a stick thrust through the cartilage of the nose, of which he bore no mark. As there is thought to be a chain in Creation, beginning with the Brute and ending with Man; were I inclined to pursue the notion, I should be at a loss where to place my Bush Native, whether as the next link above the monkey, or that below it.

Having accomplished every purpose of his Voyage, and having met with certain mortifications and disappointments in the Country, Mr. Grant left the Lady Nelson under the care of Governor King, and took his passage for England, in the Anna Josepha, Whaler, where he arrived in 1802.—His nautical observations will be found a valuable acquisition to those who may in future follow the track of the Lady Nelson.

PLATE CLXXX.

THE HYDROGRAPHER, (No. 1.)

CONSISTING OF A SERIES OF ISLANDS, HARBOURS, AND BAYS, FROM DRAWINGS BY AARON ARROWSMITH.

AT the suggestion of many of our Friends, and with the kind assistance of Mr. Arrowsmith, we intend *occasionally* to introduce such Portions of Hydrography as will correct the errors that have long existed in former Maps and Charts. Mr. Arrowsmith has favoured us with all the French West India Islands, on three Plates; the first of which, Martinico, we now insert. The beauty and accuracy of the Engraving speak sufficiently for themselves.

We have at different times, in the course of our Chronicle, had occasion to speak of this valuable Island; and we lately published a View of the celebrated Diamond Rock, (Vol. IX, p. 201,) from a Drawing by Mr. Pocock: a detailed account of which, in a letter from an enthusiastic admirer of the adjacent Scenery, appeared (Vol. XII, p. 205.) Martinico was attacked by the English in 1693, 1703, and 1759; (see Vol. II, p. 439, in Commodore Sir John Moore's Biographical Memoir); was taken by Rodney in 1762, (Vol. I, p. 363); and by Sir John Jervis

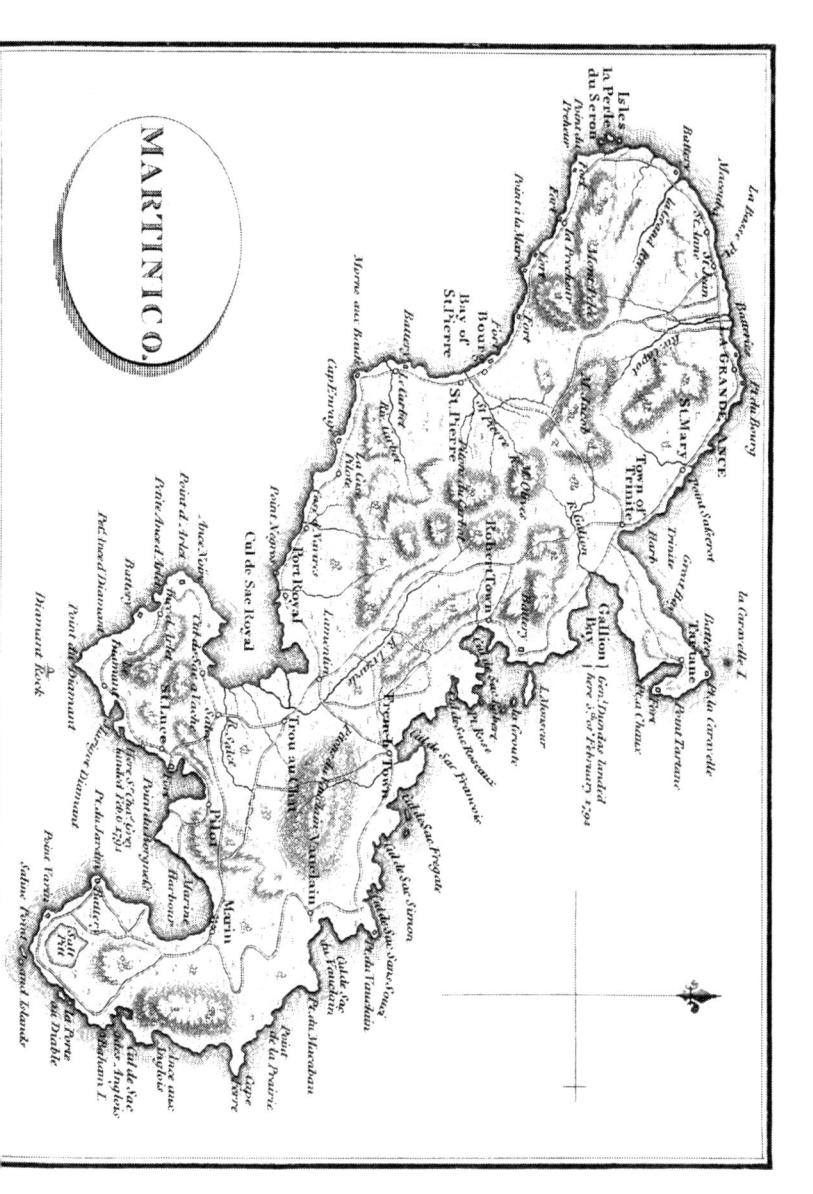

and Sir C. Grey, in 1794, (Vol. IV, p. 13.) In all of these references our Readers will find accounts of different parts of the Island.

According to Raynall, (Vol. VI, page 7,) when the exhausted French West India Company put their Possessions up to Auction, Mons. Duparquet, in 1650, paid for Martinico, St. Lucia, Granada, and the Granadines, only sixty thousand livres, or £.2,500!! Guadaloupe, Marigalante, and the Island called the Saints, had been purchased in 1619 by Mons. Boisseret for £.3,041 13s. 4d. Colbert afterwards redeemed Martinico for £.5,000; Guadaloupe, and its dependent Islands, for £.5,208 6s. 8d.; and Granada for £.4,166 13s. 4d. The French first settled here in 1635 under Desnambuc, the Chief of those enterprising Mariners, who sailed towards the Caribbee Islands in 1625, with the idea of raising there an independent State: and the sole Founders of this new Colony consisted of only one hundred Men.

Martinico, called originally by the Natives Madanina, and by the French Martinique, is about sixty miles long, and its unequal breadth scarcely any where exceeds twenty miles. Its latitude at the N.W. part is 14° 51 north, and longitude 61° 26 west. At the S.W. part the latitude is 14° 24' north, and longitude 61° 2' west. And at Fort Royal the latitude is 14° 36' north, and longitude 61° 9' west.

The Island is very uneven, and intersected in all parts by Mountains, which are marked in the Plate. It is divided, as all the Caribbees are, into Cabes-terre and Basse-terre. The former being on the windward side of the Island, is continually indented by deep Bays, which the French call Cul de Sacs: from these Ports numbers of Privateers are fitted out; and it is incredible to think what a number of Prizes they carry in, where they are sure of protection, as all the Bays are well protected with Batteries. As there are little Towns at all these Harbours, they never want People sufficient to work their guns. The two principal places in Basse-terre are, St. Pierre and Fort Royal. The whole Island is divided into twenty-one Parishes.

The principal Harbour is Port Royal, or Cul de Sac Royal, which is large and open, and the entrance free from Rocks. The most considerable Town in the Island, or indeed in any of the Caribbees, is that of St. Pierre, situated in a fine open Bay, on the leewardmost part of the Island. Viewed from the Sea, it appears seated at the foot of a steep Mountain. All the Ships loaded with the French West India produce, are obliged to repair to St.

Pierre, and clear out, where the Captain-General of all the French Caribbee Islands resides, with all the Royal Courts and Officers; owing to which, all the produce of their Colonies becomes blended under the name of Martinique.

The Settlers under Desnambuc, at first confined themselves to the culture of Tobacco and Cotton, to which they soon added the Arnotto and Indigo: that of Sugar was not begun until about 1650. About ten years afterwards, Benjamin Dacosta, a Jew, first planted some Cocoa Trees. In 1727, all the Cocoa Plantations perished; when, amidst the consternation that prevailed, the Coffee Tree was first proposed. The French Ministry had received two of these Trees, as a present from the Dutch, which were carefully preserved in the King's Botanical Garden. Two Shoots were taken from these in the year 1726, and entrusted to Mons. Desclieux, who carried them over. The Ship was greatly distressed during the passage for water, and that Gentleman shared with his young Trees the portion that was allotted to him: by which means his valuable trust was preserved. His zeal was well rewarded.

The produce of Martinico in 1775 sold for about £.790,665 : 11 : 9 but of this a little more than a quarter belonged to St. Lucia and Guadaloupe, which had sent part of their growth to Martinico.

Naval Poetry.

Bright-ey'd Fancy hovering o'er,
Scatters from her pictured Urn
Thoughts that breathe, and words that burn!

THE SAILOR.
AN ELEGY.
BY SAMUEL ROGERS, ESQ.

THE Sailor sighs as sinks his native Shore,
 As all its lessening turrets bluely fade;
He climbs the mast to feast his eye once more,
And busy fancy fondly lends her aid.

Ah! now, each dear domestic scene he knew,
Recall'd and cherish'd in a foreign clime,
Charms with the magic of a moonlight-view,
Its colours mellow'd, not impair'd by time.

True as the needle, homeward points his heart,
Through all the horrors of the stormy Main;
This, the last wish with which its warmth could part,
To meet the smile of her he loves again.

When Morn first faintly draws her silver line,
Or Eve's gray cloud descends to drink the wave;
When Sea and Sky in midnight darkness join,
Still, still he views the parting look she gave.

Her gentle spirit, lightly hovering o'er,
Attends his little Bark from Pole to Pole;
And when the beating Billows round him roar,
Whispers sweet hope to sooth his troubled soul.

Carv'd is her name in many a spicy grove,
In many a plantain-forest, waving wide;
Where dusky youths in painted plumage rove,
And giant palms o'er-arch the yellow tide.

But lo! at last he comes with crowded sail!
Lo, o'er the Cliff what eager figures bend!
And hark, what mingled murmurs swell the Gale!
In each he hears the welcome of a friend.

—'Tis she, 'tis she herself! she waves her hand!
Soon is the anchor cast, the canvass furl'd;
Soon through the whitening Surge he springs to land,
And clasps the Maid he singled from the World.

NAVAL BALLAD.

BY SAVILLE CAREY.

LIFE's like a Ship in constant motion,
    Sometimes high and sometimes low,
Where ev'ry one must brave the Ocean,
    Whatsoever Wind may blow:
If unassail'd by squall or shower,
    Wafted by the gentle Gales,
Let's not lose the fav'ring hour,
    While success attends our sails.
Or, if the wayward Winds should bluster,
    Let us not give way to fear;
But let us all our patience muster,
    And learn, from reason, how to steer.
Let judgment keep you ever steady,
    'Tis a ballast never fails;
Should dangers rise, be ever ready
    To manage well the swelling sails.

Trust not too much your own opinion
  While your Vessel's under weigh;
Let good example bear dominion,
  That's a compass will not stray.
When thund'ring tempests make you shudder,
  Or Boreas on the surface rails,
Let good discretion guide the rudder,
  And Providence attend the sails.
Then, when you're safe from danger riding,
  In some welcome Port or Bay,
Hope be the anchor you confide in,
  And care awhile enslumber'd lay:
Or, when each cann's with liquor flowing,
  And good fellowship prevails,
Let each true heart, with rapture glowing,
  Drink ' Success unto our Sails.'

COLUMBUS, AND THE DISCOVERY OF AMERICA.

(FROM CAREY'S ' REIGN OF FANCY.')

WHAT, when the daring scheme Columbus plann'd,
  Drew the warm wish, the generous purpose fann'd:
What, though he left Iberia far behind,
Bade the heart dance to rapture unconfin'd;
When faded from his sight Canary's Shores,
And the white Surge that washes the Azores,
For many a long day forc'd his course to keep,
And many a long night linger on the deep,
And still no object met th' inquiring eye,
Save one wide waste of water and the sky.
But when the magnet, guide-sta of the soul,
Swerv'd from the path, and wander'd from the pole,
And Nature seem'd from Nature to depart,
What terrors took possession of the heart!
Then came Philosophy, with aspect sage,
And bade their jarring discords cease to rage;
And still, at evening's melancholy close,
What hopes, what golden expectations rose,
When many a mountain cliff they seem'd to spy,
And fairy forest waving to the sky!
And, as they fled before the morning ray,
How rose their fears, how died those hopes away!
So melt the joys that promise still to bless,
So fly the enchanted Shores of happiness!

The day was fix'd,—the Sun's last splendours shone
Strange lustre play'd around his setting throne,
They hail'd the friendly presage with delight,
The morning gave new worlds to bless their sight:
What joys, what raptures did ye then dispense,
Ye Isles of fragrance! to the ravish'd sense!
Then did your fields their richest charms unfold,
Your rills of Amber, and your streams of Gold;
Then did your Groves their fairest liv'ry wear,
And Freedom smil'd upon the vernal year,
'Tis thus our expectations swell the sail,
Life is the Sea, and Passion is the Gale;
Long tempest-tost upon the wide expanse,
In Joy's wild chase and Hope's delusive trance,
The wish goes forth, nor finds whereon to rest,
And dove-like seeks again the shelt'ring breast;
And many a joy and fancied bliss appears,
But to dissolve like dreams of earlier years.—
The Sun goes down;—then, sent to sooth and save,
The day dawns on the midnight of the grave!
" Awake! arise! and see the skies unroll'd,
And all the flowers of Paradise unfold;
Shake off the leaden slumbers of thy rest,
And hear the mingled anthems of the Blest."
The trumpet sounds,—the curtain is unfurl'd,
The spirit wakes,—and lo! another world.

On the Gallant Exploit of LIEUTENANT YEO.

ARE Britons united, they still shall be free,
Though their Vessel be tost on a boisterous Sea;
All Dangers surmounting, the Tempest they'll weather,
By a long Pull, a strong Pull, and Pull altogether:
Then while the Waves roar, and the Hurricanes blow,
Let us all lend a hand, with a hearty *Yeo*, *Yeo!*

NAVAL BALLAD.

A SAIL on our lee-bow appears,
  She looms like a French Man of War,
Then pipe up all hands, my brave Tars,
  And cheerly for chasing prepare.
Set each Sail that will draw, ease your reefs and be mute,
   Mind how you steer,
   Don't let her veer,

>   She'll lose way if she yare,
>   So steadily down on your Enemy bear,
> And give her a British salute.
>   But now see her top-sails aback,
>   She seems making ready to fight;
>   Up hammocks! down chests! clear the deck!
>   And see all your matches alight!
> Now splice the main-brace and to quarters away!
>   Stand every one
>   True to his gun,
>   'Till the Battle be done,
> We soon shall compel them to fight, sink, or run!
>   Huzza! for Old England! huzza!

PLATE CLXXXI.
THE FRONTISPIECE TO VOLUME XIII.

THIS Engraving is a correct representation of the Monument which has been recently opened for public inspection in Westminster Abbey, to the memory of Captain James Montagu, who fell in the glorious Action of the 1st of June, 1794 *. On that memorable day he commanded the Montague, of 74 guns, and nobly sealed with his blood a Victory which, to the remotest periods, will reflect a signal lustre on the Arms of Britain.

For this specimen of national sculpture, which has been erected, by a grateful Country, to the memory of a departed Hero, the Artist † is said to have received the liberal compensation of 3,500 guineas.

On a circular pedestal stands a colossal figure of Captain Montagu, in the British Naval Uniform; behind which, rising from a Globe, is the figure of Victory, preparing to place a wreath of laurel on his head. At the base are two lions of proportionate size. On the front of the pedestal is a representation, in alto-relief, of the Engagement of the 1st of June; and at the back are two figures, in bold relief, deploring the loss of the deceased Officer.

The extreme height of the Monument, which is conceived and executed in a superior style of elegance, is upwards of twenty feet.

---

* *Vide* NAVAL CHRONICLE, Vol. 1, page 20, *et seq.*—This Monument is placed exactly opposite to that which commemorates the death of the Captains Harvey and Hutt, a description of which will be found in the Eleventh Volume of the Naval Chronicle, page 363.

† John Flaxman, Esq., R.A.

METHOD
RECOMMENDED BY
Dr. HAWES,
FOR RESTORING TO LIFE THE APPARENTLY DEAD.

The greatest exertions should be used to take out the Body before the elapse of one hour, and the resuscitative Process immediately to be employed.

CAUTIONS:

Bodies taken out of the Thames, Ponds, &c.
1. Never to be held up by the heels.
2. Not to be rolled on casks, or other rough usage.
3. Avoid the use of salt in all cases of apparent death.

WHAT THOU DOEST—DO QUICKLY.

THE DROWNED.

1. Convey carefully the body, with the head raised, to the nearest convenient house.
2. Strip, and dry the body:—Clean the mouth and nostrils.
3. YOUNG CHILDREN:—between two persons in a warm bed.
4. An ADULT.—Lay the body on a blanket or bed, and in cold weather near the fire. In the warm season air should be freely admitted.
5. It is to be gently rubbed with flannel sprinkled with spirits; and a heated warming pan, covered, lightly moved over the back and spine.
6. TO RESTORE BREATHING.—Introduce the pipe of a pair of bellows (when no apparatus) into *one* nostril; close the mouth and the *other* nostril, then inflate the lungs, till the breast be a little raised; the mouth and nostrils must then be let free. Repeat this process till life appears.
7. TOBACCO SMOKE is to be thrown gently up the fundament, with a proper instrument, or the bowl of a pipe covered, so as to defend the mouth of the assistant.
8. The BREAST to be fomented with *hot spirits:*—if no signs of life appear,— the WARM BATH:—or hot bricks, &c. applied to the palms of the hands and soles of the feet.
9. ELECTRICITY *early employed* by a MEDICAL ASSISTANT.
10. THE BREATH IS THE PRINCIPAL THING TO BE ATTENDED TO.

INTENSE COLD.

Rub the body with *snow, ice,* or *cold water.*—Restore warmth, &c. by slow degrees; and after some time, if necessary, the plans to be employed for the resuscitation of drowned persons.

SUSPENSION BY THE CORD.

1. A FEW OUNCES OF BLOOD may be taken from the jugular vein, and cupping glasses may be applied to the head and neck; leeches also to the temples.
2. THE OTHER METHODS OF TREATMENT, the same as recommended for the apparently drowned.

SUFFOCATION BY NOXIOUS VAPOURS OR LIGHTNING.

COLD WATER to be repeatedly thrown upon the face, &c. drying the body at intervals.—IF THE BODY FEELS COLD, employ gradual *warmth*, and the plans of the drowned.

INTOXICATION.

THE BODY is to be laid on a bed, &c. with the head a little raised: the neckcloth, &c. removed.—Obtain immediate MEDICAL ASSISTANCE, as the *modes of treatment must be varied* according to the state of the patient [*].

---

[*] Dr. Hawes earnestly recommends the perusal of Dr. Trotter's Essay on Drunkenness.

GENERAL OBSERVATIONS.

1. ON SIGNS OF RETURNING LIFE, the Assistants are most earnestly advised to employ the restorative means with GREAT CAUTION, so as to nourish and revive the languid signs of Life.

A tea-spoonful of warm water may be given;—and if swallowing be returned, warm wine or diluted brandy.—To be put into a warm bed, and, if disposed to sleep, will generally awake restored to health.

2. THE PLANS above recommended are to be used for THREE or FOUR HOURS. *It is an absurd and vulgar opinion to suppose persons as irrecoverable because life does not soon make its appearance.*

3. Electricity and bleeding never to be employed, unless by the direction of the MEDICAL ASSISTANTS.

NAVAL HISTORY OF THE PRESENT YEAR, 1805.

(May—June.)

RETROSPECTIVE AND MISCELLANEOUS.

AMIDST the state of distraction which still pervades the political World, and the high spirit of Party that prevails on both sides, we find it extremely difficult to select the most important documents of the Naval History of the present Year and to compress them within the bounds which our Chronicle affords. Our Readers of the present day, as well as the future Historian, will in this department of our Work find much recorded, that would otherwise have been swept away by the rapid succession of other Events; and many things are here brought together, that were scattered and dispersed among Subjects not connected with the Navy.

Our first attention has been paid to the Report of the Select Committee appointed to investigate the Tenth Report; and notwithstanding the guarded secrecy with which, on all occasions, the proceedings of the Board of Admiralty are attended, we are now able to lay some Letters of considerable importance before our Readers, which the peculiar character of the present Times has alone brought forward.

In the midst of all our late proceedings and alarms, a report of Peace still prevails, and more especially on the Continent. M. Novozilskoff, who is expected to be the Emperor of Russia's Agent in conveying to Buonaparté the new criterion of Peace, or War, is the Nobleman who was in this Country in February last, and is supposed to have received here the final determination of our Cabinet upon the subject.

The following Extract of a Letter from an Officer on board Lord Nelson's Squadron, dated May 7, gives an account of their proceedings up to that period:—

" Lord Nelson reached Tetuan * the 4th instant, intending to remain there completing his Water, &c. until the Wind became fair. The easterly breeze, which carried the Active through, failed the Amazon in the Straits four hours after; and she had the mortification to beat about the Gut five days, during which period she captured the Ceuta Packet, with 150 Troops, Arms, and Accoutrements,

---

* A View and Description of Tetuan we gave in Vol. X, p. 142, of our Chronicle.

going to that place to relieve part of the Garrison. The Gun-boats about Gibraltar are become a great annoyance, and the Spaniards were so exasperated at the Capture of the Packet, that they came out seemingly determined to attack the Amazon, but retreated as she approached them: she might have closed with them, and probably have destroyed one or two of these pests, but employed on the important mission she was, very prudently declined to risk the chance of getting a mast or yard wounded that might for a moment detain her. The Active fell in with a Spanish Squadron, of six Sail of the Line, off Carthagena, and three or four more are said to be ready at Cadiz, so that the Mediterranean will be left to the mercy of these Fellows. We yesterday heard a great deal of firing in the Straits; but whether it was a rejoicing day with the Dons only, or a little amusement between our Fleet and the Gun-boats and Batteries, is yet to be determined; possibly the latter, as the Wind was very light."

In consequence of the scarcity of Seamen in Spain, the King has issued a Decree, charging the Tribunals to set at liberty those who are not accused of murder, burglary, and other capital crimes, in order that they may be employed in the Sea Service, the Arsenals, &c.

A letter from Cadiz, dated April 4, says, " General Moreau is still here, and is much consulted in all our movements. He said the other day, ' That if he could not take Gibraltar, he would render it not worth the keeping to the English ;' and we expect that some serious attempts to burn the Town and Shipping will be made in the course of the Summer."

The following extraordinary circumstance, we learn by a letter from Husum, occurred some time since at Tonningen :—The Master of an English Vessel lying there, was ordered by the Captain of the Guardship to slack his cable, which he did, till he could slack no more: he was then ordered to cut, which he refused to do, saying, he would, or could not, if the King himself was there. In consequence of this reply, the Danish Captain sent a party of Men on board of the English Vessel, who brought the Master on board the Danish Ship, and he was there flogged severely, by order of their Captain. The Dane, in vindication of his conduct, says, the Master of the English Vessel damned the King of Denmark : this charge has, however, been refuted by a number of Witnesses who were present when the altercation took place. A petition, praying for redress, signed by about fifty English Masters of Vessels, has been sent to our Ambassador at Copenhagen.

Some outward-bound Ships to Newfoundland have been captured by a Spanish and two French Privateers. The Capture, though a great loss to the Owners and Persons concerned in the Ships, will not prove very valuable to the Enemy.

A Morning Paper says,—" Mr. Benjamin Tucker, late Deputy to the Secretaries to the Admiralty, has got a pension of 1,08 2l. per annum by the King's Warrant of the 23d May, 1805, and 300l. per annum to his Wife, Jane Tucker, if she survive him."

The Ville de Milan, French Frigate, which captured the Cleopatra, and was afterwards taken by the Leander, of 50 guns, at Halifax, is to be purchased into the Navy, and fitted out to serve on the American Station, by the name of the Milan.

A formal contradiction of the report of the loss of His Majesty's Ship Vanguard in the Gulf of Florida, signed by her Commander, Captain Evans, has been inserted in the American Journals. We are happy to find that the account of the loss of the Princess Charlotte Frigate is equally unfounded.

The London Docks were opened on the 25th of May.

A British Naval Pillar (as one of the leading Sea-marks) has lately been erected near the Low-house, South Shields. It is intended to inscribe the names of Howe, St. Vincent, Duncan, and Nelson, on each side of its square base.

The following account of the Force of our invading Enemy is thus given by a Prisoner.—There are about 3000 of their Craft at Boulogne, 800 of which are armed; the others are merely Transports for Troops, Stores, &c. There are near 1000 at Estaples, and about 600 at Vimereux, and 400 at Dunkirk, Ostend, and Calais. The Troops are in small Camps; about 8000 at Boulogne, the same number about Calais, Vimereux, Estaples, and some other Camps a little inland; in all about 50,000 Men. He seems very confident that the attempt will be made this Summer. He says, the Combined Fleet, sixty Sail of the Line, will fight our Fleet, *(Balayer la Munche,)* while the large Frigates will come up Channel to convoy the Flotilla over. The Troops are stated to be very eager to come, and entertain the most sanguine hopes of success: they are waiting very impatiently for the appearance of the Ships to set them free, and great reliance is placed on the genius of Buonaparte.

Admiralty Office, May 20, 1805.

A Return of the number of Persons promoted to the rank of Lieutenant; of Lieutenants to the rank of Master and Commander; and of Commanders to that of Post Captain, respectively, from the 1st of January 1793, to the 20th of May, 1805; specifying the number of each rank promoted in each year, and distinguishing those made at Home from those made on Foreign Service; and stating who were the First Lords Commissioners of the Admiralty during the said period, and distinguishing each change in the said Office, and the date thereof.

Year.	Captains.		Commrs.		Lieutenants.		First Lord Commissioner of the Admiralty.
	Home.	Abroad.	Home.	Abroad.	Home.	Abroad.	
1793	26	5	23	9	161	23	Earl of Chatham.
1794	41	20	73	37	283	155	Do. to Dec. 18.
		1		4		10	Earl Spencer appointed Dec. 19.
1795	59	20	91	27	247	90	Do.
1796	38	16	83	22	139	107	Do.
1797	35	12	77	31	157	123	Do.
1798	24	19	68	32	100	67	Do.
1799	27	9	48	23	166	113	Do.
1800	22	12	38	13	171	137	Do.
1801	17	3	26	3	13	19	Do. to Feb. 18.
	11	8	30	10	181	83	Earl St. Vincent appointed Feb. 19.
1802	131	15	127	18	130	167	Do.
1803	2	7	3	16	7	95	Do.
1804	19	4	33	6	73	23	Do. to May 14.
		8	3	14	10	59	Lord Melville appointed May 15.
1805	3	3	17	7	48	54	Do. to May 1.
		2	1	1	10		Lord Barham appointed May 2.
	163	34	193	50	391	368	Total by Lord St. Vincent in 3 years.
	3	11	20	21	58	113	Total by Lord Melville in 1 year.

SIR HOME POPHAM.

THE Select Committee to whom the several Papers presented to this House, relating to the Repairs of His Majesty's Ships the Romney and Sensible, whilst under the Command of Sir Home Popham, are referred, to examine into the several Matters contained therein, relative to the said Repairs; and to the Proceedings of the Admiralty and Navy Boards, and of the Commissioners of Naval Inquiry thereupon; and also to inquire into the Circumstances attending the publication of the Report of the Navy Board, dated 20th February, 1804, and into the Loss of certain Vouchers and Documents on which that Report was founded; and also into the circumstances attending the impressing of Mr. David Ewen Bartholomew; and to report the same, together with their Proceedings and Observations thereupon, from time to time to the House; and who were empowered to examine into the Expenditure and Purchase of all Stores for the use of the said Ships;—have, pursuant to the Order of the House, examined accordingly; and have agreed to the following Report:—

Your Committee having taken into consideration that part of the reference which relates to the Repairs and Stores of the Romney and Sensible, find, from the Papers referred to them, and the Evidence they have received, that there does not appear any ground whatever to impute to Sir Home Popham any fraud, or connivance at any fraudulent or corrupt practice, whatsoever. With respect to the Sensible, your Committee observe, that Sir Home Popham appears to have ordered that Ship to proceed to Calcutta from the Red Sea, (instead of sending her to be repaired at Bombay,) for the purpose of furnishing a Convoy to several Transports and Merchantmen bound to Bengal; that he gave to her Commanding Officer, Captain Sause, at Calcutta, orders dated the 11th of October, 1801, " to use his utmost exertions to repair the said Ship," and " to complete her with six months' Stores;" and that Captain Sause having never rejoined him after the execution of those orders, Sir Home Popham cannot be considered answerable for the manner in which they were executed. Your Committee do not mean, by this remark, to impute any blame to Captain Sause, not having considered any transaction relating to the Sensible as the subject of the reference made to them, further than as such transaction could be connected with the conduct of Sir Home Popham. Your Committee observe, that Sir Home Popham appears to have gone on shore from the Romney a few days after her arrival in the River Hughly, Aug. 1801, and before her arrival at Mayapour; and to have proceeded up the Country, in compliance with the desires of Marquis Wellesley, (with whom he was specially directed by his instructions to communicate,) for the purpose of conferring with his Lordship concerning certain great objects then in contemplation, in which Marquis Wellesley required his advice and assistance; that he left that Ship under the command of the First Lieutenant, Mr. Davies, an Officer on whose integrity and knowledge of the service, he stated himself to have had the utmost confidence; and that he did not return on board the Romney till after that Ship had sailed from Mayapour: it appears, therefore, to your Committee, that if the Sails and Stores of the Romney, sent on Shore at Calcutta, were not regularly surveyed before they were condemned (a point which your Committee, owing to the circumstances of the Ship having no Master, and the Boatswain being sick at the time, and of Mr. Davies, the First Lieutenant, being now absent from England, are not able correctly to ascertain,) the blame of such irregularity is not to be imputed to Sir Home Popham: and in support of this observation your Committee beg leave particularly to refer to the evidence of Captain Bowen. Your

Committee find, that the quantity of Stores demanded by Sir Home Popham, while the Romney was under repair, and supplied by Mr. Louis, who had been previously appointed, by Admiral Rainier, His Majesty's Deputy Naval Officer at Calcutta, exceeded the quantity allowed for a twelvemonth's expenditure, estimating that quantity according to the calculation made in His Majesty's Dockyards, and mentioned in the Report of the Navy Board of the 20th of February, 1804; but that Sir Home Popham has accounted for this circumstance, by stating, that he did not confine his demand to a provision of Stores for any particular period, but took on board as large a supply as the Ship could conveniently carry, having a view, in demanding such Stores, to the probable exigencies of the service upon which he was expected to be employed. Your Committee find, that Sir Home Popham, in addition to the sails which were allowed by the establishment of the Navy, ordered several to be made and supplied for the use of the Romney, which were not authorized by the strict rules of the service; but it appears to your Committee, from the concurrent testimony of several persons examined on the subject, and particularly from that of Captain Mason, who speaks from experiments made under his own observation, that those extra sails were highly advantageous in the Indian Seas. Your Committee have not thought proper to state in this Report some other instances in which Sir Home Popham appears to have deviated from the strict rules of the Service, by directing the Naval Officer to supply him with articles for the use of the Romney, which are described in the evidence, and were not conformable to the usages of the Navy; such irregularities appearing to your Committee to be wholly unworthy of Parliamentary attention, or of any other notice but that which of course they ought to have received, according to the customs of the service, in the consideration of Sir Home Popham's accounts, when any extra charge would be disallowed, unless deemed to have been expedient under the circumstances of each particular case. Your Committee, however, think themselves called upon, in strict justice to Sir Home Popham, distinctly to state, that they have not met with any instance, in effecting the repairs, or in the supply or expenditure of Stores, which has been attended with any personal advantage or emolument to himself; nor have your Committee the least reason to suspect, from the evidence before them, that his conduct, upon any occasion in which the rules of the Navy have not been rigidly observed, was influenced by any private consideration; but, on the contrary, your Committee feel it to be their duty to observe, that Sir Home Popham *appears to have been actuated by no other motive but that of an ardent zeal for the Public Service.* Your Committee do not think it necessary to state their observations, in detail, upon all the points mentioned in the Report of the Navy Board of the 20th of February, 1804; conceiving, that as far as relates to Sir Home Popham, *that Document appears to them to be materially inaccurate.* Your Committee observe, that Sir Home Popham appears to have used his utmost endeavours to obtain money for drafts on England upon the most favourable terms for the expenses of the Squadron under his Command. Your Committee have thought it their duty, in justice to the character of a meritorious Officer—*(who, so far from encouraging or conniving at any public waste, appears, in evidence before your Committee, to have effected very considerable savings),* to make a Special Report on the circumstances of his case; being the first head of their Inquiry; though the evidence, on which their Report is founded, is so blended with that which relates to the other particulars referred to them, that they must postpone reporting that evidence until the other heads of Inquiry are also brought to a conclusion.

The following Correspondence shows what knowledge Earl St. Vincent had of the Stone Expedition. We have also added some letters referred to by Lord Melville in his Speech.

It appears that Lord St. Vincent sent a secret Order, dated February 9, to Sir Andrew S. Hammond to superintend the Stone Expedition, and enclosing Sir Andrew the plan. Mr. Sullivan, Lord Hobart's Secretary, wrote also to Sir Andrew as follows:—

"*To Sir* A. S. HAMMOND.

" MY DEAR SIR,

" I hope you can report progress. I have not seen nor heard from Mr. ——— since I saw you; Lord St. Vincent approves much of the direction being with you, and will himself write to Lord Keith when the preparations are sufficiently forward. " Yours faithfully,

" *Downing-street, Feb.* 18, 1804." " J. SULLIVAN."

"*To Sir* A. S. HAMMOND.

" MY DEAR SIR,

" Lord Hobart begs me to say, that he hopes the Vessel's having taken the ground, is not an indication of her draught of Water being too great for the proposed Service. He is going to settle with Lord St. Vincent about the protections; and I am going to arrange with the Treasury about the instructions to the Custom-House.

" *Downing-street, Feb.* 21, 1804." " J. SULLIVAN."

" *To Sir* A. S. HAMMOND.

" MY DEAR SIR,

" Lord Hobart proposes to send a Messenger to-night to Lord Keith, and hopes you will send your Packet to go by him. Lord St. Vincent's letter will accompany it.

" *Downing-street, Feb.* 23, 1804." " JOHN SULLIVAN."

The above letters contain proofs that Lord St. Vincent not only knew, but even approved of the Expedition. The following Papers show that Sir Andrew S. Hammond communicated the matter formally to Lord St. Vincent, enclosing him the Secretary of State's order.

" *To Earl* ST. VINCENT.

" MY LORD,

" As I had not the honour of seeing your Lordship this morning when I waited upon you at the Admiralty, I beg to enclose, for your information, an order I received the 9th of last month from Lord Hobart; and to acquaint your Lordship, that in consequence thereof I have forwarded the service therein mentioned as far as it was in my power, and that three Ships fitted for the purpose have now sailed down the River to join Lord Keith. I beg further to acquaint your Lordship, that I have avoided as much as possible taking any People or Stores from His Majesty's Dock-yards for this Service; but, from the want of exertion of the Parties whom I was directed to controul, and the necessity which existed for extraordinary dispatch, I have been obliged to have recourse both to Woolwich and Chatham Yards, the particulars of which shall soon be laid before the Admiralty.

" I have the honour to be, &c.

" *Navy Office, March* 9, 1804. " A. S. HAMMOND."

"*Copy of an Order enclosed in Sir* ANDREW SNAPE HAMMOND's *Letter of the 9th March, to the Earl of* ST. VINCENT.

(Most secret).

" SIR, "*Downing Street, 9th Feb.* 1804.

" It being thought advisable, under the present circumstances of the War, that an attempt should be made for carrying into execution the project suggested in the enclosed paper for choaking up the entrance into the Harbour of Boulogne: and the success of such an enterprize depending in a great measure upon the secrecy and dispatch with which the preparations may be made, I have the King's commands to signify to you His Majesty's pleasure that you do take these preparations under your immediate controul, and that you do communicate confidentially with Mr. ———, supplying him with such funds, and giving him such orders for the purchase of Vessels, and providing the stone and other materials which you may judge necessary to be embarked, as shall be requisite for accomplishing the object in view. The advances you may have occasion to make for this Service will hereafter be replaced by the Treasury. As soon as the Vessels shall be sufficiently laden, you will give directions that they should proceed with all possible expedition to the Downs, where all further orders will proceed from Lord Keith. I am, Sir, your most obedient and faithful humble servant,

" *Sir A. S.* HAMMOND, *Bart.,* " HOBART."
Comptroller of the Navy."

" *To A. S.* HAMMOND, *Bart., Comptroller of the Navy.*

" SIR,

" I have received your letter of yesterday, enclosing an instruction which you had received from Lord Hobart for the execution of a Secret Service, and which I have no doubt will be well performed; but as the whole expense is to be defrayed by the Treasury, I do not see occasion for any part of the detail being submitted to the Admiralty Board. I return herewith Lord Hobart's letter, and have the honour to be, Sir, your most obedient humble servant,

" *Admiralty, 10th March,* 1804. " ST. VINCENT."

Here is Lord St. Vincent's own hand-writing, to show that he knew of the Expedition, and did not discountenance it. By other letters it appears he had further information of its progress. On the 26th of March, Mr. Sullivan informs Sir A. S. Hammond he has shown Lord St. Vincent further Papers respecting the Expedition. On the 12th of April he again writes to Sir Andrew, to say he has shown the First Lord more papers respecting it. This was the *only* secret Expedition and secret Naval Service during the whole of Lord St. Vincent's Administration. It appears, that during three months his Lordship was at least six times consulted on the subject. We subjoin the answer of Earl St. Vincent before the Commissioners of Naval Inquiry:—

" *Extract from the Examination of the Right Honourable the Earl of* ST. VINCENT, *K.B.; taken upon oath, the 2d November,* 1804."

" It appearing that the sum of fourteen thousand pounds was advanced by the Navy Board to Messrs. T. Hammersley and Company, between the 18th of February and 21st of April, 1804, for a Secret Service; was the Comptroller of the Navy authorized by you to perform any Secret Service for which this money was advanced? or had you any knowledge of the transaction?—He was not; nor have I any knowledge of the transaction.

" ST. VINCENT."

The following Papers laid before the House of Lords, show that Earl St. Vincent was at one time desirous of employing the Merchants' Yards:—
(Copy not kept.)

"*Substance of a Letter written by Sir* A. S. HAMMOND, *Comptroller of the Navy, to the Earl of* ST. VINCENT, *28th December*, 1802.

"Not having heard from your Lordship on the subject of our conversation on Thursday, the 16th instant, respecting the Merchant Builders, I cannot help feeling anxious thereupon, and therefore take the liberty of writing to your Lordship this Letter, to prevent any unnecessary delay, not having had any communication with them on the subject."

(No. 2. in 14.)

SIR, "*Rocketts*, 29th *Dec.* 1802.

"It must be fresh in your recollection that I have seldom conversed with you on any subject without introducing *the urgent necessity of entering into Contracts for building as many 74 gun Ships as you could find fit Persons to undertake in every part of the Kingdom*; I cannot therefore refrain from expressing considerable surprise at the favour of your Letter to me of yesterday, which requires that should repeat in the strongest terms the opinion I have so frequently given.

"I am, Sir,
"Your most obedient humble servant,
"*Sir A. S. Hammond.*   " ST. VINCENT."

The above Letter is decisive of Earl St. Vincent's desire to build in Merchants' Yards, and Sir Andrew Hammond accordingly advertised in the Newspapers for Tenders to build by contract, and wrote Letters to the Admiralty and to Earl St. Vincent on the subject; when he received the two following Letters:—

(No. 5. in 14.)
"SIR,   " *Rocketts*, 2d *January*, 1803.

"You appear to have misconceived the reply I made to your suggestion of my seeing the Merchant Builders, the propriety of which I felt doubts upon; and certainly nothing passed between us in the conversation alluded to, that could be considered as tying your hands from holding any communication with the Merchant Builders that you might think necessary or likely to be advantageous to the Public.

"*I was not a little surprised at seeing in the Newspapers an Advertisement from the Navy Board for the building of* 74 *gun Ships, which my Letter neither authorized nor directed,* having gone no further than to show that I continued in the opinion I had so frequently given upon the subject of building Ships of the Line by contract; but a regular communication ought to have taken place between the two Boards, and an official order given by the Admiralty to the Navy Board before any steps were taken. From what you represent, I wish *this precipitate Advertisement may not add to your impediments* in procuring a supply of Timber for the King's Yards.   " I am, &c.

"*Sir A. S. Hammond.*   " ST. VINCENT."

"SIR,   " *Admiralty Office*, 3d *Jan.* 1803.

"Having communicated to my Lords Commissioners of the Admiralty your Letter of the 1st instant, relative to a Letter which you received from the Earl of St. Vincent, directing you "not to lose a moment's time in contracting for the building some 74 gun Ships," I am commanded by their Lordships to request that you will transmit to me, for their information, copies of the Letters which have passed on this subject between the Earl of St. Vincent and you, and which occasioned the Advertisement from the Navy Office, inserted in the Newspapers of Saturday last, for the building Ships of the Line by contract.

" I am, Sir,
" Your most obedient humble Servant,
" Sir A. S. Hammond, Bart., &c. " EVAN NEPEAN."

The Board of Admiralty desired the Navy Board to transmit all the Tenders for building Ships of the Line which had been sent in consequence of the advertisement. Some of these tenders were as low as 25l. per ton for a 74 in three years; others offered to build upon being allowed a fair valuation on the materials and labour, with a reasonable profit. The following is a copy of the answer of the Board of Admiralty to the Navy Board after perusing these tenders:—

(No. 17 in 14.)
" GENTLEMEN, " Admiralty Office, Jan. 13, 1803.
" Having laid before my Lords Commissioners of the Admiralty your letter to me of the 10th instant, enclosing tenders which you had received from the Merchant Ship Builders, I am commanded by their Lordships to acquaint you, that *it is not their intention that any of the tenders should be accepted, or that any Line of Battle Ships should now be built in Merchants' Yards.*

" I am, Gentlemen, your most humble Servant,
" EVAN NEPEAN "
" P.S. Herewith return the Enclosures.
" Navy Board."

To these Letters we add the following from the Navy Board to the Secretary of the Admiralty:—

(Secret.)
" SIR, Navy Office, 31st Jan. 1805.
" We request you will inform the Right Honourable the Lords Commissioners of the Admiralty, that in conformity to their Lordships' order, dated the 22d instant, we have contracted with the following Merchant Builders in the River for eight 74 gun Ships, distributed in the manner, and to be completed in the time respectively expressed against their names.

		YEARS.
Mr. Wills	2 74 gun Ships..........	3½
—— Pitcher,	2	3½
—— Barnard,	1	3½
—— Dudman,	2	3½
—— Brent,	1	3½

It is however with much concern we have to inform their Lordships, we have not been able to prevail with the Builders to abate more than the fractional sum of eleven shillings per ton in the price they demanded for building these Ships; they resisted every proposition made to them, that fell short of the price we have at length agreed upon, which we are sorry to say is 36l. per ton, exceeding the estimate which had been made by the Surveyors of the Navy in the sum of 2l. 5s. per ton, after the most liberal consideration of the statement of particulars which had been delivered in by the Merchant Builders, and which statement we required of them, in order that we might ascertain the grounds upon which they demanded so great an increase as 10l. per ton on the price at which some of them had tendered to build 74-gun Ships in January 1803, but which tender their Lordships at that time did not deem it advisable that we should accept.

" Notwithstanding the excess of price demanded by the Builders beyond the estimates of the Surveyors of the Navy at first view may seem unreasonable, we cannot but acknowledge that it appears less so, when all the circumstances they have stated in vindication of their demands are fairly considered.

" They represented that they had nothing now to look to but the litera execution of their contract, having no expectation of any recompence, if, in case of their fixing too low a price, they should sustain a heavy loss in the completion of the Ships, which they could not foresee at the time of entering into the contract, and which might result from an alteration of circumstances during the time the Ships are in hand; a consideration which operated with this Board on the occasion of the loss which the Builders sustained in building the six 74 gun Ships contracted for in January 1800, when in consequence of the same having been proved to the Board, we had pledged ourselves to indemnify them to a certain extent, but which the Lords Commissioners of the Admiralty did not deem it proper we should make good to them in any degree.

" They represented that, for some time past, the Overseers employed in superintending the work, appeared to be actuated by a different disposition from that which used to govern them; namely, a fair, reasonable, workmanlike principle, that had for its object the good of His Majesty's Service, without oppressing the Builder; instead of which they now seemed to be actuated too generally by a spirit of strictness which gives rise to many difficulties and impediments in the execution of their contract.

" They represented that, in justice to themselves and families, it must be expressly stipulated, that the Certificate which has been invariably given by His Majesty's Officers of the Ship being completed agreeably to contract, should be final on the part of Government, in order that they may not be subject to vexatious prosecutions years afterwards, as in the case of the Ajax.

They also represented, that the great provision we had made for furnishing the Dock-yards with a large stock of timber (in consequence of the exhausted state in which they had been of that article) must operate most powerfully to increase their difficulties in procuring their supplies, and consequently raise the price very considerably. At this part of the conference one of the Builders begged we would inform them, if a report which had reached them was founded in truth; viz. that we had Agents in the Country employed with Government Money, to the amount of 40,000l., in purchasing Timber of the next fall; for, if so, it would be impossible for them, without ruin to themselves, to undertake the contract which was now in agitation. We could have no hesitation, in answer to this question, to say we had no Agents employed in purchasing Timber in the Country. But as we wished to know the authority on which such a report was founded, we desired them to tell us from whom they obtained this information. *In reply, Mr. Dudman, one of the Builders, stated, that he had received the information from Sir Thomas Troubridge, in order to put him on his guard in his transactions with the Navy Board.*

In consequence of it appearing to us, from what the builders said upon the subject, that they might suppose (or at least make a plea of it hereafter, unless informed of the real state of the case) that the assistance we afforded to two of our principal contractors, to enable them to extend their purchases and deliveries to replenish their reduced stores might operate to their (the builders) prejudice, in their provision of timber for building of these Ships, we deemed it proper confidentially to inform them of the real nature of the transaction alluded to; viz. that we had no agent in the country employed in the purchase of timber on commission, but that we had found it necessary to advance, by way of loan, at five per cent. interest, and on ample security, a sum of money, short, however, of what the builders stated to two of our principal contractors, to enable them to extend their purchases (beyond what their own capitals would reach) to a large quantity of timber which we had been informed would otherwise fall into the hands of country dealers, and be applied to country purposes; which timber, or any other they might purchase by means of our loan, was to be delivered under the terms of their existing contracts; but that the effect of this transaction was nearly, if not quite terminated, and at all events would, we conceived, extend in a very trifling degree to the ensuing fall, of which they appeared to be satisfied.

Upon this subject it may now only be necessary for us to add, that the resolution of the Board to make the advance to the two contractors (to which there was only one dissenting voice) was made on the 20th of July, 1804, and the knowledge of the transaction the Board believed to be confined to the parties, to the Board, and two of their principal Clerks, and to their Lordships, communicated by the Comptroller of the Navy to the First Lord of the Admiralty, who approved the measure.

Their Lordships will observe, that we have not as yet been able to agree for more than eight of the ten Ships ordered to be contracted for. And, as an agreement, that the price demanded by the builders, though large, is not unreasonable; we beg leave to call their Lordships' attention to the circumstances under which Mr. Bernard and Mr. Brent have consented to contract with the Board. They are known to possess premises sufficiently ample, and adequate means and ability to enable them to execute our orders to a large amount; yet they would, on no account, undertake more than one Ship each, upon the terms of the intended contract,

We are, Sir, your very humble servants,

A. S. HAMMOND, H. HARMOOD,
H. DUNCAN, S. GAMBIER,
J. HENSLOW, F. J. HARTWELL,
W. RULE, H. LEGGE.
W. PALMER,

P. S. Since writing the above, we have agreed with Messrs. Adams of Bucklershard, to build a 74 Gun-ship, in three years and a half, which will be the subject of a future letter.

W. Marsden, Esq.

ARRANGEMENTS OF THE WESTERN SQUADRONS BY THE PRESENT ADMIRALTY,

Exclusive of Downs and North Sea Fleets, and that under Lord Nelson, down to the 20th of June, 1805; viz.

21 Sail of the Line, off Brest, under Admiral Lord Gardner.
5   do.   Coast of Ireland, under Rear-Admiral Drury.
7   do.   off Rochefort, under Rear-Admiral Graves.
9   do.   off Ferrol, under Vice-Admiral Calder.
9   do.   off Cadiz, under Vice-Admiral Collingwood.

51 Ships of the Line, all highly fitted, manned, and equipped for any Service, Home or Foreign.   F. F.

Letters on Service,

Copied verbatim from the LONDON GAZETTE,
[Continued from page 414.]

ADMIRALTY-OFFICE, MAY 18, 1805.

Copy of a Letter from Captain Mitchell, of His Majesty's Sloop Inspector, to William Marsden, Esq.; dated Yarmouth Roads, May 14, 1805.

SIR,

I HAVE to inform you, that His Majesty's Sloop Musquito has sent in this morning the French Privateer Orestes, Dogger rigged, mounting one long 24 pounder and six swivels, and manned with thirty-four Men.

I am, Sir, &c.
E. J. MITCHELL.

JUNE 1.

Copy of a Letter from Commodore Sir Samuel Hood, K.B., late Commander in Chief of His Majesty's Ships and Vessels at the Leeward Islands, to William Marsden, Esq.; dated at Barbadoes, the 28th of March, 1805.

SIR,

I enclose herewith, for the information of the Lords Commissioners of the Admiralty, copy of a letter from Lieutenant Barker, commanding His Majesty's armed Brig Grenada, giving an account of the Capture of l'Intrepid Privateer.

I am, &c. SAM. HOOD.

SIR *His Majesty's Brig Grenada, March 16, 1805.*

I have the satisfaction to acquaint you, that at two A. M. the Union Island bearing east six miles, I discovered a suspicious Vessel to the S.W., and after a Chase of two hours came up with and captured the French Schooner Privateer l'Intrepid, commanded by Citoyen Jean Durand, mounting four six-pounders and sixty-two Men. I have likewise the satisfaction to acquaint you, that we have not sustained any loss of Men, as she struck upon receiving a few shot and two or three vollies of musketry. The Privateer was fitted out at Cayenne, and had been twelve days at Sea, and not taken any thing.

I have the honour to be, &c.
JOHN BARKER.

Copy of a Letter from Captain Richard Thwaits, Commander of the Duchess of Bedford Defence-Ship, to William Marsden, Esq., dated in Hoseley-Bay, the 28th of last Month.

SIR,

I herewith forward a letter from Lieutenant Blow, of the Charger Gun-brig, informing me of his having captured one of the Enemy's small Cruisers.

I am, &c. RICHARD THWAITS.

SIR, *His Majesty's Brig Charger, Hoseley-Bay, 28th May, 1805.*

I beg leave to inform you, for the information of the Commander in Chief, Orfordness bearing W.N.W. fourteen leagues, I captured the de Zenno, a small Cutter Privateer, commanded by Lodwick Peffer, out two days from Flushing, but had made no Captures. She had on board thirteen Men and a chest of arms.

I have the honour to be, &c.

Captain Richard Thwaits, His Majesty's J. A. BLOW.
Armed Ship Duchess of Bedford.

JUNE 8.

Copy of a Letter from Captain Snell, Commander of His Majesty's Sloop the Avon, to William Marsden, Esq., dated at Lisbon, the 17th May, 1805.

SIR,

I have the honour to enclose herewith, a copy of a letter received by me from Lieutenant J. C. Carpenter, commanding His Majesty's Schooner Milbrook,

And am, &c.
F. J. SNELL.

His Majesty's Schooner *Millbrook, off the Bayonna*
SIR,   *Islands, May* 9, 1805.

I beg to inform you, that His Majesty's Schooner under my Command captured on the 6th instant, off Oporto, the Spanish Lugger Privateer la Travela of three guns, with small arms and forty Men; she had the day before captured a Brig, laden with wine, from Oporto: on receiving the information, I made sail for Vigo, to which Port I concluded she was sent. This morning, the Bayonna Islands bearing east about eight leagues, I observed a Brig standing for the Northern Passage; I immediately made sail for the Southern Passage, and succeeded in capturing her within the Bayonnas, at the entrance of Vigo River. She proved to be the Stork English Brig, bound to Newfoundland, laden with salt, had been captured from the Newfoundland Convoy on the 9th ultimo, by the Phenix Spanish Privateer Brig of twelve guns.

I have the honour to be, &c.

JOHN C. CARPENTER.

To F. J. Snell, Esq. Commander of His
Majesty's Sloop Avon, Lisbon.

Copy of a Letter from Sir Richard Bickerton, Bart., Rear-Admiral of the Red, to William Marsden, Esq., dated on board the Royal Sovereign, at Gibraltar, the 13th May, 1805.

SIR,

I herewith transmit to you, to lay before the Lords Commissioners of the Admiralty, a copy of a letter, dated the 8th instant, from the Honourable Captain Boyle, of His Majesty's Ship Seahorse, to Vice-Admiral Lord Viscount Nelson, giving an account of his having attacked a Spanish Convoy, from which he succeeded in capturing an Ordnance Brig, laden with powder. The conduct of Lieutenant Downie, who commanded the Boats on this occasion, as well as of the other Officers of the Seahorse, is highly spoken of by Captain Boyle, as their Lordships will observe.

I have the honour to be, &c.

R. BICKERTON.

His Majesty's Ship Seahorse, Gibraltar Bay,
MY LORD,   *May,* 8, 1805.

On the 4th instant, I learnt that a Spanish Convoy was on the Coast to the westward of Carthagena, chiefly loaded on Government account, with Gunpowder, Ordnance, and Naval Stores for the Gun-boats at Malaga, Ceuta, and Algeziras. Conceiving the destruction of the same of consequence, I kept close along Shore with the hope of falling in with them, and effecting my wishes. At two P.M. they were discovered from the mast-head; at five I observed them haul into S. Pedro, an anchorage to the eastward of Cape de Gatte, under the protection of a Fort, two armed Schooners, and three Gun and Mortar Launches, where I determined to attempt to destroy them. The Vessel of greatest consequence to get out was an Ordnance Brig loaded with one thousand one hundred and seventy quintals of Powder, and various other Stores, commanded by Don Juan Terragut, Master in the Spanish Navy; and which was effected by Lieutenant Downie, First of the Seahorse, in a six-oared Cutter, in the most gallant and well-judged manner; whose conduct on this, as well as on every other occasion, I feel it my duty to mention to your Lordship as that of a most zealous Officer; and I beg leave to add, that Lieutenant Downie assures me he met with every possible assistance from Mr. Thomas Napper, Midshipman, who accompanied him in a four-oared Boat. The Seahorse during the time kept up a quick and well-directed fire on the Fort, Gun-vessels, and Convoy; and having every reason to believe I had sunk one of the Gun-launches, and damaged and sunk several others of the Convoy, night coming on, with light Winds, the main-top-gallant-mast, sails braces, bow-lines shot away, I felt it imprudent any longer to attempt the destruction of the whole by exposing the Ship to the well-directed fire of the Gun-vessels, which latterly struck her every shot. For the exertions, on this occasion, of Lieutenant Ogle Moore, Lieutenant Charles Brown Yonge, who had not received his confirmed Commission; Mr. Spratt, Master; Lieutenant Clarke, of the

Royal Marines; Lieutenant Hagemeister, of the Russian Navy, I feel severally indebted; and indeed I should do injustice to every other Officer and Man on board, did I not mention them in the same manner.

It would give me greater satisfaction could I inform your Lordship we met with no loss on this Service: however I feel that sustained in having only one Seaman killed, as trifling, considering the well-directed fire in so many different directions of the Enemy. Trusting that my proceedings will meet your Lordship's approbation, I have the honour to be, &c.

C. BOYLE.

Right Hon. Lord Viscount Nelson, K.B.,
&c. &c. &c.

(A Copy.) R. BICKERTON.

JUNE 15.

Copy of a Letter from Rear-Admiral Dacres, Commander in Chief of His Majesty's Ships and Vessels at Jamaica, to William Marsden, Esq.; dated on board His Majesty's Ship Shark, Port Royal, 8th of April, 1805.

SIR,

I herewith transmit, for their Lordships' information, the copy of a letter received from Captain Mudge, of the Blanche, acquainting me of his having captured a French Privateer.

I am, &c. J. R. DACRES.

His Majesty's Ship Blanche, off Cape Tiberon,
SIR, *April 5, 1805.*

I beg leave to acquaint you with having, this day, captured the French Schooner Privateer le Hazard, mounting three guns and fifty-eight Men, after a chase of twenty-six Hours.

I am, &c. Z. MUDGE.

Rear-Admiral Dacres, Commander in Chief,
&c. &c. &c.

Copy of another Letter from Rear-Admiral Dacres to William Marsden, Esq.; dated on board His Majesty's Ship l'Hercule, Port Royal Harbour, April 12, 1805.

SIR,

I have the honour to enclose, for their Lordships' information, the copy of a letter I have received from Captain le Geyte, of the Stork, acquainting me, that the Pinnace and Cutter had cut out a Dutch Privateer: also another letter from Captain Ross, of the Pique, to Vice-Admiral Sir John Thomas Duckworth, stating that he had captured His Catholic Majesty's Corvette Orquijo.

I am, &c. J. R. DACRES.

SIR, *His Majesty's Sloop Stork, off Mona, March 25, 1805.*

I have the honour to acquaint you, that the Pinnace and Cutter of the Stork, with eighteen Men, under the Command of Lieutenant Robertson, assisted by Lieutenant Murray, on the night of the 23d instant cut out of the Harbour of Cape Roxo, in Porto Rico, the Dutch Schooner Privateer Antelope, of five guns and fifty-four Men, forty of which only were on board, and of that number but fifteen were made Prisoners, the rest making their escape by jumping into the Water.

As the Antelope was prepared to heave down on the following day, her guns, &c. were on board a Brig, alongside of which she was lashed; and from the circumstance of her Crew being divided between the two Vessels, and prepared to defend themselves, it became necessary to board them both at once, which was effected in a very gallant manner, without any other accident on our part than that of Lieutenant Murray, and one Seaman, being slightly wounded.

Lieutenant Robertson, whom I have always found an active and valuable Officer, appears to have conducted himself upon the present occasion with great

great steadiness; and I have much pleasure in acknowledging the sense I entertain of his merit, as well as that of Lieutenant Murray, and the Seamen employed. The Antelope is a fine Vessel and a remarkably fast Sailer.

I have the honour to be, &c.

G. LE GEYTE.

To Rear-Admiral Dacres, Commander in Chief.

His Majesty's Ship Pique, off the Havana,
8th February, 1805.

SIR,

I have the honour to inform you of our having, this afternoon, captured His Catholic Majesty's Corvette Orquijo, of 18 guns and 82 Men, commanded by Don Manuel Degongra, from Carthagena to Havana, with dispatches, which were thrown overboard before we took possession. I have the honour to be, &c.

CHARLES B. H ROSS.

To Sir John Thomas Duckworth, K.B., Vice-
Admiral of the Blue, Commander in Chief,
&c. &c. &c.

Copy of a Letter from Captain Dashwood, of His Majesty's Ship Bacchante, to William Marsden, Esq.; dated on board the said Ship at New Providence, 13th of April, 1805.

SIR,

I avail myself of the opportunity of a Packet sailing for England to enclose you a copy of a letter which I have this day transmitted to Rear-Admiral Dacres, Commander in Chief at Jamaica, giving an account of my having captured His Catholic Majesty's Schooner la Elizabeth, commanded by Don Josef Fer Fexeyron, of 10 guns and 47 Men. Also of a most gallant Exploit performed by Lieutenant Oliver, in storming and taking a Fort, in order to effect the Capture of three French Privateers, supposed to be laying in the Harbour of Mariel, on the Island of Cuba; and who, from their piratical depredations, had much annoyed the Trade of His Majesty's Subjects, as well as the Commerce of Neutral Nations: and although the object of the Expedition was not fully obtained, in consequence of their having sailed the evening previous to the Attack, yet still, I trust, the bold and manly conduct displayed by Lieutenant Oliver will be honoured with the approbation of my Lords Commissioners of the Admiralty: and although Lieutenant Campbell had not the good fortune to share in the glory of this well-intended enterprise, yet great credit is due to his intentions and exertions. Lieutenant Oliver speaks in the highest terms of commendation of the spirit and alacrity of the Honourable Almeira de Courcy, as well as the whole of his intrepid Crew. I have the honour to be, &c.

H. DASHWOOD.

SIR, *Bacchante, New Providence, April 13, 1805.*

I have the honour to acquaint you, that, on the 3d instant, His Majesty's Ship under my directions captured, off the Havana, His Catholic Majesty's Schooner la Elizabeth, of 10 guns and 47 Men, commanded by Don Josef Fer Fexeyron. She was charged with dispatches from the Governor of Pensacola, which were thrown overboard previous to her surrendering.

Having received information that there were three French Privateers in the Harbour of Mariel, (a small convenient Port, a little to the westward of the Havana,) which had annoyed most considerably the Trade of His Majesty's Subjects, transiently passing through the Gulf, I determined, if possible, to rout this Band of Pirates; for, from their plundering and ill treating the Crew of every Vessel they met with, most particularly the Americans, they were nothing better; and Lieutenants Oliver and Campbell having, in the most handsome manner, volunteered their Service on this hazardous occasion, I dispatched these excellent Officers, accompanied by the Honourable Almeira de Courcy, Midshipman, on the evening of the 5th instant, in two Boats: and as it was absolutely necessary to gain possession of a Round Tower near forty feet high, on the top of which were planted three long twenty-four-pounders, with loop-holes round its circumference for musketry, and manned with a Captain and thirty Soldiers, I gave directions to attack and carry the Fort previous to their entering the Harbour, so as to enable them to secure a safe retreat. Lieutenant Oliver, the senior Officer, being in the headmost Boat, finding himself discovered, and as not a moment was to be lost at such a critical period, most nobly advanced, without waiting for his Friend, landed in the face, and in opposition to a most tremendous fire, without condescending to return the salutation, mounted the Fort by a ladder which he had previously provided, and fairly carried it by a *coup-de-main* with thirteen Men, leaving Mr. de Courcy, with three others, to guard the Boat, with an accident to only one brave Man (George Allison) wounded, who was unfortunately shot through the body before the Boat touched the ground; but I am happy to say, from the care and attention of Mr. Williams, the Surgeon, he is already rapidly recovering. The Enemy had two killed and three wounded.

Lieutenant Oliver, leaving Serjeant Denslow, of the Marines, (who, from his bravery and good conduct, deserves great praise,) with six Men to guard the Fort, and having been rejoined by Lieutenant Campbell, dashed on to attack the Privateers, but to their great mortification found they had sailed the day previous on a Cruise; he was therefore obliged to be contented with taking possession of two Schooners, laden with sugar, which he most gallantly brought away from alongside a Wharf, in spite of repeated discharges of musketry from the Troops and Militia, which poured down in numbers from the surrounding Country.

I should not have been thus particular in recounting a circumstance which was not attended with ultimate success, were it not to mark my admiration of the noble conduct of Lieutenant Oliver in so gallantly attacking and carrying a Fort which, with the Men it contained, ought to have maintained its position against fifty times the number that were opposed : but nothing could withstand the prompt and manly steps taken by that Officer and his gallant Crew on this occasion: and as, in my humble judgment, the attempt was most daring and hazardous, and had the Privateers been there, I doubt not but success would have attended them, so I humbly solicit the honour of notice to this most gallant Officer.

I have the honour to be, &c.

To Rear-Admiral Dacres, Commander   C. DASHWOOD.
in Chief, &c. &c. &c. Jamaica.

Copies of two Letters from Captain Lake, Commander of His Majesty's Ship the Topaze, to William Marsden, Esq.

SIR,   *Topaze, at Sea, May* 7, 1805.
I have the honour to transmit, for the information of the Lords Commissioners of the Admiralty, a copy of my letter to Admiral Lord Gardner of this date.
William Marsden, Esq.   I am, &c.   W. T. LAKE.

MY LORD,   *Topaze, May* 7, 1805.
I have the honour to acquaint you, that His Majesty's Ship under my Command has just captured the Spanish Ship Privateer Napoleon, of St. Sebastian, pierced for 20 guns, and mounting 10 nine-pounders, and four eighteen-pound carronades, with 180 Men on board.

She sailed 57 days since from Bourdeaux, and has taken in this her first Cruise, the Westmoreland, an outward bound Letter of Marque, of Liverpool, after a smart Action, and the Brig Brunswick from Honduras.

I have the honour to be, &c.
Admiral Lord Gardner, &c. &c. &c.   W. T. LAKE.

SIR,   *Topaze, at Sea, May* 20, 1805.
I enclose herewith, for their Lordships' information, a copy of a Letter I have written this day to Admiral Lord Gardner. I have the honour to be, &c.
William Marsden, Esq.   W. T. LAKE

MY LORD,   *Topaze, at Sea, May* 20, 1805.
I have the satisfaction to acquaint you, that His Majesty's Ship under my Command has been again successful, having this day captured el Fenix, a Spanish

Privateer Brig, of 14 guns and 85 Men, of St. Sebastian ; out from Vigo ten days, without making a Capture. I have the honour to be, &c.

Admiral Lord Gardner, &c. &c. &c. W. T. LAKE.

JUNE 18, 1805.

Copy of a Letter from Rear-Admiral Drury, to William Marsden, Esq. ; dated on board the Trent, in Cork Harbour, the 10th Instant.

SIR,

Enclosed I transmit you, for the information of my Lords Commissioners of the Admiralty, a letter from Captain Losack, of His Majesty's Sloop Helena, giving an account of the Capture of the Santa Leocadia, a Spanish Privateer, of 14 guns and 114 Men. I am, &c.

W. O'B. DRURY.

SIR, *His Majesty's Ship Helena, at Sea, 9th June,* 1805.

I have the honour to acquaint you, that on the Station prescribed by your order of the 21st of March, His Majesty's Sloop under my Command captured on the 5th instant, after a Chase of ten hours, and a smart exchange of shot for fifteen minutes, the Santa Leocadia Spanish Ship Privateer, pierced for 20 guns, 14 nine-pounders mounted, and a complement of 114 Men. I am happy, Sir, to add, that no person was hurt on board the Helena, although the Enemy's guns were well supplied with grape and langrage; she was 54 days from St. Sebastian, not having made any Capture, perfectly new, coppered, sails well, and in my opinion calculated for the King's Service. Could I venture, Sir, on this short trial of the Officers and Crew I have the pleasure to command, to mention their conduct, I should certainly recommend them to notice ; among whom Lieutenant Hugh Wylie, First of the Helena, and Messrs. Watson and Willitts, who have both passed for Lieutenants, and anxiously waiting their Lordships' patronage.

I have the honour to be, &c.

WOODLEY LOSACK.

JUNE 22, 1805.

Copy of a Letter from Rear-Admiral Drury to William Marsden, Esq.; dated on board the Trent, in Cork Harbour, the 13th Instant.

SIR,

You will please to acquaint the Right Honourable the Lords Commissioners of the Admiralty of the arrival, this day, of His Majesty's Ship Loire, and three Privateers, two Spanish and one French.

I herewith transmit Captain Maitland's letter, enclosing one from Lieutenant Yeo, First Lieutenant of the Loire, giving an account of the Capture of the above Vessels, as well as of his most judicious and prompt decision in entering the Bay of Muros; and by the most active and daring gallantry on the part of Captain Maitland and Lieutenant Yeo, and the Officers and Ship's Company of the Loire, taking the Forts which defended the Bay ; the particulars of which are therein detailed ; also another letter from Captain Maitland, describing the very gallant attack made by Lieutenant Yeo, in the Boats of the Loire, on a Spanish Felucca and small Privateer, under the enemy's Batteries, accompanied with lists of the killed and wounded, and a list of Vessels captured and destroyed.

I have the honour to be, &c.

W. O' B. DRURY.

His Majesty's Ship Loire, off Cape Finisterre,
SIR, *June 2,* 1805.

I have to inform you, that, after delivering the dispatches Lord Gardner charged me with to Sir Robert Calder, in stretching to the westward to regain my station, a small Vessel was discovered standing into the Bay of Camarinas, to the eastward of Cape Finisterre. Being quite calm after dark, I sent the Launch and two Cutters, under Mr. Yeo, First Lieutenant, assisted by Lieutenant Mallock of the Marines, and Messrs. Clinch, Herbert, and Mildridge, Midshipmen, to endeavour to bring her out. From the Intricacy of the Passage, the Boats did not get up till break of day, when they found two small Privateers moored under a Battery of ten guns; undaunted, however, by a circumstance so little expected, Mr. Yeo ordered the Launch, commanded by Mr. Clinch, to board the smallest, while he, with the two Cutters, most gallantly attacked and carried the largest, a Felucca armed with three eighteen-pounders, four four-pounders brass swivels and fifty Men.

The Launch had the same success in her attack; the Fort immediately opened a fire; so ill directed, however, as to do little damage. Being still perfectly calm close under the guns of the Battery, and no possibility of receiving assistance from the Ship, Mr. Yeo was under the painful necessity of abandoning the smallest Vessel, a Lugger of two six-pounders and thirty-two Men, to secure the Felucca, which, I am happy to add, was effected with only three Men, William Turner, James Gardner, Quarter-Master, and John Maynes, Marine, slightly wounded.

The loss on board the Lugger cannot be ascertained. When the Crew of the Felucca was mustered, nineteen out of fifty were missing, some of whom had jumped overboard, but the greatest part were killed by the pike, there being no weapons used but the pike and sabre.

When we call to mind the inequality of force, Officers included, there being not more than thirty-five of the Loire's opposed to eighty Spaniards, with their Vessels moored to the walls of a heavy Battery, it must be allowed to confer the greatest credit on the Officers and Men employed on the Service.

Mr. Yeo, in coming out, took possession of three small Merchant Vessels, but finding their Cargoes consisted only of small wine for the enemy's Squadron at Ferrol, I have destroyed them. The name of the Privateer captured is the Esperanza, alias San Pedro, of Corunna. She is quite new, only out four days, and was victualled and stored for a Cruise of one month.

Mr. Yeo assures me that he was assisted by Mr. Mallock with the greatest bravery, and gives the highest praise to Mr. Clinch for the gallantry and promptness with which he carried his orders into execution in the Launch. He also speaks in the warmest terms of the Officers and other Men under his Command.

I have the honour to be, &c.
FRED. MAITLAND.
Rear-Admiral Drury, &c. &c. &c. Cork.

His Majesty's Ship Loire, at Anchor, Muros Road, Spain,
SIR, *June* 4, 1805.

Being informed that there was a French Privateer, of twenty-six guns, fitting out at Muros, and nearly ready for Sea, it struck me, from my recollection of the Bay (having been in it formerly, when Lieutenant of the Kingsfisher), as being practicable either to bring her out or destroy her, with the Ship I have the honour to Command. I accordingly prepared yesterday evening for engaging at anchor, and appointed Mr. Yeo, First Lieutenant, with Lieutenant Mallocks and Douglas, of the Marines, and Mr. Clinch, Master's Mate, to head the Boarders and Marines, amounting, Officers included, to fifty Men (being all that could be spared from anchoring the Ship and working the guns), in landing and storming the Fort, though I then had no idea its strength was so great as it has proved. At nine this morning, on the Sea breeze setting in, I stood for the Bay in the Ship, the Men previously prepared being in the Boats ready to shove off. On hauling close round the point of the road, a small Battery of two guns opened a fire on the Ship; a few shot were returned; but perceiving it would annoy us considerably, from its situation, I desired Mr. Yeo to push on Shore and spike the guns, reminding the Men of its being the anniversary of their Sovereign's birth, and that, for his sake, as well as their own credit, their utmost exertions must be used. Though such an injunction was unnecessary, it had a great effect in animating and raising the spirits of the people. As the Ship drew in, and more fully opened the Bay, I perceived a very long Corvette, of twenty-six ports, apparently nearly ready for Sea, and a large Brig, of twenty ports, in a state of fitting, but neither of them firing, led me to conclude they had not their guns on board, and left no other object to occupy my attention but a heavy Fort which, at this moment, opened to our view, within less than a quarter of a mile, and began a wonderfully well-directed fire, almost every shot taking place in the hull. Perceiving that, by standing further on, more guns would be brought to bear upon us, without our being enabled to near the Fort so much as I wished, I ordered the helm to be put down; and when, from the way she had, we had gained an advantageous position, anchored with a spring, and commenced firing. Although we have but little doubt that, before long, we should have silenced the Fort, yet from the specimen they gave us, and being completely embrazured, it must have cost us many lives, and great injury to the Ship, had not Mr. Yeo's gallantry and great conduct soon put an end to their fire.

I must now revert to him and the Party under his Command. Having landed under the small Battery on the Point, it was instantly abandoned; but hardly had he time to spike the guns, when, at the distance of a quarter of a mile, he perceived a regular Fort, ditched, and with a gate, which the enemy (fortunately never suspecting our landing) had neglected to secure, open a fire upon the Ship, without waiting for orders he pushed forward, and was opposed at the inner gate by the Governor, with such Troops as were in the Town, and the Crews of the French Privateers. From the testimony of the Prisoners, as well as our own Men, it appears that Mr. Yeo was the first that entered the Fort, with one blow laid the Go-Governor dead at his feet, and broke his own sabre in two; the other Officers were dispatched by such Officers and Men of ours as were most advanced, and the narrowness of the gate would permit, to push forward; the remainder instantly fled to the further end of the Fort, where, from the Ship, we could perceive many of them leap from the embrazures upon the Rocks, (a height of above twenty-five feet); such as laid down their arms received quarter. For a more particular account of the proceedings of Mr. Yeo and his Party, I beg leave to refer you to his letter enclosed herewith, and have to request you will be pleased to recommend him to the notice of the Lords Commissioners of the Admiralty; being a very old Officer, and in the two late instances has displayed as much gallantry as ever fell to the lot of any Man; he speaks in the strongest language of the Officers and Men under his Command on Shore; and I feel it but justice to attribute our success wholly to their exertions; for, although the fire from the Ship was admirably directed, the enemy were so completely covered by their embrazures, as to render the grape almost ineffectual.

The instant the Union was displayed at the Fort, I sent and took possession of the Enemy's Vessels in the Road, consisting of the Confiance French Ship Privateer, pierced for twenty-six twelves and nines, none of which however were on board; the Belier, a French Privateer Brig, pierced for twenty eighteen pound carronades; and a Spanish Merchant Brig in ballast. I then hoisted a Flag of Truce, and sent to inform the inhabitants of the Town, that if they would deliver up such Stores of the Ship as were on Shore, there would be no further molestation. The proposal was thankfully agreed to. I did not, however, think it advisable to allow the People to remain long enough to embark the guns, there being a large body of Troops in the vicinity. A great many small Vessels are in the Bay, and hauled up on the Beach; none of them having Cargoes of any value, I conceive it an act of inhumanity to deprive the poorer inhabitants of the means of gaining their livelihood, and shall not molest them. On inspecting the Brig, as she had only the lower rigging over head, and was not in a state of forwardness, I found it impracticable to bring her away, and therefore set fire to her: she is now burnt to the water's edge. I cannot conclude my letter without giving the portion of credit that is their due to the Officers and Men on board the Ship. They conducted themselves with the greatest steadiness and coolness; and, although under a heavy fire, pointed their guns with the utmost precision: there being hardly a shot that did not take effect. To Lieutenants Lawe and Bertram I feel much indebted, as well as to Mr. Shea the Purser, (who volunteered his Services, and to whom I gave the charge of the Quarter Deck Carronades in Mr. Yeo's absence,) for the precision and coolness displayed by the Men under their Command in pointing the guns, as was their exact attention paid to my orders, and ceasing fire the instant the Union Jack made its appearance on the Walls, by which, in all probability, the lives of several of our Men were saved. Mr. Cleverly, the Master, brought the broadside to bear with much quickness and nicety, by means of the spring. I send you herewith a list of our Wounded on board and on Shore, with one of the Enemy's Killed and Wounded; and an account of their Force at the commencement of the Action.

I have been under the necessity of being more detailed than I could wish, but it is out of my power, in a smaller compass, to do justice to the exertions and conduct of the Officers and Men employed on the different Services. It is but fair at the same time to state that, much to the credit of the Ship's Company, the Bishop and one of the principal Inhabitants of the Town came off to express their gratitude for the orderly behaviour of the People, (there not being one instance of pillage,) and to make offer of every refreshment the place affords.

I am now waiting for the Land Breeze to carry us out, having already recalled the Officers and Men from the Fort, the guns being spiked and thrown over the parapet, the carriages rendered unserviceable, and the embrazures, with part of the Fort, blown up. I have the honour to be, &c.

FRED. MAITLAND.

Rear-Admiral Drury, &c. &c. &c. Cove.

SIR, *His Majesty's Ship Loire, Muros, June 4, 1805.*

I have the pleasure to acquaint you, that I proceeded on Shore with the Party you did me the honour to place under my Command, for the purpose of storming the Fort on the Point agreeable to your orders, which, on our approach, the Soldiers quitted. On my arrival, I observed a strong Fort at the entrance of the Town, opening a heavy fire on the Ship; and, judging it practicable to carry it by storm, from a thorough knowledge I had of the determined bravery of all the Officers and Men, I ordered them to follow me for that purpose, which was obeyed with all that energy and gallantry which British Seamen and Marines are so well known to possess on such an occasion, and, in a very short time, reached the outer gate, when the French Centinel fired, and retreated into the Fort, which we instantly entered, and was met by the Governor and all the Garrison, &c., when, after a dreadful slaughter on the part of the enemy, the remainder surrendered, and I instantly ordered the British Colours to be hoisted.

I feel it my duty, as well as the greatest pleasure, to mention the great support I received from Lieutenant Mallock, of the Royal Marines, and Mr. Charles Clinch, Master's Mate, as, from their being near me all the time of the Action, I was enabled to observe their very cool and gallant behaviour, as also of Lieutenant Douglas, of the Royal Marines, who, though engaged at different parts of the Fort, I have no less reason to be highly pleased with.

I must now beg leave to say how much I am indebted to every Seaman and Marine of the Party, who behaved so unanimously brave nothing could withstand them; and to their credit as Englishmen as well as their profession, the instant the Fort was in our possession, they seemed to try who could be the first to relieve and assist the poor wounded prisoners, who were lying in numbers in different parts of the Fort; and I had the pleasure to see their humanity amply repaid by the gratitude the unfortunate Men's friends expressed when they came to take them away.

I have the honour to be, &c.

JAMES LUCAS YEO.

To Captain Frederick Maitland, &c. &c. &c.

A List of the wounded on Shore belonging to His Majesty's Ship Loire, at Muros, the 4th of June, 1805.

Lieutenant J. L. Yeo, slightly; Mr. Clinch, Master's Mate, ditto; Henry Gray, Seaman, ditto; Martin Hendrickson, Seaman, ditto; John Payne, Seaman, ditto; John Leonard, Marine, ditto.

On Board.

James Caldwell, Seaman, dangerously; Magnus Johnson, Seaman, lost his right leg above the knee; Christian Wilson, Seaman, calf of his leg shot off; John Whitecomb, Seaman, severely; John Plummer, Seaman, slightly; Mark Archer, Seaman, ditto; Thomas Lloyd, Seaman, ditto; John Moulds, Seaman, ditto; James Gillett, Seaman, ditto.—Total, 2 Officers, 12 Seamen, and 1 Marine.

Spaniards killed and wounded.

The Governor of the Fort, and a Spanish Gentleman who had volunteered; the Second Captain of the Confiance, and nine others, killed. Thirty, amongst which were most of the Officers of the Confiance, wounded.—Total, 12 killed and 30 wounded.

FRED. L. MAITLAND.

Enemy's Force at the Commencement of the Action when opposed to His Majesty's Ship Loire, in Muros Bay, the 4th of June, 1805.

A Fort of 12 Spanish eighteen-pounders, mounted on travelling carriages; 22 Spanish Soldiers, several Spanish Gentlemen and Townsmen Volunteers, and about 100 of the Confiance's Ship's Company.

The small Battery on the Boint, 2 Spanish eighteen-pounders, one mounted as above, the other on a Ship Carriage, manned by 8 Artillery Men and 10 other Spaniards.

In the Bay.

La Confiance of Bourdeaux, pierced for 26 guns, twelves and nines (not on board), 116 feet long on the main-deck, 30 feet wide, measures about 450 tons, is in good order, and a very fit Ship for His Majesty's Service; is reckoned to sail excessively fast; was to have gone to Sea in a few days, bound to India, with a complement of 300 Men : brought away.

Le L lier, of Bourdeaux, pierced for 20 guns; also fitting for Sea ; was to have carried en h'teen-pounder carronades, and 180 Men ; supposed to be destined to cruize to the westward of Cape Clear : burnt.

The guns on the Fort and Battery spiked, and thrown over the Parapet. The carriages broke, and rendered unserviceable. The embrazures blown up. Forty barrels of Powder brought on board, with two small brass cannons, and fifty stand of arms.

FRED. MAITLAND.

Copy of a Letter from Rear-Admiral Dacres, Commander in Chief of His Majesty's Ships and Vessels at Jamaica, to William Marsden, Esq; dated on board the Hercule, at Sea, the 2d May 1805.

SIR,

I have the honour to enclose, for their Lordships' information, the copy of a letter from Captain Coghlan, of His Majesty's Sloop Renard, acquainting me of his having brought to Action the General Erneuf Privateer, late His Majesty's Sloop Lilly, which, after a close Action of thirty-five minutes, took fire and exploded. It is an additional proof of the steady and decisive conduct of Captain Coghlan, who speaks in high terms of his Officers and Ship's Company, all of whom will, I am sure, meet the approbation of their Lordships.

I am, &c.   J. R. DACRES.

His Majesty's Sloop Renard, Port Royal, Jamaica,
SIR,   *April 27, 1805.*

Having escorted the Chesterfield Packet to the latitude directed in your order of the sixteenth of March last, and being on my way to carry into effect the latter part of it, I have the honour to acquaint you, that at eleven A. M. on Friday the twentieth ult., being in latitude twenty-one deg. fourteen min. north, and longitude seventy-one deg. thirty min. west, a Ship was seen to leeward standing (under easy sail) to the north west: all sail was instantly made in chase, and the stranger soon discovered to be an Enemy, who, upon our approach, shortened sail, evidently with an intention to engage us: at twenty minutes past two P. M. having reduced our sail, I closed with the Enemy, who opened his fire upon us, but not a gun was fired from this Ship until within pistol shot, at which distance she was placed on the Enemy's weather-bow, when a fire commenced that reflects infinite praise on the Officers who directed it ; for at the short period of thirty-five minutes, the Enemy was discovered to be on fire and in ten minutes after blew up with a dreadful explosion: every possible exertion was now made to get the only Boat that could swim to the relief of the few brave, but unfortunate survivors, who had just before so gallantly defended themselves, and were now seen all around us, on the scattered remnants of the Wreck, in a mangled and truly distressing state: but it is with pleasure I add, that of the few who escaped the flames, not a Man was drowned, amounting to fifty-five.

The Ship proved to be the General Erneuf, a Privateer, late His Majesty's Sloop Lilly, commanded by Monsieur Paul Gerand Pointe, seven days from Basse-terre, Guadaloupe, carrying eighteen twelve-pounder carronades, and two long guns (four more than when in His Majesty's Service), with a complement of 160 Men, (thirty-one of whom were Soldiers,) going to cruise for the homeward bound Jamaica Fleet.

The Enemy's loss was great before the melancholy scene that put an end to the Action, having between twenty and thirty Men killed and wounded; and I am singularly happy to acquaint you that mine is inconsiderable, nine Men only being wounded, some slightly, I hope none dangerously. The steady, cool, and determined conduct of the Officers and Men serving under my orders, was truly meritorious, and gives them just claims on every commendation that is in the power of their Commander to bestow. Our sails, running and standing rigging, have suffered much, the Enemy's fire being principally directed against them. The Second Captain and one Lieutenant are the only surviving Officers. This Ship cruised with great success against the Trade of His Majesty's Subjects, having made six valuable Captures on her former Cruise.

I have the honour to be, &c.
JEREMIAH COGHLAN.
To James Richard Dacres, Esq; Rear-Admiral of the Red, &c. &c. &.

Copy of another Letter from Rear-Admiral Dacres to William Marsden, Esq.; dated on board l'Hercule, at Sea, the 9th May 1805.

SIR,

I have the honour to enclose you the Copy of a Letter I have received from Captain Hardyman, of the Unicorn, acquainting me of the Boats of that Ship having captured the Tape-a-bord, Cutter Privateer.

I am, &c. J. R. DACRES.

SIR, *His Majesty's Ship Unicorn, at Sea, May 6, 1805.*

I beg leave to inform you of the Capture of the French National Privateer le Tape-a-bord, mounting four six-pounders, well armed, and carrying forty-six Men, commanded by Citizen Hemigueth, by the Boats of His Majesty's Ship under my Command. On the North Side of St. Domingo, Cape François bearing S. W. by S., distance eight or nine leagues, on the morning of the 6th Instant, a strange Sail was seen on the larboard bow, distance seven or eight miles, having then light airs, and inclinable to calm, and perceiving the stranger was using every effort with his sweeps to escape, and apparently full of Men, and no hopes of my closing with His Majesty's Ship, I directed Henry Smith Wilson, First Lieutenant, with four Boats, assisted by James Tait and Henry Bourchier, Second and Third Lieutenants, backed by the volunteer services of Thomas Tud, or Tucker, a Passenger belonging to His Majesty's Ship Northumberland, Walter Powell, Lieutenant of Marines, and Charles Rundle, Purser of His Majesty's Ship under my Command, to proceed with the Boats, and endeavour to come up with the Chase. The cool and determined manner in which this service was performed, after a pull of many hours, and the strong opposition they met with from the well-directed fire of the guns and musketry, kept up by the Privateer, induces me thus publickly to express my approbation of every Officer, Seaman, and Marine engaged on this Service; and I am happy to add, that no Lives were lost upon the occasion.

This Privateer was from Samana, on a Cruise; out ten days, without taking any thing. I am, &c.

L. T. HARDYMAN.
To Rear-Admiral Dacres, &c. &c. &c. Jamaica.

Promotions and Appointments.

Capt. Codrington is appointed to the Orion; Capt. S. Warren to the Glory, *vice* Aylmer; Capt. Simpson to the Wasp; Lieut. Talbot to the Encounter, a new Gun-vessel; Captain Stephens is appointed to the Captain; Captain Lawford to the Audacious; Capt. Lechmere to the Thunderer; Capt. Fane to the Hind; Capt. M'Namara to the Dictator; Mr. Rose to be Purser of the Sardine; Capt. Worth is appointed to the Tourterelle; Capt. Beaufort to the Woolwich; Capt. Fahie to the Amelia; Capt. Woolcombe, to the Hyæna; Capt. Clinch to the Osprey; Capt. Byam to the Busy; Lieut. Pringle to command the Pert, (late Buonaparté); Lieut. Dodd, of the Royal William, to the Pickle Schooner; Capt. Shortland, of the Trompeuse, to the rank of Post Captain, by the death of Capt. Brawn, of the Squirrel, on the Coast of Africa.

His Royal Highness the Prince of Wales has been pleased to appoint the Rev. James Stanier Clarke, F.R.S., and Chaplain to the Household, to be his Royal Highnes's Librarian.—Mr. Clarke was formerly Chaplain on board the Impetueux, commanded by the late Admiral Payne; is Author of the " Naval Sermons," and " History of the Maritime Discoveries from the earliest Periods."—We understand Mr. Clarke has another Naval Work in the Press, to be called the History of Shipwrecks, &c. From our knowledge of the abilities of the Author, and the information we have received relating to this latter Work, we doubt not but our Readers will be as anxious to see it as we are.

Capt. P. Campbell is appointed to the St. Fiorenzo Frigate, in the East Indies; Captain Buterfield to be Agent of Transports afloat, and to command the Division now at Cork; J. Barlton, Esq. to be Secretary to Admiral Stirling; and J. Lake, Esq. to be a Lieutenant at Haslar Hospital, in the room of Lieut. Parke, deceased.

Lieutenant Yeo, of the Loire Frigate, who fought the late gallant Action in Muros Bay, is promoted to the rank of Commander.

MARRIAGES.

At Lymington, Hants, the Hon. Colonel St. George, of Switéerland, to Miss M. Carteret, second Daughter of the late Admiral Carteret, formerly of Winchester, and Niece of the Recorder of London.

Lately, at Jersey, S. Champion, Esq., Secretary to Sir James Saumarez, to Miss E. Pipon, Daughter of the late T. Pipon, Esq., Chief Magistrate of that Island.

Captain Mansell, of the Navy, to Miss Thorold, Daughter of the Rev. J. Thorold.

OBITUARY.

On the Coast of Africa, Ernest Brawn, Esq., Captain of the Squirrel Frigate. Ths Gentleman was honoured with a Medal for his Services in Egypt last War, and was promoted to the rank of Post Captain in 1802.

Miss S. Montagu, third Daughter of Admiral Montagu, Commander in Chief at Portsmouth.

At Grenada, Lieutenant H. Bateson, of His Majesty's Ship Amelia; Lieutenant Strong, of the Marines, of His Majesty's Ship Galatea; Mr. Gascoyne, Master of His Majesty's Ship Beaulieu.

At his House, at the Royal Hospital at Haslar, Lieutenant T. Parke, an Officer who, in his professional character, was happily possessed of the qualities which usually command respect and esteem, and who, in the circle of social and domestic life, fulfilled the amiable duties of an affectionate Husband, a kind Father, and a faithful Friend.

Monday, June the 10th, Mark Milbanke, Esq., Admiral of the White. He was leaning over the hand-rail of his stair-case, and unfortunately fell into the vestibule. Mr. Heaviside, the Surgeon, was immediately sent for, but before he arrived, the Admiral had expired. Admiral Milbanke, who was in his 84th year, was the second on our list of Admirals, after Sir Peter Parker, Admiral of the Fleet. He was made a Post Captain as far back as the year 1748; was advanced to the rank of Rear-Admiral in 1779; to that of Vice-Admiral in 1780; and to be a full Admiral in 1793. He had seen much Service, and we shall take an early opportunity of presenting our Readers with a sketch of his professional progress.

INDEX

TO THE

MEMOIRS, HINTS, PHILOSOPHICAL PAPERS, MEDICAL FACTS, NAVAL LITERATURE, POETRY, REMARKABLE INCIDENTS, &c. &c. IN VOL. XIII.

A.

ACTION; a gallant one performed by the Merchant Ship Scarborough, 353.

ADMIRALTY BOARD appoints Sub-Lieuts. to such Brigs as are commanded by Lieuts. 69.

ADMIRALTY of Copenhagen orders three Beacons to be placed in the Categat, 287.

AMBASSADOR, the British, makes a spirited remonstrance at the Court of Portugal on the subject of the Spanish Prizes, 207.

AMERICA engaged in Hostility with the Algerines, 158, 159. State of America, as contained in the Message of the President of the United States, 158. Proceedings in the House of Representatives, 159. Orders of the Prefect of Guadaloupe to all American Captains, 160. Unfortunate mistake of the Captain of the Leander armed Ship, ib. The Mate of an American Vessel murdered at Cape François, ib. Bill brought into the House of Representatives for regulating the arming of Merchant Ships, 161. The Port of Dominique closed against all American cargoes, ib.

ANECDOTE of Captain William Chambers, 113. Of the Royal William, ib. Of a Game Cock, 116, 438. Of Captain Campbell, 169. Of a British Tar, 195. Of Captain Nesham, 262. Of Lord Howard, ib. Of the Duke of Ossuna, 268. Of Sir Thomas Rich, 339. Of Captain Lord Cochrane, 357.

ANNE; detail of the loss of the Ship so called, 59.

ANSON, Lord; his expedient to prevent a Ship from driving, 113.

APPENDIX, Nos. I, II.

ARROW; extract of a letter from an Officer on board that Ship, 381.

ATTACK; French account of Captain Francis Mason's on le Vinereux Privateer, 352.

B.

BARCELONA; French account of the Blockade of, 74.

BATTERY; some account of a floating mortar one, 193.

BICKERTON, Rear-Admiral Sir Richard, Bart.; portrait and biographical memoir of; viz. Some particulars of his Family, 337–339. Commences his Naval Career on board of the Medway, 339. Removed to the Enterprise Frigate, ib. Communicates the first intelligence of hostility on the part of the French in 1776, 340. Promoted to be a Lieutenant, and appointed to the Prince George, ib. Made First Lieutenant of the Jupiter, of 50 guns, which engages a French Line of Battle Ship, and compells her to bear away with great loss, 341. Made a Master and Commander, and appointed to the Swallow Sloop, 341. The Combined Fleets escape the notice of the British Fleet, ib. Captain Bickerton, in company with Captain Inglefield, captures the Black Prince, a large American Privateer, 342. His eagerness to engage exposes him to imminent danger, ib. Assists Commodore Fielding in detaining Dutch Ships, ib. The Commodore detains a Dutch Squadron, ib. Captain Bickerton is at the taking of St. Eustatius, 343. Made Post by Sir G. Rodney in the Gibraltar, afterward removed into the Invincible, and is in the Action off Martinico, under Sir Samuel Hood, in 1781, ib. Sir Samuel speaks highly in praise of his Officers and Men, ib. Disparity of the British and French Squadrons engaged, ib. Captain Bickerton comes home in the Amazon, ib. Appointed to the Sybil Frigate, and ordered to the West Indies, where he remains till 1790, and brings home the West India Fleet, 344. Appointed to the Ruby in 1793, and afterwards to the Ramillies, which sails with Lord Howe's Squadron, to cruise in the Bay, ib. Sir Richard chases a part of the Squadron which was afterwards taken by Sir John Borlase Warren, ib. Promoted to be Rear-Admiral of the Blue, ib. Appointed Second in Command, as Port-Admiral at Portsmouth, 345. Joins Lord Keith in the Mediterranean, and is appointed by his Lordship to command the Blockade of Cadiz, ib. List of the blockading Squadron, ib. Lord Keith collects his Fleet at Gibraltar, in order to attack Cadiz, ib. Sir Richard proceeds with Lord Keith to the Blockade of Alexandria, ib. List of the Fleet, 347. Vigorous Attack made on Alexandria, 348. Alexandria capitulates, 349. Honourable mention made of Sir Richard in Lord Keith's Official Dispatches, 350. The Thanks of both Houses of Parliament voted to them, ib. Sir Richard is complimented by General Menou, and invested with the Imperial Ottoman Order of the Crescent, ib. Advanced to be Rear-Admiral of the Red Squadron, and hoists his Flag on board of the Royal Sovereign, as Second in Command in the Mediterranean, 351. Heraldic particulars, ib.

BLIGH, Admiral RICHARD RODNEY; portrait and biographical memoir of, 425. Commences his Naval Career under the immediate auspices of his Godfather, Lord Rodney, ib. Made a Lieutenant, and afterward promoted to be a Commander in the Virgin Sloop of War, and captures several of the Enemy's Privateers, ib. Raised to the Rank of Post

INDEX.

Captain, 426. Appointed to the Excellent, and afterward to the Alexander, in which Ship he falls in with a French Squadron, and forced to strike to very superior Force, *ib.* His official letter respecting the Engagement, *ib.* The French Ships are so much damaged, as to be compelled to return to Brest, 428. Promoted to be Rear-Admiral of the Blue, 429. Tried by a Court Martial for the Surrender of the Alexander, and most honourably acquitted, 429. Hoists his Flag under Sir Peter Parker, at Portsmouth, *ib.* Appointed Second in Command. under Sir Henry Harvey, in the Windward Islands, *ib.* Assumes the Command on the Jamaica Station, where he is actively employed till 1799, when, having been previously appointed Vice-Admiral, he returns to England, *ib.* Appointed to the Command of the Naval Force in Scotland, and afterward promoted to be Admiral of the Blue, *ib.* His defence of the Alexander not surpassed in our Naval Annals, 430.

BOAT; some account of a curious one made of sheet iron, 278.

BOMBAY; extract of a letter from thence, stating a singular fact, 289.

BOUSFIELD, Captain DANIEL, Commander of the Ship Ceres; his Letter respecting the Engagement which he had with the Buonaparté Privateer, 383. The Commander of the Buonaparté's Letter to Capt. Bousfield, 384.

BRITISH GENEROSITY; instance of, 357.

——— TAR; fortitude and humour of one, 195.

BUCKINGHAM; generosity of her Officers and Crew to the Dutch Prisoners on board her, 69.

BUONAPARTE; the private expenses of his Coronation, 65. Conjectures on the Motives of his pacific Message to his Majesty, 133. His Consecration brings a *bon-mot* to remembrance, *ib* Curious conversation which took place betwixt him and the Dutch Admiral Verheul, 287.

BUONAPARTE Privateer beat off by Merchant Ships, 156. List of the killed and wounded on board the Merchantmen, 157. Further particulars of the Engagement, 272.

C.

CENTURION, 50 guns, beats off the Marengo of 80 guns and two Frigates, 218, 288.

CHRONOMETRICAL REGULATION, 50.

COCHRANE, Admiral; his Conduct ably vindicated in the Courier against some aspersions in the Morning Chronicle, 134.

COMMISSION under the Great Seal commences its labours, 133.

COMPASS, Mariner's; account of some improvements lately made on it, 196

CONSTANCE; account of the loss of the Tender so called, 207.

CONTAGION; removal of, 191.

COPENHAGEN; historical sketch of the battle of, by a Native of Denmark, 463.

CORRESPONDENCE, 51, 196, 268, 363.

COURTS MARTIAL, Naval; proceedings of, in the Trials of Captain Bennet, 238. Of Captain Pickmore, 331.

D.

DANCE, Sir NATHANIEL; liberality of the Bombay Insurance Society to him, for his gallant Action with Linois, 360. Correspondence which took place on the occasion, 361—364.

D'AUVERGNE, Commodore PHILIP, Duke of Bouillon; portrait and biographical memoir of; viz. Some particulars of his entrance into the Navy, 169. Makes several Voyages as a Midshipman in the Flora Frigate, and is introduced to the Empress of Russia, *ib.* Sails with the Hon. Captain Phipps on a Voyage of Observation, *ib.* Some account of the Voyage, 170. His conduct highly approved of by Captain Phipps, 171. Narrowly escapes being made Prisoner by the Americans, 172. Made Acting Lieutenant of Admiral Shuldham's Flag-ship, 173. Sails with Sir Peter Parker against Rhode Island, *ib.* Lord Howe promotes him to the rank of Lieutenant, and appoints him to the Command of the Alarm, 174. Appointed Brigade Major to the Seamen and Artillery doing duty on Rhode Island, *ib.* Made First Lieutenant of the Arethusa Frigate, is shipwrecked, and made Prisoner, *ib.* Recognised and claimed by the reigning Duke of Bouillon as his Relation, *ib.* Rejects the tempting offers made to him by one of the French Ministers, *ib.* The Duke of Bouillon and the Admiralty approve of his conduct, *ib.* Appointed to command the Lark, and sails in the Expedition against the Cape of Good Hope, 175. Leads the Attack against the Dutch East India Ships in Saldanha Bay, *ib.* The object of the Expedition against the Cape is frustrated, *ib.* Success of the Squadron against the Dutch Ships, *ib.* Lieut. d'Auvergne is made a Master and Commander, 177. Cruises in the Rattlesnake, under Captain Paisley, and ordered to verify, &c. the position of Trinidad, *ib.* Is shipwrecked on that Island, *ib.* Ordered by Commodore Johnstone to maintain possession of Trinidad, *ib.* His conduct highly approved of, and Post rank conferred on him, 178. Returns to England with Sir Edward Hughes's Dispatches, and finds the Duke of Bouillon waiting for his arrival, having ascertained his relationship to him, *ib.* Passes the Winter at the Duke of Bouillon's Seat in Normandy, who adopts him as his Son and Successor, 179. Makes the Tour of the Western Provinces of France, in company with Lord Sydney, and presented to Louis the XVIth at Fontainbleau, *ib.* Returns to England, and is appointed to the Command of the Narcissus Frigate, *ib.* His ill Health obliges him to relinquish the Command of his Ship, and he passes some time with the Duke of Bouillon, 180. The Duke dies, and is succeeded by his only Son Prince James Leopold, *ib.* The oaths of fidelity and allegiance are taken to him and to Captain d'Auvergne, as his Successor, *ib.* Appointed Captain of the Nonsuch, and Commander of a Flotilla of Gun-boats, for the protection of Jersey and Guernsey, *ib.* Succeeds the Earl of Balcarras in the controul and direction of the bounties granted to French lay Emigrants in the above-mentioned Islands, 181. Invested with the supreme direction and inspection of the military Corps of Officers raised from those refugees, ib. An Address presented to him by the French Emigrants for the delicacy of his conduct towards them, ib. Consults his Patron, Earl Howe, and receives a long and detailed letter from that distinguished Commander, ib. Honoured with the distinction of a broad pendant, 182. After the Definitive Treaty of Amiens he obtains permission to go to Paris for the purpose of applying for restitution or indemnity for his alienated domains, as Successor to the Dukes of Bouillon, ib. Rudely seized by some of the French police, and hurried before the Minister of Police, 183. Conducted to the Prison of the Temple, 186. Sees a person of shocking appearance in the Temple, ib. Caution given to him by the Turnkey, 187. Is liberated, 188. Infamous request made to him, ib. Receives equivocal Passports, 189. Submits his case to the British Ministry, and hoists his broad Pendant on board the Severn, ib. The States of Jersey vote liberal bounties to such Seamen as would serve under his Command, 190. Elected a Member of the Grand Cross of the Capitulary Order of St. Joachim, ib. Heraldic particulars, ib.

DOCKS; the London ones opened for the reception of Ships and Merchandize, 136.

DOCK YARD at Woolwich; observations made of the gradual rising of the tide at the, 68.

DOMINICA; Letter from General Prevost, giving an account of the French having effected a Landing on that Island, 326.

DORIS Frigate; loss of the, 123.

DROWNED PERSONS, &c. Method recommended by Dr. Hawes for restoring them to life, 481.

DUQUESNE Man of War ordered to be broke up, 133.

DUTCH PRISONERS on board the Buckingham generously treated by the Officers and Crew on board of that Ship, 69.

E

EARL OF ABERGAVENNY; loss of the East Indiaman so called, 194. Names of some of the persons who were saved from the wreck, 128. Further particulars, 188, 386.

EAST INDIA DOCKS at Blackwall; their foundation stone laid, 286.

EMBASSIES; supposed intention of Government respecting some splendid ones, 133.

ENGLISH GRATITUDE; instance of, 194.

———— MERCHANTMAN; the Master of one ill treated by a Danish Captain, 399.

ENTERPRISE; account of a gallant one, 353.

EUROPEAN SHIPPING; Scale of, 195.

EXPEDITION; account of part of the Force to be employed in the intended one, 65. Preparations for it carried on with activity, 133.

————, Catamaran; some account of the one which was first attempted in 1693, 275.

F.

FAUST, ST.; his Letter to the Editor of the Delft Courant, 47

FEVER; cause and cure of the Jail, 193.

FILTERING MACHINE; account of a newly invented one, 354.

FISGARD; remarkable success of that Frigate off Cape St. Vincent, 66.

FLEET; List of the English and French Fleets at Louisbourg in 1757, 114.

FLOATING MORTAR BATTERY; some account of a newly invented one, 193.

FLORA; loss of the Brig so called, 122.

FRANCE; interesting letter from la Peyrouse to the King of, 434.

FRENCH account of the Blockade of Barcelona, 74.

———— CRUELTY; instance of, 264.

———— FLEET; List of the, at Louisbourg, in 1757, 114.

———— SCHUYTS; eight of them brought into the Downs, 400.

G.

GIBRALTAR; the King issues a Proclamation respecting the infectious disease at, 144.

GRANT, Lieut.; observations on his Narrative of a Voyage of Discovery to New South Wales, 201, 469.

GRATITUDE; English; instance of, 194.

GREAT BRITAIN; the Correspondence between the Court of, and those of Petersburg and Stockholm, conducted with uncommon activity, 65.

GREENWICH HOSPITAL; button worn by the Officers at, 49.

GUERNSEY; account of the late Gale at, 78,

H.

HAMMOND, Sir A. S.; correspondence betwixt him and the Earl of St. Vincent, &c. 487

HAWES, Dr.; method recommended by him for restoring to life the apparently dead, 481

HYDROGRAPHER, the, (No. I,) 474

HUNTER, Lieut. WILLIAM; portrait and biographical memoir of; viz. Some account of his entrance into the Navy, 1. Embarks on board the Neptune Letter of Marque, which is captured by an Algerine Zebec, 3. Good conduct of the Algerine Captain, 4. They proceed to Port Mahon Harbour, and are put into Quarantine, ib. Sail to Smyrna, and return to England, ib. Mr. Hunter embarks on board the John and Zachariah, and sails to the West Indies, 5. Is struck by his Captain, and leaves him in an extraordinary manner, ib. Accidentally meets with his Captain again, and renews his engagement, 6. Applies to a Friend of his Father, ib. Hypocritical conduct of his Father's Friend, 7. Leaves the house of his pretended Friend with indignation, and takes a night's lodging in a watch-house, ib. Sails to the East Indies, and is shipwrecked, 8. Hard case of Seamen when discharged, 9. Mr. H. again sails to the East Indies, and afterwards returns to his native Country, where he makes some proficiency in the Mathematics, 11. Appointed a Midshipman of the Bedford, ib. Exerts himself with the other Mids in rigging the Ship, 12. Arrives at Lisbon at the time of the great Earthquake there, in 1755, 13. Extraordinary escape of a sailor from imminent danger, 14. Account of a dreadful and destructive Hurricane, 15. Mr. H.

INDEX.

sails in the Expedition to America in 1758, 16. Attacked by nine Canoes, 20. Gallant conduct of a Soldier, 22. Mr. H. is disappointed in his expectation of Promotion, 24. Sails to Quebec, 25. Proceedings of our Squadrons, 26—29. Employed in very fatiguing service at the Morro, 30. Returns to England, and is paid off, *ib.* Becomes acquainted with the Poet Falconer, 31. Returns to his Father, and receives a letter from the Secretary of the Admiralty, *ib.* Relates a curious circumstance respecting the Ramilies, *ib.* Receives a flattering letter from the Secretary of the Admiralty, 34. Appointed to command the Gaspee Brig, 35. Ordered to the Gulph of St. Lawrence, to superintend the Fisheries, 36. While cruising off the Gulph of St. Lawrence an unlucky circumstance takes place, *ib.* Tried by a Court Martial, and honourably acquitted, 38. Attacks an American Battery, and is forced to capitulate, 40. Sent prisoner to Albany, and afterwards exchanged, 41. Presents a Memorial of his Services to the Earl of Sandwich, 42. Disappointed again in his expectation of promotion, 43. Appointed Lieutenant of Greenwich Hospital, 45. Facsimile of his hand writing, *ib.*

J.

JAIL FEVER; Cause and Cure of, 193.
AMAICA; Speech of Lieutenant-Governor Nugent on opening the General Assembly of, 157.
JAMES, Commodore Sir WILLIAM, Bart.; portrait and biographical memoir of, 89. Enters the Navy at twelve years of age, 90. Appointed Commander of a Ship, and is taken Prisoner, *ib.* Is shipwrecked, but escapes, after experiencing extreme hardships, 91. Enters into the East India Company's Service, *ib.* Low state of the Company at the time Mr. James entered into its service, 92. Brief account of the origin and progress of the East India Company, *ib.* Mr. James performs two Voyages as Chief Mate of a Ship, and is afterward appointed to command the Guardian, 96. Ordered to protect the Trade on the Malabar Coast from the depredations of Angria and other Pirates, *ib.* Some account of Angria, *ib.* Captain James attacks a Fleet of Angria's Ships, sinks one of them, and compels the remainder to take shelter in Gheirah and Severndroog, 98. Description of two kinds of Vessels employed by Angria, *ib.* Their mode of attack, 99. Captain James is appointed Commander in Chief of the East India Company's Marine Forces, 100. Pursues Angria's Fleet, *ib.* Attacks Severndroog, 101. Blows up two of Angria's Magazines, and takes about 100 Prisoners, 102. Four of the Enemy's Forts subdued in one day, 103. Sails with Admiral Watson against Gheriah, 104. Order in which the Fleet attacked Angria's Forces, *ib.* Gheriah surrenders, 106. Angria's Wife and Children, and other Relatives, taken Prisoners, 107. Affecting Interview betwixt Admiral Watson and Angria's Relations, *ib.* A handsome Sword presented to him by the East India Company, *ib.* Appointed Chairman of the Company, *ib.* Created a Baronet, and returned a Member to serve in Parliament, 110. Elected one of the Elder Brethern, and Deputy Master, of the Trinity House, and Governor of Greenwich Hospital, *ib.* Plans the Capture of Pondicherry, *ib.* A valuable Service of Plate presented to him by the Company, *ib.* His health rapidly declines, and he dies suddenly on the day of his Daughter's marriage, *ib.* Superb Monument erected to his Memory, 111. Inscription on the Monument, *ib.* Heraldic Particulars, 112.

INVASION; Debate in Parliament respecting it, 148. Catalogue of all the Descents for the purpose of invading Britain from 1066 to 1096, 430.

K.

KING'S BENCH, Court of; Trials interesting to the Navy in; viz. Rack and others *v.* Mackay, 67. Jones *v.* an Officer on the Impress Service, 234. Stowe *v.* a Lieutenant in the Navy, 235. The King *v.* Herriott and others, 236.

L.

LANDER, Captain, with two of his Officers and some of his Crew, murdered at Penang, 287.
LAUNCH of the Hebe Frigate at Deptford; some account of the, 68. Ship of War launched at Dartmouth, 69.
LA PEYROUSE; interesting letter from him to Louis XVI of France, 434.
LETTER; curious one extracted from the Rotterdam Courant, 47. Official ones from Admiral Saunders, 439.
LIFE BOAT; some account of one built on a new construction, 261.
LIGHT HOUSE; Plan of a new invented one for Flamborough Head submitted to the inspection of the Trinity Houses, &c. 68.
LINOIS, Admiral; some account of, 115. Beat off in the Marengo of 80 guns, by the Centurion of 50 guns, 218.
LOUISBOURG; List of the English and French Fleets at, in 1757, 114.

M.

M'ARTHUR's (Mr.) Naval and Military Courts Martial; observations on a new edition of, 55.
MACHINE; dreadful explosion of one called the INFERNAL, 276.
MARINE DESIGNS, Naval Portraits, &c. in the Exhibition of the Royal Academy in 1805, 396.
MARINE LIST (Lloyd's) of Ships lost, destroyed, captured, and recaptured, &c. 87, 167, 247, 336, 424.
MARINER'S COMPASS; account of some imprevements lately made in it, 196.
MASON, Capt. FRANCIS; French account of his Attack on le Vimereaux Privateer, 352.
MATTHEWS's, (Mr. GEORGE) observations on the means that would have prevented the loss of the Venerable, 51.
MEDICAL ESTABLISHMENT in the Royal Navy, 212.
MELVILLE, Lord Viscount, writes a Letter to the Commissioners of Naval Inquiry, 284. Answer of the Commissioners, 286. Resigns his Situation as First Lord of the Admiraly,

INDEX.

287. Interesting Debates in Parliament respecting him, 289, 417.
METALLIC RIGGING ; observations on, 48.
MIDSHIPMEN ; those who have served their time are to be employed as Sub-Lieuts. 84.
MOORE, Major-General Sir JOHN, lands at Lisbon on a secret Mission, 67.

N

NABEY ; loss of the Ship so called, 120.
NATIVE OF GERMANY ; extract from his Tour in Zealand, 463.
NAVAL ACTION ; gallant one performed by Capt. Lind in the Centurion, 218, 288.
NAVAL ANECDOTES, COMMERCIAL HINTS, RECOLLECTIONS, &c. 46, 113, 191, 259, 352, 430 ; specified under their various subject words.
NAVAL ENGAGEMENT ; account of a spirited one fought in 1756, 278.
——— EVENTS ; chronological sketch of the most remarkable in the year 1804, 62.
——— FORCE for the protection of Ireland, 65
——— HOSPITAL about to be established at Barbadoes, 155.
——— HISTORY of the present year, 1805, 65, 133, 206, 284, 399, 482.
——— REFORM. Ninth Report of the Commissioners of Naval Inquiry presented to the House of Commons, 152. Notice of a Motion to be made in Parliament for continuing the Act for Naval Inquiry, 153, 154. Lord Melville's letter to the Commissioners, 284. The Commissioners' Answer, 286. The Lord Mayor is solicited to convene a Common Council on the subject of the Tenth Report, 284. A similar request made to the Sheriffs of Middlesex, 287. Interesting Debate in Parliament respecting the Tenth Report, 289. Account of Mr. Trotter's funded property, 360. Further Debates in Parliament in regard to Lord Melville, 417. Petition presented to Parliament from the Navy Board, 418. Motion made for the production of Papers while Lord St. Vincent was First Lord of the Admiralty, ib. Motion made relative to Sir Home Popham, 419. Notice taken in Parliament of the Eleventh Report, 421 —Fifth Report of the Commissioners of Naval Inquiry,—(continued from Vol. XII,) 452.
NAVAL LITERATURE. See M'Arthur, Woodward, Grant, Native of Germany.
——— MECHANIC ; some account of a self-taught one, 261.
——— POETRY. Dibdin's Charming Kitty, 392. The Bells of Ostend, 393. Ballad, 394. To the River Wye, 395. Sonnet, 396. The Sailor ; an Elegy, 476. Naval Ballad, 477. Columbus, and the Discovery of America, 478. On the gallant Exploit of Lieut. Yeo, 479. Naval Ballad, ib.
——— SURGEONS ; regulations respecting their pay, 163.
——— STATE PAPERS, SPANISH. Appendix, Nos. I and II.
NAVIGATION of the Thames, 46.
NAVY ROYAL ; estimates respecting it ordered to be laid before Parliament, 152. Sir Evan Nepean moves certain Resolutions respecting the number of Seamen, &c. to be employed in the Navy, ib. Naval Medical Establishment, 212. Hints for improving the British Navy, 268. List of the Ships which at present compose the French Navy, 269. Interesting Account of the Danish Navy, 264. List of the efficient Force of the British Navy in April, 1805, 365. Some account of the American Navy, 356.
NAVY BOARD ; the Commissioners of it present a Petition to Parliament for the production of two of their letters to the Admiralty, 418.
ONSLOW, Admiral Sir RICHARD, Bart.; Portrait and biographical Memoir of; viz. Some particulars of his Family, 249. Commences his naval career very early in life, 250. Made a lieutenant, and afterwards advanced to the rank of Commander, ib. Promoted to be a Post Captain, and appointed to command the Humber, ib. Convoys the outward-bound Baltic Fleet, and on his return to England loses his Ship on the Haysborough Sands, ib. Tried by a Court Martial for the loss of the Ship, and honorably acquitted, ib. Appointed to command the St. Albans, and sails under the Orders of Commodore Hotham, to reinforce Admiral Barrington in the West Indies, ib. They are attacked by a very superior French Fleet, which they repulse, 252. Captain Onslow is appointed to the Bellona, and sails with the Fleet under the Command of Admiral Geary to prevent the junction of the French and Spanish Fleets, 253. They capture twelve Sail of Merchantmen, ib. Captain Onslow captures a Dutch Ship of 50 guns, ib. Sails with the Fleet for the relief of Gibraltar in 1781, 254. Is also in the Fleet which sails under Admiral Howe for the relief of Gibraltar, and is in the Engagement with the combined French and Spanish Fleets, 255. His Advancements, 256. Appointed to be Port-Admiral at Plymouth, and afterward to be Second in Command of the Fleet under Admiral Duncan, ib. Distinguishes himself greatly in the Engagement with the Dutch Fleet, ib. List of the Ships which composed his Division, 257. The Dutch Vice-Admiral surrenders to him, 258. Number of the Ships taken in the Engagement, ib. The Vice-Admiral is created a Baronet, and receives the Thanks of both Houses of Parliament, ib.
ORDE, Sir JOHN, captures several valuable Spanish Ships, 133.

P.

PARLIAMENT, Imperial ; his Majesty's Speech on the opening of, 71. Debates interesting to the Navy in, 148, 224, 289, 415
PLATES. See page at back of Dedication.
PLYMOUTH REPORT from Dec. 15, 1804, to January 8, 1805, 78 ;—from January 9 to Feb. 19, 239 ;—from Feb. 24 to April 1, 329.
POPHAM's (Sir HOME) exhortations and injunctions to the Company of his Majesty's Ship Diadem, 50. Extract from the Courier respecting him, 137. Notice of a Motion to be made in Parliament in regard to Sir

INDEX.

Home, 152. Proceedings with respect to him, 226, 419. Report of the Select Committee respecting him, 485

PORTSMOUTH REPORT, from December 11, 1804, to January 13, 1805, 81;—from Feb. 1 to 20, 244;—from Feb. 25 to March 22, 329;

PRESERVATION; two remarkable instances of, 263, 355.

PRESS GANG; a whimsical circumstance happens to one, 357.

PRINCE OF WALES ISLAND; Motion made in Parliament for the Papers respecting the Establishment of that Island to be produced, 153. Manner in which it came into the possession of the British, 154.

PRIVATEER; a French one beat off by an English Brig of inferior Force, 66.

————— fitted out in 1744 by the Gentlemen who used White's Chocolate House, 277.

PRIZES; account of those taken at the beginning of the War in 1744, 267.

PROCLAMATION by the King respecting the infectious disease at Gibraltar, 144.

PROMOTIONS by different First Lords of the Admiralty from 1793 to 1805, 484

Q.

QUARANTINE ACT; Bill presented in Parliament for the Amendment of it, 153.

R.

RAVEN BRIG; account of the loss of the, 385.
REPORTS, FOREIGN, 73, 154, 325.
————— HOME, 76, 162, 239, 327.
REVOLUTIONNAIRE; Answer of M. la Bross to the Invitation of some of the Officers of that Ship, 161.
RIGGING, METALLIC; observations on, 48.
ROCHEFORT SQUADRON escapes on the night of the 11th of January, 136.
ROCK, LADY'S; interesting story relating to the one so called, 443.
ROUGE, FORT; Attack on, 75.
ROYAL SOVEREIGN and Royal Charlotte Yachts; dimensions of the, 61.
RUSSIAN VOYAGE OF DISCOVERY; some account of, 433. Singular Adventures of four Russian Sailors, 445.

S.

SAUNDERS, Admiral; official letters from, 439.
SCHANK, Capt. JOHN; some account of the Sliding Keels invented by him, 201.
SEA; dreadful sufferings of some deserters at, 368. Hardship experienced by some Seamen belonging to the Sussex Indiaman, 433.
SEAMAN; remarkable cure of a blind one, 115 A Seaman pardoned at the place of execution, 400. Singular Adventures of four Russian Seamen, 445.
SEVERN; account of the loss of the, 56.
SEXTANT; account of one newly invented, 196.
SHIPPING, EUROPEAN; Scale of, 195.
SHIPS; number of these in Commission in 1805, 133. List of Ships remaining at Spithead on the 20th of February, 1805, 244. List of those under the Command of Sir J. T. Duckworth at Jamaica, and also a List of of the Ships under the Orders of Sir Samuel Hood at the Leeward Islands, 357. List of Vessels building at Rochefort, 357.
SHIPWRECKS; correct relation of, 56, 69, 120, 385, 441
SHOAL near Dungeness; account of the, 356.

SLIDING KEELS; advantages resulting from their use, 201. The Lieut. and Master the Trial Cutter examined respecting the uses of Sliding Keels, 204.
SMUGGLING: abstract of a Bill for the more effectual prevention of, 358.
SPAIN; declaration of War against, 70. The British Government issues Orders that a neutral Vessel shall be molested in going thither with Grain, 136.
SPANISH SHIPS; Embargo on, 65. Great success of the Fisgard against Spanish Vessel, 66. Sir Richard Strachan captures a large Frigate, ib. List of Ships captured by the Fisgard previous to the 3d of Dec. 67. A valuable Vessel captured by the Phen Frigate, 67. Very valuable one taken by the Neptune of Greenock, 68. The property belonging to the Officers and Crew of the captured Frigates restored by Order of Government, 136. Debate in Parliament respecting them, 148. Singular custom observed on board of Spanish Galley 263. Spanish Naval State Papers; Appendix, Nos. I and II.
SPEEDY; account of the supposed loss of, 59
ST. FAUST, JEAN de; some account of, 355
ST. VINCENT, Earl of; justification of his conduct with regard to the prosecution commenced by him against the Publishers, &c. of the Sun and True Briton Newspapers for a Libel, 208. Motion made in Parliament for the production of several Naval Papers written when his Lordship presided at the Admiralty, 118.
SUB-LIEUTENANTS; appointment of, by the Lords of the Admiralty, 69.
SURGEONS and their Mates; fixed provision made for them, 134. Regulations respecting their Pay, 163.

T.

TARTARUS; particulars of the loss of the, 5
THAMES; Navigation of, 46. Observations on the gradual rising of the tide-waters of the Thames at Woolwich Dock Yard, 68
THUNDERER; dangerous situation of the, 67
THURNHAM, Lt., writes an affecting letter to his Father immediately before his death, 25
TRIEST; description of the Town and Harbour of, 436.
TUCKER, Mr.; his letter to Mr. Marsden Secretary to the Admiralty, in reply to letter from the Navy Board respecting the Accounts of the Romney, &c. 368—381.

V.

VANCOUVER, Capt. GEORGE; singular inscription on his tomb-stone, 277.
VOYAGE OF DISCOVERY; some account of Russian one, 433.

W.

WALES, Princess of, is present at the Launch of the Hebe Frigate, 63.
WALTON, Admiral Sir GEORGE; his laconic letter to Sir George Byng, 249
WAR, Declaration of, against Spain, 70. Declaration respecting it, 136.
WATER; how to preserve it sweet at Sea, 27
WOODARD, Mr.; interesting and melancholy Narrative of, 130. Makes a Discovery, 131

Y.

YACHTS, Royal Sovereign and Royal Charlotte; dimensions of the, 61.

INDEX to the GAZETTE LETTERS in VOL. XIII; containing Accounts of the Captures, Proceedings, &c. by and of the under-mentioned Officers and Ships.

BARKER, Lieut. John, 493
Bayley, Capt. T. 406
Bettesworth, Capt. G.E.B. 403
Bingham, Capt. Joseph, 220
Blow, Lieut. J. A 493
Bouverie, Capt. D. Pleydell, 217
Boyle, Hon. Capt. C. 494
Cadogan, Hon. Capt. George, 146
Carpenter, Lieut. John C. 494
Carteret, Capt. Philip, 405
Coghlan, Capt. Jeremiah, 502
Colby, Capt. David, 413
Cribb, Capt. R. W. 404
Dashwood, Capt. C. 497
Dashwood Capt. H. 496
Elphinstone, Capt. C. 73
Farquhar, Capt. Arthur, 222

Fyffe, Capt. J. 414
Gardner, Hon. Capt. F. F. 217
Geyte, Capt. G. Le, 495
Hardyman, Capt. L. T. 503
Heywood, Capt. P. 220
Honeyman, Capt. Robert, 412
Hood, Commodore Sir Samuel, 403
Impey, Capt. John, 414
Jackson, Capt. S. 413
Kerr, Capt. Lord Mark Robert, 147
Lake, Capt. W. T. 216, 497
Lamborn, Capt. J. 402
Langford, Capt. Frederick, 411
Lawrie, Capt. Sir Robert, 409
Lind, Capt. James, 218, 221
Losack, Capt. Woodley, 498
Maitland, Capt. Fred. 499

Mitchell, Capt. E. J. 493
Mudge, Capt. Z. 495
Musgrave, Mr. Thomas, 221
Nicholson, Lieut. James, 148
Nourse, Capt. Joseph, 73
Owen, Capt. 146, 401
Page, Capt. B. W. 220, 221
Poynts, Capt. S. 148
Price, Lieut. W. 413
Rainier, Vice-Admiral, 147, 221
Rose, Lieut. James, 216, 405
Rose, Capt. Jonas, 222
Ross, Capt. Charles B. H. 496
Selby, Capt. W. 401
Shirley, Lieut. Thomas, 411
Talbot, Capt. John, 407
Wallace, Lieut. W. R. 145
Yeo, Lieut. James Lucas, 501

INDEX to the PROMOTIONS and APPOINTMENTS.

ALDRIDGE, Capt. 163
Baker, Capt. J. 245
Baker, Lieut. 334
Ball, Capt. 163
Banes, Mr. 423
Barham, the Right Hon. Charles Lord, 423
Barlton, Mr. J. 504
Barton, Capt. 423
Beaufort, Capt. 504
Bedford, Capt. 163
Bennet, Hon. Capt. 245
Bickerton, Rear-Admiral Sir Richard, Bart. 84
Bissell, Capt. 163, 245
Bland, Capt. 423
Bligh, Capt. W. 423
Bogue, Lieut. 84
Bouchier, Capt. 84
Boyles, Capt. C. 423
Brace, Capt. 245
Bradley, Capt. 334
Brenton, Capt. E. P. 84
Bromley, Mr. E. 245
Brown, Capt. 163, 423
Browell, Capt. 163
Buchanan, Lieut. J, 84
Butterfield, Capt. 504
Byam, Capt. 504
Byng, Capt. 245
Campbell, Capt. P. 504
Carden, Capt. 84
Clarke, Rev. James Stanier, 504
Clement, Capt. 245
Clinch, Capt. 504
Codrington, Capt. 504
Coffin, Sir Isaac, Bart. 245
Coghlan, Capt. 163
Colpoys, Vice-Admiral Sir John, 163
Cooke, Capt. J. 334
Curry, Mr. Samuel, 84
Curry, Capt, 423

Curtis, Admiral Sir Roger, Bart. 84
Darby, Mr. J. 84
Davie, Capt. 84
Dobbin, Lieut, 335
Dodd, Lieut. 504
Domett, Rear-Admiral, 84
Donne, Rev. H. 245
Douglas, Admiral, 163
Down, Lieut. 84, 163
Drummond, Capt. 84
Duncan, Hon. Lieut. H. 84
Dundas, Capt. 423
Ekins, Capt. 163
Elliott, Hon. Capt. 245
Ellison, Capt. 163
Fahie, Capt. 504
Fane, Capt. 504
Forbes, Capt. 84
Fordyce, Mr. 84
Forster, Capt. 245
Foster, Capt. 163
Freemantle, Capt. 423
Gardner, Admiral Lord, 245
Gascoyne, Capt. 245
Gore, Capt. 84, 163
Granger, Capt. 84
Grant, Lieut. 84, 164
Grant, Capt. 423
Hall, Capt. H. 245
Halstead, Capt. 245
Hanwell, Capt. 334
Hardinge, Capt. 84, 163
Hardy, Capt. J. J. O, 423
Harris, Mr. George, 84, 423
Hawker, Capt. E. 245
Hill, Mr. C. 84
Home, Major, 245
Hope, Capt. W. 163
Houston, Lieut. 245
Hunt, Capt. 423
Hunter, Capt. 423
Inman, Capt, 84

Irwin, Lieut. 84, 163
Keith, Lieut. Sir George, 335
Kelly, Capt. 423
Ker, Dr. Charles, 335
King, Capt. 334, 423
Lake, Mr. J. 504
Laroche, Capt. 245
Lawford, Capt. 504
Lechmere, Capt. 504
Lee, Capt. 423
Lind, Capt. James, 423
Linzee, Capt. S. H. 423
Livingstone, Sir T. 84, 163
Lobb, Capt. 84
Lock, Capt. 245
Loring, Capt. J. W. 84, 334
Losack, Capt. G. 84
Louis, Admiral, 163
Lumsdaine, Capt. 423
Macdonald, Mr. 84
Mackenzie, Capt. 163, 334
M'Namara, Capt. 504
Malbon, Capt. 84
Mends, Capt. 84
Middleton, Sir Charles, Bart. 84, 334
Mitchell, Mr. 84
Moorsom, Capt. 334
Murat, Marshal, 245
Nagle, Mr. F. 84, 423
Nepean, Sir Evan, Bart. 84
Oldham, Capt. 245
Oliver, Capt. 163
Packwood, Lieut. 423
Paget, Capt. 423
Parker, Capt. 334
Parsons, Sir Lawrence, 245
Patterson, Mr. W. L. 84
Pearson, Capt. 245
Pellew, Sir Edward, 245
Pender, Capt. 334
Phillips, Lieut. 245
Pigot, Capt. 334

Prevost, Capt. 163
Pringle, Lieut. 504
Pritchard, Mr. 84
Raggett, Capt. 163
Rodd, Capt. 423
Rose, Mr. 504
Row, Mr. N. 84
Royen, M. H. Van, 423
Sawyer, Capt. 423
Sayer, Capt. George, 84
Seator, Capt. 84, 163
Serle, Mr. 84
Short, Capt. 334
Shortland, Capt. 504
Simpson, Capt. 84, 504
Simpson, Lieut. 163
Simpson, Mr. Thomas, 423
Skinner, Lieut. 84, 163
Smith, Sir Sidney, 245
Snell, Capt. 245
Somerville, Sub-Lieut. G. F. 423
Souter, Rev. Mr. 84
Stanhope, Admiral, 163
Stephens, Capt. 504
Sykes, Capt. 245
Talbot, Lieut. 423, 504
Thompson, Mr. 84, 423
Thornborough, Rear-Admiral, 334
Tremlett, Lieut. 84
Trowbridge, Sir T. 163, 245
Tyler, Capt. 163
Walker, Capt. 245
Warren, Capt. S. 504
Westbeach, Capt. 84
White, Capt. T. 423
Whitebread, Mr. G. 245
Wilby, Mr. John, 84
Wilkes, Mr. James, 163
Woolcombe, Capt. 84, 163, 504
Worth, Capt. 504
Yeo, Lieut. 504
Yorke, Capt. 423

INDEX to the MARRIAGES.

BEVAN, Major, 85
Campbell, Rear-Admiral, 164
Champion, Mr. S. '504
Cooper, Mr. J. 246
Croft, Capt. 335
Duncan, Lord Viscount, 85
Ferris, Capt. 423
Finling, Capt. Charles, 85
Hall, Mrs. E. 86
Hamilton, Mr. Augustus, 335
Hanchet, Lieut. 163
Harvey, Capt. Thomas, 335
Hatley, Capt. 163
Hill, Capt. 85
Hood, Commodore, 85
Humphreys, Capt. 245
Kerr, Capt. 85
Lackington, Mr. G. 245
Luckey, Capt. D. 245
Mansell, Capt. 504
Monro, Mr. James, 335
Morris, Lieut. 423
O'Bryen, Capt. E. 164
Paget, Hon. Capt. C. 245
Pearson, Sir R. 86
Penrose, William, 164
Rogers, Mr. 164
Rolles, Capt. 85
Seymour, Capt. M. 163
St. George, Hon. Col. 504
Stone, Lieut. J. C. 423
Stevang, Capt. 245
Waring, Capt. Henry, 335
Welsh, Capt. 245
Winthrop, Capt. 85
Young, Lieut. E. 85
Young, Capt. T. 85

INDEX to the OBITUARY.

ASHLINGTON, Lieut. John 335
Baker, Lieut. J. E. 335
Barwell, Mr. 246
Bateson, Lieut. H. 504
Battier, Mr. G. 86
Bellamy, Lieut. John, 164
Berkeley, Miss S. E. 166
Bertie, Mrs. 246
Betty, Mr. Z. 335
Bird, Dr. 85
Brace, Mr. Uppington, 164
Brawn, Captain Ernest, 504
Bruce, Mr. R. 86
Bruix, Admiral, 335
Callaway, Mr. J. 86
Cameron, Mr. 246
Chappe, Mr. 246
Church, Miss, 86
Clarke, Mrs. 246
Courcy, Miss de, 86
Cresswell, Major, 246
Cumberlege, Capt.; the infant son of, 246
Dalyell, Lieut. William C. C. 166
Davis, Mr. Owen, 86
Day, Mr. 335
Delafons, Capt. 335
Domville, Mr. 165
Douglas, Lieut. James, 246
Elliott, Lieut. 246
Furbor, Mr. Thomas, 85
Furmidge, Lieut. 246
Gascoyne, Mr. 504
Geary, Capt. 166, 246
Greig, Mr. J. S. 166
Haddon, Lieut. B. F. 165
Hales, Sir Samuel, Bart. 85, 165
Hall, Mrs. E. 86
Hardyman, Miss J. 246
Harland, Dowager Lady, 166
Harris, Mr. 246
Hedley, John, 165
Heron, Mr. 423
Hotham, Montagu, Esq. 246
Huddart, Capt. John, 164
Jervis, Capt. 165
Jones, Capt. C. B. 86
Kilbeck, Mr. 246
Kirk, Mr. 166
Liardet, Mrs. 86
M'Donald, Mr. 166
Matson, Mr. R. 166
Maxwell, Mr. 166
Mechain, M. 86
Milbanke, Admiral Mark, 504
Mitchell, Mr. John, 86
Montagu, Miss S. 504
Mouat, Capt. S. P. 166
Mulcaster, Lieut. 165
Nicholson, James, 165
Nightingale, Sir E., Bart. 164
Palgrave, Mr. Robert, 86
Parke, Lieut. T. 504
Paul, Capt. 335
Pearson, Sir R. 86
Redpath, William, 165
Renou, Capt. A. 165
Richards, Lieut. 165
Saradine, Capt. 166
Simmonds, Mr. 166
Stephens, Mr. F. 166
Strong, Lieut. 504
Sullings, Edward, 165
Templer, Capt. 423
Thurnham, Lieut. 166
Urquhart, Lieut. 85
Wallis, Mrs. M. 166
Watt, William, 165
Willes, Capt. John, 165
Williams, Mr. S. 246
Wooldridge, Capt. F. 246
Wordsworth, Capt. 335
Young, Mrs. 246

END OF THE THIRTEENTH VOLUME.

APPENDIX.

No. I.

SPANISH NAVAL STATE PAPERS.

EXTRACTS FROM

NAVAL STATE PAPERS

LAID BEFORE PARLIAMENT JANUARY 24TH,

RELATIVE TO

THE WAR WITH SPAIN.

Extract of a Dispatch from Lord HAWKESBURY *to* J. H. FRERE, *Esq. dated Downing Street, 2d June,* 1803.

I SHALL now proceed to signify to you his Majesty's pleasure with respect to the conduct which it will be proper for you to observe at the Court at which you reside.

It is the King's sincere and earnest desire that the Spanish Government may be enabled to maintain the strictest neutrality in the War which has commenced between Great Britain and France. You will therefore endeavour, by all the means in your power, to impress upon the Spanish Ministers the expediency of their adopting this system; and you will assure them, that if it be adopted, his Majesty will respect it with the most scrupulous good faith.

His Majesty's Government having no means of deciding how far his Catholic Majesty may consider himself as bound by the Treaty of defensive and offensive alliance, which was concluded at St. Ildephonso on the 9th of August 1796, it is indispensably necessary that you should lose no time in ascertaining this important point. If the Spanish Government should state to you, that they conceive themselves to be under the obligation to furnish to France the number of Troops and Ships which are stipulated in the Treaty above mentioned, but that their co-operation will extend no further, you will refrain from giving any opinion upon this measure, but will content yourself with signifying that you will transmit the information of it to your Court. You will however watch, with the most unremitting vigilance, the progress of any preparations which may be made for carrying it into execution; and you will, from time to time, transmit such intelligence as you may be able to acquire upon the subject, to the Commanders of his Majesty's Ships in the Mediterranean, at Gibraltar, and at Lisbon, in order that those Officers may be enabled to pursue such measures as may be best calculated to intercept the Spanish Auxiliary Ships, on their attempting to sail from the Ports either of the Mediterranean or of the Atlantic; a proceeding which would be in strict conformity to the most rigid principles of Neutrality, and could not be construed into an act of direct aggression against Spain herself.

If, however, you should learn from the Spanish Ministers, that the French Government will not be satisfied with the definitive succours stipulated, but will require his Catholic Majesty to place a greater proportion of his Naval and Military Force at the disposition of France, you will state to them, unreservedly, that his Majesty will consider a compliance with this requisition as equivalent to a Declaration of War, and as justifying his Majesty in proceeding to immediate hostilities against Spain.

The next object to which his Majesty has commanded me to direct your particular attention, is the situation of Portugal.

Having now stated to you such proceedings on the part of Spain, as would render it expedient for his Majesty to commence hostilities against that Power, I have to signify to you his Majesty's pleasure, that if any of these events should occur, you should make the strongest representations against them; and in the case of your not receiving a satisfactory answer, you will quit Madrid and proceed to Lisbon, whence you will return to England. Previously to your departure, you will apprise the Officers commanding his Majesty's Ships in the Mediterranean, at Lisbon, and at Gibraltar, of your intention, in order that they may proceed to hostilities against Spain without delay.

Dispatch from J. H. FRERE, *Esq. to Lord* HAWKESBURY, *dated Aranjuez, 3d June,* 1803.

In this Letter nothing occurs particularly connected with the objects of our CHRONICLE.

A Note from Don PEDRO CEVALLOS *to* J. H. FRERE, *Esq. dated Aranjuez,* 9th *June,* 1803, *in answer to the above.*

[Then follows Mr. Frere's answer alluded to, and described in his preceding Note.]

Dispatch from J. H. FRERE, *Esq. to Lord* HAWKESBURY, *dated Madrid,* 12th *September,* 1803.

MY LORD,

The enclosed Note was sent in consequence of my being informed that General Bournonville had obtained permission for about 1500 Men, between Sailors and Artillerymen, to pass to Ferrol to man the Ships there. I can hardly flatter myself that my remonstrance will be attended to, but I thought it useful and necessary to enter a protest against a proceeding contrary to the principles of the Neutrality hitherto professed by this Government, and which came so nearly within the scope of the instructions which I received from your Lordship.

J. H. FRERE.

[The Note alluded to is sufficiently described in the above. It adds, besides, that England had respected the Neutrality of Spain so strictly, as to allow a French Frigate recently pursued to escape into Ferrol the moment it was within the limited distance of the Spanish Shore.]

24th *Nov.* 1803.—Lord Hawkesbury gives instructions to Mr. Frere to preserve Neutrality if possible, and to watch the extent of the pecuniary succours given to France. Large Succours, he says, are subsidies, and just ground of War. If such Succours are only a temporary measure, they may be passed over at present; but if continued, they may be regarded as a just ground of War whenever Great Britain shall choose to take up that ground. The instructions nearly repeat what has already been set forth.

27th *Dec.*—Mr. Frere to Lord Hawkesbury, describing his interview with Cevallos the Spanish Minister, on the above subject, and inclosing the following Notes:—

Mr. FRERE *to* CEVALLOS *the Spanish Minister.*

SIR,   *Escurial,* 13th *Dec.* 1803.

I obey the orders which I have just received from my Court, by transmitting to your Excellency, in an authentic shape, the declarations which I have frequently had the honour of making verbally, and in a manner less positive and less precise.

Since the commencement of hostilities, his Majesty has never ceased to consider the preservation of good understanding with the Court of Spain as a principal object of his political views. This Court, indeed, has never refused to acknowledge the justice of his

Majesty's intentions and good will towards it. But it is equally manifest, and the Court of Spain itself cannot but admit it, that the effect of this good will, and of these intentions, must depend upon that of the efforts which Spain is bound to make on her side; in the first place, *to maintain a system of absolute Neutrality;* and, secondly, *to cause it to be respected by the other Belligerent Powers.*

With regard to the former, his Majesty is perfectly sensible of the difficulties of the situation in which Spain is placed, as well by reason of her ancient ties with France, as on account of the character and habitual conduct of that Power and of her Chief. This consideration would induce him to act with forbearance to a certain degree, and particularly to overlook such pecuniary sacrifices as should not be of sufficient magnitude to force attention on account of their political effects. But it is expressly enjoined me to declare to your Excellency, that pecuniary advances, such as are stipulated in the Convention recently concluded with France, cannot be considered by the British Government but as a War Subsidy: a Succour the most efficacious; the best adapted to the wants and to the situation of the enemy; the most prejudicial to the interests of his Britannic Majesty's Subjects; and the most dangerous for his Dominions: in fine, more than an equivalent to every other species of aggression.

Notwithstanding his personal sentiments, imperious necessity, and that first duty which compels a Prince to consider, above and before all things, the Nation whose interests are committed to his care; have prescribed to his Majesty that conduct from which he cannot depart.

With regard to the Second Article, that of causing this Neutrality to be respected by the other Belligerent Powers, it appears superfluous to repeat to your Excellency the declarations which I have already made on the subject of Portugal; nevertheless, sinc this object is again pointed out in my last instructions, I cannot refrain from repeating to your Excellency the declaration, that the passage of the French Troops through the Territories of Spain would be considered as a violation of her Neutrality, and that his Majesty would find himself compelled to have recourse to the most decisive measures, in consequence of such an event. Such, Sir, is an abridgment of the instructions which I have just received from my Court, and which I communicate nearly in the same terms. There are others, of inferior importance, upon which I shall have the honour to converse with you in the conference of to-morrow.

Whilst I attach the utmost importance to these interesting subjects, it affords me much satisfaction to think that your Excellency will at length be persuaded that I have been far from exceeding the views and sentiments of my Government in the declarations which I have formerly made; and that the advice which I have thought it right, in consequence, to suggest, has been founded upon ideas sufficiently correct, and inspired by the sincerest desire of perpetuating the continuance of harmony and good understanding between the two Countries.

(Signed)   J. H. FRERE.

Translation of a Note from Don PEDRO CEVALLOS *to* J. H. FRERE, *Esq. dated Escurial,*
16*th December,* 1803.

SIR,

As soon as the War began between France and England, Spain was required by the former Power to furnish the defensive Succours stipulated by the Treaty of 1796, the execution of which, in as much as it is a consequence of engagements previously contracted by Spain, and a fresh proof of the King's good faith, presents in no degree an obstacle to the continuance of friendship and good understanding with Great Britain, with whom his Majesty has endeavoured to maintain them by every means of conciliation; Great Britain corresponding to the same object, by punishing the Privateers who transgress the law of Neutrality, according to repeated official accounts, and chiefly those of the 29th November, a later date than the expedition of the Courier who has given rise to the Note which you have just sent me.

Although the Spanish Cabinet is penetrated with the maxim, that the idea of aiding France is compatible with that of Neutrality towards England; his Majesty has thought that he could better maintain these two objects by a method, which, without being disagreeable to France, strips her Neutrality towards Great Britain of that hostile exterior, which Military Succours necessarily present; which sometimes, in spite of friendly protestations, leads the minds of Neutral Sovereigns to mistrust, to the hazard of the wished-for Peace.

Such have been the King's political views in agreeing to a Treaty of Subsidy to France, equivalent to the Military Succour.

Neither before, nor since this Treaty, has the Spanish Government omitted any of those means which lead to the preservation of good understanding with Great Britain, as is proved to you by the imprisonment inflicted upon the Spaniard who had dared to insult the British Flag.

The British Cabinet in its conferences with the Spanish Minister, has not considered that Spain violated her Neutrality by the act of assisting France with the Military Succour stipulated for her defence.

The pecuniary aid substituted in its place, besides that it carries no hostile appearance, neither compromises the good understanding of those who are neuter, nor gives to France such ready and expeditious means of hostility against Great Britain.

The King has employed his offices with the French Government to avoid the entry of her Troops into Spain, and to calm the apprehensions of the Court of Portugal, obtaining from the First Consul that this point should become an object of Negotiation between the two Governments, and his Majesty offering to co-operate with his good offices for the conclusion of a Treaty which is to shelter the Kingdom of Portugal from any attack; the favourable effects of which that Monarchy has already began to feel, and it is in his power to derive from it all the advantage which she desires.

In this situation of things I receive your Note; which represents that Spain, in having substituted pecuniary supplies for her defensive engagements, has displeased the English Cabinet in a degree the most unexpected, under pretext that they exceed her engagements; whereas to represent them under this point of view, it would be necessary to know their amount, which is not known; or knowing it, to compare it with the expense of furnishing the defensive Succours due to France.

This comparative statement of what has been hitherto executed by Spain, and the contents of your Note; and what is more, the contradiction which there is between the equitable and conciliatory conduct of Great Britain in sentencing to punishment the Privateers who have violated the Spanish Flag, according to the accounts of the 29th November, and the alarming expressions in which your Note of the 13th instant is conceived, obliges the Spanish Cabinet to require of you more clear and decisive explanations of the ideas of your Cabinet, which I hope you will be pleased to communicate to me with the dispatch which their importance demands.

(Signed)   PEDRO CEVALLOS.

Mr. FRERE *to* CEVALLOS, *the Spanish Minister.*

SIR,   *Madrid, 26th Dec.* 1803.

I comply with your Excellency's request, in communicating to you the explicit and decisive explanations of the ideas of my Cabinet, mentioned in my Note of the 13th inst. They are nearly the same with those which I had the honour verbally to address to you in our conference on this subject. Your Excellency then remarked, and the same observation again occurs in your Note of the 16th instant, that the furnishing the Succours stipulated by the Treaty of 1796, being but a consequence of engagements previously contracted, is in fact only a fresh proof of the good faith of his Catholic Majesty, and can in no wise be prejudicial to the continuance of good harmony with his Britannic Majesty.

I confess to your Excellency, that without having too favourable an opinion of my own abilities, I could not nevertheless help feeling a degree of humiliation, on seeing that a Person, whose judgment I infinitely respected, set so little a value on mine; and that he thought he might hazard with me a sophism, from which, if the gravity of the subject could allow of it, it would not be difficult to draw the most absurd consequences.

In fact, it remains to be known, whether a Power can acquire the right of attacking another, and at the same time impose on her the obligation to abstain from every species of reprisals. It cannot surely be necessary seriously to discuss a similar question. It suffices simply to say, that such a right cannot exist; that nature and common sense reject it; that all political combinations are inadequate to bestow it; and that most certainly no Nation can acquire it by an act of its own judgment, such as the signature of a Treaty concluded voluntarily, and without necessity.

But, it may be asked, should not the stipulations of a Treaty be complied with? I do not examine, if in the present case the stipulations of the Treaty, which binds Spain to France, have not been annulled by reiterated acts of this very Power. It may be granted that this Treaty is of the utmost validity; it may even be admitted that it is most strictly obligatory; and that the Spanish Government is bound to execute most scrupulously all its articles; but after all these concessions, it remains for me on the

SPANISH NAVAL STATE PAPERS.

other hand to remark, that this obligation is absolutely foreign to Great Britain, and that its Government is not bound to respect the execution of a Treaty to which it has been far from contributing, which has been made without its knowledge, against its consent, and even in opposition to its power. An individual who yesterday was free, enters to-day a Volunteer; to-morrow he receives orders to march to the attack of a place; his honour and his engagement oblige him to fulfil his duty; but he would be in the wrong to suppose that this obligation ought to be respected by the besieged, or that it will protect him against the natural consequences of a vigorous resistance. If in fact any misfortune should befall him, he ought to consider it solely as the consequence of the engagement he had entered into.

The same reason applies to the substitution of pecuniary Subsidies, and still more strongly, if these Subsidies, by their amount, or by the effect of other circumstances, become more than an equivalent for the stipulated contingent; but in the present case, France has shown a marked eagerness to obtain this substitution; the Court of England has lately declared, in a formal manner, that it considers such a substitution as more prejudicial than would be the supplying the contingent itself. These two Governments are assuredly the best and only judges of what is conducive to their respective interests and their opinions, so unequivocally declared, render it unnecessary for me to reply to your Excellency's arguments. There still remains one remark more to make on this subject; and your Excellency will the more readily pardon me, as it may in some degree be considered as necessary to my personal justification.—When your Excellency expresses to me the surprise which the declaration I made on the 13th of this month had caused, you will allow me to call to your recollection, that this declaration merely contained the formal expression of the same ideas and of the same language which I had held on every occasion when I had the honour of speaking to you on the subject of the enormous subsidies lately demanded by France. It was perhaps natural, that your Excellency should at that time have referred to other information, rather than to verbal assurances on my part. I certainly regret it; but neither my Government nor myself can be responsible for it. With respect to that part of your Excellency's Note, which says, that the British Cabinet, in its conferences with the Spanish Minister, was not of opinion that Spain infringed its neutrality by affording the stipulated Succours, it appears to me no easy task to understand clearly the precise force of the expression made use of by your Excellency in the original; but if I am to understand it, as alluding to any declaration whatever on this subject on the part of his Majesty's Ministers, I will venture to take upon myself, under the most formal responsibility, to deny the existence of such a declaration.

Not to omit any thing on the several points contained in your Excellency's Note, it will be necessary to say a word on the subject of Portugal. At the very commencement of hostilities, I obeyed the orders of my Court, by declaring both to your Excellency and to Mon Seigneur the Prince of the Peace, that his Majesty, in pursuance of his alliance with the Court of Portugal, found himself obliged to consider the non-passage of the French Troops through the Spanish territories as indispensable to the maintenance of the neutrality of that Court. It appears, then, that in a Convention, the ostensible and acknowledged design of which were to secure the tranquillity of Spain, it would have been natural to introduce an article that might secure her against a similar infraction of her neutrality; it being manifest, that such an infraction would determine the British Government no longer to consider Spain as a neutral Power. On the contrary, it appears, that the Treaty contains only one article, by which Spain engages herself to interpose her good offices with Portugal, in order to prevail upon her also to furnish France with a subsidy against her own ally. I have just stated to your Excellency the sentiments of my Court on the granting of these subsidies by Spain, in reply to your Excellency's arguments, which dwelt solely upon the existence of prior Treaties. It may therefore be permitted me to remind your Excellency, that Portugal is bound by prior Treaties to furnish Succours to England. That Portugal has no neutrality to purchase: that if Portugal is to conform to the system adopted by Spain, that is to say, the substitution of Pecuniary Succours for a contingent, these Succours are due to England. If, on the contrary, her neutrality is to be purchased by furnishing Succours to the enemy of her ally, as is now proposed to Portugal to do, it would thence result that Spain should likewise furnish Succours to England, and not to France: if Spain should reject such a demand as an insult, she ought not to endeavour to induce Portugal to submit to it. Two opposite principles can never be admitted in two cases precisely similar. Let not insinuations, founded on a pretended disparity between the forces of the two Belligerent Powers, be put in opposition to this just and natural consequence! Such considerations have not been admitted by England. She has, by a solemn defiance, proved the falsehood of the vain and groundless assertion, that

England was unable to cope single-handed with France. She has given this defiance. She will maintain it, or she will fall gloriously. Never will she admit the idea of an humiliating inferiority, either as the basis of her own conduct, or of her relations with foreign Powers. Too well I know the respect which is due to a great and powerful Monarchy, to dwell upon injurious comparisons, especially in an official and permanent form: but your Excellency will doubtless recollect the observations which I have verbally made to you respecting the relative situations of Portugal and Spain, with regard to France and England. If I do not think it proper to repeat them on this occasion, I can assure your Excellency that I am far from concealing them, or from apprehending that they can be disavowed by my Government.

It appears to me, that the above statement will answer your Excellency's ideas: but I cannot close it without affording myself the satisfaction of rendering justice to the upright and friendly intentions of his Catholic Majesty, manifested on several occasions, and almost uniformly in your Excellency's language and conduct.

Your Excellency has likewise afforded the same testimony in favour of the principles and conduct of his Britannic Majesty's Government. Such is, unfortunately, the temper of mankind, that rivalry and hatred are not the sole motives which give rise to hostilities. Doubtless, had a national hatred, or an opposition of interests been necessary, one might have expected an uninterrupted continuance of that harmony, which is so perfectly suitable to the habits and interests of the two nations. In all cases, and under all circumstances, his Majesty will be very far from laying any thing to the charge of his Catholic Majesty's wishes, or of the intentions of his Government. He will attribute it to a fatal combination of circumstances, and to the consequence of the unfortunate engagements which have re-united a friendly Power to his natural enemy.

J. H. FRERE.

Extract of a Dispatch from J. H. FRERE, *Esq. to Lord* HAWKESBURY, *dated Madrid, 27th December,* 1803.

The reports which reach us here from other quarters, have determined me to confine myself to the strong protestation contained in the Note enclosed in my former dispatch; and for the rest, to watch their conduct; contenting myself with reporting it to your Lordship, unless circumstances should arise which would render my further forbearance incompatible with the observance of your Lordship's instructions. Since this time I have learnt that this Government have already advanced to France the eight millions of livres, and that they are on the point of furnishing a further sum of four millions. Besides this, the recruiting for the army, which had been going on briskly, has been stopped, or, at least, suffered to stop of itself; while a greater activity prevails in the marine department; though I conceived it my duty to make a strong remonstrance upon this head, and even to stake my continuance here, agreeably to your Lordship's instructions, upon the absolute cessation of these naval armaments.

J. H. FRERE.

[*The discussion is pursued in various long Notes, without any satisfactory information being given, or much novelty occurring in the dispatches. After Mr.* PITT *came into power, the following Papers passed:*]

Copy of a Letter from Lord HARROWBY *to* J. H. FRERE, *Esq. dated Downing Street, 22d May,* 1804.

SIR,

It being extremely desirable, in the present state of the political relations between this country and Spain, that his Majesty's Government should obtain the most accurate information with respect to the actual condition of the ports and arsenals of Spain, I have to signify to you the King's pleasure, that you transmit to me a detailed statement, in as far as it can be procured, not only of any warlike preparations which may be carrying on in any of those Ports, and of the Ships of War both in commission and in ordinary, but also of the state of the Royal Arsenal, and of the extent of the means existing in them to increase their present Naval Establishment. You will likewise instruct the Consuls to endeavour to discover any measures which may have been adopted by the Spanish Government for the purpose of obtaining supplies of Naval Stores, the amount of such supplies, the countries from which they are to be shipped, and the manner in which they are to be conveyed to the Ports of Spain. With a reference to this subject, it is also important

SPANISH NAVAL STATE PAPERS.

that his Majesty's Government should be furnished with an account of the specie imported into the Ports of Spain in the course of the last year, and with an estimate of the probable amount of the Shipments of the present year, as well as with information of the periods at which they may be expected to arrive in Europe.

HARROWBY.

Copy of a Dispatch from J. H. FRERE, *Esq. to Lord* HARROWBY, *dated Madrid, 5th July,* 1804.

MY LORD,

I have to acknowledge the receipt of your Lordship's dispatch, No. 1, of the 22d May; and though there has not yet been time to satisfy the inquiries which your Lordship directs me to make, yet your Lordship will see from the tenour of my other letters of this date, that there can be no reason to apprehend that this Court are disposed to renounce their present System of Nominal Neutrality; and I should apprehend that the French Government are as little disposed, for the sake of a momentary assistance, to exchange an useful tributary for a burdensome ally. The accounts which I receive from the Ports do not indicate any preparation on the part of this Government, and Mr. Cevallos' language is in the same tone as before, speaking of the neutrality of this country as a thing settled and admitted, and seeming to wish to lead me on to similar language. Thus when I thought it my duty to question him respecting the situation of the Ports, saying that though I had no reason to believe that any preparations were going on, yet that I had learnt that some reports to that effect were in circulation, and that I wished to be able to explain to my Government the ground and origin of such reports; he replied that they were wholly without foundation; that the British Government had insisted upon the non-armament, as one of the conditions of neutrality; that he had informed me in an official note that Spain consented to desist from any further armament; that she had done so; and that every thing remained at this moment upon the same footing. I then questioned him upon the subject of Mr. Lebrun's mission, respecting which he did not seem disposed to give me any explanation.

The object of this mission still remains unknown; though, from the circumstance of Mr. Lebrun's having visited the Port of Ferrol in his way, and being himself a Naval Officer, there can be little doubt of its being connected with some Maritime project.

J. H. FRERE.

Copy of a Dispatch from J. H. FRERE, *Esq. to Lord* HARROWBY, *dated Madrid, 29th August,* 1804.

MY LORD,

Having been informed by Admiral Cochrane of the arrival of reinforcements through Spain to the French Fleet at Ferrol, I wrote to Mr. Cevallos the Note of which the enclosed is a copy; and after some days having received no answer, and having learnt positively from other quarters, the passage of such reinforcements through the Spanish territory, I made a second application to Mr. Cevallos upon the subject. He has as yet returned me no answer, and I think it right not to wait any longer for his explanation, before I acquaint your Lordship with the circumstance; more especially since there being no doubt of the fact complained of, no very satisfactory explanation can be expected.

J. H. FRERE.

Mr. FRERE *to* CEVALLOS, *20th August,* 1804.

SIR,

The Captain-General of Galicia will not have failed to communicate to your Excellency the representations which have been made to him by the Commander in Chief of his Britannic Majesty's Fleet stationed off Ferrol, with regard to the reinforcement of Soldiers, and Sailors who traverse Spain, in order to reach the French Squadron now in that Port. Admiral Cochrane, on his side, has transmitted to me his correspondence; and although I should have desired to be enabled to verify with more precision what foundation there might be for these complaints, before I laid them officially before your Excellency, I have thought it more conformable to the dispositions of my Government, to endeavour to prevent, by remonstrances, which may be premature, an act so decidedly hostile to England, than to risk being under that still more painful necessity which the certainty of its having been performed would impose upon me. I will also confess to your Excellency, that the private information I possess on the passage of French Soldiers from Malaga to Ferrol, has seemed to me to confirm the other accounts which have been given to Admiral Cochrane. And it is possible that, as this Government did not oppose this indirect violation of its territory, France may have been encouraged to try a still more open and flagrant one, by obtaining a passage through Spain for Troops going from France itself, in order to reinforce its Squadron at Ferrol.

As the Commander in Chief, in communicating to me his correspondence with the Captain-General of Galicia, informs me, that he at the same time transmitted it to his Government, I hope that your Excellency will soon enable me to quiet the uneasiness which they must feel from the project in question, by giving me the assurance that efficacious measures have been taken to prevent its being carried into execution.

J. H. FRERE.

Mr. FRERE *to* CEVALLOS, *27th August*, 1804.

SIR,

I flatter myself, that your Excellency will not blame my impatience to receive some satisfactory answer on the subject of my Note of the 20th of this month. I have since that day received authentic accounts of the passage of several small detachments of Frenchmen going to Ferrol; and I believe that this circumstance is not at this moment unknown to his Catholic Majesty's Government; but in any case, should they think proper to make inquiries into the fact, it would afford some satisfaction to me to receive, in the mean time, your Excellency's assurance that measures were already taken to put a stop to this abuse, of the continuance of which, the Spanish Government must henceforward charge itself with the consequences.

J. H. FRERE.

Copy of a Dispatch from Lord HARROWBY *to* J. H. FRERE, *Esq. dated Downing Street, September* 29, 1804.

SIR,

Information has been received from Rear-Admiral Cochrane, that orders have been given by the Court of Madrid, for arming without loss of time at Ferrol four Ships of the Line, two Frigates, and other smaller Vessels; that similar orders have been given at Carthagena and Cadiz; and particularly, that three first-rate Ships of the Line are directed to sail from the last-mentioned Port; and as an additional proof of hostile intentions, that orders have been given to the Packets to arm as in time of War.

In consequence of this information, I am commanded to signify to you his Majesty's pleasure, that as soon as you receive this dispatch, you should request an audience of M. de Cevallos.

You will express to him the surprise and concern with which the intelligence of these unexpected and unjustifiable measures has been received in this country.

You will recall to his recollection of that Minister, the grounds upon which his Majesty has hitherto forborne from considering Spain as an enemy. That nothing could have induced him to continue this forbearance, but a sincere desire to avoid extending the calamities of War, and a willingness to confide in the assurances of the Spanish Government, that the payments made to France were only intended to gain time, until circumstances should enable them to adopt measures more consistent with their interests and their wishes. That his Majesty had repeatedly required a communication of the engagements entered into with France; but had only received in answer to such demands an indefinite assurance, that whatever might be the amount of the payments to be made by Spain to France, they had been calculated with a reference to the expense of the Military and Naval Succours stipulated by Treaty. That no means had been afforded to his Majesty of judging whether the payments were in fact only an equivalent for the Succours, or whether they so far exceeded that amount as to make it impossible to consider Spain otherwise than as a principal in the War.

That his Majesty therefore had been under the necessity of expressly reserving to himself the full right of regulating his conduct towards Spain, according to the appearance of existing circumstances; but that the abstaining from all Naval preparations on the part of that Power had been distinctly declared to be one of the indispensable conditions annexed by his Majesty to the continuance of his forbearance.

[*To be concluded in our next.*]

APPENDIX.

No. II.

SPANISH NAVAL STATE PAPERS.

[Continued from our last.]

WE will state to M. de Cevallos, that after such declarations had been made, it would be difficult to suppose that any explanation could be given of the present Naval preparations, which would render such a proceeding consistent with the neutrality which is professed; but it is manifestly impossible to consider it, unaccompanied as it has been by any previous explanation whatever, in any other light than as a menace directly hostile, and imposing upon his Majesty the duty of taking, without delay, every measure of precaution; and particularly of giving orders to his Admiral off the Port of Ferrol, to prevent any of the Spanish Ships of War from sailing from that Port, or any additional Ships of War from entering it.

The whole conduct of his Majesty towards Spain has abundantly proved his earnest desire to carry that forbearance to the utmost limit a due regard to the safety and interests of his people would admit: but he cannot depart from the declarations he has already made; nor allow Spain to enjoy all the advantages of neutrality, and, at the same time, to carry on against him a double War, by assisting his enemies with pecuniary succours, to which no limit is assigned; and by obliging him at the same time to divert a part of his Naval Force from acting against those enemies, in order to watch the Armaments carried on in Ports professing to be neutral.

You are, therefore, directed to require from the Spanish Government the immediate recall of all orders for the Naval Armament at Ferrol, Cadiz, and Carthagena, as well as for sending reinforcements from some of those Ports to others; and you will apprise M. de Cevallos, that, unless you receive a satisfactory answer without delay, you are ordered to quit Madrid. If positive and unequivocal assurances are given, not only that the present Naval Equipments shall be discontinued, but that the Naval Armaments in the Ports of Spain shall be placed upon the same footing on which they were previously to the commencement of hostilities between Great Britain and France, you will engage to transmit such assurances to his Majesty; and you will take upon yourself to answer for its being the intention of his Majesty, in case there appears sufficient reason to believe that they will be strictly fulfilled, to send a Minister to Madrid, for the purpose of entering into an amicable discussion of all other points of difference.

It must, however, be distinctly understood, that no such discussion can be entered into unless the Court of Spain is prepared to give such an explanation of its engagements with France, and of the system which it intends to adopt, as may enable his Majesty to ascertain the nature of the relations which are to subsist between himself and his Catholic Majesty.

If the answer given by M. de Cevallos should be negative or equivocal, you will demand your passports, and leave Madrid.

I am, &c.

HARROWBY,

Mr. FRERE to CEVALLOS, 27th Sept. 1804.

SIR,

An indisposition, which still confines me to my bed, has prevented me from addressing your Excellency sooner, on the subject of the Naval Armament which is carrying on at Ferrol. The total cessation of all preparations in the Ports having been the principal condition required by England, and agreed to by Spain, as the price of the continuance of that system of forbearance which England has hitherto observed, the violation of this condition, against which I now protest, can be considered in no other light than as a hostile aggression on the part of Spain, and a defiance given to England.

J. H. FRERE.

Note from Don PEDRO CEVALLOS *to J. H.* FRERE, *Esq. dated Escurial, 3d Oct.* 1804.

SIR,

I have made a report to the King my master of the contents of your Note of the 27th ult. in which you speak of a Naval Armament which you suppose to be fitting out in Ferrol. His Majesty being informed of your representations, orders me to answer, that he has never thought of being wanting to the agreements entered into with the British Government that the cessation of all Naval Armament against Great Britain shall be observed as it has been hitherto; and that whatever information to the contrary may have reached you, is wholly unfounded, and offensive to the reputation which the Spanish Government justly enjoys.

I take this opportunity of renewing to you the assurances of my wishes to oblige you, and I pray God to preserve your life many years.

P. CEVALLOS.

Copy of a Dispatch from Lord HARROWBY *to J. H.* FRERE, *Esq. dated Downing Street, October* 22, 1804.

SIR,

The Lively, Captain Hammond, arrived at Portsmouth on Wednesday morning, with the Fama, a Spanish Frigate, laden with dollars from Rio de la Plata, and brought information of the action which took place on the 5th inst. between four of his Majesty's Frigates and the same number of Spanish Frigates, in which three of the latter were captured, and one unfortunately blew up. Although, from the situation of the Ships when this action happened, it is probable that the event is known at the Court of Madrid, I have thought it necessary to give you this information without loss of time, in order that you may be able to explain to the Spanish Government the principles upon which the orders given to his Majesty's Naval Commanders are rested, and the effect which this event is here considered to have upon the relative situation of the two countries. As the subject was fully discussed in a conference which took place yesterday between the Spanish Minister and myself, I cannot point out to you more distinctly the language which his Majesty thinks proper to be held upon this occasion, than by stating to you the substance of this conversation. In answer to the first question of the Spanish Minister, in what light this event was to be considered? I informed him, that it was an act done in consequence of express orders from his Majesty, to detain all Ships laden with treasure for Spain. That such orders had been issued as soon as intelligence was received of the equipment of Naval Armaments in the Ports of Spain, and particularly at Ferrol, without any previous explanation. That the Court of Madrid could have no reason to be surprised that such a step was taken, as it had been repeatedly stated to the Spanish Government, and particularly in a note delivered by Mr. Frere on the 18th February last, that as long as they continued in a situation of merely nominal neutrality, any Naval Armament in their Ports must be considered as putting an immediate end to the forbearance of England, and as necessarily producing consequences that were distinctly pointed out. I added, that upon the first intelligence of the Armament, Admiral Cochrane had been directed to communicate to the Governor of Ferrol the orders he had received to oppose the sailing of any Spanish Ships of War to or from Ferrol; and Mr. B. Frere has also been directed to inform the Court of Madrid, of the orders given by his Majesty, that all necessary measures of precaution should be taken, and particularly those notified by Admiral Cochrane. The Spanish Minister then observed, that his Court was not apprised of the orders given to detain the Ships laden with Treasure, which being Ships of War, their resistance to any attempt to detain them must have been foreseen. I observed in reply, that this was the first and most obvious measure of those measures of precaution which had been announced. That it had been thought right to announce precisely the intention of engaging the Ships of War which might attempt to sail to or from Ferrol, because it would depend upon the Spanish Government, after receiving such an intimation, to give such orders as to their sailing as it might think proper, **and to prevent a hostile meeting between the two**

SPANISH NAVAL STATE PAPERS.

Squadrons; but that to have announced more particularly the intention of detaining the Treasure Ships, must either have been perfectly useless, if the Spanish Government had no means of giving them notice of such intention, or must have afforded the opportunity of rendering it completely abortive. That Spain having violated one of the conditions upon which the forbearance of his Majesty depended, it became immediately necessary for him to prevent the continuance of those Succours, which were furnished by Spain to France. That these Succours were of two kinds; Naval Armaments and Treasure.—That his Majesty had hitherto submitted, with unexampled moderation, to connive at the payment of a subsidy by Spain to France, upon the grounds which have been often stated; but that, from the moment Spain had manifested the intention, instead of confining herself to pecuniary assistance, to add her Naval Forces to those of France; and had manifested it in the least equivocal manner, by equipping a considerable Squadron in the Port of Ferrol, where it would be ready to join a Squadron of French Ships, and to outnumber the British Force employed in blockading them; from that moment his Majesty could no longer delay carrying into execution every measure of necessary precaution; and he had as just a right to detain Treasure destined to increase the means of his enemies, as to attack the Ships of Spain sailing in conjunction with those of France. I expressed in strong terms his Majesty's concern at the loss of so many valuable lives in the conflict, and particularly at the unfortunate accident which destroyed one of the Spanish Frigates (the Mercedes), with nearly the whole of her Crew. I did not controvert his observation, that it was impossible for those Frigates not to resist, when they were met by so equal a Force; and I thought it right to avow, without hesitation, that although it was hoped the Treasure might have been brought in single Ships of a force so inferior to his Majesty's Squadron, as to justify the expectation that they might be detained without violence, yet that his Majesty's Government were aware that this expectation might be disappointed, and as the act itself was thought necessary, had determined to incur the hazard of what might follow from resistance. To the question put by the Spanish Minister, in what state the Spanish Frigates and their Crews were to be considered? I replied, in the same state as Ships and Crews detained under similar circumstances upon former occasions. That the Officers and Men would be treated with every possible attention, and the Treasure would be transported to a place of security, to await such orders as the issue of the present discussions with the Court of Madrid may appear to his Majesty to require. After these points had been discussed, the Spanish Minister desired to know whether this event was to be considered as putting an end to all further explanation, and placing the two countries in a state of War? To this I replied, that it was certainly by no means so considered on our part; that it was still the earnest wish of his Majesty, that such explanations, assurances, and securities might be given by the Court of Madrid, respecting their Naval Armaments, present and future, and respecting all other subjects of discussion between the two Governments, as might not only maintain an amicable intercourse between them, but establish it in future upon a more distinct and permanent footing. An explanation of the Naval Armaments alone would not, then, (replied M. d'Anduaga,) now satisfy the English Government? To this I answered, that such an explanation alone would not now satisfy us, nor would it have been satisfactory at any former period. The Court of Madrid had repeatedly been informed, that his Majesty could not be satisfied without being made completely acquainted with the relation in which Spain stands with France, in order to be enabled to judge, upon a full view of all the circumstances, in what relation he could consent to consider Spain as standing with respect to Great Britain.

In reply to several observations which fell from Chevalier d'Anduaga, that assurances had been given as to the amount of the subsidy, which was stated to be only an equivalent for Military Succours; as to the contents of the Treaty with France, which was alleged to contain nothing injurious to Great Britain; as to the innocent destination of any Armaments which might be made; as to the decided intention of his Catholic Majesty to preserve the strictest neutrality; and as to the injustice of any suspicions which could attach to Spanish honour and veracity. I assured him, in return, that both the Government and the Nation had the highest value and respect for Spanish honour and veracity; but that we had too much ground from experience to be slow in trusting the ability of Spain to act up to the honourable and independent principles by which her conduct would naturally be guided. That I sincerely wished the Armaments in question might prove to have been really, as he had endeavoured to represent them, only the consequence of an order given under the pressure of necessity, for the purpose of transporting Troops to subdue the revolters in Biscay; but that if this were really the intention of the order, it was inconceivable, that no notice should have been given to the British Minister at Madrid, or to the Admiral off the Port of Ferrol, who might have conveyed the explanation of the Armament at the same moment with the news of its existence. That it was singular if Ships of the Line were to be used for this purpose, that they should not have been equipped merely as Transports. That although the orders were received at Ferrol on the 7th of last month, and must consequently have been given at Madrid some days earlier, yet up to this moment he was possessed of no direct information from his Court, was authorized to give me no explanation, and was reduced to state upon this subject, his own conjecture, founded upon inlperfect intelligence, and upon his own earnest wishes to explain the transaction in a manner calculated to prevent a rupture between the two countries. Having dwelt upon the various grounds which made this explanation improbable and unsatisfactory, I concluded the conversation by expressing my fears, that the orders would be found to have proceeded from that influence which had unfortunately so long diverted the Spanish Councils from an attention to their real interest and dignity; that the measure, if dictated by that influence, would probably be persisted in; and that a breach would then become inevitable; but that the moderation and forbearance of his Majesty's conduct hitherto, (to which the Spanish Minister bore the fullest testimony,) would be a sufficient security, that no reasonable means of accommodation would be rejected; and I should be equally desirous with himself to be the instrument of re-establishing between our respective countries a greater degree of harmony and cordiality than could exist between a nominal neutrality on the one side and a jealous forbearance on the other.— I am in daily expectation of hearing from you what passed at Madrid upon the receipt of the communication made by Admiral Cochrane to the Spanish Governor off Ferrol: until that information is received, I have nothing to add to my former instructions.

P. S. Since this was written, an account was received of the arrival of his Majesty's Ships the Amphion and Indefatigable, with the Spanish Frigates the Medea and Clara.

I am, &c.

HARROWBY.

Dispatch from B. FRERE, *Esq. to Lord* HARROWBY, *dated Escurial, October 27th,* 1804.

MY LORD,

Your Lordship's dispatches, Nos. 1 and 2, were delivered to me by the Messenger Smith, on the night of the 18th, in consequence of which I lost no time in coming down to the Escurial, where the Court are resident at present; and having demanded an audience of M. Cevallos, which he gave me on the 21st, I told him that I believed he would find by his letters from England, that the sensation which the late unexpected Armament at Ferrol had caused there, had been by no means over-rated in the Note which I had addressed to him upon the subject some weeks ago; that I was now charged to declare to him formally his Majesty's surprise and concern at such a measure having been adopted, without any previous communication to him, and unaccompanied by any explanations of its object; and to require the immediate recall of all orders which might have been given at Ferrol or elsewhere, for increasing their Naval Force, or for altering its position; and that it should be reduced to the state in which it was at the beginning of the War. M. Cevallos said, that he found that there had been a great deal of misrepresentation and exaggeration upon the subject of this Armament, which he affected to treat very lightly: he said, that the expedition consisted of a few Ships, which were already armed at the time, whose destination I must be well acquainted with; that the project was now given up; and he wished to infer that there was therefore no ground of complaint for what had passed. I replied, that I knew no more of the destination of this expedition, than what I have learnt from public report, which was, that it was meant to convey Troops to quell an insurrection in Biscay: but that it appeared to me so incredible that Ships of War should be armed to carry Forces to a Province which had no ports to receive them, which was already in possession of their Troops, and which was so situated, that the march by land might be performed in a much shorter time than was necessary for preparing the making the Voyage; that I had not ventured to write this report home to my Government. M. Cevallos however assured me, that this was the design; and, extravagant as it was, the march by land into Biscay of the Troops before destined for the embarkation seems to confirm this assurance. I observed, that whatever might have been the object of this Armament, it was equally a breach of the Convention which Spain had entered into with England; and as M. Cevallos maintained that the engagement had been only contracted for not arming against Great Britain, I referred him to my brother's note of the 18th February, in which the cessation of all Armaments is demanded in the clearest terms. I told him at the same time, that if he was now inclined to dispute this point, I

SPANISH NAVAL STATE PAPERS.

must revert to the instructions upon which the demand was framed, and which were to the full as positive as those which I had now received. He protested against the extravagance of such a pretension, which he said would reduce them to the lowest state of humiliation if Spain could not arm to repel the insults of a foreign enemy, or to quell her own rebellious subjects. I repeated the assurances of his Majesty's disposition to make every possible concession in favour of Spain; but that this was an engagement which the security of this Kingdom called for, and that Spain might rely upon its being pushed no further than that object required. Finding that it was needless to attempt to draw any satisfactory assurance from M. Cevallos in conversation, I told him that my instructions related likewise to some other important points; that if he pleased I would read them over to him; after which, if he thought it necessary, I would deliver to him in writing a summary of their contents. In treating of the subject of the money furnished to France, he affected much surprise at its being considered merely as a temporary measure, and asked from whence my Court could have got that idea, of which he himself disclaimed any share. I told him I knew my brother had repeatedly received several assurances at the very time when the Treaty was negotiating, from a person high in authority, whose assurances were then esteemed authentic, and that as such he had transmitted them to his Government. M. Cevallos repeated, that they had no such views; that the Treaty was concluded for the whole of the present War; that it contained no article whatever hostile to Great Britain; and as to the amount of the Subsidies, he could only repeat what he had already said, and what M. d'Anduaga had stated to your Lordship, that they are calculated with a reference to the expense of furnishing the Succours stipulated by Treaty. This assurance, he said, he trusted I should think sufficient, and that England would so far do justice to the good faith of the Spanish Cabinet as to pronounce herself satisfied with such a declaration—I observed to him, that my Government was already in possession of thus much information upon the subject when my present instructions were forwarded to me, and therefore that I must expect a more explicit answer, or comply with the orders to demand my passports; that in the terms in which he stated it, the amount of the Succour stipulated was without any limit, since the Treaty provides, that in case of necessity, the auxiliary Power is liable to be called upon to assist her ally with all her forces; in which situation there would be no bounds to the sums which Spain might furnish to the enemy under the denomination of an equivalent for these Succours. I did not, however, succeed in obtaining further explanation upon the subject; and there was in M. Cevallo's manner a more decided determination not to give way upon this point, and more disposition to ill humour at being pressed upon it, than upon that of the total cessation of all Armaments in the Ports. He took no other notice of the orders given to Admiral Cochrane to shut the Port of Ferrol to their Ships of War, than by asking me to read that paragraph a second time; and when I had finished the dispatch, he said, that Spain would continue to act with the same good faith which she had always hitherto done; that England ought to be perfectly at ease upon the subject of the Armament, which had never been of any consequence, and was now laid aside; that upon the question of the Subsidies, she had all the satisfaction that she could reasonably require; and that it was time that she herself should give some assurance of her own dispositions, without which a neutrality, restless and disturbed as that which Spain now possesses, would prove as prejudicial to the Country as War itself. I answered, that the dispositions of my Government towards Spain were not less friendly than they had always been, and that it was to the conduct of Spain herself that he must attribute the unsettled state of the connexion between the two Countries; nor could it be otherwise, as long as she maintained this reserve upon a point which affects so essentially the interests of Great Britain as that of her pecuniary engagements with France: and I left him, by saying, that I hoped that upon consideration he would see it in the same light, and that I should receive a more satisfactory answer to the Note which I should transmit to him, than I had been able to obtain from the conference. Your Lordship will observe an interval of some days between this conference and the date of my Note, during which I have been confined by a return of indisposition, which disabled me from writing; having, however, stated so fully beforehand the nature of my instructions to M. Cevallos, I am in hopes that no time will have been lost by this circumstance, and that I shall receive his answer as soon as if my Note had been presented immediately after our conference.

I have the honour to be, &c.

B. FRERE.

[The discussion continues to be pursued in several long Notes, without much novelty.]

SPANISH NAVAL STATE PAPERS.

Translation of a Note from Don PEDRO CEVALLOS, *to* B. FRERE, *Esq. dated*
S. Lorenzo, Nov. 3, 1804.

SIR,

I have received the two Notes which you were pleased to address to me, dated the 30th October last, and the 2d inst., and having given an account to the King, my master, of their contents, I have the honour to declare to you, that Spain has given constant proofs of good correspondence with Great Britain, of her fidelity in observing the Treaty of Neutrality, (called by you a suspension of hostilities, though they have not disturbed the state of Peace since the Treaty of Amiens,) and has completely done away the apprehensions which England founded upon vague accounts of Armaments which neither did exist, nor, if they had existed, had any tendency prejudicial to the tranquillity of Great Britain.

And although these three points are satisfied in my Note of the 29th of October last, still his Majesty is willing to make a fresh sacrifice to Peace, carrying his royal condescension to the point which you desire, and ordering me to satisfy your questions, as I do, in the most unequivocal manner; saying,

To the First. That Spain, in consequence of the Treaty of Neutrality concluded the 19th October, 1803, will make no Armament contrary to the said Convention.

To the Second. That there is not a greater number of Ships armed, than there was at the epoch of the said Convention.

To the Third. That no change, infractory of the Neutrality, shall be made in the distribution of the Ships already armed; nor is it likely that there should be any need to change the said distribution, under the supposition of Neutrality.

To the Fourth. That the Treaty of Subsidies with France contains nothing offensive to our Neutrality with Great Britain; and that the Subsidies are equivalent to what would be the expense of the Naval and Military Succours stipulated in the Treaty of Alliance with the French Republic.

As my answers are not less distinct than satisfactory, for they have been formed in no other stile than that of good faith, I think I have a fresh right to be satisfied by you in regard to the measure taken by the British Cabinet, in order that the Commander of its Forces before Ferrol should prevent the entrance of the Spanish Ships in the said Port; a complaint which I have not had the honour to see satisfied by you, as becomes a measure which carries with it mistrust of the Spanish Government, and offends its honour and dignity, by shackling the exercise of its domestic authority.

I do not believe that you will have any difficulty in recognising the violence of which this measure of your Government partakes, when I observe, by your Note of the 30th, (which did not reach me till after a delay of two days,) that your good faith and conciliatory spirit have prompted you to do away the equivocation which there was in the instructions of your Court with regard to the epoch which is to regulate the reduction of the Maritime Forces of Spain, making a due appreciation of my observations, which were founded in the express determination of the compact of Neutrality.

PEDRO CEVALLOS.

Mr. FRERE *to* CEVALLOS.

SIR, Madrid, Nov. 3, 1804.

I have just had the honour of receiving your Note of this day, and I am concerned to remark, that upon the two principal points it is as equivocal and as little satisfactory as those which preceded it. Your Excellency gives me no answer whether you will, or not, enter into an engagement that no Armament whatever shall be fitted out in the Spanish Ports, referring me only to the terms of a Convention, upon the force of which we are by no means agreed, your Excellency maintaining that the engagement not to arm was not a general one, (which I require,) but that it merely referred to Armaments against Great Britain. I see also with regret that I have not advanced a single step on the question of the Subsidies granted to France. The answer which your Excellency now gives me is the same which was returned to the first representations of my Government on this point, and it is absolutely impossible for me to transmit it as satisfactory, or to withdraw my requests for Passports.

B. FRERE.

SPANISH NAVAL STATE PAPERS.

Nov. 5. Mr. Frere peremptorily insists on receiving his Passports; and Nov. 7, Cevallos sends them. Here all intercourse ceased. At this time the detention of the Spanish Frigates was unknown at Madrid.

Several orders to our Commanders at Sea, and extracts of Letters from them, are given; but the following are the most important:—

Extract of a Letter from Rear-Admiral COCHRANE *to the Hon. Admiral* CORNWALLIS, *dated on board his Majesty's Ship Northumberland, off Ferrol, the 21st of October,* 1804.

The Spanish Ships here are in the same state as when I wrote last. I now enclose the most correct list that can be obtained of their situation, by which you will perceive that they are all in a state fit for Service.

A List of all the Spanish Ships of War in the Port of Ferrol, October 1804:—

La Conception, 120 guns, in good order, without masts; guns all on board, in the Arsenal.
La Prince d'Asturia, 120 guns, newly repaired, ditto, ditto, ditto.
La Mexicano, 120 guns, in good order, ditto, ditto, ditto.
La St. Fernando, 90 guns, an old Ship newly repaired, ditto, ditto.
La Neptano, 84 guns, rigged, and in good order, in the Arsenal—complete.
La Monarco, 74 guns, ditto, ditto, ditto.
La St. Augustin, 74 guns, ditto, ditto—sails fast.—Old Ship—ditto.
La St. Juan Nepanesceno, 74 guns, just out of Dock.—In good order.
La Mantanes, 74 guns, in good order—ten years old.
La St. Yldefonso, 74 guns, thirteen years old.
La St. Francisco d'Asis, 74 guns, in Dock, and has had a thorough repair.
La St. Felino, 74 guns, sails very fast.—Old, but in good order.
La St. Fulgencia, 64 guns, old, but in good order.
L'Oriente, 74 guns, ditto, but in order for Service.
La St. Julian, 64 guns, ditto, ditto.
L'Esmaralda, 44 guns. Frigate.
La Flora, 44 guns, ordered to be docked for immediate Service.
La Prueba, 44 guns, new.—Never been at Sea.—Completely rigged.
La Vengenza, 40 guns, rigged and ready for Sea.
La Diana, 40 guns, in good order. About ten years old.
La Pila, 40 guns, in good order.

In the Arsenal there are sixteen or eighteen Gun-Boats, carrying a long 24-pounder, and thirty Men belonging to each. During the last War they had Floating Batteries carrying from eight to ten long 24-pounders, with a furnace for heating shot. One of them lay at Rides the most of the War.

Extract of a Letter from Rear-Admiral COCHRANE *to the Hon. Admiral* CORNWALLIS, *dated on board his Majesty's Ship Northumberland, off Ferrol, the 25th October,* 1804.

The Spanish Line of Battle Ships are in a state so as to be ready in a few days. The baking of biscuit goes on; all their ovens are at work; most of the water is on board; and the Ships are kept in a more immediate state for Service than they have been for a twelvemonth past.

The Duguay Trouin will be out of the Dry Dock next spring tide. When the Redoutable goes in the Fougueux will be nearly ready to come out of the Bason. I have reason to think that they have now a sufficiency of Men for four of their Line of Battle Ships, if not the whole. Parties continue to arrive from France.

SPANISH NAVAL STATE PAPERS.

Some additional Papers respecting the Negociation with Spain, were laid before Parliament. They relate to the Naval Armaments in the different Ports of Spain. Mr. Duff's communications from Cadiz upon those Armaments are extremely valuable and decisive.

THE FOLLOWING ADDITIONAL PAPERS WERE PRESENTED TO BOTH HOUSES OF PARLIAMENT.

No. IV.—*Extract of a Letter from* JAMES DUFF, *Esq. his Majesty's Consul at Cadiz, to* WILLIAM MARSDEN, *Esq. dated Oct.* 14, 1803.

I am assured this day, orders have been received at the Island for the arming at that Arsenal of two Three-deckers, an Eighty-four, and three Seventy-fours; and at Carthagena three large Frigates. It has even been said some Line of Battle Ships have been ordered to be fitted out there, also at Ferrol, but I believe not with certainty; and the fact is, several months must elapse before those at this department can be in any readiness to put to Sea. My next will probably convey you more pointed information on this head.

Our Captain General is called to Court; and as a considerable number of Troops have assembled at Zamora and Valladolid, it may be inferred with a view to his inspecting them, or giving him some command.

No. VI.—*Extract of a Letter from Rear-Admiral Sir* EDWARD PELLEW, *Bart. dated on board his Majesty's Ship Tonnant, off Ferrol,* 24th *October,* 1803, *to the Hon. Admiral* CORNWALLIS.

Much increased activity prevails since the last dispatches from Madrid, and they worked night and day until the sixteen Gun-boats were ready. It may be possible that these Spanish Ships are fitting to embark Augereau's Army. I shall use every means to discover that measure if it should be adopted, and forward the earliest intelligence of it to you.

No. VII.—*Naval Occurrences for October* 1803, *reported by Mr.* DUFF.

Ships ordered to be fitted out at Cadiz:—Trinidad, 130 guns, Capt. Brigadier Don Francisco Ureart: Santa Ana, 112, Capt. Dionisio Alcala Galean; San Rafael, 84, Don Ijsh. Arambure; Terrible, 74, Don Ijsh. de la Guardia; Soberano, 74, Don Juan Carranza; America, 64, Don Jose Melendez; and Amphitrite, 40, Don Jose Varela; destined for Vera Cruz and Havana.—Rusina, 34, Don Jose Novales, destined for Lima.

Ships fitting out at Carthagena:—Reyna Louisa, 112 guns; San Carlos, 112; Bahama, 74, arrived at Cadiz the 4th of November; Argonauta, 84; Matilde, 34; and Vanganza, 34.

The Ships ordered to be fitted out at Ferrol are five, though hitherto the following only are named: Prince d'Austuria, 120 guns; Neptune, 84; and San Augustin, 74.

The place of rendezvous, it is asserted, will be this Port; but from all appearances the earliest possible they can assemble will be February or March next. The French Ship and Corvette have not yet got into Dock.

No. VIII.—*Naval Occurrences for November* 1803, *reported by Mr.* DUFF, *his Majesty's Consul at Cadiz.*

In the Carracca, the fitting out of the six Ships is going on. The America of 66 guns is the only one of them which is completed, and is gone out of the Arsenal; as to the others, three of them (one of which is the Trinidad) are in Port; some time will elapse before they come out of it, and can be equipped as well as the others.

At Ferrol they are occupied in the Armament of the five Ships to be fitted out there, the Neptune, Don Antonio Vaides; Monerca, Don Antonio Argomosa; Sn. Augustin, Don Antonio Pareja; Sn. Fulgencia, Don Jocechin Rivera; Prince, Don Conne Charruca; the Ships as fitted are expected to come here.

Of the four Ships fitted out at Carthagena, the Argonaut, of 84 guns, Brigadier Don Bufael de One, and the Bahama, 74, Captain Don Limode Truxillo, have been some time arrived here; the two remaining, Sn. Carlos, 112 guns, Brigadier Don Louis Musias and Reyna Luisa, 112 guns, Brigadier Don Antonio Pastigo, were preparing to folley.

[*To be continued.*]

Lightning Source UK Ltd.
Milton Keynes UK
18 September 2010

160050UK00001B/63/P